SOUTH OF MY DAYS

SOUTH OF MY DAYS

A BIOGRAPHY OF
JUDITH WRIGHT

VERONICA BRADY

Angus&Robertson
An imprint of HarperCollins*Publishers*

Angus&Robertson
An imprint of HarperCollins*Publishers*, Australia

First published in 1998
by HarperCollins*Publishers* Pty Limited
ACN 009 913 517
A member of the HarperCollins*Publishers* (Australia) Pty Limited Group
http://www.harpercollins.com.au

Copyright © Veronica Brady 1998

This book is copyright.
Apart from any fair dealing for the purposes of private study, research,
criticism or review, as permitted under the Copyright Act, no part may
be reproduced by any process without written permission.
Inquiries should be addressed to the publishers.

HarperCollins*Publishers*
25 Ryde Road, Pymble, Sydney, NSW 2073, Australia
31 View Road, Glenfield, Auckland 10, New Zealand
77–85 Fulham Palace Road, London, W6 8JB, United Kingdom
Hazelton Lanes, 55 Avenue Road, Suite 2900, Toronto, Ontario M5R 3L2
and 1995 Markham Road, Scarborough, Ontario M1B 5M8, Canada
10 East 53rd Street, New York NY 10032, USA

National Library of Australia Cataloguing-in-Publication data:

Brady, Veronica, 1929–.
 South of my days: a biography of Judith Wright.
 Includes index.
 ISBN 0 207 18857 2.
 1. Wright, Judith, 1915–. Biography. 2. Poets, Australian – 20th Century – Biography.
 I. Title.
A821.3

Typeset in New Caledonia 11/15pt
Printed in Australia by Griffin Press Pty Ltd on 80 gsm Econoprint
Cover photograph of Judith Wright reproduced with permission from the National Library
of Australia.

5 4 3 2 1
02 01 00 99 98

CONTENTS

Acknowledgements • vii
Introduction • ix
List of Abbreviations • xiii

CHAPTER I
The Generations of Men • 1

CHAPTER II
The World and the Child • 21

CHAPTER III
Do Not Weaken For Their Grief:
Do Not Give In • 38

CHAPTER IV
Where Is Home, Ulysses? • 59

CHAPTER V
South of My Days … • 84

CHAPTER VI
"Senses That Spoke and Mind That
Shaped a World" • 102

CHAPTER VII
The Gateway • 123

CHAPTER VIII
Change and Distance • 152

CHAPTER IX
Shadow • 199

CHAPTER X
Look at the News from the Other Capitals • 242

CHAPTER XI
A Kind of Weaving • 284

CHAPTER XII
Moving South • 313

CHAPTER XIII
Towards a Treaty: A Juster Justice • 358

CHAPTER XIV
Phantom Dwelling • 424

CHAPTER XV
I Choose Fire – Not Snow • 468

Notes • 529
Index • 563

ACKNOWLEDGEMENTS

There are very many people who need to be thanked for their help in writing this book.

First of all there is Judith Wright herself, who first thought of this book and throughout has shared her time, her memories, her papers and her inspiration. Her family, too, have been unfailingly generous and helpful, ready to put up with all kinds of intrusive questions and to share their knowledge with me. It is invidious to single anyone out, but I must especially thank Caroline Mitchell and Tina Lister for their help with photographs as well as for their friendship.

In Armidale, Joe Massingham, the Master of Wright College in the University of New England, not only introduced me to family members but also acted as my chauffeur. The Headmistress of New England Girls' School – Judith Wright's old school – Anne Abbott was also generous with her time as well as with the school records. Shirley Walker, who wrote the fine study of Judith Wright's poetry, not only made me very welcome to Armidale but shared her knowledge with me with scholarly generosity.

Judith Wright's many friends also took me into their confidence and friendship, and I owe a particular debt to Kathleen McArthur, Barbara Blackman and Len Webb, long-term friends of Judith's, and to others like Rodney Hall, Tom Shapcott and Peter Skryznecki. During my stay in Canberra Dymphna Clark, Heather Rusden and Anne Edgeworth did everything they could to share their own memories and introduce me to others.

Librarians, as always, were invaluable. Without the generosity of the National Library of Australia which awarded me a Harold White

Fellowship it would not have been possible to spend the time which was needed in the National Library. The staff of the manuscript section, where I spent most of my time working on the Wright papers, not only went far and above the call of duty in looking after my needs but also set an example of scholarship. I must also thank the staff of the special collections section of the Baillieu Library at the University of Melbourne who made the Meanjin papers available to me, and the staff of the Reid Library at the University of Western Australia.

Finally, I must thank my own community and my many friends for their patience and support and my colleagues in the Department of English at the University of Western Australia, especially Sue Lewis, our administrative officer, who made so many things happen, Pauline Dugmore who typed a messy manuscript with skill and patience in the midst of many other claims on her time and energy, and Denise Hill who helped at critical times.

There are many others who helped along the way. They know who they are, and I hope they will realised how grateful I am to them all.

Veronica Brady

INTRODUCTION

"You need to live to ninety to realise all the stories that
are tucked away in your background."

Oral History, 1/17

A poet's life, any life, is a process of unfolding realisation. For Judith Wright there has also been the question of responsibility, not only for others – something inherited from her family – but also for what Owen Barfield (a thinker she and her husband Jack admired) calls poetic values[1]: poetry as a way not only of knowing but also of living in the world, straining towards fullness of consciousness in which what is outside is fused with what lies within the self. Today we are more likely to call them environmental values, an awareness of our relationship to and responsibility for the living world around us, and this awareness and this responsibility lie at the centre of Judith Wright's concerns and her career.

A life, someone has said, is often more of a haunting than a history. From childhood Judith's life has been filled with unseen presences – of her ancestors, of trees and flowers, birds and animals all instinct with some mysterious life. The land, too, for her is a living force, bearing with it a past we have not spoken but to which she has attuned herself – the memories of Aboriginal people and their culture, "a dream the world breathed sleeping and forgot"[2] which nevertheless remains with her as a kind of melancholy longing for a vanished space, a grief for a lost country, a lost paradise, an image of some past she will never be able to recover and from which she is and always will be shut out. "The further I went, even in my first book [as she told Jim Davidson] the more I became aware I was writing poetry on the theme of the white occupation, and it has become a rather strong one in my life."³

The clearest expression of this melancholy is to be found in the poem she wrote to Oodgeroo Noonuccal (then Kath Walker) "Two Dreamtimes".⁴ It is a poem about loss and division. In this she was breaking new ground. "I don't know of anyone else who was doing this [writing about Aboriginal people's culture even in the early 1940s] when I began and now I think," she reflected, looking back, "I can possibly claim to be rather original";⁵ though it is true that Mary Gilmore, whom Judith used to visit in Sydney in the late 1930s, used also to write occasionally about Aboriginal people and their culture but in a more elegaic and sentimental vein. Judith was to carry this concern much further.

She was also to break new ground intellectually, influenced by her husband, the philosopher Jack McKinney. At a time and in a place in which what general intellectual life there was put all its emphasis on the mind, and Australian intellectual life, such as it was, could be seen as the last outpost of the Enlightenment – secular, analytic, sceptical and confidently rational – Judith was exploring the intuitive and bodily; what Hélène Cixous was to call the "feminine economy"⁶ in which meaning has to do with what is bodily and with the natural world, not just with abstract reason.

Thus from the beginning of her career Judith was to appeal away from history, experienced as a growing series of disasters threatening the very continuance of life, to the world of myth, of the archaic and so-called "primitive".⁷ Yet, paradoxically, she was and is a strikingly modern figure, aware of the challenge of the immediate present in ways most of her Australian contemporaries were not. Despite, or perhaps because of, the sense of tradition she inherited from her family she was curiously unprotected by the "halo effect" of history which enabled so many Australians, then and now, to live in a kind of innocence . Like many European thinkers, and Auden and Isherwood in England, she stood imaginatively at the end of the old world, anticipating the void which was to open up with World War II and its appalling culmination at Hiroshima and Nagasaki.

Others might look for consolation from these harsh realities, retreating into distraction or collapsing in despair. But Judith has lived most of her adult life on the edge, refusing to give up belief in the "holiness of the heart's affections" and of the body's splendours and pains, "bearing it out even to the edge of doom", and on the other hand insisting on the need to change and to make beliefs issue in action. Throughout her life, therefore, Judith has sustained a faith in the living world and in love, that interplay between sexuality and dream, idealism and ordeal. It is a faith at once peculiarly womanly and peculiarly and courageously passionate.

But she has also been politically active and passionately concerned for the environment. The founding president of the Wildlife Preservation Society of Queensland, which saved the Great Barrier Reef from destruction in the 1960s and in effect initiated the environmental movement, later helping to preserve large areas of rainforest and coastal lands, Judith was also long-term Council member of the Australian Conservation Foundation. In the 1970s she was member of the Enquiry into the National Estate instituted by the Whitlam government, and in the 1980s a founding member of the Aboriginal Treaty Committee, a culmination of her work as long-term champion of Aboriginal people and culture. She is a woman of public achievement therefore, not prepared to live a merely private life as a poet, but a woman whose philosophical convictions drive her to act in the public domain.

With all that, Judith Wright is one of our major poets, recipient of numerous awards both national and international: the Grace Levin Poetry Prize for 1949, the Encyclopaedia Britannica Award for Literature in 1964, the Christopher Brennan Award for 1974, the 1984 World Prize for Poetry, to name only a few. She has also been awarded honorary doctorates from the Australian National University, Monash University, the University of New England, the University of Melbourne, the University of Sydney and Griffith University and is generally regarded as one of our most substantial poets – she has even been nominated for the Nobel Prize for Literature.

"Time and trouble", Dorothy Sayers wrote, may "tame an advanced young woman, but an advanced old woman is not controllable by any earthly force."[8] As she has grown older, Judith Wright seems to have become more not less passionate in her thought and social commitments. When she was young, women – especially women of her class – were expected to leave questions of power and public affairs to the men. But she had more opportunity and more self-confidence and more determination than most and she refused to submit, using the measure of economic security she managed to win for herself to live an emancipated life, to live it passionately, powerfully and lovingly, discovering new stories not just for women – though that is crucial – but for Australians generally. It is a life of monumental significance. I can only hope to capture something of its passion, power and flair.

ABBREVIATIONS

ABC	Australian Broadcasting Corporation (until 1983, Commission)
ACF	Australian Conservation Foundation
AIAS	Australian Institute of Aboriginal Studies
AIF	Australian Imperial Force
ALP	Australian Labor Party
ANU	Australian National University
ANZAAS	Australian and New Zealand Association for the Advancement of Science
ASA	Australian Society of Authors
ASIO	Australian Secret Intelligence Organisation
ATSIC	Australian and Torres Strait Islander Commission
BBC	British Broadcasting Corporation
C.P.	*Collected Poems* (1994 edition)
CSIRO	Commonwealth Scientific and Industrial Research Organisation
FAW	Fellowship of Australian Writers
FIDO	Fraser Island Defence Organisation
M.A.	*Meanjin* Archive
N.L.	National Library
RSL	Returned Services League
WEL	Women's Electoral Lobby

CHAPTER I

THE GENERATIONS OF MEN

> The Generations of Men run on in the tide of time,
> But leave their destin'd lineaments permanent for ever and ever
>
> William Blake,
> epigraph to *The Generations of Men*

Judith Wright was born under the shadow of war on 31st May 1915, just a few weeks after the landing at Gallipoli. Her mother's two brothers were in the Australian Imperial Force (AIF). One was to be captured by the Turks and the other to survive three years in France. This shadow fell on her childhood even after the fighting ceased – in 1919, pregnant with her third child and second son, Peter, Judith's mother caught the Spanish influenza and never recovered from its consequences, remaining an invalid until she died in 1927, when her daughter was twelve.

Wright's unpublished autobiography opens with two images from this time, two moments of awareness, what Jung called "islands of consciousness",[1] which help to define the person she was to become. In the first – recalled also in a poem written over fifty years later – aged about three or four, she has wandered away from a family party and, coming to the woodheap not far from the kitchen, forbidden territory, she decides to climb it. Halfway up, however, she runs a large and painful splinter into her knee. Blood, "astoundingly red blood",[2] spurts all over her best white dress, her blue sash and her new white socks. As the poem remembers it:

> *The world went scarlet with shock*
> *and shook with appalling noise*
> *like the yell of a branded calf*[3]

as she sobbed out "I has hurt myself",[4] her first use of the first-person singular, her first awareness of being herself. But it was a self who was vulnerable and aware of being an individual;

> It was the sudden knowledge of my separateness from everything else that was making me howl so loud. I had been enclosed in what I might now describe as a space-time continuum which included myself, now I was alone, in pain and trapped in a single limited person. There I would have to stay until I was old and died – as old as my grandmother.[5]

This is a moment of attestation, of saying "It's me here",[6] but one which recognises that she is not pure consciousness that, as Paul Ricoeur puts it, "possessing bodies is precisely what persons do indeed do … (is) what they actually are".[7] It is the challenge she was to take up for the rest of her life:

> *Die? Die? Die?*
> *Like a fly or a sheep? A word*
> *to strike you dumb on a sob.*
> *If dying is what will happen*
> *how shall I manage this trap*
> *of a skin so ready to bleed,*
> *and this hurtable bagful of red*
> *in a world of sting and slap*
> *and cut and knock and stab?*[8]

But she was to live vividly, excitingly and richly – and to become a major poet of the body's joys also.

The second memory is also about dissent. It must have taken place in November 1918, if not on Armistice Day, 11th November, or on Guy Fawkes Day, then sometime around those dates.

> A great vivid wall of flame springs up into a darkness of shifting shadows and wincing leaves, sending out flights of sparks and

volumes of rolling smoke. Over it wobbles, with a terrible moustached grin, a white giant. Fire licks his bulging stomach, eats into his glowing, slowly splitting guts of straw, springs up to balance on his shoulders. Surely somebody will save him?

I bury my face in something, perhaps my mother's skirts, crying for the poor ugly giant, now bowing, grinning still, into the flames. But everyone around is laughing and talking, and nobody makes a move to rescue him. It's only the old Kaiser, they say, we're burning the Kaiser because it's the end of the war, and now your uncles can come home.[9]

Another moment of attestation. But this time Judith is aware of the body and person of another and is responsible for them. Elsewhere, throughout Australia and the British Empire, people were rejoicing at the end of the war. Even in Armidale, not far away, people seemed to have gone mad. One woman, a former student at the New England Girls' School (where Judith herself was to be educated later), recalls the frenzy of the day:

Peace was declared on November 11th at 11 am 1918. Excitement ran wild and tears of happiness and joy were shed; and no lessons were done that day. When we were preparing for bed that evening, we heard marching and singing, and we looked out of our bedrooms from the Main Building windows to see all the Armidale School boys shouting loudly, 'We want the girls – we want the girls.' Then Miss Lyon said, 'I will allow this walk on two conditions – first that you don't leave the main road; and second, when I blow my whistle you will all stop and turn round to come back to the NEGS.'

Immediately all the Armidale School boys clapped, and sang 'For She's a Jolly Good Fellow'. Miss Lyon then instructed us to dress in our uniforms and come down, and how the boys welcomed us, grabbing at any of us, in case there were not enough girls to go around. We all had a super gay walk, singing all the loved War songs – 'Rose of No Man's Land'; 'Keep the Homefires Burning'; 'The Red Cross Nurse'; 'Tipperary'; 'There's a Long Long Trail', and many others.

Of course we all had a few little squeezes and kisses, and Miss Lyon with two mistresses (and torches) walked behind us, joining in the singing.

When we were nearly back at NEGS' entrance, the boys let out a terrific yell – 'Look, why here comes old Polly Perkins in his buggy and horse, and a master to help him.' Mr Perkins was the headmaster of the Armidale School, and was very worried as he had searched all over Armidale looking for his boys. Then he had the bright thought – could they have gone to NEGS? Miss Lyon and Mr Perkins then let us sing a few more songs, and we ended our wonderful evening with 'God Save Our King'. The boys left, Miss Lyon called the roll, and all were present; then she said, 'Now girls, hot cocoa and biscuits are waiting for you, and then bed.' Three cheers for Miss Lyon – it certainly was a night never to be forgotten.[10]

Judith Wright responded differently; she felt for the figure writhing in the flames. Even at this stage she resisted the emotions of the crowd, implicitly understanding that life ought to be based on relationships between people, not on slogans. Born into privilege, she was beginning to sense that, as Emmanuel Levinas puts it, her "being in the world, her 'place in the sun'" might be at the expense of others.[11] Later she was to shock her father, a firm believer in the glories of the British Empire, by feeling sorry for Ghandi, when she read of his imprisonment for his opposition to British rule in India, and, during the Great Depression of the 1930s, was to worry about the shabby figures tramping the country roads in their broken boots, looking for work.

At this moment in childhood she caught a glimpse of the mystery of love, which was to fascinate her for the rest of her life; in fire is the mystery of love as creation and destruction. The epigraph to her fourth collection of poems, *The Two Fires*, points to this mystery. It is a quotation from Herakleitos.

> The World, which is the same for all, no one of gods or men has made; but it was ever, is now, and ever shall be an ever-living Fire, with measures of it kindling, and measures going out.[12]

The saying has it that poets are born not made. From the beginning, Judith Wright seems to have lived inside the inheritance of her birth, but also outside it with a certain amount of tension. What was this inheritance?

She was born, as she wrote later, into a family which "made a great ring, a magic circle of conservatism",[13] around her, born to a "sure and conceded ground" where "a certain consensus of echo, a sanctioning sound/supported our childhood lives".[14]

On her father's side she was descended from a solid Wiltshire county family, the Wyndhams – a Wyndham had been the speaker of the Long Parliament which precipitated the English Civil War in 1639.

In 1828 her great-great-grandfather, George Wyndham, emigrated from "Dinton", the family home to New South Wales. A younger son destined for the Church, he decided to try his luck in the colonies instead. When he arrived, the Governor made him a substantial grant of land in the Hunter Valley. He was also assigned twenty convicts to work for him and with their help transformed the land into a large estate, draining the swamps and cutting down the forest to plant the wheat and vines for which the estate "Dalwood" was to become famous.[15] As Wright describes it, the house he built there was an Antipodean version of "Dinton", "a great house of cool stone corridors and high-ceilinged rooms [with] ...wide iron barred doors opening into a stone-flagged courtyard where servants pumped water splashing into pails".[16]

After the end of convict transportation, however, things went awry for lack of labour, and with bad seasons to add to that, many settlers abandoned their farms. But George Wyndham was not a man to give up. With all his household, his cattle and horses and a few trusted ex-convict servants, he closed "Dalwood", leaving it in charge of a caretaker, and set out to the north-west through virtually unknown country inhabited by hostile Aboriginal tribes. For three years they travelled, his wife Margaret and the children in one wagon, the stores in another, and the cook and his equipment in the third, up to the virtually unexplored New England Tableland (where his descendants were to settle), down again to the coastal plain and to the Richmond River where Aborigines drove off the cattle and Margaret and the children hid in the wagons until George and the men returned in triumph with the "stolen" herd. There they took up land and prospered for a time, but the depression of the 1840s over, they returned to "Dalwood". Prices for wine, wool and hides rose, and with the new runs to add to "Dalwood", they become increasingly prosperous.[17]

As a young man in England, George Wyndham had been something of a radical who dreamed of equality and a new kind of society. But, as his great-great-granddaughter observed, in the new country his innate conservatism asserted itself, and "Dalwood" became a "bulwark, a protection against the very ideas he had come to realise".[18] His children were brought up in the tradition of family duty he had learned, a tradition which insisted on the rights of property and the responsibilities of children to their parents. "Dalwood ... made its own world and imposed its own rules; presided over by George and Margaret, those apparently serene figures of achievement, it left no room for question."[19]

Questions, however, arose for the next generation. One of George and Margaret Wyndham's daughters, Weeta, married Arthur Mackenzie. Dashing, handsome and a good horseman, he did not, however, have his father-in-law's business acumen or luck. Hoping to do better elsewhere, he set out from the Hunter Valley for Queensland to take up land there and soon afterwards sent for his wife and children to join him. But the climate, poor land, hostile Aborigines and poor prices defeated him and within a few years they returned. Broken in health and in spirit, Mackenzie was no longer able to support his family and they lived more or less as mendicants in a cottage on the "Dalwood" property. One of their daughters, May, was to marry Albert Wright and become Judith Wright's grandmother and heroine of *The Generations of Men*.

Albert Wright came from a family not quite as distinguished as the Wyndhams but more romantic. Originally Scottish, of the clan MacGregor, the family had been outlawed for their support of Bonnie Prince Charles in the uprising of 1745 and had fled to France where one of them married a Frenchwoman and settled there. Around 1770, one of the MacGregor sons crossed the Channel and settled in Cornwall at Totness under the name of Wright. It was his grandson, Philip Wentworth Wright, who emigrated to Australia in 1840, some years after the Wyndhams. His arrival was much less privileged.

Philip Wright had brought from England only as much money as was appropriate to launch a younger son from a not particularly wealthy family. This he lost almost at once, being unwise in the ways of the world, to a confidence trickster. He was left almost destitute, stranded in a strange country which was itself passing through difficult times, and his young wife was about to bear her first child.[20]

He was determined, however – a quality he passed on to his great-granddaughter – and managed to steer his way through the booms and busts of the 1840s and 1850s to become the owner of a flour mill and inn at Aberdeen on the Hunter River (the setting for one of Judith Wright's novels for children, *The River and the Road*), and eventually of a farming property, "Bickham", near Blandford (which still belonged to the family when his grandson Phillip Wright, Judith's father, was writing his memoirs in the 1960s).[21]

He was sufficiently prosperous to send his eldest son, Albert, to the King's School in Parramatta, then regarded as the best school in the colony. But the desperate shortage of labour which followed the gold rushes of the 1850s obliged him to bring his son home to help after only a year at the school. Albert was a brilliant student and the headmaster wrote, begging his father to allow him to stay on and offering to find him a scholarship. "But there was no chance of that with almost every able-bodied man in the country swarming to the gold fields and the value of pastoral properties sinking daily."[22]

Philip Wright had recently invested in two isolated and undeveloped stations in the north-west, a considerable distance from "Bickham". The shepherds and stockmen he had employed to run them had gone off to the goldfields. So Albert was sent off to manage these stations, more or less on his own in the bush, and he stayed there until his father managed to sell them. By this time he had turned twenty. It was too late to go back to school, even if his father had been prepared to support him there, and Albert accepted the invitation of a family friend who had bought a number of stations in Queensland during the slump to manage one of them, "Nulalbin" on the Dawson River, while his younger brother, Fred, was to manage "Avon Downs" in the Isaac River country.

Once again, in this venture Albert was successful and working hard, efficiently and honestly, managed to buy "Nulalbin". He could now think of marrying.[23]

Albert was naturally introspective, and the years alone in the bush had made him even more shy than he might have been. But for some years he had corresponded with the daughter of neighbours, Sallie Dickinson, and when he next came south for a holiday he proposed to her. She refused him however, and he returned alone to "Nulalbin". His next trip south was in 1871 to attend a family wedding. There he met May Mackenzie, a friend of his sister, Mary. The train had been delayed and he was late for the wedding but in time for the reception where he and May met. It was love at first sight, and a few days later Albert proposed. May was only sixteen, and after their own experiences in the north her parents were aware of the hardships she would face. But eventually they agreed to the marriage. Albert returned to "Nulalbin" to build a house more suitable for his young bride than the rough quarters he had been living in. In September 1872, they were married and set out for the north.

"Nulalbin" was in harsh country with extremes of heat, drought and flood, tropical diseases and hostile Aboriginal inhabitants. May felt herself under constant surveillance,[24] though Albert seems to have been more sympathetic and less brutal than most in his dealings with the local people. He was interested in the Wadja, and began compiling a dictionary of their language. He also paid wages to the Aboriginal stockmen who worked for him – something very unusual for that time and place. Nevertheless he was a white man and part of the vanguard of settlement in an area in which the Aborigines were resisting particularly strongly. On one occasion, for example, as the local Justice of the Peace, he learned about a massacre of the Wadja in retaliation for the killing of a white man. It is not clear how he responded – he made no entries in his diary for several weeks precisely at that time. Most likely he did nothing, unable or unwilling to bring to justice the white men involved.

It was a battle for him and his young wife, and soon for their children, to survive, physically as well as economically. The country was not really suitable for cattle being subject to droughts and floods; markets were distant and prices fluctuating and unreliable. It was an extraordinarily difficult life for May. Apart from the heat, the snakes, the insects and tropical diseases, water was short and unsuitable for drinking. The garden she planted refused to flourish, so they lived mainly on meat and bread. She was frequently ill, but she bore Albert four children here, Bertie, Arthur, Elsie and Weeta – the youngest, Phillip, Judith's father, was born in New England – and stood by him valiantly.

When Bertie, their eldest son, fell mysteriously ill and the doctors were unable to diagnose his illness, they were agreed that he should not remain in the tropics. In *The Generations of Men* Judith Wright imagines Albert's feelings at this verdict:

> It was the old story, Albert thought. The country raised all kinds of hopes, only to frustrate them; prospectors, pastoralists, speculators, all followed the will-o'-the-wisp, and when it vanished only the land remained – obstinate and wild as ever, but now strewn with the bones of sheep, cattle and men. He had been a fool once, but now he would be wiser.[25]

Considering the general difficulties May and Albert were facing, they decided to cut their losses and move south, and the news from Sydney where Bertie was being treated by a new doctor encouraged this decision. He was improving, and they talked of his going to stay with his grandparents at "Bickham". But not long after this news, as they were beginning to hope that he was cured, a telegram arrived to say that he was dead.[26]

After this, at "Nulalbin", things went from bad to worse with drought, disastrous bushfires and mounting debts. In November 1888 they left "Nulalbin" for New England where Albert had bought a run on the eastern fall of the plateau. It had a bad reputation since the country was rough and mountainous, still thickly wooded and open to wild weather from the east and south, and for that reason they were able to get the land cheaply. But they were determined to make a go of it, and May called the property "Wongwibinda", meaning "Stay here always" in the local Aboriginal language.[27]

It was a hard battle at first, with dingoes and with bad seasons and poor prices for wool and beef. But May was happy to be back in the kind of country she knew. She planned and laid out much of the garden, and the avenue of pines which led in from the road and the orchard.[28] Writing her story years later her granddaughter sympathised with her as she settled into:

> *The house closed in with sycamore and chestnut*
> *fighting the foreign wind.*
> *Here I will stay, she said; be done with the black north,*
> *the harsh horizon rimmed with drought. –*
> *Planted the island there and drew it round her.*[29]

She was not quite done with "the black north". They had not sold "Nulalbin" but had put in a manager. Albert had to keep an eye on it and their other station further north in the Gulf country, "Vena Park", which they had bought with a partner. Still struggling to make "Wongwibinda" pay, towards the end of 1889 they decided to sell the full share of "Vena Park" to their partner. Albert was to go there to discuss, and if possible, finalise the deal and visit "Nulalbin" on the way.

As Judith Wright tells the story (based on Albert's diaries), he was exhausted when he set out on the long journey, partly by sea and partly by stagecoach and horseback. In a long passage in *The Generations of Men*, as he sets out she also has him musing about the enterprise of settlement itself, particularly about its effects on the Aboriginal people whose lands they had occupied:

> He thought of one man who had spent his life laying strychnine baits of flour-cakes wherever he went, wiping out whole tribes, whole camps of blacks, insane, obsessed by a terror far beyond anything that the reality could have inspired, he died warning the world against 'those treacherous devils'.

She also makes him reflect on the effects of the white settlers, on

> the mortal wound that the blacks had known how to deal in return for their own dispossession. 'You must understand us or you must kill us,' they had said; and understanding would have meant – something beyond the powers of the white men, some renunciation impossible to be made ...

> He imagined a whole civilization haunted, like a house haunted by the ghost of a murdered man buried under it ... Yes, they were all haunted.

Whether or not Albert actually put it this way in 1889 this intuition was to be at the centre of his granddaughter's sense of herself and her inheritance and was to follow her throughout her life.

> To forgive oneself – that was the hardest task. Until the [whites] ... could recognize and forgive – that deep and festering consciousness of guilt in themselves, they would not forgive the blacks for setting it there. The murder would go on – open or concealed – until the blacks were all gone and the whites forever crippled.[30]

Albert reached "Avon Downs" eventually and concluded an agreement with his partner, Haydon, though not very amicably – the two men had never got on very well – and then set out on the long journey home. It was a difficult and exhausting one. On board ship sailing south from Townsville, he became seriously ill and when the ship arrived at Rockhampton he was taken to hospital with pneumonia. His brother-in-law, Arundell Mackenzie, was summoned, realised how ill Albert was and sent for May, who arrived just before he died.

According to his granddaughter, who never actually knew him but who became more and more interested in him years later when she read his diaries, Albert was a man who had never quite reconciled the two worlds within him, the

> world in which a man must be respectable and successful, a good hand at a bargain, with a shrewd eye for horses and cattle, and the dark lonely world in which he was still haunted by the dingoes' howling and the last struggles of the child he had had to disown and trust in himself too early.[31]

May, his wife, was still a young woman with five children to care for – their last child, Phillip, Judith's father, had been born not long before Albert had set out for the north. Everyone expected May to sell up and leave "Wongwibinda" and return to her family in the Hunter Valley.

But she was not a conventional woman – like her granddaughter she did not "believe in female submission and … male domination". She and Albert had worked as partners, and whenever she could she would join him looking over the flocks and the state of the land; she also had a good head for figures. The thought of her own mother's situation as a poor relative may have influenced her, also, so she decided to stay on at "Wongwibinda", determined, in her granddaughter's words, to "dictate her terms to life and model it according to her will".[32]

With the help of Arthur, her eldest son, she not only survived but prospered, adding two more properties in New England, "Wallamumbi" and "Jeogla", to the family holdings, and later buying several others in western New South Wales and southern Queensland.

Later, prosperous at last, she enjoyed success and took the family overseas on the imperial tour that was the custom and prerogative of successful colonials, visiting the Wyndham relatives and claiming her imperial inheritance. This was the strong woman, the matriarchal presence, her granddaughter recalls:

> Beloved, beneficent, dogmatic and more than a little feared, it is not possible even for her grandchildren to forget where she [was or] is, to dismiss her as old and negligible … A great deal has happened as she planned – more, perhaps than she herself knows. The world that she has built, the century that she encloses, combine to warm her with the sun of this last autumn.[33]

Judith's father, Phillip, was particularly close to May since he had been born only a few months before his father had died. His eldest brother, Arthur, however, was his mother's right-hand man and stayed at home to look after the properties when the rest of them went on their imperial tours. His other brother, Cecil, seems to have been more independent: when he came of age he set up on his own, marrying Madeleine Delpratt, from a prominent Queensland family who lived at Tamborine (where Judith was later to settle), and managing his affairs separately from the family company. But Phillip, as the youngest, had a deep sense of family and loyalty to the tradition. All his life, for instance, he extolled the virtues and values of Herefords, becoming President of the Hereford Society, a position he held for many years, a tribute perhaps to the fact that earlier in their Queensland venture his father had bought some Herefords descended from the original cattle George Wyndham had brought from England in 1827.[34]

Phillip was very proud of his imperial inheritance, having made three overseas trips before he was twenty. On the first of these, in 1902, he sailed with his family across the Pacific to North America and then to Canada where they had Wyndham relatives to visit, after which they went on to England. Apart from "bringing out" her two daughters, May Wright had two main purposes there: to attend the Coronation of Edward VII and to look for letters written home by George Wyndham and his wife, Margaret, in their first years in Australia. Several years earlier, a pillowcase full of letters from the family in England had been found in the ceiling at "Dalwood", and she was eager to find her great-grandparents' replies. When she arrived in England, however, she found that they had been destroyed – the aunt who had kept them had died only a year or so earlier, but since she had left no instructions about them in her will, they had been thrown out. That was a disappointment, but later the most interesting of the letters found at "Dalwood" were published as *The Dinton-Dalwood Letters*, and the whole collection was lodged with the Mitchell Library in Sydney.[35]

The Coronation was a splendid occasion. Phillip had been put into school while the rest of the family toured the Continent – he stayed with relations, the Gores, and went with their sons to Bedford Grammar School, but he was determined to get to the Coronation. "Britain was at that time in her heyday", he recalls in his memoirs, "and no effort was spared to make the event one of world-shaking importance." The school had refused his mother's request to let him attend the Coronation, but Phillip was determined to be there and when the day came he sneaked out, took the train to London and threw himself on his mother's mercies. For once her sense of duty gave way to her imperial feelings, and he was allowed to stay. Stilted as his account of the occasion is, it nevertheless captures his excitement:

> Kings and Princes from all over the world took part in the procession, and contingents of troops from all parts of the widely-flung Empire lined the streets. The populace was beside itself

> with excitement, and the noise deafening. Other spectators on the stand with us could not contain themselves and there were numerous cases of people fainting with excitement.[36]

The Wrights returned home to Australia to a disastrous drought which so seriously depleted the family finances that Phillip was not sent to school the next year, as had been planned, though in 1904 he had a year as a boarder at "North Shore Grammar" [sic].

> I cannot say I was entirely happy at school, and chafed at the restraints and limits of school life. However, I understood the boys much better than I did the English boys at Bedford and made many friends.[37]

He liked sports and managed to get into the second XV at football and the second crew as an oarsman, hoping to become stroke of the first crew the following year. But money was still scarce and he did not go back to school. In this way his formal education was fairly limited, but for the rest of his life he respected learning and was to be proud of his daughter's achievements.

By 1907, family finances were sufficiently restored to send Phillip to Ceylon (now Sri Lanka) with an English cousin, Max Wright, who had been ordered to the tropics for his health. There, once again, he bathed in the glories of Empire. The Viceroy of India, Lord Kitchener, was paying an official visit to Kandy, the capital, and the two young men witnessed the welcoming procession "composed, together with musicians etc, of many elephants, heavily caparisoned and adorned, carrying gorgeous howdahs containing members of the nobility and other notables". They followed the crowds as the Viceroy visited the Temple of the Tooth, one of the most sacred of Buddhist shrines since the tooth was said to be the Buddha's. Normally seen by only "the highest personages and on the rarest occasions", it had been brought out for the Viceroy. Slipping past the guards and expecting at any moment to be challenged and expelled, the two young men followed the path through long dark passages to a room in the centre of the temple:

> There, on a silk cushion on a table, was 'the Tooth'. It was held up by a thick gold wire, one end of which was twisted around it,

and the other was set in a flat gold base or stand. It was quite unlike a tooth and appeared to be a cylindrical piece of bone; yellow with age, and about an inch long. It is kept in a bell shaped golden casket, lined of many ... covers, each of which is set on top of the other and closely fitting. Each of these covers has an individual lock and key, the keys being kept by individual monks. To open it therefore meant that every monk had to be present to turn his particular key.[38]

Afterwards they set out on their own to explore the ruins of the ancient palace of Anhuradapura and climbed the highest point of the island, Adam's Peak, concluding their stay at a hill Rest House managed by a German. A jarring note intruded here, however: the manager boasted to them that Germany was planning a war against Britain to despoil her of her Empire, which at the time must have seemed unthinkable.

A few years later, in 1911, there was another trip with the family (again, without the hard-working Arthur) to London by way of the Suez Canal, arriving at Naples where a car, ordered in Australia, was waiting for them with an Italian chauffeur to drive them overland to London. For Phillip, however, the most vivid memory of that trip was not of museums and monuments, but a brush on the French–Italian border with the French customs who refused them entry because they did not (according to the guards) have all the papers they should have had for the car. The problem was solved by waiting until three o'clock in the morning and then driving across the border at high speed. The French customs gave chase, but the Italian chauffeur entered into the spirit of the thing and out-distanced the pursuers on the narrow and winding coastal road.[39] After that, social life in London must have seemed a little tame. The family returned home by way of Canada, where they once again visited relations.

It was time for Phillip to settle down. The year 1912, he recalls, "passed without much activity of general interest". But it was "a red-letter year for me. I became engaged to be married to Ethel Bigg of 'Swallowfield' near Armidale." They had known one another from childhood but "apart from short social visits" had seen very little of each other.[40] They were married on 2nd April 1913, though not in the

Armidale Cathedral as Phillip says in his memoir, but in the little chapel on the main Bigg property, "Thalgarrah", near Armidale.

The Bigg family also came from English gentry, though there seems to be a more romantic and less steady air about them. According to family legend, a Bigg on his way to the Crusades stole the priest's chair from a parish church in France and was pursued down the main street by the priest shouting a curse that ever after each generation would lose its money and have to make it all over again.

Whatever the truth of that story, Henry Edward Bigg, the eldest son of a clerk in the East India Company who had to leave England for his health, came to Australia in 1857 and set out for the north to make his fortune in Queensland. There, after breaking his leg in a fall from a horse, he fell in love with the daughter of a stockman, Burraston, who brought him back to his hut to look after him. Burraston was an ex-convict, and thus, according to Judith Wright, "firmly kept in the dimmest background when any of us talked about ancestry".[41] His daughter seems to have been a remarkable woman, "although never mentioned in polite society",[42] travelling with her new husband through dangerous country with a mob of sheep to Rockhampton, though that venture failed as did several others. She lost her first baby, a son, from diphtheria in remote Queensland, helped her husband survive fevers, floods and droughts when they finally settled on the Isaac River and was a good mother to the rest of their children. Their luck turned in 1875: a Bigg aunt in England committed suicide and left money to her nephew not long after he and his wife had come south to settle in New England and become members of New England society.

There were other interesting and shadowy figures on Judith Wright's mother's side: John Dougan, for instance, who belonged to a well-connected English family, went to the West Indies just before the end of slavery there and is said to have freed his own slaves before slavery was officially banned and to have lost £180,000 by doing so. He married a Creole woman, part-Spanish and very beautiful. Her great-granddaughter married and came to Australia in 1870 where her elder daughter, Angela, married the ship's doctor, Percy Spasshat, probably from a Huguenot family. He set up a practice in Armidale, built a house which still survives there, and fathered three daughters before dying of typhoid after a 100-kilometre ride to look after a patient. One of these daughters, Mabel, married Alfred Edward Bigg, and their eldest daughter, Ethel, was Judith's mother.[43]

This great-grandmother, Angela, was still alive in Judith Wright's childhood. She was a very beautiful woman, even in her eighties, and cultivated. Angela was a different kind of figure, however, from the powerful May Wright, being relatively poor. When her husband died she opened a small boarding school in the house her husband had built in Armidale, teaching the daughters of the local gentry the basics, but also extras like music and French. As Judith Wright remembered her in her old age, Angela lived in genteel poverty and Judith's mother used to bring her fruit, eggs and cream from "Wallamumbi". Judith also remembered the beautiful dresses this grandmother used to make for her, especially one, "a lovely petunia colour, done in feather stitch" which her mother would not let her keep, making her give it away because it was "too grown up".[44]

To counterbalance this exotic strain in their inheritance, however, the Bigg family also cultivated religion. At "Thalgarrah" they built the little weatherboard church (still standing) in which family weddings, christenings and funerals took place and in which Ethel Bigg was married to Phillip Wright on 2nd April 1913.

One of Judith Wright's poems reflects on her parents' wedding photograph:

> *Ineloquent, side by side, this country couple*
> *smiling confettied outside the family house –*
> *he with his awkward faun-look, ears spread wide,*
> *she with her downward conscious poise of beauty;*
> *surrounded, wished-for, toasted by your clans*
> *in the last threatening calm before the wars.*[45]

Judith recalls her mother's "lovely long black hair and her beauty", an echo perhaps of her Creole ancestry.[46] As for her father, he was a young man of great expectations, the favourite son of his formidable mother.

Phillip and Ethel's honeymoon was suitably imperial. They went to Japan, travelling on the *Empire* which called at Thursday Island, Darwin, Manila, Hong Kong and Shanghai, reaching Japan in cherry blossom time. There they stayed for five weeks, travelling around the country, Phillip marvelling at the pace at which Japan was "quickly assimilating Western ideas". The return trip, however, was not so pleasant. This time they were on a German ship, the *Scharnhorst*, and, according to Phillip, they found the Germans "offensive and disagreeable". Every night the officers would drink a toast to "Der Tag", the day on which war would be declared on England. Nor did the ship come up to British standards of hygiene, being infested with cockroaches, or to British standards of decency: steaming along the Chinese coast to Hong Kong, the *Scharnhorst* rammed and sank a large sampan. Instead of stopping to pick up the crew struggling in the water, however, the ship sailed on. No doubt the sailors would have been picked up by one of the other sampans nearby but this behaviour confirmed Phillip Wright's views of the "arrogance" of Germans and the "over-bearing" way in which they treated native peoples.

The Wrights did not enjoy their time ashore in FooChow. Not only were the streets "the repositories of the rubbish and filth" of the surrounding houses, but the people there were hostile, regarding them "with obvious dislike as 'foreign devils'". Even the "hordes of mangy mongrel dogs ... bared their teeth and growled at [them] in a most alarming manner, thus doubly emphasizing the general antagonism."

The elements seemed to be against them, too. While they were in the city a storm blew up and by the time they got to the waterfront it was so bad that the owner of the sampan they had engaged to bring them to and from the ship refused to take them until the winds died down. The ship was due to sail within the hour and would not wait for them, so the situation was desperate. Then Phillip remembered the Police Chief, who had come on board when they first anchored to check their papers, "a fat genial Chinese with a gorgeous long pigtail". Finding out where he lived, they went there and appealed to him. He ordered his own sampan man to take them back to the *Scharnhorst*, which the man did, though obviously terrified and reluctant.

Thence they sailed to Singapore where they boarded a Dutch ship for Batavia, connecting with the appropriately named *Empire* which took them back to Sydney. They took the train to Armidale and then returned to "Wallamumbi", which had been added to and altered for them while they were away.[47]

Not long after their return, Phillip's eldest brother, Arthur, died of pneumonia, having contracted sunstroke on a visit to one of the family's new stations, "Kindon" in the Goondiwindi district. He had been his mother's right-hand man and had managed the family's affairs with her since his father's death. Now, since his other brother, Cecil, had moved out on his own, Phillip had to take over. It was, as he put it in his memoirs, "a big assignment",[48] taking him away from home a great deal to travel between the different properties the family owned. It also involved him in a court case to get possession of a mob of cattle he had contracted to buy during the drought of 1914, but which the previous owner refused to sell when the rains came.[49]

The outbreak of war in 1914 increased Phillip's burdens as men flocked to join the forces. "Those who held back," he recalls, "were treated as cowards and given the treatment of the white feather by zealous patriots ... Most of my friends and contemporaries offered their services, and as time went on my position became almost unbearable."[50] But he felt that he had to stay and look after the family interests. A bad knee, the result of a football injury at school, also meant that he probably would have been rejected anyway. It was not an easy time, especially as two of his wife's brothers had enlisted and were soon to go overseas. When the Conscription Referendum was held in 1916, however, he campaigned in favour of a "yes" vote, hoping that "if carried, I would be told where my duty lay".[51] In fact it was not carried. But when the Great Waterfront Strike broke out in 1917, Phillip went to Sydney and worked driving cargo wagons to and from the wharves to keep the war effort going.[52]

For his wife, Ethel, this must have been a lonely time. "Wallamumbi" was some fifty kilometres from Armidale – a considerable distance in those days when the roads were poor and travel slow – and the mail came only once a week. They did have a telephone, but it was a party line – one ring for the post office, two for "Wongwibinda", three for "Wallamumbi" and so on, so that a ring was heard in all these places and anyone who cared to do so could eavesdrop. May Wright was a formidable mother-in-law and Ethel Wright often hesitated to get in touch with her own family, believing that May listened to the conversations. She was probably also waiting anxiously for her daughter-in-law to produce a child, which did not help. It was not until 31st May 1915, two years after Phillip and Ethel's marriage, that a child was born at "Thalgarrah", Ethel's family's home, a girl, Judith Arundell Wright. Two and a half years later Ethel bore a son, Bruce, and in 1918, another son, Peter. The dynasty was secure.

So Judith Wright was born into the heart of the pastoral tradition, one of settlement, energy and prosperity, though a prosperity won against the odds. As she wrote in "For a Pastoral Family", she owed much

> *to the forerunners, men and women*
> *who took over as if by right a century and a half*
> *in an ancient difficult bush ...*

She was never to forget this debt, however she was to be troubled by its ambiguities. As she wrote to her brothers:

> *Our people who gnawed at the fringe*
> *of the edible leaf of this country*
> *left you a margin of action, a rural security,*
> *and left to me*
> *what serves as a base for poetry,*
> *a doubtful song that has a dying fall.*[53]

In a way, this "doubtful song" had begun in her two earliest memories, at the woodheap and at the bonfire; memories of ambiguity:

> *For the good of the Old Country,*
> *the land was taken; the Empire had loyal service.*
> *Would any convict us?*
> *Our plea has been endorsed by every appropriate jury.*[54]

Implicitly, even then, however, she was not so sure.

CHAPTER II

THE WORLD AND THE CHILD

> ... Nothing is named;
> nothing is ago, nothing is not yet.
>
> from "The World and The Child",
> *Collected Poems*, p. 36

We learn who we are by being in place, even more perhaps than by being in time. All her life Judith Wright has related to the landscapes of childhood. Parents are crucial, too. She recalls her father as "a very impressive person",[1] gentle as well as strong. Her cousin, Tina, remembers hearing him comforting his wife, Judith's mother, helping her through an asthma attack one night when Tina was staying with them.[2] Judith's memories of him are similar:

> ...*the smell of a tweed shoulder sobbed-on,*
> *through picnics, scoldings, moralities imparted*
> *shyly, the sound of songs at a piano —*
> *through all I had to learn and to unlearn.*[3]

The bond she established with him was to remain for the rest of her life. Judith's relationship with her mother was more painful. Spanish influenza contracted when Judith was four left Ethel more or less an invalid for the rest of her life. Her daughter's recollections of her are poignant:

> *... pointing out birds or pansies' eyebrows,*
> *gentle, fighting increasing pain – I know her*
> *better from this averted girlish face*
> *than in those memories death cut so short.*
>
> *That was the most important thing she showed us –*
> *that pain increases, death is final,*
> *that people vanish.*[4]

The story of Ceres and Persephone is reversed: it is the mother, not the daughter, who is fading away into the darkness. There were also moments of extraordinary joy, however. When she was well Ethel would take the children into the orchard to pick fruit. As Judith remembers these times:

> Planted, evidently, years before I was born, the orchard was in its full beauty of flowers and fruit ... From mid-spring to the fall of the last pears and apples, it was a kind of Eden, with more variety than the first reported garden had. Cherries, peaches, apricots, yellow and brown-skinned pears, sweet red Jonathan apples and green cooking apples all grew there on the innocent days before the Fall and the arrival of fruitflies and other pests which spoiled its harvests.

There they "picked and picked until the house's baskets were full, and [their] hands and faces sticky with juice".[5]

But most of the time Judith's mother spent indoors, directing the work of the household when she was able to do so, or when she was ill lying in her room or on the sofa in the living room. As a result, many of Judith's memories of her are "sort of blacked out":[6] "there was always this pain, this sense of being cut off from her in a way because often when I wanted to talk to her she was just not available".[7]

The house was her domain, the woman's domain in the country. But for Judith it was not a place of intimacy, a cradle where life begins and then is enclosed and protected, but cold and dark. Partly there were architectural reasons for this. The house at "Wallamumbi" faced south, away from the sun and light and was freezing in winter. It was rambling and uncomfortable. The original house, having been built in the early days as a kind of fortress against the weather and the Aborigines, had been added to several times, so that now it was on a series of levels with draughty passages and corridors connecting them. In Judith's memory it seemed in this way to be turning its back on life:

> With a whole landscape to choose from, it [faced] ... to the southeast from which the more chilly and damp weather blew, and was divided by a corridor, the hall, which conducted the cold air from the front right through to the back. The rooms each side of this hall were surrounded by deep verandahs, which shaded them from all sun and, like its south-east aspect, seemed to assert that the house had been built in a tropical climate ... The darkness of the whole house was depressing.[8]

There were a few warm places in it, however: the kitchen was welcoming not only because of the "long iron range, polished to black satin and hazed with heat for the fire that burned all day and was banked with heavier wood at night" but also because of the "girls" who worked there – orphans who had been brought out from England by May Wright on one of her visits to England as a "sort of private Fairbridge Foundation", as Judith put it. The Foundation was an English scheme to assist disadvantaged young people by bringing them to Australia. At "Wallamumbi" they were trained as domestics as well as being educated – and properly paid for their work, which was not always the case elsewhere. The laundry where they worked, pushing "great white hills of sheets down into the soap-foamed copper or heav[ing] them out again, or thump[ing] wool-greasy work-clothes over the wash boards",[9] was also warm and welcoming. The child loved their lively company and their gossip – much more interesting than anything she heard at family gatherings.

But mostly she did not feel happy indoors. "Outside and Inside were clearly divided into layers separating people and functions",[10] and she preferred Outside. Inside everything had to be clean "since a fear of germs had ... overtaken us, with [her] Mother's illness ... attributed vaguely to those malicious influences".[11] Inside she was supposed to be a good girl, to learn to sew and knit, help with the housework and play with dolls and keep scrapbooks. Judith found this boring, especially as, ill as she was, her mother seemed "inactive and lacking in authority"[12] – already, as her earliest memories suggest, Judith was claiming the authority to be herself. Although looking back, she realised that this must have added a great deal to her mother's isolation and loneliness as her illness got worse,[13] she had no intention of being a "good little girl", especially as she was aware that the fact that she was a girl had been a disappointment to her parents.

Outside was the men's world where girls were not really supposed to go but which Judith was determined to share. She used to follow the men about as they worked close to the house, and was even allowed from time to time to go with them when they rode out over the property checking on the stock or on the state of the fences or, even more occasionally, when they went mustering. Later, even after she became deaf, she could still recall their voices yarning around the camp fire. So it is the voice of Jack Purkiss, a stockman who worked for them for many years, "one of the most conscientious men I ever had to do with", according to her father,[14] which speaks in "South of My Days".[15] Ted Chalker, "an unusual character and one of the old school of bushmen"[16] was also the model for the much misunderstood poem "Bullocky". As Judith realised later, she must have been a nuisance, but she was a lonely child, especially when her brothers were small, and the men were kind and let her tag along.

When she was old enough to do so, she learned to ride. She was never as good with horses as were her cousins, her Uncle Cecil's children, but after her morning lessons she would spend most of her free time exploring the property on horseback taking her lunch with her, though her pony Tommy had an unfortunate habit of eating it when she was not looking. But while she was small she spent most of her time around about the house and the way she describes this time in her autobiography suggests the sense of stability and of belonging to the life of the station which the various outhouses gave her. If as "The World and the Child" puts it,

> *Out of himself like a thread the child spins pain*
> *and makes a net to catch the unknown world,*[17]

here she found a series of rich and abiding images to soothe the pain.

There was, first of all, the storehouse, with its lead-lined boxes of tea, bags of flour and of white and brown sugar, tins of treacle and

"Cocky's joy" (golden syrup), bars of yellow, mottled, homemade soap and other household goods. Upstairs was another storeroom, reached by an outside staircase, where apples and other fruit and vegetables were stored on long shelves. Next door stood the little sentry smokehouse for curing bacon and ham, "with its atmosphere treacly and deep, mixed with the smells of the various spices of enticing perfumes,"[18] and next to it the dairy where she learned to make butter, turning the handle at an even pace to separate the cream from the skim milk which then went to the pigs. Country children learn to work early, and this may be why when Judith had a child of her own she was determined that her daughter would be allowed to enjoy herself.[19] Beside the dairy was the shed where the bags of bran and pollard for the fowls were stored.

Judith's favourite was the blacksmith's shop under the pine trees beyond the house where the horses stood shifting, uneasily, waiting their turn to be shod while inside, the mysteries of fire, which had always fascinated her, were celebrated:

> The suck and sigh of the bellows, the glowing and fading of the charcoal, and of the iron heating in it, the black soot which darkened the iron walls and the roof and the earth floor where my bare feet were soon blackened too, and the holes in the iron of the walls and roof which shone like stars in the dark height of the roof.[20]

Not every place was so sympathetic. She did not much like the machinery shed where the ploughs, the carts, the big old four-wheeled wool wagon and the car, which took them to Armidale to shop or on her mother's frequent visits to the doctor, were housed.

> The cold metal [of the car] smelt unwelcoming, like the chilly underground smells of petrol and oil in the drums that stood near them. I regretted the warm wood smells of the weathered old wagon and cart, their flaking paint and tall wheels with tapering spokes.[21]

Even then, it seems, she was dubious about the values of "progress".

Nor was she fond of what she calls "the deathly side" of station life, "tough, relentless and frightening". The butcher's shop belonged to that side:

> Its earthen floor was piled with sawdust to catch the last drops of blood and fluid from the carcasses on the hooks, but the meat house and its surroundings had a sick smell that never went away however often the place was washed and the sawdust changed.[22]

The sheep and cattle were slaughtered at some distance from the house but the carcasses had to be bled and hung on tall gallows where she could not avoid seeing them. Nor could she ignore the noises of the animals about to be slaughtered. The pigs were the worst. "Unlike the sheep and cattle [they] seemed to know their fate early, and their screams even before the knives appeared were so piercing that everyone knew what was happening." These pigs had been her friends, coming to the edge of the sty to be scratched with a stick or gobbling the kitchen scraps, buttermilk from the dairy and the rotten apples which she and her little brothers fed them. Worse, the little floored slat shed in which they slept with its iron roof looked like a little house, so that "their deaths ... were a little like human deaths".

Like most country children, Judith was familiar with death and blood from an early age. Their violence even invaded the orchard where she and her brothers picked fruit with their mother from time to time:

> Parrots loved the orchard too ... and great flocks of eastern rosellas with their brilliant colours, pounced on it before the fruit was properly ripe and were shot in numbers by my father and whoever else had access to the guns which hung on the office wall. This often made a visit to the orchard a grief for parrot-lovers like myself.[23]

There are two kinds of beginnings, one which is a beginning of a world and another which is a beginning in the midst of a world.[24] Judith Wright's was obviously of the second kind: she grew up in a world which was already given, solid and substantial. Around the house, especially, had been made by her ancestors and was her inheritance. But the land beyond was different, although not, of course, untouched by change:

Invasions of sheep and cattle, ringbarking gangs, fences and timbergetters had altered [the landscape] severely during the seven or eight decades of occupation before I was born. But in the days before machinery, cultivation, artificial pastures and aerial agriculture had changed them, they seemed to me as close to Eden as humans could reach.[25]

It was a very beautiful area, and she "always knew it",[26] her "blood's country", the New England Tableland, with its

> *...high delicate outline*
> *of bony slopes wincing under the winter,*
> *low trees blue-leaved and olive, outcropping granite—*
> *clean, lean, hungry country,*[27]

its trees leaning all one way because of the wind and its dancing grasses and its creeks and rivers

> *fed by white mountain springs*
> *beloved of the shy bird, the bellbird,*
> *whose cry is like falling water*[28]

Then further, beyond the encircling hills at the edge of the plateau, lay

> the great blue sweep of the view from ... Point Lookout to the sea, the mysterious darkness of the rainforest below, the birds and animals whose names and habitats my father knew, the glimpse of the sea beaches beyond as a far horizon, and in the early morning the sight of a level ocean of cloud top lapping to the very edge of the plateau and luminous with dawn rose.[29]

Yet it was also, she felt obscurely even then, a haunted land. It had never been very thickly populated by the Aborigines but because it was high country, ceremonies used to be held there. Many sacred places existed, like the Bora Ring she wrote about in her poem,[30] and a very old carved tree which stood near the woolshed at "Wallamumbi", "signs of an occupation stretching many thousands of years into the past".[31] She was to become more aware of this past later, but even as a child she sensed strange powers within the land. When her brothers were small she would marshal them by the gate and march them down the hill and over the road across the creek to a group of dramatic rocks standing out on the rise. There she would strike the rocks with a piece of iron, striking a spark from them, declaring that that meant she had magical power and from now on they must obey her.[32]

Never a conventional little girl, Judith always wanted to test the boundaries – as her first memories suggest. So a few years after the incident at the woodheap, she decided to climb to the top of the tankstand where the windmill tank stood, "a big iron affair hoisted far above us ... [and] reached by a vertical wooden ladder". It, too, was out of bounds, but she intended to get to the top and did so. Unfortunately, "on the fearful descent" she took too long, was seen, captured and scolded.[33]

Punishment did not daunt her, however. Shortly before this she had gone off by herself to visit the family of one of the stockmen who lived on the other side of the creek some distance away:

> After quite a long walk which entailed crossing the creek – a shallow friendly sandy-bottomed stream with a few deep holes and without a bridge – I arrived at the Cundys' cottage. I was disappointed not to be welcomed as a playmate for the boys, who stood around staring while Mrs Cundy politely served me tea and asked whether my mother knew where I was. It hadn't occurred to me to wonder about this, since in my experience my mother always knew what I was doing, so I replied that she did.[34]

She did not, of course, but the "Big House" was informed immediately and Judith was escorted home in disgrace and shut in the bathroom for punishment. The "Lost Child" was a fear even in the 1920s and all available hands had been out looking for her; the anger was a measure of this anxiety. But she was learning about questioning and longing:

> *Yet what is it that moves? What is the unresting hunger*
> *that shapes the soft-fleshed face, makes the bones harden?*
> *Rebel, rebel, it cries. Never be satisfied.*
> *Do not weaken for their grief; do not give in or pardon.*
> *Only through this pain, this black desire, this anger,*
> *shall you at last return to your lost garden.*

For the moment, however, this "lost garden" was all about her:

> *Where the wild harebell grows to a blue cave*
> *and the climbing ant is a monster of green light*
> *the child clings to his grassblade. The mountain range*
> *lies like a pillow for his head at night,*
> *the moon swings from his ceiling. He is a wave*
> *that timeless moves through time, imperishably bright.*[35]

This was the beginning of her poetry, this world in which

> *I see became I am,*
> *I am became I see.*

As she looked, as Blake would have said, not *with* her eyes but *through* them:

> *In winter dawns of frost*
> *the lamp swung in my hand.*
> *The battered moon on the slope*
> *lay like a dune of sand;*
>
> *and in the trap at my feet*
> *the rabbit leapt and prayed,*
> *weeping blood, and crouched*
> *when the light shone on the blade.*
>
> *The sudden sun lit up*
> *the webs from wire to wire;*
> *the white webs, the white dew,*
> *blazed with a holy fire.*[36]

It gave her a profound sense of belonging. At times, she remembers, she felt as if her father and with him, of course, the whole family, owned the world, "practically the whole of New England".[37] With her brothers she often climbed a tree to watch the sun setting, glorying not only in its splendour but also in the thought that it was setting over their land.[38]

Like all children, however, she had to be educated. They were too far away to attend the local school, though Judith later suspected[39] that the presence of children of Aboriginal itinerants at the school from time to time may have explained why the Wright children were kept at home, learning by correspondence, supervised by their mother when she was well enough, or by one of a succession of governesses who came and went, or by their Aunt Weeta. Lessons arrived every week with the mail from the Blackfriars Correspondence School in Sydney – the work they had done marked and corrected and new work for the coming week. Judith looked forward eagerly to this day. She was good at her work and since her mother was keenly interested in her education, she could at least please her in this.

It was her mother also who first introduced her to poetry, though her grandmother read poetry to them from time to time as well. True, the poetry Ethel Bigg liked was mostly about war or lost love and mostly from newspapers or women's magazines – she had good taste in most things, Judith recalled, but not in poetry.[40] Journals like the *Bulletin* did not come into the house since they were regarded as "lower class".[41] But her mother did encourage her to send her poems to the children's page of the *Sydney Mail*, the first of them being published when Judith was seven. The editor, Ellen May McFadyen, a writer herself, encouraged Judith and kept on publishing her work – letters she wrote about life on a New England station, as well as poems.[42]

Her mother also encouraged her to read. Most stations had a library – "to stop people going mad", as Judith said later – and theirs was a good one. There was, for instance, a full set of Kipling, "not a bad influence on the whole", she thought, "as long as you take him with a grain of salt".[43] But there were also Australian books for children, May Gibbs' stories, for instance, and Norman Lindsay's *The Magic Pudding*, which she loved. There was also a first edition of Miles Franklin's *My Brilliant Career*, whose heroine, Sybylla Melvin, inspired Judith early on with a determination to break away from life in the country and become a writer.[44]

Books offered an escape into another world where she could think and feel what she liked and explore what was forbidden and unknown. Reading also made Indoors inhabitable. Judith would spend hours with a book in some corner she had made her own, alone "away under the furniture … in dusty privacy" or, if the weather was fine enough, outside in a corner of the tankstand or beside the kitchen wall shaded by a friendly tree.[45] But books could also get her into trouble. On one occasion, leafing through Shelley's *Collected Works*, she came upon *The Cenci*, which is a play about incest, and was reading it with interest when her mother discovered her and confiscated it, horrified. Some time later, however, Judith found it on the top of her mother's wardrobe, took it down and finished it.

> Like many women at the time, [Judith wrote later] Ethel Wright was preternaturally embarrassed by the subject of sex, about which I knew virtually nothing before I went to school (and little after it) though I did know enough to know she was evading the subject. No child brought up on a station where cattle were bred could be as without anatomical knowledge as she seemed to assume I was, let alone some inkling of physiology. But in spite of the fact that Outside was ... my favourite ambience, I failed to connect it with Inside, and I suppose a good deal of my ignorance was connected with my mother's own obvious reluctance.[46]

There was one last warm image, however, which she associates with her mother. Ethel's health continued to deteriorate and in 1925 when Judith was nine and a half the doctors pronounced that her mother might not live through another New England winter and needed to go away to a warm climate. A tropical cure was proposed. With a relation as companion to look after the invalid, the family took the train to Brisbane and sailed from there to Singapore, then to Surabaya in what was then the Netherlands East Indies.

Sailing along the Queensland coast, Judith saw the Great Barrier Reef for the first time. Afterwards she recalled "the marvellous blue of calm waters, the green islands of the Whitsunday Passage rising out of them and passing by".[47] The tropics also made a profound impression on her, the people of Surabaya especially: "I was in raptures. All this strange vegetation and those marvellous dark laughing people ... and the strangeness of it", though she disliked the colonisers, "those rather awful Dutchmen stalking the streets", the imperial masters.[48]

She came back full of stories but nobody listened to them or to her. Her mother's illness continued, and so did the work of the station and the wider world to which it was linked. But their private world was absorbing. From time to time their father would take them for picnics or camping and would then share with them some of the strange stories he had been told by his Aboriginal nurse, Minnie, whom he had loved. Itinerant Aboriginal people, shearers, station hands or rabbiters, passed through "Wallamumbi" occasionally. On one occasion, told that she must not have anything to do with them because they were "black", she fetched a bucket of whitewash and was about to pour it over them until someone stopped her.[49] Whether or not this really happened, even as a child it seems she was interested in Aboriginal people and their culture and was prepared to cross the boundaries between "them and us".

Beyond "Wallamumbi", almost the only people Judith knew were family. She was close to her cousin, Tina, the one of her Uncle Cecil's five children nearest to her in age. His wife Madeleine was fond of Judith and took care of her often when her mother was ill, so Judith spent a good deal of time at "Dyamberin", their station. Thirty kilometres away, it was at the farthest reaches of Outside in rough country on the edge of the Tableland, in the Falls country. But they seemed to live in a different world. As she recalls, her uncle and her aunt

> *... spoke the tongue of the falls-country,*
> *sidelong, reluctant as leaves.*
> *Trees were their thoughts:*
> *peppermint-gum, black-sally,*
> *white tea-tree hung over creeks,*
> *rustle of bracken.*
> *They spoke evasively,*
> *listened to evident silence,*
> *ran out on people.*

Her aunt was a musician and painter, and her piano

> *scattered glittering notes*
> *of leaves in sunlight,*
> *drummed with winter rains,*
> *opened green depths like gullies.*

Her Uncle Cecil, however, was a great horseman, more of a dare-devil figure than Judith's steady and responsible father. She associated him with

> *... the galloping storms of hoofs*
> *like eucalypts chattering,*
> *or stones hopping on slopes.*
> *Enclosed in the dust of mobs*
> *or swinging and propping*
> *among those ribbony holes*
> *he was happy.*
> *His eyes were as wary,*
> *as soft as a kangaroo's.*[50]

"Wongwibinda", however, was the centre of the family, a place of order, presided over by May Wright, now an old woman but as powerful as ever. Judith remembers her strolling in the garden

> *Flowers of red silk and purple velvet grew*
> *under the humming may-tree; the huge pines*
> *made night across the grass, where the black snake*
> *went whispering in its coils; and moving sunlight drew*
> *copper fingers through the apple-trees.*
> *Warm is the light the summer day refines,*
> *and warm is she, whom life has made secure.*
> *Walking slow along her garden ways,*
> *a bee grown old at summer's end, she dips*
> *and drinks that honey.*[51]

But she also recalls her at work, competent still, in her office

> dark and crowded ... filled with the documents and tied-up bundles of papers, with paperweights and ornaments brought back from trips overseas, from Italy, from England, from France and America; too thickly hung with photographs of prize bulls with ribbons hanging from their necks, with old pictures of tennis-parties, picnic-parties, family gatherings (the ladies in high necks and narrow waists) fossilized for the incurious stare of a new generation.[52]

Life at "Wongwibinda" was ceremonious. May Wright presided over meals in "the long dark room with its great cedar table", its French windows opening onto the verandah with its climbing roses and wisteria and, beyond, the luxuriance of the garden. She

> always liked meals to have a certain dignity, the solemnity of a family ritual. Even in the hardest years, she had managed to preserve something of that dignity in her household, a reminiscence of the great family dinners at Dalwood, where she had once sat as the least of the hierarchy and observed the ceremonies on which [her grandparents] had always insisted.[53]

As a result, Judith knew that, however much she might question that inheritance, she and all the rest of the family would "carry a certain stamp, a mark that singles out even the most distant or rebellious of them for her own".[54] But she remembered her grandmother as "a very beneficent person ... [though] you had to do things right, use elbow grease and no flicking dusters about".[55]

Her strength could be crushing. There was Uncle Arundell from whom Judith took her second name, for instance. He was seldom seen at "Wongwibinda" since he had spent his life in the north looking after the family holdings there – it was he who had sent the telegram from Rockhampton to May Wright telling her that Albert was dying. He had never married. Judith recalls him as

> *an empty cross old man,*
> *alien, denied by all*
> *but the old clocks on the wall.*

Yet she also sensed his loneliness and sense of loss as

> *day by day [he] sat*
> *intent and desolate,*
> *with sharpened lip and eye.*[56]

Aunt Weeta was an even more troubling figure, not only because Judith saw more of her, but also because she was a woman. Her sister Elsie, like her brother Cecil, had broken away, marrying Claude Rowland, who was serving in the Royal Navy during World War I and only returning to Australia much later. But Weeta had never married and lived in the shadow of her aging but still imperious mother.

> *Her room was large enough – you would say, private*
> *from the rest of the house, until you looked again*
> *and saw it supervised by her mother's window.*[57]

Her niece recognised her talent, realising that when Weeta played the piano it was "different from the usual tinkle of ladies".[58] Gradually, Weeta played less and less, and no longer Beethoven but

> *... the pieces her mother liked to hear –*
> *Chopin and Chaminade, In a Persian Market.*

She was also given charge of the practical details of the house, so that her hands were "pricked and blackened" with sewing and household chores, no longer a musician's hands. Her gift for painting had been crushed, also. As a young woman Weeta had won prizes locally and had visited the galleries of Europe. But now she no longer painted.

> *... When they said to her,*
> *"Why not take up your sketching again? So pretty – "*
> *she was abrupt*

and in her room the paintings in which she had taken most pride had their faces turned to the wall:

> *Brushes, paints, Beethoven put aside*
> *(for ignorant flattery's worse than ignorant blame),*
> *she took her stance and held it till she died.*[59]

One senses her niece's admiration at her stand, however little Judith understood it as a child.

Weeta was the spinster aunt, at everyone's service, governess to the family when no other governess was available, and constantly at her mother's beck and call. But her niece sensed a courage and an independence, admiring her stand:

> *I praise her for her silence and her pride;*
> *art lay in both*

even as she was aware also of

> ...a small unnoticed flame –
> grief too unseen, resentment too denied.[60]

It is satisfying to know that when at last in 1929 May Wright died, Weeta learned to drive and used to career around the countryside in a large black Buick visiting her friends, free to enjoy herself as she pleased.[61]

Judith appears to have seen less of her mother's side of the family, probably because her mother was so often ill. What tended to predominate there was "this pain, this sense of being cut off from her in a way because often when I wanted to talk to her she was just not available."[62] So Judith does not write much about "Thalgarrah", the main Bigg station where her parents were married and she was born, or "Swallowfield", where her mother grew up. True, there are the memories of visits to her maternal grandmother Spasshat and the beautiful dresses she used to make. But generally, the Biggs seem not to have interested Judith so much. For one thing, they were religious and often entertained the clergy who came every so often to conduct services in the little church at "Thalgarrah". Judith did not like these clergymen:

> I noticed that though the Good Shepherd and the Lamb of God figured a lot in the church services and the afternoon-tea conversation of the visiting clerics, as they sat in their wicker chairs and took little iced cakes from the best china plates, they didn't seem to know about the real fate of sheep and the duties of those who bred them. The life of action and the life of rather perverted feeling did not match.[63]

For her it was the world of action which mattered, and her feelings came out of it. But memories of this other world returned later.

For the time being it was a privileged but lonely childhood, full of energy, the energy described in "Child and Wattle-tree":

> *Strong as the sun is the golden tree*
> *that gives and says nothing,*
> *that takes and knows nothing;*
> *but I am stronger than the sun; I am a child.*

*The tree I am lying beneath is the tree of my heart,
and my heart moves like a dark bird
among its birds and shadows.*[64]

CHAPTER III

DO NOT WEAKEN FOR THEIR GRIEF: DO NOT GIVE IN

> Yet what is it that moves? What is the unresting hunger
> that shapes the soft-fleshed face, makes the bones harden?
> Rebel, rebel, it cries. Never be satisfied.
> Do not weaken for their grief; do not give in or pardon.
> Only through this pain, this black desire, this anger,
> shall you at last return to your lost garden.
>
> from "The World and The Child"
> *Collected Poems*, p. 36

Ethel Wright died on 3rd September 1927, when her daughter was twelve. As Judith wrote later:

That was the most important thing she showed us –
that pain increases, death is final,
that people vanish.[1]

Her father was to live long and remain important for her, especially as she got to know him better as she grew older. But he had his own loss to cope with. In its stilted way, his autobiography expresses something of his pain:

> To anyone who has not had the experience the sense of deprivation and loneliness following such a loss would be

impossible to realise and for a time I felt there was nothing to be worthwhile living for except my children.[2]

Yet he had his responsibilities, and the woman of the house is essential to the life of any property. He married again, to Dora Temperley of Ballina in November 1928. She, too, came from a colonial background. Her great-grandfather had been the first vicar of Port Macquarie in convict days, and her father was a notable local figure, proprietor of the *Richmond River Times*, founder and chairman of the Independent Cable Association and – something his new son-in-law would have respected – "credited with having been the first to introduce paspalum grass which revolutionised the dairying industry on the north coast".[3]

Judith did not take to her new stepmother; twelve is not the best age for this kind of adjustment. Always close to her father, she must have resented this new woman who was so different from her mother. Where Ethel Wright had been reclusive, "gentle, fighting increasing pain"[4], her stepmother insisted on her position, perhaps because she was not entirely sure of it. A family story has it that the person Phillip Wright really wanted for his second wife was a family friend who had come to look after the household after Ethel's death. She had always admired Phillip and the children liked her. But Phillip bungled the matter, shyly asking her whether she would consider "staying on". She misunderstood, thinking he merely wanted her to stay on as housekeeper, refused and left "Wallamumbi". Not long afterwards, he proposed to Dora Temperley and was accepted. So Judith felt very much on her own.

A succession of governesses had come and gone, though the children had also spent some time with their grandmother, now an old woman, and with their Aunt Weeta, who had also given them lessons. But after her mother's death, reading, writing and her own company became more and more important to Judith, though frightening also, as one of her later poems suggests:

> *To be alone in a strange place in spring*
> *shakes the heart. The others are somewhere else;*
> *the shouting, the running, the eating, the drinking –*

never alone and thinking,
never remembering the Dream or finding the Thing,
always striving with your breath hardly above the
    water.[5]

To others poetry might seem just another ladylike accomplishment and certainly it gave her some standing; before her father married again Judith won first prize in the senior section of the *Sydney Mail*'s poetry competition for the children's page. But poetry was more than that for Judith; it helped her sustain herself and her bond with the world around her, to find her own adolescent energies there:

To hide in a thrust of green leaves
with the blood's leap and retreat
warm in you;
burning, going and returning
like a thrust of green leaves
out of your eyes, out of your hands and your feet –
to turn and to look up,
to find above you the enfolding, the exulting
may-tree
shakes the heart.[6]

At this stage, of course, she could not express these feelings so eloquently as she did later. But the poems she published in the *School Chronicle* when she went to school suggest that these later poems draw on her earlier experiences. "The Gift of Life", for instance, is about spring as her own awakening:

A new translucent green
    From each brown wrapping breaks,
And each new leaf cries to his brother,
    "This is youth, and life, and no other".[7]

It was an awakening also into a largeness of experience beyond the self, as another poem written at school implies:

Children of men go,
    Wondering ever.

> *The words of that music*
> > *Their hearts shall know never.*
> *Sisters are we of the skies and their wonders.*
> > *We, the frail greenlings that wince from the deep*
> *waters thunders.*[8]

She was still an explorer even if now as an adolescent the territory lay within herself. There is pain in these poems, the sense of vulnerability which had been with her since childhood also, and intensified by the loss of her mother, which compounded the normal adolescent fears of death:

> *There's fear in my heart tonight*
> *And Fear chills my hands.*
> *For something walks the house to-night*
> *From unknown lands.*
>
> *I was walking down the hall,*
> *And blue the candle shone.*
> *I turned the corner of the hall*
> *And stood like a stone.*
>
> *There on the door step*
> *As true as I shall die,*
> *Stood a gold-haired woman;*
> *That woman was I.*
>
> *She looked at me smiling.*
> *And I was cold as death.*
> *She slipped past me to the dark*
> *Without a sound or breath.*
>
> *I turned to the empty hall,*
> *But no one was there.*
> *I called myself, I sought myself,*
> *And found the empty air.*[9]

Writing and reading poetry, of course, was associated with the mother who had always encouraged her and thus drew her more powerfully towards these "unknown lands". But it also offered a way out into a larger "real" world. Writing had liberated Sybylla Melvin in *My Brilliant Career*, Miles Franklin's novel, which Judith admired, and she wanted it to do the same for her.

The first step to liberation was education. In the last term of 1928, Michaelmas term, she was sent to board at the New England Girls' School in Armidale. Her favourite cousin, Tina, went with her, but apart from her Judith knew no-one else. At this late stage of the year the other girls had already made their friends and knew the ways of the school, so it was not an easy beginning. Judith's isolated and introverted life so far had not prepared her for a closed community of girls, though she was not alone in feeling like this; many of the girls came from even more isolated stations in Queensland and Western New South Wales. Judith felt awkward and unattractive, "bulging with adolescence, spotty and most uncertain of herself",[10] in contrast with Tina, who was good-looking, gregarious and popular with the boys at the Armidale School, their brother school.

A short story written years later, "Save the First Dance", probably expresses Judith's feelings – a mixture of loneliness and self-defensive patrician disdain:

> What I felt most, when I left home for the boarding-school, was above all how thin, how limited is human character. Brought up deep in the countryside, but fed through a sometimes almost Gothic bookshelf, I had expected more of my companions. Those daughters of department-store owners, businessmen, squatters, whose forbears had driven hoofed herds to … possess an unpassable country, or of politicians too narrow and unused to practice a politics based on anything but sheer self interest … seemed bent only on reflecting their parents' bored commercialism, and finally serving the equally limited men they would marry to their best advantage.
>
> I looked at them, despaired, and became sullen and ugly to protect what was in my own heart. Spinning my cocoon of camouflaged dislike, I learned to live in it.[11]

For all that, NEGS seemed to be unusually enlightened for its time. The curriculum was wide ranging, the teachers well qualified and there was an excellent library. The school also had a strong theatrical tradition and nearly every year staged a large-scale production, ranging from Shakespeare to recent West End successes. There were also smaller productions during the year. Even more unusually, the girls could spend their spare time more or less as they pleased. They could go riding, for instance, or play golf – a nine-hole course had been opened in 1926 by the Chief Justice of New South Wales. Judith was never interested in sport so she spent most of her free time in the library if the weather was wet or cold, or outside among the trees overlooking the golf course if it was fine. She also loved gardening and used to cultivate a plot of her own – illegally, with the connivance of the school gardener. Gardening was not a recognised sport. But she was found out, and that activity ceased, though she still enjoyed talking to the gardener as she had enjoyed talking to the men about the place at "Wallamumbi".

She shone at all her school subjects except mathematics, to which she was "hopelessly resistant",[12] though the fact that later on for a brief time in the late 1940s she was the statistician at the University of Queensland and all her life managed money shrewdly suggests that this might have been an exaggeration. As well as English, French and Latin, at which she excelled, she enjoyed Botany, Zoology and Geology – subjects which had to do with the land she loved. She seems to have been fortunate, too, in her English teacher, Ruth Young, who had joined the staff in 1928, the same year as Judith herself, and recognised the talent of the shy and awkward new girl and encouraged her interest in poetry. Judith also became a member of the *School Chronicle* Committee, which accepted for publication one or two of her poems during her time at the school.

As well as their taking conventional academic subjects, the Headmistress, Miss Dumolo, believed the girls ought to be politically educated. Every year a mock election was held, with returning and presiding officers, poll clerks, rolls and so on. Candidates represented the political parties of the day: the United Country Party, the United Australian Party, the Australian Labor Party and there were one or two Independents. Each candidate had to have a campaign committee and was expected to hold election meetings and defend her position. According to the local newspapers the enthusiasm generated was at least as great as that of a real election.[13]

There is no record that Judith ever stood as a candidate. She was not particularly outgoing and not particularly popular, and she had a reputation for being "a swot" so it is unlikely. As she recalled in the book published to celebrate the school's centenary in 1995, nobody was "much interested in me plagued by acne, grief and social problems" whose only claim to fame was "a capacity for writing verse and ... answering the hard questions in English class".[14] Even if she had been involved in these political exercises, however, judging by one of her poems published at the time, "A Call To Arms", she might not have been a radical; in this poem for once, she seems to have succumbed to imperial feeling, exhorting the "children of the Empire" to

> *Rise up and take your place*
> *With the strong undaunted courage*
> *and fire of your race.*[15]

For most, the real highlight of the year was the school dance in midwinter to which the boys from the Armidale School came. "Save the First Dance" describes the scene:

> The dining hall, cleaned of its tables and draped with bunting in the school colours and pictures of the Royal Family, waited in silence that smelled of polish and French chalk. The mistresses (we would never have said "teachers", which smacked of the town High School) ... [sat] along the north wall below the High Table, greeting the masters of the opposite school only when the heads had met, like liners, in mid-ocean, hooting slightly.[16]

She probably spent much of the night by the wall since, as well as being shy and feeling plain, she wore glasses. Her short-sightedness she had been born with, but "people don't look much at a child, you know",[17] as she said somewhat ruefully. Her problem had only just been discovered, and the glasses made her all the more self-conscious.

In "Save the First Dance" the girl "lost, miserable and defenceless against humiliation" watches the others, in particular the exotic newcomer at the centre of the story, Gisela, "like a splendid pigeon or bird of paradise", the daughter of Dutch-Javanese parents, "sent from somewhere far north to these cold bare buildings". In the story she shatters all the rules and proprieties by wearing jewels, a dress of deep ruby-red velvet with a plunging neckline and rouge, and dancing defiantly with one of the mistresses, "a tall, willow-wand redhead" who had a good degree in science and was reputed to be brilliant and to have "a past".

Whether or not something like this actually happened, the story captures the feelings of a girl sitting by the wall while the others dance, catching glimpses of passionate freedom and beauty she can only dream of, shut out from it by her own awkwardness. When she is finally asked to dance she manages to ladder "immensely, a black stocking severely kicked by a small grey-jacketed partner who tripped and fell in [her] very arms".[18]

School was not a happy time, then, and when her cousin Tina left in 1931, not wanting to stay on to matriculate, Judith felt all the more alone. Tina had been popular not only with the boys at the Armidale School but also with the other girls, so that Judith had relied on her reflected glory. Nevertheless school was a means to the end of liberation. Determined to get to university, she stayed on to get her matriculation, settling down grimly to work.

During the first term vacation something happened which nearly wrecked her plans. One day, as she often did, Judith rode out to meet Tina halfway between "Wallamumbi" and "Dyamberin" where Tina lived, to spend the day together with her in the bush. Judith was never as fearless a rider as her uncle and cousins. A few years earlier, when she was out mustering with them she had fallen and broken her arm on a mountain road when the girth had snapped and she had been thrown off her horse. That accident had left its mark since the arm had mended crookedly, though when the doctor proposed breaking it again to straighten it she had refused to go through it all again. For the rest of her life one arm was slightly out of kilter. But what happened on this ride in the autumn of 1932 was to affect her life even more seriously.

As usual Tina was riding ahead, when suddenly Judith's new pony, Jill, a gift from her father, propped – she had had a heart attack – and crashed to the ground, falling on top of her rider who had just enough presence of mind to shout to Tina to go for help before she lost consciousness.

The nearest help was at least eight kilometres away at "Maiden Creek" where the Frasers, subject of the poem "Brothers and Sisters",[19] lived. So it was a while before they arrived in their rickety old car. In the meantime, lying beside the dead horse, covered with flies and aware that she was badly hurt, Judith drifted in and out of consciousness. When the Frasers arrived the first thing they did was to pour brandy down her throat. This brought her back to consciousness and she recalls swearing as she had never sworn before as the brandy went down and she was aware of the pain before losing consciousness again. With the help of two timber cutters who had been working nearby, Judith was moved into the shade to wait for an ambulance, though during that operation, fortunately, she was unconscious.

It was several hours before the ambulance arrived, her father with it – there was only one ambulance in the town and it had been out on call on the other side of Armidale. When they finally got Judith to hospital, the case was too complicated to deal with there, so she was sent to Sydney by train under the care of the NEGS matron, Sister McGuffog. Judith still remembers being manoeuvred through a window, strapped to a stretcher, into the train.

For the first few days in hospital in Sydney she was in "a wild delirium infested with black spiders ten times more real than actual spiders ever were".[20] That was followed by three tedious months as she lay in bed with a contraption the surgeon had devised to ensure that the bones knitted properly; "a complicated harness and a plaster cast with a billy-can of shot hanging off the end of her leg, twenty pounds of it"[21] to encourage the bones to knit straight. Unable to move, Judith spent her time looking at the birds and the changes of light in the big old Moreton Bay fig outside her room and reading. A schoolfriend of her mother's, Jan Holt, used to visit her nearly every day and bring "everything from Dickens to *The Hunting of the Snark*".[22]

There was plenty of time to think. The accident to her pelvis meant that it would be dangerous for Judith to have children. She would not, as she put it, "be a good breeder"[23] and thus not a good grazier's wife.

This made her all the more determined to get away and become a writer. But she had missed a term at school and fallen behind in her work. She had never liked mathematics, so she decided not to bother with that subject and to concentrate on the others. She did well in them, especially in English, in which she got honours, and was dux of the school. Unfortunately, however, maths was a prerequisite for matriculation and thus entrance to university.

This was another serious setback. But Judith reflected that since she had no intention of becoming a teacher she did not really need a degree. What she wanted and needed was to get away to spend as much time as she could reading in the library in preparation for a career as a writer. So she determined to go to university in any case. It was the height of the Depression, and even though families like hers were not as badly hit as most, wool and beef prices were down and there was little money to spare. May Wright came to the rescue. Her death may have represented an end of an era,[24] but even in death her influence continued. In her will she had left a bequest for her granddaughters' education – the men got the land, so she wanted the women to have education; that bequest would enable Judith to go to university. The assets May Wright had left were mostly in land, however, and it was difficult to realise on land during the Depression when prices were so low.

But Judith's father was an honourable man, determined to honour his mother's will as his brother Cecil, the other executor, also was. They managed to sell some land to raise the money that was needed for Judith. Like many country people, Phillip Wright regarded the city as a wicked and dangerous place and believed his daughter was still too young to go there. So they struck a compromise: she would stay home for a year and help her Aunt Madeleine with the education of her younger daughter. After that she could go to university in Sydney.

In January 1934, Judith Wright left home to enrol in the University of Sydney. She had visited the city from time to time with her father or to stay with her mother's friend who had looked after her when she was in hospital, but she knew it "only round the edges".[25] Now she looked forward to exploring for herself. Her father was anxious and came with her to make sure that she was settled in safely. Remembering how unhappy she had been at boarding school she refused to go to Women's College and would have liked to have found a room for herself. But her father would have none of that. She was to stay with a relation of her stepmother, a Mrs Louat, who ran a boarding house in Mosman, in Military Road not far from the ferry wharf. From there she could go by ferry to the Quay and then catch the tram which ran along Parramatta Road to the university. Her father carefully rehearsed this route with her to make sure. He also arranged an interview with the registrar of the university, noting in his diary that he was "very emphatic in telling Judith that she will be sorry that she did not matriculate and thus cannot take a degree".[26] After that, "fairly well pleased" and confident that she was in "safe hands" and that it was, as she put it, "safe to let [her] loose",[27] her father returned to New England.

Judith, too, was pleased. At the boarding house, where most of the other boarders were clerks or other city workers, she felt that a new world was opening up. She was also, she felt, in touch with the literary world through the elderly lady and her daughter who occupied the top floor. This lady had another daughter, Nina Murdoch, who had published two books of verse and a travel book and was thus "actually an authoress". She was also the founder of the Australian Broadcasting Commission's Argonauts' Club and had travelled in Europe. Though Wright did not ever meet her, the association, she felt, gave "a halo of splendour to the house".[28]

Travelling up Parramatta Road to the university, Wright observed another side of the city and of the Depression. In New England she had seen shabby men, often in broken boots, carrying their swags along the roads looking for work. But in Sydney it was much worse. The Depression there was "grimy, grim and despondent", and its effects were much more evident. The streets in the suburbs around the university were "haunted by hopeless-looking men whose toes showed through their boots, shivering in the winter cold", and the women looked even more desperate, shabbily dressed with hungry looking, raggedly dressed children. As Judith recalled in her autobiography:

> Parramatta Road, with its few private cars (once the more prosperous of the businessmen had got to work), its broken-down

market trucks and the general sootiness and paintlessness condition of its buildings, was bad enough. But to venture beyond it, into fabled Redfern and Newtown, Glebe and Balmain, was to see what the Depression really meant. After one or two such explorations I was glad to leave exploration to itself, at least in the neighbourhood of the University.[29]

Even as a child she had questioned the status quo, but what she was seeing here troubled her much more profoundly. Many of her family and their friends in New England were moving in the opposite direction, to the right. When the New South Wales Premier, Jack Lang, subsequently dismissed by the Governor of New South Wales, repudiated the State's debts to the Bank of England in order to use the money to relieve unemployment, many of them had joined the New Guard, a right-wing organisation which admired the strong-arm methods of dictators like Hitler and Mussolini. But Wright's experiences were making her more aware of life on the "other side of the tracks", so that when she came home for holidays her opinions "turned many of the family into firecrackers".[30]

During the year, unbeknownst to Judith's father, Mrs Louat's boarding house closed down. So Judith found a room for herself near the university on the other side of Parramatta Road. It was pretty basic:

> There was a sort of shower room downstairs, but one had to move out some of the mops and buckets first, and hot water came in a bucket from the wood stove. The dunny in the backyard was not inviting either; and the landlady and her man whose name I never learned were chary with the cleaning and laundry.[31]

But she paid only fifteen shillings a week for it and felt independent at last. There were no cooking facilities, but she ate at the student union or, when it was closed, at a working-man's café nearby. Like George Eliot's Dorothea in *Middlemarch*, she was beginning, she felt, to be aware of "the largeness of the world and the manifold wakings of men [and women] to labour and endurance".[32]

This independence did not last long. Judith's father became uneasy about her and sent a family friend who lived in Sydney to investigate.

When she tracked her quarry down, the friend was horrified: quite apart from its location, Judith's room had only one piece of furniture, a rather frowsy double bed, and papers and pens were scattered everywhere. Though she was not enrolled for a degree, it was exam time and she was taking her work seriously. Defending herself, Judith pleaded economy as her justification and pointed to the church next door with its message to sinners to repent as a sign of respectability. But the game was up and in the new year Judith had to move into Women's College.[33]

Nevertheless, it had been an interesting year. She had spent a good deal of time in the library reading contemporary poetry and fiction as well as the French Symbolists. For academic subjects she took English, History, Philosophy and Psychology. Of these she soon parted company with History, or with the way it was taught – Britain and the Empire, with Australia figuring only as part of the Empire. This was the way she had been brought up to see things, but even as a child she had questioned the right of Empire. She disliked the approach of the Professor, Stephen Roberts, who had little time for things Australian, and she later called his pioneering *History of Australia* "that bloody book. Not a word about anything but trouble with the natives … and not a word about our justification or otherwise for taking the land".[34]

Judith did not like Psychology much either, since it was mainly an introduction to statistical method and was behaviourist in its approach. But it was a prerequisite for Anthropology, which she took in second year, and the methods she learned were to prove useful later in her career. She also found English, her other first-year subject, fairly conservative, since it concentrated on Chaucer and Shakespeare and the history of the English language – honours students also studied Anglo-Saxon. There were two professors: Sir Mungo McCallum was approaching retirement, but Professor Waldock was younger. Like most of the other women students Judith was fascinated by him:

> It was [he] we fixed our eyes on. Tall, youngish (or so he seemed), pale with a gesture that raised the wings of his academic gown in angelic flight. Shakespeare with him was more of a passion than a subject … Sitting with the other women in Arts I sometimes heard some collective sighs rising at the more moving declarations.[35]

She could not, however, imagine him even knowing the name of Nina Murdoch or of any other Australian writer for that matter – Australian writing was not regarded as literature.

But another lecturer, Guy Howarth, was interested in contemporary literature and introduced his students to

> daring modern authors like Eliot and startled us into argument. There was no arguing with Waldock and Shakespeare; but *The Waste Land*, patients etherised on tables as images for sunsets, smells of steaks in passageway, were new notions of poetry to struggle with. I didn't find any other students who had come to University with the idea of being poets, and our arguments were not very informed, but I brooded over Eliot and Hopkins with real excitement.[36]

Howarth was later to complain that none of his students was influenced by his lectures, but Wright seems to have been. She was even secretly experimenting with "free verse and linguistic entanglements I fondly imagined were Hopkinsian" and trying to get them published and when they were rejected consoling herself with the thought that "Australia was no place for experiment".[37]

Her other first-year subject was Philosophy, taught by Eric Partridge, John Anderson and John Passmore (who recalled her later as a keen and proficient student[38]); she was to remain interested in philosophy for the rest of her life. Her teachers were stimulating and went on to distinguished careers. John Anderson, perhaps the best known if not necessarily the best philosopher, was just at the beginning of his controversial career. He used to take his students to the Trades Hall where they would listen to fiery speeches and sing "The Red Flag" and to the New Theatre for readings of left-wing plays like Clifford Odet's *Waiting for Lefty*. But he was always the enemy of dogmatism and his scepticism about the high political passions of the day seems to have had its effect on her.

Besides, she had many other interests. A young woman from the country, for the first time she was beginning to enjoy herself socially.

> There was a lot of living to be done [she wrote in her Autobiography] and as I moved into my 19th year I felt I was well

behindhand with this. Fairly astute over how to get where I
wanted to be, I made friends with beautiful girls ... tagging along
... picking up male crumbs from their table.[39]

One of these was Cecily Nixon. With her "extraordinary depths of green eyes and her wide white smile in a tanned face"[40] she was usually surrounded by admirers, and some of them, Judith discovered, were prepared to console themselves with her company. Cecily's mother liked her daughter's friend and encouraged her to bring Judith home. A graduate and an "advanced woman", she talked frankly about sex and social life generally, teaching Judith more than her mother ever could or would have done – important for a young woman determined to enjoy herself.

In those days there were only about five thousand students at the university and most students who were socially inclined got to know one another even if they were in different faculties. Living in college, as Judith did after first year, was a help also. As Donald Horne remembered it, Sydney University was a privileged place:

> Most [students] were there because their parents had enough money to buy them careers as doctors, lawyers, dentists or engineers. At its top the University was embedded in the gentility of the Establishment; its governing body was largely controlled by important judges and doctors from downtown and some of the professors were members of Sydney society. Orthodoxy was prized and most University men and women were expected to keep their feet solidly on the firm base provided by the unchallengeable wisdom of Sydney ... Most student activities seemed to be dominated by the more conventional men and women from the private schools and the "good suburbs".[41]

Wright came from the country, but she belonged to this world, however much she questioned it. Most of her boyfriends were privileged also, studying medicine or law – she preferred medical students, she said, because in those days before the contraceptive pill they knew how to be "careful".[42]

There were still some social difficulties, with money and clothes especially. The dresses Judith had brought with her from the country were decidedly unfashionable, mostly made by aunts or bought by her stepmother, who could not sew or knit. Judith decided to spend money, very quickly acquiring "a dress-maker and a knowledge of Farmers' store". Even if "not beautiful like [her] friends" she was soon fashionably dressed. But she forgot that her bank statements went to her father. When he discovered her extravagance he was horrified and "pulled [her] up sharply". Nevertheless she felt she was "ahead of the game"; and the "clothes were worth the money" and the dressing down by her father.[43]

To her surprise, too, Women's College proved different from boarding school; much more agreeable socially and a free place. In June of her first year there, Camilla Wedgwood was appointed principal to succeed Susannah Williams, who had been in that position since 1919. Wedgwood was a remarkable woman, and a fine role model. She came from the distinguished English family which had also produced Charles Darwin and, in the twentieth century, Ralph Vaughan Williams. She had read Anthropology at Cambridge and later at the London School of Economics under Bronislaw Malinowski, and after a temporary lectureship at Bedford College in 1928, had come to the Department of Anthropology in Sydney. When that contract expired she went to the University of Cape Town and then to do field work in New Guinea, returning from there to Sydney to the Anthropology department in 1935.

She was an inspiring figure to any young woman interested in ideas: there were very few women working in universities those days but she had been successful there. Moreover, she seems to have been relaxed as a college principal. According to Judith, she "did not care what you did so long as you did not forget your poetry" for the poetry readings held in the Common Room every Sunday evening.[44] Wedgwood's Quaker inheritance had also given her a social conscience. She was aware of what was going on in Nazi Germany and elsewhere in Europe, and as one of the founders of the German Emergency Fellowship Society, she tried to bring Jewish victims of Hitler's persecution to Australia and help them settle here. She influenced Judith's thinking on the matter.

It may also have been Wedgwood's influence which turned Judith to Anthropology, which she took in second and third years. The only Anthropology course in the southern hemisphere, it concentrated on

Aboriginal culture and society, something Judith had begun to be aware of as a child listening to her father's stories. Professor P. R. Elkin was one of the pioneers in this field, and his interests were sociological and even political, not merely academic, as he tried to draw the attention of governments and bureaucrats to the plight of Aboriginal people – though, it is true, with limited success. He did however, give his students an appreciation of the richness and diversity of Aboriginal cultures.

He was a dry lecturer, Judith recalled, but "a good man if ever there was one" and passionate about his subject, and when he was roused about the injustices from which Aboriginal people suffered, "like the Uniting Church in full flight".[45] In retrospect she realised that his approach was assimilationist, though it was his argument that "we non-Aboriginals had to assimilate to them, not the Aboriginal people to us".[46] The other lecturer, William Stanner, was doing ground-breaking field work in the Northern Territory, studying the complex systems of Aboriginal kinship which were only just beginning to be recognised. As Judith remarked later, though she may not have realised it then, he understood that "Aborigines and higher mathematics had been friends from the beginning".[47]

All this was of great interest to a young woman from a pastoral family whose father had a feeling for the Aboriginal past and whose paternal grandfather (as she later discovered) had been unusually interested in the Aboriginal people, the Wadja on whose land he had settled along the Dawson River in Queensland. This interest in and commitment to Aboriginal people and their culture was to stay with her for the rest of her life. She continued her reading and met Stanner again when he worked with her and Nugget Coombs on the Aboriginal Treaty Committee in the 1970s. She was also in touch with Elkin from time to time until his death, asking his opinion, for instance, about a book of Aboriginal legends she had been asked to edit in the 1960s, and accepting his advice that to do so would be an act of appropriation.

Judith's other subject was Oriental History, taught by Professor Sadler, a scholar who had lived in Japan and had married a Japanese woman. An enthusiast for his subject, from time to time Sadler would invite students to lunch to meet his wife and enjoy his Japanese garden and collection of Oriental art. At the time the newspapers were full of the Japanese invasion of Manchuria and soon afterwards of China and of talk about the "Japanese menace". Sadler gave them a different view of Japan, indeed of the world, an alternative to the British imperial history on which Judith had been brought up, though, to be fair, her father had liked Japan when he was there on his honeymoon trip. She also came in contact with Japanese aesthetics for the first time.

After she moved into Women's College Judith also became involved in the general life of the university. Despite her glasses, she joined SUDS (Sydney University Drama Society) and appeared in the chorus in one or two plays as well as in the Women's College play. She was not a theatrical success, though she did get to know fellow students like Nigel Lovell and Lyndall Barbour, who were later to become well-known actors, and met Doris Fitton of the Independent Theatre, who came from time to time to help with SUDS productions. Judith was more successful with her writing, however, and became a reporter for the student newspaper *Honi Soit*. In second year she was given charge of a column – "under a pseudonym, of course; women were not regarded very highly"[48] – and next year was made one of the subeditors, though she was to deal only with social reporting, the area to which women journalists were usually confined. The editors, Hugh Gilchrist and Alan Crawford, leading university "intellectuals", were, as she remembers it, "very upstage", and paid little attention to someone who was "just a woman from the country".[49]

She had some poems published during this time, not just in the Women's College magazine but even in *Hermes*, the student literary magazine in which other young writers such as James McAuley and A. D. Hope also published. Judith had not found her real voice yet, and most of her poems were fashionably melancholy or about love. But some of the themes of her mature work were beginning to emerge, and her feeling for the natural world marked her poems out from most of the others who were more modishly influenced by Eliot's *The Waste Land* and urban themes. One of these poems, published anonymously in the Women's College magazine, is typical:

I have made lyrics about Love,
and the white birds on the green tree.

> *I have made lyrics about Love*
> *and lambs in springtime and their glee.*
> *I have made lyrics about Love,*
> *But what is this that has come to me?*
>
> *Oh, is it with such anguish then*
> *That the bird struggles from its sheath?*
> *Is it such struggle and agony when*
> *The young lamb draws its first free breath?*
>
> *I have made lyrics about Love*
> *and flowers swaying with the bee.*
> *I have made lyrics about Love.*
> *But what is this that has come to me?*[50]

Politics was becoming important also in Judith's life. Many students were concerned about events in Europe after Hitler swept to power in Germany in 1933, and later when Mussolini invaded Abyssinia; another world war seemed to be brewing. *Honi Soit* reported a range of lectures and debates about these events, some defending the fascists, impressed by their growing power and passion for efficiency, but most of them highly critical. Memories of the carnage of World War I were still strong and most students echoed the sentiments of the famous motion of the Oxford Union at the time that "in no circumstances would this House die for King and Country". In the ballot held in Sydney in 1935 forty-seven per cent of those who voted, for instance, said they were pacifists, even though they also believed that "war was inevitable under capitalism".

Like many of her contemporaries, Wright was moving to the left. She admitted that the Russians "had made a mess of things" – as her family no doubt pointed out – but she believed that it was "possible to have a more just society". She liked the ideal that communism seemed to her to represent, that "you don't need to do your neighbours in to survive" (which, she thought, was "what it came to in the Depression") and that it is possible to share rather than compete for resources of a social, economic and human kind. Judith was also reading Marx – "not to have Marx on your bookshelf was a sign of a fool in those days" – and regarded Marxism as an "intellectual feat".[51] The war in Spain, which broke out when the army under Franco moved to overthrow the Republican Government, brought these feelings to a head. To many it seemed the beginning of the struggle between left and right – those who wanted change and the defenders of an old, unjust world.

In the meantime, Judith and her friends found time to enjoy themselves. She particularly loved the surf and would often spend days, and sometimes whole nights, on the beach at Bondi. Living in the country and spending only a week or two at her grandmother's cottage at South West Rocks on the Coast near Kempsey, with its "sweet slope of grass edged with the sea",[52] she had never learned to swim, but she loved the water. Years later, when she first saw people water-skiing, she wrote enviously that she had been "born too early. I would have loved it – also I'd love to go under-water fishing".[53] "The Surfer" expresses this fascination with the ocean and for the daring of the swimmer whose

> ...*brown strength drove through the hollow and coil*
> *of green-through weirs of water!*
> *Muscle of arm thrust down long muscle of water;*
> *and swimming so, went out of sight*
> *where mortal, masterful, frail, the gulls went wheeling*
> *in air as he in water, with delight.*[54]

She always enjoyed pushing the limits, and the memory of the daring and erotic freedom of those times have remained with her, as another poem (published in *Poet's Choice 1974* but never reprinted) makes clear:

> ...*Forty years older*
> *I still go surfing, Johnny, still go in*
> *even near sunset. But time's turning over...*
> *Forty years from the first to the last lover.*
> *Lord, what a span for wrestle and kiss to cover.*
> *Who were you then?*
> *Not sure that I remember.*[55]

Judith finished her third year at university at the end of 1936, and since she could not take a degree there was no question of going on to graduate work, which few women did in any case. The world outside was growing even more menacing as Hitler's armies began to mass and the Japanese invaded Manchuria and then China. Time seemed to be running out for her generation:

> *...on the sand the grey-wolf sea lies snarling,*
> *cold twilight wind splits the waves' hair and shows*
> *the bones they worry in their wolf-teeth.*[56]

CHAPTER IV

WHERE IS HOME, ULYSSES?

> The hard inquiring wind strikes to the bone
> and whines division.
>   Many roads meet here
> in me, the traveller and the ways I travel ...
> Where's home, Ulysses?
>
> from "For New England",
Collected Poems, p. 22

After all she had seen, learned and done, Judith could not go back to live in New England. There was nothing, she felt, for her there. But where to go? Without a degree she could not go on to further study, though she would have liked to have done graduate work in anthropology. But she did not see herself as an academic. To her, academics seemed merely to circle "around the things [she] wanted to know"[1] and to live limited lives. Yet she wanted and needed to be independent and did not expect the family to support her. She could not support herself, she knew, as a writer, and certainly not as a poet. But jobs were still scarce, especially for women. Apart from teaching and nursing, which did not appeal, for middle-class women there was only secretarial work, and that was not plentiful; though newspapers were saying that the Depression was nearly over, unemployment was still around seventeen per cent and far higher for women.

Before she settled down to earn her living, she wanted to see the world – there was still enough of her grandmother's legacy to get her to

Europe, though she would have to be frugal. It would not be the kind of Grand Tour taken by earlier generations of the family, whose relics were in the trunks in the storeroom at "Wallamumbi". But as Judith and her friends realised, war was coming, a war which would affect them all, and "overseas was where it was all happening".[2] It was important to see Europe before it disappeared. In any case, there seemed to be little for intelligent young people to do in Australia, and many of Judith's friends were also going away – Christina Stead's *For Love Alone* captures the desperation which drove them to do so. Judith, it was true, was not quite so desperate. For one thing, even if she was not yet able to express it, she felt she belonged to the land; as she was to put it later,

> ... *the long slopes' concurrence is my flesh*
> *who am the gazer and the land I stare on*,[3]

and this feeling bound her, however much she might want to break away. Besides, going overseas was not such a declaration of independence for her as it was for many others. By now it had almost become a family tradition for each new generation – her cousin Tina, for example, had just left for London. With her inheritance, going to England was part of finding out who she was and where she came from:

> *Sullenly the jealous bones recall*
> *what other earth is shaped and hoarded in them*,[4]

calling her to explore the other side of the world from which her family had come. For once, tradition was on her side.

In 1937, King George VI – who had succeeded his elder brother Edward, forced to abdicate over his love for a divorced woman, Mrs Simpson – was to be crowned, and the *Sydney Morning Herald* reported breathlessly that the coronation was to cost £454,000, adding loyally that this would provide work for the unemployed. As a boy Judith's father had revelled in the glories of an earlier coronation, Edward VII's, and it pleased him to think that his daughter would keep up the imperial connection. He bought her a ticket for the ceremony (though there is no record that she actually used it), thinking it a good year for her to visit England. Often in the past, standing "deserted on the wharves", she had *watched the ships fan out their web of streamers,*[5]

taking friends or relatives away to the other side of the world; now she was to follow them. She sailed in February 1937 on the *Moreton Bay*, a one-class ship, accompanied by a distant relative, Grace Cardale, fifteen years older, but someone she had always liked. Grace had looked after Judith and her brothers sometimes as children when their mother was ill. In any case she seems to have left Judith free to enjoy herself on the ship, and they parted company when they reached London, Grace to visit relatives and Judith going her own way.[6]

The "double tree" was beginning to branch out, and Judith decided to explore its Scottish as well as its English roots. Growing up she had heard mostly from Grandmother May Wright about her side of the family, the Wyndhams, but now Judith wanted to find out more about the Wrights, her dead Grandfather Albert's family. She set out in a battered little car with her university friend, Cecily Nixon, who had reached London after her, to tour the MacGregor country (the Wrights had originally been MacGregors before they fled to France after the collapse of the 1745 rising). They drove through the Highlands, staying at little inns, talking to the local people, posing for photographs by lochs and in picturesque glens, coaxing the aging car up and down mountains and along narrow roads until it finally broke down for good.

Cecily went back to London, having things to do there. But Judith decided to take "a sort of walking tour" of Scotland, hitchhiking since money was short. She enjoyed herself thoroughly, catching rides mostly with truck drivers, travelling in this way from Aberdeen to Edinburgh and then south through Yorkshire back to London.[7] Whether she reported these adventures to her father we do not know, but one suspects not.

On her way south Judith called on some of the Wyndham relatives. They welcomed her but, she suspected, found their young Australian relative "a bit shocking". Reflecting on the letters George Wyndham and his wife Margaret had written back to England from the Hunter Valley in the 1830s and 1840s, which had been destroyed not long before on the death of Great Aunt Charlotte who had looked after them, Judith felt that "a great deal of history [had thus] vanished up the spout",[8] beginning to suspect that the Australian connection mattered less to the English side of the family than the British connection did to the Australian side – May Wright had treasured the letters from "Dinton", the family seat in Wiltshire, which had been discovered at "Dalwood". In this way, Judith was beginning to realise where her own deepest loyalties might lie, and this realisation was to underlie her poems in the 1940s. It also gave her sympathy for the remittance man she wrote about in one of those poems:

> *The spendthrift, disinherited and graceless,*
> *accepted his pittance with an easy air,*
> *only surprised he could escape so simply*
> *from the pheasant-shooting and the aunts in the close;*
> *took to the life, dropped easily out of knowledge,*
> *and tramping the backtracks in the summer haze*
> *let everything but life slip through his fingers.*[9]

She then made another foray into family history, a trip to Cornwall where her MacGregor ancestor and his wife had settled under the name of Wright when they returned clandestinely to England, and loved the coast, the little fishing villages and the legendary Arthurian countryside. From Cornwall she returned to London, where she stayed until she left for the continent with Cecily Nixon.

In London she met up again with a young New Zealander, Tony, whom she had first met on the ship coming over. He was very different from most of the young men she had met previously; he was a farmer, from the south of the South Island, but not like the country men she had known. During the long winters when there was nothing much else to do, he used to knit Fair-Isle sweaters from his own wool to sell. Judith found him "very undemanding and pleasant to be with".[10]

London was an exciting place, crowded that year with people from all over the world. As well as the coronation an Imperial Conference was held that same year, attended by Indian and African potentates in splendid traditional robes as well as the blue-suited politicians and officials from Canada, Australia, New Zealand and South Africa. The Depression seemed far away as Judith and Tony explored London, went to parties and dances, sometimes sleeping the night on the Embankment as many others were doing that warm and festive summer.

When Judith left for the continent Tony went on to the United

States and then later to South America where he gained his flying licence – his aim all along. But when war broke out in 1939 he returned to England, enlisted in the Royal Air Force (RAF) and was later shot down over the Baltic. She remembered him in a poem, "To A. H., New Year 1943", published in *Meanjin* in 1943 but not republished after that:

> *In an uneasy year, in a loaded spring*
> *there yet was laughter and dancing and some kindness.*

The poem also recalls him as someone "with a direct mind", who,

> *. . . intolerant of madness,*
> *found everywhere the pleasant and the gentle*
> *and made them your friend,*[11]

a figure of ironic self-possession. But later, in "Letter to a Friend", published in *Meanjin* in 1949 after the first atomic explosions at Hiroshima and Nagasaki, she remembered him differently, recalling his memory almost enviously since he no longer lived in "a time bomb world", mourning someone who had become a legend rather than an actual person:

> *Darkness the enemy, flowering upwards*
> *from the sea-depth, from the earth bottom,*
> *enfolded you; night has eaten*
> *your blood and your bones and your words;*
> *night the old enemy, rising*
> *to swallow the light of our day.*[12]

Despite the glitter of London that coronation summer there was also a sense of this darkness approaching. Germany's military might was growing, and Hitler's parades and frenzied speeches were becoming more and more aggressive. Italian bombs were raining down on Abyssinia and with the war in Spain going badly for the Republicans, the British Prime Minister, Neville Chamberlain, announced that Britain would spend £1,500,000 on armaments – a huge sum then – over the next five years. Picasso's agonised painting, *Guernica*, inspired by the destruction of the Basque town by Nazi dive-bombers, spoke of the sense that gripped many at the time that some new and dreadful savagery had been let loose and that a world war, even more brutal than the last, was coming.

Nevertheless Judith had not forgotten her ambition of becoming a writer. She had no contacts in the literary scene, but she was reading what was being published and trying to meet writers in London. The Australian writers, Vance and Nettie Palmer, were in London at the time, just back from Spain where their daughter Helen was driving an ambulance for the Republicans. Judith did not know them, however, and probably did not meet them, though they were to become friends in the late 1940s. But she did meet briefly the poet and editor John Grigson and some friends of John Cornford, the young poet just down from Cambridge who had gone to Spain to join the International Brigade and was killed there. Like most of the people she met, she was deeply concerned about this struggle and read W. H. Auden's long poem "Spain", written to help the Republican cause. As she wrote later, this war was to them a kind of test case;

> the first real break in the conscience of Europe ... Should a government be pulled down just because it was Socialist! Should people support dictators because they have property themselves and dictators represent property. To pull down a whole government just because you had something to protect [is] to impose the rule of the monied. These are still important questions.[13]

The kind of patriotism which had gloried in burning the Kaiser in effigy in 1918 was still abhorrent to her so that when later, on the outbreak of war, Auden and his friend Christopher Isherwood left England to live in the United States, she defended their decision, even though she was no great admirer of Auden's poetry (privately she regarded him as "one of the great destroyers of language",[14] and thought Robert Graves and Louis MacNeice much better poets). But she was no mere aesthete either: "A poet who isn't involved in the questions of his day in some way or another which provides some kind of basic contact with people," she thought, "becomes detached from what ought to be his audience."[15] For this reason she would have liked to attend the International Congress of Writers to be held in Madrid towards the end of the year to support the Republican cause. But the logistical and ethical problems for an unknown young poet from Australia with little money were too great, and she did not go: "You would have had to go past the frontier guards, and you didn't want to be involved in things you didn't want to be involved in."[16]

Instead, she and Cecily set out for a tour of Europe, "travelling hard" and staying with families who took in paying guests or in cheap pensions. It was important, she thought, to see Europe before war came and shut them out. In Holland they stayed with people Cecily knew of, who showed the young women the cosmopolitan and friendly city; Judith worried about them later when the Germans occupied Holland. From there they went on to Germany, which she thoroughly disliked with its Nazi flags and slogans everywhere and men in black and brown shirts swaggering through the streets. There were "crude posters on lamp-posts and walls ... chalk scrawlings on doors ... broken windows in the ghettoes" and she was appalled by the stories of Jews beaten up and even killed.[17] The Rhineland she found particularly unpleasant. She and Cecily stayed with what Judith remembered as "a ghastly family, an ancient baron ... [and] his two nasty sisters", "very Nazi people indeed" who gloried in the thought of the coming war[18] rather like the officers on the ship on which Judith's father and mother had returned from their honeymoon in Japan on the eve of World War I.

The baron and his sisters were also anti-Semitic. Judith recalled one particular incident with disgust. In his halting English the old baron asked her whether there were any "ewes" in Australia, to which she replied that "we had a lot of sheep". Then, realising what he was really saying, she added that she had many Jewish friends.[19] Her German was not fluent, so she did not always comprehend what was being said, though she did often have to bite her tongue – as on this occasion. Dissent could be dangerous, and she realised later that she had been "lucky to get away with what [she] did". "Clearly there were terrible things going on in Germany. It was a miserable place really."[20]

Austria was also unpleasant. Judith was conscious of "the jackboots marching on the other side of the border", and, hiking in the Alps near the Austro-German border, she and Cecily saw German troops massing for the invasion which was to come in March 1938. Everywhere the local Austrian Nazis were boasting of victory; obviously it would not be long before the invasion occurred. They felt "tension all the time ...

Everywhere you felt on the edge of an explosion. It was not a very happy time at all."[21]

Hungary they found more sympathetic. In many ways, with its sweeping plains and easy-going people, the country reminded Judith of Australia, especially the families they stayed with near Lake Balaton. But war was on everyone's mind here, too, and people were particularly worried about the forthcoming harvest in Germany, believing that if it failed Hitler would sweep through Austria and help himself to theirs.

Their three days in Budapest, however, were the climax of the trip. There Judith met a young chemistry student, Endre, the friend of a friend who had asked him to show her the city.

> It was early summer, the trees along the Bude streets in new green plumes and feathers; a smell of peach brandy, the scent of female American tourists, the scent of the racing brown river ... Endre gambolled; we went to the Museum, to the cafés, to the galleries, we boated on the Danube; we drank curious drinks on terraces above the river where the little cafe tables glittered under their canvas umbrellas.[22]

But Endre had a Jewish grandmother. "My brother and I, we loved her," he confessed. "But now – we are afraid. Is it not cruel, that my grandmother, so kind, should be a fear to me? Hungaria – poor Hungaria!"[23] Judith recognised the fear she had sensed in Germany and Austria, but her friendship with Endre brought it home, made it personal. He was ugly, "comically ... ugly; small, square, with a face like a dog, a shy, anxious dog eager to please, who if encouraged will probably jump up and tear your stockings", but she felt for him, perhaps especially for this reason.

They spent only three days together. "Like a rubber ball he bounced beside me down the river-bank and over the long bridge to my pension, talking with his entire person" or taking her to expensive restaurants where they and his friends danced, "drunk with gipsy-music and the csarda richly scented with expensive brandy."[24] On the last night he "proposed one last moonlight walk through the ... miniature wood" on one of the islands in the river and kissed her. The next morning he saw her off at sunrise on the train, presenting her with a bouquet of flowers.

After that she and Cecily had planned to return to England by way of Italy, but frontiers were closing all around them. Sanctions against Italy, imposed because of the invasion of Abyssinia, made it impossible for them to go there, so they returned to London more or less uneventfully by way of Switzerland and France. Money was running out, and it was time to return to Australia. Other Wright women had stayed on and married; her Aunt Elsie, for example, and Tina, her cousin, who also married an Englishman and saw the war through in England, only returning to Australia with her husband to settle in the 1950s. But Judith's experiences in Europe had shaken her. In comparison with the violence she saw in Germany, Austria and Hungary, Australia looked to her "like a far off haven of freedom" – Endre in Budapest had been especially envious of her for living there. When many of her contemporaries, like her distant relation Patrick White, stayed in London, she went home.

On the way back, however, she had a final experience of the British Empire in its last imperial days. Her mother's younger sister had married a tea planter in Sri Lanka (then Ceylon), and she stayed several weeks with them there. As a young man her father had gloried in the trappings of empire, but Judith found them distasteful and thought her aunt, her husband and their way of life "pretty ghastly".[25] They were intent on upholding British rule, but she was aware that there was "a great deal of rebellion", muted though it might be, going on around her and sympathised with it, as she had earlier sympathised with Gandhi and the Indians' struggle for independence. She would have liked to have gone out by herself to see what was happening but that simply was not done – white people, white women especially, did not "mix with labour".[26]

Not long before, a well-born young Englishman, son of a former aide-de-camp of the Governor-General of Australia, had shocked the planters and their wives by talking with "the natives" and even living briefly amongst them. Worse, he had made "inflammatory remarks" about their pay and conditions.[27] Wright had actually met his father at a dance in Canberra when she had been there the previous year with her own father, president of the Hereford Society, to lobby on behalf of the cattlemen. But as a woman and as her aunt and uncle's guest there was no way in which she could have behaved as this "disgraceful youth" had done. Instead, she had to spend her days at the club, drinking gin and tonic, dancing with the planters and gossiping with the wives.

At that time many young Australian women of her class came there to do just this in search of suitable husbands – they were unkindly called "the fishing fleet". This kind of life appealed to Judith even less than life as a grazier's wife. Even as a child visiting the Netherlands East Indies she had disliked what she saw of colonial rule, the "awful Dutchmen stalking the streets". She disliked having to listen to gossip and criticism of the "natives" and disliked even more being "indoctrinated into what you could and could not do", having to behave like a mem-sahib, forbidden even to pick up a needle if you dropped it: "You had to say 'Boy!' and he would come running to pick it up. You weren't allowed to do anything."[28]

On the ship home Judith met a young Jewish man. Australian born, he, too, had been appalled by what he had seen in Europe, and they became friends. Even more aware through him that the world was drifting, almost inexorably, towards war it became more than ever impossible for her to return to New England to plant an "island there and [draw] it round her" as her grandmother had done.[29] The question of what she was to do and how she was to earn her living returned with urgency. She arrived in Sydney in the sweltering summer of 1938. On 14th January, the hottest day for more than fifty years, bushfires swept through the North Shore, covering the city and harbour with a pall of smoke through which the sun shone like a red balloon; in places the asphalt melted.

This year also marked the 150th anniversary of the first white settlement at Sydney Cove. Judith came home from London's coronation year to more patriotic celebrations, though these are not mentioned in her autobiography. Nor is there any mention of the Aboriginal issue, to be so important to her later. It was raised, however, by the Aboriginal people themselves who staged a counter demonstration, protesting at the celebration of what they saw as invasion. It was not an issue that interested most people, even thinking people then, though the Jindyworobak movement, which looked to Aboriginal cultures as a source of our understanding of ourselves as Australians, was beginning to appeal to some artists, writers and intellectuals. The general view was that the Aborigines were "a dying race" and that the best that could be done was to express regret and "soothe the dying pillow". This passage from the *Australian National Review*'s essay on the significance of the sesquicentenary was probably more sympathetic than most:

> The poor Aborigine is the saddest chapter in our history ... They are a dying race and it is for us to do what we can to save the remnants ... The problem [however] ... is that they ought to be our special thought and attention at the present time ... [but that] they are wiping themselves out with tribal fights.[30]

For Judith, however, there was the question of a career to settle. Without a degree it seemed that the best she could do would be to become a secretary, so she went to business college to learn typing and shorthand. The two women who ran it were "too old for the jobs they had once had among predatory business men",[31] but they were shrewd as well as intelligent and taught more than mere typing and shorthand. From time to time, as Judith remembered it, they would call a halt "to the clatter of typewriters hammering out sentences about the quick brown fox" to deliver "a short but useful talk on office deportment and how to protect your virtue". But they did not forget the art of pleasing the boss either: "you might suggest quietly an alternative word or sentence if [he] was stuck in dictation; if he accepted it, you didn't remind him that it was your wording or idea, for that was dangerous to your job". Flirting was "not for office hours unless it was the top boss who initiated it, in which case you had to be both compliant and resistant enough to remain *virgo intacta*. Remember that jobs were scarce. Always retain personal freshness and make sure your stockings were invisibly mended."[32]

Judith had the advantage of a university education and she had been overseas, so that as soon as she could type well enough to pass muster, a job was found for her as assistant secretary to the young and rising second-in-command of an oil company. Unfortunately, she was also expected to look after the filing system, something she knew nothing about, and since the senior woman in his office "had no intention of sharing her knowledge", within a few weeks Judith found herself back at business college "for further training".[33] Judging by the meticulous way she has handled her correspondence and her business affairs in later life this training seems to have been very successful.

The first position Judith looked for subsequently was as a journalist: she had had some experience at university working for *Honi Soit*, and journalism seemed the sort of profession to suit a writer. Through family connections she got an interview with the editor of the *Sydney Morning Herald*, who sent her on to the social editor, Constance Robertson, daughter of A. G. Stephens and revered for that connection. Constance, however, accepted that a woman's place was with the social pages, and told Judith that she would have to serve at least two years' apprenticeship "reporting social events and the clothes of the socially acceptable before she moved on to anything else". She would have to learn other skills also, like social tact. The Depression was not over yet, and some people who traditionally featured in the social pages were still short of money, which had to be concealed:

> So a backless dress in white satin had to be transformed in the reporting into a "daring creation in white angel skin", a "deep-cut model in cream silk" or whatever description the reporteress [this was how she was to be described] could dredge up, once it had been described for the first time.[34]

The position did not appeal. But in any case, Judith was not likely to be employed. There were few openings, she was told, and they usually went to young city women "of good social background", not young women from the country.

The other possibility was the newly created Australian Broadcasting Commission (ABC) where some of her university contemporaries, Margot McCallum and Dorothy Auchterlonie (later Green), for example, already had jobs. But here, too, Judith drew a blank. Eventually, however, she found work with the big American advertising firm of J. Walter Thompson, which had recently opened an office in Sydney. Apart from copywriting and preparing ads, the firm had just moved into the new area of market research, using the Gallup Poll method, and Judith was employed in this area.

There were a number of well-qualified women on the staff, amongst them Margaret Piddington who had also been a university contemporary and became a good friend. The work was interesting, and it taught Judith a great deal – far more than working on the social pages of the *Sydney Morning Herald* would have done. Much of this work was done outside the office, interviewing people at home, and for interviewing purposes the suburbs were classified, ranging from A-class suburbs like Rose Bay and Woollahra, where the wealthy lived, to D-class ones like Redfern and Golden Grove. They ignored the E-class suburbs Judith had glimpsed when she first came to Sydney, where people were living under bridges or in corrugated tin humpies and "were really desperate".[35]

Like most of her colleagues, Judith preferred the C and D allocations to A and B, where it was nearly always a maid who answered the door. It was very difficult to get past her to interview the "Mistress of the House", and even if they did, these wives of doctors, lawyers and prosperous businessmen were usually suspicious of the interviewers or snobbishly disdainful of questions about their favourite radio station or brand of soap. "Moreover to knock on an upper class door without previous introduction was to be automatically classified as working class" – something Judith did not find appealing. On the other hand, people in the poorer suburbs often resented a woman with a job who was comparatively well-dressed – going there, Judith used to wear her shabbier clothes, not relishing being judged "upper class and an oppressor".[36] Her favourite suburbs were lower middle-class/upper working-class, where she was often invited in for a cup of tea and a yarn, and people were only too happy to talk about radio programs and the brand of soap or washing powder they used. Radio then was the equivalent of television today, so there was plenty to talk about.

Judith was seeing a different world from the one in which she had grown up. In some of the poorer suburbs, for instance, the radio might have been picked up from the local dump and then reconditioned or even made from spare parts found there – Sydney was still, as Christina Stead described it, a place where "people fought and struggled and were poor". But it was also very beautiful and very picturesque. There were almost no buildings more than four storeys high, so the harbour seemed to be everywhere, glittering in the sunshine. As refugees from Europe began to arrive the city was also becoming more cosmopolitan. Coffee shops were opening and new kinds of goods were appearing in the shops: European cheeses supplementing the ubiquitous Kraft cheddar, and salami, liverwurst and other smallgoods adding to the range of foods in the delicatessens. Different languages could be heard in the streets, and poor as many of them now were, the refugees displayed a new sense of style in the way they dressed.

Judith was living in Darlinghurst Road, not far from Kings Cross, in the heart of these developments in a flat in a block called "Havilah". Her room, a mere "flatette" (since it had no kitchen, only a gas stove in the corner), would not have impressed her father, nor would the area itself. She told him that she was living in the next suburb, Elizabeth Bay, which was eminently respectable – a B-class, if not A-class suburb, in fact. "Havilah", however, was definitely not respectable. "Those who lived there were much given to noises in the night and the early morning snatching of other people's milk bottles."[37] But it was within easy walking distance of her job in the city, down the steps and across Woolloomooloo, with plenty of sights to enjoy on the way. At that time many gypsies still lived in Woolloomooloo, noticeable for their graceful bodies and beautiful clothes. Some lived in old vans and others were so poor that they camped under the bridges with the Aborigines.[38]

This was still a limited world for anyone with ambitions to be a writer. Few books were locally published. According to the *Australian Quarterly* for May 1939 (which relied on a list supplied by the National Library) only ten books were published in Australia in 1938, and only two of these were novels, one about a future invasion of Australia and the other "about the influence of a woman on a man's life". There was only one collection of poems noted: *So They Played Together*, a collection for children illustrated by the author who, the *Australian Quarterly* said, "could not draw for nuts".

Old attitudes were changing a little, however, and Australian writers were gaining some recognition. In 1935 the Melbourne *Age* had published a series of articles on Australian literature and its possibilities. The first in this series, by the Professor of English at Melbourne University, G. H. Cowling, was typical of older imperial attitudes. There was little possibility of any literature worth the name emerging here, he wrote, because the country was still "too new, too raw", lacking "ancient churches, castles and ruins"[39] – the sort of thing which had been said since the beginnings of white settlement. Vance Palmer's essay, however, the next in the series, spoke with a new confidence:

> We have to discover ourselves – our character, the character of the country, the particular kind of society that has developed here – and this can only be done through the searching explorations of literature ... It is one of the limitations of the human mind that it can never grasp things fully till they are presented through the medium of art ... and so unless a country has its life fully mirrored in books it will not show a very rich intelligence in the business of living.[40]

He also noted a "surprising growth" in local publishing, though he lamented the lack of "lively and intelligent criticism".

P. R. Stephensen's *The Foundations of Australian Culture* was published the following year, and its subtitle, *An Essay Towards National Self Respect*, echoed Palmer's confidence. The sesquicentenary of 1938 also helped to generate interest in Australian writing. A prize of several hundred pounds was offered for a long poem as part of the centenary celebrations – won by F. D. Fitzgerald's *Essay on Memory* – and novelists like Eleanor Dark and M. Barnard Eldershaw were beginning to explore Australian history in their fiction. The visit of an American Professor of English, Hartley Grattan, from the University of Texas, an enthusiast for Australian literature, made some people at least realise that Australian writing could attract international interest: "The producers of literature," he wrote in an essay published in the *Australian National Review*, "must seek their basic inspiration in the life of man on the Australian earth ... All culture is somehow rooted in the natural earth."[41]

This was rhetorically comforting but not very practical for a young woman like Judith who wanted to write poetry, since few journals apart from the *Bulletin* and the more up-market *Australian Quarterly* and the short-lived *Australian National Review* published poems. On the advice of a friend, Jeannie Clunies-Ross, she concentrated on the more serious journals, managing to get two poems into the *Australian National*

Review, "Earth" in 1938 and "City Rain" in 1939. Mary Gilmore published in this journal as did younger poets just beginning to make their name like A. D. Hope, Ian Mudie, Paul Grano, Martin Haley and C. B. Christesen, who was to found *Meanjin* some years later. Neither of Judith's poems was particularly memorable. But at least they met Hartley Grattan's criterion, being preoccupied with "the spirit of the land". "Earth", for instance, begins:

> *Men breed the marvellous, but earth breeds man.*
> *We build as she directs, and all our thoughts,*
> *Our truths, our lies, our loves, return to her.*[42]

She did not frequent literary circles then – or indeed later. But from time to time she would visit Mary Gilmore in her upstairs flat not far from her, just down from the Cross in Darlinghurst Road. She was "very much an institution", and Judith would usually take her a bunch of violets as a tribute.[43] Though she was not much impressed with her poetry which she regarded as "Georgian" – a word of condemnation she had picked up in London – she admired Gilmore's stories of pioneering days in the bush which drew her attention to her own background; "you have to live to be ninety to realise how many stories are tucked away in your background," as she reflected.[44] Gilmore's feelings for Aboriginal people and their culture, especially for the Wiradjuri people she had known as a child, and for the beauty of their land also spoke to her: "simply by going on living Mary Gilmore became part of one's life".[45]

There were also a number of lively and gifted young artists in Sydney at the time, and Judith particularly admired Margaret Preston, even then drawing on Aboriginal influences, and Rah Fizelle. The de Basil Ballet came to Sydney in 1939, and Judith went to it, even though it meant going without a few meals and sitting in the back row. At the same time she kept up her interest in politics and would from time to time attend play readings at the New Theatre, sitting on "chairs of excruciating hardness",[46] or listen to speakers like Dr Evatt and Eddie Ward, occasionally catching a glimpse of Miles Franklin, "very small, brown-haired, not very impressive, but a good speaker".[47]

She was still more left than right in her politics. For one thing, what she was seeing in her work in Sydney's poorer suburbs convinced her that "something had to be done". Though she was not clear what this might be, it seemed obvious to her that "greed is a poor basis on which to run a society".[48] Even more importantly perhaps, what she had seen in Germany "still stuck like a thorn in her mind".[49] Several of her university friends had been Jewish, and the young man with whom she had become friendly returning from Sri Lanka, for whom being Jewish was increasingly seeming "a fate rather than a nationality",[50] kept her aware of what was happening.

Many Australians admired Hitler, even some of her extended family, for the way he had restored the German economy and its people's self-respect and dealt with what they saw as the "threat of Communism". In January 1938 the *Australian National Review* had published an essay by the founder of the National Colonial League of Germany and head of the Colonial Board of the National Socialist Party on "Germany's Needs for Space and Raw Materials". Judith could not agree with these views. But although another of her friends, a physicist, was a communist, she was suspicious of dogmatism. Perhaps this was the result of John Anderson's influence at Sydney University but more likely it was temperamental: the child who sympathised with the defeated Kaiser in 1918 was hardly likely to support dictators either of right or left. At the same time Colin Badgery's essay in defence of the Left Book Club, published in the *Australian Quarterly* for June 1939, probably reflected her thoughts. It was true, he wrote, that the Club's

> books signally fail to present both sides of the case. But the intellectual has come to doubt the virtue of presenting both sides when the other side is Fascism. He is learning to see that truth is not necessarily to be found exactly and squarely in the middle ... He has, moreover, learned from experience, not all of which has been vicarious, that those who sit on fences form an admirable target for the sharp-shooters on both sides.[51]

In March 1938 British Prime Minister Chamberlain signed a non-aggression pact with Hitler, which guaranteed his occupation of Czechoslovakia as well as Austria and convinced many people, Judith amongst them, that nothing could stop Hitler but war. "The likely fate of [her] generation" haunted her as "a sort of hysteria ... [woke] people from their contented slumber ... the news became grimmer every day."⁵² Using the polling skills she had learned at work, Judith and a group of friends conducted a survey of people's expectations and sold it to a popular newspaper. The published results were grim: the majority expected war, and a war that would be even more destructive than World War I. True, there were some lighter moments. One question, for example, asked people which weapons they would most fear if war came: high-explosive bombs, poison gas or bacteriological warfare. Most nominated bacteriological warfare, but one woman chose poison gas, writing in explanation that gas was "more dangerous in the kitchen than people realise".⁵³

For many the threat was still distant. Judith, however, was soon to be involved more intimately. Not long after she got back to Australia in 1938 letters had begun to arrive from Endre, the young Hungarian she had met in Budapest:

> Busy with my own life and its various problems I found them an amusing reminder of a few pleasant days; their schoolroom English was always good for a laugh, the foreign stamps were impressive. I answered them, though it was often hard to think of anything to say. Our worlds did not touch anywhere ... but the warmth of his confidences ... pleased and flattered me ... [At] a time when, friends drifting into marriage, and I myself struggling for a foothold in an alien city world, I felt the need of some impersonal far off confidant.⁵⁴

Suddenly, however, Endre and his world became demanding. One rainy and cold day Judith arrived home wet through. "The electric heater would not work, my city job seemed more than ever nauseating and pointless" – but there was a letter, a fat one, from Endre. In it he told her that he had graduated, paid off his debts and was now free to come to Australia as he had dreamed. But Australian migration laws were complex and discouraging and he was allowed to take only a very small amount of money out of Hungary. The only way he could get into Australia would be for someone in the country to put up a £50 guarantee that he would not become a charge on the state and would remain gainfully employed. Would she do this for him? Then they could be reunited, he said, adding that he had a "box painted special for you my Darling with all Hungarian embroidery, laces and other such and will give you when we meet".[55] Suddenly the distant world drew closer: someone who had been part of a kind of fantasy became a real human being. "It was as though some pleasant and familiar piece of furniture had suddenly put on human attributes and problems and made some fantastic demand on one's time and affection."[56] He was no longer a "pen friend", a memory of pleasant times in the past but a person whose demands were painful, possibly dangerous and certainly costly.

The sum of £50 was appallingly large to her then. Besides, what did she really know of this man with whom she had spent a mere three days in a foreign city? She was vexed with herself for having used him as she had and then for letting them both drift into this situation. But she was aware also of what a Nazi government in Hungary would mean for him as a Jew – she had seen and heard enough in Germany. Not sure what she should do and afraid of committing herself, she procrastinated, writing to him about the difficulties of migrants in a new country, the problems of getting a visa and her own lack of money. On his side, Endre's letters grew "sad and short". But in the midst of her indecision an enormous parcel arrived, containing a length of white Hungarian lace, "a wedding-dress length" which must, she realised, "have cost [him] more than I dared conjecture". It had been sent at the same time as his first letter, in which "he had so joyfully announced his freedom" and his intention of joining her in Australia.[57]

Shortly after that, in September 1939, war broke out and she heard no more from Endre apart from two messages from the Red Cross in Lisbon, "one to say that he was well, the next a garbled note, of which all I could understand were the words My Darling (which he had not used for some time) and farewell". It was, she felt, "a Shakespearian tragic note".[58] But this was not happening on stage, rather in real life. He disappeared without trace; "into a concentration camp, a front-line regiment, a labour camp", she never knew, and no further news ever came. Nor after the war could Judith find out what had happened to him. As for the length of lace, she sold it later, sending the money to "some refugee appeal or other ... Nothing remains but the guilt".[59]

In the midst of growing fanaticism she looked back on him as a figure of vulnerability yet also, despite everything, of ironic self-possession. Thinking of him she recalled the saying of another of her friends at that time:

> "Liberty" is a word with many meanings most of them false. Each country builds its frontiers in the name of freedom, destroying freedom; and each man fortifies his single soul in the name of freedom not understanding that liberty is love and has no frontiers.[60]

Perhaps these words came to her mind also as she listened to the radio in a friend's flat and heard the news that Hitler had invaded Poland, and that Britain had declared war, and shortly afterwards Australia.

> The whole of life shifted like a Kaleidoscope; everything took up a new position, everyone changed place. Though the first troops did not sail for more than four months, streets seemed to fill with uniforms almost at once. Friends vanished, and news of what they were doing and where they were became difficult to get.[61]

Judith's Jewish friend had already moved away, not wanting to involve her in the tragedy of his people. He enlisted early in the war and was to be seriously wounded later at Tobruk; other young men she knew began to disappear into the armed forces. But Judith was uneasy with patriotic fervour. A physicist friend had shared with her his fears of the new and more terrible weapons which were being developed – an essay on Lord Rutherford's work on radioactivity had appeared in the *Australian Quarterly* – and she began to fear what war might mean. Visiting Mary Gilmore she could not agree with her view that "one could only support one's man in this coming battle". It seemed to Judith, amongst other things, to imply that women "had always been subjects, not actors in the game of living"[62] – something she could not agree with even if she believed in war.

For the first few months, however, nothing much seemed to happen – this was the time of the "Phoney War" as the Germans gathered their forces to sweep through Belgium, Holland and France in 1940. But Judith was growing increasingly restless in her advertising job, which seemed to her "more and more irrelevant and destructive, relying ... for its impact on greed, fear and vanity".[63] Realising this, her father suggested her name to the Professor of Geography at the University of Sydney, Macdonald Holmes, who was in need of a new secretary. Worried about the erosion gullies on his property which were tearing great scars along the edges of the escarpment, Phillip Wright had called Holmes in to advise him on a new soil contour plan which he had developed, so he had some influence with the Professor.

Judith welcomed the idea of the move and of returning to the university, hoping even as a secretary to find herself in a "rather more creative ambience". She got the job but in fact she was sadly disappointed. There were jealousies amongst the staff and, while she had assumed that she would work for all of them, that was not the Professor's view, so she sat for unoccupied hours in her small room waiting for work, smoking "too many cigarettes and [flirting] with one of the staff, having nothing else to do most of the time and nobody else in mind".[64] Besides, the university in wartime was depressing. There were few students to be seen in the quad, staff were depleted and the lack of groundsmen left the lawns uncut and the grounds littered with rubbish.

In other ways, too, her life was increasingly unsatisfactory. The trip home to New England to spend the Christmas of 1939 with the family put paid to any notion she might have had of marrying a grazier. The son of a New England family she knew offered her a lift home from Sydney. He had come to the city to buy a new utility and since, in those days, engines had to be run in by travelling slowly for the first few hundred miles, he welcomed company on the drive back.

They left Sydney on "Black Friday", a day of record heat and bushfires; the streets were already sizzling when the young man called for her at six a.m. The Blue Mountains as well as the Victorian forests were alight so they had to keep the windows closed as scorched leaves, twigs, dust and smoke swirled around them in a violent westerly wind as they crawled along. Early on they drained the remains of their water bag, but the young man plugged on stubbornly, refusing to stop, convinced that when they reached the New England Tableland it would be cooler. Only once did he relent, stopping at the pub at Murrurundi at the head of the Hunter Valley. Even there the water from the well was so warm that it was undrinkable and the two beers Judith downed before she could face anything to eat did little to improve her temper.

If there ever had been any chance of her doing what was expected of her and marrying this young man, that drive ended it. She was angry at his determination to keep on driving and the heat made her fretful. "Soaked with sweat and grey with smoke and dust", she was "by no means an attractive proposition". Soon after they left the pub they quarrelled badly, and she slept for the rest of the way.[65]

The next year, 1940, the war began to go badly; as the German offensive drove through Holland, Belgium and France, the British army retreated across the Channel and the Battle for Britain began. Judith was worried about the fate of the friends she had made in Holland and even more worried about her cousin Tina, whose husband had given up his academic career to serve in the Royal Navy, and who was living in London. The poem, "The Hanging Avalanche of Days", which she published in *Southerly* that year, expresses something of the "still and dreadful threat"[66] she felt at the time.

In Australia the *National Security Act* had given the government power to regulate just about every aspect of life in the interests of the war effort and to impose draconian penalties on anyone who refused to cooperate. Even the gypsies of Woolloomooloo were affected; the men were drafted into the armed forces or into munition factories, their splendid necklaces of gold coins and medals were requisitioned and their caravans taken away, forcing the women and children to live in squalid houses which they could not afford.[67] The war effort, however, was increasingly thought to justify everything. By mid-1941 Hitler had invaded Russia, his troops controlled Greece, and the Allies were seriously threatened.

On the home front, refugees who had fled from Hitler's growing power were now regarded as enemy aliens, in many cases simply because they spoke German. Many were interned, though most of them were released quite soon, but even then they were required to register and report regularly to the local police. People were also urged to keep an eye on one another and to report any unusual activity. Judith had recently moved to Springfield Avenue in Kings Cross where she shared a room with another woman who was particularly zealous, wanting to report a woman who lived on the top floors of the flats opposite because she used to brush her hair every night leaning out of the window, which, her flatmate thought, probably meant that she was signalling to the enemy.[68] News was censored and wild rumours of spies, who were supposed to be everywhere, and of submarines and warships waiting off the coast to attack flourished.

In the middle of all this, Judith's job at the university seemed more and more pointless, and she thought of enlisting in one of the women's services. But she was beginning to go deaf, which would have made her medically unfit. At first she put this deafness down to wax in the ears. But her current boyfriend noticed it also, and he and her father persuaded her to see a specialist who diagnosed it as ostosclerosis, a condition which could get progressively worse. Judith was worried that the condition could be hereditary. At this news, her boyfriend who had been talking of getting married – he was in the army and was soon to go overseas – began to distance himself and once again, as Judith reflected later, in this way she was saved from marrying someone she did not really love.[69] Very soon they lost touch.

News also came from time to time about other young men she had known who had been wounded or killed in action like Tony, the New Zealander she had known on board ship and in London. Meantime, as she wrote later, she

> entered on one or two irrelevant love affairs. Uniforms were a potent concealer of realities and incitement to sex, as indeed is war itself, and there seems no reason for saying no, when Armageddons are in prospect or are actually occurring.[70]

When Japan entered the war on 7th December 1941, bombing Pearl Harbor and destroying most of the American Pacific Fleet and later taking Singapore and sinking the two great British battleships of the Eastern Fleet, the *Prince of Wales* and the *Repulse*, "those supposedly impregnable defenders of the impregnable and glorious British Empire in which Australia had been taught to put its trust",[71] Armageddon seemed close. Judith had given up her work at the university and taken a temporary position in the building section at the

Sydney Town Hall, expecting to be called home to help her father in New England; now that both her brothers were in the army he was trying to look after all the family properties by himself. But suddenly the job at the Town Hall took on a new importance.

As the Japanese continued to sweep southwards, invading Indonesia and bombing northern Australian towns like Darwin, Broome and Townsville, panic gripped Sydney. Gun emplacements and concrete pill boxes appeared on the foreshores and there were tank traps on the beaches where she and her friends used to surf. "Australians were incredulous. Such things simply did not happen in our cosy shelter."[72] But now it looked as if Sydney might be bombed. The building section at the Town Hall was besieged with inquiries. There were only three of them in the section – the section head, his secretary and Judith, who was the junior typist – and they were at a loss to answer the anxious questions directed at them: "How to prepare a building for a bombing raid, against high explosives? Against fire-bombing? Against a gas attack? Nobody had told the Town Hall". Judith suggested to the section head that she should go to the Public Library and find out what British sources and newspapers had to say on the subject. The idea struck her boss as "a little outlandish; he had never taken any action not prescribed by the City Council ... But the times pressed, and no directives came from above".[73] So Judith spent three days in the library, summarising all she could find and after this answered all inquiries, enjoying her new power. She also enjoyed some of the inquiries. One woman, for example, had problems with the advice to organise a roof-top team to put out fires with sand and water buckets: "We got no men in the house in the day time," she explained, "plenty at night but they got other things in mind and I don't know if I can organise them into teams."[74]

Judith was now a key member of Sydney's Air Raid Precautions Centre. As the Japanese moved closer it was decided to move this centre underground to a tunnel near Wynyard Station, part of the unfinished eastern suburbs railway line, reached by a series of very grimy concrete steps. The tunnel, "hastily lined with plywood, connected to telephone and electricity lines and stocked with rickety camp tables and canvas chairs", smelt strongly of mushrooms, and at times they felt almost like mushrooms themselves since they lived and worked there day and night, on the alert for possible enemy attacks.

But gradually their hearts retreated "from [their] mouths to their normal place, at the phone switchboards at which a couple of very young telephonists sat, taking turns on the switches". Gradually, too, even though their work and whereabouts were supposed to be secret, khaki and navy-blue uniforms began to appear in the tunnel at night and stretchers were spirited in. "Sometimes these held members of the Air Raid Centre, but more often [they] accommodated more than one; love had once more triumphed, if not over locksmiths, at least over instructions." That was one way of looking at it. But, "The Company of Lovers", first published in the second number of *Meanjin* for 1942, sets these meetings in a more tragic perspective:

> *We meet and part now all over the world.*
> *We, the lost company,*
> *take hands together in the night, forget*
> *the night in our brief happiness, silently*

as around them

> *Death marshals up his armies . . .*
> *Their footsteps crowd too near.*[75]

But then Judith's war took a different turn. Her father had just been appointed to oversee Civil Defence for the whole New England region. This time when she offered to leave Sydney and come home to help in running the family properties he accepted.

> *Time and the world that faster spin until*
> *mind cannot grasp them now or heart take hold*[76]

were bringing her back to where she began.

CHAPTER V

SOUTH OF MY DAYS...

South of my days' circle, part of my blood's country,
rises that tableland, high delicate outline
of bony slopes wincing under the winter.

from "South of My Days",
Collected Poems, p. 20

It was April 1942 and the trip to Armidale was very different from the one Judith had made with the young pastoralist in his new utility at Christmas 1939. Until now, however much she had loved it as a child, she had more or less taken the land for granted. Family attitudes, reflected in the name "New England", suggesting that it was somehow secondhand and "not really English", had also influenced her, however unconsciously[1] – though her visit to England had changed that a little.

> But now, as the train panted up the foothills of the Moonbis, and the haze of dust and eucalypt vapour dimmed the drought-stricken landscape I found myself suddenly and sharply aware of it as "my country". These hills and valleys were not mine, but me, the threat of Japanese invasion hung over them as over me; I felt it under my own ribs. Whatever other blood I held, this was the country I loved and knew.[2]

The land was as vulnerable as she had felt herself as a child. In a world at war

> ...there is no end to the breaking –
> one smashed, another mocks from your enemy's eye –
> put that out, there's a world in every skull.

But she was returning here to

> ...the green world of a child;
> the infinity of day that closed in day,
> the widening spiral turning and returning.[3]

She was returning, too, because she was needed. Her father had only an old man, Jack Purkiss, and a land army girl who knew very little about the land to help him look after three properties and manage the civil defence of the region.

The sense of crisis was strong. The Japanese were moving south through New Guinea, and the week after Judith left, two of their submarines got through the defence nets into Sydney Harbour, sank a ferry, narrowly missing an ammunition ship, and shelled a block of flats in the eastern suburbs. The fact that, as so often in war, the danger was combined with farce did not reduce the threat – in the panic during the submarine attack no one thought to inform the Air Raid Precautions Centre where she had been working, which was supposed to oversee the safety of civilians![4]

Heavily censored, the newspapers might talk of "heavy enemy losses", "the inspired leadership of General MacArthur" and run stories of Allied heroism – the headline "Lone Plane's Big Victory; Enemy Impasse in New Guinea" is a good example. But it was clear that the Japanese were perilously close and invasion seemed imminent. Nor were those who knew the real situation very optimistic. The best that one American commentator, Cecil Brown of the American CBS network, could say was that the recent arrival of General MacArthur who had escaped from the Philippines gave the Allies "a reasonable chance of holding Australia". In his view, however, "the picture in the Pacific" was "not bright" and he concluded that "it would be hiding the facts to say other than this: the US at the moment is in its most serious position in history".[5] The position of Australia was even more serious of course.

The second section of "The Moving Image" expresses something of this mood with its image of the world seen from the air looking

> ... evil and small
> like a dried head from the islands with a grin of shell,
> brittle and easy to break.

It seemed that there might be

> Nothing left but to pray, God save us all.[6]

Since one of Judith's former boyfriends was serving in New Guinea, she had a special sense of the horror of the war being fought there.

When the train finally arrived in Armidale there was no one to meet her – there was no petrol to spare – so she took the mail car, travelling through a landscape whose emptiness made her feel the land's vulnerability all the more. The few cars they met, with their protuberances (charcoal gas burners used to produce fuel in the absence of petrol), emphasised a sense of weirdness and menace; the only other vehicles were a few of the army trucks and jeeps still left in the south.

When she finally reached "Wallamumbi", it too seemed "empty and rather dishevelled", and her father was just back from "a mysterious excursion about which we were ... not to ask questions".[7] He was to be away a great deal for the rest of the year and into the next. Judith found even more fear here perhaps than in Sydney. One of her father's friends, an aristocratic German but also a sympathiser with the Nazi cause, had been imprisoned as a spy. Shortly afterwards a swastika was found carved into a pole of the rose trellis at "Wallamumbi"; a sign, the family thought, that the enemy had put in a claim for their property.[8]

The coastal towns were in terror of invasion. Coffs Harbour was thought to be the most likely target, and Judith's father and the one or two others responsible for civil defence were ordered to organise for an evacuation if and when the Japanese made a landing. They were to follow a "scorched earth" policy on the lines the Russians had been using against the Germans. The farmers were to burn their crops, destroy their stores of hay and grain, muster all their livestock and then drive them up to the New England plateau. Not surprisingly, they were not enthusiastic about this plan, but it was her father's task to persuade them to it and then, if necessary, carry it through.

Even at the time Judith realised that the plan was even more farcical than the debacle with the Air Raid during the submarine raid on Sydney had been.

> Since all roads from the coast to the tableland were to be mined and defended by the military services, there could be no route for the exodus except up the steep and trackless spurs of the Dividing Range. It was doubtful if even the Army had convinced itself that this enormous conglomeration of cattle, pigs, sheep, horses, and for all I remember, fowls and ducks and geese as well would ever reach the 5000 feet high plateau through that wild and tangled rainforest and up those spurs. The farmers, with practical knowledge of the ways and feelings of their livestock, knew it wouldn't. After a few meetings with the outraged farmers, my father was thankful when the invasion scare began to fade and the Army ceased to press the scheme.[9]

All this kept her father very busy and he was grateful for Judith's help in managing the three stations for which he was responsible.

For the time being she enjoyed being outdoors again on the land. Indoors, which she associated with her mother's illness and death, still depressed her, especially as it was the domain of her stepmother, and she resented having to help her with the housework when there was so much to do outside. Nor did Judith like the office work which her father handed over to her – she had not left Sydney with these things in mind. But outdoors was different. She learned again the tracks from paddock to paddock and across the Oaky River to "Jeogla", her brother Bruce's domain, where his wife was living with her baby daughter. "Mustering and drafting the cattle had always been a joy" and even the chill of the winter winds as autumn came to an end did not lessen it. She was working her way "back into the country [she] more and more recognised as [her] heartland".[10]

Years later she recalled it as a time in which she was rediscovering the ground on which she was to build her life.

> When fifty years of absence should have dimmed it, I can take my horse in memory across those hills and valleys, with the Snowy Range closing off the horizon with blues and purples, and taste the water in the creeks we once drank from.[11]

She was reconnecting with her childhood and with the springs of creativity there:

> As a poet you have to imitate somebody [she told an interviewer], but since I had the beautiful landscape outside that I love so much and was my main subject from the start ... It comes to me naturally ... But when you live in very close connection with a large and splendid landscape as I did you feel yourself a good deal matters more than just "I".[12]

She was drawn again into this larger life, looking after the land and the work of the station as well as helping to get her father's garden, his pride and joy, back into order, making butter and cheese and feeding the pigs. Although she did not share the panic of some and could not imagine Japanese bombers recognising the lights of "Wallamumbi" or "Jeogla" and raining bombs down on them, on the family principle, "one in all in", she faithfully kept the blackout and looked for enemy aircraft. It might seem peaceful but even here she was conscious of

> *...that new and harsher tune;*
> *[Saw] crimson stars of danger travel the sky*
> *and the shadow of the bombers across the moon.*[13]

It also made her see the country more vividly, as "beloved and imperilled and my own blood and bone".[14]

Out of these feeling she was beginning to make poems which were more substantial than those she had written so far, more deeply rooted in a world and a tradition to which she belonged, finding a voice which was no longer a mere echo of others.

"Waiting" belongs to this time, contrasting the anxiety of listening to the radio for the latest news with the abiding and seemingly inviolable life of the land as

> *From starfrost to starfrost the folded hills lie bare*
> *and the sheep move grazing or stand...*
> *From the houses on the hill the small smoke rises*
> *in patterns of vague peace from dawn to night.*[15]

"Soldier's Farm", too, turns the sense of war's futile slaughter expressed in poems like "To A. H., New Year 1943" into a sense of some larger unity as the dead soldier's spirit becomes part of the land:

> *...his willing blood moves in these trees*
> *that hold his heart up sunwards with their arms.*[16]

Poetry for her had always been something "feminine"; her mother had read poetry to her, encouraged her to write it and sent off her first poems to the *Sydney Mail*, and her grandmother had read poetry to her also. But the major Australian poets of the time, Kenneth Slessor and R. D. FitzGerald, had seemed to her either "masculine and tough or glittering and self-absorbed" and she had rebelled against their "masculine order of things".[17] But now, returning to the maternal presence of the land, she was finding herself and her voice. In her case, Hartley Grattan's emphasis on the importance of the land, a view echoed by H. M. Green when he wrote that "the future is full of possibilities, provided that ... our younger writers can be brought to realise that literature is a growth of the soul,"[18] struck home. Moreover, in contrast with most of her contemporaries, she did not have to work at finding feeling for the land in an artificial way, as some of the Jindyworobaks were doing. For her the land was part of herself, part of a meditative, almost ceremonial, recall of childhood as something living and powerful.

She had also begun to mine the vein of family history which was to be so important for her later. At her father's suggestion she began a novel on the subject, wrestling with it for several months and then putting it aside, deciding that after all poetry was her metier. A decade later, however, she would come back to this material and produce *The Generations of Men*, after discovering her grandparents' diaries. She was also learning more about her mother's family.

But all this writing was done under difficulties. As she told Clem Christesen, the editor of *Meanjin*, when she was thinking of escaping to

Brisbane: "there is a lot of work on a country station", it is "a dawn to dusk affair and no days off either".[19] The only time she had to write was at night. To add to her problems, the winter of 1942 was exceptionally cold, and since there were no men to spare to chop the firewood there was little to heat the house, which was as cold as she remembered it from childhood. But it was dark as well since the shortage of fuel for the generator meant that there was electricity only for a few hours a day, so mostly she had to read and write by candlelight.

In the middle of winter news came that her maternal grandfather was ill and perhaps dying.[20] There was no petrol to spare, so she took the mail car to "Wongwibinda" to catch another mail car from there to "Thalgarrah". She was the only passenger on the first leg of the journey and a great snowstorm had covered the country. The car's struggle with the snowdrifts on the Doughboy Range took hours, and frequently they sank into deep patches of snow from which they had to dig the car out. By the time they finally reached "Wongwibinda", long after midnight, Judith was shivering uncontrollably – cars were not heated in those days and it was impossible to keep the weather out. To make matters worse, her Aunt Weeta had given up waiting and gone to bed, the hot-water bottle she had left was cold and the fire had gone out.

When Judith reached "Thalgarrah" the next day it was just as cold and even more depressing, with her cousin Win, "as always accustomed to the drudgery of a spinster aunt", looking after the old man. The big old house was almost all closed except for the kitchen quarters and the corridor that led to his bedroom, and even the hottest fire could not keep him warm. Outside the snow lay thick and drifted under the house, and when Judith left at last after a few days it was only just beginning to melt.

> I felt as though the whole world had somehow vanished under that chill white and might not come back at all – or come back forever frozen. Kissing grandfather goodbye, his cheek seemed as white and cold as the country. I was not to see him again.[21]

But she did take away with her more than she had ever known of her mother's family since the old man showed her his grandfather's diaries. As a young man in the 1860s he had been on one of the expeditions looking for the lost explorer Ludwig Leichhardt and later, was one of the first settlers on the Isaac River in Queensland until he was driven out by Aboriginal resistance. All this added to her growing realisation that Australia was not just England at second-hand but had a history of its own which mattered and generated its own kind of responsibilities. Some of this history, of course, was already speaking in poems she was writing at the time.

As winter gave way to a dry spring and a summer of drought, however, Judith began to feel more and more oppressed by the "boring nature of country living and country jobs".[22] The

> ...sick dust, spiralling with the wind,
> [was] harsh as grief's taste in our mouths
> and [had] eclipsed the small sun.

As if the war was having its effect even here:

> the steel-shocked earth has turned against this plough
> and runs with wind all day, and all night
> sighs in our sleep against the windowpane.[23]

Meantime the war was moving north as the Battle of the Coral Sea removed the immediate threat of invasion of Australia and New Guinea became the main battleground. But the innocence of her childhood had gone, the innocence of

> ...those enormous years I half recall,
> when between one blue summer and another
> time seemed as many miles as round the world,
> and world a day, a moment or a mile,
> or a sweet slope of grass edged with the sea,
> or a new song to sing, or a tree dressed in gold.

A world at war seemed bound to history in its "endless circle of time and star/that never chime with the blood". Time

> like a bushranger held its guns on us
> and forced our choice. And the clock begins to race

though she had not given up hope that a "lovelier distance [lay] ahead".[24] For the moment, as poems like "Battle Station, New Guinea" published in the *Sydney Morning Herald*[25] but not republished after that suggest, she thought of friends in New Guinea sinking in mud as they "clawed their way north against the Japanese"[26] and these thoughts increased her sense of entrapment and even of panic. "The Trains" describes this sense as the trains "in a splendour of power" go north with guns:

> *Strange primitive piece of flesh, the heart laid quiet*
> *hearing their cry pierce through its thin-walled cave*
> *recalls the forgotten tiger*
> *and leaps awake in its old panic riot.*[27]

Nevertheless things were changing. Her father's civil defence work was lessening as invasion seemed less likely, and Judith was no longer so badly needed at "Wallamumbi". Wanting to get back into the centre of things she made a trip to Sydney, hoping to enlist in one of the women's forces. But she was turned down on account of her deafness, and she returned to New England. The journey through the drought-stricken land increased her worries; the land was in trouble also.

This concerned her father too. The time they spent together in the paddocks was drawing them closer than they had been since she was a child. Her tribute to him after his death gives a glimpse of this growing intimacy:

> If more men on the land had been as truly of the land as Phillip Wright was, we today would have fewer problems of the results of bad land use ... more respect for the land's own natural capacities and a better appreciation of the use of its ecosystems ...
>
> He was a child of his times – we all are limited by them ... [But] his most important legacy ran counter to the worst aspect of those times and tried to reassert more lasting values.[28]

As they worked together she learned more from him about family history but also more about the story of white settlers' dealings with the land's Aboriginal inhabitants. One day, not long after she had first arrived, he took her with him on one of his civil defence assignments.

Looking for an old track which led from the coast up to the tableland, which might be used for the evacuation from the coast he was trying to organise, they came on a sheer cliff, "Darkies' Head" or "Nigger's Leap" (the name she gave it in the poem she wrote about it), and he told her the story that lay behind its name. In revenge for the killing of some cattle, a whole group of Aboriginal men, women and children had been driven over the cliff.

"I don't even know now why he told me the story," she reflected later. But as he told it she sensed his disquiet: on the one hand his family now owned the land to which these Aboriginal people had belonged and on the other, apart from being appalled at the brutality of the story, he remembered his childhood love for his nurse, Minnie, and his friendship with the Aboriginal stockmen with whom he had worked as a young man. To them

> he owed such Aboriginal lore as fire-making and finding honey in the native bee-trees. I think that even though he did not betray the attitudes in which he had been brought up, which attempted to justify the past with a scorn and contempt for Aborigines, his own feelings betrayed them.[29]

As Judith was to point out later in her own writing and conversation, the early pastoralists had depended heavily on Aboriginal stockmen, and this was so in New England as well as elsewhere. The Cohen family, for example, who, despite their name were Aboriginal, worked for several generations for the Wrights and were part of the extended family. In January 1900, May Wright's diary records a family picnic on which Jack Cohen and another Aboriginal stockman, Paddy Ross, came with them and caught fish for them to eat.[30]

Judith thought that her father was somehow relieved that the story of Nigger's Leap had been told, though he made no comment when he read the poem she wrote about it.

In this way she was becoming aware of a profound "gulf between us and the Aborigines: the Aborigines are the land, we merely think we own it",[31] and the family history she was exploring made her more aware of this gap. In "Bora Ring", for example, she writes about coming on a deserted sacred place out riding one day and being suddenly aware that

> *The song is gone; the dance*
> *is secret with the dancers in the earth,*
> *the ritual useless, and the tribal story*
> *lost in an alien tale*

but aware also of

> *...a sightless shadow, an unsaid word*
> *that fastens in the blood the ancient curse,*
> *the fear as old as Cain.*[32]

Later, reading through documents for her history of the Aboriginal side of settlement in Queensland, *The Cry For the Dead*, she copied out the words of one historian, that it is on the frontiers of an advancing society "that [the] radio-activity [of violence] concentrates itself. Rumours, second thoughts, belong to the established community and cannot be maintained outside it".[33] In poems like "Nigger's Leap", "Bora Ring" and "Half-caste Girl", all written at this time, her imagination was entering into this radioactive zone.

The story of Nigger's Leap "had sunk more deeply into her life than [her father] would perhaps have liked; and was to influence it to the end". Though it is the kind of story most would prefer to forget or "shuffle back into a violent and miserable past", for her "that dark cliffhead, with the depth of shadows below it in the gulfs, is still a potent place"[34] – as the Danish philosopher Søren Kierkegaard said, we tend to live our lives forward and understand them backwards.

In a piece Judith wrote for the Tasmanian Wilderness Calendar for 1982, for example, she reflects on the twin strands which have run through her life: love of the land and a sense of some "darkness" in it, or at least in the history of our relations with it, and of her own complicity within it.[35] At the time, of course, this sense was more inchoate than it was to become. But already it was cutting her off from childhood innocence on the one hand and on the other from the romanticism of writers like the Jindyworobaks, who were prepared to appropriate Aboriginal culture as a means of getting in touch with what they called "the spirit of the land". Brought up in a tradition of duty as she had been, Judith could not divorce knowledge from responsibility.

Her time in New England was important. But even though she had returned home to help her father, she now felt something of a stranger. Her experiences at university, in Europe and working in Sydney had put a distance between her and the rest of the family. Her "childhood spent almost in ignorance of city life"[36] was receding, and the beginnings of her uneasiness about the past were troubling her. But, more practically, the cold was having an effect. Not long after her grandfather's death her much loved little white dog, William, "now old but still brave and resourceful", died of age and cold. "I found him lying outside my father's office and wept as I hadn't wept since my grandfather died." She was later to remember him as the chief character in the children's book she published in 1958, *Kings of the Dingoes*. His death, following that of her grandfather, her last direct link with her mother, "seemed to close off [her] own youth".[37]

Judith was also beginning to feel that her usefulness at "Wallamumbi" was coming to an end. She still did not get on with her stepmother and spent some time with her sister-in-law and niece at "Jeogla". But she was missing the social life of Sydney. With the war still on, there were almost no young men left in the district and the routine of country life became increasingly oppressive. There was hope that the elder of her two brothers, Bruce, might soon be released from the army where he seemed to be doing nothing more than sitting in a suburban army depot in Brisbane. A sergeant major, he was supposed to be overseeing the reception of wrecked or broken-down army vehicles from northern bases or from New Guinea, but this was not a very demanding job and for much of the time he had little to do. In contrast, the escalation of the Pacific war meant that Australian farmers had an increasingly important role to play feeding the Allied armies; there would be plenty for him to do at home since their father had large commitments in food production. Long and tedious negotiations began with the army. Phillip Wright was by this time an influential man, so the family members hoped for success if they kept "annoying the authorities" and "moving everything that could be moved".[38]

For months they were "entangled in red tape – the army is a maddening career",[39] but it looked as if Judith might soon be able to get away without seeming to betray her father and the family. This was all the more important because she was beginning to be noticed as a poet, having had her work published in the *Sydney Morning Herald*, the *Bulletin* and the newly founded *Meanjin*. Douglas Stewart, the editor of the *Bulletin*'s Red Page, had written to her encouragingly and taken her to lunch when she was in Sydney to consult a specialist about her rapidly increasing deafness, and they had had a "good talk about poetry".[40]

In these poems Judith seemed to have expressed what many people were feeling, casting a new light on the land and its history at a time of crisis, observing it clearly and lovingly, and letting people speak in such a way that it made the story of settlement at once more heroic and more human. She was giving the land a new significance, creating a sense of the relationship between human beings and their environment and turning the simple legend of the bush into something much more monumental, as, for instance, in lines like these, describing a simple country landscape in which

> ... Evening and the earth are one,
> and bird and tree are simple and stand still.[41]

It was not accidental, of course, that this flowering had occurred when she went back to New England. In the city she had experienced a negativism and disassociation from the world, but here, returning to "the green world of a child"[42] she felt in touch with a "whole human reality which is much more than we are at any time conscious of possessing".[43] For that reason, even though she wanted to get out of the narrow circle of the family and their friends, she was not sure that she wanted to get back to Sydney – cities had always seemed dehumanising to her.

Meanjin, a new literary journal, drew her attention to Brisbane, at that stage something of a frontier town. But it was also the city closest to the war in the north and thus still somehow dangerous with the urgent passions of war, intensified by the American forces who had virtually taken it over. She began to think of going north, as earlier generations of her family had done, and helping with *Meanjin*, which seemed to her aware of the crisis of their time as no other journal in Australia then was.

Its founder, Clem Christesen, had been a radio broadcaster during the Depression and had published poems in the *Australian National*

Review in the late 1930s. But he was to prove that his great gift was as an editor. Rejected by the army in 1940 on account of asthma, he was working for the Queensland government writing tourist brochures when he and a group of friends launched their new journal in December 1940.[44] The first issue, a mere 250 copies and costing £4 10s to print, had a distinctive cover – four black footprints – and its title was Aboriginal, "Meanjin" being the name the local Aboriginal people gave to the neck of land on which Brisbane was originally founded. There was also a drawing of an Aboriginal child on the title page. However romanticised the image might be – Lynne Strahan describes the child as "a dark Christopher Robin, clutching his boomerang and dangling his catch behind him"[45] – the fact that it was there at all appealed to Judith. There was nothing like this in the *Australian National Review* or the *Australian Quarterly*. As for the *Bulletin*, its notorious slogan, "Australia for the White Man", and its cartoons representing Aborigines, if they were represented at all, as Jacky Jacky, a half comic, half incompetent, childish and inferior figure, confirmed all the old racist stereotypes she was beginning to question.

Meanjin's mood also echoed her feelings. In his explanation of the symbolism of the footsteps on the cover, Elkin, the Professor of Anthropology she had admired as an undergraduate, wrote that they were a reminder that

> we have to place our feet firmly in the heroic steps, and go forward to build an Australia, not only economically just, democratically free, educationally wide and morally strong, but also culturally alive – an Australia in which we shall live our own "dreamtime" myths, sharing them with all men of vision, courage and truth.[46]

Many of the essays in these early issues were about the horrors of war, "global bloody slaughter" as one writer called it, and the need for a transformation of value which Judith was also looking and hoping for. A quotation from Stephen Spender, which served as the epigraph to the second number in the journal's second year, 1943, in which "Soldier's Farm" was first published, spoke about the task she was also beginning to think about:

> In a world in which the system in which we have lived is collapsing all round us, and in which our religions and faiths are too bound up with the past and with the interests of that civilisation to adapt themselves to new circumstances, there is still the faint possibility that a poetry of poets who did not quibble, and divide themselves into small opposing schools, might remind men of the meaning of the dignity of life. Without becoming directly involved in politics themselves, it might create a picture of the nature of man's spiritual and physical being, around which a new political structure might crystallise. The poets might retain the values of the past, unconnected with vested interests and blind conventions, which would enable what is living and valid in the past to live into the future.[47]

There is a nice irony in the fact that a Brisbane relative of Judith's stepmother introduced Judith to *Meanjin*, sending her a copy of the first issue. But she soon became a regular contributor as well as a subscriber, and for a time there was a poem of hers in almost every issue. For her, *Meanjin* not only offered the opportunity for publication but also the inspiration she was looking for. As she told Christesen in her first letter;

> I very much admire the work that you and your staff are doing in continuing the publication of *Meanjin* ... under what must be extremely difficult conditions. More than ever at present it seems important that Australian poets should have some means of reaching the public, if the regimentation and mental brutalization of war are not to overcome us altogether.[48]

The mention of *Meanjin*'s staff – in fact until Judith became the unpaid secretary, Christesen *was Meanjin* – suggests a certain romantic or perhaps aristocratic misapprehension of life in the real world of literary journals, especially in wartime Brisbane. But *Meanjin* did seem to offer something for her there.

At that time she was not yet free to leave New England and in any case there were wartime restrictions on interstate travel. But in the meantime she could help financially – her father was paying her for her work, and where she was there was nothing much to spend it on. At first Judith offered this help diffidently since she realised it could seem as if she were buying publication.[49] Christesen seems to have had no such scruples and accepted the cheques she sent fairly regularly without query. In June 1943, going further, she offered to send £2 per quarter to help pay contributors. If she had not been so far away, she said, she would also have liked to help with the secretarial work.

As "Waiting", a poem written at this time suggests, she was feeling more and more constrained and that constraint did not only have to do with the way

> ...*the circling days weave tighter, and the spider*
> *Time binds us helpless till his sting go in.*
> *Moving in a dazed routine, we hardly wonder*
> *what hour ahead waits with a basilisk grin.*
> *Only the radio, like a seashell held to the ear,*
> *gives back the echo of our own blood's fever;*
> *its confused voices like the body's urgent warning*
> *of a disease that it may not recover.*[50]

She needed ideas as well as excitement and wrote frequently to Christesen, whom she was soon addressing as "Clem" while she became "Judy". But she was also deferential, telling him that she was "at the moment merely a Jackeroo" and assuring him when she asked his opinion of a poem – it happened to be "Waiting" – that "you can judge better than I can".[51]

Towards the end of 1943 Christesen wrote that he might pass through Armidale on a trip to Sydney that he was hoping to make, and she wrote back eagerly inviting him to break his journey there. "The country is marvellous to see at the moment," she told him, and she thought she would be able to get into town to see him even though they would be shearing at the time. Judith also advised him that the best hotel at which to stay was Tattersall's, "both for beer and bedding".[52] In fact he did not get to Armidale, but that only increased her hopes of getting to Brisbane.

Although Judith's interest in *Meanjin* was literary, Christesen's politics were also more sympathetic than those of the people around her in New England. "I am not interested in any party," she told him, "but I am considerably more left than right, though my family is rather the opposite."⁵³ She was also growing more critical of the way the land was being used – or misused. "Dust", written at this time, expresses this sense. The drought questions the achievements of the family and pastoralists like them, so assured of their importance to the country:

> *We counted the beautiful money*
> *and gave it in our hearts to the child asleep …*

But now,

> *the dust accuses. Our dream was the wrong dream,*
> *our strength was the wrong strength.*⁵⁴

This is a note which was to sound through the rest of her life.

On the larger scene, as the Allies pushed northwards in the Pacific and in Europe advanced on Berlin, the war seemed to be drawing to an end. Judith's brother, Bruce, was due home very soon and she would soon be able to leave. Sydney was too big and too complicated, and many of her friends were now "in prison camps, or mutilated, or dead".⁵⁵ The choice, therefore, was Brisbane, although she did not know anyone there apart from Christesen and her stepmother's relations. But it seemed interesting. General MacArthur had moved his headquarters there from Melbourne so that, instead of merely listening to the radio, Judith would be much closer to the war, if not involved in it. Brisbane would also be warm and, in contrast with the austerity of the New England landscape, tropically lush, perhaps like the tropics she remembered from the childhood trip to Surabaya – they had sailed from Brisbane on that trip.

To get there, however, Judith needed a job, otherwise she would not be given a clearance to travel interstate. She had had enough of advertising and of working for local government. But seeing an advertisement for a clerk for the Australian Universities Commission branch based at the University of Queensland, she applied for it successfully. Late in 1943 she took the train north with her ticket and credentials and two prewar suitcases packed with her prewar clothes (she had worn mainly work clothes in New England) and books.⁵⁶

The eighteen months she had spent in the country had made her see the land with new eyes, "as beloved and ... my own blood and bone"[57], and had also changed her and set her on a different track, making her more secure in the distance she felt between herself and the rest of the family. Leaving them now, she felt she had made a choice. As she put it in "The Moving Image", written in 1944:

> ...the lovelier distance is ahead.
> I would go farther with you, clock and star,
> though the earth break under my feet and storm
> snatch at my breath and night ride over me.

She was also beginning to be recognised as a writer at last, which gave her a new confidence, a new sense of energy:

> I am the maker. I have both time and fear,
> knowing that to yield to either is to be dead.
> All that is real is to live, to desire, to be.

She was looking for something more, the "dangerous music" with which "The Moving Image" concludes:

> Yet listen, the music grows around us, before us, behind,
> there is sound in the silence; the dark is a tremor of light.
> It is the corn rising when winter is done.
> It is the madmen singing, the lovers, the blind;
> the cry of Tom of Bedlam, naked under the sun.[58]

Perhaps when she wrote these lines she had already met the most important person in her life, the man who, like Tom of Bedlam in the poem,

> ...makes one word of the song all life is learning.[59]

CHAPTER VI

"SENSES THAT SPOKE AND MIND THAT SHAPED A WORLD"

from "The Moving Image",
Collected Poems, p. 5

The trip north to Brisbane was a trip into the war zone. The sedate rhythms of country life where she had spent so much of her time and which had shaped her childhood –

From the houses on the hill the small smoke rises
in patterns of vague peace from dawn to night[1]

– faded away and the syncopations increased. At Wallangarra, on the border where the rail gauges changed, the difficulties of loading and unloading "moved the American forces to incredulous oaths". Military guards patrolled the platforms and endless lines of railway trucks going north with supplies and guns, like the trains of her poem, shunted and groaned.[2]

It was a long journey, and when Judith finally arrived Brisbane was very different from the sleepy beach town, "the Cinderella town in [the] Cinderella state" of family tradition.[3] Many people had fled in the days of panic when the Japanese were advancing south and Darwin, Broome and Townsville were bombed and there were rumours that the whole north above the Brisbane line was to be abandoned. Schools and other institutions had also packed up and gone inland and rural families found themselves entertaining relations from the city, come to stay for the duration.[4] But as civilians moved out the military moved in. At the height of the crisis there seemed to be almost as many men in uniform as civilians, and even in 1944 it was still a town at war.

Judith recalls the streets crowded with the "well-filled olive and blue uniforms of the US Army and Airforce and the dough-boy caps and skittish sailor collars of the Navy" besides whom the "sloppy and worn khaki" of the comparatively few Australian soldiers not fighting in New Guinea seemed shabby in comparison with the sleekly fitted opulence of the Americans. The city was also filled with the camp followers, black marketeers and suppliers of goods, legitimate and illegitimate, to the servicemen. Many of the people who had fled in 1942 and 1943 had not returned, partly because it was nearly impossible to find accommodation and many were living in garages or tar-paper shelters under houses. But that was part of the ramshackle air of the place; with manpower scarce, even for street-sweeping and cleaning, the whole town seemed shabby and rakish.

The problem, then, for Judith was to find somewhere to live. Before she left New England Christesen had invited her to stay with him and his Russian-born wife, Nina. But wanting to be independent she refused. The Christesens, however, found her a room at 100 Sydney Street, New Farm, which had previously been rented by Dorothy Auchterlonie (later Dorothy Green), a contemporary of Judith's at university. Though they had seen very little of one another since – Auchterlonie had been an evening student – they were to become friends and allies later. Auchterlonie had been working for the ABC but was now leaving Brisbane for Sydney. It was a nice coincidence, and Wright was grateful to have somewhere to live, even if it was by no means luxury accommodation:

> It was a narrow and windowless room, with a stretcher, a table and chair and cupboard and little else, but it was luxury compared with what I might have found for myself. The tram to and from the city ran beside the house, clanging and clashing blue sparks on its way across the points towards the river at the end of Sydney Street. Over the road, New Farm Park with its rows of crimson-flowering poinciana trees and its palms and roo-garden stretched to the river. It contained a tumbled-down

dunny with unclean buckets and with a variety of graffiti on the ladies' side, offering advice to girls about pregnancy and the Yanks, probably not taken by the struggling forms I passed on my evening walks.[5]

The house was owned by friends of the Christesens, John and Ada Ward. Ada was the widow – "or at least that was the accepted view"[6] – of Randolph Bedford, a once wealthy mining entrepreneur who was also a writer who had published in the *Bulletin*. Although he seemed a slightly raffish figure, Judith had heard of him in Sydney and at "the prim-lipped (Local) University",[7] so that did not worry her. Besides, Ada's previous association with Bedford gave her a certain standing in Brisbane's literary circles, something in which her boarder could share. John, Ada's new husband, had no such pretensions; he, too, was in touch with the racy side of life, being a taxi driver – a profitable if not entirely respectable occupation in a city largely occupied by American soldiers, sailors and airmen. Taxi drivers could become as rich as they cared to since the Americans seemed to have no idea of money and were easily conned into tipping lavishly. As Judith observed, "money more or less fell into his pocket".[8] Ada's daughter, a medical student, had her own income, so there was no need to rent out their spare room, and they probably let it to Judith as a favour to Clem, who also claimed to have been a friend of Randolph Bedford. It was pleasant enough, however, even if cramped, and Brisbane's warmth encouraged her to sit outside and write, basking like a lizard in the sun under a big old tree in the backyard.[9]

When she first arrived her brother Bruce was still in Brisbane, seething under the restrictions and idiocies of the army and of his job, and longing to get back to his wife and little daughter in New England. They would often meet for meals, though since Bruce was only a sergeant major and good restaurants were expensive and usually open only to officers, these were not luxurious affairs. A family friend, also stuck in the army in Brisbane where his young wife and baby had joined him in a squalid little room, was also company.

At work Judith was the sole representative of the Universities Commission. Her desk, grudgingly provided by the "overcrowded little

University",[10] was in a temporary annexe, a shed occupied by the examinations section which consisted of three or four typists and one Val Ward, "a cheerful heavily built young man" who appeared to be her nominal boss but disclaimed any connection with the Universities Commission and professed no interest in what it did. Judith had as little to do as she had had at Sydney University but much more to interest her.

There was little reason, therefore, for complaint. She was well paid, and Brisbane, if corrupt, was lively and cheerful and if dirty, was warm. As a city it seemed disposed to enjoy life and she rejoiced in its flamboyant vegetation and flowers, "the electric-blue of morning glories scrambling over unpainted fences, the flaming yellow of cassias and the magenta of bougainvillea and the palms with their languid dirty feather-dusters, disguised its sins".[11] She found it a rumbustious place after New England. So did her friends. Years later, Barrie Reid, a distinguished literary man who became State Librarian of Victoria, recalled those years. He had been younger than she but precociously enjoyed what he saw:

> How extraordinary Brisbane was in the war years – segregation with the black town and jazz clubs in South Brisbane, the black girls coming up from the Northern Rivers; powdered MacArthur and equally powdered Mountbatten striding out the side door of that bank at the corner of Queen and Edward; the bloody fights between the Yanks and our lot on so many street corners, the parks full of people fucking; your trains going North with guns.[12]

This was a different world from anything Judith had known before. But its energies appealed to her, too. She liked the tropical warmth, the flowering trees and the gardens, not of roses, delphiniums, petunias and decorous lawns shadowed with hedges and conifers as they were in New England but of tropical flowers with a "richer depth of colour" and the kind of fertile luxuriance which had fascinated her on her childhood family visit to the Netherlands East Indies. It was the kind of beauty she wrote about in the unpublished short story "Save the First Dance" and attributed to Gisela, the exotic schoolgirl from the tropics whose presence transformed the drab boarding school with her beauty. In the story it promised freedom on the one hand and on the other highlighted the "fear and dislike of natural beauty that animated the Church authorities who laid down the roles of our dress and of our days and ruled the school".[13]

Now Judith was in this tropical world, in the last hectic but confident stages of the Pacific war, and her own woman at last. Here the air seemed "more golden and warmer" than she had known before, and beyond the city she imagined a "darker depth of forests and a deeper blue of mountains and sea" to be explored. She also liked the cheerful and unashamed shoddiness of the poorer suburbs on the city side of the Botanic Gardens with their dingy factories and small businesses and broken-down houses under rusty tin roofs by the "muddy brown snake" of the river. Most of the brothels were here also, with the girls in kimonos and open dressing-gowns sitting on rickety chairs on the pavement and doing a roaring trade with the servicemen.[14]

Where Judith had come from, cleanliness and order were the marks of decent people but from childhood she had rebelled against them. Here, however, everything flourished and sprawled, and cockroaches and rats were an unavoidable part of life. She did not enjoy finding a dead cockroach one day in a milkshake she had ordered from the kiosk in the Botanical Gardens where she had lunch, but that was Queensland she reflected, and even if there had been a Department of Health to which she could complain, which she doubted, it was "probably almost without staff or rules to be appealed to".[15] Soap was scarce, things grew rapidly, flowered and decayed and everywhere "there was a lingering smell of grease and human odours,"[16] and the urgency of war:

all that is real is to live, to desire, to be.[17]

Untidiness did not trouble her much, though she felt for the young wife of the New England family friend who was posted there in the army, who used to sit up all night for fear that the huge rats which infested their room might attack the baby. But for Judith the easygoing air of the place appealed after the strenuous years she had been through.

Even the divisions between rich and poor, which had been evident when she was growing up in New England, and even more evident in Sydney during the surveys she did for J. Walter Thompson, seemed different and less troubling here since the gentility principle that exaggerated these divisions did not seem to operate in Brisbane; people did not "seem to want any other views of life than those they already had."[18] Aboriginal people, too, were far more numerous than in Sydney or New England, a

> visible presence, a background of dark sorrowful faces, as [she] travelled between the north and south sides of the river, the train carried [her] through suburbs where they seemed to predominate in numbers, as they had not done in the south ... In Sydney, it had been possible to forget their existence – they did not come to the city proper, and suburbs like La Perouse were out of sight and presence, while Redfern and Surry Hills were more or less taboo areas.[19]

Physically fertile as it was, however, Brisbane was not a centre of intellectual energy. In New England Judith had thought about the kind of world she wanted when the war was over and had hoped in Brisbane to be in touch with others who shared her hopes for the future and "to break away from old ties and disappointments".[20] But here most people seemed to see "the war's end as a chance to resume the old priorities, not to begin building a war-free world".[21] Even at *Meanjin* things were not quite as she had hoped. From New England she had written to Christesen that she was looking forward to "plenty of chances to talk",[22] but when she arrived she found that she was merely expected to be the secretary. The magazine was Christesen's creation and he kept a tight hold on it. Judith had little to do with policy or content, spending most of her time editing material he had already edited. From a distance *Meanjin* had seemed a force for the new order she and many others looked for as the war drew to a close, but at close quarters what she found was a struggle for funding and quarrels between Christesen and his patrons and collaborators.

Nevertheless, the Christesens' house at Dutton Park was the centre of as much intellectual life as Brisbane had at the time and Judith spent many evenings there, coming by tram across the city from New Farm. Like most people, she loved Nina, Clem's wife, "curved and sweetly made, kindness beamed out of her, and her blue eyes were trustworthy",[23] but she did not find Clem so easy to get on with. He was a good editor and had a lively mind, but she found him volatile, inclined to enthusiasms and too easily impressed by people who were better educated than he was, especially if they were American – very different from the kind of man she most admired, quiet, steady and thoughtful like her father. Judith's recollections are probably coloured by the tensions which later grew up between them but they suggest she was disappointed in the man she had admired from afar: "Clem was thought lucky to have married Nina; there was about him a combative peevishness that seemed to twitch his moustache and line his forehead with marks of self-defensive and retaliatory emotions that I didn't much like".[24]

While handling the correspondence at *Meanjin* Judith got to know writers she admired like David Campbell and Rosemary Dobson (who later became friends) and William Hart-Smith whom she never met but whose imagistic style she enjoyed.[25] She was also in touch with the Jindyworobak movement to whose anthology she contributed. She thought that Flexmore Hudson was "on the right track" with his interest in Aboriginal culture, but she was fair-minded enough to acknowledge that he was not as good an editor as Christesen and that he encouraged what she regarded as "some unsatisfactory writing"[26] – intellectual integrity was always important for her.

At *Meanjin* she was also close to the Ern Malley affair. When Max Harris, editor of the avant-garde journal *Angry Penguins*, received a bundle of poems by an unknown new poet, Ern Malley, he had written to Christesen telling him that he had discovered a significant new talent and was sending some of them to him for his opinion. In turn, Christesen then consulted Judith. Always interested in experiment, she liked them and insists to this day that there were some good poems in the collection: "You can't sit two poets down over a quantity of beer with paper in front of them and not get some pretty remarkable phraseology out of it whatever the intention".[27]

The atmosphere at *Meanjin* was also more receptive to women than at the *Bulletin*, and Judith was treated more or less as an equal, meeting other writers like "the good James Devaney", a poet who had published, as she had, in the *Australian National Review* before the war and had befriended John Shaw Neilson who was then living with him and his wife in Brisbane. Unfortunately he was trying to protect the old man from the local literati, so to her regret Judith did not meet Neilson, remarking that she "was not seen as the sort of person who would interest him, so no one took me".[28] Years later, however, she played an important role in reviving interest in his poetry, editing two collections – one of them of hitherto unpublished poems – and writing extensively and enthusiastically about his work, especially in her seminal *Preoccupations in Australian Poetry*. At *Meanjin* she also met Paul Grano, another poet published in the *Australian National Review*, "a semi-failed Catholic with the painful conscience that the Church inflicted on sinners and backsliders".[29]

Americans posted in Brisbane or on leave there also came sometimes, "looking for signs of literary ability among the natives whom they were defending from Japan's ambitions". Christesen was impressed by them, especially the poets, and several became *Meanjin* contributors, most notably Karl Shapiro. Judith was less impressed, however, perhaps because she felt patronised, noting somewhat tartly that "Pearl Harbor wasn't a subject they brought up".[30] But they were generous with their books, lending them and sometimes leaving them behind when they moved north into the war zone, in this way introducing the *Meanjin* circle to American poetry, until then very difficult to come by, in Brisbane especially. On their side some young American writers became interested in Australian writing and were to keep up this interest.

There were also a number of older and much more conservative writers who had held sway in Brisbane since the 1930s – called the "Arthurs and Marthas" by some of the *Meanjin* group – but Judith had little to do with them. She was more interested in a lively group of young writers, the Barjais. While still at school in 1943 Barrie Reid started a magazine, *Barjai* (the name for a meeting place for youth in the local Aboriginal dialect), "designed to further cultural activity among the youth of today", as he pretentiously put it. It appeared bi-monthly and survived until 1947 when its editor and founding members moved away. They were a lively group, and many of them later made their names as writers or littérateurs.

They met every second Sunday afternoon at the "ladylike Lyceum Club rooms" on the second floor of a Queen Street building in the centre of the city to listen to invited speakers, drink tea and read their own work. Barbara Patterson (later Blackman), one of the group, remembers Barrie Reid as "the essential romantic hero ... straight, handsome, with a fall of blond hair above engaging blue eyes" and with a rascally wit. His lieutenant was Laurie Collinson, the personification of "avant-garde subversion ... as pale and consumptive as a poet should look, Jewish, homosexual and Communist". As well as reading his own poems Reid gave serious papers about "The Artist And The Modern World Crisis", for example, and introduced them to the novels of Rex Warner, the poetry of Sidney Keyes and George Borcheu's "Say No To Wax". Collinson's contribution was less solemn, "pithy Audenesque poems" which played with references to Freud and other thinkers then regarded as shocking.

In those days other members of the group were Barbara Patterson, Grace Perry and Thelma Forshaw. Thea Astley came occasionally, "an elder member, good looking in an angular way, who looked down from her height, read pieces generally crackling and arid". Laurence Hope, "gentle, impish, Aboriginal in lankiness and hair foliage" would also appear from time to time, bringing in a "few wet paintings of northern cane fields on his return from road-gang work there". Charles Osborne, from a serious Bible-reading family, was drawn in, too, to become a serious literary man in later life and editor of the *London Magazine*. There were more exotic members of the group, like Patricia Maria Therese O'Rourke, who had been to Brisbane's most elegant Catholic school where the students were expected to speak French, but who lived in the Regatta Hotel on the river where her father was the publican and wrote poems of "appropriate mystery and elaboration".[31]

Judith was over twenty-one so she was not eligible to publish in *Barjai*, but she was invited to speak at their meetings. One of these occasions was in November 1945, not long after the war had ended. Guy Howarth, her former English lecturer, had been the speaker at the previous meeting but the impression he made was nothing in comparison with hers. Barrie Reid recalled it as "a brilliant afternoon. Her talk was electrifying. Every one of us still speaks of it. Despite the indecisive delivery and her shyness she had the attention of everyone. It was a triumph". What most appealed, moreover, was that she spoke about "the personal, the existential" – a fashionable word then – and that she attacked "the neurotic luxuriation, [the] self-pity and [the] carefully nurtured ailments" they found in so many contemporary intellectuals, "the irresponsibles, the moaners", he called them. This was what many of the group were looking for:

> She believes [he went on] that the crisis today is psychological; it cannot be solved by science. We can only be rescued by complete understanding, by being completely honest not only intellectually but also emotionally. We must discover and understand the real value of life. We must be emotionally intelligent – only thus can this world-wide psychological distress be cured and the world saved from centuries of no light ... We are the disease. Until we are ourselves this sickness will roar about the world. The responsibility rises hugely before us.[32]

This was only a few months after the first two atomic bombs dropped on Hiroshima and Nagasaki had brought the war to an end but also cast the shadow of annihilation over the world. Judith's mood was apocalyptic, but rational. She would not join the stampede to the left, and her talk, according to Reid, "strengthened [his] wobbly anarchic resolve not to be captured by the Communist Party", then riding on the crest of popularity because of the heroic resistance of the Russians during the war and because, to many, communism seemed to offer the promise of a new world.

Judith had always been suspicious of easy answers and dogmatic systems. Besides, her patrician sense was offended by the communists whom she found not only "one eyed" but "tough and abusive also".[33] Even as a child she had disliked conformity, especially conformity with some kind of absolute sanction, and many were turning to communism as to a system of belief. This dislike and this suspicion were strengthened by her friendship with Jack McKinney, who also spoke to the Barjais.[34] She had met him at the Christesens', where he came from time to time to borrow books from Clem's library. A self-taught philosopher, he occasionally contributed to *Meanjin* and interested Judith at once by the range and originality of his ideas. When they met he was living contentedly in a little house at Surfer's Paradise, then a small fishing town, keeping himself by gardening and selling vegetables, but spending most of his time reading and thinking. His marriage had broken down and his wife had gone south when the Japanese threat was at its height. A spry small man with sharp blue eyes and a little goatee beard, he seemed strangely self-sufficient.

He was more than twenty years older than Judith, and he seemed to know where he was going, even if he was not entirely clear how he would get there. But he shared her sense that something had gone very seriously wrong with Western civilisation and her suspicion of ideology. In contrast, Christesen had been publishing articles by overseas writers like Arthur Koestler and Alex Comfort, which she found "rather propagandist, if interesting enough". In her view they had not got to the heart of the matter, the need for another set of values, a redefinition of what "reality" might mean and a sense of the "lovelier distance ahead" which "The Moving Image" looked for.[35] "What a mess those serious-minded poor devils are in", she had written to Christesen after reading one of these articles, "up against basic contradictions wherever they turn, and quite unable to solve them on their premises".[36]

Commitment was in the air. *Meanjin* had published Sartre's "We Write For Our Time: For An Engaged Literature" that year, 1945, and a series of articles in successive issues on "the future we mean to have", written by people like C. E. W. Bean (who wrote the history of Australia's part in World War I), Vance Palmer and Manning Clark, then a young academic. Christesen was clear that this was the way to go: "the times demand certain loyalties", he wrote to a friend,[37] and his editorial for the first number of *Meanjin* for 1945 also made this clear:

> We feel the majority of people understand that this war is not a war only but an end and a beginning, an end of things known and a beginning of things unknown ... This new drive is coming mainly from the younger people ... largely untouched by the between-wars disillusionment. In the work of these young writers and artists a strong socio-political consciousness is evident ... To them art and politics are interlocked. They challenge present-day education, advertisement and propaganda, which ... has helped to produce some criminal social disintegration.[38]

In a sense, of course, Judith was one of these younger writers, and she had interrogated the present order of things, in poems like "Country Town":

Where do the roads lead? It is not where we expected.
The gold is mined and safe, and where is the profit?
The church is built, the bishop is ordained,
and this is where we live: where do we live?
And how should we rebel? The chains are stronger.[39]

But nobody seemed to be asking, much less to have any idea of how to answer these questions until she met McKinney, whose ideas, complicated but strangely compelling, exploded into her uncertainty. Not only was he preoccupied with the questions which concerned her, about war and the general direction of Western culture, but he also believed that women and artists were the ones best able to answer them, assuming, as she did, that

All that is real is to live, to desire, to be.[40]

The articles he was publishing in *Meanjin* about the need for a "transvaluation of value" spoke to her as nothing else she was reading did.

He was old enough to be her father, having been born in 1891, and came from a different background – and at this stage perhaps this was the role he played for her. His father had been a journalist working on country newspapers in Victoria, becoming president of the Country Press Association and ending his career as a senior journalist with the Melbourne *Argus*. But on his mother's side he was related to the explorer Robert O'Hara Bourke, who was his mother's brother. He was proud of this, perhaps because in his own way he was an explorer, and one never "put off by lack of knowledge of the terrain",[41] as Judith observed.

After leaving Scotch College, which he disliked, he became a journalist like his father. But, sent on one of his first assignments to interview the widow of a man killed in a gruesome industrial accident, he threw in his job and set off on his bicycle into the bush, getting as far as Broken Hill. The journey all but killed him, however. It was midsummer, so hot that the tyres on his bicycle melted and he nearly died of exhaustion and heat. Recovering, he became an opal miner at White Cliffs, then a station hand in Western New South Wales and Southern Queensland, finally saving enough to buy his own plant and set up as a drover. When World War I broke out, however, he worked his way back to Victoria to enlist in the light horse.[42]

But he suffered from a birth defect, Achilles heel, which was likely to disqualify him medically. So he persuaded a friend already in the army to provide him with a uniform. That done, he issued himself with a regimental number, a crime sheet and a medical history record. This unusual way of getting into the army also meant that he avoided having to swear the oath of allegiance – something which was to please him for the rest of his life.

His training, such as it was, finished, he sailed for Egypt with reinforcements for the 13th Light Horse but, fortunately for him, he arrived too late to take part in the Gallipoli campaign. In Egypt he was transferred to the bicycle corps and sent to France where he served, with occasional breaks for leave, until the end of the war in November 1918, being promoted to company sergeant major in 1917. It was only when his bad heel finally gave out and he was wounded in September 1918 that his disability and his unofficial presence in the army were discovered and he became something of a conundrum to the bureaucratic mind. He was sent back to France, however, and after the Armistice was sent to a course in wool-classing to prepare him for civilian life. He was finally discharged in February 1920 with a clean bill of health, despite the fact that he was to suffer not only from shellshock – something the army took little account of – but also from gastric and heart troubles for the rest of his life. For the rest of his life, too, he had to fight the army to keep even the very small disability pension he had managed to secure.

Those years in the trenches continued to haunt him with terrible nightmares, and even sometimes in broad daylight he would have attacks of terror, going white and trembling all over. Very often when an aircraft flew over, he would fling himself to the ground in fear. But he was not a man to surrender to nightmares.[43]

He was determined to work out why Western civilisation had collapsed into the shambles of this war, teaching him and thousands of others how to reduce "a delicately constituted, living, loving, thinking piece of human mechanism (known in this instance as the enemy) to such a condition of bloody unrecognisability as would unfit him for further uses of war".[44] The novel he wrote in 1935, *The Crucible*, which won first prize in a competition instituted by the Victorian Returned

Servicemen's League (RSL) for the best novel about the war and is dedicated to "the memory of all those good fellows (which includes many officially 'bad' fellows) whom we left behind on the other side", is part of that attempt. To him, the war was a work of "colossal insanity"; "men turned into machines, slaves to the guns"... "Science! Civilization. It all came to this. A gigantic game of skittles."[45] In this context "life's ideals" seemed a hollow sham.[46] As he wrestled with these questions, he became more and more interested in philosophy and convinced that our whole civilisation needed to be set on a new and different footing if humanity were to survive. This was the point he had reached when Judith met him.

After returning to Australia in 1920 he had married Myrtle Gallagher, the daughter of a saddler who lived in Wentworth on the New South Wales–Victorian border and a former teacher and nurse who had served overseas with the army. They had four children, two boys and two girls. After the marriage McKinney worked first as the manager of a large maize plantation near Kingaroy in Queensland and then took up a soldier–settler block nearby, raising pigs and running a dairy farm. But the work of clearing and fencing as well as running the farm was too much for him and the Depression of the 1930s broke them financially. They retreated to Surfers Paradise on the coast where he supported the family by writing short stories and a long-running radio serial, *The Noonans*, about a family of Irish settlers. He was also shortlisted to write the famous series *Dad and Dave*. But it was a battle to survive, and the army refused to give him more than seventy-five per cent of the pension he should have been entitled to. The prize money from *The Crucible* temporarily saved the day, however, enabling him to buy the fibro shack he was living in when he first met Judith.

In 1943, when the Japanese threat was at its height, his wife finally left, taking the two younger children. McKinney was left virtually penniless since he sent his pension to her, but he was free to concentrate on his philosophy, reading through the history of Western thought to see where it had gone wrong and then to work out how it might be set on a different basis, one which would stand for the values of life rather than the values of death. Obviously this was a huge and ambitious project, especially for someone with no academic training and so few resources. In Queensland, libraries were few and far between and starved of resources; in the course of a debate in State Parliament on the allocation of funds for training one of the two librarians at the Brisbane Public Library, for instance, one member angrily rejected the idea, declaring that funds would be requested soon for training rubbish collectors.[47] To make things worse, the war had made books and paper very difficult to come by.

The main reason why McKinney visited the Christesens was to borrow books – thanks to his American friends, Christesen had one of the best libraries in Brisbane. But McKinney was also hoping that Christesen would help him find a publisher for the book he was working on, an examination of the failure of Western philosophy and an attempt to find an alternative to it. Christesen was talking of setting up a *Meanjin* publishing house, so he might be interested in his project, McKinney thought, especially as Christesen professed to be interested in new ideas and new responses to the challenge of the postwar world.

Judith had never met anyone quite like him. He was asking the kind of questions she had been asking for some time and she soon decided that the answers he was suggesting might make the radical change she was looking for. But she also found him fascinating as a person. He was witty, famous for his Irish jokes, which he would tell with his blue eyes sparkling, and she found him "a joy to be with". His mind, too, was "like none I had come across in its quickness of apprehension, its surprising and, to me, often illuminating, comments on books and theories I thought I knew about".[48] Others might see him condescendingly as something of a crank, but the difficult and abstruse questions he was exploring interested her, though she had not formulated them so clearly or so ambitiously.

As the war moved north and then came to an end Brisbane was reverting to the sleepy beach town it had been previously. But in McKinney Judith found the intellectual challenge she was looking for:

> I hadn't had my mind so stretched for many years – it was a challenge I enjoyed more and more. It began to set me, too, off on new tracks of thinking and to put those years of Andersonian philosophy in quite new lights. The thinkers most people revered

were being turned upside down and their pockets rifled and they seemed to begin to mean something more than they themselves, and my teachers had apparently known.[49]

She found an integrity in him, a "certainty, passion and peace"[50] that was immensely attractive. Unlike her, he seemed to have few doubts about his own integrity and purposes, and in this way may have reminded her of her father. It mattered, too, that she could be useful to him with her philosophical training and also with her secretarial skills. In her own way, like her distant relation Patrick White at this same time, she was tired of being aimless.

At *Meanjin* Christesen still relied on Judith as his unpaid secretary. But he did not seem prepared to give her any more responsibility and she disliked the constant preoccupation with money and the tensions which had grown up between Christesen and many of his former friends and supporters. *Meanjin*'s financial situation was becoming desperate. Dr Duhig, the patron who had largely financed the magazine, was no longer prepared to go on doing so, and it seemed as if it would have to cease publication. Just at this point, however, Colin Badger, director of the extension service at the University of Melbourne, approached Christesen. Interested in acquiring a literary journal for the university, he invited him to bring *Meanjin* to Melbourne where he would be given an office and a university position and salary. The university would also pay a secretary's salary. Christesen offered that position to Judith, thinking that her growing reputation as a poet would also be an asset, pressing her to accept.

But, quite apart from her dislike of the cold weather she would find in Melbourne, Judith and Clem were no longer at ease with one another. Partly this was temperamental, due to Clem's refusal to regard her as anything more than a secretary, but possibly it was also partly because of the growing tension between him and McKinney. Christesen seems to have disliked the way McKinney was taking up more and more of the time of his unpaid secretary and supplanting him as her intellectual mentor (which seems to be how he saw himself). McKinney was aware of this, and a letter he wrote to Christesen about this time implicitly defends his friendship with Judith in a way which suggests how important she had become to him:

> The situation might be described as follows. A person, A, who has been following a certain line of inquiry for several years, comes in contact with a person, B, who has followed a similar line of inquiry and has worked out the answer. Naturally A (being the frank and generous [sic] person A ['B' is crossed out here and 'A' substituted] is) is impelled to make available to B the information etc. which she has gained in the course of her own independent inquiries, and this being in the nature of the case, precisely what B is in need of he takes the fullest possible advantage of the aid offering. The inevitability of the situation becomes all the more obvious when it is realised that the answer to which B has arrived is of a far-reaching nature that goes infinitely further in its implications than any personal considerations of either A or B.[51]

Evidently this was not the first time the matter has been discussed since he concludes: "It was the inevitability that I was intending to convey which I spoke of B having been 'sent' to Brisbane, which was not really as mystical as it sounded." The tone is not particularly romantic; what he seems to appreciate is Judith's usefulness to him in "digging up all sorts of stuff in which notable people – Dunne, Eddington and others – are trying to formulate what is reduced to simple terms in Towards The Future". But masculine culture then tended to be even more shy of emotion than it is now, and in any case the two men never got on really well. Nevertheless it is clear that McKinney counted on Judith, and she decided to stay on in Brisbane.

She was certainly helpful to him. Working in the university, she had access to the library and through one of her friends there, arranged inter-library loans for him of works he would have otherwise been unable to get hold of, works by contemporary philosophers and scientists such as Jeans, Broad and Einstein, and journals of philosophy, science and mathematics in which new developments in those areas were being discussed. Judith also had accounts with bookshops in Sydney where she could buy books for him which were not available in Brisbane. Whenever McKinney came to Brisbane they would spend hours discussing this reading and she would often spend her weekends at Surfer's Paradise, staying with a neighbour down the road; once or twice, when her brother Bruce was in Brisbane, he came with her and they could with propriety – an important matter then – stay with McKinney in his little house. Fortunately, the two men got on well, and McKinney's elder daughter, Lucy, also liked Judith.

McKinney's experiences had made him wary of personal commitment. All his energies were directed to his philosophical work, and his correspondence with Christesen does not suggest any deep feeling for Judith at this stage. He was also emotionally fragile. In 1943, when he had only just met Judith, he confessed to Christesen that he was "in a pretty bad plight at the moment, my brain is not functioning" and he could not "get on with work", adding that "my brain goes like that periodically".[52] Later, probably in late 1944 or early 1945, he was also longing for "anything that can contribute to clarity of thought and calmness of nerve, in no matter how humble a way ... to be given right of way".[53] But he was beginning to take a certain pride in Judith's growing reputation, writing to Christesen in 1945: "Say, our Judith is forging ahead isn't she?... and she is doing good work", though he thought her most recent poem published in *Meanjin* (probably either "Nigger's Leap" or "Eli, Eli") "wasn't her best".[54]

Suddenly, however, with the war over, his wife returned to Surfer's Paradise. Trying to finish his book, and faced with the need to make a choice, McKinney took flight. What he said to Judith we do not know. But he did write to Christesen, entrusting his daughter Lucy and his manuscript to him, writing that: "My domestic affairs have come to a stage of finality and I'll be a wanderer on the face of the earth for a while, till I find a spot to settle in ... I'm going on that biking tour I once spoke of ... Herewith Lucy and the manuscript – both precious".[55]

Judith's thoughts are not recorded. But McKinney kept in touch with her, writing from the different places he visited about the books he had discovered in the local library – the first place he visited – and in her spare time, she got on with typing his book and the articles he was writing. When he got back, his wife was still in the house at Surfer's Paradise. Leaving her there and settling his pension on her, he gave his address to Christesen as c/- Indooroopilly Post Office. For the next year or so he earned his living as a gardener, living where and as he could, and sometimes going away on his bicycle as he tried to finish his book. But Christesen was distancing himself from his promise to publish the book. Academic philosophers to whom he showed parts of it were not impressed – McKinney had had no formal training in philosophy and in any case he was questioning the premises of the discipline as they knew it. Christesen himself had little understanding of the difficulties of what McKinney was trying to do. So he came to depend on Judith. She was not only the only one who understood and appreciated what he was trying to do but could also discuss his ideas with him.

Poems like "The Moving Image", first published in 1945, express her sense at this time of being in transition. She had been, she felt, "dwarfed by the dark", by the horrors of the war just finished when she had felt that there was "no end to the breaking" and by its horrifying conclusion, the annihilation of Hiroshima and Nagasaki. Yet that poem concludes with a sense of new life and new hope:

> *Yet listen, the music grows around us, before us, behind,*
> *there is sound in the silence; the dark is a tremor of light.*
> *It is the corn rising when winter is done.*
> *It is the madmen singing, the lovers, the blind;*
> *the cry of Tom of Bedlam, naked under the sun.*[56]

This figure of the fool, Tom of Bedlam, came from *King Lear*, of course. But the poem's description of him,

> *One word in his mouth spread open like a fan,*
> *the sound of it dwarfed the stars and stole his breath*
> *as a million voices shouted it to each;*
> *and through the web of all their lives he ran*
> *to grasp a glory never in one man's reach*[57]

in its own way prefigures what she was to write later of Jack McKinney after his death:

> *There was a sureness in your contemplation,*
> *a purity in that closed look you wore,*
> *as though a godwit, rising from its shore,*

> *followed alone and on its first migration*
> *its road of air across the tumbled sea,*
> *containing its own angel of assurance*
> *that far out there its promised home would be.*[58]

However that may be, his thinking was clarifying her own. She was beginning to have doubts about the way she had been brought up to see the world, beginning to feel that, as she put it in her autobiography:

> The language and culture I was brought up in ... had nothing to do with the land my relatives had taken. It was wholly imported, a second skin that never fitted, no matter how we pulled and dragged it over the landscape that we lived in. Nor, of course, did we ourselves fit. That fact was growing more obvious as the land changed under our hand.[59]

McKinney was beginning to suggest, however, that this was true for the Western world generally, that our definitions of reality and value had got it wrong. "What we call the world," he wrote, is "an experiential construction", the product of our perception, not necessarily something absolutely given.[60] But, he argued, the world picture we have thus created, based on rational thought and empirical measurement and trust in what we call the "facts" was no longer working; indeed, it threatened to destroy us and the world with us – the atomic bomb, after all, is a scientific triumph. This was the way Judith had been thinking also. It seemed to her that our world view suffered

> from one-sided masculinity and a linear narrowness of thought; their culmination in logical positivism and materialism seemed inevitable, and those developments ... struck me as leading nowhere but to a world scarcely worth living in, and one, clearly that was on a slide to its own destruction.[61]

When McKinney wrote that we can "only be saved by a change of our whole outlook on life, or, to use a now discredited but still useful term, by a change of heart ... a new way of looking at things, a new attitude to life that emerged spontaneously in men's minds",[62] Judith was in total agreement. But he also had an ironic approach she appreciated: "The case is urgent," he told Christesen, "The only hope is ... a sort of cosmic courage on the part of those prepared to take a pusch [sic] as part of the cosmic adventure," adding, characteristically, that, in this, we must also "have the backing of fact".[63]

For all his single-mindedness McKinney had a modest, even quizzical, attitude to himself. What mattered most to him was not what he discovered but what came to him, the kind of illumination he wrote about to Christesen, saying that "at last 'I' have accomplished something that 'I' always wanted to accomplish, and do you know what was stopping me all the time? 'I' was. There's more trouble caused by 'I' than anyone else I know."[64] He was also endearingly unworldly, quite indifferent to money and happy to live simply as he imagined a philosopher should. "In our family," he told his daughter Lucy, "we don't bother about money balances."[65] In this sense also he was the "wise fool" of "The Moving Image", the hidden face of the true identity Judith had always been looking for, someone more intent on the inner than on the outer life, and someone mercifully exempt from the "territorial quarrelling and the internecine warfare" she had observed in academia. His "limpid view of life" was "that if you were speaking the truth in a way which people could understand, that truth would be understood."[66] She knew enough about "academic methods and defensive in-fighting" to see that this integrity would not be enough if his work were to gain acceptance. It "would have to be backed up with more acceptable authority than he was yet able to give it". Even if Christesen did publish his book, who would "listen to a wayside philosopher in those sophisticated, professional, institutionalised times"?[67]

However quixotic the attempt, Judith was determined that McKinney would be heard. He would "have to find what the thinkers were thinking and take them unawares in their own domain". Afraid that "the barbed-wire entanglements of academia might destroy him",[68] she would accompany him in his task. How complicated as well as difficult this task was to be would emerge during the next twenty years.

CHAPTER VII

THE GATEWAY

> For the new locus is never
> Hidden under the old one
> Where reason could rout it out
> Nor guarded by dragons in distant
> Mountains where Imagination
> Could explore it; the place of birth
> Is too obvious and near to notice
>
> from W. H. Auden, "The Age of Anxiety"

With the war over, the men were returning. "It was a quiet return, devoid of fanfares and parades. Most preferred it that way, slipping back into families, jobs and the slow rhythm of life with ease",[1] returning to hot and steamy Brisbane or to the wide dusty streets of inland towns. Finding refuge in a familiar world, from their memories of New Guinea and the Middle East or bombing raids over Europe in the pubs and corner stores, the family gatherings, sports meetings and races, they took up their old jobs – if they had had them – or walked easily into new ones as the postwar economy boomed. Food and clothes were still rationed and petrol, cigarettes and beer were in short supply. But for most people it was "easy as it goes". The war was over at last, life was beginning again; Australia was safe and secure, "the country of the future". Women who had worked while the men were away were returning home, having babies and looking after their husbands and their houses. With a car of their own, a Holden, the "people's car", in the garage, a new washing machine to put an end to much of the household drudgery, new clothes and money for holidays away for the family, for most people the late 1940s were good years.

The war had "left a dreadful hole in people's lives",[2] Judith's included. For her many things were still unresolved, most importantly her relationship with Jack. But she was troubled also by the way the war had ended: "If the US President had given the O.K. to wipe out whole cities at a blow, clearly none of us were going to be very civilized in the years ahead."[3] Nor at first was she alone in this anxiety. As Geoffrey Blainey put it in his review of these years: "The new era of the atom bomb was expected to be unsafe."[4] But for Judith it was a violent end to the years of violence.

With Jack she had been reading about contemporary developments in science and mathematics which had made these bombs possible, and she understood better than most the threat they posed. "Night after Bushfire", for example, published in 1946, was an attempt to visualise the consequences of atomic war, translating them into a familiar frame of reference. Its opening lines express the horror she felt:

> *There is no more silence on the plains of the moon*
> *and time is no more alien there, than here.*
> *Sun thrust his warm hand down at the high noon,*
> *but all that stirred was the faint dust of fear.*[5]

Knowing, too, what war had done to Jack, she was aware of its human cost, aware as others might not have been of "Manjack home from the wars", who

> *...walked down the street –*
> *bent like a bow his body round its great scar –*
> *and held his head upright. I saw his eyes*
> *flaring and fixed, a tiger or a dark star.*[6]

Although it was a cheerful and comfortable time for most, she felt unsettled:

> *How reconcile the alien eyes,*
> *the warring life how reconcile?*

On the lean slope and dripping hill
the sheep move slowly, single-file.
Where is it the heart's country lies?[7]

Women might be going back to the home and to their men, but for the moment she had neither. True, she was one of the fortunate ones who still had a job, though not the same one. With the expansion of the universities as men back from the war flooded into them under the Commonwealth Repatriation Training Scheme, her job with the Universities Commission became more important so it went to a man. But someone in the university administration remembered that she had often helped colleagues in the examination section to draw up statistics and make diagrams of future projections. So, despite the fact that she had not even sat for mathematics in her final school examination, she was appointed university statistician. It was quite a well-paid position, especially for a woman, and guaranteed her independence.

But Judith had no intention of working in an office for the rest of her life. Besides, her growing deafness was making this difficult. In her new office, for instance, the desk faced the window with its back to the door, so she was often not aware of someone coming in to talk to her because she usually did not hear them enter the room – she could only hear someone facing her. Although she solved that problem by putting a mirror on her typewriter, communication was becoming a strain. The work she was doing, dealing with statistics and projections, was also a long way from her real interests – her poetry and the work she was doing with Jack. So with the money she had saved during the war – her father had paid her for her work in New England, and there had been little to spend money on during wartime – Judith bought, indeed "paid cash down", as she was proud to say,[8] a little timber-cutter's house for sale at Mount Tamborine, a small town high up in the rainforest overlooking the Gold Coast. At that time the area was still quite "undeveloped" and Judith hoped to use the house as a place in which to write in her spare time.

Since his wife's return to their house in Surfer's Paradise, however, Jack had nowhere to live when he returned from his wanderings through Queensland. Judith suggested that he use this house at Mount

Tamborine and get on with his work there. It was by no means luxurious, with only three rooms and no water or electricity laid on. But it was "quiet and secluded behind a lot of lantana hedge, good for writing"[9] in the middle of the forest, then more or less untouched, and looking down on the few small farms below. Having been reading quantum physics at the time, Jack christened it "Quantum est" (it is enough) and spent most of his time there while Judith would come up to stay most weekends.

Gradually their relationship deepened. Always shy, Douglas Stewart recalls Judith as a loner[10] – with Jack she felt at home. Outwardly she might seem assured but inwardly she felt "chaotic ... all over the place",[11] but the autonomy and centredness of his existence and the power of his thinking were profoundly reassuring. For his part Jack was also becoming increasingly dependent on her emotionally as well as for the intellectual sympathy and material support she gave him. Barrie Reid recalled how "shy Jack" would sit silently at their gatherings, waiting until she noticed him, and they would then go out together.[12] Her deafness was also making her more awkward socially, and her hearing aid only seemed to make it worse since it depended on a large battery which had to be strapped to her thigh, from which wires went up to her ear. She tried to conceal them under her clothing but they were pretty obvious and, to make matters worse, from time to time if she fiddled with the volume, the aid would emit strange shrieks. Spare parts were hard to come by too, even after the war. So Judith spent more and more of her spare time at "Quantum" with Jack.

Together they would read and discuss works about contemporary physics and mathematics as well as new philosophers and scientists like Wittgenstein, Jeans and Eddington. They also discovered Jung, Lévy-Bruhl's work on "primitive" thought and the aesthetician Owen Barfield whose *Poetic Diction* dealt with the mythical, intuitive and "primitive" areas of consciousness Judith was already exploring in her poetry. Though they came from different backgrounds, she and Jack also had much the same attitude to the land, which he saw, as she did, as the manifestation of a deeper and more abiding reality. Like her, too, he regarded our treatment of it as an index of our values, or rather of our lack of proper values, and like her he regarded the end of the war as a challenge, not a signal for relaxation.

> We are faced in all departments of life with bewildering problems [he wrote]. These problems are many and complex, but for the purposes of a general survey we may take the atomic bomb as typifying them all, and in fact threatening to render them meaningless by its own overwhelming menace.

Moreover, he was prepared to face this threat steadily and realistically. For him

> the most significant fact about the atomic bomb is that there is nothing whatever that we can do to protect ourselves from it. This is not intended as an exercise in pessimism. It is an exercise in objectivity.[13]

Most people might be intent on restoring the "normal" world they had known, cultivating family values and building up their material possessions as a guarantee of security. But he insisted that they were in the midst of a crisis, a time of transition, and that the craving for security and normality was part of the problem. "We ourselves, our thoughts and emotions, are the crisis."[14]

This was the "challenge of reason" which was the burden of the book Jack was writing and hoped – in vain as it turned out – that Christesen would publish. But this "reason" which preoccupied him was not the logical linear thinking of the Enlightenment but rather "a new way of looking at things, a new attitude to life that emerged ... in men's minds", emerging creatively and intuitively as something "that happened to us"[15] – something much closer to poetic thinking.

Obviously Judith was deeply sympathetic. She had long felt that something was wrong with the direction Western civilisation was taking and with its desire to dominate the natural world, to accumulate material things and its implicit belief that force is the ultimate arbiter of truth – that might, in effect, is right. This belief, she thought, accounted for the way most people had rejoiced when the atom bombs had ended the war. But neither she nor Jack could accept this view. Nor did he subscribe to the belief in "progress" and "development", the new catch-cries. What was needed instead, he thought, was "a law to guide us and a mystery to move about in" and "understanding and enlightenment". For him the way to this "mountain-height of understanding and true power [lay] through the valley of renunciation",[16] not the pursuit of material progress they saw all around them.

According to Judith, then, Jack "had a belief and had a mind, two things I needed".[17] More expansively, she wrote in her autobiography:

> The challenge he gave me somehow fitted into my life. All those years (I was almost in my thirties) spent looking for some kind of elucidation and base for my work (I still felt myself primarily a poet) seemed to have been leading to [working with him]. I wriggled, argued, tried to get out of it, but already felt that if I didn't accept the challenge, I would never find another opportunity to do something worthwhile or to set my life on a proper footing.[18]

True, as this passage suggests, there were plenty of difficulties. First of all, there was the question of propriety. Although her brother had got on well with Jack when they first met at Surfer's Paradise, it is not likely that the family would have approved of their living together. Jack, after all, was still married and his wife still refused to contemplate divorce. Sharing a house was therefore regarded as something scandalous. Judith herself might not care about public opinion. But her father was by now a public figure in New England, elected president of the Graziers' Federal Council in 1947, a position he was to hold for over a decade. He was also a prominent member of the Country Party and an advocate of the New State Movement of New England and of the establishment of the University of New England; when it was set up, he became deputy chancellor and later chancellor. Even if Phillip Wright was not embarrassed by the relationship he could hardly be expected to see Jack as the best match for his daughter, of whom he had always been so protective.

Jack was almost penniless, too, since what little money came to him from his army pension he sent to his wife. He was much older than Judith and not in very good health. Nor did he have any prospect of earning money – philosophy is not a paying proposition and with no formal training he stood no chance of a university position, even if he had wanted it. More tellingly perhaps, he was still suffering from the trauma of his years in the trenches. His letters to Christesen suggest that, at least until he settled down with Judith, he was sometimes very edgy. Even after that, he still had bad nightmares and occasional attacks of sheer panic. "You could always tell," Judith recalls, "he turned pale and sweaty and his eyes would go away."[19]

She does not say anything in her autobiography about conflict with the family but some of the poems she was writing at the time, "The Builders", for example, express a sense of beleaguerment, though lines like the following may also have something to do with the way Jack had lived his life, against the grain of commonsense:

> *Only those men survive*
> *who dare to hold their love against the world;*
> *who dare to live and doubt what they are told.*
> *They are the quick of life;*
> *their faith is insolence; joyful is their grief.*

In view of the fact that it was to mean so much to her later on it is significant that she uses the metaphor here of the Great Barrier Reef and in particular of the creatures who are its builders and who are still part of it in their death. But the concluding lines, speaking as they do of risk and endurance against odds, suggest that for her risk was the way forward, not the conventional way of settling down comfortably:

> *This is life's promise and accomplishment –*
> *a fraction-foothold taken.*
> *Where dark eroding seas had broken,*
> *the quick, the sensitive, the lover,*
> *the passionate touch and intergrowth of living.*[20]

But there was no rift with the family – that was not the way Wrights behaved – and in any case they had a tradition of strong women. Nor would Judith have wanted a break. As "Birds", published not long afterwards in 1952, tells us, her family feeling was strong, if sometimes painful. She might wander away from them as she did even as a child but she would always return, knowing that, despite everything, this was her centre;

> *The blood that feeds my heart is the blood they gave me,*
> *and my heart is the house where they gather and fight for*
> *dominion –*
> *all different, all with a wish and a will to save me,*
> *to turn me into the ways of other people.*[21]

Nevertheless as far as she was concerned, Jack was the one with whom she wanted to spend the rest of her life. In 1947 she applied for and got a grant for one year from the Commonwealth Literary Fund to write a book on family history, based on the documents she had been exploring in New England in 1943. This was the book which was to become *The Generations of Men*. With this grant to support them, in 1948 Judith took a year's leave of absence from the university and lived more or less permanently with Jack at "Quantum". As it became clear to the family that they were together to stay, Jack was accepted, becoming part of the family gatherings in New England at Christmas time.

The men of the family liked him; Judith's father had "a great respect for people who thought",[22] perhaps because he had not had very much education himself. For their part, however, the women did not always approve of the way Judith seemed to dance attention on Jack, though they, too, found it difficult to resist his charm.[23] This acceptance was to be important later on when Judith and Jack were very short of money: wool prices were booming after the war and Judith's shares in the family company helped to keep them afloat. From time to time, too, her father would help out when emergencies occurred.

Their love, as some of the poems suggest, at first did not always come easily, perhaps because it was so complicated and so unconventional:

> *All things conspire to hold me from you –*
> *even my love,*
> *since that would mask you and unname you*
> *till merely woman and man we live.*
> *All men wear arms against the rebel –*
> *and they are wise,*
> *since the sound world they know and stable*
> *is eaten by lovers' eyes.*

> *All things conspire to stand between us –*
> *even you and I,*
> *who still command us, still unjoin us,*
> *and drive us forward till we die.*[24]

But these poems also express a deep contentment:

> *How to live, I said, as the flame-tree lives?*
> *– to know what the flame-tree knows; to be*
> *prodigal of my life as that wild tree*
> *and wear my passion so?...*
>
> *How shall I thank you, who teach me how to wait*
> *in quietness for the hour to ask or give:*
> *to take and in taking bestow, in bestowing live.*[25]

The famous "Woman to Man" and other poems like "Woman to Child", "Conch-shell" and "The Maker", which appeared in her second volume, *Woman to Man* (1949), have to do with birth and pregnancy, and the lesser known "The Unborn" about being haunted by a child who never was, a

> *...footless darkness following where I go,*
> *[a] lipless drinker at my drowsy breast.*[26]

Her daughter, Meredith, was not born until 1950, and Judith insists that these poems were not written as yet out of personal experience but out of the sense of having at last met a man with whom she really wanted to have a child. Certainly the poems written when she was actually pregnant with Meredith are different in tone and, as she says, "it is a ridiculous idea to think you have to have experienced something to write about it"[27] – we do not say that Shakespeare must have committed murder since he wrote *Macbeth*, for instance, as she also said to me.

What is more likely is that in these poems she is exploring her discovery in her relationship of the "not-I" within her which gave her a new relationship to herself, her body and her writing.[28] "You have a poem," she was later to say, "as you have a baby."[29] Her language was coinciding now with her body and she was writing with a new intensity, aware also of the kinds of realities "The Unborn" explores, her "own not-voice", the realities she and Jack were reading about in Jung's writings.

They were also a first intuition of what she was to discover later in Aboriginal culture. In the 1970s, for example, reading for *The Cry for the Dead*, she copied a passage from Elkin's *The Australian Aborigines and How to Understand Them* which discusses the belief that the spirits of the unborn have existed from the beginnings, the Dreaming, when the tribal heroes and cult ancestors first travelled through the world and made it what it is,[30] which might have something to do with the "dark sound/that made no word" of the poem "The Unborn".[31] Thinking seriously about having a child, as she was doing now, seems also to have brought her up before the danger it involved as a consequence of her riding accident – hence perhaps the conclusion of "Woman to Man",

Oh hold me, for I am afraid.[32]

The "not I" was speaking, too, to the sense of vulnerability she had known as a child but had suppressed for so long.

In the meantime she was maturing as a poet. *The Moving Image*, her first collection, was published in 1946 after a certain amount of hassle with Christesen. She might have been a poet and a woman, but she insisted on being professional about the arrangements. Christesen seemed to have been content with the loosest of arrangements, but Judith pressed for a contract, "as a protection for both of us ... Poets shouldn't, I know, be business-like," she wrote, "but me father brought me up strict, and my solicitors are carrying on the process."[33] Later, when the printing was held up by one of the many strikes of the late 1940s, Christesen still did not want to talk about terms, suggesting that they wait until she had seen the galley proofs. But she demurred, reminding him that this was "not the regular practice". She did not think that he was "trying to drive a bargain". But she wanted to "have all things on a proper footing" even though she was "fairly short of money" at the time, having been "embroiled with doctors" in Sydney, from where in fact she wrote to him. But when Christesen began to talk of letting her have all the profits, she replied somewhat brusquely:

> I have seen too much of business deals: friendly concerns turn sour. So if you have a contract form handy, let's get the matter tidy, shall we? I'd much rather *Meanjin* had a bit of extra profit than that we should have any misunderstanding.[34]

Nor did she have any inflated ideas about the importance of the book. It was, she reminded him, "the first book of a virtually unknown writer", and the market was "fairly glutted with poetry".[35]

When it did appear, however, it was received enthusiastically. "No book of poems," one critic declared later, "had received such an enthusiastic reception since O'Dowd's *The Bush*"[36] – a judgement which is not as far off the mark as it may seem today since O'Dowd also articulated a sense of the land and of being Australian which spoke for his time as Judith's poems did for hers. According to Douglas Stewart, editor of the prestigious Red Page of the *Bulletin*, these were poems which "promise anything, everything, the world".[37]

As if to confirm this, the collection was even noticed in England, something very unusual in those days. Before the book appeared, Alex Comfort had published in his *Poetry Folio* one of the poems, "Bullocky" (a poem she now thoroughly dislikes, incidentally, for the way it has been read as a celebration of the myth of the heroic pioneer – she is now at pains to point out that the bullocky is in fact mad). He also wrote to tell that "a well known English poet" had pronounced it "one of the best pieces of Colonial verse he had seen". Judith refused to be patronised like this, remarking in a letter to Christesen that she felt "tempted to withdraw, with a cry of 'God stone me up a gum tree'".[38] She was never one to overestimate – or indeed underestimate. For her the book was, in a sense, a work of piety (in the proper sense of the word) – she sent the first copy to her father, "to whom it rightfully belongs"[39] – so she was grateful for the good reviews: "It's nice of them not to tear it limb from limb," she told Christesen.[40]

The book made her reputation, and many of the poems in it were anthologised and set for schools – something she did not entirely approve of since she disliked the way poetry was usually taught – which continued to bring in a steady, if small, income. When she came to publish her next collection, *Woman to Man*, which appeared in 1949, it was published by Angus & Robertson, then Australia's largest and most prestigious publisher. With various ups and downs she remained with them for the rest of her career as a poet, though she published her prose elsewhere.

The Brisbane literary scene was changing, with *Meanjin* removed to Melbourne and the Barjais moving away – the journal *Barjai* itself had ceased publication in 1947 for lack of money. Barrie Reid was now at university and complaining that most of his fellow students were selfish careerists. "None of the young," he wrote loftily to Christesen in Melbourne, "know what a poet is – they keep confusing him with a politician, a divine, a philosopher."[41] He and Charles Osborne had opened the Ballad Bookshop and this occupied him until he went to Melbourne in the early 1950s to become a librarian part of the group of artists and writers who gathered around John and Sunday Reed at "Heide" in Eltham. From there Barrie still occasionally kept in touch with Judith and Jack (whom he also admired).

Through him they heard about developments in painting taking place in Melbourne and elsewhere, especially with the work of Albert Tucker, Sidney Nolan and Arthur Boyd (whose work was to inspire some of Judith's poems, notably "Eli, Eli" and "The Harp and the King"). When Nolan held an exhibition in Brisbane in the early 1950s the press attacked it as "obscure" and even "obscene" but Judith wrote a letter to the *Courier Mail* defending it. It may also have been through her, indirectly at least, that Nolan's interest in Fraser Island was kindled since he went there with Barrie Reid not long after she and Jack did.

Others of the group were also drifting away. Charles Osborne had moved to London where he was eventually to become the editor of the *London Magazine* and an important figure in the literary scene. In that respect, later he was able to help Judith find an English publisher for Jack's second book, *The Structure of Modern Thought*, published in 1971 after his death. Thea Astley went to North Queensland and then to Sydney, and Barbara Patterson had left for Melbourne with the young artist Charles Blackman whom she was to marry there. Propriety, which seemed to have gone missing with the refugees who fled from the war, was returning. Brisbane was relapsing into its provincial pieties again and the avant-garde and the unusual were once more suspect.

Barbara Blackman recalls an afternoon about that time when Charles and another young artist, Laurie Hope, also one of the Barjai group, were walking down the street arm in arm, Charles carrying a bunch of flowers. Two young painters enjoying themselves flouting the respectable. However, a policeman on the beat was not amused, scenting two homosexuals. Pulling them up, he sternly ordered them to separate and go in opposite directions, watching them to make sure that they did so!

In the circumstances, Judith and Jack were well off at Mount Tamborine, reading and minding their own business. Not that they had given up thinking. Indeed, while most people about them were busy settling back into suburban life they were exploring what Patrick White called "the deep end of the unconscious"[42] from which, White thought, most of us shy away. Many other Australians were taking refuge in an imaginary past and even more imaginary future. Judith and Jack were prepared to face the immediate present – a more solitary task. In this they were the "Moderns" Jung describes in *Modern Man in Search of a Soul*; standing

> upon a peak, or at the end of the world, the abyss of the future before [them] above ... the heavens and below ... the whole of mankind with a history that disappears in primeval mists ... leaving behind all that has been discarded and outgrown, and acknowledging that [they stood] before a void out of which all things may grow.[43]

This sense of being on a kind of frontier is the mood of poems Judith was writing at the time, "Eli, Eli", for instance, which was inspired by Arthur Boyd's painting *The Mockers*, though it also seems to echo the Buddha's sorrowful sense of living in a time of wars, with people killing and wounding one another, preyed on by desire.

But other poems move beyond history, attempting to express a primal vision of a world beyond conscious thought, hence the opening lines of "The Bones Speak", published in *Meanjin* in 1947:

> *Great images of silence haunt me*
> *in the visible darkness bowed in unseen stone.*

> *It is a thousand years and all are one:*
> *great rocks of silence lie upon my tongue*
> *and idols carved by no man rule this cave.*[44]

So even when she wrote about familiar Australian landscapes, as in "Night after Bushfire" and "The Bushfire", she saw them, as she explained later, from a double vision, that of commonsense and that of contemporary physics which she was reading with Jack. This gave her an angle of vision which was no longer purely human but sub-linguistic, being preoccupied with the energies which can destroy the world as they have contributed to making it. In poems like this, she says, she was moving from her "own situation of love and human connection" to try to "visualise the horrors of Hiroshima and Nagasaki", by translating them into another frame of reference,[45] one in which, as she wrote in "Night after Bushfire",

> *Man, if he come to brave that glance alone,*
> *must leave behind his human home and name.*[46]

Even in looking back to childhood, in "Stars", for example, her recollection of her parents,

> *she to whom I cling*
> *and he who fathered me,*

is set in this double context, caught up in larger currents of existence in which the stars become a "storm of honey bees" or a

> *...flight of golden birds*
> *or swarm of motes in a beam*
> *or fish in a dark sea.*[47]

This was not the way most people around them were looking at the world, but many writers and thinkers elsewhere were. Owen Barfield, whose *Poetic Diction* they read and admired, for instance, argued that

> the possibility of man's avoiding self-destruction depends upon
> his realizing before it is too late that what he let loose over
> Hiroshima, after fiddling with its exterior for three centuries was
> the force of his own unconscious mind.[48]

So long as a "nothingness within [matched] the nothingness without",[49] he argued, the world would be in danger. What was necessary was "to live in harmony with the unconscious depths of [our] being", and the way to this was through the "participant knowledge" of poetry, which enables us to "live in harmony with nature, as distinct from riding – or being ridden – roughshod"[50] over it, which is characteristic of our culture. Read in this light the poems in *Woman to Man* take on a different complexion. They are not just poems about "women's experience", though they begin there, but attempts also at the "felt change of consciousness" Barfield speaks of, "the full meanings of which are flashing iridescent shapes like flames ever flickering vestiges of the slowly evolving consciousness beneath them".[51]

As a child Judith had rebelled against the women's world she was supposed to live in, but now, ironically, critics were calling her the poet of "women's secret experience", making her, as Vincent Buckley put it, little more than "a high-brow Dorothy Dix".[52] The epigraph to the collection should have given the lie to this over-simplification. It is from Francis Bacon's *The Wisdom of the Ancients*: "Love", it begins, "was the most ancient of all the gods, and existed before everything else, except Chaos, which is held coeval therewith", and concludes, taking us into the prelinguistic world Judith was trying to explore, the spectacle of Chaos which the atom bombs had opened up, with the thought that "the summary or collective law of nature, or the principle of love ... can scarce possibly find full admittance in the thoughts of men, though some faint notion may be had thereof".[53]

In poems like "Woman to Man" and "Woman to Child" therefore, Judith was not necessarily writing only about personal experience but trying to move back to this source of things, the darkness and light at the heart of existence. "Midnight" is obviously about this quest:

> *Darkness where I find my sight,*
> *shadowless and burning night,*
> *here where death and life are met*
> *is the fire of being set.*

> *Watchman eye and workman hand*
> *are spun of water, air and sand.*
> *These will crumble and be gone,*
> *still that darkness rages on.*[54]

For her, as Jung put it, the psyche was "not a question mark but a door that opens upon the human world from a world beyond", putting the individual in touch with "strange and unrecognizable realities" that were not merely subjective but illuminated the crisis of contemporary history. This kind of thinking was to make her receptive to Aboriginal culture later on. But it grew out of the childhood experiences in which, as she wrote in "To a Child",

> *I see* became *I am*,
> *I am* became *I see*.[55]

For her, personally, her important work, then, was her poetry. But the Commonwealth Literary Fund grant, which had made it possible for her to take a year's leave of absence from the university, obliged her to get to work on the family papers she had discovered in New England. The material was difficult to shape, however, and was proving harder to interpret than she had expected. But she had a sense that the clue she was looking for lay in the land if she could get closer to it.

She still remembered the austerity of New England, her sense of "something sad", a view of history different from the one she had been brought up with – the story of heroic pioneering, and another kind of memory contained in "those granite rocks [and] holy areas of stone which link up with stones across the country all the way to Western Australia".[56] This is the kind of memory hinted at in "Half-caste Girl", one of the poems in her first collection:

> *Against the world's stone walls she thrust her heart –*
> *endless the strength of its beating –*
> *atom of flesh that cannot move a stone.*
> *She used her love for lever;*
> *but the wall is cunningly made.*[57]

In Queensland she found a new warmth and luxuriousness which she wanted to explore. Jack understood – he, too, had spent a great deal of time in the bush – and they decided to explore the country. Wartime travel restrictions had been lifted so they set out for the central Queensland country through which her grandfather and before him his less successful father-in-law, Arthur MacKenzie, had driven their flocks, and to a greater or lesser extent had been defeated by it. Jack and Judith had little money and travelled hard by train or bus or by hitching rides, often camping out or putting up in the cheapest accommodation they could find, going as far north as Rockhampton.

On their way north they stayed a few weeks with Jack's daughter, Lucy, who was married to the lighthouse keeper on Lady Elliott Island, travelling over on the supply launch. This was Judith's first real experience of the Great Barrier Reef. When she was ten, sailing with the family to what was then the Netherlands East Indies, they had passed through the Reef's waters and she still remembered "the marvellous blue of calm waters, the green islands of the Whitsunday Passage rising out of them and passing by", but not much more. Now, however, there was time to explore the beaches and the reef with its water gardens. Although the island itself had been damaged by "development", the offshore reef was more or less untouched:

> I wandered over it amazed at the colours of the corals, the shell
> fish and the tiny darting fish and crimson and blue slugs and stars
> and clams in its pool gardens, and stared down from a small boat
> at its shelf and coral crags. I fell in love with the Reef then.[58]

Returning to Gladstone on the mainland by another supply launch they went on to Rockhampton where her grandfather, Albert Wright, whose story became an important part of *The Generations of Men*, had died and was buried.

In contrast with the robust figure of May Wright, so important to her as a child, Albert had been until now only a shadowy presence. But as the poem she wrote about it, "The Morning of the Dead" (which she did not publish until 1956) suggests, the encounter with him, though it was imaginary only, became part of a "pilgrimage".

The poem begins as she and Jack arrive at the cemetery where Albert had been buried. Above them

> *Out of the sky that is always astonished by dawn*
> *move the enormous unconscious clouds,*
> *blindly becoming, being, undoing their being;*
> *like the clouds of sleep that want what they are and no*
> > *more,*
> *untouched by future and past.*

But she is here to make contact with the past, on a pilgrimage

> *with my hand in the hand of another, to look for a grave,*
> *in the blazing day of a town in the far north,*
> *among pale toppling stones.*

Under "the clouds of the mango-trees" they came on a gravedigger,

> *a thin dark muscular man deep in the soil,*
> *shining with sweat, clay crumbed in his stiff hair . . .*

> *"What are you looking for?" "A grave, sixty years old."*
> *The grave of somebody dead long before I was born;*
> *the grave of a man I had met as part of myself;*
> *a man silenced by death but speaking still in my life –*
> *my dark grandfather's grave.*

> *But he was not to be found. He had crumbled away,*
> *and the wooden tablet had gone and the rose had gone;*
> *probably some other stranger was buried there now,*
> *bone nudging old bone.*

The grave digger is sceptical,

> *(putting away a stiff in time for the Saturday racing)*
> *gave us a twist of a smile. Sixty years old?*
> *Cripes, it's a long way to come for a long while ago.*
> *Why can't you leave him alone?*

But somehow her grandfather's story seems part of her own. In that place, under the clouds melting with each other,

> *he and I met, bowed in our sleep like clouds;*
> *touched untouchedly; clouds that melt into each other;*
> *shapes that need not strive, because their event is their*
>   *truth;*
> *found each other in love.*

She has reached a new stage of her life

> *(changing, altering, sleepily under the sun of love)*

and has a new sense of answers to questions she has asked all her life, so far waiting for her in this encounter. "The eyes of the dead" perhaps

> *... reflect light more truly than pools or lakes*
> *relating it to being in a new way,*
> *till earth shuts on them and takes in their sight.*
> *In them light generates some new complexity,*
> *able to answer.*

Somehow she feels his eyes on her now:

> *this is what the dead desire – their meaning.*[59]

Already, reading his diaries in New England during the war and more thinking about the book which was to become *The Generations of Men*, Judith had realised that Albert was different from most pioneers, introspective, more aware of the ambiguities of settlement, interested in rather than contemptuous of the Aboriginal people whose land he was invading, and something of a writer. As she learned more about him, she imagined him as someone never

> really [able] to reconcile the two worlds that existed side by side within him: [the] world in which ... a man must be respectable and successful, a good head at a bargain, with a shrewd eye for horses and cattle, and the dark lonely world in which he was still haunted by the dingoes howling and the last struggles of the child he had to disown and crush in himself too early.[60]

She imagined, that is to say, someone with a much more ambiguous sense of self than her formidable Wright grandmother, or indeed most of the other Wrights, had ever been.

Standing at his grave, she imagined his voice, the voice of someone who had died a comparative failure.

> "I was borne down; my work was left unfinished;
> alive I turned to stone; my love was ruined;
> ignorance, oppression, pain left my sight tarnished,
> my world corrupt and dying.
>
> "Oh make me perfect
> Burn with a fire of sight the substance of my sorrow.
> Take what I was and find in it that truth
> the universes on their holy journey.

Somehow, his life, his interest in and sympathy for the Aboriginal people whose land he occupied, has meaning for her:

> All those old tribes, dark trees endowed with sight,
> found new replies to night and day. Their glances
> forged a meaning between man and creature,
> creature and nature.

For her, too, there is work to do.

> ...Meaning cannot rest or stay the same.
> Meaning seeks its own unthought-of meaning,
> murders and is murdered, travels on
> into new territory past touch or sight –
> is dark entreating light.

She has heard

> ...The dead
> cry, Bear my children; follow out my thought;
> live for me, since you wear my life.

The task lies ahead, to "take life further", to work at "the passion/of vision that is art".

Becoming seeks for being.
Learning desires so to transcend itself
that nothing's left to learn. Time seeks eternity.
The flesh continually works towards its ending.
Earth stares with all its eyes upon divinity.[61]

Then they turned south, returning home. It had been a long trip and by this time they were tired and dirty so, a day out of Maryborough, they decided for once to be extravagant and telegraphed ahead, booking a room in the town's best hotel. It proved to be very grand, with servants in livery and a dignified and solemn receptionist with a feeling for "good family", who had booked them into the best room, the bridal suite – they were mistaken for a well-known family, also named McKinney, who lived in Toowoomba. But the grandeur was overwhelming. They were so dirty that they hardly dared get into the magnificent bath with its gold taps and fittings, much less wash their filthy clothes in it and when they asked the receptionist where they might wash them he was shocked at the very thought of their wanting to do anything so menial. So they gave in, their clothes remained filthy and the next day they were on the road again.[62]

These next few days were significant in another way. From Maryborough in those days timber barges used to wind their way down the Mary River to the coast and then across to Fraser Island to bring back trees cut down from the tropical forest which still flourished there. Judith and Jack decided to make the trip to Fraser Island by one of these barges.

Fraser Island had featured in her grandfather's diaries in an incident which had long fascinated her. It happened during his first trip north when he was still a young man and unmarried, sailing north to Rockhampton where he was to disembark and make his way inland to manage a new station on the Dawson River, "Nulalbin", which he later bought and to which he was later to bring his young bride May Wright.

Sailing between Fraser Island and the mainland they had seen a group of naked black figures run down a headland, dancing and waving at the ship and shouting "Sugar-bag! bacca!" As Wright retold the incident in *The Generations of Men*: "The long lazy days had made the men tolerant, they waved and shouted back, holding up their tobacco plugs; 'Bacca, here come and get it!'."

Led by a tall bearded man, the blacks dived in to make the long swim out to the ship, which was moving away from them. Swimming strongly, they began to overhaul it, and the captain entered into the spirit of the thing, slowing the ship down. As the swimmers approached, the passengers began betting on who would be the first to climb on board. It proved to be the big man who had first taken the plunge, and when he climbed on board he was showered with plugs of tobacco which he shared with his friends who now crowded behind him on the deck. "Just for a moment," Judith imagined, "it seemed the two races merged, the blacks for once were equal and comrades and there was no ill-will."

The incident, a moment of "truce in a long and unrelenting war" she believed, had troubled her grandfather, "reviving in him certain questions of conscience most of the men he knew had long since ceased to ask or perhaps had never asked", questions to do with their occupation of the land and of the massacres, rapes, traffic in grog and all the other brutalities of the frontier. After this experience of fellowship, he had "promised himself further exploration of their culture and language".[63] In fact there had been little opportunity for this exploration and he himself had been caught up in the story of conquest and settlement. So she was interested to see Fraser Island.

Jack managed to get a job as a deckhand and Judith was engaged as cook. In one of her short stories she was later to describe a similar trip, but that story turned rather on the loneliness of a woman who lives by the river whose only glimpse of the outside world is the barges going by and who has a brief affair with the captain. Jack and Judith's trip was much less romantic. The barge was small, dirty and smelly, and they suffered from mosquitoes and sandflies. But they were fascinated by the island itself, the largest sand island in the world and a crucial area ecologically. In the 1960s and 1970s it was one of the areas environmentalists fought to protect, eventually succeeding in having it listed as a World Heritage Area. Even then, however, they saw signs of damage from "development"; the magnificent trees and shrubs being chopped down for timber, depriving the birds and animals of their habitat, and vegetation on the dunes uprooted. But there was still an abundance of bird and animal life in the scrub, especially around the inland lakes, and the beaches were very beautiful, though the Aborigines had all been taken away to reserves and missions. Sidney Nolan's paintings would later capture something of this melancholy beauty, and in their turn inspire Patrick White's *A Fringe of Leaves*, based on the story of the white woman, Eliza Fraser, wrecked in *The Stirling Castle*, who lived with the Aboriginal people there until she was "rescued".

On the trip back to the mainland the mosquitoes and sandflies continued to attack, and by the time they reached Maryborough Judith was in agony and her feet were so swollen that for weeks the only shoes she could wear were a pair of golden shoes she had bought for a wedding. So once more they decided to splash out and, seeing flights advertised from Maryborough to Brisbane, decided to fly and from there take the bus home to Mount Tamborine.

The trip had given her a feeling for Queensland and for her family's struggles in the north. But the book was proving to be a larger project than she had bargained for. At the end of 1948 it was still not finished. So she applied – successfully – for an extension of the grant for another year. Anti-communist suspicions were beginning to be voiced in parliament and there had been some criticism of grants awarded to "well-known communists", but her family name and her father's public standing probably protected her, as well as her growing reputation as a poet: in 1949 she was awarded the Grace Leven Prize for poetry. The grant meant that they had money for the coming year, so there was no need to go back to work at the university, and she and Jack settled down to writing and reading.

Towards the end of 1949 she became pregnant. In June of that year she had written to Christesen that she had been "embroiled with doctors",[64] though by December of that year she reported herself "very well thanks – very healthy in fact." There must have been some gossip about her health, however, since she also told him that his "informant must be six months out of date".[65] She was always jealous of her privacy, so she kept the news to herself and close friends as long as possible. Besides, this pregnancy, which she very much wanted, was likely to be difficult and dangerous. The break to her pelvis was likely to cause problems and she also experienced kidney trouble, as her mother had done. To add to this she was worried about the interruption to her writing since she was the main breadwinner. Jack left the decision to her whether or not to go on with the pregnancy, and in her mind there was no question that she would. Ever since she had met Jack she had wanted a child by him. As she wrote in "The Promised One", she had

> ... lived in a wind of ghosts; a storm of hands
> beat at my flesh. The Lazarus at my gate
> demanding life.

But now

> ... the dream each night renews –
> the runner on lonely roads, whose face is turned away,[66]

was coming towards her, taking flesh in her. "A Song to Sing You" gives some sense of her joy:

> When I went out in early summer
> the creeks were full
> and the grass growing;
> the bat's-wing coral-tree stood in flower
> and the lake of my heart
> was clear and peaceful.
>
> I began to make a song
> to sing you some day ...
>
> My heart made it,
> my blood bore it,
> my tongue spoke it,
> the song of the child yet to be born.[67]

"Dark Gift", however, reflects the sense of danger which was also with her:

> The flower begins in the dark
> where life is not.

> *Death has a word to speak*
> *and the flower begins.*
>
> *How small, how closely bound*
> *in nothing's net*
> *the word waits in the ground*
> *for the cloak earth spins.*[68]

But she felt herself drawn at last into the "truth of [her] body", the mystery of fertility which "Ishtar" explores (Ishtar is goddess of childbirth):

> *When in fear I became a woman*
> *I first felt your hand.*
> *When the shadow of the future first fell across me*
> *it was your shadow, my grave and hooded attendant.*
> . . .
> *You neither know nor care for the truth of my heart;*
> *but the truth of my body has all to do with you.*
> *You have no need of my thoughts or my hopes,*
> *living in the realm of the absolute event.*[69]

It was not an easy pregnancy and its last months were spent in Brisbane. As she wrote to her friend Kathleen McArthur, she disliked having to "pack [her] goods and chattels and trail down and start the waiting process",[70] to be near the best medical attention – her father had insisted on helping financially. She was also still worried that she was "not getting any writing done at all – too much sewing for that". But there was nothing much she could do about it, especially as she felt "awfully domestic" and not poetic at all, "though", she reflected, perhaps that was "a good thing".[71] "Waiting Ward" belongs to this time:

> *Some wore fear like a wound,*
> *some wore hope like a flower.*
> *Some waited for the touch of joy*
> *and some for the summons of terror;*
>
> *But I would have her remembered,*
> *the girl with the red hair.*

> *She wore fear like a flower*
> *and carried death like a child.*
>
> *All the other women*
> *overmastered by life*
> *contained besides their terror*
> *that terror's gentle answer;*
>
> *she was the ace of spades,*
> *she knew the future early –*
> *the girl who sang and smiled*
> *and carried a black secret.*

She was the girl who died, and her memory was to remain.

> *Face of grey stone*
> *I have turned you into a mountain*
> *to oppose in me for ever*
> *the world of pleasure and grievance,*
> *the world of winning and losing.*[72]

On the surface, however, she seemed confident, very much her own woman. As Barrie Reid recalled in a letter written not long before his own death, to her friends she even seemed almost a reproach to their anxieties:

> Do you remember how anxious we (not you, or you concealed it beautifully) were when you went to hospital?... Jack came to Highgate Hill, taking his cue from your matter-of-factness, tried manfully to be the usual Jack but his face got white and drawn – I slipped a sleeping pill into his glass of milk at night.[73]

Meredith McKinney was born eventually and safely on 21st April 1950, by caesarean section, "the girl I had longed for",

> *...the dark baby hung*
> *in a nurse's arms,*
> *seen through a mist – your eyes*
> *still vague, a stranger's eyes;*

> *hung in a hospital world*
> *of drugs and fevers.*[74]

Her birth was "the clincher", she said, in her relationship with Jack. He had a "deep respect for life" and was a loving father, so the baby drew them even closer. Language had always interested him, and he was fascinated as the baby's language skills unfolded; he took great delight in teaching her preposterous new words. Their friends were happy for them also. Mary Gilmore and Nettie Palmer both wrote congratulations and others came visiting. For Judith, it was as if some continuity, security and purpose had been established at last in the midst of a threatening world. She could now dream, she told a friend,

> of handing over to Meredith when she is 21 everything that time has accumulated around me and going away and sitting on some lonely beach (if such things exist then) and catching up on the universe.[75]

The baby's arrival did raise practical problems. "Quantum" might have been just large enough for the two of them, and Barrie Reid might have enthused in romantic retrospect about "lovely little 'Quantum' where we were all so poor",[76] but it was too small for three. Drying nappies festooned the kitchen and living room, and there was no quiet place left for either of them to work. Once again, however, family came to the rescue. A legacy from one of Judith's mother's relatives, her Great Aunt Rose, reached them from England, and with it and the last of their savings they were able to buy another and larger house, 303 Long Road, also at Mount Tamborine.

When they had lived at "Quantum" they had often walked past, marvelling at "the amount of space some people had to live in"[77] and they had also liked its cheerful disarray: it was occupied by a family whose father worked in Brisbane during the war and had access to "surplus equipment" so that "under the house" (which most Queenslanders used as a storeroom) was cluttered with surplus, nails, screws and hardware. When the war ended, and with it the father's job, they had moved away, leaving the house empty, but cheerfully so; neighbours used the acre of land around the house to pasture weaned calves and the garden had become a riot of kikuyu grass and hardy shrubs. They felt at home immediately.

They called it "Calanthe", the name of a rare rainforest orchid, popularly known as the flying dove orchid. As Judith wrote later, it was wooden, as most Queensland houses were, "a shy house ... nearly invisible from the outside with all the green it hides behind",[78] a hedge of lantana contained by a long white fence which concealed a large and luxuriant garden, and full of birds. Indoors the house was roomy, if rambling, "all doors and odd corners" – something they liked. They also liked the space. Now they could run to a study as well as a spare room, and a divan bed in the study meant that, if needs be, they could accommodate several guests. In its "spaces and awkward corners", as she wrote in a long poem when she was about to leave it many years later, they were to "spread [their] lives out, fitted and grow together". It was to be a generous place:

> *Your old trees dying warmed as with winter fires.*
> *Your bird calls, mice in cupboards, snakes in the garden,*
> *made welcome nuisances for us, panics and symbols.*
> *We ceased to be strangers.*[79]

It was also a good investment. The house itself was well and solidly built and also had "wonder of wonders in those days – an actual hot-water system and refrigerator – no doubt (also) 'surplus requirements' for the services". There were no less than five water tanks and the house was near the school Meredith would be going to. From the back steps, too, there was a fine view down over the cunjevoi and crinum-lined creek that ran along the gully to the height above dominated by the magnificent flame tree which was to inspire several of Judith's poems.

They were settling down, and this panorama seemed to celebrate it:

> *Out of the torn earth's mouth*
> *comes the old cry of praise.*
> *Still is the song made flesh*
> *though the singer dies.*[80]

Theodor Adorno had been more pessimistic when he wrote that in the world we live "the blossom tree lies" if we see its bloom "without the shadow of terror".[81] But for Wright now, there was a guarantee that in a midst of a world threatened with destruction the fires of creation were burning still:

> *flesh of the world's delight,*
> *voice of the world's desire,*
> *I drink you with my sight*
> *and I am filled with fire.*[82]

CHAPTER VIII

CHANGE AND DISTANCE

> For only change and distance shape for us
> some new tremendous symbol for the soul.
>
> from "The Harp and the King"
> *Collected Poems*, p. 158

If the 1930s had been the Age of Anxiety, for most Australians the 1950s was the Age of Certainties. It got off to a good start with the fiftieth anniversary of Federation, duly celebrated with a general sense of patriotic self-congratulation – though Aborigines were not mentioned; they were, after all, not regarded as citizens. The ABC ran a series of talks on Great Australians, and there were re-enactments of heroic events like Sturt's expedition into the Centre one hundred years earlier, events which were said to have laid the foundations of the "progress" and prosperity in which Australians were rejoicing. In the Snowy Mountains, thousands of migrants, newly arrived from the ruins of postwar Europe, were building what was seen as the great monument to a new industrialised future, the Snowy River Hydro-Electric Scheme. People were settling down after the war, and the future was looking good.

But it was also a strangely confusing time. As Elizabeth Harrower describes it:

> In the cities, great wealth was masked by naivety one would hesitate to call childlike. A contradictory striving after perpetual adolescence, sophistication and an accumulation of wealth were

the motives of action. The chief conviction was one of superiority. This was brought about by the Pacific isolation of the continent and by trips to a Europe where all the famous treasures were old and frequently dirty, where there were peasants and the city dwellers were peculiarly poor. What the fuss was few Australians could imagine. Not all of them believed in its existence.[1]

Put in slogan form, this was the "Great Australian emptiness" which Patrick White was also railing against.

Judith Wright disliked the mindlessness and the obsession with comfort and security, but neither she nor Jack looked down on ordinary Australians – they reserved their scorn for leaders at home and abroad. Like ordinary people, they were trying now to settle down. They had their home, "Calanthe", and a child to look after and in some ways were beginning to behave more conventionally. At "Quantum", for example, they had made do with what Jack used to call "literary tablecloths", newspaper spread across the table, which they could read as they ate. But now, thanks to Barbara Blackman who gave them a real tablecloth for Christmas, their table was much more commonplace. Having cleared some of their wild growths of tobacco bush and lantana from the block and arranged their books, typewriter, "the few paintings they had bought from Laurie Hope, and our scanty supply of crockery and saucepans", they felt, Jack remarked, as if they had become "imitation landed gentry".[2]

Meredith was making them more aware of practicalities, too, particularly about money. Not long after Meredith's birth, in June 1950, Judith was writing to Clem Christesen inquiring about the royalties from *The Moving Image*, which was still selling well.[3] Until now, like most of their friends, they had been cheerfully poor, but looking after a baby and later providing what she needed for school or to keep up with friends or with Judith's own memories of childhood made things more difficult.

When Meredith wanted a pony, for example, they sold a painting they had bought at Nolan's first exhibition in Brisbane, one of the first Fraser Island paintings, of the ghostly figure of a convict wading ashore. It hung on Meredith's wall, but she did not like it, finding it frightening, so the sale was no sacrifice to her. Jack and Judith worried about Nolan's feelings, however, and wrote asking whether he would mind their selling it. He replied saying that he liked his paintings to circulate.[4] Meredith got her pony and Judith an extra chore since children are not always good at the details of looking after pets.

Judith was also determined that Jack should not be distracted from his work, so the task of keeping the family fell on her, too. By writing short stories, mostly for the *Bulletin* (which paid relatively well), and doing educational broadcasts for the ABC and giving lectures for Adult Education she hoped they could survive. Occasional windfalls from the family – pastoralists were doing well in the 1950s – helped also.

Poor as they were, it was probably just as well that they were living more or less in a world of their own on the mountain. Down below it was a troubling time for many of their friends and acquaintances. Barrie Reid, for instance, felt "enormous anti-life forces" around him,[5] complaining that they all seemed to be in the midst of a "slow dying" and facing a "following midnight".[6] This sounds flamboyant, but quite apart from the threat of nuclear destruction vast changes were underway. The old empires were collapsing. The Dutch had been driven out and the new Republic of Indonesia appeared. The British had left India, communist insurgents were for a time in control in Malaysia, and in Indo-China the Vietnamese were challenging French rule. Communists had taken over from the Nationalists in China and communist forces crossed the Kalu River into North Korea, beginning the Korean War when the American army under General MacArthur, former Allied Commander-In-Chief in the Pacific during World War II, moved against them, threatening to use atomic weapons.

For many Australians, these changes were deeply disturbing: the war seemed to have let loose forces they could neither understand nor control. At home, too, changes were afoot. Chifley's Labor Government talked socialism and proposed to nationalise the banks. Industrial unrest was widespread, culminating in the coal miners' strike of the late 1940s, which paralysed industry, leading many ordinary Australians to believe that communists had taken over the trades unions and were threatening to destroy the "democratic way of life". Although Chifley brought in the army to crush the miners' strike and union funds were frozen and their leaders jailed when they refused to hand over these funds or say where they had been hidden, their fears brought down his government in the elections held in December 1949.

The long reign of the conservatives under Menzies began. Fear of communism swept the country, echoing the mood in the United States and setting off a witch hunt against "leftists", splitting the Labor Party and leading to the creation of the Democratic Labor Party, dedicated to the destruction of communist influence in the trade unions and elsewhere. Matching the hysteria whipped up in the United States by Senator Joe McCarthy and his Committee for Un-American Activities in 1951, the Menzies Government attempted to outlaw the Communist Party but was blocked by the High Court and was only narrowly defeated in the referendum brought in to change the constitution to enable it to do so. This hysteria reached its peak in 1954, with the Petrov Royal Commission, "a carefully stage-managed ... mixture of fact and farce worthy of a B-grade movie"[7] in which many well-known writers and thinkers on the left, including Clem and Nina Christesen and Vance and Nettie Palmer, were accused of being communists and their careers threatened.

It was a frightening time for people trying to think things through coolly for themselves, as the McKinneys were. Because they had distanced themselves a little they were not so directly threatened, though the recent release of the relevant Australian Secret Intelligence Organisation (ASIO) files of the time indicates that they were under surveillance. They remained concerned, and in July 1952 Judith wrote to Christesen asking him to include her name in a peace appeal signed by a group of Australian writers.[8] The next year, short of money as she and Jack were, she sent a small donation.[9] Nevertheless, both she and Jack disliked the growing dogmatism, on the left as well as on the right.

By now Judith was a significant name in Australian writing, and her family connections may have added to that significance, so the Establishment attempted from time to time to recruit her. She was approached by Sir John Latham, chair of the newly founded Australian Committee for Cultural Freedom, apparently an eminently respectable organisation but now known to have been secretly funded by the Central Intelligence Agency (CIA). Its doctrinaire anti-communism troubled her, however, and she declined the invitation.[10] Not long afterwards, the English writer Stephen Spender, then editor of *Encounter* and member of the London Committee for Cultural Freedom and on a tour of Australia, visited her at Mount Tamborine. Judith and Jack gave him lunch at a local café and then took him and his entourage for a walk in the rainforest. But that was all. She valued her independence and had no desire to be involved in the ideological warfare of the times.

She was also cool about overtures from the poet James McAuley, whom she had known slightly at university (where he had been famous for his jazz piano playing) and who was now a prominent member of the Committee and a recent convert to a vigorously anti-communist Catholicism. He sent her an early draft of his long poem, *Captain Quiros*, about the Spanish sailor and religious visionary who sailed across the Pacific from South America in search of the Great South Land and who thought he had found it when he made landfall on what was in fact one of the islands north-east of Australia, probably the New Hebrides (now Vanuatu). Judith found the tone of the poem didactic, triumphalist and unappealing. Its dogmatism seemed to her part of what she called "forgetting how to read", the tendency to take up entrenched positions which made her and people like Jack McKinney feel not only that they were "no longer wanted" but also that they wanted to keep their distance. This was difficult, however, as she wrote years later, with a touch of hauteur; "in that awful *galerè* [a French word for a sentence to the galleys] we did not engage on such bloodied ground – we had other work to do and a daughter to bring up on nothing much at all".[11]

For most of her life, as she told Christesen in the 1940s, Judith had been more left than right in her politics, but she also distrusted the new popularity of the Communist Party. Their politics seemed to her extreme and their bullying insistence on the party line offended her. This, and the tensions which had grown up between them, made her less than sympathetic to Christesen (who seemed to her to have flirted with communist ideas) when he appealed for help in defending himself against the charges laid against him during the Petrov Royal Commission. Apart from his left-wing views, the fact that his wife Nina was Russian-born made him suspect. It did not matter that her parents were White Russians, anti-communists who had fled from Russia; the fact that she was Russian was enough to condemn him. Judith's reply was determinedly detached:

> I don't regard the modern techniques of "charge and counter-charge" and complicated political manoeuvring by whatever "side" as likely to reach any solution of the world's problems which seem to me solvable only on quite other terms ... [This solution] makes a demand upon self-discipline, inner sincerity and capacity for feeling which ... seems impossible for most people to compass, and less and less possible the more such "charges and counter-charges" are indulged ... I am returning your copy of the letter to Latham [Sir John Latham, Chancellor of Melbourne University to whom Christesen had asked her to write]; you may find some other use for it.[12]

This may seem hard but Jack's influence had made her less and less sympathetic to short-term politics – and she reflects this influence when she adds in parenthesis; "By the way have you seen Jack's article 'Philosophy East and West?'"

In their view Western culture had reached an impasse and the only way out was the "change of heart" Jack was writing about. Whereas the political quarrels and debates around them seemed to be conducted on the same old ground, together they were looking for something different.

> There is after all, another method of approaching the present crescendo of fear and insecurity; but since it involves the development of an objectivity which lifts the view somewhat above the sinister dust of the immediate confusion, it's scarcely likely to gain any recognition in the present mood.[13]

From their detachment on the mountain it was possible to see this crescendo as mere "froth on the foam of history"[14] – a phrase of Jack's – and refuse to be distracted by the swirling currents around them. But for people like Christesen and the Palmers and many others it was not so easy. Nevertheless, what they saw convinced the McKinneys that they wanted no part in what was going on. They were also determined to resist the tide of "progress" sweeping the country. For Judith a sense of the past, of tradition, was always important, and now with Meredith the "notion of a sacred responsibility for continuance", especially for the "continuing future of our children",[15] enhanced this.

On the mountain they were by no means "out of it" – they were too concerned with the crisis they were thinking and writing about. But geographically they were rather isolated. In those days relatively few people owned cars, and Mount Tamborine was several hours away from Brisbane in any case. After the brief excitement of the US camp which had been located there during the war the locals settled down to life as usual: a few timber cutters and small farmers battling for a living on small blocks in the valleys cut out from the forests, people like Judith and Jack trying to get away to think, write, paint or just to live their own lives, and a few Aboriginal people, mostly at that stage disguising their real identity. There was only one bus a day, which rattled up and down along the winding road through the rainforest and across the coastal plain below. During the war new buses and spare parts had been unavailable and maintenance minimal so that breakdowns were frequent and the trip often took much longer than bargained for, though the bus driver, whom Jack nicknamed – for obvious reasons – "Have-A-Chat" provided entertainment on the way.

So far as the local community was concerned, Jack and Judith were free to get on with their lives, Though, even here some were infected by the rage for "development". One of the locals, for instance, told Jack that he loved seeing the smoke going up from the trees which had been cut down, declaring that he had been "fighting trees all his life".[16] But by and large, as Judith reflected looking back twenty years later in the poem "Habitat", which she wrote when she was about to leave "Calanthe",

> *We were fortunate, house; in a world of exiles*
> *stateless, homeless wandering, spying, murdering,*
> *wars, bewilderments, losses and betrayals,*
> *we found each other.*
> *In your spaces and awkward corners*
> *we spread our lives out, fitted and grew together.*

In New England she had sometimes been haunted by the Aboriginal past her family had helped to destroy. But what she found at "Calanthe" was much simpler, relics of ordinary people like themselves:

> *Digging the garden*
> *I used to ponder their remnants:*
> *crockery bits, smashed bottles,*
> *iron bolts, shoesoles,*
> *lost toys.*[17]

The garden flourished too, and helped to keep them supplied with food. Very soon Judith was boasting to Kathleen McArthur of "two ten-foot rows of potatoes, six rosellas, six red-pepper plants, a dozen tomatoes, a bed of cabbages – the mind reels at enumerating what more".[18] It was a hospitable house, too:

> *An eight-foot carpet-snake*
> *used to winter in the ceiling.*
> *We heard him roll and stretch*
> *when the evening fire was lighted*

and it also sheltered possums, mice and spiders. With the cloud of atomic destruction hanging over the world it seemed reassuring that still here

> *Mud-wasps built cells*
> *in hollows under books,*
> *cicadas left horny ghosts,*
> *split-backed, hooked to weatherboards.*[19]

It was a tough house, surviving cyclones, rolling "like a wooden ship/in waves of violence", enduring tropical rains and heat waves when the

> *Wood cracked and shrank,*
> *tank-water ebbed to the bottom.*
> *Air itself seemed flammable;*
> *we were scared to scratch a match.*[20]

It gave Judith a sense of permanence she had not known even at "Wallamumbi", and certainly not in the various places, mostly rooms or flats, she had lived in since then.

True, there were problems. They were constantly short of money. Jack was also quite often ill and Judith's hack work – short stories,

ABC broadcasts and lectures – did not bring in very much. But Judith was a shrewd businesswoman who kept a sharp eye on the royalties from her poetry, for example, and worked hard at her other writing, which paid better.

But 1956 was a particularly bad year – Judith had been seriously ill and unable to work – and at the end of it, with an overdraft of £700 (a great deal then) it looked as if they would have to sell up and go to Brisbane where Judith could get a job.[21] But Jack was getting on with his work, and Meredith, after her series of childhood illnesses, was well again and settled at school and the last thing Judith wanted was to have to move to Brisbane with all the upheavals that would entail, and getting a job would be difficult at her age. The only solution seemed to be to find a way of making a little more money from their one-acre block. Someone had drawn her attention to the pamphlets being put out by the Agriculture Department on keeping hens in cages – an American idea which repelled her. Nevertheless it might help them survive.

> The ten or eleven hens and the rooster [they] already had were producing well enough on the little bit of land allocated to the henshed. If I could acquire more hens, the gap between living expenses and earnings would close – but that, I worked out, would need about 300 producing hens and the poultry I already had were destroying the soil in the yard, even though the kikuyu grass cover was rampant and the big hedge protected the fenceline.[22]

She felt that she could manage the physical work, though she worried that it might be difficult to prevent Jack from pitching in also and overtaxing his strength. Just at that time a commission for a film script for the Department of the Interior, to be filmed at "Jeogla" and "Wallamumbi", gave them a bit of extra money, so with that and a loan from the bank, they launched out as poultry farmers. Water was to be pumped from the creek, the old chicken shed was renovated to accommodate three hundred layers, and they were in business.

It was hard work, and the price of feed seemed to be always rising and the price of eggs always falling, but for the time being it kept the banks at bay. Judith did not like the work. She complained to Kathleen that she smelt "henny ... just faintly but all the time"; the smells and feathers seemed to "seep into one somehow – little bits of chicken fluff in lungs and eggs before your eyes instead of spots".[23] But at least her conscience was not as troubled as she thought it might be. The hens sang "so happily about eggs and poultry mash that it's a pleasure to hear them ... Nature clearly intended hens to live in small cramped cages".[24] She gave them the best of food and greenstuffs and not only did they seem contented but also laid well.

She also kept slogging away at her literary hack work and giving lectures for Adult Education which took her to various parts of Queensland. This was tiring but could be entertaining. One night, at Warwick, a "beery gentleman" wandered into the hall, sat there bemused for a few moments and then staggered out complaining that he "hadn't heard a word about the British Empire".[25]

As her poems make clear, people interested her – as a child she had loved listening to the yarns of the men who worked at "Wallamumbi". But Jack was even better than she at getting on with people. As the Blackmans said, his was a "peculiarly potent personality,"[26] interested in everyone and everything and someone who loved listening as well as talking. Language fascinated him in particular, and he delighted in the conversation and sayings of the locals. On one occasion their neighbour described a particularly splendid sunset he had seen in which the "pink buggers had mixed in with the gold and red buggers", and afterwards Jack would entertain visitors with a recital of this speech and of other flights of vernacular eloquence.[27]

It helped, too, that he was an "ex-digger" and a handyman who could talk knowledgeably to anyone about most things – one he liked to boast about was the fact that he had managed to convert the local vicar's wife to composting.[28] Judith may well have had him in mind in "The Poet", first published in *Meanjin* in 1956:

> *Simplex Simplicior Simplicissimus*
> *stood like a shouldering crystal under the sun*
> *and changed its light into all the colours of love.*
> *Great heavens, they said to him, look what you've done;*
> *you've turned What Is into There's No Such Thing;*

> *now we must turn it back. And the butterfly's wing*
> *dropped at his feet and the bird sang business only.*[29]

Children loved him; he had a whole set of tricks, like whistling on two notes at once,[30] but also showed an unfailing interest in and respect for them. With his philosopher's gift of taking nothing for granted he got on very well with the artists, writers and other people who came visiting from Brisbane and elsewhere. As the Blackmans recalled;

> Many who visited the Mountain in those years poet-hunting ... found themselves instead haunted by this spry old man with the white, clipped beard, keen blue eyes, who had something witty and relevant to say to everyone he met, and a determined interest in finding out something new about each person who crossed his doorstep.[31]

So it is not surprising perhaps that the local people accepted Jack and Judith's relationship, even though they were not legally married.

He also got on well with Aboriginal people they met on the mountain or on their travels. Before the 1967 referendum, Aborigines were not regarded as citizens and were thus officially invisible, supposed to be out of sight on government reserves and missions, but McKinney had no respect for the ways of bureaucracy and regarded them as people like himself. He also had a strong sense of justice and was appalled at the way they were treated. His daughter Lucy worked as a nurse on the Palm Island reserve, and he returned from a visit there disgusted at the way a beautiful island had been turned into a prison. "No white official," he told Judith, had "the slightest interest in them."[32] He was usually cheerful and easygoing, but his anger so impressed Meredith that when he returned later for a second visit she was very worried, telling her friend Nettie Palmer, "I don't want my Daddy to be in trouble."[33]

Jack was much older than Judith, turning sixty in 1951, and might, as the Blackmans put it, "have aged away in invalidism", but at "Calanthe" he seemed to become "young again".[34] He also grew more confident in his work, largely perhaps because of Judith's support. Christesen's interest in publishing his book, *The Challenge of Reason*, never very strong, faded away with Clem's move to Melbourne. But believing that Jack had important things to say, Judith set up their own press, Mountain Press, and published it in the same year that Meredith was born, 1950. Free copies were sent to the university libraries throughout the country and Judith managed to persuade a few bookshops in Brisbane to stock the book. To her disappointment there were few sales, no reviews and almost no responses.

Jack was, after all, an outsider. He objected to what he saw as the irrelevance of the intellectual games played by most professional philosophers, believing that what was needed was a new way of looking at things, a new attitude to life. In his view the world had reached a crisis point: "Reason [which for him involved the intuitive and emotional, not mere rationality] has ceased to influence men's actions, men no longer have faith in themselves, in one another, or finally the value and meaning of life itself" – hence he thought, the materialism, acquisitiveness, competitiveness and individualism which was becoming a way of life throughout the Western and, increasingly, the non-Western world. The only answer to this crisis, he argued, was "a new cooperative enterprise of the spirit at a new and higher level of understanding". But this involved asceticism, the opposite of the consumerism beginning to take hold: "The way to the mountain height of understanding and true power lies through the valley of renunciation."[35]

His vision went beyond the narrow confines of philosophy as it was then practised and was closer to the older idea of a philosopher as someone in search of wisdom. His book had attracted almost no attention, but determined that he would be heard, Judith encouraged him to contribute articles to international philosophical journals. There he had a good deal of success, publishing seven articles in the distinguished British journal *Mind*, for example. He also worked on a series of philosophical dialogues along the lines of the dialogues of Socrates to submit to the British Broadcasting Corporation (BBC), at that time broadcasting similar material. But the series was discontinued before he could submit them.

Judith worried at Jack's lack of recognition elsewhere, but his thought and her growing reputation as a poet was making "their citadel at Tamborine an intellectual outpost".[36] Their partnership was crucial.

At once intellectual and deeply personal, it gave Judith a renewed sense of hope and purpose and joy. She was living in a way that was unconventional – something her upbringing would not have approved of entirely – and often difficult materially, but she had found someone with whom she could share her deepest concerns and who invigorated her: Jack's "jokes and conversation kept [her] happy as well as in love".[37]

Her background was very different from his and she did not find it quite as easy as he did to fit in to the local community, telling a friend on one occasion that "we have to use all of ourselves to reduce our conversation to the eighth of oneself that is allowable in social chit-chat".[38] This was true even of her own family, who seemed to be more and more engrossed in their property and in their overseas travels, reporting to the same friend after the 1956 Christmas visit to New England that they were "lyrical about the USA, two-tone cars, and supermarkets and state highways".[39] Nevertheless she tried hard for Meredith's sake, especially after she started school, to be a conventional wife and mother.

> I'm a member of the Parents and Citizens Association [she wrote] and apparently accepted as a respectable member of society, or at least one whose cakes are not despised. I find this rather funny, but it can't be helped. Jack wisely refuses to be drawn into the magic circle.[40]

Meredith herself, she reported, was not "a natural school girl but she seems to recognise that one must [submit] and doesn't complain at all".

With all this, the housework, the hens, her stories, articles, the work on *The Generations of Men*, which at that stage she regarded as a biography novel, Judith was hard-pressed:

> I seem to be halfways through everything at present, like a goat stuck in a fence; the flower-garden, the vegetable garden, Meredith's new clothes for school, revising the school anthology (*New Land, New Language*), my correspondence file and about six other domestic agonies.[41]

None of this came easy – she had spent too long as a child rebelling at women's rituals to be at home in them – and something of her exasperation comes through in an article on her in the *Sydney Morning*

Herald in 1958 when she was in Sydney to give a Commonwealth Literary Fund lecture:

> "When you're a house-wife, and a gardener and also a poultry farmer, you just have to fit your writing in the cracks", she smiled. As for reading: "I can only prop a book against the sugar bowl at breakfast and hope nobody talks to me!"
>
> That might not be difficult for her husband, Mr J. McKinney, a philosopher and an author himself, but her eight-year-old daughter, Meredith, naturally has things that must be said to mother at breakfast.
>
> Meredith is a Brownie, and more interested in ballet than in poetry at the moment.[42]

Demands from others seemed to mount up also. A retired anthropologist who lived nearby, she reported, for example,

> has gone into hospital determined to die as soon as possible and won't even talk. She handed over the business of [Aboriginal] legends which is still hanging fire with Melbourne University Press before she left, and I am to make all the decisions and do all the work (not get any of the cheques, however); and as it hasn't got to page-proof stage yet I can see trouble ahead. I couldn't very well decline the job however, as [she] insisted I was the only person qualified to deal with it (I'm not) and simply walked out from under.[43]

She was also more aware than Jack was of their anomalous position, perhaps because she was a woman:

> People will come up to you in the country and ask what you do, or what your husband does rather ... When you answer we're writers there is a very perceptible total back-off, and that's something you feel surrounded by. You feel as though you're bacteria on a plate ... It's quite an interesting experience, useful insofar as you can pride yourself on it and write. You don't feel any pressure to go out and justify what you are saying or doing in the country because you know what you can't do.[44]

She had never been a conventional woman, and was not about to become one. True, she put Jack's needs first but in this she resembled other women of her time and before it. Nettie Palmer, for instance, had once told her that "what Vance wants comes first"[45] and Margaret Preston, whose painting Judith admired, believed that her "first duty was to her husband".[46] But she had no intention of annihilating herself, being quite aware of her situation. As Miles Franklin had put it, "a woman writer, except in rare circumstances, has no protection as enjoyed by men who use their wives and mistresses ... and save themselves from the wear and tear of interruption".[47] "If there was a budding Marie Curie, or a female Pasteur or Einstein, or a Charlotte Brontë, in Australia," she told a friend, "she would still be condemned to be a charwoman."[48]

Nevertheless, Judith was convinced that women had an intellectual contribution to make and that it needed to be acknowledged. When she edited the annual *Anthology of Australian Poetry* for Angus & Robertson in 1948, she included an unusual number of poems by women, upsetting some reviewers who suggested that she was "undermining the established views of poetry in Australia, and should be thoroughly slapped down for so doing".[49] Much as Judith loved Jack and deferred to him, she was the one in charge. As she told a reporter from *Cleo* in the 1970s, "I have no respect for [most] women ... They have no guts. I'm what you might call a Woman's Libber from way back." Women should be independent, but most of them "don't think for themselves very much. To be fully human, you have to take responsibility for yourself."[50] Her friendship with Kathleen McArthur, another independent woman, was an important one, therefore. But even there she kept an eye on Kathleen, advising her before she went for a holiday in Melbourne to "find something to do ... If you go in for Canasta parties I'll sorrow over you".[51]

Her situation kept her under pressure. She could only get down to her real work, her poetry, at night after the others were asleep, and she had "night terrors" that she might never be able to write good poetry again – for her a poet was not someone to whom poems happened but someone devoted to the craft as well as the art and was prepared to work at it. No wonder, then, as she told Kathleen, that from time to time she longed "to get away from everyone except my family and dwell in one room on Stradbroke Island away from cars and telephones and never do anything I don't want to do".[52] She might write: "It's Monday ... and the washing's done and dried and sorted and waiting to be ironed and to hell with it ... I'm getting sick of oughts, of which my life at present is made up", but she had been brought up to do her duty, and could only hope that "perhaps when I'm 50 [that] stern goddess, daughter of the voice of God, will let up on me", though, with a characteristic note of self-awareness, reflected that "she'll probably be tougher than ever".[53] But she did not feel entirely frustrated:

> It has been a week of moderate achievement [she wrote on another occasion]: Meredith's new wool dress and hood and pyjamas made, half of Ursula's beastly galley proofs corrected for her, two indexes done for the anthology, Jack has done the final revision of his dialogues and they are ready to type, and yesterday I listened to three acts of *Parsifal* and knitted a cardigan sleeve for Meredith. Meanwhile I feel a moderate pride, too, in a poem I wrote today.[54]

No wonder, then, that she wrote, "I cannot think what is happening to time, for though I do twice as much work in a day I'm sure I can never catch up with the creature ... I wish I had some of the nice long days I used to have when I was eight or nine."[55]

Nevertheless it was an important stage. As one of Drusilla Modjeska's characters in *The Orchard* puts it; "there are passages that everyone of us must traverse on our entry into life. It is the journey of the soul that makes us ... or not,"[56] or as Judith herself put it; "You don't know where you are until you know what you are,"[57] and she was certainly getting to know who she was and where her loyalties lay.

Living on the mountain did give them a sense of distance from what was going on around them, though their deepest concern was with the nuclear threat. The first nuclear, as distinct from atomic, bomb was detonated in 1951, and shortly afterwards the British began nuclear testing at Maralinga in Central Australia. As Judith wrote in her autobiography:

> That program was kept under heavy wrappers, but rumours still crept through; testing was rumoured to be going wrong, plumes from the tests were moving in unexpected directions, and the question of their effects on white populations was sometimes muttered. Their effects on Aborigines were simply not raised, nor would anyone bother to ask.
>
> But to me, the whole enterprise of nuclear testing, let alone the bomb itself, was a deeply negative and destructive development in the human psyche.[58]

These anxieties were reflected in her poetry. The title poem of "The Two Fires", for instance, contrasted the natural world and the drive to creation with "the denial of the very basis of life which was at the root of the Bomb, and of the militaristic uses of nuclear physics – that latest and deepest exploitation of the material world itself".[59]

Experience seemed to confirm her anxieties. During the tests, Meredith developed a mysterious rash which the doctor could not identify, and Jack succumbed to a particularly virulent form of flu which lingered for months. There was also a series of disastrous droughts and storms. She blamed all these on the tests during which it was rumoured that "something had gone disastrously wrong".[60]

> Even during the war itself [she wrote in her autobiography] when the huge American Army staging camp below the mountain had added health hazards in the form of camp followers and escapees, people said there hadn't been as many illnesses as now ... I, being a sceptic, believed that the haste with which we were reassured about the effects of bomb testings and pesticides had something suspicious about it.[61]

Meredith made Judith even more concerned since her daughter was growing up in a world faced with annihilation. "Two Songs for the World's End" express these fears:

> *Bombs ripen on the leafless tree*
> *under which the children play.*
> *And there my darling all alone*
> *dances in the spying day.*

> *I gave her nerves to feel her pain,*
> *I put her mortal beauty on.*
> *I taught her love, that hate might find*
> *its black work the easier done.*[62]

This sense of danger followed her everywhere. On one occasion, for example, she flew from Brisbane to Armidale to give a lecture at the University of New England, taking Meredith with her. Flying then was not as safe as it is now, nor was it so comfortable, and the aircraft was a converted Hudson bomber with no radar.

> At Glen Innes the pilot came to warn us of a cyclone. He was going on [but] any one who did not want to could stay. I didn't have enough money for a hotel room so I decided to go on. At the Queensland border we ran into a dense swirling cloud; and suddenly just beside the plane a steep green mountainside appeared. I was later ashamed to remember, that so far from attempting to shield my infant daughter from what looked like an imminent crash, I held her up to admire the view (and incidentally to shield myself). We sheared upwards so sharply that my seat-belt almost cut into my ribs ... When we arrived at the airport the pilot asked; "Was anyone frightened back there?" We all shook our heads politely. "My God," he said, "I was."[63]

As someone said of Sylvia Plath, she was prepared "to look with unnerving steadiness at the Gorgon". But she did not lose her feeling for people.

"The Precipice", published in *Meanjin* in 1953, is about the story of someone devoured by the Gorgon, a story which actually happened nearby. It is about a woman who took the bus to Mount Tamborine and then a taxi to the edge of the National Park. There

> in the darkness of the evening, she walked down the path through the rainforest and jumped, with them in her arms, over the cliff at the path's end. The whole family had died and were found only after a long search, clasped in her arms.[64]

Her husband had returned from the war an emotional and physical wreck, and she could not endure anymore his violence or the threat of a nuclear holocaust. It was a story which touched Judith's own deep fears, as the poem's conclusion makes clear:

> *Now, and for years to come, that path is seared*
> *by the blazing headlong torrent of their direction;*
> *and we must hold our weathercock minds from turning*
> *into its downward gale, towards destruction.*[65]

Internationally these fears were not unusual. Sylvia Plath's poems and works like Henry Miller's *The Air-Conditioned Nightmare* (which the McKinneys read and were impressed by) expressed a similar sense of impending apocalypse, the sense articulated by Einstein and Russell in their 1955 manifesto, which concluded: "Here then is the problem we present to you, stark and dreadful and inescapable. Shall we put an end to the human race, or shall mankind renounce war."[66] In Australia, however, most writers, with the exception perhaps of James McAuley and Vincent Buckley, seemed unaffected. So it is not surprising that Wright told Kathleen McArthur that she was able to read less and less of the work of her contemporaries and was concentrating on writers like Shakespeare and Villon and, more recently, Rilke. Jack was also keeping her up with contemporary philosophy, mathematics and science. The mindlessness around her distressed her. As she wrote in her autobiography:

> Nothing overrode the money nexus. Australians were as rootless and mindless as ever in spite of the upsurge of feeling during the war, and the various declarations of politicians. Most of us seemed to be natural real-estate agents, an eye to the main chance, and not to the good of the land.[67]

But at least Jack's philosophy gave her some understanding of the situation and the hope of a way out of it, suggesting that a first step was to understand the nature of the problem they faced which, he suggested, had to do with the separation between body and spirit but was also bound up with the question of language. What was necessary, he thought, was to put an end to this separation and redefine what was meant by reality.

Judith echoed these views in two essays she wrote which were published in a journal, *Language*, which appeared in 1952 and then disappeared after the second issue, possibly because it announced itself as determinedly neutral, a journal "with no axes to grind. The editor dislikes the sight of axes"[68] – not a popular view in the 1950s.

> Our picture of the world is altering [she wrote] ...The current of events which forms the life-stream of the individual escapes – and we can now see, has in its essential form always escaped – fixation and description. The word tree, for instance, is only a label – the tree seen, the momentous living event, slips through it as through a sieve; it is part of the flow of our relative individual experience, and our perception of it is no more lasting than a dream-perception.[69]

What Jack called "the common high fever" which seemed to have seized the Western world could only be cured by courageous and careful thought and being humble enough to put oneself in tune with the living world of nature. Like Adorno, both of them believed that:

> The only responsible course is to deny oneself the ideological misuse of one's own existence [evident in the passion for material possessions and comforts], and for the rest to conduct oneself in private as modestly, unobtrusively and unpretentiously as is required, no longer by good upbringing but by the shame of still having air to breathe, in hell.[70]

"The Harp and the King", first published in *Meanjin* in 1953, is about this shame. Inspired by Arthur Boyd's painting of David playing before Saul (which Jack and Judith had "bought on tick" at his exhibition in Brisbane), the poem sets the creative power of the imagination over and against the destructive madness of imperial power:

> *Old king without a throne,*
> *the hollow of despair*
> *behind his obstinate unyielding stare,*
> *knows only, God is gone:*
> *and, fingers clenching on his chair,*
> *feels night and the soul's terror coming on.*[71]

To "the self-betrayed", "the world's a traitor" and he remains imprisoned in his own violent fantasies. But the harp, the symbol of creative power, sings "the praise of time", of the privilege and panic of mortality, of the need to face the truth of our times and the obligation to go on searching:

> ... *[We] betray all truths that we possess.*
> *Time strips the soul and leaves it comfortless*
> *and sends it thirsty through a bone-white drought.*
> *Time's subtler treacheries teach us to betray.*
> *What else could drive us on our way?*
> *Wounded we cross the desert's emptiness,*
> *and must be false to what would make us whole.*
> *For only change and distance shape for us*
> *some new tremendous symbol for the soul.*[72]

Together she and Jack were trying to take this journey and to shape this symbol. She had always been uneasy with the world of consciousness, always, as she put it, something of a heretic.[73] But being with Jack, a fellow heretic, gave her new confidence. Meredith, too, strengthened her determination, gave her "something to fight for. I didn't matter, she did".[74]

The poem "Unknown Water" makes this dedication clear, picking up the traditional rural images of her earlier poems but turning them in a new direction. It is about a time of drought which is not only physical but spiritual also and centres on the image of

> ... *the old man, part of my childhood,*
> *who knew all about cattle and horses.*

But the water he and she used to know

> ... *is dried up now. All dried,*
> *and the drought goes raging on. Your own sons and*
>   *daughters*
> *have forgotten what it is to live by a water*
> *that never dries up.*

So the task to which the poem dedicates itself is to renew this tradition, to discover the water which is still there underneath the surface, concluding with these words to the old man:

> ...*I am not you,*
> *but you are part of me. Go easy with me, old man;*
> *I am helping to clear a track to unknown water.*[75]

This track led by way of a renewal of language back to the living world. The kind of poetry she was writing at the time reflected the call by Owen Barfield (whose *Poetic Diction* she and Jack were reading) for an end to the language which deals with "solid chunks, with definitions, boundaries and limits to which other chunks may be added as occasion arises",[76] replacing it with a language of "flashing, iridescent shapes, like flames – the ever-flickering vertigo of the slowly evolving consciousness beneath them".[77] In the light of these ideas, the strange flickering fires and shapes of poems like "The Two Fires" take on a new significance.

This is the kind of poetry which, Barfield said, is "straining towards a plenum of consciousness [expressing a] ...knowledge which would bring about its own destruction ... like a ship that is wrecked on entering harbour".[78] The critics who found these poems didactic and lacking in inspiration did not understand this, nor did they understand the impact upon her of the fires of Hiroshima and Nagasaki. Fire had always fascinated her, but these fires, a manifestation of the possibility of ultimate destruction, seemed to her to represent "a deeply negative and destructive development in the human psyche. I could not keep [them] out of the poems if I wanted to."[79]

Other poems, however, took a more positive path, trying to let the world, threatened with destruction, speak itself. In these poems she was writing what the French poet François Ponge, another writer who interested her, called the "poem thing", an attempt not to dominate nature but to be attuned to it. This, too, was a way of reacting to the sense of crisis she felt since, as Ponge pointed out, poetry of this kind moves to preserve a world threatened by "radiation war".[80] The earlier French Symbolists, whom Judith had read and admired as an undergraduate, had talked of the need to "purify the language of the tribe" but as one of the few who understood what she was trying to do pointed out in an essay which links her work with Ponge's, "the tribe is much changed after two world wars and some previews of a third".[81] The great task of poets now was thus to be "the heralds of a silent world", putting it in "possession – through men – of a language". And doing this by starting "with the simplest things carefully worded".[82] In this way poetry would "help to preserve ... the treasures of the past" also.[83]

The collection, *Birds* (1962), which Judith wrote for Meredith who had begun school loving poetry but had very soon begun to dislike it, is written on this principle, a principle with which children are familiar – as Judith said in these poems she tried to write "the kind of poetry kids would enjoy ... to look through their eyes a bit".[84] But it was a method which was very demanding, as "For Precision" suggests:

> *Let me be sure and economical as the rayed*
> *suns, stars, flowers, wheels: let me fall as a gull, a hawk*
>
> *through the confusions of foggy talk,*
> *and pin with one irremediable stroke –*
> *what? – the escaping wavering wandering light,*
> *the blur, the brilliance ...*
> *... speaking with a pure voice.*[85]

Learning a language, as Jack wrote in *The Structure of Modern Thought*, quoting Wittgenstein, is not learning to give names to objects but learning the names of objects.[86] As "Gum-trees Stripping" has it,

> *Words are not meanings for a tree.*

The task is rather to learn the language of the tree.

> *... wisdom shells the words away*
> *to watch this fountain slowed in air*
> *where sun joins earth – to watch the place*
> *at which these silent rituals are ...*
>
> *If it is possible to be wise*
> *here, wisdom lies outside the word*
> *in the earlier answer of the eyes.*[87]

She was in search of the forces of life and to speak for them in a situation in which, in the last words of "The Two Fires", otherwise

> *The world's denied.*[88]

This search kept her from the despair which shadows many of her poems at the time, especially when she thought of Meredith – as in these lines from "Two Generations":

> *What do you learn of the world? I hold your hand;*
> *but even my touch is cancelled by that wind;*
> *because the wind is my own breath,*
> *whispering that the heart of man condemns the world to*
>   *death.*[89]

Nevertheless it would be wrong to suggest that they lived lives of gloom. Their friends from the *Meanjin* and *Barjai* days had mostly moved away but many still kept in touch. Laurie Hope came often, and Barbara and Charles Blackman became particular friends, often looking after "Calanthe" when the McKinneys were away. Charles liked to paint there, and did most of his "Alice in Wonderland" series there, drawing on the tropical luxuriance of the rainforest and images of Meredith wandering in the garden at "Calanthe". He also painted a fine portrait of Jack, mostly done when he was sitting absorbed in his reading and paying no attention to anything else,

> *... tracing out a pattern to its core*
> *through lovely logics of the octagon*
> *and radials' perfect plunging.*[90]

Barbara had admired them both from the *Barjai* days when they "lifted her sky high". "Thereafter," as she wrote in her autobiography, they "became lifetime friends and sky heroes for me in the Aboriginal sense." She enjoyed visiting them at Mount Tamborine, "loved their wordiness and their quirky humour. They read me Jung." Nor did the fact that Judith was deaf and Barbara blind seem to matter: "She of the faraway voice and I of the faraway face did not find our lacks obstructive to the deepening roots of friendship."[91]

Jack especially enjoyed the company of the artists, believing that contemporary art was exploring much the same territory as physics and mathematics, though from its own point of view, of course, as relativity and quantum theory began to supersede the world created by Newton. Whether or not the artists understood Jack, they found his conversation fascinating; Judith remembers Albert Tucker, for instance, sitting silent and absorbed as he talked. Sidney Nolan came, too, in the early 1950s, fresh from their visit to Fraser Island which was to inspire a memorable series of paintings.

They had many literary visitors, also. A. D. Hope, then a young lecturer at the University College in Canberra, later the Australian National University, was one of the earliest, and he proved "a most co-operative guest, even praising the breakfast eggs" – the staple diet when money was scarce. He also arranged later for Judith to give some lectures at the College – a useful supplement to their income as well as giving her intellectual exercise and introducing her to people like Leonie Kramer, then a young lecturer whom she later recalled as a young mother with her two children clinging to her.

"Good Alan Marshall" came, too, fresh from a trip to the north in search of Aboriginal stories. Younger writers like Tom Shapcott and Rodney Hall looked to Judith, as the Barjais had done, as an inspirational figure. Tom Shapcott, for instance, recalled a visit with his family to "Calanthe" in the mid-1950s when he was still working as an accountant but determined to become a poet, as if visiting Judith Wright was like a visit to the Muse herself, though Jack's personality and sparkling intelligence also fascinated him.[92] According to Rodney Hall, Judith Wright and John Manifold, founder of the Realist Writers, were the two great inspirations of his life as a young poet. Manifold was more directly involved politically but Hall found in Judith a presence which became the embodiment of the values he believed in and struggled for politically and socially.[93]

Perhaps the most extraordinary of the visitors to "Calanthe" was Francis Barbazon, a poet and, in Judith's view, "the last manifestation of the Barjais". He had been a friend of Melbourne painters like Nolan and Tucker and had been on the fringes of the group who gathered at "Heide" around John and Sunday Reed where he had also met Barrie Reid. Always interested in mysticism, Barbazon had become a Sufi and a disciple of an Indian guru Meher Baba, and he visited Jack and Judith in 1958 looking for land in Queensland on which to build a centre to welcome the Master when he came to Australia. Judith had included one of his poems in *A Book of Australian Verse* and Barrie Reid had often talked about her to him, so he called in on them at Mount Tamborine. Judith was not particularly impressed. Barbazon

> arrived in a most extraordinary vintage car, too long to fit across our lawn, which blocked our exit to the garage ... and left leaving a number of expensive books he was selling on behalf of his mentor on the lawn, crushed by those solid rubber wheels.

She and Jack were interested in Indian philosophy, but Jack, who had been reading in a more disciplined way, "soon retired from all attempts at pinning him down to earth and went back to his books", leaving Judith to occupy hours of her time in poetic and spiritual argument. He may have been, as she said, "a spiritual plus", but he was a "practical nobody", managing not only to lose the bathplug – which was a nuisance – but himself when he went walking along "well-tracked and trodden rainforest paths". He also spent much of his time in "unsuccessful proselytising".[94]

The older generation like Mary Gilmore and Marjorie Barnard stayed in touch too, and Barnard visited, giving Judith useful advice about placing her short stories. Vance and Nettie Palmer, who had a little beach house at Caloundra, also became friends. Jack had known Vance in the 1930s through his novels and radio plays but they had lost touch when Jack's interests turned to philosophy. Now, however, the persecution they were enduring because of their left-wing (but by no means communist) views, meant that they spent more time in Caloundra. When the McKinneys went to the coast they would often call in, and later, when they bought a house at Boreen Point, they saw even more of one another. Nettie, who loved children, was especially fond of Meredith whom she called "Miss Pony Tail", and they would often go walking together, Nettie "paddling along in an old pair of sandshoes, exclaiming at the wild-flowers". Judith remembers her waiting for them, sitting on the kerb outside her house, wearing this "most extraordinary old pair of busted shoes and an enormous hat ... picking little bits out of the sandshoes. She didn't care how she looked". Meredith loved her and her conversation, "down to earth ... and full of jokes".[95]

In the meantime Judith's reputation as a poet was growing, even if the critics did not always understand or appreciate the new philosophical weight of her work. On occasion, Prime Minister Menzies quoted from her poetry in a speech – she was piqued that he did not ask permission or pay for the right to quote – and wrote to her saying how much he had enjoyed the sequence "Flesh". Stephen Spender's visit and the lunch they had together at the local café has already been mentioned, but not her recollection of his entourage, a "flanking bodyguard of sinister black-suited guides or guards who didn't as far as I remember even buy us a coffee".[96] She found John Betjeman, another international visitor, more agreeable and entertained him at home – in his letter of thanks he praised her avocado salad. Like most of their visitors he was also fascinated by Jack's conversation.

One visitor proved especially important – Frank Eyre, newly arrived from England to manage Oxford University Press in Australia. The Press was determined to win back the Australian market from American publishers who had begun to take an interest, and it was planning an ambitious publishing program. One of Eyre's projects was to be an anthology of Australian verse – Oxford still refused to use the word "poetry" for Australian writing – and he wrote offering Judith £150 to edit the anthology, saying that he would like to come and talk about it. It was a large sum then, and they needed the money. Judith was looking for a publisher for *The Generations of Men*, which she had just completed – Melbourne University Press had rejected it as "too fictional" and Angus & Robertson as not fictional enough – so the news of his arrival sent them into a spin. There was, she wrote, much "cleaning up of the premises and tucking the beer bottles (left by the previous owner) in the garage ... so as to make a favourable impression on the employer".[97]

When Eyre arrived they got on very well. He took to Jack and his conversation and, impressed by Judith as well as by her work, went away with the manuscript of *The Generations of Men*, which Oxford was to publish after some delay in 1959. Later, he also commissioned a critical monograph on Charles Harpur, published in 1963, whose work and ideas Judith discovered in her reading for the anthology, and the pioneering study *Preoccupations in Australian Poetry* (1965), which also came out of this reading and the lectures she was giving in the 1950s to make ends meet. Oxford was also to publish the first of Judith's books for children, *King of the Dingoes* (1958), whose hero was her beloved

Judith with her mother, Ethel Wright,
and brothers Bruce and Peter, circa 1926.
(Courtesy of Judith Wright)

Phillip and Ethel Wright (née Bigg), wedding photograph, 1913.
(Courtesy of Caroline Mitchell)

Ethel Wright (née Bigg), wedding photograph, 1913.
(Courtesy of Caroline Mitchell)

Judith Wright with her brother, Bruce, circa 1920.
(Courtesy of Caroline Mitchell)

Judith Wright (left) with her cousin, Margaret Wright, 1919.
(Courtesy Margaret Lister (née Wright))

Judith, Bruce and Peter Wright
on the front drive of "Wallamumbi", circa 1929.
(Courtesy of Caroline Mitchell)

Family picture – Bruce, Peter, Ethel and Judith Wright (Judith standing).
(Courtesy of Caroline Mitchell)

Judith Wright in the 1930s.
(Courtesy of Judith Wright)

dog who had died of old age and the cold during the grim winter she had spent in New England in 1943.

The McKinneys appreciated "the peace of the mountain" but they also needed good minds and good discussion and people on their wavelength. But, for Judith at least, Kathleen McArthur was the friend she saw most often and later, when Judith moved away from Queensland, they shared a correspondence that lasts to this day. Born within eleven days of each other, they came from similar backgrounds. On her father's side Kathleen's family were Brisbane industrialists, but through her mother she was a Durack; Kathleen and Judith both liked to think that the Duracks had passed by Judith's grandparents' property "Nulalbin" when travelling westward.

They first met in 1951 not long after the McKinneys had settled into "Calanthe", when a book arrived from Kathleen in the post for Meredith's birthday – *The Way of the Whirlwind* by Mary and Elizabeth Durack, Kathleen's cousins. A book was a little premature since this was Meredith's first birthday; what Judith and Jack gave her was a playpen and sandpit. Nevertheless Judith wrote back thanking Kathleen and inviting her to come and see them, which she did not long after the Brisbane Show – before that they had been busy entertaining Judith's father on his way to Brisbane where some of his cattle were to be shown. "We are awfully bad-mannered people and not in the least like Buckingham Palace", Judith wrote.[98] But in the event they hit it off.

Kathleen was also unconventional; her marriage had broken up and she was living with her three children at Caloundra (where she knew the Palmers), in a house named "Midyim", barely visible in its garden of wildflowers, shrubs and trees. She was also an artist, passionately interested in wildflowers, which she drew with delicate accuracy, and her interest sparked Judith's, who at that stage knew little about the wildflowers of Queensland – flowers, as she said, could always lift her spirits, "even if we're headed for the gates of hell".[99] On one occasion some years later, driving to Brisbane on business, Judith suddenly had to stop the car

> to investigate a patch of purple flowers, about fifty of the most enormous and brightly-coloured Bugles I have ever seen,

growing under a gum tree and surrounded by equally enormous and brightly-coloured hare-bells and bachelors' buttons. It's a wonderful year for flowers ... All the scents I love vaguely pushed into the garden over the past years and forgotten all about have sprung to life ... bewildering me completely.[100]

Her friendship with Kathleen gave her licence to indulge herself. Significantly, too, Kathleen associated their first meeting with flowers. "It was a year of great blossoming of the Mountain's Flame Trees ... [though] a very dry year", and she remembered especially the view from "Calanthe's" back steps (where Jack liked to sit), which looked out over the gully to "the most inspiring of all Flame Trees in the paddock above" on the opposite hill. Like most people, Kathleen was impressed by Jack. He "was a great and fast talker and I was flat out keeping up with him in the sleepy mountain air", so that she had to wait for the walks in the rainforest with Judith and the children to get to know her properly. Judith's deafness was a problem at first, but she was learning to lip-read at the time which meant that, walking in the forest and unable to face her, Kathleen had to let Judith do all the talking, giving her "the advantage of being a listener to one who had much to tell".

Their love of flowers drew them together and in their walks they would rejoice in the "patches of yellow, some white, dampiera blue, boronia pink ... blown purple irises so quick to wither and scented clusters of heath interspersed with single blooms to watch for all crowded with blossoms" – flowers which were not valued by most people because they "didn't look like New Farm Park or the tulip beds of Holland".[101] Judith also loved Kathleen's drawings, which helped her see the wildflowers more vividly. One letter thanked her for some prints Kathleen had sent her:

> I want to tell you how beautifully they "come through" – what a successful mixture of flowers and shrubs they are en masse. I was truly moved by them as I always am by your flower drawings ... [The] Phaius [orchid] is extra – and how well the nunyium and bugle and sun orchid with that delicate colour have come through the printing.

She also shared what she had seen for herself on the mountain:

> Such flame trees out up here! One on the hill opposite over the creek, a big one, one huge blaze; and I can't get away to go on a pilgrimage to it because we're so desperately busy. I must try to wake up really early and sneak off: it's something not to be repeated.

Concluding with a request for more drawings to send to friends which she insisted on paying for – Kathleen was nearly as short of money as they were and Judith had told her she had hopes of finding some rich people who would buy her drawings – she enclosed a poem of her own "as inadequate return for all this joy".[102]

But their friendship did not always exist on these lofty heights; two women together, they could also enjoy "a good old natter about obstetrics" and it was Kathleen who came to Judith's rescue when she was ill in 1956. Brought up in a fairly disciplined way, Judith enjoyed her friend's spontaneity, remarking that she and the "goddess Gaia may have ... a lot in common ... a refusal to be straitlaced into mere description and illustration". They both like to "wander, reminisce, recall and enjoy".[103] In this way she introduced Judith once again to the flowering, fertile world she had known briefly with her mother when they were picking fruit in the orchard, though Kathleen had little of the care for appearances which had characterised Judith's childhood world.

Jack was provoking Judith to think more strenuously, but Kathleen helped her to see – something very important for a writer. As *Preoccupations in Australian Poetry* put it:

> Before one's country can become an accepted background against which the poet's and novelist's imagination can move unhindered it must first be observed, understood, described, and as it were absorbed. The writer must be at peace with his landscape before he can turn confidently to its human figures.[104]

Jack enjoyed Kathleen's company also and would occasionally add a postscript to Judith's letters to her, like the quirky one he wrote when he was deep in a philosophical problem, the fact that the data of individual experience is known and the only starting point of our common world picture conflicts with the fact that the world picture cannot be shown to be demonstrable from the individual's experiential data. The answer ... is no. But perhaps you don't think about it, for which I don't blame you.[105]

Judith was probably the more tough-minded of the two and more interested in politics and the larger world, but Kathleen was to become a firm ally in later battles to save the environment they loved, and it was she who first broached the idea of agitating to have the area around Cooloola declared a National Park.

It was the kind of friendship which can grow up between two strong women who share a similar background, and not only see eye to eye but are also driven by a similar restlessness, a similar sense of the contradictions between their desires and the forces pressing on them. But it was the kind of friendship, also, which gave rise to a whole new poetry of existence.

This whole new poetry was very important in the midst of the Cold War and the threat of nuclear annihilation Judith felt hanging over them, and it was significant perhaps that their meeting with Kathleen followed not long after a holiday they had spent on Stradbroke Island to introduce Meredith to the sea, which she loved. Judith was also typing up a collection of her poems which were to be published in England, as well as Jack's latest article, but it was nevertheless an idyllic time.

> Point Lookout is so lovely [Judith wrote], and having no cars on the island makes it a sort of modern paradise. Meredith took to the sea and the rock pools and got very spoiled by everyone but is settling back to normal now.[106]

They later discovered that one of those who had spoiled her most, the yardsman at the guest-house at which they stayed, was a convicted murderer. But that does not seem to have lessened their enjoyment, and they loved the coast, exploring it sometimes with Kathleen and sometimes by themselves. On one of these expeditions they discovered the little town of Boreen Point, not far from Caloundra where Kathleen lived.

It was poor farming country – the few farmers "scratched for survival like starving fowls" – but beautiful, and Judith wrote about it several times, once in a short story and once in a memoir published many years later in *Overland*. Excerpts from that memoir give a vivid sense of the place:

> The Point was a small outcrop of pink-cream rock stretching into the various blues of the lake. Tides struggled upriver through the series of little lakes, to die out where the river entered the big lake at its upper end. A couple of fishermen made a living out of its shallow sandy reaches, but the mullet-run in spring was the only small surge of wealth the fishery offered. Maybe twenty holiday cottages, the post-office, the store that one-legged Martin kept (he was a sawmill casualty), and two small boarding-houses were dotted along the sand roads; for sale notices studded the trees on most of the other too-small allotments.

Here on their first visit they met

> Bert ... the local man of destiny, a developer with grandiose dreams, and almost nothing in the kitty. He had somehow got himself to the USA at the end of the war, seen the first rush of the motel business into avid little towns, come back with ideas beyond his capacity. He had crashed and bankrupted himself with a first attempt, a series of concrete cottages built out of unsecured bank loans, above a beach so dangerous that nobody, after the first few drownings, wanted to live there. Still unquenched, he moved up the river to the lovely but nearly roadless lake country, built another cottage with his own hands and no money, sold it and was now engaged in his second venture. Land there – because of the state of the only two access tracks – was astonishingly cheap; cottages, on Bert's method at least, were quick and easy to build; the sand of the Point was full of silica and needed little cement to build walls and floors. He now had visions – having sold two more cottages – of a chain of motels all up the coast to Cairns and a fortune ahead. He was employing one man to help him pour concrete and lug timber from the sawmill, and living on credit he didn't have.[107]

Bert's dreams did not appeal to them, but they loved the place. Jack hated the winter, and here they would be able to escape the cold and enjoy its warm and lazy climate. Meredith, too, was enchanted by the place, by "the little hut ... the creek and pink sands by the lake and their paperbarks and [the] tiny waves" which meant that although she had not yet learned to swim she would be quite safe. As Jack said, quoting the local barber, it was "the most peacefullest place".[108] They decided to be reckless and buy the house. The next task was to make it habitable:

> We mixed buckets of whitewash with a bit of red powder and slapped them on the thirsty concrete surfaces; the cottage looked like something made of coconut ice and had a holiday air. Warm winds came whiffing in with a sea-smell, we could buy fish cheap under the counter (not declared to the Fish Board and sent off south to go stale), and pineapples from the farms. It was a good place to write in, no telephones, no proper roads, no bus except the daily school bus and the weekend tourist bus that held maybe ten or twenty tourists.[109]

When they were not there they hoped to be able to let the house, though that proved difficult. The place was not only unfashionable but also difficult to get to since the road was very bad, especially in wet weather.

In one of her letters Judith described a "nightmare trip" back to Mount Tamborine. Alf Wesson, who worked with Frank Eyre at Oxford University Press, had been staying with them and followed them. Meredith who "went with him in case he got lonely" later implored Jack when they finally arrived safely at "Calanthe" having been "seriously bogged" on the way not to drive so fast because it made Alf nervous.[110] Nevertheless they loved the place and managed to hang on to it through thick and thin for many years.

They had not lost their taste for exploration, though Meredith's arrival meant that they could no longer travel as lightly as they used to. In 1952 Jack heard from one of his friends, the local garage mechanic, of a little panel van for sale second-hand. They bought it and, with a rubber mattress in the back, could now go off camping in it. For a time, too, they discussed painting J. & J. McKinney on the side – registration for commerical vehicles was cheaper than for private cars – but honesty prevailed over economy.[111] It was by no means the kind of grand car Judith's relations owned, but at least they could now drive themselves to the Christmas family gatherings in New England as well as go off exploring in it.

One of these trips took them through the coastal plains around Noosa which they were later to try and save from the developers. Kathleen was with them and recalled Judith's delight:

> At the time Noosa had an extended sandpit on the southern side of the bar where there were lots of sea shells left by the tide. Judith could be seen enjoying them singly as she placed each on the palm of her hand, felt them with her finger-tips and opened her hands on them, "the white empty shells come out of the scour of the sea," and only a bird-call from the precious Noosa Wood.[112]

Many poems, such as "Wild Flower Plain", "Phaius Orchid" and "Nameless Flower", were evidently inspired by this country. Behind the "marble-dazzling beaches" were the sandy swamps and

> *the bitter and thorny moor*
> *that sets its bar between*
> *hill's green and sea's glitter*[113]

and the "tame hills" leading up to the high country and its magnificent views:

> from the top of Mount Timberweel we could follow the distant coastline, up Laguna Bay, around Cook's Double Island Point into Wide Bay and Tin Can Bay, what appeared as unadulterated wilderness, the lower section of what is now termed the Great Sandy Region extending to Sandy Cape on Fraser Island, to be nominated for World Heritage.[114]

Even then, however, they sensed its fragility, and it was Kathleen who suggested that they should try and have the area declared a National Park. In Brisbane, on their way back to Mount Tamborine, Judith made some enquires about this while Kathleen investigated ways of getting in to explore the area more closely. As Judith was to point out later on, the environmental movement of the 1960s and 1970s grew out of this kind of feeling for the land:

> Few of the people who became involved in the 60s and early 70s in the struggle to set off a change of heart did so with any wild optimism that the direction of things could be radically changed. Rather their indignation ... [was inspired by] some particular piece of violence, cruelty, indifference or outright vandalism, [seeing] for example the clean and delicately moulded coastal dunes, with their banksias and casuarinas and trails of flowering plants, and the beaches they loved, being passed through the machines of sand miners ... They were simply too revolted to put up with any more of it. They took action as one might take action to rescue a child from wilful torture.[115]

On one of their trips Jack and Judith met David Fleay and his wife, who had run a celebrated wildlife sanctuary outside Healesville in the Dandenong Ranges near Melbourne, but had fled to Queensland to escape the "development" which was destroying the Victorian forest to set up another sanctuary, delighting in the richness and variety of the tropical coastlands. They became friends and the Fleays would visit "Calanthe" from time to time, supporting them in their environmental concerns – Jack shared Judith's passion, even if he was less involved at the public level. She recalled him, for instance, sometime in 1955 "leaning on the bulldozer in which the driver was lunching, while he used all his Irish inheritance of blarney to convince the unwilling driver of the importance of trees"[116] – successfully, too.

The McKinneys travelled inland, also, and it was on one of these trips that Jack decided it would be a good idea if Judith learned to drive. In those days in Queensland all that was necessary was to convince the local policeman that you were able to manage a car. So after a few lessons from Jack they fronted up at the local police station. Judith was asked to drive up the main street, where she made a few awkward turns, and was given her licence. But a licence is not everything. Not long afterwards, driving on a gravel road, she lost control and the car skidded and crashed into a tree. Fortunately the tree was riddled with white ants and collapsed under the impact so there was no great damage done either to themselves or to the car. But for some time Jack did most of the driving.[117]

One of the most memorable of their journeys was along the route taken by Judith's grandfather, driving north as far as Charters Towers and then back through Townsville along the coastal road. Early on they travelled through the brigalow country, generally regarded as worthless – the Queensland Premier, Bjelke-Petersen, was beginning to clear it with tractors and chainsaws – but which Judith loved, as her father had done:

> No tourist would look twice at it ... Yet the plain has its own beauty. The shimmering haze of light and glare reflects itself from the silvery blue and green of iron bark and poplarbox leaves in intricate patterns of light and shade. By night the stars are dazzling.[118]

Many of the survivors of the Aboriginal tribes driven off their lands elsewhere had taken refuge here before being herded into reservations or missions in the 1930s, and the poems she wrote witness to their lost and melancholy presence.

In the Carnarvon Ranges, where the Kairi Nuri, Karingbah, Longabilla, Jinan and Wadja peoples used to meet, there were still Aboriginal paintings in some of the more remote caves. But otherwise in the 1950s "the tribes were silent", their "complex musical languages", as she wrote later, "had vanished and would not be heard again", though later they were to revive. The land was changing, too, damaged by white occupation; the caves, the sacred places with their paintings and fertility symbols were desecrated by "the scrawls of the initials, dates, hearts and arrows of literate occupation". Bloody massacres had also happened here. The second poem of the sequence "Seven Songs from a Journey", "Brigalow Country", turns on an image of a ghostly figure of an Aboriginal girl

> *Haunted and alone*
> *with the tribe of the brigalows ...*
> *dances*
> *to the singing of the dingoes.*

> *Living lost and lonely*
> *with the tribe of the brigalows,*
> *don't want to stay*
> *but never can go*[119]

"Canefields" presents an image from the present:

> *The coloured girl leans on the bridge,*
> *folding her sorrow into her breast.*
> *Her face is a dark and downward mirror*
> *where her eyes look, and are lost*

since around her

> *The old land is marshalled under*
> *the heavy regiment of green cane;*
> *but by the lagoon the paperbarks*
> *unroll their blank and tattered parchment,*
> *waiting for some unknown inscription*
> *which love might make in ink-dark water.*

This image was so truthful, that when they became friends the Aboriginal writer Kath Walker (later Oodgeroo Noonuccal) told Judith that when she first read the poem she thought it was about herself as a young woman, expressing a sense of the girl's longing and of her sense of what is sacred, hidden still in the land profaned by alien occupation as

> *...in that water the great lily*
> *sets her perfect dusk-blue petals*
> *in their inherited order of prayer*
> *around that blazing throne, her centre.*
> *There time shall meet eternity*
> *and her worship find its answer.*[120]

Implicit here, too, is the sense that it is the Aboriginal girl who holds the key to this "order of prayer".

Other poems express a feeling of being on the edge of an abyss of space and time. Camping out gave an almost mystical sense of the dark as a source of light and intensity, a "personal experience, almost unbearable, of being part of the galaxy"[121], similar to the one she and Jack experienced on occasion in the garden at "Calanthe":

> *Night is what remains*
> *when the equation is finished.*
> *Night is the earth's dream*
> *that the sun is dead . . .*
>
> *Night blocks our way, saying,*
> *I at least am real.*[122]

Against the destructiveness and vulgarity of the consumer society growing up around them it seemed like a rock, absolute, like the land itself. So, too, was the sea

> *Mountain, wall and tree*
> *bear witness against our lives . . .*
> *. . . No one has marked the sea.*[123]

This intuition that, despite everything, there is an abiding power in the natural world was at the centre of Judith's life. So, too, was the belief that, as another poem in the "Seven Songs from a Journey" sequence, "The Prospector", puts it, this is a "land to be won by love only". Our occupation, however, has been loveless:

> *. . . here there's none*
> *but the fire's black kiss, and the lonely*
> *print of skull and bone.*[124]

This is echoed in one of her stories published in the *Bulletin* in 1953, but here it also links the feeling of desolation to the fate of the land's Aboriginal inhabitants.

The story concerns a man trying to find out more about settlement (as she was at the time in her researches for *The Generations of Men*), who arrives at a remote station somewhere in Queensland. He is met by the housekeeper, an Aboriginal woman, "bare footed and hideously dressed . . . half-limp[ing], half-hop[ping] on a withered leg". The image of the original station buildings, a hut near a big old tree made of split slab, echoes the feeling that settlement has meant destruction rather than creation, and the housekeeper's comments reinforce this: "Roof used to be bark, now tin ... Nearly fallen down, you see."[125]

"At Cooloolah", another poem which dates from this time, connects Judith's uneasiness with the history of her own family. Seeing a piece of driftwood, like a "spear/thrust from the water" of one of the lakes on the sand plain, the poem recalls a passage in her grandfather's diary, in which, riding in broad daylight he had suddenly seen ahead of him

> *a black accoutred warrior armed for fighting.*

Just as suddenly, however, he had disappeared, "sank into bare plain" as if he were a ghost. The image returns here, reminding her that she is "a stranger, come of a conquering people", aware as she watches a blue crane fishing in the pool,

> *... the certain heir of lake and evening*
> *... [who] will wear their colour till he dies,*

that she is "unloved by all my eyes delight in" and must feel "uneasy, for an old murder's sake" – her grandfather had been relatively sympathetic to the Aboriginal people whose land he had occupied, but he, too, had found himself on the fringes of a massacre. Increasingly convinced that there was "not only ... some deep incompatibility between us and the country but in our relations to the Aborigines whom ... we had dispossessed",[126] the poem realises how little, despite everything, she belongs here:

> *Those dark-skinned people who once named Cooloolah*
> *knew that no land is lost or won by wars,*
> *for earth is spirit: the invader's feet will tangle*
> *in nets there and his blood be thinned by fears.*[127]

These journeys through the outback were important therefore. They also pointed to the alternatives in the conclusion of the last of the "Seven Songs from a Journey" in the image of two trees beside a pool on the flanks of Mount Mary, "the solitary mountain ... as tall as grief":

One wept long branches full of withering stars,
and one, naked of leaves, held up a crown;
a great fierce blossom yellow as the sun
taken out of the sky at his heat's thirsty noon.[128]

The fires of creation were burning still, and Judith would continue to serve them. But to do that she needed also to come to terms with her inheritance, and in her thinking she was beginning to rewrite it to include also the story of the Aboriginal people they had displaced. *The Cry for the Dead*, not published until 1981, was to be her attempt to rework *The Generations of Men* from this point of view.

As she wrote in *Preoccupations in Australian Poetry*, "The true function of an art and culture is to interpret us to ourselves, and to relate us to the country and society in which we live."[129] But this involved healing "the scar left by the struggle to conquer [the land] and waken a landscape that had survived on its own terms until the world's last days".[130] That meant looking again at the history of the Aboriginal peoples who had lived in such close relationships with the land, reworking the "Australian legend", moving away from its "over sentimentalized emphasis on 'mateship'" to get to "the truth last lies behind it".[131] Like Patrick White, she thought that that involved making it "a country of the mind" or, as Jack would have put it, bringing together the subjective and objective worlds, matching the outer reality of the land, its austere power, with some inner equivalent. In the struggles to survive and settle "something had left us, something had died".[132] Now we needed to go back to recover it.

This was something to do with the land itself. Her poetry had long been concerned with this search, but she was realising more and more that it also demanded a new understanding of our dealings with Aboriginal people and a new appreciation of their culture. If we managed to do that Australia might "become something new in the world ... [as we fashioned] a new kind of consciousness out of our new conditions".[133] Her travels through Queensland, and her readings in pioneering history, had made her aware of this need as she reflected on the dispossession of its Aboriginal inhabitants, bound to the land "by the indissoluble link of religion and totemic kinship, so that our intrusion on the land itself became a kind of bloodless murder, even where no actual murder took place".[134]

Judith was also learning more about Aboriginal people themselves. In the 1950s, for instance, at Kathleen's suggestion she and Jack had gone to see the film *Jedda*, one of the first to deal with Aboriginal people and to feature Aboriginal actors. Then in Brisbane in 1951 she had attended a lecture by a German priest and anthropologist, Father Wurms, who was then working in the north-west, and been very impressed by it. "A rare and intelligent priest indeed", he believed that the first task of any missionary or anthropologist was to live among the people for four or five years being ministered to or studied and absorb their culture thoroughly. Only then was it possible to begin to understand. This was a different approach from any Judith had come across at university — "anthropologists don't usually go native",[135] as she said — but it struck her as "the way to go". She also read Alan Marshall's and Roland Robinson's collections of Aboriginal stories at this time.

But Judith was beginning to realise the difficulties involved in this work and how easy it was for non-Aboriginal people to use Aborigines for their own ends. When Oxford University Press asked her to edit a book of Aboriginal legends for a series they were producing, she decided after reflection that she must refuse. In a letter to Kathleen, she said:

> The more I read the more I realise what a strenuous task it is to try to change them into European yarns to amuse the kids. So many of them are tied indissolubly to one piece of ground and one tribe and even a few special persons in that tribe; so many more though they can be made to sound like stories are really not stories at all but religious dramas, and so many are from a point of view that Europeans could never come near understanding.[136]

She and Jack needed the money the anthology would bring, but she needed her integrity more.

Something which happened at Boreen Point, and which Judith wrote about in a short story and later included in her memoir of the place, also made her aware as never before of the plight of contemporary Aboriginal people. It happened to an Aboriginal family they had got to know, but for obvious reasons all the names were changed. When they were at the Point during school time, Meredith went to the school there, catching the school bus outside the sawmill about eight hundred metres from their house. Judith walked with her and, waiting for the bus to arrive, they got to know an Aboriginal woman, Lola, who lived nearby and whose children also caught the school bus. One of these children, Rosie, became a firm friend of Meredith's, while the other two, Donnie and Alan, who were older, protected her from the other boys on the bus.

Lola and her husband, Joe, lived with their children in the smallest of the cottages, "a fibro three-roomed affair up on high stumps with an array of broken bottles and tin cans under it, which Joe intended to take to town and sell for scrap one day". Joe was very black, though Lola was "a pale glowing brown, velvety-eyed, with a mop-shaped head of Kanaky hair and a smile like sunlight on a white beach". Somehow they had managed to get away from life on the reservation – possibly "for good behaviour and earning power ... If he hadn't somehow got permission to stay where he was ... for the resentment of their presence ... was more than enough for him to have been reported to the police station and ordered back to the reservation they had come from."[137] Lola made baskets which were sold – at a huge mark-up – at the local store, and Joe worked at any job he could find, supplementing their income by fishing.

They were determined, as far as they could, to give their children a better chance in life than they themselves had had. But the locals were not sympathetic, regarding them as "no-hopers" because they were Aborigines. Meredith had a hard time of it at school, especially in the playground where the other children jeered at her for mixing with "dirty Abos", at one stage threatening to boycott her altogether unless she gave them up. To Judith's relief, however, she refused to do so.

One holiday weekend Judith took them all to the local show.

> The wonders of the Show kept us spellbound for awhile, wandering from sideshows to swings and merry-go-round and horses and goats and cattle. Then we climbed the steps of the so-called pavilion – an unpainted timber structure with a series of display tables for crafts, cookery and flowers and a groundfloor (literally) for vegetables and the Pet Show. Upstairs, Donnie and Rosie dragged me to inspect the rows of school plasticine sculptures and the Art display. 'Look, look Donnie,' cried Rosie, 'I've won the Art prize!'

> Sure enough, it appeared, she had; though the pictures were unsigned and the teachers, perhaps with such questions of discrimination in view, discreetly didn't name the winners on the cards. When Rosie pointed out her own, with its blue card attached, it was certainly much better than the rest. But Donnie grabbed her hand and shushed her fiercely. "If they know it's yours they'll take the prize away."
>
> We dared not stand long to admire it, for Donnie moved on and dragged us with him. No doubt he was right.[138]

It was not long after this, however, that Joe had an accident with an axe which left him lame and thus made it more difficult to find work. The McKinneys went back to "Calanthe" and it was only when they came back for the summer that they heard what had happened. Less and less able to get work, Joe had started drinking and spent more and more time away from home. Desperate to provide for the children, Lola began living with a white man, a timber worker who lived nearby. Joe came home one day and, finding them together, in his rage took the axe to Lola and killed her – "a wonder he didn't murder the lot of them and you too", the locals told the McKinneys, warning them against "lett[ing] niggers into [their] house again". Joe went to jail for life and the children were sent to Palm Island to "learn their place".

It was a grim story and made a deep impression on the McKinneys.

> Long ago, Joe had confided in Jack, when asked why he was living at the Point where he had no kin or friends and the family was isolated from any kind of support beyond seasonal jobs. "They tell us on the Reserve that we got to go out there and get simulated," said Joe; "we got no right to get supported by other people with taxes and that, we got to prove that we can live like everyone else. We thought we'd try, that's all."[139]

They had tried and they had failed.

"The two threads of [her] life, the love of the land itself and the deep unease over the fate of its original people were beginning to twine together and the rest of [her] life would be influenced by that connection."[140] Something new was beginning, but a phase of her life was ending also.

In the early months of 1956, Judith realised that she was pregnant again with "Meredith's much meditated brother or sister". Meredith was enchanted, though we do not know what Jack thought. Judith herself was happy, even though she worried about Jack since, as the pregnancy went on, "much would fall on his shoulders".[141] He had been over-working and his old headaches and gastric troubles had returned, so she persuaded him to accept an invitation from his daughter Lucy to stay with her on Palm Island. He left in early July but was back within a few weeks.

The pregnancy was not proving as easy as Judith had hoped and the fact that she, too, was exhausted from all she had been doing did not help. Early in August the doctor told her that she would lose the baby if she did not have complete rest. The McKinneys decided to go to Boreen Point, asking the Blackmans to come and stay at "Calanthe" to look after the house and garden and – not least of their chores – the hens.

On their way to the Point they stayed with Kathleen. By this time Judith was "feeling decidedly off-colour in some unidentifiable way". Kathleen realised that something was seriously wrong, but Judith insisted on going to Boreen. There, however, "after a few increasingly miserable days", she finally went to the little country hospital at Cooroy, where at last, on the doctor's urging, she gave in and accepted a curette. But even after this she was no better, and a few more days at Boreen convinced them that she would have to go back to Brisbane to her doctor there. They asked Kathleen to look after Meredith for the time being and headed south.

The doctor was not communicative, only telling Judith that he would book her into hospital for "further treatment" in a fortnight. In the meantime they went back to Mount Tamborine where the Blackmans, obliging as ever, made way for them until Judith returned to Brisbane to be operated on. By then she was desperately ill, and it may be that the poem "Double Image" owes something to that time:

> *The long-dead living forest rose*
> *as white as bone, as dark as hair.*
> *In rage the old protagonists*
> *fought for my life; and I was there.*[142]

In any case, she remembers very little of that time in hospital. She badly wanted to have the baby and "the little beggar put up a determined struggle". But when she was out of danger she was told it had been an ectopic pregnancy that had been terminated, only just in time to save her life.[143]

Back at "Calanthe", after several weeks in hospital, the Blackmans looked after the cooking until they had to go back to Melbourne where they were now living. But it was months before Judith was free of pain and able to work again – she had been driving herself hard for years and the convalescence was a long one. They went back to Boreen for warmth and quiet, where she spent most of her time lying on the couch, trying to write a series of public lectures she had agreed to do. Writing to Kathleen to thank her for looking after Meredith she told how much she "loath[ed] being a semi-invalid still. However, I'm all right in the mornings." She worried about Meredith, knowing what it had meant to her as a child to have a sick mother. And she worried also about "poor Jack [who] seems to spend his time fixing up the light-engine and looking after useless women", though she took some comfort from the fact that the proofs had just arrived from *The New York Journal of Philosophy* for an article of his which they were about to publish, and from the fact that she was to go to Armidale soon, taking Meredith with her – "he can be a bachelor for a while".[144]

This expedition, however, was not for pleasure but for the purpose of receiving an honorary doctorate of literature from the University of New England at the end of October (earlier that year she had been given a doctorate from the University of Queensland), and the public lectures were to be given at the university after the award of the doctorate. Judith had to drive herself hard to get them done. But after a trip to the Border Ranges to see the wildflowers she finally managed to finish them, writing to Kathleen to tell her so and to share her plans and anxieties:

> Meredith and I leave by plane; Jack will drive down for us in a fortnight. Just as long as I don't get a major pain in the middle of them ... but I find that if one lives on painkilling tablets all is well; hope and pray that in six months or so I'll be past that nasty necessity.

In the event, the lectures went off, she thought, quite well, "though everyone sat at the very back of an enormous room and I had a cough and a sore throat on account of going to 10,000 feet and not being pressurised". It was also "a confusing audience" to whom she spoke,

> composed of schoolgirls, third-year English students, my old school mistresses taking notes, and quantities of my aunts, uncles, cousins, brothers and parents. I can't think of anything that would have pleased them unless I had been Ruth Draper or a strip-tease artist.[145]

These lectures were to become *Preoccupations in Australian Poetry*, published ten years later by Oxford University Press, and in this sense new possibilities were opening out for her as a critic as well as a poet. But other possibilities were closing: 1956 ended with the knowledge that she must not become pregnant again and that Meredith must remain an only child. "Old Woman's Song", not published, significantly, until it appeared in the *Collected Poems*, gives some sense of what this meant. Its opening line, "The moon drained white by day" is also the title she gives to this section of her autobiography.

The poem turns on two images, the moon and an old pear-tree, fallen in a storm. Both are white and still and both seem barren, and she identifies with them:

> *Women believe in the moon.*
> *This branch I hold*
> *is not more white and still than she*
> *whose flower is ages old.*[146]

Yet both still live: the old pear-tree still puts out blossom, still puts out "obstinate tokens still/of fruit [they] cannot bear" and she will go on with her life. As the poem which follows in the *Collected Poems*, "Age to Youth" makes clear, love remained the centre of her existence:

> *...whatever we repent*
> *of the time that we live,*
> *it is never what we give –*
> *it is never that we love.*[147]

Nevertheless the way ahead would be somehow colder. Jack was growing old and the world about them was as troubled as ever – 1957 saw the Russian invasion of Hungary, trouble was brewing in Vietnam and the split in the Labor Party assured the continuance of the "suave and conservative rule of Menzies".[148] Most of the McKinneys' friends had moved away, some of them to become rich and famous like Sidney Nolan and Charles Blackman, who was now "painting portraits for the *Australian Women's Weekly* at fifteen hundred pounds"[149] and was soon to have an exhibition in London. On the mountain the McKinneys were feeling more isolated. But they kept on working

> with just enough success for both of us to feel that a breakthrough might be around the corner. But always, when we turned to each other for talk and comfort, our real coincidences of thought and feeling brought us together even more closely. I was troubled over his health, he over my pressure of work, but we were each other's complements in many ways.[150]

Nevertheless, what was between them was enough:

> *…perilously joined,*
> *lighted in one small room,*
> *we have made all things true.*
> *Out of the I and the you*
> *spreads this field of power,*
> *that all that waits may come,*
> *all possibles be known –*
> *all futures step from their stone*
> *and pasts come into flower.*[151]

CHAPTER IX

SHADOW

> Come now; the angel leads.
> All human lives betray,
> all human love erodes
> under time's laser ray;
>
> from "For One Dying",
Collected Poems, p. 259

Patrick White did not like the poem Judith Wright wrote on turning fifty in 1965. He found it depressing, too domestic, and would have preferred something more stylish than the cup of coffee which features in the opening lines:

> *Having known war and peace*
> *and loss and finding,*
> *I drink my coffee and wait*
> *for the sun to rise.*
>
> *With kitchen swept, cat fed,*
> *the day still quiet,*
> *I taste my fifty years*
> *here in the cup.*

He did not sense or respond to the weight of experience which makes the poem move so gravely. But he also missed the passion which was soon to flare out in the public life she was to live, the battles for the environment and all that they would lead to. In a sense, she was like the "green birds" outside;

> *Their wings wait for the sun*
> *to show their colours*

as, perhaps unconsciously, she was waiting to "show [her] colours too."[1]

Over the last few years this weight had been increasing. Her own deafness was a growing handicap, though she handled it with a mixture of humour and irony, writing to Kathleen, for example, about a reception at the University of New England (where her father was now chancellor) after the honorary Doctorate of Letters which the university had awarded her. In a room "full of screaming relations" she could not understand what anyone was saying, least of all the waiter, who brought her three gins in swift succession, though happily, she said, she stayed upright and coherent.[2]

But in other ways being deaf was not funny. It was difficult looking after a child and being deaf. On one occasion, Barbara Blackman remembers when Meredith, still a baby, fell out of her cot on to the floor without Judith noticing, and it was only by accident that she found her, already blue in the face from screaming.[3] Deafness also cut her off from people, even from Jack, because she could only hear when facing the person she was talking to. To cope with this when she and Jack were out walking, he would often run ahead and talk to her walking backwards.

Far more serious, however, was Jack's declining health though he kept on writing and reading and refused to become an invalid. But in mid-1966, Meredith had an attack of bronchitis which she passed on to him. Judith describes what happened in a letter to Barbara Blackman:

> It knocked him flat for weeks, and just when he was beginning to look alive again we had a night of terror with Jack having an Awful Pain in the tummy, and of course I thought it was a perforation, which always haunts me. He chose just the most difficult moment at the end of a long-weekend, when all the doctors who come up for week-ends had moved off to Brisbane again and when all the doctors in Beaudesert were out at a big holiday motor-accident there. I spent a frantic half-hour dialling doctors and at last ordered the ambulance up from Beaudesert. Then a friend of ours went scouring the mountain in her car and

collected the last doctor left, who hadn't a telephone and was only an anaesthetist anyway, but came and said he thought it wasn't a perforation but a gall-bladder, which was thankful to hear. Anyway Jack went off in ambulance and spent a couple of days in hospital, but revived fairly well by then (after bewildering the men's ward by writing madly all the time he was in there).[4]

Not long after he was discharged Judith had to go to Warwick to give a lecture for Adult Education – "ten pounds in it", she told Barbara[5] – and Jack insisted on coming with her. That revived the bronchitis, and he was ill again for some time afterwards. He continued to crack hardy but Judith knew that he was seriously ill. "I feel my heart is gradually bleeding to death. But cannot write about that," she told Kathleen McArthur. She also dared not leave him for more than a few minutes and worried that Meredith might have to give up her ballet lessons because she could not leave him to take her there.[6]

This time, however, Jack made a good recovery, helped by the appearance of one of his articles in *Mind,* next to one by Bertrand Russell. But in September the pain returned and he had to spend several weeks in bed. "I don't get used to it," Judith wrote. Even though after a few weeks he was able to walk a little, she knew how precarious his health really was. "It is almost incredible to have him more or less safe and sound and looking and talking like himself ... I keep going and looking at him to make sure even now."[7] Another "very deadly attack" followed, however. Again he recovered. But she was increasingly afraid and could hardly "believe that he came back to us".[8] For a while, however, things seemed to be improving and she was able to write to Barbara Blackman quite cheerfully about "a crazy pet Currawong, found as baby by Meredith on the road, which flies suddenly out of the blue and lands on my shoulder with a scream and pulls my hair".[9] But the fear remained, as poems like "The Histeridae" make clear, beginning with the smell of a decaying carcass in the backyard and concluding with an appalled vision of the carrion which swarm from it when it is burnt. "For One Dying" puts it more coolly, but gives us perhaps a deeper sense of Judith's pain as she watched Jack's health decline:

*Green places and pure springs
are poisoned and laid bare –
even the hawk's high wings
ride on a fatal air.*

*But come; the angel calls.
Deep in the dreamer's cave
the one pure source upwells
its single luminous wave.*[10]

Ill as he was, Jack went on working. Another poem tells about watching him

*...with a kind of fear,
moving untaught and yet with such precision,
as though on bridgeways tested long before.*

*There was a sureness in your contemplation,
a purity in that closed look you wore,
as though a godwit, rising from its shore,
followed alone and on its first migration
its road of air across the tumbled sea.*[11]

But Jack was not only interested in philosophy. At Boreen Point one wet weekend in 1958, fascinated by the lives and conversations of the local people, he sat down and wrote a play, produced by the Twelfth Night Theatre in Brisbane the next year. About a group of ordinary, inarticulate Australians, it reflects the conviction that made him interested in everyone, from professors to barbers, that

> they're human beings, whether they can express their thoughts or not – whether they have any thoughts to express or not ... Because of their very spiritual nakedness, they might have something to tell us about ourselves, about our own inner workings, of which we are usually quite unconscious.[12]

As Eunice Hanger said in her introduction to the play, it was the work of a man who had "a serene respect for individuals as individuals", but who also had a "creative gift ... the capacity to realize ... individuals, doing and saying what they must because they were that kind of person in that kind of situation".[13] The play was a success at the box office, and there was talk of putting it on at the Adelaide Festival in 1962. This fell through, however, on account of problems in casting and perhaps for other reasons.

Jack's heart was playing up seriously and his gastric problems were growing worse and Judith lived with constant anxiety. When she had to go away, she always left someone to watch him in case he had another attack. Their friends were worried for him, also. Vance Palmer, himself to die of a heart attack the following year, wrote saying how sorry he was to hear that Jack's heart had been "playing tricks". For his part Jack insisted on making light of these problems, declaring, as Judith reported, that he was "very well and plunging about",[14] but then another gastric or heart attack would send him back to the edge between life and death.

Shortly after Jack's first big attack in 1956, the McKinneys were obliged to go to Boreen Point to get the cottage ready for a "steady young Christian couple" who wanted to rent the place at three guineas a week for a year – an opportunity they could not afford to miss. Alf Wesson from Oxford University Press, who had become a friend,

> wanted to come for that week-end so we took him in tow, and as soon as we got there for the week-end and settled in down came the rain in floods and torrents and waterfalls. We waited one day and saw the Christian Couple and signed an agreement with them and then fled for Tamborine before the rain cut us off. Drove all afternoon and far into the evening with poor Alf and Meredith behind in Alf's car in a high state of nervous tension because of the rain cutting them off from us every now and then and their not knowing which was the road home. Then we all got bogged together on Long Road because as usual the grader had just paid us its annual visit just before the rain, and George the milkman pulled us out. Anyway having reached "Calanthe" poor Alf was too done in to think of going for another day or two, and then I had to set to and write a public lecture to give in Brisbane.[15]

She "got it finished on Monday, [however,] with a great burst and darned a hole in my grey dress and shot down and gave it with great éclat, no less than five hundred people ... came and sat on the lecture-hall steps and stood at the back, though it was a freezing night." The lecture was on Harpur, Kendall and Brennan, and she herself found it "so boring I nearly threw the whole thing in halfway through" – understandable enough in the circumstances. But the audience was appreciative and "it earned us twenty quid".[16]

Travelling was not always easy. On one occasion, camping in the Warrumbungle Mountains, as they often did, a sudden rainstorm soaked them through. Insisting that Jack and Meredith get into the car and keep dry, Judith put on her swimsuit and struck camp. As they "wriggled out on to the road in streaming tempests", however, she realised that somehow she would have to change back into her clothes before they went much further. But the road was too muddy to risk stopping until they got out of the mountains. When they did, the only thing for it was to stand beside the car in the middle of the road and change – "mercifully no one came along".[17]

Despite all their precautions, by the time they reached Inverell Jack had developed flu and was put into hospital for several days. Judith made light of the adventure, writing that she and Meredith had lived "happily and pleasantly in a scruffy hotel with a charming landlady, visiting relations who lived nearby and swimming in the 'river-like' local swimming pool".[18] But the anxiety about Jack's health was constant.

Her father, too, was in failing health and was taken to hospital at this time with heart problems. As she remarked to Kathleen McArthur, "Men seem terribly vulnerable these days". With all this, the demands on her time did not lessen; writing and giving lectures, finalising the manuscript for *The Generations of Men* and *Preoccupations in Australian Poetry*, working on the children's books *King of the Dingoes*, *The Day the Mountains Played*, *Range the Mountains High*, *Country Towns* and *The River and the Road*, seeing her volume of short stories, *The Nature of Love*, through the press, and doing the research for her book on Charles Harpur in the Mitchell Library. Reading "those pathetic notes in old shaky hand", was rather like finding love letters, she thought, "from someone you used to know with a suicide note attached",[19] so this became a labour of love.

Harpur's vision of Australia as a place where a more decent and humane society might be possible and in which people would gradually learn to live with the strange new land seemed increasingly important in a time in which, it seemed, "progress was the only thing ... If you could knock something down or something like that it was regarded as a tremendous contribution", and history seemed more and more like a nightmare from which, however hard they tried, they could not awake. "It struck me that we must have started off in Harpur's time with very much the same kind of hang-ups as we've got now."[20]

In the meantime she kept house, looked after the poultry farm, paid the bills and did their income tax, looked after Jack and typed his work, drove Meredith to ballet lessons, took care of her pony, ran her birthday parties and attended to school sports and parents' functions. But she was increasingly troubled by what was happening to the rainforest as bulldozers and tractors with chains cleared yet more of the original trees and plants for "development". Elsewhere, too, rumours began to circulate about plans to exploit Fraser Island and the sandy coastal plain around Cooloola. All this obliged her to attend an increasing number of meetings to oppose these developments.

Some years earlier she and Kathleen McArthur had founded the Wildlife Preservation Society of Queensland (WPSQ), a more or less amateur organisation. But now it looked as if they had serious professional work to do, not just organising protests but thinking the issues through.

> The very words "conservation", "ecology" and "pollution" were unfamiliar. The problem of soil erosion – largely because of the publicity given to it through the dust-bowl disasters of the United States – was known and discussed. But few people had read or heard of famous conservationists like Aldo Leopold, who in 1933 wrote: "Civilisation is not ... the enslavement of a stable and constant earth. It is a state of mutual and interdependent cooperation between human animals, other animals, plants and soils, which may be destroyed at any moment by the failure of any of them."[21]

Judith was president of the WPSQ and several times a month had therefore to drive down to and back from Brisbane for meetings – since

Jack was not well she came back the same night. She also kept up a growing correspondence with environmentalists in Australia and overseas as well as writing to the newspapers to alert public opinion to the growing threat to the environment. She was aware that she was challenging powerful interests and this often made her uneasy, though she had no intention of giving up.

She did not like the direction in which things seemed to be moving intellectually either. The *Nation*, one of the few journals of intelligent comment, had closed, and the *Bulletin*, whose Red Page had been so important to her and Australian writing in general, had been taken over by Kerry Packer, to be turned into Australia's version of *Time*. Douglas Stewart, the *Bulletin's* long-term literary editor, she predicted, would "soon be out on his ear". Far from being a solution to society's problems, material and technological progress seemed to her to be intensifying them. As she wrote in a poem published in the *Sydney Morning Herald* in June 1966, computers

> ... *make me nervous*
> *because they're eating us;*
> *here a muscle, there a mind,*
> *an action or a vision.*

She was not a Luddite, however. In her view the fault was not in the machines but in the human beings, in our inability to find values or solutions other than merely material ones:

> ... *Perhaps we make [computers]*
> *because we're sick of humans.*[22]

Although Jack was never one to attend meetings and in any case was unable to do so on account of his health, he was as concerned as she was about these issues, seeing the attack on the environment and the growing preoccupation with money as yet another sign of the crisis. He was supportive, insisting that he was quite able to look after himself and Meredith when Judith had to go away – though, in 1962 when she began secondary school, Meredith became a boarder.

But Judith's worries about Jack did not diminish. As she wrote to Barbara Blackman:

> Jack is not as well as I'd like, though really he's very lucky. He is sensible and doesn't do too much, and he doesn't now get any pain to speak of and can work for hours at a time at his writing, but he tires very easily and has rather lost confidence. After all, it was a very bad illness, and he is sixty-seven now. I wish for his sake especially that he could get a really good break-through with his job; it would hearten him no end.[23]

In everything Judith did she counted on his support. Neither of them could accept the complacency which allowed most people to float contentedly on the tide of "progress". Security was something by which they had always set little store and she was always ready to commit herself. Those who refused to ask questions disgusted her:

> Do you notice how everything is hardening up? – how much of a grip the hypocrites and the grabbers have now? Is it hire purchase, is it Billy Graham, is it TV or is it destiny? But to be liberal or to be different or to be creative is getting more and more precarious. Safety, safety, that's the cry. When I look back on my undergraduate days in 1934 and on, and look at today's undergraduates and teenagers, I think both how innocent we were and how full of belief in the soul and disbelief in the Church; and these believe in what? That the soul doesn't exist and the Church is safety, or that nothing exists? I like the violent ones best, but then it's such an empty violence, not for anything and not really against anything either, just violence. Am I looking at them wrong? But I haven't heard or seen a word spoken by the young (I don't count those over forty) that implies a hope of anything at all. That's what is against us, in the end; the lack of hope for anything different; it means that the stranglehold of the official views on everything is never to be broken. Nobody believes them ... but nobody believes anything else either or that there is anything to believe.[24]

Judith was interested in and sympathetic to the protest movements in the United States and elsewhere at the end of the 1950s and early 1960s, as most of her contemporaries were not. In the 1950s she had come across Henry Miller's *The Air-Conditioned Nightmare* and passed it on to Kathleen McArthur, enthusiastically telling her that she had "read the book straight off, and my goodness, what a man! He comes through like a thunder-bolt. [It's] a most profound experience reading it."[25] In comparison Katherine Mansfield, whose letters she had also read recently, seemed tame and limited;

> [She] writes such huge self-analytic letters, finds out just what is wrong, goes through enormous chastenings and radical changes, ceases to be an intellectual and learns to live, and the next letter is as bad as ever... She is like a snake half-way out of its skin and stuck there, and probably always will stick.[26]

The sense of disaster implicit in these responses set Judith at odds with the academic establishment whose detachment from the actual world (as she saw it) troubled her. That kind of security was not for her; the world she lived in and the way she saw it, she knew, was very different, much more urgent, more disillusioned perhaps. Looking at the moon one night, she wrote to Barbara Blackman that it seemed as if she had "pulled a tattered yashmak over her face and [had] a very weak and dirty rainbow in it. She reminds me of Margot Fonteyn."[27]

But it was not all gloom. The natural world could still give her life purpose and meaning:

> ... *in the rockpools of the shore*
> *creatures like flowers and jewels*
> *wait dumbly for my eyes' translation,*
> *decked for our moment's meeting and no more.*
>
> *I cannot know my beauty*
> *– say all the creatures –*
> *till you interpret me in god-made words.*[28]

Watching Meredith grow up meant a great deal also. Like most of her friends she succumbed to the Beatles craze. But she was at school in Brisbane when two of them, Paul and George, paid a visit to Tamborine to see the rainforest, coming incognito and then dropping in to the Eagle Heights hotel for a late lunch. Judith's account of the occasion, to Barbara Blackman, then living in London, is entertaining:

It so happened that that was our beer-picking up day, but when I arrived at the hotel in all innocence, there were four ecstatic girls and one brother from the Marist school with a camera waiting outside, the bar was full of obvious Security Men drinking deep, and the front door was shut. I had to browbeat Bernie Muller into giving me my liquor order and he forgot the price of rum. I didn't wait, feeling that it would hardly be fair to do so on their day off, and anyway if I had waited I would have had to ask for an autograph for Meredith and my hair is now too silver for me to contemplate asking young men for their autograph, with any decent dignity. But I haven't dared tell Meredith how near [them] I actually was![29]

As this suggests, she was a tolerant parent, confident of the bond between them, believing, as she wrote in a poem about Meredith, home for holidays, that "you will come here all your life for renewal and meeting".[30]

Then, quite suddenly, in 1962, Judith and Jack got married. One day Mrs Patterson, Barbara Blackman's mother, who was very fond of Judith and Jack, met them both in Brisbane, looking very spruced-up in a countrified way, awkward in their best clothes. When asked what they were doing in town, they shyly confessed that they were going to be married. New Federal legislation had made divorce possible without fault.[31] So Meredith being at school and Jack "splendidly well", they had decided to regularise their relationship. A financial windfall helped them celebrate. Judith's father had been reorganising his affairs and had given her a parcel of shares in the family company at the same time as some money had come from her mother's side of the family. So they went "gallivanting to Brisbane, to plays and lectures, staying at expensive motels in a way we could not before Meredith went to school. The money won't last for much more of this but it's been fun" she told a friend.[32]

Most of the time, however, Judith was living in two worlds, working still but aware of Jack's growing frailty:

> *The self that night undrowns when I'm asleep*
> *travels beneath the dumb days that I give,*
> *within the limits set that I may live,*
> *and beats in anger on the things I love.*
> *I am the cross it bears, and it the tears I weep.*[33]

She had to keep on with her daily chores, her critical writing and editing, answering an endless stream of letters and managing to write some poetry of her own in the time left over. "If I had the initiative," she told Barbara, "I'd go out and find some unemployed junior to come in once a week and type the lot for me, all the permission to print under the following conditions ones, all the no I haven't a photograph ones, all the no I'm so sorry I can't ones, all the business about this wild life thing I'm involved in . . . all the boring ones in fact."[34]

But she could never forget Jack, writing, for instance, about watching him walk up the road in spring.

> *[The] elm puts on a glory, lit yet dim*
> *with mingled light and leaf; there is a thrust*
> *of irresistible budding. On the road*
> *he walks, head up, just balancing its load.*[35]

Death seemed everywhere, as she watched a kestrel, for instance, dive on a lizard which swerved aside, miss and fly into the power lines, becoming

> *a channel for the spark*
> *that in an instant made*
> *life into death, his wreck*
> *too violent for a bird*[36]

– a glimpse of "death's excess,/life's helplessness". Even burning the leaves in autumn became a portent and a ritual:

> *When twigs are built and match is set,*
> *your death springs up like life; its flare*
> *crowns and consumes the ended year.*
> *Corruption changes to desire*
> *that sears the pure and wavering air,*
> *and death goes upward like a prayer.*[37]

What she had been expecting and dreading finally happened on 6th December 1966, though when it came, it came unexpectedly, Jack's death. Earlier in the year he had been in misery with rheumatism and later developed bad stomach pains; Judith had suspected cancer. Nevertheless he kept on working on his book. She was very busy with her own work – the environmental battle was hotting up, *Wildlife*, the journal the WSPQ had founded, was in financial straits and she was involved in discussions which preceded the foundation of the Australian Conservation Foundation (ACF). She was also threatened with a "dirty big op", possibly the mastectomy she was to have some years later and so paid less attention to this illness than she might have done; something she regretted later. Eventually, however, Jack was ordered to the Greenslopes Repatriation Hospital in Brisbane for x-rays.

> [It was] a terribly hot December [as she recalled it] and the Repatriation Hospital was truly dreadful at that time, a lot of old soldiers cramming themselves into hospital for their last years. There were something like 24 men in his ward – you could hardly make your way through the beds. There was no air conditioning, not even a fan ... The free hospital system did not allow any luxuries.[38]

Meredith was also ill at the time with glandular fever, so Judith was not able to spend much time with him, though she did buy him a fan. In any case she told herself that she would "drag him out at any cost" as soon as the x-rays were over. But during the second x-ray session, he died of a heart attack. When she saw him in the mortuary she was overwhelmed by how frail and small he looked:

> *...I touched you where you lay*
> *(for it was not goodbye I had to say)*
> *and made a kind of promise. What it meant*
> *was: I am only I, as I was you.*[39]

Judith "had to do everything one does when someone dies",[40] settle Jack's affairs, such as they were, and arrange the funeral at the crematorium in Brisbane – it was too difficult to get the body to Tamborine. Quite a lot of people came, family and friends. Then sometime later she organised a small private ceremony at Mount Tamborine at which only close friends were present. Jack's ashes were buried in the little cemetery looking out over the valley below, next to his old friend, "Have-A-Chat", the bus driver who had driven them up and down the mountain to Brisbane in their early days – friends agreed that the two of them would probably spend eternity talking. On the tombstone a line from Traherne, a poet Jack and Judith both loved, was engraved:

> *Let the spirit of Truth be with me.*

It was Traherne, as she wrote, who had seen

> *... the depth of darkness*
> *shake, part and move,*
> *and from death's centre the light's ladder*
> *go up from love to Love.*[41]

Meredith was sent off to stay with friends and then to the family in New England, where Judith followed her for Christmas – it "seemed necessary to get away from the house at that time". After that they went for a holiday on the coast: Judith needed a break and Meredith was about to face her final year at school.[42] Like Jack, she did not look for "religious comfort ... It seems to me that what you've got is what you've got", but she did not divide "things into religious and non-religious" either, agreeing with Jung that "we are emotional, thinking, physical, intuitional all at once".[43] As for life after death, she did not believe in the survival of the personality but she did believe in "Karma", which "involves all sorts of up and down movements" and thus had its own kind of justice: There are "certainly people alive at the moment", she thought, "who would benefit from a spell as a cockroach and some as an albatross."[44] In the long run, as she saw it,

> *... incomprehensible energy*
> *creates us and destroys, all words are made*
> *in the long shadow of eternity.*
> *Their meanings alter even as the thing is said.*

As her poems make clear, she felt sometimes close to despair at her loss:

> *I sighed for a world left desolate without you,*
> *all certainty, passion and peace withdrawn;*

> *men like furious ants without the ant's humility,*
> *their automatic days led in by a mechanical dawn.*
>
> *Voices all round me witnessed your unknown absence.*[45]

But there was also a sense that Jack's life had somehow been triumphant:

> *Time may be gaoler, set until we die;*
> *but you were gaoled, and made your breakaway.*
>
> *And left a truth, a triumph, as you went,*
> *to prove the path.*[46]

It was this sense which gave her fortitude. And she kept her sense of style. Tina, the cousin who had shared many crises with her, remembered Judith leaning out the front window at "Calanthe" waving a whisky bottle when Tina arrived there shortly after Jack's death.[47]

The old grandfather clock at "Calanthe", extraordinarily, had stopped almost at the moment of his death,[48] and for a while Judith kept company with the clock as a "silent memento" before she decided to get it working again. For some time she had "some rather odd experiences". For several months, the house "seemed to be haunted by black butterflies landing on [her] shoulders and sphinx moths coming out of the night to sit on the rim of my glass and have a whisky". Some might have seen them as "a sign from heaven which may or may not exist". She did not know about this, but she did believe in some kind of justice: "people who have been crushed into corners, beaten up and generally denied do get their due". Whether or not there is life after death "there's a law of conservation of matter and thus of all other aspects of matter [she believed] – through which we come to be able to think, love and even think about something beyond the self", a law she liked to call the "conservation of everything".[49]

The image of butterflies in "Wings", written about this time, thus takes on new significance:

> *Between great coloured vanes the butterflies*
> *drift to the sea with fixed bewildered eyes ...*

> *Poor Rimbauds never able to return*
> *out of the searing rainbows they put on,*
>
> *their wings have trapped them. Staring helplessly*
> *they blow beyond the headland, to the sea.*[50]

But her memories of the man Jack had been and the way he conducted himself gave her comfort. She also treasured the memory of a man, also a patient in the hospital, who sought her out after Jack's death to tell her that even though he had only known him for the few days he was in hospital, Jack had impressed him as a magnificent human being.[51]

> *What I remember of you makes reply.*
> *Your eyes, your look, remain, all said and done,*
> *the guarantee of blessing, now you're gone.*[52]

She was not Ceres watching Eurydice receding into the dark, as she had been as a child watching her mother dying, but herself Eurydice, left in the hell she felt the world was becoming while he had gone free, hearing

> *the King's long shout of triumph, and a voice*
> *that cried "All's lost". And silence fell.*
> *I grope my way through silences like clouds.*
> *And still that phrase of music always murmurs,*
> *but fainter, farther, like your eyes receding.*
>
> *Your all-creating, all-redeeming song*
> *fades, as the daylight fades.*[53]

But he had left an image of integrity. So another poem concludes with a kind of prayer:

> *Renew the central dream*
> *in blazing purity,*
> *and let my rags confirm*
> *and robe eternity.*

> *For still the angel leads.*
> *Ruined yet pure we go*
> *with all our days and deeds*
> *into that flame, that snow.*[54]

But "death's part of life, dammit," and life had to go on. She had vowed on her fiftieth birthday to

> *... show my colours too.*
> *Though we've polluted*
> *even this air I breathe*
> *and spoiled green earth*[55]

and she would go on contesting this pollution. There was Meredith to care for also.

In January 1967, not long after Jack's death, they moved to a small flat in Brisbane at 1/15 Cedar Street, Greenslopes, near Meredith's school where she could now be a day girl. But Judith could not bring herself to sell "Calanthe", the place she and Jack had made for themselves and Meredith. It had grown as they had grown:

> *A kind of weaving*
> *goes on all the time in houses, its pattern*
> *determined by the years of taking and giving.*
>
> *And we were fortunate, house, to have your shelter.*
> *Your roof crouched among trees on the turning planet,*
> *part of a surface receiving rain and sunlight,*
> *kept off the shrieking*
> *speed of space, the bad weather,*
> *enclosed our portion of time, our pattern of making.*

It had sheltered

> *Storms beat in from the west, from eastward cyclones.*
> *The traffic outside, the wars and rumours of wars,*
> *the sad lost voices, the glow and rumble of cities,*
> *you muted for us ...*

> *Inside the books were read and the words were*
>   *scribbled,*
> *the talk went on, the friends and enemies came*
> *and went; but we were content, coherent, employed*
> *on our true affairs.*
> *Our sicknesses, love and quarrels*
> *continued in and around your beds and chairs.*[56]

Now it was time to leave, to come down from the mountain to the city, to a small flat and to live closer to the currents of history:

> *And outside – ah, outside!*
> *The juggernaut machines,*
> *the blue drifting gases,*
> *the crashing aircraft!*[57]

And all the time Jack's memory could still seize her with the sudden anguish expressed in "Rosina Alcona to Julius Brenzaida" (a poem referring to one of the love poems in the Brontës' Gondall cycle), sparked by the sight of an old wooden pub

> *Where you and I once*
> *in an absolute present*
> *drank laughing*
> *in a day still living,*
> *still laughing, still permanent...*
>
> *...*
>
> *"These days obscure but cannot do thee wrong."*[58]

But she had to get on with life. Offered a position in the English Department at the University of Queensland she accepted it, so that money was not such a worry. Her reputation was growing nationally and internationally, and she had already been awarded an honorary Doctorate of Letters from the University of New England. *Preoccupations in Australian Poetry*, which had been published in 1965 and reprinted in 1966, had been well received.

Judith enjoyed university teaching since she had always got on well with young people, being open minded and non-judgemental.

> I am fond of the young all round [she told a reporter when she was awarded the prestigious *Encyclopaedia Britannica* Prize for Literature]. They are very much better than people say. It is more difficult now to grow up – there are more things to drag one off the track. They are making a good job of growing up.[59]

She also liked their passion and sense of historical urgency. This was the 1960s, and change was coming to Australia, even to Brisbane. Racial rioting had exploded in Los Angeles in 1965, the Civil Rights movement was growing, challenging segregation, and President Johnson had declared that equality was not just a right or a theory but a fact which must be made a social reality in the United States. Meantime the war in Vietnam, begun as a covert operation, was escalating, and with it protests. Young people, students especially, moved out into the streets, colliding with authority. Sit-ins, drugs and the sexual freedom that came with the contraceptive pill seemed to herald the new revolutionary Age of Aquarius.

In Brisbane, students were becoming politicised not only by Australia's involvement in the Vietnam War but also by a new mood amongst Aboriginal Australians. The young Charles Perkins had galvanised awareness with his Freedom Rides, inspired by the American example, throughout New South Wales country towns, challenging racial prejudice on the one hand and inspiring Aboriginal people on the other. And there was a new mood of hopefulness as the referendum of 1967 returned a "yes" vote, acknowledging Aboriginal people at last as Australian citizens. Many of Judith's students and friends among the younger writers were involved, notably Rodney Hall, who was working for the ABC. He belonged to the group, Realist Writers, which had formed around the poet John Manifold, member of a Western District of Victoria grazing family who had nevertheless become a member of the Communist Party, though an idealistic somewhat eccentric member, it had to be said, and whose views were rather different from the orthodox party line which at that time was strictly Stalinist. Living in Queensland, as far as possible from the rest of his family and their privileged background, Manifold was an inspiration to young writers like Hall.[60]

Until now, living at Mount Tamborine, looking after Jack and running the household, Judith had been a little apart from other Queensland writers. But now, living in Brisbane and teaching at the university, mixing with graduate as well as undergraduate students, Judith was becoming more actively involved. She had already been drawn into the environmental movement by what she had seen around her on the mountain, on the coastal plain below, and in the coastal country around Cooloola and on Fraser Island. Now she was becoming involved in Aboriginal issues.

In 1963 she had met Kath Walker (later to be known by her tribal name, Oodgeroo Noonuccal), Aboriginal poet and activist, when Jacaranda Press had sent her the manuscript of Kath's first collection of poems. They were not conventional in language and style, being passionately political and speaking out of the pain and anger of Aboriginal people, "a galvanising set of demands",[61] as Judith described them in her tribute to Noonuccal after her death and quoting her:

> *We want hope not racialism,*
> *Brotherhood, not ostracism,*
> *Black advance, not white ascendance.*
> *Make us equals, not dependents.*

> Those demands, and many more, [Judith continued] rang out against a background of long accepted silence, and they seemed to me imperative. This poetry had to be published and listened to, for it was a challenge and a warning as well as a new achievement.[62]

In contrast with most of the poetry she was reading for Jacaranda Press, "the general run of largely boring and cliché-ridden verse that thudded on to publishers' desks", she found this stuff was alive[63] and recommended, indeed insisted, on its publication. The mournful voices that spoke in them troubled her, especially as she realised that what they spoke about was for many Aboriginal people either as present reality or heart-breaking memory. But lines like these from "We are Going"

> *The bora ring is gone.*
> *The corroboree is gone.*
> *And we are going*[64]

also reminded her of the deserted bora ring she had come upon at "Wongwibinda", the memory out of which her own poem "Bora Ring" had come.

> For me, who ... knew from my father the fate of New England Aborigines driven by white men with whips and guns over cliffsides for "trespass" or cattle spearing, but had never known the "pure cultures" the anthropologists were now beginning to study, the poem was more moving than any elegy in an English country churchyard.[65]

When academic critics declared that this was "not poetry at all" and that it had neither the polish of English poetry nor the "authentic voice of the song-man", Judith passionately defended it, noting also that "the gender distinction [in this verdict] was clear".[66] In her view many of the poems, notably "Tree Grave" and "Dawn Wail", stood out by any standards. As for the "political" poems, "they worked as they were intended to do, their sharply pointed comment could hurt and startle readers who had never encountered such criticism before [there were many at the time] ... They had a clarity, an incisive quality, that clung to the mind like bindi burrs. That is to say, they were functional as poetry should be."[67] As she was to say later, they made a point important for criticism generally: "the conscientious critic now has to find ways of becoming also a critic of conscience".[68]

In other ways, too, she was becoming increasingly radical. Though she seldom went on marches or demonstrations – that was not her style – in her tutorials Judith related the texts they were studying to these concerns of conscience, to the questions of war and peace which had always exercised her and to the environmental crisis. Together, she believed, young and old must work to find "a way out of the mess we have got ourselves in" – something, she said, that "no one had been game before to do".[69] Her classes were popular; students found her a stimulating teacher, though her deafness meant that she tended to talk while they listened. She enjoyed teaching, finding it very different from lecturing in country halls and to the audiences of academics she had also been used to addressing. As Meredith would, Judith hoped, be at university soon, she had an extra interest, though she worried about the fashion for drugs. "The problems of prosperity were coming into focus"[70] in this way it seemed.

Judith was not always at ease with her academic colleagues, though some of them, like Val Vallis, were people she had met through the Christesens. The return to the "Great Tradition" of English literature advocated by A.D. Hope and James McAuley and other university poets like Vincent Buckley did not appeal to her. She saw it as the literary equivalent of the importation of foreign flora and fauna which had so damaged the physical environment. As *Preoccupations in Australian Poetry* makes clear, she believed that the great task of Australian writers and critics was to resolve the contradiction, the inner argument between the transplanted European and his new country, to engage with the land itself and make it into what Patrick White called "a country of the mind", and thus make "Australia into our real spiritual home".[71] This demanded both commitment and a sense of reality beyond the merely material and rational, which was unfashionable. As Jack had argued in his last book, which Judith was at that time preparing for publication, "contemporary philosophy is the philosophy of non-commitment, the philosophy of asking no questions and making no mistakes".[72] "Advice to a Young Poet" expresses her dissatisfaction with this view:

> *There's a carefully neutral tone*
> *you must obey;*
> *there are certain things you must learn*
> *never to say.*
>
> *The city may totter around you,*
> *the girders split;*
> *but don't take a prophetic stance,*
> *you'll be sorry for it.*[73]

She refused to accept that poetry existed in its own separate, largely academic enclosure apart from the world. At the University of New England Summer School from 25th January to 2nd February 1965 she had agreed with Clement Semmler's attack on what he called "sinister signs of professionalism", a reference perhaps to Vincent Buckley's paper, also given at the Summer School, which argued that Australian literature might not be "suitable" for university teaching.[74]

Nor did she like the vogue for long discursive poems championed by Hope and McAuley. For her the poetry that the current situation called for was sharp, clear and incisive, the kind of poetry in which the image becomes a symbol, transforming experience and taking the reader beyond commonsense to the intuitive and unconscious – the kind of poems she herself had been writing. In a verse debate with Hope in the *Sydney Morning Herald* in November 1965, she not only makes this clear but points to the political consequences she looked for. The poems she wanted would be like

> *small things that flower and waft their seed*
> *and die to make a soil again*
> *on sand laid bare by human greed –*
> *a soil to hold and breathe the rain,*
> *and clothe the dunes, and change their air.*[75]

For her the individual counted, not the mob. As Jack had put it, we needed to "see the world with unflinching clarity and act upon it".[76]

Apart from her students, however, now that Jack was dead few people seemed to share her sense of urgency. In fact they seemed to find it strange. "People just thought, she's being philosophical again", Judith told Heather Rusden, dismissing it as "the influence of that husband of hers".[77] "Tool", not published, significantly, until it appeared in her *Collected Poems* in 1971, expresses the sense of beleaguered defiance she was beginning to feel as a result.

> *When I say, Oh, my love*
> *there's none to hear the cry*
> *but the opposing dark*
> *that begs, but does not speak,*
> *the rock that hides the spark.*

> *I crowd against that rock*
> *my act, affirm, oppose,*
> *I forge myself as tool*
> *that tempers under toil,*
> *to file this night . . .* [78]

Nevertheless she was being recognised elsewhere, winning the annual award of the Poetry Society of Great Britain for 1967, for example. The most important, prestigious and useful, however, was the *Encyclopaedia Britannica* Literary Prize that had come to her in 1964. It was worth £5000, which was very welcome. When Judith got the news she was marking Senior English examination papers for the University of Queensland at 6/- a paper – the long drought of 1964 which continued into 1965 meant that there were no dividends from the family company, and that year the McKinneys had to rely entirely on what Judith could earn. The prize promised "some financial freedom to get on with the job", she told the Australian *Women's Weekly* in an interview headed: "'Imagine a Poet Winning £5000 Prize' said Judith Wright". She would not be marking examination papers next year:

> I might get a motor-mower to relieve my husband, who has heart trouble. This will allow him to get on with his philosophical writing, and be a worry off my mind. I will get a few comforts for the house, and I will certainly buy the long-play record our 14-year-old daughter, Meredith wants. Yes, it's a Beatles record, and I fully approve. I like the Beatles. They are quite a good influence on the young. Look at the way they insisted, on their American tour, that the concerts be unsegregated. Courage is a good thing.[79]

Though she did not tell this to the reporter, she also planned to buy some land nearby in "lyrebird country" and donate it to the government so that it could be added to the National Park. She would also buy "books, books, books, books".[80]

The award ceremony had been held in Canberra in January 1965. Amongst the people she had met there were Frances James the journalist, and Gough Whitlam, whom she had met with her father on the train to Canberra nearly thirty years ago and had bet him a box of chocolates that he would be prime minister within twenty years – a prophecy soon to be fulfilled. She had also given a Commonwealth Literary Fund Award lecture on William Baylebridge in which she had upset a number of people, including Patrick White, by saying that Australian literature seemed to her to be in the doldrums at the moment and needed a new impetus.[81] Certainly her own interests were moving in a different direction.

The media focused, however, on the fact that she was a woman or a "bush poet" – the *Courier Mail*'s headline, for example, was "Lover of the Bush is Our Top Writer"[82] and the *Sydney Morning Herald*'s was "£5000 Award To Woman Poet"[83] – but the international recognition the award implied was a welcome vindication. Earlier in that year, reviewing her latest collection, *Five Senses*, one reviewer, Evan Jones, had pronounced condescendingly that as a poet she suffered from "limitations ... Her unique resources are limited to the landscape of 'my blood's country', to flora and fauna, and to motherhood".[84] International opinion, however, was obviously different. But the money mattered, too, and after buying what she wanted, Judith put the remainder aside for Meredith's education in case she did not get a scholarship to take her to university.

The honours were to continue. Two years later in 1967 Judith was invited to a World Poetry Conference to be held in Montreal as part of the International Exposition, Expo '67. She agreed to go – she needed a break after Jack's death. She was the only Australian included, and the conference theme, "Le Poète et la Terre des Hommes" (the Poet and the World of Humankind), was calculated to appeal to her. Reporting her departure, however, the media did not seem to appreciate either the honour or the drift of her recent work. The *Courier Mail*, for example, reported tartly that "Queensland's major poet flew to Canada yesterday leaving 'the poverty of public imagination' and 'the horrors of poetry in Queensland schools' behind", concluding with an image of her "picking up her umbrella with housewifely concern as she boarded the aircraft".[85] Even good critics did not seem to appreciate the new direction she had been taking. R. F. Brissenden, for example, wrote in a review of *The Other Half* that she had "allowed the responsibility of the poet as a public figure to weigh rather too heavily on her".[86] But in Montreal she found many other poets who were also attempting to wrestle with what Dorothy Green, one of the few critics who understood Judith's work, referred to as "the most baffling problem, the problem of reconciling the active and the contemplative, the body and the spirit, the event and the concept ... or whatever name is given to the dualisms of human consciousness".[87]

She had not, however, realised the problems of jet travel for someone as deaf as she was, and with the hip injury which was the legacy of her riding accident. Her only other trip abroad, thirty years earlier, had been by ship. This time the journey took thirty-six hours and she arrived "a jet-lagged wreck",[88] in the hallucinatory state expressed in the poem she wrote about the conference:

> *This was the dream that woke me*
> *from nembutal sleep into the pains of grief.*
>
> *I had no hemisphere, yet all four hemispheres*
> *reeled in a number-neoned sky,*
> *over the grieved and starving, over the wars,*
> *over the counter-clicking business corporations.*
> *And round the cliffs of one grey vertical*
> *squares of uncurtained light*
> *showed all the sad, the human ends of love –*
> *not springtime fulltime love but one-night stands*
> *paid for with juke-box coins ...* [89]

She revived as the conference went on and enjoyed meeting poets from all over the world: Japan, China, India, Madagascar, Lebanon, the USSR, Cuba, Brazil, France and, of course, large numbers from Canada and the United States. Robert Lowell was amongst them and she found him "nice if egoistic", though she was not really taken with his poetry whose "self engagement" troubled her. But she shared his horror at what was happening in Vietnam and elsewhere – the huge anti-war march on the Pentagon in which he and Norman Mailer figured so prominently was to take place only a few months after the conference in October. As she recalled, in fact, "there was less poetry than politics in the air".⁹⁰ Denise Levertov, for instance, told the audience that they must be prepared to oppose "the war machine" with their bodies as well as their mind.⁹¹

Judith was in tune with this mood. Her paper, one of the three given at the opening session – the others were the Frenchman André Frénaud and the Polish poet in exile, Czeslaw Milosz – declared that the poet's task was to accept reality, look hard at it and alert people, always ready to evade the truth, to the crisis we faced. They must, she said, affirm life against death and the threat of destruction and try to make the technological nightmare more liveable. In cities shrouded by

> ... *chemical mist*
> *mist from incinerators for the dead,*
> *mist from the dollar-mints and automobiles,*
> *mist from the cities grown*
> *from crystallizing chemicals*⁹²

the poet must make images of spring reaffirm the living world.

Frénaud, who spoke first, had sounded a similar note, arguing that the poet should present "images of liberty" in his work and that this responsibility came from the "moral authority" of poetry itself. But Milosz, the third speaker, now living in the United States and marked no doubt by his experiences under the Soviet regime, went in a different direction. For him the poet's place was as far away as possible from history and social concerns. In the discussion which followed, the Canadian poet, Irving Layton, took up this point, launching a vigorous attack on the poetry of commitment. "Poetry is love, solitude and prayer," he insisted, "or it is nothing", challenging those with left-wing sympathies to denounce the attacks on poetry and freedom of expression in the Eastern bloc. He was troubled, he said, by the large claims which were being made for the poet's place in the world since they made him "think ... of funeral orations or of ... a mutual admiration circle".⁹³

The debate, a lively one, was drawn to a conclusion by French poet Pierre Seghers who recalled the arguments in France about the poetry of commitment which followed the experiences of World War II, arguing that it had been his view at the time and was still his view, that it was the poets of the Resistance, committed poets, who had helped, perhaps enabled, French people to recover their identity and their dignity after the humiliations of the Occupation. "For me [he said] ...this [kind of] poetry can be the equivalent of metaphysical poetry, a poetry of depth" – something with which Judith passionately agreed. Nevertheless, in the long run the only issue worth consideration, he concluded, was "the quality of the poem itself".[94] According to the newspaper report, "the applause which greeted this declaration and that of others who spoke for the social responsibility of the poet showed where the feelings of the majority lay."[95]

Many of the poets there were in fact involved in political struggles; Pablo Neruda, for instance, in Chile, and some in other parts of South America and Cuba. Most of the French and Germans also argued strenuously for commitment, and many from the United States agreed with them. The escalation of the war in Vietnam increased this feeling – it had prevented the South Vietnamese poet, Phan Van Ky, from getting to the conference – and the crisis in Czechoslovakia, the brutal ending of the "Prague Spring" by the Russian invasion which was to see the imprisonment of writers like Wacek Havel, was then at its height. Thus at the end of the conference a group of poets issued a declaration demanding the right to freedom of expression, whatever the political or economic system in which the writer might live, adding at the same time, however, that they had "no desire to add to the uprisings, the violence and animosity with which the world is already filled".[96]

If one is to judge by the attitude of many of the newspapers, especially the English-speaking (as distinct from the French) press, however, the general public was not in sympathy. The Toronto *Telegraph*, for example, was not impressed with the idea of having a poetry conference in the first place, opening its report:

> So you think only Conservatives and Shriners have Conferences?
> Well at Expo even poets can have them. This week they came
> from all over the world to attend. Barry Callaghan kept a diary.[97]

Nor did Mr Callaghan think much of Judith Wright; he had more to say about her physical condition – presumably the consequence of her long flight – than the substance of her paper:

> Judith Wright of Australia ... apologises for being a minor poet from a minor country. Her voice quavers, and her right leg shakes badly, the calf muscle wags back and forth. She talks of the terrors of science and technology as if they were the devil incarnate. Ms Wright struggles through the explication of her argument, while Czeslaw Milosz of Poland, the next speaker, watches her with a curious detachment.[98]

But perhaps these condescending attitudes were understandable since the real focus of Expo '67 was on science and technology, not poetry. Pavilions glittered with high-tech shows of sound and light, state of the art video cameras, experimental films and previews of the coming computer age, all promising the kind of world Judith was attacking:

> *To keep the crowds amused*
> *they calmed them with the curves of lovely fireworks,*
> *each arc exact, prefigured and agreed-on*
> *by chemists and by weapon-builders ...*
>
> *"Rockets!" the crowds cried. "Wars!"*
> *and every window opened, every poet*
> *began to burn with napalm flames.*
> *and fires detached and fell into the crowds,*
> *fires of a human flesh.*
> *Here a hand fell, opening like a flower,*
> *a firework breast, a glowing genital.*[99]

It also seems as if the newspapers disliked the poets' opposition to the war in Vietnam. Another Toronto newspaper, the *Star*, reported that Denise Levertov had "urged everyone to get up, leave for California and lie on the docks to obstruct the munitions ships on their way to Vietnam"[100] – a good example of distortion by simplification. Reading reports like this it is easier to understand the anger Judith's poem expresses in the contrast it draws between the crowds calling for war and the poets looking down from their hotel windows:

> *Each in their planned and floodlit window-spaces*
> *the poets stood and beckoned to the crowds.*

> *"Language!" they cried with their wild human breath,*
> *but in the squares beneath the crowds cried "Numbers!"*
> *"Words," cried the poets from their past, "Fires! Forests!"*
> *the chemical greens of plastic leaves behind them.*[101]

As she had said in her paper, "most poetry today amounts to a more or less minute description of or a reaction to Hell or to a turning inward for reassurance that Hell is not all that is possible ... [since] now that Heaven's impossible, we are left with nothing to set against Hell but our inner convictions".[102] The sense of disaster here all but overwhelms conviction as the poem concludes emptily with the crowds dispersing:

> *Now under midnight's sign*
> *there's nothing but the dark, the nembutal sleep,*
> *the hemispheres are flattened by Mercator*
> *projections; folded like fans.*
> *The sweepers issue from their corners*
> *and that show's over.*[103]

She had to fly straight home as soon as the conference was over – not something she was looking forward to. But she had left Meredith, about to sit for her final school exams (and she needed a scholarship if she was to get to university), with Rodney Hall and his wife, Beth, and did not want to impose on them, especially as they were rather poor at the time. She arrived after another "dreadful long flight ... with a fierce chest complaint", and it was over a month before she recovered.[104] But she had met a number of poets and made several friends, including a group of politically active young French poets – since her time at university she had been interested in contemporary French poetry, and a colleague in the Department of French in the University of Queensland, Antoine Denat, had dedicated his essay on François Ponge to her.[105] She had also made friends with an Indian poet, a woman with whom she had long discussions about Hindu philosophy which also interested her. Jack had thought it might offer an alternative to the Western philosophical paradigm which, in his view, was manifestly breaking down – the Vietnam War was another symptom of this.

Since childhood, fire had fascinated her. "Fire Sermon", written about this time, links Buddha's vision of the destructive fires of desire with the figure of Shiva, dancing in the fires of destruction and creation. In the poem a voice, presumably a supporter of the South Vietnamese regime, speaks of "sinister powers" moving south into their ricefields. But the poem's centre lies instead in the television image of a child weeping under the "chemical rain descending . . . blacken[ing] the fields" and then moves to the temple where

> . . . *the great gold Buddha*
> *smiles inward with half-closed eyes.*
> *All is Maya, the dance, the veil,*
> *Shiva's violent dream.*
>
> *Let me out of this dream, I cry.*
> *I belong to a simple people*
> *and all we want is to live.*[106]

As this suggests, Vietnam for her was much more than a political issue; it represented a crisis of value. It was not enough merely to contest the war therefore; one must also keep going the "song of praise", the praise of life which is the poet's task. As she had written some years earlier:

> *Out of the torn earth's mouth*
> *comes the old cry of praise.*
> *Still is the song made flesh*
> *though the singer dies.*[107]

Despite everything, she still affirmed this cry in the midst of death. The flame tree in the garden at "Calanthe", which Jack had planted eighteen years ago, had only now begun to bloom:

> *suddenly, wholly, ceremoniously*
> *it puts off every leaf and stands up nakedly,*
> *calling and gathering,*
>
> *every capacity in it, every power,*
> *drawing up from the very roots of being*

> *this pulse of total red that shocks my seeing*
> *into an agony of flower.*[108]

The war in Vietnam, like the atomic bomb and nuclear weapons and the destruction of the environment, was the product of a culture of death. But leaning on the sill, watching the tree bloom, the "past years feeding it", she committed herself to life. "Massacre of the Innocents", which she had sensed even as a child born a few weeks after the landings at Gallipoli, was still going on, but as a poet she had to speak for these innocents:

> *We speak with the voice*
> *of your daughters, your sons,*
> *We look through the eyes*
> *of all innocent ones.*
> *We are spring, which soon dies.*
>
> *We are hope, and you kill us.*[109]

"Christmas Ballad" is about the human cost, not only for the children and peasants dying in the fields but also for the soldiers fighting it. It is a poem about a soldier returning home, and its opening stanza makes this point clearly – some might say too clearly:

> *Then they retrieved the walking dead,*
> *wiped his eyes clear of blood,*
> *replaced his heart with a nylon one*
> *and dry-cleaned his uniform.*[110]

Our civilisation seemed to have surrendered to the imperatives of technology:

> *The will to power destroys the power to will.*
> *The weapon made, we cannot help but use it;*
> *it drags us with its own momentum still.*
>
> *The power to kill compounds the need to kill.*[111]

But the answer, as Jack had never tired of saying, lay in the renewal of imagination, the power to figure forth images of life, not those images of death. War was an ancient and continuing problem, but the power which technology had given us to destroy the natural world posed a new and even more terrible threat, the destruction of the sources of life as a culture which, as Judith put it, was "trying to mould the landscape to our desires rather going along with what it wanted".[112] It was this conviction which was to provide the energy she was to put into the environmental movement in the next few years.

In the late 1950s, watching "developers" clearing the rainforest on Mount Tamborine, cutting up the Gold Coast into blocks and then ravaging the even more fragile coastal areas to the north for economic gain, she had decided that something must be done and, as we have seen, with Kathleen McArthur and David Fleay, had founded the WPSQ. There was already a tradition of concern for the environment in Queensland and in her family. A cousin by marriage – Judith's Uncle Cecil had married into his family – Romeo Lahey had been one of the pioneers, even though, or perhaps because, the family fortune had been made from timber mills. He had worked tirelessly and finally succeeded in having the Lamington area declared a National Park, and his influence had perhaps inspired Judith's father to push for a National Park in New England.

The society had become aware of the need for education. There seemed to be little concern with our rich variety of plant, animal, bird and insect life or of the threat to them, and Queensland was probably just as little concerned – at school, Meredith's nature study lessons had consisted of cutting up a lemon. Brian Clouston, the proprietor of Jacaranda Press, had suggested publishing a magazine dealing with environmental issues, to be distributed through the Education Department but also for public sale, suggesting the name *Wildlife*.

The first issue, which had appeared in June 1963, was largely the work of Judith Wright and Kathleen McArthur with a great deal of help from Stan and Kay Breedon, John Orrell and George Knight. It was professionally produced, a glossy magazine, with a life-size cover photograph (taken by Stan Breedon) of a ringtail possum, one of the rich chestnut-brown species found in Queensland and included articles like "The Vanishing Dunes" (by Kathleen McArthur), "The Life Around Us" (David Stammer), "Living Areas for our Fauna" (C. Roff) and

"Nature was First" (John Orrell). David Fleay had two articles introducing readers to the northern quoll and the crested hawk. John Orrell asked people to "Be Sensible About Snakes" and A. M. Duncan-Kemp linked interest in nature with respect for Aboriginal culture in his article, "Bush-Flowers in the Aboriginal Clock".

Judith herself had contributed four articles, one on the work of Romeo Lahey (who kept an interest in the WPSQ and its magazine and wrote encouragingly to her), another on spring in the rainforest, "The Season Begins", the third on the rainforest in summer while the fourth was a review of a new book on Australian birds and animals. Living in the city now she might feel that

> ... *I've applied to the wrong place.*
> *The more I walk round this city*
> *(though I know it, you might say, like I know myself)*
> *the less I like the look of it*[113]

but the natural world for her was still the source of life and renewal and on the top of her other concerns she had thrown herself into work for it. *Wildlife* was produced by volunteers, but most of the editorial work fell on Judith. In her work for *Meanjin* in the 1940s she had had some editorial experience, but *Meanjin* had few, if any, illustrations whereas photographs, some of them in colour, were a feature of *Wildlife*. Moreover, many of the articles contained Latin terms and names for the flora and fauna being discussed and she had had no formal training in botany or biology and sometimes got them wrong — to the disgust of one of their best contributors, John Orrell, who wrote from his home in Cairns that "no one at headquarters could be a naturalist".[114]

Other problems also had begun to develop. The Queensland Education Department appears to have been less than enthusiastic about distributing the magazine, despite several letters from Judith as president of the WPSQ appealing for help. Circulation was growing, but slowly, and since production was expensive and Jacaranda was only a small and struggling press, Clouston let them know that it could not continue to carry the burden. *Wildlife* was making its way, however. In October 1965, for instance, they received a letter from Buckingham Palace from the

Duke of Edinburgh thanking them for the copy of the magazine and saying how much he enjoyed it. But they desperately needed financial assistance if the magazine was to continue. It was decided to apply for funds from the Myer Foundation. Judith's name was an asset here, but it meant that she had to spend even more time lobbying.

In July 1965, Baillieu Myer was in Brisbane and invited her to dinner with him at Lennon's Hotel. In February 1966 the Foundation offered a subsidy of £256 a quarter to cover the losses on each issue, to be paid every six months for two years or for as long as the society continued to publish *Wildlife*, whichever was the shorter. Since it was contrary to the Foundation's policy to grant money to magazines, officially the money was awarded to the WPSQ for its work for the environment.

All this had been going on as Jack's health had continued to deteriorate, so the demands on Judith's energies had been very heavy. Early in 1966, when Stan Breedon offered to take over as editor, the committee accepted his offer, an arrangement which was not entirely successful. In October the previous year, however, well-known naturalist Vincent Serventy had arrived in Queensland from Western Australia, and had written to Judith from the caravan park in which he was staying expressing his enthusiasm for *Wildlife* and asking to meet her.[115] His enthusiasm continued and towards the end of 1966 he offered to take over as editor from Breadon – at a distance since he was based in Western Australia. But he was to prove a conscientious, efficient and successful editor.

That was one problem more or less solved. But in the same year, 1966, Judith had become a foundation member of the Australian Conservation Foundation (ACF), which had grown out of a seminar on wildlife conservation she had attended at the University of New England. At this seminar she had met Len Webb, an expert in rainforests and a pioneering ecologist who was to become an ally and friend, and Geoff Tracey, a botanist. Both of them worked for the Commonwealth Scientific and Industrial Research Organisation (CSIRO) but Francis Ratcliffe, also from CSIRO, an Englishman whose *Flying Fox and Drifting Sand*, first published in 1935, had become a classic account of the flora and fauna of Northern Australia, was the moving spirit in the idea of establishing a national conservation body. The visit to Australia of the Duke of Edinburgh in 1966 had given new impetus to the idea – Ratcliffe was very much an Establishment man.

Ratcliffe had warmed to Judith's passion for the environment, writing to her in January 1965 not long after their first meeting that she seemed "to touch something to which I instinctively respond",[116] and had invited her to become one of the first counsellors of the Foundation which had been set up with a grant of £1000 from Prime Minister Menzies. He was also confident that business would contribute. This was a policy which was to cause trouble later on, at least as far as Judith was concerned. But for the moment, she had accepted his offer, suggesting also, as practical as ever, that he put his mind to getting tax deductibility for donations to the Foundation.[117]

By the end of that year, December 1966, the WPSQ had also been invited to affiliate with the ACF, and Ratcliffe had boasted that the council now included academics, businessmen and government officials as well as environmentalists – a strange conglomeration in Judith's view – reporting also that donations to the ACF were non tax-deductible. Judith had been a little suspicious. As she wrote later: "everyone [seemed to be] ... jumping on the conservation band wagon".[118] But the matter in her view was urgent so she had accepted the alliance.

A letter written to the Blackmans in March 1966 expresses her sense of urgency, pointing also in the direction of a battle which was to take up much, if not most, of her time, and energy over the next few years. Charles Blackman had just expressed his interest in going to the Great Barrier Reef when they returned to Australia, to which Judith had responded, writing to Barbara that

> If [he] really wants to see [it] he'd better hurry. It's all being eaten away by rampaging tourists and crown-of-thorns starfish in conjunction. Our Wildlife Preservation Society is unable to stop either. Nor do I recommend you to go to Stradbroke which is being eaten away by rutile-sand mining, despite our best efforts ... Progress is on the forward move, Queensland's vast potential is being exploited, say the politicians.[119]

In *The Coral Battleground,* published in 1977, Judith tells the story of the battle which had now begun to save the Great Barrier Reef, a battle which was peculiarly local and therefore peculiarly urgent, and very close to her heart, from the time she had first seen it sailing to Surabaya as a child. In one of the poems written in the late 1940s, for instance, she had used the Reef as an image of her then embattled love for Jack. As she began to realise the extent of the threat, she felt a personal responsibility for it, writing that:

> If the Great Barrier Reef could think, it would fear us ... We have its fate in our hands, and slowly but surely as the years go on, we are destroying those great water-gardens, lovely indeed as cherry-boughs in flower under the once-clear sea, but far more complex, far more alive, teeming with myriads of varied animal lives.[120]

She could not do much about the world crisis of war, nuclear weapons and power, ever-escalating technology, the population explosion, and so on. But this, she and her friends believed, was a battle they could perhaps win, and the Foreword to the 1977 edition of *The Coral Battleground* claims that in fact they did:

> There are not many success stories in the attempts we make to save especially important elements of the natural world from our own greeds and needs ... but the story of the rescue of the Great Barrier Reef still throws light on the present and gives hope for the future, and because of the rescue many people have been able to experience and enjoy the marvellous stretch of sea and reefs and islands, and the intricate patterns of living beings, which make up its existence.[121]

It is true, the Foreword to the second edition, written twenty years later, in 1996, is less optimistic, writing this time that "this story has no real beginning and no one knows what its end will be".[122] Whatever the verdict, however, it was a struggle which was to take up much of the next stage of Judith's life.

In 1963 some members of the WPSQ had become concerned at reports that coral collectors, shell collectors and an increasing number of tourists were threatening the Reef. One of the people most concerned had been the photographer Noel Monkman, who lived with his wife Kitty on Green Island offshore from Cairns and saw at close hand what was happening. Someone in the society suggested that they work to have the Reef gazetted as one great underwater park.[123] Certainly it was clear that responsibility for ensuring its safety lay with government. In the meantime, however, a growing number of people had begun to share their concern. By mid-1966 the society had more than six hundred members, most of them willing to get actively involved, and from being "a small collection of cranks labelled as anti-progressive visionaries", conservationists were becoming significant.

They were also gathering support from scientists like Len Webb and Geoff Tracey, and a group of young graduate students at the University of Queensland led by Des Connell, who was researching water pollution, and Eddie Hegerl of the Department of Zoology. Early in 1967 they formed the Littoral Society, to defend the Reef, and joined forces with the WPSQ. Len Webb had also recruited a powerful ally, Melbourne-born artist John Büsst, who now lived on Bedarra Island off the coast near Innisfail. He and his wife Alison were passionate environmentalists and had already formed an organisation "consisting only of himself, as president, secretary and treasurer, with its own letterhead", to save the nearby forest around Innisfail. Büsst was a personal friend of politician Harold Holt, soon to become prime minister of Australia, who had been to school with him. Others in the area, like Mrs Billie Gill, an amateur ornithologist and a farmer's wife, and another friend of Len Webb joined in.[124] In mid-1967, just before Judith left for the Poetry Conference in Montreal, the WPSQ had heard from these members of the Innisfail branch that pollution on the Reef was assuming dangerous proportions. Even more disturbing, John Büsst had noticed a limestone mining application advertised in the local papers, which proposed to remove coral from Ellison Reef, offshore from Innisfail.[125] The Innisfail branch had lodged a protest with the Mining Warden's Court as had the ACF. Would the whole WPSQ join them? he asked. Thus, Judith wrote later, "was the first stroke in a battle which was to occupy our minds and time for years ahead ... we were plunged at once into a mystifying controversy".[126]

Shortly after that, Judith had left for Montreal. But for her, conservation was not an issue she could take up or put down. Once committed to the cause, it became part of her life. Soon after her return she flung herself in earnest into the battle for the Reef. Although she had had no scientific training, over the years with Jack she had been educating herself, aware of the need for integrity and accuracy in debate. In 1962, for example, she wrote to Kathleen wanting to "find out a bit about this insecticide thing" – Rachel Carson's *Silent Spring* had just appeared – if they were to be effective in their opposition to farming methods which were damaging the environment. She worried that some of the committee thought that "saving wild life" was "to sit contentedly around looking at slides". Since government was more and more "run by international technologists ... [and] apparently more people read the financial pages than the literary", they must be well informed and professional in their approach. Thus the committee had conducted a poll gauging reactions to the use of insecticides, using the skills Judith had developed in advertising, and the results – which suggested that a large number of people were worried about the possible effects – had been broadcast on the ABC's "This Day Tonight".

Even then, Judith was becoming a public figure on account of her work for the environment as well as for her writing. She did not enjoy it, however, writing to Kathleen that

> being interviewed on TV is funny but not enjoyable. Those darn great monsters swelling around in the dark outside and peering down from the ceiling and two interviewers (one not at all bright) asking rather foolish questions: it was rather like a three-cornered game of tennis where two who know the rules take on a mug who doesn't. However, I did get my own back at least twice. I shan't go and look at it; it would be eerie.[127]

All this had had its effect; Judith noted in the same letter, as a result of the program on "This Day Tonight", "a small wound [had] been made in the rhinoceros hide". But they needed more professional allies. Len Webb had become chief of these allies. "A vital and urgent man with a love for the magnificent forests he studied" [as she describes him, he] "travelled to and fro, talking to people and making himself unpopular, but also being heard by those with foresight". His sense of "the urgency, even the tragedy", of what was unfolding resembled her own as "the rainforest continued to be felled and burned, and plants and animals unknown, or almost unknown, to science, and never to be replaced, went up in smoke."[128]

Crisis is a way of thinking about a situation not necessarily inherent in that situation itself,[129] but the two of them shared this way of thinking and a disgust with what was going on. As Judith put it, "Progress was the cry, and progress [they] got, no matter how destructive and planless."[130] Len's work in the rainforest had made him a pioneer in the new science of ecology. Its central theme, according to Charles Birch in a paper Judith kept in her files for years, is "its declaration of interdependence ... All living things and all the business and technology that go on over the face of the earth are utterly dependent upon the cyclical processes of the 20 odd elements that make up living things." This echoed the sense of being part of a living whole which Judith had known since childhood and which Jack's philosophy and her growing interest in Aboriginal culture had confirmed, the sense that the land problem is the root of all socio-economic problems. Webb agreed, remarking in a letter to her that "land is the common heritage of all mankind, not to be owned by individuals".[131]

Judith was coming to know John Büsst also and to enjoy his company. "A slender, enthusiastic man full of laughter, a compulsive smoker and lover of good company",[132] he had mostly spent his life painting, boating and swimming, exploring the Reef and the rainforest, occasionally selling his paintings to tourists or to galleries elsewhere – he had a private income which meant that he did not have to worry too much about money. In 1957 he and his wife Alison had moved to the mainland, to Bingal Bay – hence the name he liked to give himself, "the Bingal Bay Bastard" – not far from Innisfail and built there "a splendid tropical bungalow, complete with hand-made furniture of local bamboo, on the side of the hill with magnificent views of the Pacific" in the midst of spacious grounds teeming with bird and animal life. But now he was becoming seriously involved in the battle for the Reef.

He had liked to say that anyone living south of Cairns was off his (or her) head. But events were proving that he was not a mere drop-out and certainly not a hermit. With his many friends, including Holt, who had a smaller cottage out of sight around the Bay, he was discovering his political skills, and he used his friendship with Holt to advantage. Holt loved the Reef – it has been said that he was drowned at Portsea because he was secretly envious of Büsst and was trying to do in the cold waters off Portsea what Büsst used to do in the warm tropical waters – and was prepared to listen to the environmentalists' concerns.

The young scientists of the Littoral Society who loved the Reef also fought hard for it, and many Queenslanders joined in. As the WPSQ's newsletter for 1967 put it: "We in Queensland have a particular responsibility, as we virtually hold the Great Barrrier Reef in trust for the rest of the world",[133] and many were determined to live up to this responsibility.

Most of Judith's life could be seen as leading up to this battle: her love for the land, her father and environmental concerns as early as the 1930s, memories of brief childhood holidays by the sea and the days and nights on Bondi Beach when she was a student, Jack's belief in the relationship between human beings and the natural world, Kathleen's friendship, the trips she and Jack had made along the coast as well as into the interior – all these things had prepared her for it.

It is not surprising that her account of the battle is so passionate, presenting it more or less as a struggle between good and evil, between life and death. On the one side were those who loved the world and on the other, those who were destroying it, the mining companies, international investors, politicians and devotees of progress, whom she linked with the war-makers and the "sinister powers" of technology, the

> ... *conquerors and self-poisoners*
> *more than scorpion or snake*[134]

she was to write about in the angry poem, "Australia 1970", people themselves dying of the venom they manufacture as they kill the earth.

The skirmish which began the battle was the application to mine coral from Ellison Reef for limestone, used in the sugar-cane industry and therefore a promising proposal from a commercial point of view. The developers argued that Ellison Reef was a "dead" reef so that mining it would do no harm to the Reef as a whole. But this was an argument the environmentalists rejected. In their view, there was no such thing as a "dead" reef; Ellison Reef and others like it had only entered into a different phase of life, one moreover which was necessary for the Reef as a whole system.[135]

Determined to prove that this was so, Büsst took counsel with local fishermen and also flew out with them over that part of the Reef. From the air it looked like any other reef, and the fishermen agreed with him. At this stage they also gained a new ally, a medical man, Dr Barnes, who had become interested in the Reef in the course of his research into the causes of a disease known as ciguatera, which he believed was caused by eating fish from areas in which algae growths were concentrated on "dead" coral boulders. These areas were scattered all over the Pacific and in his opinion Ellison Reef was no more "dead" than they were.

The problem was, however, that neither Barnes nor Büsst nor the local fishermen counted as scientific witnesses before the Warden's Court, which had to decide whether or not to allow the mining to go ahead. The environmentalists asked for a postponement of the hearing to allow them to find such witnesses, and this was granted. At an urgent meeting of the Council of the WPSQ and the Littoral Society, representatives made a suggestion.

> They were young men with no money to speak of but they were experienced divers and some ... already had qualifications as biologists and marine collectors. If [the WPSQ] could raise the money, the transport, the accommodation and some of the equipment, they were willing to apply for leave from the University to go north and organise a dive on Ellison Reef and a count of species.[136]

Judith's account suggests the mounting excitement as they marshalled their slender financial resources to organise the dive. Through Büsst's influence they obtained sponsorship from the airline, TAA, and Avis Rent-A-Car, whose Innisfail manager was a friend of his, and the young scientists, denied official leave, took time off anyway. The dive took place and the weather stayed calm, allowing them to dive every day. The locals also joined in enthusiastically – boat-owners and crews refused to be paid for their work – and the dive was a success, identifying 88 species of live coral, 60 species of mollusc and 190 species of fish. They got their evidence that Ellison Reef was not "dead".

Then another stroke of luck occurred. The director of the ACF, Don McMichael, a trained marine biologist, had had an interest in this area of the Reef in the past and was prepared to give evidence in court that mining would cause serious damage to the life systems of the Reef, which were all interrelated. The weight of all this evidence was conclusive and the court upheld their objection.[137]

The decision took time. When it was handed down in December, Judith was in the middle of the Pacific beginning a few months' travel abroad. But the case had roused a great deal of interest and alerted people to the growing threat to the environment posed by the advocates of "development". In particular the *Australian* had given the issue generous coverage, thanks to Judith and Büsst, who had personally visited the newspaper's Brisbane office and convinced a young reporter, Barry Wain, of the importance of the issue. Other newspapers became interested also, and the ABC took up the cause as well. The battle was only just beginning, but they had allies.

CHAPTER X

LOOK AT THE NEWS FROM THE OTHER CAPITALS

> Look at the news from the other capitals ...
> ... here the air gets darker (I can't stop coughing)
> and the river smells like death.
>
> "The City",
> Collected Poems, p. 274

Judith was very tired. On her return from the conference in Montreal in September 1967 she had gone straight back to work at university, exhausted and suffering from a lung condition, the result of the long flight.[1] Jack's death and the move from "Calanthe" had been painful and there had been little time for grief with the battle for Ellison Reef.

It was all very well, not long after his death, to vow to make herself

> *A keen and useful tool*

in the battle for life against the frowning darkness, a tool that

> *shows shining at its edge*
> *of wear against the world*

and to

> *Affirm, oppose and give*
> *brighten and wear my edge.*

> *[To] strike that there may live*
> *one spark's affirmative*
> *to answer ... oh, my love.*²

But the strain was beginning to tell. There was the Vietnam War to oppose and the destruction of the environment, and the long reign of Premier Joh Bjelke-Petersen was beginning its attack on civil rights. Looking back, she remembered wearily how few there seemed then to be who dared to face these issues.³

The shadow she had been aware of from childhood seemed to be growing bigger. Poems like "The City" reflect the fear that civilisation itself was in decline, and not just by the attacks of politicians and the advocates of "progress" but by something more insidious:

> *Do you know that the art-gallery's been burned down*
> *and they're building some kind of temple? ...*
> *All night long the side-streets*
> *ring with the queerest noises, they call it music;*
> *people wear blankets and leather.*⁴

She was worried, too, for Meredith who was growing up in this increasingly unsafe world:

> *Perhaps we should have trained you*
> *in using weapons,*
> *bequeathed you a straight eye,*
> *a sure-shot trigger-finger,*
>
> *or that most commonplace*
> *of self-defences,*
> *an eye to Number One,*
> *shop-lifting skills,*
>
> *a fibrous heart, a head*
> *sharp with arithmetic*
> *to figure out the chances ...*

In such a world how to keep one's humanity?

*How write an honest letter
to you, my dearest?
We know each other well –
not well enough.*[5]

Still not over Jack's death, Judith needed a break. There was some money left from the *Encyclopaedia Britannica* Award and she had had a recent windfall, a small legacy from a relation, so she decided to take an overseas trip. On 3rd December 1967 she and Meredith set out for a Pacific cruise on the *Himalaya*, after which they were to work their way around Australia, with Judith speaking at both the Adelaide and Perth festivals, and then sail for Europe. She also hoped to enlist international help for the struggle to save the Great Barrier Reef.

The trip began well. In mid-Pacific a cable arrived telling them that the Mining Warden had upheld the objection to mining Ellison Reef, thus establishing a precedent, as she put it, "not for mining the Great Barrier Reef, but for not mining it".[6] News came, too, that Meredith had done well enough in her examinations to get a Commonwealth Scholarship. It would ease their money worries and was "very useful indeed. [It] means we can bring back a souvenir or two". She could relax while Meredith enjoyed herself "down there with juke boxes and boys in the teenagers' end, and [she] saw some islands and had some sleep".[7]

Some weeks later they were back in Australia, spending Christmas as usual in New England. Judith had decided not to go to Europe by way of the United States – the route the family had often taken in the past. As she told a friend, "[I] don't want to drag a 17-year-old through riots and murders", and she was looking forward to travelling around Australia. She enjoyed herself "sitting on the verandah at 'Wallamumbi' brushing the flies away, bird-watching in the garden, and answering a beer-carton of mail that was waiting for me when I landed … No car, no house, no job, no responsibilities except organising our travels." Even writing was "practically out of [her] life except for necessary lectures to help us round the world". Elizabeth Perkins of the English Department at the university, a good friend, had taken over the car and the care of "Calanthe" which had not yet been sold. She "assures me that she is keeping the place clean and not allowing student orgies in it", Judith wrote, "Not that I'd mind that." In this relaxed mood she felt like "a passing butterfly migrating from country to country".[8] The first step in her migration, however, was the Adelaide Festival to which she had been invited as a guest to run a poetry workshop with Bruce Dawe.

She liked Dawe and respected his poetry and political views, and they got on well. Judith had never been a "literary person in the sense of going to writers' gatherings" and had always disliked the academic exploitation of literature, so she found running a workshop rather bemusing, "rather like running a pottery class", she thought. Not sure that poetry could actually be "taught", she spent most of her time just reading it to the class, though she did try to teach them the craft to write haikus, short poems on the Japanese model of five-to-seven syllable lines based on a single image or concept, which she thought "fun to do". However, by good fortune Ann Elder, already a fine poet, was in the class, and Judith found that very rewarding, remarking to Heather Rusden that she thought her "a better poet than me".[9]

Later that month she was in Perth for the festival there. But this time she managed to ruffle feathers when the *West Australian*, under the heading, "Schools Don't Help, Says Australian Poet", reported on 27th February that she had attacked the teaching of poetry in schools – one of her hobby-horses. Teachers murdered poems by dissecting them line by line, she said, preventing students from experiencing poetry for themselves. She also made herself more unpopular by putting in a plea for conservation, mourning the destruction of the native fauna and the unique local flora – another aspect of the destructiveness she saw also in teaching and the examination system.

Even though she was on holiday her concern for the natural world and for justice remained. Not long before she and Meredith sailed for Europe, Judith signed a letter attacking the South African regime, "to all intents and purposes a police state", published in the *Sydney Morning Herald* on 20th March. The Chancellor of the Australian National University, the Anglican Archbishop of Newcastle, James McAuley, Edward St John, Patrick White, Kylie Tennant and Gough Whitlam were amongst the other signatories.

On this trip Judith and Meredith did not visit Ceylon (Sri Lanka), perhaps because of her memories of the time she had spent there on her way back from Europe in 1937.

Meredith loved their trip through India, however, rejoicing especially in "Sikh boys with turbans and motorbikes". But they were only passing through on their way to Pakistan where they had been invited to stay with the poet Jocelyn Ortt-Saeed with whom Judith had corresponded for some years. She was comfortably off – her husband was the proprietor of a sugar-mill – so they were well looked after. Despite this, they managed to contract "some fly-borne disease", and by the time they arrived in Rome several weeks later Judith had developed "pretty severe gastroenteritis" and was "a bit of a wipe-off". All that she saw of Rome was the interior of the hotel, which was unfortunate because it was the first time she had been in the city – in 1937, international sanctions against Mussolini, because of his invasion of Abyssinia, had kept her out. At first she also thought it unfortunate that the hotel into which the travel section of her bank had booked them was "highly expensive". But it paid off since the staff looked after her very well. Meantime, Meredith enjoyed herself with the "handsome young Italians", spending more time sitting with hippies on the Spanish Steps than in galleries or museums – rightly so, her mother thought, remembering her own travels.[10]

When Judith was better, Italy began to do its work on her, also. She and Meredith set off by train, travelling to Florence and then on to Venice where they spent Easter, finding the city, the people and the ceremonies "marvellous". From there the train took them through the Dolomite Mountains and the Alps to Vienna, travelling along the flowering valleys of the Austrian countryside in springtime. In Vienna Judith was to give a lecture for the British Council on Australian literature, but illness continued to dog them. It was Meredith who fell ill this time, with bronchitis, so that there was little opportunity to explore the city, though Judith did go by herself to the opera.

From there they crossed into Germany and sailed by steamer along the Rhine. Beautiful as it was, Judith was haunted by memories of what she had seen and heard in 1937. Neither did the Germans' pursuit of economic development appeal to her so that on the whole she found the country "horrid" and "not much better than in 1937".[11]

As she had said in an article published in *Quadrant* just before she left Australia, for her the environmental movement represented a "groping movement towards a new kind of understanding",[12] and in this visit she was making contact with others involved in this movement who would sympathise and, she hoped, support Australian environmentalists as they continued to fight what she saw as "our dramatic losing battle".[13] She was given "a courteous hearing" by the director of the International Union for the Conservation of Wildlife in his unpretentious house on the shores of Lake Geneva. He was horrified when he heard of the threat to the Reef. The scientific importance and the fame of the Reef were such that he could hardly believe that any government would willingly risk those for the chance of an oil or mineral strike.[14] But the organisation had little money and so could not help financially, and in any case the director felt that it could not interfere in Australian affairs. He did undertake, however, to write, expressing the organisation's concern, to scientists throughout the world and also to the Australian prime minister and the premier of Queensland – "not much use the latter", Wright remarked.[15] He also suggested that the French might provide help by organising a research survey. Events were to prevent her from talking to French environmentalists, but Judith was heartened by the meeting.

Leaving Germany, she and Meredith took the train north to Scandinavia where the winter snows were only just melting, enjoying the spectacular scenery of mountains and fjords and valleys where the flowers were just beginning to appear. Then they went south to Holland, staying in Amsterdam. We do not know whether the friends she had made there in 1937 survived the war and the German occupation, since Judith did not mention them. She and Meredith enjoyed the free and fair-minded city – Meredith, of course, was particularly taken by the Dam, the central square where hippies from all over the world congregated. It was here that they first heard rumours of an "uprising" in Paris, but since no one could tell them exactly what was happening, they decided to keep to their original plans. In any case, Judith was always interested in such developments and saw no need to change arrangements (they had been booked into a hotel on the Left Bank, the student quarter), as more cautious people advised them to do. She had never been afraid of radical people or radical thought and was more in sympathy with students and trade unionists than with the government of Charles de Gaulle, which they were challenging.

She and Meredith "finally dragged into the Gare du Nord" in May on one of the last trains into Paris "just before the whole place broke down",[16] and were lucky enough to get one of the last taxis to their hotel. She had hoped to meet some of the young French poets whose company she had enjoyed the previous year at the Poetry Expo in Montreal. But the whole city was on strike and the *navettes*, the ferry boats which ran up and down the Seine, were the only public transport still running, so it was difficult to get about. In any case, Judith assumed that her young poet friends, all of them radicals, would be in the midst of the demonstrations, marches and discussions.

In the circumstances the only way to get about was to walk, which they did, managing to explore a good deal of the inner city this way. They both had good walking shoes – "shoe leather was very important in Paris at that time"[17] – so they rather enjoyed themselves, having places like Notre Dame, the parks and museums more or less to themselves. Since most tourists were too frightened to venture out the streets were more or less deserted, so they "had a wonderful view of the architecture". They were also fascinated by the graffiti scrawled everywhere on the walls. One in particular, *"Dix ans est assez"* (ten years is enough), especially appealed, as she applied it in her mind to Bjelke-Petersen, the arch-enemy of conservationists and Aborigines who was to be in office for many years.

They had originally planned to spend only a week in Paris, but the strike detained them. Although their hotel was fairly basic, they were comfortable enough. "Gas and electricity were okay for domestic consumption and there was still food," she told Kathleen McArthur, "So apart from the smelly garbage cans it wasn't too unpleasant, and I found great excitement in struggling through the newspapers, student and otherwise, and the various inflammatory leaflets we were handed everywhere in the streets."[18] There were clashes, some of them serious, between police and the demonstrators, but they did not see any of them or any real violence. In any case her sympathies were with the radicals, which made her different from most other foreigners, few of whom had any sympathy for them. They had several adventures, however.

On one occasion, they had arranged to meet one of Judith's colleagues at the University of Queensland, Kathleen Campbell-Brown, a senior lecturer in the French Department who was on study leave in Paris, staying with her former professor, a Parisian. She invited them to meet her at his flat. When they arrived, the professor was not home, but not long afterwards he burst in, dishevelled and flustered, having just emerged from the sewers where he had taken refuge from angry students. Kathleen, it seems, had not noticed the strike or that the students and unionists had risen against teachers and the government. She was outraged, declaring that she would find out "what was going on" and was determined to "get to the bottom of all this". Her researches, however, did not get her very far. Aware that there was no transport, the McKinneys walked to the restaurant where they had arranged to eat that evening, having allowed plenty of time. But Kathleen, unaware that she, too, would have to walk, arrived very foot-sore – she had come out in high heels.[19]

A few days later, Judith had to take to her bed again, this time with bronchitis, and Meredith was left to her own devices. This was a "great education for her",[20] as she went out exploring by herself and bringing back newspapers, pamphlets and manifestos. But by now Judith was beginning to be anxious, since there was a deadline to meet, a lecture to give in London for the British Council and there seemed no hope of getting out. There were no trains and no flights in or out of Paris. The only possible way was to catch a bus to Brussels and fly from there to London. But there was only one small bus to Brussels, and tickets were almost impossible to come by.[21]

Judith was still not well enough to go out, so Meredith went off, day after day, to try for a ticket at Cook's Travel Agency, which was "full of terrified tourists". The Americans were especially agitated since they had never been very popular in Paris and were now being shown that very clearly. They had plenty of money, however, so they were the ones who managed to get tickets. Small as she was and not very assertive, Meredith had no chance competing against their size, agitated aggression and money. But after several days a sympathetic clerk noticed her in the scrum, beckoned her forward and she got the tickets.

The next problem was to reach the bus, which left some distance from their hotel. Their luggage was heavy and with no transport available, it looked as if they would have to walk, dragging their luggage over the cobblestones. In the end, the hotel proprietor offered to drive them in his own car, though only part of the way since petrol was scarce. After that they "staggered [several kilometres] along the street with [their] enormous suitcases ... and finally managed to load themselves on to the bus",[22] exhausted. In Brussels when they finally got there, there were the same crowds of panicky tourists, mostly Americans, at the airport, clamouring for tickets to London. By spending the night at the airport the McKinneys finally managed to board a flight and arrived, somewhat the worse for wear, at Heathrow.

It had been an interesting time, for all its difficulties, and Judith looked back with interest, keeping copies of the newspapers, cuttings from them and many of the pamphlets Meredith had brought back from her forays. Judith read French, so had been able to follow what was happening, concluding that the students had wanted to go further than the workers who had finally come to an agreement with the government. Their lives and livelihoods were at risk, she understood, as the students' were not, and she drew the somewhat gloomy conclusion that "revolution is practically impossible now that money is power and power is money". The original French Revolution had brought down the French royalty and aristocracy. But the power which the 1968 revolutionaries challenged was not only worldwide but also more or less omnipotent. "To bring down the whole world's trade and interest", Judith concluded, "is beyond the scope of any new movement."[23]

That did not bode well for environmentalists in their struggle against international as well as national financial interests. Nevertheless in England Judith visited Peter Scott, the renowned naturalist and environmentalist, at his wildlife sanctuary on the banks of the Severn River, hoping to convince him of the need for international support, financial support especially, in the struggle to save the Reef. Alison Büsst, John's wife, on an overseas trip with Harold Holt's widow, Dame Zara, was also to visit him on the same mission, later. Judith did not find Scott very encouraging since he believed that the fact that the earth's resources were dwindling was making international companies and their allies more desperate to exploit whatever they found. Environmentalists, therefore, were up against overwhelming odds. In the present struggle the best they could do was to save parts of the Reef. But its exploitation, he thought, was more or less inevitable.

After this depressing meeting, a trip to Scotland lifted Judith's spirits. There she revived her "MacGregorhood", which she had first explored in 1937. The most interesting moment of this exploration occurred on a trip in a "broken-down-bus-line" through the Braes of Balquhidd, an area "long lost to the MacGregors" and now "infested" by Campbells. As they passed a ruined fort on an island that once belonged to the MacGregors a "lady arose in the back of the bus", announcing "I'll have ye know that I'm a Campbell and anyone speaking' ill o' the Campbells will have ME tae reckon with." According to Meredith, Judith muttered "And I'm a MacGregor" but Judith herself doesn't think she would have dared to do so: "They remember long in Scotland as in Ireland."[24]

In other ways, however, Scotland felt different from the country Judith had known thirty years earlier, "peculiar, like a left-over from the Stuarts as far as arguments and complexities go", apart from the rest of the world, as it had not seemed thirty years earlier. There were strikes here, too, but the poverty (before the North Sea oil boom) and the sense of old wars and grudges troubled her. London, when they returned, was troubling also. The weather, too, was depressing: the skies "seemed like an old grey sponge most of the time" and their coughs returned. But Judith had business to do there.

After Jack's death she had put together the manuscript of the book he had been working on and in London she hoped to find a publisher for it – there was little chance of publishing a work of philosophy in Australia. Charles Osborne, a friend from Barjai days in Brisbane, was now an important figure in the literary scene, editor of the *London Magazine*, amongst other things, and with his help she managed to place the book, *The Structure of Modern Thought*, which appeared in 1971.

Meantime Meredith had bought a knapsack and gone off on her own. Once again, Judith thought that "fair enough". Young people needed adventure and independence, she believed, remembering her own travels. True, the world now seemed much more dangerous than it had been when she had hitch-hiked through Scotland and slept on the London Embankment, but she refused to impose her fears on her daughter. They parted in Stratford whence Judith went off to Ireland to stay in Cork with a Wyndham cousin living there. Somewhat to her surprise she enjoyed herself, responding to the free and easy pace of life and the beauties of the countryside. It was a break from the sense of crisis, the hope and despair she had sensed elsewhere, the uprisings, strikes and mass protests against the Vietnam War.

In the United States Martin Luther King had been murdered on 4th April and the Columbia University student demonstrations had broken out at the end of that month and continued on into May, predating the Paris students' demonstrations. Then on 5th June Robert Kennedy was assassinated, and at the end of August the Democratic Convention in Chicago took place in the midst of violent anti-Vietnam demonstrations and social and sexual protests of all kinds. In Europe, on 21st August, Russian troops had invaded Czechoslovakia, putting an end to the "Prague Spring". In London, however, Judith had not felt "much revolutionary fervour, except for a few Vietnam groups", though she admitted that where they had been staying, Earls Court, was "no place to observe the reactions of the ordinary Londoner since there aren't any here; we are mostly black, brown and yellow". Ireland seemed a world of its own and she was able briefly to relax there.

When she returned to London to meet up with Meredith again, Judith found it dirty and overcrowded, very different from the glittering city she had remembered in 1937. There were "too many people" who seemed much too docile, "lined up [in queues] for hours". She was beginning to long for home, to get back to "Calanthe" "in time to plant spring vegetables: oh joy".[25] Their money was running out, too. Meredith, who was having a good time, would have liked to stay on, but she, too, missed "home".

On the return trip, she flung herself with gusto into shipboard life while Judith spent most of her time in a deckchair writing, getting back to work, enjoying her solitude and preserving her equanimity – on the ship there were "rather too many people [she] didn't want to communicate with".[26] Since the Suez Canal was still closed they returned by way of the Cape of Good Hope, where Judith agreed to join a trip through the vineyards outside Cape Town. But the glimpses she caught of the squalor in which the blacks were forced to live under the apartheid system appalled her, even though she had tried to "avert her eyes".[27] She decided to make no further trips ashore. Judith was equally appalled when the whites she met told her complacently that South Africa and Australia were alike and that the whites of the two countries had a great deal in common. At their next port of call, Durban, Judith hoped to meet Helen Jacob, one of the leading white opponents of apartheid. She was looking forward to the meeting, but when the ship arrived in Durban she found that Jacob was under house arrest and was not allowed visitors. So Judith stayed on board, leaving Meredith and her friends to enjoy themselves ashore.

Arriving back in Australia and disembarking in Fremantle, one of the first sights to greet them was a car with a "Save the Barrier Reef" bumper sticker – one of the stickers produced by the Littoral Society. It was a reminder of the struggle and the work that lay ahead. The thought of this work had been with Judith throughout their travels and she was keen to catch up with developments, so she arranged to return to Mount Tamborine by way of.Cairns, flying through the north-west and around the Top End. In Cairns she arranged to see John Büsst, who would brief her.

But first there was a literary luncheon in Perth, organised jointly by the *West Australian* and the University of Western Australia's Extension Department. Writing to her in June about arrangements for the lecture, the director of extension had told that he envied her her experience of "the French Revolution", and echoed her distaste for consumer society which seemed to him to be "destroying the consumer", urging her to be radical in what she said and in particular, "to continue [her] attacks on academics ... Be a poet and woman", he wrote, "not an obstinate old Black Orpington (grey feathered) in the pecking order of our wretched pedagogic fowl yard."[28] Judith obliged, attacking once again the insensitivities of teachers and academics and pleading for the preservation of the environment, especially the forests of the south-west. Once again the *West Australian* reported her as doing so, troubling local sensibilities.

Leaving Perth, Judith and Meredith flew north to Port Hedland, where the development of the iron-ore resources of the Pilbara was just beginning. Lang Hancock, the mining entrepreneur largely responsible for these developments, was a champion of nuclear power and proposed using it to deepen the harbour, then under construction – not a proposal to please Judith. Nevertheless, they stayed for several days since she wanted to meet some of the local Aboriginal people. This did not happen, however, since the mine had increased tensions between Aborigines and non-Aborigines in an area where tensions already existed – the Pilbara had seen one of the first strikes by Aboriginal stockmen in the 1950s, organised by the legendary Don McLeod who was still alive and still encouraging Aboriginal people to claim their rights. These tensions were to continue and even escalate in the 1970s. When the Whitlam Government made it compulsory to pay Aboriginal stockmen the same as whites, most Aborigines were turned off the stations, usually the land on which they had lived from time immemorial which they regarded as theirs, even though they had been prepared, perforce, to share it with the pastoralists. Alienated, unemployed and embittered, they drifted to the fringes of towns nearby. Things became difficult for the pastoralists also, short of labour and faced with new costs. So it was not surprising that during her brief stay Judith was offered a station nearby for $2000. Interested at first, she discovered that the area was part of the port development, so the deal fell through.

After that, hopping from stop to stop, some of them outback stations where the plane landed to deliver mail and sometimes take on passengers, and sometimes staying overnight, Judith and Meredith went on their way, arriving at Cairns several days later. The holiday was over.

According to John Büsst, there was still a sense of euphoria over the success in stopping mining on Ellison Reef. But they had lost an important ally when the Prime Minister, Harold Holt, had drowned off Portsea in Victoria in 1967. No one knew which way his successor, John Gorton, would go, whether he was sympathetic to the environmental cause or not. But Büsst was keen to honour the memory of his friend Holt with a travelling scholarship for marine biology and ecology. He was also hopeful that if Gorton was sympathetic they might have the whole Reef declared a National Park and in each State a National Wilderness Area gazetted, fronting onto a Marine National Park.

It was clear, however, that these long-term goals would have to be put off for the moment because of more immediate concerns. The

Queensland Government seemed determined to press ahead immediately with the economic exploitation of the Reef. Even before Judith had left Australia, Büsst and Arthur Fenton, secretary of the WPSQ, had reported that most of the 1900 kilometres of the Queensland coastline had been quietly leased to developers by the Queensland Government, as they had discovered in a prospectus for Planet Metals they had accidentally come across.[29] To add to their worries, the oil crisis of the early 1970s was looming, and oil exploration was the latest fashion in "development". Disturbingly there were thought to be significant resources of oil in the Great Barrier Reef area. As Kathleen McArthur wrote, looking back:

> In the sixties and early seventies the conservation ethic had not yet become trendy; its numbers were small and of uncertain strength due to opposition. "Ratbag" was the usual tag attached to anyone who championed the conservation cause and who were earnestly warned against being branded so. In time it became a party-political mud-slinging pastime to the ridiculous extent of being accused of being paid by the KGB! ... Male chauvinism added to the insult, for a macho could not be expected to discuss anything on the ecology of a coral reef, coastal management, biological divinity, etcetera, with a woman. For the next decade [therefore environmentalists like themselves were] under great pressure.[30]

But Judith had been roused by the sight of the land below her as she flew north from Perth. It was, and always would be, part of her:

> *Rose-red a thousand miles*
> *my country passed beneath.*
> *Curved symmetry of dunes*
> *echo my ribs and hands.*
> *I am those worn red lands.*[31]

For its sake and for Meredith and her children she would continue to fight.

The meeting with Büsst confirmed this determination, and so did the return to "Calanthe", to live there for the first time since Jack's death. The butterflies were still there in the garden,

> ...*Lifted by air and dream*
> *they rose and circled into heaven's slipstream*
>
> *to seek each other over fields of blue.*[32]

The flame-tree Jack had planted was also still standing, with its

> *extravagant fans; sheltered in it the spider weaves*
> *and birds move through it ...*
>
> *every capacity in it, every power,*
> *drawing up from the very roots of being*
> *this pulse of total red that shocks my seeing*
> *into an agony of flower.*[33]

This return and this pulse of life reminded her also of the future of her responsibilities to young people like Meredith, whose voices speak in "Massacre of the Innocents" written about this time:

> *We speak with the voice*
> *of your daughters, your sons,*
> *We look through the eyes*
> *of all innocent ones.*
> *We are spring, which soon dies.*[34]

So she decided not to go back to university teaching, though she was asked to do so, but to concentrate on conservation issues. The fact that for the moment poetry seemed to have deserted her helped this decision. As she said later:

> When your husband dies this makes an awful gap in your life ...
> Jack had always been my audience, the person I wrote for. [So] I
> could not start writing poetry again for some time.[35]

Meredith had decided to take a year off, learning typing and shorthand in Brisbane before she went to Canberra to the Australian National University to do Asian Studies. Judith found her a flat in Brisbane – useful to Judith as a pied-à-terre when she came to WPSQ meetings on Tuesday evenings; there would be no need now to drive back alone in the dark to Mount Tamborine. Money, as usual, was a consideration. For the moment Judith's books were selling quite well and she had enough to live on, but she needed to look to the future. She wrote to Frank Eyre at Oxford University Press, telling him that she would like "to get another book or two on your lists", though writing might be difficult. She was "plagued with visitors who just drop in to see what a poet looks like",[36] but she told Eyre that she was confident she would come up with something

> if the telephone would stop ringing, the post stop coming, visitors forget my address and all my multifarious commitments straighten themselves out. I feel like the Pigeon in "Alice" who, if you remember, built his nest in the tree tops to get away from Serpents, only to find them come wriggling down from the skies.[37]

For the moment it seemed as if Judith would have to concentrate on prose. Poems would still come from time to time, as she told Finola Moorhead, "like butterflies flitting by her nose", but she was "too busy [and] had to look away" and get on with her other work. In 1969 she worked with Val Vallis on a manuscript of John Shaw Neilson's unpublished poems, assembled by Ruth Harrison, which was published the next year as *Witnesses of Spring* with an introduction by Judith. She returned to the lecturing circuit and addressed the Fellowship of Australian Writers at the invitation of Manning Clark in Canberra. Judith was also invited to contribute to a Sydney theatrical group, Flashpoint, who were commissioning a series of short plays to "stimulate thinking", though there is no record that she wrote anything for them.

But the environment was claiming more and more of her energies, and these claims seemed to be everywhere, even in apparently trivial matters, like an advertisement for Qantas she had noticed not long after her return from Europe which featured as tourist attractions the Ord River (where the Court Government's dam was, she believed, having disastrous effects on the environment) and the brigalow belt in Queensland, also being wrecked by "development". As she wrote tartly to the airline, she thought it "undesirable to give the impression overseas that Australians have little concern for the conservation of their natural heritage … A surprising number of people overseas want to see the natural Australia".[38]

What was happening to both of those areas in fact provoked two of her angriest poems, "Jet Flight over Derby" and "Australia 1970", which opens:

> *Die, wild country, like the eaglehawk,*
> *dangerous till the last breath's gone,*
> *clawing and striking. Die*
> *cursing your captor through a raging eye.*[39]

– the latter poem inspired by the sight of the brigalow country she loved, and which her father also loved, being cleared by bulldozers and tractors with chains.

A new attack on the Reef was also beginning. The Great Barrier Reef Committee, a small committee of scientists, for many years the only organisation concerned with the Reef as a whole, had asked the State Government to fund a biological survey of the Reef, thinking that biologists would be unlikely to favour "development". Instead the government commissioned a survey by an American geologist who had no biological qualifications, apart from the fact that he collected shells as a hobby.[40] His report had not been released when Judith visited Büsst on her way home, but they feared the worst since a geologist was likely to be sympathetic to mining – as the report proved to be. It was strenuously attacked, however, by scientists of international repute like the American, Dr Fred Grassle, then working in Queensland, who later returned to the Woods Hole Oceanographic Institution in the United States, and Professor Joe Connell, also an oceanographer, from California. Grassle, in particular, was to become a firm ally and an important resource in the battle. But their attacks seemed to be having little effect either on the State Government or on the oil companies already at work surveying the Reef.

The crown of thorns starfish epidemic was also spreading, with disastrous consequences. The wreck that year of an oil tanker, the *Torrey Castle*, off the south coast of England and the damage it did to the environment had dramatised the disastrous consequences oil drilling might have for the Reef and also pointed to the threat posed by the growing number of tankers navigating the dangerous waters of the Reef. But the advocates of "development" were stepping up their efforts and attacking environmentalists. Premier Bjelke-Petersen accused them of being in the pay of "Communists" working "to overthrow the Australian way of life" and these attacks were gaining some credence. Kathleen McArthur, for instance, reported being confronted by a complete stranger in the street demanding to know, "Who pays you?"[41]

The threat to the Great Barrier Reef was not the only one which troubled Judith and her friends; the area around Cooloola was in danger also. Early in 1967 a permit to mine for mineral sands had been granted, involving 11,500 acres of the dunes. Later that year the company involved issued a prospectus preparatory to listing on the stock exchange, stating that "after 1974 ... the company will also commence mining high dune areas around Gympie".[42] Kathleen McArthur alerted the WPSQ to this proposal and they began working to oppose the granting of any mining licences and to stop this particular project. Despite this, towards the end of 1968 further proposals were put forward to "develop" the low-lying part of the Cooloola State forest between the high dunes and the Noosa River by stocking it with cattle, the developers arguing that it was an empty space which could be rendered productive. From an ecological point of view it was no such thing, being crucial to the ecology of the whole region, providing "an essential wildflower and honey flora component".[43] It was also extremely fragile and would, they believed, be destroyed by grazing.

There was a clear clash of values. Bjelke-Petersen's Government was intent on economic development: "Where there are minerals," the Minister for Mines declared, "it is our duty to encourage extraction",[44] and he quoted figures showing that the mineral sand industry had already earned the State $3,458,385. Similarly, supporters of the cattlemen pointed to the contribution that industry made to the economy. In their opposition to these proposals, the environmentalists did not deny that they might generate wealth. But they questioned "the wisdom of ignoring the values of the future for the sake of the quick profit of the present",[45] quoting a range of scientific opinion which testified to the uniqueness of the ecology and vegetation of the area and also to its tourist potential, pointing out that sand dunes like those of this area were "found nowhere else in Australia, and, indeed, nowhere else in the world". They also cited scientific evidence. Dr F. W. Whitehouse, for instance, a consulting geologist, wrote that the dunes had been "formed in a bygone age and are not being formed today. They are irreplaceable."[46] Len Webb also testified that this was an essential area for the study of coastal and rainforest growth on low fertility sands and an important ecological junction since it marked the northern limit of distribution of a large number of plant species.[47]

Judith agreed with these scientific arguments, but her feelings were also personal. This was the area she had travelled through with Jack in the 1950s, and which had inspired the poem, "At Cooloolah". As she had written then

> ... no land is lost or won by wars,
> for earth is spirit: the invader's feet will tangle
> in nets there and his blood be thinned by fears.[48]

For her the issue was a life and death matter, but her growing friendship with the Aboriginal writer, Kath Walker, was also making her more sensitive to these issues as Aboriginal people began to make claims on land which had been taken from them. Shortly after Jack's death, Kath had shared with Judith her dream of establishing an Aboriginal Culture Centre where her people might recover their roots and also share something of their culture with non-Aboriginal Australians.

At the time this seemed an almost impossible dream. Quite apart from lack of money, in Queensland Aboriginal people could not legally own land, even if they had the financial resources. This discovery shocked Judith and she determined to do all she could to help Kath get the land and her centre established. For the next year or so she drove around with Kath looking for suitable places – when they found one, of course, the next step would be to get legal possession.

Judith learned a great deal from this time. On one occasion, she took Kath to a bora ring she had discovered some years earlier on the Queensland–New South Wales border. When they got there, however, a road and several fences had cut across the site, virtually destroying it. They were shocked at this vandalism. Another time, further down the Border Ranges they came upon a rock shelter, which had evidently been a ceremonial place of some importance, but there had also been a massacre there – the ground was strewn with the remains of spent cartridges. In this way Judith was beginning to see more and more of the other side of the history of pastoral expansion, in which her family had been involved and which she had written about.

From time to time Kath would come to stay at "Calanthe" to write or just for a break, and at night they would have long sessions talking on Judith's verandah or in her kitchen over a bottle of Scotch. In this way she learned more about Kath's feeling for the land, coming to understand more fully the Aboriginal sense that people do not own the land but are owned by it. In this way the differences between their views and those of non-Aboriginal Australians were growing clearer, and with it an awareness of the ways in which Aboriginal people and the land had suffered. As far as the land was concerned, as Judith put it some years later in the Tasmanian Wilderness Calender, she now realised that:

> We owe [the land] repentance and such amends as we can make, and one last chance of making those amends is to keep as much of it as we can, in the closest state we can to its original beauty ... a place where we can find some kind of rest, joy, and even forgiveness.[49]

None of these arguments carried much weight with the advocates of "development" or with the government. Indeed, speaking in Parliament in 1969, the Queensland Minister for Mines showed how little he understood the nature or drift of this kind of argument, which was based not only on these Aboriginal beliefs but also on the fact that the whole area constituted a complex ecosystem and that to damage any part of it was to damage the whole. In his view the environmentalists' opposition was merely aesthetic, inspired by a love for wildflowers and wildlife. Defending the developers he assured "hon. members that if one gets into the centre of eight acres of scrub one sees just as much as it is possible to see from the centre of a 48,000 acre area of scrub ... I would rather see an attractive orchard laid out by man than scrub left standing".[50] In Judith's view, this was a good example of what she called the "slash and burn mentality", which seemed to be the mentality of the Queensland Government.

But many ordinary people were beginning to share the environmentalists' view. One group, for instance, composed "The Cooloola

Conservation Song", expressing their feeling for the land (although not necessarily in high poetic terms). It begins:

> *We tell you, Mister Minister, before the axe goes through*
> *If you do to Cooloola what you say you're gonna do*
> *And desecrate a wonderland to please a wealthy few,*
> *We tell ya, Mister Minister, we will not vote for you.*[51]

All over the rest of Australia, too, similar groups were springing up, equipped with little but enthusiasm but determined to make a difference. In the event, the Cooloola Campaign became a model of grass roots action. It was led by the Caloundra branch of the WPSQ and by Kathleen McArthur, its indefatigable secretary, who organised a campaign of postcards to the Premier. The wording was simple:

> Your Government's failure to declare the whole of Cooloola a National Park, in the face of mounting public pressure, is deplorable.
>
> The only acceptable use for this unique wilderness is its immediate dedication as a National Park.[52]

People had only to sign the card, give their address and, encouraged by the slogan, "Spend Five Cents to Save Cooloola", post it. WPSQ members throughout the State were also mobilised for local action, knocking on doors to gain support and encourage people to send postcards as well. With an election in the wind, the campaign was successful: Bjelke-Petersen was nothing if not a good politician and since, as Judith remarked, "a lot of people would have lost their seats over Cooloola,"[53] he gave way. A secret ballot on the issue was held in Parliament and the "developers" were defeated.

Disgruntled, the general manager of the mining company Conzinc Rio Tinto abused the campaign as "the greatest example of mob psychology since Julius Caesar".[54] But Judith and her friends, especially Kathleen McArthur, were jubilant. As Judith had written to Kathleen several years earlier, she preferred "long battles on the right or romantic side, like ours, to winning ones on the nasty side. I suppose it's my Highland blood",[55] but this sweet victory was very pleasing. The campaign also increased her popularity and, at its height, someone wrote to the *Courier Mail* to suggest that if the Cooloola area was saved and made a National Park it should be called the Judith Wright National Park.

In the midst of all this Judith had her worries as the mother of a teenage daughter enjoying her independence. Not long after returning from Europe, Meredith had decided to get her driving licence, asking her current boyfriend (who drove a Mini at racing circuits) to teach her. Judith was a little apprehensive. "Needless to say this paralyses me with terror," she wrote to Barbara Blackman, "but one must venture one's all".[56] But she was prudent also and insisted on paying for professional driving lessons. When she had her licence, of course, Meredith became more independent. But there was no time to lament this, even if Judith had been inclined to do so, since she herself was increasingly busy, "shuttling around the country",[57] addressing meetings and rallies to save the environment. What time she had to spare she spent on her edition of John Shaw Neilson's poems.

All this meant that she was often away from "Calanthe". She felt a certain sense of betrayal, telling Barbara Blackman:

> The cat weeps when I leave, the birds all beat vainly on my window, with young in nest and a dry spell cutting down their foodstuffs, and my mail piles up ... But now I swear to stay round for a bit. I have two swamp pheasants living in the nut trees barking away quietly most of the day, and the whip birds and bowerbirds survived a nasty yellow tomcat somebody dropped on my doorstep, which I keep trying to entice into humane traps to take it away to a vet and which lives in the laundry and makes horrid messes in the washing machine.[58]

But it was difficult to stay at home as the Great Barrier Reef battle intensified and, with it, the need to mobilise public opinion. The Littoral Society was running a campaign of bumper stickers, "Save the Barrier Reef", and by October 1969 15,000 had been sold. They also organised a petition calling on the Queensland Government not to permit any further drilling for oil or gas on the Reef without a proper environmental impact survey and detailed plans for its protection. The petition gained 13,000 signatures in only a few weeks.[59]

There was also good news from Canberra. The new Prime Minister, John Gorton, seemed sympathetic to the cause and on 21st November 1968 the Federal Parliament passed the *Continental Shelf (Living Natural Resources) Act* which went part of the way to claiming the Continental Shelf, and therefore the Great Barrier Reef, for Australia as a whole and gave the Commonwealth responsibility for sedentary living species on the Reef, not only within the twelve-mile limit but up to the outer boundaries of the Reef.[60] Ominously, however, the Minister responsible, Doug Anthony, said nothing about mining in his speech. Equally ominous was the fact that new iron foundries at Kwinana in Western Australian had just been opened to process the iron ore from the Pilbara and that limestone was essential for this process – the Reef was a source of limestone.

In the same month news came of a joint Japanese–Australian survey of the Reef. A small Japanese submarine, the *Yomiuri*, was to carry a number of scientists through Reef waters. This might have been good news, since a survey of the Reef as a whole was something the environmentalists had been pushing for, but the submarine was owned by a Japanese newspaper magnate who also had considerable oil interests.[61] Then, in April 1969, news broke that an American mining company was also about to conduct a survey of the Reef, this time from the air.

There was also talk of new developments elsewhere, in particular woodchipping in Tasmania, and the "first unpleasant reports" began to circulate amongst environmentalists of the way it was devastating the forests there. It seemed that the "true religion" Judith wrote about in a poem published in the *Australian*, October 1969 (to be sung to the tune of "The Church's One Foundation"), was spreading, the religion of the

> *... You Beaut Country*
> *so quality controlled,*
> *with not a dune or forest*
> *that can't be bought or sold.*

The poem concludes by giving the last word to two Queenslanders enthusiastic for "development":

> *So join our congregation;*
> *Australia is our pigeon.*

> *Raise high the hymn to Camm and Sim*
> *"The Buck's the True Religion."*[62]

Judith would contest these attitudes to the end, but was less confident than she had been that the Reef could be saved: international as well as national interests had their eyes on it, and at home the rage for development went from strength to strength. As she wrote later:

> We knew . . . that we were up against an almost impossible task fighting not only international oil companies on the Reef question, but international mining interests too, over the Cooloola mining applications. With our pitiful resources it was very much a David and Goliath job.[63]

To make matters worse, not all of their allies were standing firm – Judith had no time for compromise. The ACF held a symposium on the Reef in May 1969 but, determined to be "non-partisan", they also invited representatives of the oil and mining industries. An "unfortunate statement" by a Queensland member of the Foundation gave the impression that it might not object to drilling on the Reef, provided a scientific study had been made. This kind of fair-mindedness might be all very well in the laboratory or lecture room, but as far as Judith was concerned, they were in the middle of a war. What was at stake, she believed, was survival, and in a battle of that kind no quarter could be asked for or given.

It was also a matter of belief. As she wrote in her essay, "Conservation as a Concept": "what we do with the power given us by the scientific investigation of the basis and processes of nature ... is necessarily and inevitably a moral question, a question of the values we adopt in life as a whole."[64] Her position was clear: as she told the *Australian*, "they'll have to shoot me to stop me".[65]

She was ready to go anywhere to speak or lobby for the cause, directly or indirectly. In September 1969 she was an invited speaker in Melbourne on "Man and His Science", organised to honour Sir Macfarlane Burnet. Other speakers included international figures like the philosopher Peter Medawar and distinguished scientists like Neil Jons and Australian Frank Fenner. In this exalted company Judith argued that the environmental movement held the key to survival, and insisted on the question of values, arguing that the notion of a science that is "value-free" was not only illusory but dangerous. The environmental movement was not something marginal, she argued, but central to the search for

> a new kind of understanding which shall take into account actual living processes and interdependences, and can see man as part of a wider process and subordinate to its laws. What is more, this interest also seems to represent a point at which a new spark can perhaps jump across the gap that at present separates the arts and sciences – to the great detriment of each – and allows a new kind of understanding and cooperation to grow up between them.[66]

It was hard work. But public opinion was becoming more sympathetic, helped by events like the oil spill off Santa Barbara in the United States which occurred in January 1969, drawing attention once more to the damage that could be done to the Reef if something similar occurred there. Closer to home, a blow-out in the Esso oilfield in Bass Strait reinforced that lesson. Judith and her friends kept at it. In August the WPSQ ran a stall at the Brisbane Exhibition which attracted a great deal of interest and a large number of new members. Then, following on from that success, on 2nd October the society launched a "Save the Reef Campaign" at Toowong Town Hall, attended by a large and enthusiastic crowd. Five days later the committee commissioned a poll on the subject of drilling for oil on the Reef, to be conducted with the help of the Psychology and Mathematics departments of the University of Queensland and the scientists of the Littoral Society. Judith drew on her experience with J. Walter Thompson before the war to ensure that the polling was done thoroughly and professionally.

In the meantime the ABC and the quality newspapers were also taking up the cause. The *Australian* commented with heavy sarcasm in an editorial that:

> Conservation this week took a historic step forward ... Mr Camm [Queensland Minister for Mines] revealed that the only way to save the Great Barrier Reef for Australia is to drill it full of oil-wells with the greatest possible speed ...

> The next action must be increased naval patrols to prevent international poaching of our prized Crown of Thorns Starfish, nurtured so carefully on the reef by skilled Governmental vacillation.

All of which suggested, the editorial concluded, in a more serious vein, "that no time need be lost in putting the defensive plan into action".[67]

In October, news came that drilling was about to begin at Repulse Bay, off Mackay, and that drilling permits were still being issued by the Queensland Government. On Christmas Eve, in an editorial the *Australian* once again attacked what it called the "political dereliction", "buck-passing" and "apathy" of the Queensland Government in this matter where public interest and concern had been so thoroughly demonstrated. The Great Barrier Reef, it declared, "must be regarded as a touchstone ... The solutions are not beyond the wit and resources of the nation. All they demand is the will."[68]

Despite this support, over the summer the situation was looking desperate for the defenders of the Reef. There were no Christmas holidays for Wright and her friends and the strain was beginning to tell. Arthur Fenton had been their indefatigable secretary but his health was giving way. He and his wife, Hilda, had given over most of their house to stacks of letters, files and articles on conservation, working night and day at their correspondence and organisational chores. As a result, their private lives as well as their health were suffering and they needed a break.[69] Kathleen McArthur, too, was feeling the strain and suffering from bad attacks of migraine, and Vincent Serventy wrote to Judith expressing his concern for her health. John Büsst, always a heavy smoker, was now threatened with cancer of the throat and his doctor ordered him to rest himself, his voice especially, and keep away from all public activity for several months. Though he refused to give in, he was at least slowed down and made a little less vocal. At a meeting held in Brisbane early in January, when he was on his way through to Melbourne to see a specialist, John talked only "in a semi-whisper to save his threatened larynx".[70]

At this desperate stage, however, new allies appeared. In January the Queensland Trades and Labour Council (John Büsst had been working on them before he became ill) imposed a black ban on all drilling on the Reef. This would effectively stop it since without transport and union labour the mining companies would not be able to proceed. Moreover, the *Australian* noted, this was, for once, a union ban which was likely to "have an unprecedented measure of public support [which] it deserves to".[71]

The State Government, according to Judith's account, was now "thoroughly alarmed" and began its own counter-propaganda, reminding people of the financial cost of the ban to Mackay and the jobs and general contribution to the economy which the oil companies would make. The government also declared that compensation would have to be paid to mining companies if the leases were not available to them and that this would put a burden on taxpayers. But public opinion stood firm, and even in the Mackay area 1304 people were prepared to sign a petition against drilling.[72] Supporting this opposition, the *Australian* referred its readers to recent events in the United States where the people were "insisting on a reordering of national priorities". In Australia, too, it said, "we ignore or miscalculate the significance of this movement at our peril", predicting "that the quality of the environment will become a major issue of our time".[73]

The general mood certainly seemed to be changing. Even the Great Barrier Reef Committee, hitherto relatively quiet, but the only organisation officially charged with the Reef's protection, spoke out against mining through its Chair, Dr Bob Endean, who warned of the incalculable damage that would be caused by oil spills. The *Australian* backed this up with a long article by the scientist Eddie Hegerl, one of those who had been involved in the original dive to prove that Ellison Reef was not "dead", detailing the dangers drilling posed to the Reef. The Federal member for North Queensland, Dr Patterson of the ALP, joined the debate, demanding that the Commonwealth Government give an unqualified assurance that it would not ratify any permits already issued by the State to drill on the Reef. Support was also coming from overseas, not only from scientists but also from people like the residents of Santa Barbara, shocked by the devastation caused by the oil spills along their coastline.

In Melbourne tests were to show that Büsst's throat condition had almost completely cleared up. He was triumphant, writing that "I feel like The Man They Could Not Hang", announcing that he was back to work and was about to talk to Sir John Barry (who had coined the phrase, Australia would soon be "a quarry surrounded by an oil slick"). He was also to give evidence in Canberra to a Senate Select Committee on Offshore Petroleum Resources which was being conducted by the Federal Parliament. The reprieve, he wrote, had given him "an enormous increase in useful energy". In any case he had no intention of giving in to illness or keeping silent, joking that he "must have talked too much or swallowed too much 'dead coral' over the past year [but that] you can't keep a good man dumb". If he should fall ill again, he intended to "get them to graft a loud hailer on to my navel". "The Bingal Bay Bastard" still had plenty of fight left in him. "I don't give a bugger for anybody," he declared, "and I'll stick my neck out to the limit."[74]

Help came from other quarters also. Judith's old friend Charles Blackman, now an artist of note, contributed a drawing of a forest of derricks and pepperheads sprouting from the Reef to the *Sydney Morning Herald* on Saturday 10th January 1970 as an illustration of some lines from a poem Judith was working on at the time:

> *I crush the Reef. Its coral cool*
> *darkened where my shadow fell.*
> *The fronded live anemone*
> *furled itself and shrank from me.*
> *For death's my servant and my tool*
> *and, like my shadow, follows me.*[75]

Both Judith and Charles donated what they were paid for their contribution to the Save the Reef Campaign.

Judith's standing as a poet was also an asset, of course, and she was not afraid to use this influence to confront politicians. In reply to one of her presentations, for instance, Prime Minister Gorton wrote a personal letter to say that although constitutionally the Commonwealth had little power over the States, he would do all he could to preserve the environment. Nor was this influence only at the Federal level. That year Judith confronted the Queensland Minister for Justice over the case of someone arrested for bringing firearms into a National Park – forbidden under the Act – and who then had been let off without facing trial.[76]

Quite apart from the political interference she suspected here, she was outraged by the lack of concern for the inviolability of National Parks which needed protection from careless intruders. As Queensland's "Famous Australian Poet", she was not afraid to speak out, despite the repressive atmosphere.

Not all her friends understood her position. Some thought she was exhausting herself and wasting her time and talents on political issues, and that she ought to give more time and energy to her poetry. Even Dorothy Green, herself an activist, told her that she hated "to read of you vanishing under the wild waves of conservation".[77] But this kind of criticism had little effect, especially now that, with the intervention of the trade unions, the tide seemed to be turning in the battle for the Reef. "For once", she wrote, "it seemed, Australia was not only up there with the best of them, but a jump ahead. No trades union in US, that we knew of, had considered taking this kind of action."[78]

Just at this dramatic point, Judith left for a visit to India with a group of writers and academics: Leonie Kramer, James McAuley, George Russell (Professor of English at the Australian National University), and the poet Rodney Hall. The visit had been arranged sometime earlier and Judith had been delighted then to think of meeting Indian writers, visiting Indian universities and attending a five-day seminar in New Delhi. It was a curiously assorted delegation. Leonie Kramer (whom she had first met when she was a young lecturer at what was then University College in Canberra) and George Russell were academics pure and simple, James McAuley, whom she had known at University, was a poet as well as an academic but someone whose politics were very different from hers, while Rodney Hall was an old friend and ally, especially in the fight against racism. Judith was interested to revisit India – she and Meredith had passed through on their way to Pakistan a few years earlier, and she and Jack had been very interested in Hindu thought in the 1950s. Meredith came with her since she was to do Asian Studies in the New Year at the Australian National University.

Nevertheless, Judith's thoughts as they set out were mixed, and she saw India with half her mind on the battles she had left behind in

Australia. Most Australians, she reflected, saw India as a country with "unsolvable problems", but in her view our problems would "be as bad, very soon, though differently so" if the environmental crisis and other problems she was becoming aware of, like the treatment of our Aboriginal and Islander peoples, were not resolved. Perhaps things might even be worse since, unlike India, non-Aboriginal Australia "had produced no religion, no philosophy and little art". Our brief history was "a rage of purely material exploitation", and our treatment of our "Aboriginal precursors was at least as bad as India's treatment of the lowest of its outcasts". We thought of ourselves as educated and enlightened, but in Judith's view, unless we drastically changed direction, we, too, would soon reach "their . . . point of poverty, land exhaustion and over-population. And in doing so, we would have contributed far less to the world than India had done."[79]

On their way north to Singapore they had flown over the Centre, and what she had felt flying over the north-west after her return to Europe – her love for the land and grief for it – came back, as she looked down on the land below her:

> *I cross this ravelled shore*
> *and sigh: there's man no more.*
> *Only a rage, a fear,*
> *smokes up to darken air.*
> *"Destroy the earth! Destroy.*
> *There shall be no more joy."*[80]

In fact, India did her good. At the Poetry Conference in Montreal she had had long discussions about Hindu and Islamic philosophy with poets from India and Pakistan, and had been corresponding with several Indian academics who were admirers of her poetry, regarding her as something of a guru – many of the themes of her poetry, especially her preoccupation with fire, seemed to them in tune with Indian culture.

Leonie Kramer, George Russell and James McAuley were "firm upholders of the Raj", enjoying themselves as distinguished visitors. But Judith and Rodney Hall were determined to see and learn as much as they could of the life of the ordinary people and in their free time would explore the streets and bazaars as well as the museums. The heat, the smells, the lithe bodies and dark faces, the colours of the women's saris, the "magic of it all", fascinated Wright as Indonesia had done as a child, though she found the poverty appalling. They even dared eat and drink from time to time from street stalls. Ironically, however, it was not they but the other members of the party, who were much more careful, who fell ill. James McAuley in particular was unwell for much of the time, and on his return he was found to be seriously ill.

The group travelled mostly by train, from Delhi to Bombay first of all and then across India from Bombay to Mysore in the South. But this travel was not always as exclusive as their hosts had meant it to be. On one occasion, Judith, Meredith and Rodney arrived before the others to catch the train to Mysore to find that a carriage had been reserved for "Mrs Judith Wright and Party". This kind of segregation did not appeal, so Rodney removed the notice and "people streamed in, sat at our feet, fed their babies and so on", to their enjoyment,[81] though presumably to the discomfort of other members of their party. This desire to mix with the people was not mere romanticism, however, since Judith really wanted to understand the country; any alternative to the aggressive materialism she saw developing in Australia seemed worth exploring. As she put it to a friend after her return:

> India blows your mind and is in many ways the end ... I made friends there with writers and mystics and would like to end my days sitting in contemplation on a Himalayan foothill ... It was very downcasting ... to come back to the materialist society.[82]

Nevertheless she also saw and remembered the other side of it: "the little girls begging in the streets of Bombay, obviously never washed in their lives, and the occasional corpses". Nor could she get out of her mind the ragged forests around Bangalore or the state of game park near Mysore and of the remnants of the hill tribes they saw there. But the religious sense which pervaded culture and society attracted her: "You can't escape the gods in India where, of course, they all congregate if they have got good enough Karma in their past lives, before they move into the infinite." At the same time she remained a sceptic, writing to Len Webb that:

> I'm not against gods myself, nice engaging creatures some of them, but their intellectual capacities never seem to have been developed in line with their divinity and I can't believe in divine morons ... though divine fools are okay.[83]

For all that, the culture she glimpsed on this trip appealed far more than the technological destructiveness which seemed to her to be the mark of contemporary Western culture, the coldness of which she summed up in one of her poems in the figure of a dead astronaut circling the earth, "a hollow wingless seed, a seed of death".[84]

Despite our affluence, she felt Australians were "in the claws of far more sinister predators than the tigers [which were] rapidly being eaten out" in India,[85] especially in Queensland where the government seemed hell-bent on economic development, whatever the human and environmental cost.

The Barrier Reef battle, however, seemed to have reached a stalemate for the time being. No one was clear about the exact extent of the Commonwealth's power over the actions of State governments, or indeed which of them had ultimate authority for the Reef itself, so a conference had been called. But public opinion was on the environmentalists' side. In February a by-election was held in the State seat of Albert on the Gold Coast, traditionally a very safe seat for Premier Bjelke-Petersen's National Party, a three-cornered contest between the Country Party, the Liberals and the Labor Party. In the campaign, however, the Reef became the crucial issue, with both Liberals and Labor distancing themselves from the State Government's policies of "development". As a result the Liberal candidate was elected, though Labor had also put up an unexpectedly good showing. Clearly opposition to mining the Reef was a vote winner.

Not long afterwards, the State Government set up a Royal Commission to investigate the whole issue. The mining and financial companies' interests involved would be able to pay the best lawyers to represent their interests, but the WPSQ decided that they must also make submissions, although their resources could not match their opponents. A well-known Brisbane law firm, Lippiatt and Company, however, offered to prepare their case pro bono. So for several months the WPSQ coordinating committee, which Judith chaired as president of the society, met once a week with the lawyers to prepare their case – a time-consuming business but one which ultimately paid off.

In the meantime, at the beginning of the year, Judith travelled to Adelaide as a guest of the Writers' Festival to speak about poetry in the 1970s, insisting on the need to return to belief in the value of human beings and of the natural world. They were essential, she declared, to the growth of the imagination, which was in turn the key to our survival. During the festival she also spoke at a seminar organised at Adelaide University on Conservation and Politics, seeing these concerns as an aspect of her work as a poet. Poetry, she insisted, was

> a human creative activity, not an academic subject of study ... [which] works against the dehumanising effects of science, technology and the urban industrial society. The time is short if we are to reimagine a world again worth living in. We are deprived of the life of the senses and feelings [and] a change of heart is more and more urgent.[86]

This change of heart, which Jack had looked for, also meant putting the living world back at the centre of things, not to be dominated and destroyed, but to be respected and conserved. The poet's contribution was central if this change was to occur; she must be a kind of ambassador and spokeswoman for the natural world, otherwise silent, which they must fight to preserve. Accordingly, in November she wrote an open letter to Prime Minister Gorton and the Premier of Queensland, asking for "a complete policy change towards the use and misuse of this country, its soils, waters, forests, air, littorals and wild life, before it is too late", declaring that we needed a new legislative approach, demanding that finance be set aside for conservation: "We must no longer allow this country to be overridden by the demands of short term exploitation for the few or for local profits".[87]

Judith was becoming something of a national figure. In April she was elected a Fellow of the Australian Academy of Humanities for her international reputation as a poet and for her critical and scholarly work – she had just delivered the Chris Brennan Memorial Lecture, one of the first scholars to honour his significance as a poet, as she had been one of the first to write about Charles Harpur, Henry Kendall and John Shaw Neilson and rehabilitate their reputations. Her austerity, energy and integrity also inspired many young poets, young women especially. As Finola Moorhead recalls her impact:

> The daydream, the emotionality of belief and hope, the grand themes, the abstract themes [dear to many who wanted to be poets] bore no resemblance to her clarity. The word-craft, the rhythm, serenity. The authority.

For young women like her, Judith's political persona added to this authority, giving her work a moral, not merely aesthetic dimension. As Moorhead continues:

> Her political work on the environment and for the indigenous peoples of the world, so indefatigable, so compassionate, so thorough, infused the poems she did capture ... She has the wisdom of age and living ethically.[88]

But this political work did get in the way of poetry, and she was writing less and less of it, with so much other writing to do. She was in frequent correspondence with the Federal Government and Opposition, for instance, and in April was even asked to write a speech for a member of the Queensland Country Party on the kangaroo question, having, as she put it, "worked on him for some time".[89] In the same month she was keynote speaker at a Queensland Liberal Party seminar on environmental conservation and also spoke in Sydney at a meeting organised by the Ryde Municipal Council, chaired by Sir Garfield Barwick, then President of the ACF, on the problems of pollution in Sydney Harbour and the Parramatta River. Later, in June, she took part in two panels, one on the importance of the environment generally for the newly founded Women's Electoral Lobby, and the other on specific conservation issues for the Queensland Institute of Engineers.

True, the prophet was not always honoured in her own country. A protest to the Shire Clerk of Beaudesert about a proposal to chop down trees in the main street of Mount Tamborine to make way for "improvements" only resulted in a letter in which he "advised [that her] ... views would be taken into account".⁹⁰ Yet small gestures by many local people suggested how important she was to them. At a bush picnic organised at Advancetown, not far from Mount Tamborine, for instance, she was presented with a magnificent bouquet to thank her for her "inspirational leadership".⁹¹ Despite all her other commitments, in reply she wrote thanking by name each person who had signed the card.

Involved as she was at the national level, she did not forget her own territory, and at the end of May she embarked on a six-week lecture tour of the Queensland coast with her friend, the poet Nancy Cato, speaking about the dangers of soil depletion. It was not an easy trip since it took her as far north as Cape York and through some difficult country. As she wrote to Barbara Blackman when she was planning the tour:

> [It] sounds very alarming, and I have to take a fan-belt extra for the car and a whole lot of other things whose uses I have no notion of, such as gaskets and valves and spark plugs in case of accident. But I hope to survive. I will be alone part of the journey, Nancy Cato Norman is coming for some of it. Nancy is so cat-like nervous and so frailly beautiful I fear she will break up somewhere and have to be put together by a psychiatrist ... I on the other hand am made of Spanish leather.⁹²

In the event they both survived, and the trip at least provided a break from all she had been doing.

The forthcoming Royal Commission had been demanding a great deal of time and energy; in particular the weekly meetings with the barristers of Lippiatt and Company involved hours of work beforehand, preparing evidence. The WPSQ were also desperately short of money to pay the fares to Brisbane of the expert witnesses they would need to call. All they had in hand was $3000, though they hoped for help from the ACF whose influential patron, the Duke of Edinburgh, was firmly opposed to mining on the Reef. Much time had to go to fund-raising.

The mining companies had the money but the WPSQ felt that they had right on their side. Moreover, the union blockade was proving successful and public opinion was supportive. So Judith could write to Barbara Blackman:

> All goes like a merry-go-round here with tanker spills and marine biologists ringing up about evidence for royal commissions, and states of utter confusion reigning everywhere. Our Premier is now catching it hot from the churches over Sunday drinking but is noticeably more polite to churches than to conservationists from whom he catches it hot over other matters. Conservation now being a bandwagon I have to answer the telephone all the time while previously indifferent people and institutions try to catch the bandwagon too, people like the Victoria League and the Rotary Clubs and the awful bourgeois in general whom I hate from the bottom of my soul all purr their requests for a nice talk. Come Monday luncheon, no pay nor expenses but it is very nice of us to ask you. I kick them circumspectly where it hurts. They waste a lot of my time.[93]

The Royal Commission, when it finally opened, "looked like being a very long job, and a demanding one for us as well as for the commissioners". In the first seven weeks, twenty-three witnesses were heard, and there were more to come.

> Sitting on the benches and chairs along the walls, [they] knew this would be the beginning of a new, but at least as hardworking, phase of the Reef battle [they] had just gone through. [They] had won the battle for public opinion and for a halt of drilling. What lay ahead was another matter.[94]

But the personal cost was beginning to tell. Arthur Fenton, "a quiet mainstay, one of those who never asked for honours", was ill and to die not long afterwards, largely as a result of overwork. His death, Judith said, "darkened and saddened the battle; much of what we ... managed to achieve," she wrote, "was due to him."[95] John Büsst, whom she had visited on her northern trip, was ill again also. Despite the hopeful prognosis he had been given earlier, he was now clearly dying, but undaunted and happy to be at home overlooking his beloved Bingal Bay and the Reef. As the journalist who had covered the Reef story for the *Australian* and knew him well wrote after his death, "happiness was one more year without a sealed road into his private paradise". This feeling, he also wrote, was "infectious; he made so much sense the rest of the world was crazy ... Even the prospect of death was not going to upset his priorities."[96]

Büsst was too ill to come to Brisbane to give evidence at the Royal Commission and died quietly some months later, early in 1971. In his obituary, headed the "Bingal Bay Bastard", published in the *Nation* on 1st May, Barry Wain paid tribute to him:

> The Australian Conservation movement lost an able, dedicated strategist and the human race one of its finer members. He was a man who believed passionately in conservation and was truly outraged at the thought of Nature's destruction.

A memorial was built to him on the hillside overlooking the ocean in front of his home and the piece of rainforest which in his will he left to James Cook University of Townsville. At the request of his wife, Alison, and the Innisfail branch of the WPSQ, Judith wrote the inscription for it:

> *John Büsst*
> *Artist and Lover of Beauty*
> *Who Fought That Man and Nature Might Survive*[97]

Sitting with him on his verandah during the trip, "calm blue seas [stretching] far out to the Barrier", Judith had perhaps remembered her first time on the Reef, staying on Lady Elliot Island with Jack. Certainly she invokes this memory in *The Coral Battleground*:

> On a still blue summer day, with the ultramarine sea scarcely splashing the edge of the fringing reef, I was bending over a single small pool among the corals. Above it, dozens of small clams spread their velvety lips, patterned in blue and fawns, violets, reds and chocolate browns, not one of them like another. In it, sea-anemones drifted long white tentacles above the clean sand, and peacock-blue fish, only inches long, darted in and out of coral branches of all shapes and colours. One blue sea-star lay on the sand floor. The water was so clear that every detail of the pool's crannies and their inhabitants was vivid, and every movement could be seen through its translucence. In the centre

> of the pool, as if on stage, swayed a dancing creature of crimson and yellow, rippling all over like a wind-blown shawl. That was the Spanish Dancer ... For me it became an inner image of the Reef itself.[98]

Their mutual sense of the threat to it had inspired them both.

> Not a town but was putting undiluted and untreated sewage into creeks and rivers. Oil slicks from ships' tanks were often reported. The Reef was suffering; the illnesses of civilization were already changing it. What chance had we of keeping it as it had been, or even as it is now.[99]

Judith and her friends were determined to continue the struggle.

On the political scene, the situation was beginning to look more hopeful. At the end of June, Prime Minister Gorton promised to help the environmentalists with their legal costs, despite opposition from within his own party, troubled not only by his support for environmentalists but also by his apparent readiness to override States' rights to preserve the Reef – States' rights, of course, were a central article of conservative belief. Not long afterwards, Gorton lost the leadership to William McMahon. But the environment cause, by now, had too much support to be ignored. Besides, at Federal level the conservatives' long reign was coming to an end and a revitalised Labor Party was promising new policies to protect the environment. The general feeling was that change was in the air, summed up in Labor's slogan, "It's Time", and with the Royal Commission in progress even the Queensland Government was obliged to go slowly on its plans for "development".

As it dragged on, moreover, the Royal Commission was proving embarrassing to the government, revealing, for instance, that it had no body of offshore drilling operations in operation and that even the draft regulations which had been prepared were highly inadequate. Other damning pieces of evidence came to light: that the Repulse Bay drilling was to have been conducted from a ship not a platform, for example, and this, "in a region of very high tidal variation and cyclones where a fixed platform would clearly have been safer".[100] Nevertheless, "time wore on and the words piled up, [and] the fate of the Reef lost its immediacy for many, even for environmentalists with other problems to face".[101] The final report of the Royal Commission did not appear until several years later, in 1974, not long before the end of the Whitlam Government. By that time it had not only lost its immediacy but was also a divided report: the chairman maintained that all drilling should be postponed and permitted, if at all, only after further research into its consequences and the other two members accepting that drilling might be permitted in certain parts of the Reef under stringent conditions.[102] It was, as Judith said, a "finale without an ending".[103] A great deal had been achieved, however. The preservation of the Reef had become a matter for national and international concern, and the Whitlam Government had declared the whole Reef a Marine National Park.

In the winter of 1970, in the midst of the battle, Judith's father had died, giving a blessing before he did so on the work she was doing. Always concerned for the environment, even in hospital for the heart problems from which he was to die, he had written to Judith congratulating her on her work to save the Reef and for the environment generally, though, characteristically prudent, he also hoped that she would not have to bear the expense of appearing before the Royal Commission. He told her of his pride as chancellor that some students from the University of New England had appeared at the Royal Commission, though he was equally proud that there had been "no untoward incidents" amongst the student body when the Queen had visited the university[104] – he was always a law and order man. Close, as ever, to his daughter, he also enquired about the progress of Jack's book, which was to be published in London by Chatto & Windus early in the New Year.

Family had always mattered to Judith, however much she might have disagreed with them from time to time, and so had a sense of pride in their achievements – it pleased her that the name the poet Harpur gave to the hero of his unfinished epic was Egremont (the Wyndhams of Dinton were related to Lord Egremont). Especially after Jack's death she had always felt secure in the fact "you could always call on the family".[105] Now her father, the patriarch, was dead. As she had written:

> *Fathers and mothers enter an old pattern,*
> *whoever they are; assume it for the children's*
> *dependent and rebellious eyes.*

But for her this pattern was bound up with memories of

> *... the smell of tweed shoulder sobbed-on,*
> *through picnics, scoldings, moralities imparted*
> *shyly, the sound of songs at a piano –*
> *through all I had to learn and to unlearn,*
> *absorb and fight against; through your love and kindnesses.*[106]

This had shown itself practically, also, in the financial help her father had given her from time to time. In return she had achieved a great deal and made a name for herself in the public world, something which mattered to him.

In his last years he had written his autobiography with her help, and it was published after his death. He had missed out on the kind of education Judith had had, but in its own stilted way the book enabled him to sum up his life:

> I feel that my life has been a more than ordinarily interesting one ... I have lived from the bullock dray horse and buggy period through to the time the world and humanity have undergone tremendous changes, even to the point where the fact that people have landed on the moon is taken for granted ... I have been blessed to an extent that happens to few people. Both of my marriages have been happy ... My children have been all healthy and strong and are taking a foremost part in public and other affairs ... carrying on in many cases the projects that I had a hand in helping along and ... branching out into new fields.[107]

For him it was a satisfactory conclusion. But his death, like his life, left Judith wondering:

> *... He lived long –*
> *so long, I knew him well. Or so I thought;*
> *But now I wonder.*[108]

Yet his influence remained in a world threatened with destruction, in which words like "honour" and "loyalty" had no currency amongst politicians "sliding like [rats]", "profitmakers cheating for position", "these muddy men" she so disliked, in which men like her father and Jack remained unforgettable, a "burst of glory in the world of man". One of her poems written around this time expresses what this memory meant:

> *I call you up, true men who lived and died,*
> *my dead beloved, my guides, my living friends.*
> *I say your names, I sing you to my side.*
> *Keep far from me the sickness of despair.*
> *Even on the last black slope*
> *among mad images that rave or weep,*
> *let all your voices call me back to air:*
> *show me my true beginning and their ends.*[109]

Because of them, she felt, it is "not truly possible to lose faith in life. It's so very much bigger than we are and its purposes aren't the same as ours."[110]

These purposes were beginning to manifest themselves in other, darker ways. Judith had to spend time in hospital, undergoing tests for suspected cancer, and "Communication", written at this time, tells of an encounter there with a woman who was dying:

> *Three days and nights we talked out to each other*
> *our separate pains, deeper than strangers do.*

All the many other things she had been doing fell away:

> *Die as we must, we two were then related*
> *in human honesty and suffering,*

reminding her of her mortality and of her humanity:

> *"The heart is one" (sang Baez); it can get through.*
> *Through the impersonal gabble of exchanges*
> *lights suddenly flash on, the circuit pulses,*
> *joins us together briefly, then estranges.*

Shortly afterwards the woman died, but the memory of the relationship remained:

> *The line goes dead, but still the line is there,*
> *for our reality is in relation.*[111]

Judith was growing older, moving in a new direction, but undaunted:

> *Yes, we still can sing*
> *who reach this barren shore.*
> *But no note will sound*
> *as it did before...*
> *Not the heart directs*
> *what happens to the heart...*

She was aware that she was no longer completely in control of her life, if she ever had been. Perhaps, too, no-one should any longer

> *...take for truth*
> *any word we said.*

But the saying would continue, however austerely:

> *Let the song be bare*
> *that was richly dressed.*
> *Sing with one reserve:*
> *Silence might be best.*[112]

CHAPTER XI

A KIND OF WEAVING

> A kind of weaving
> goes on all the time in houses, its pattern
> determined by the years of taking and giving.
>
> from 'Habitat' IX,
> *Collected Poems*, p. 309

There was a "kind of weaving" going on in Judith's life at this time, between the inner and the outer life, the private and the public, the aesthetic and the ethical. The poem which concludes the first edition of her *Collected Poems*, published in 1971, "Shadow", sums up the process. For a long time, since childhood perhaps, her imagination has been preoccupied with death – paradoxically one of the reasons perhaps why her poetry is so full of images of light. The first atomic bomb and then the development of nuclear power, which opened out the horrifying possibility of annihilation of life as we know it, had intensified the preoccupation, and Jack McKinney's death had brought it home personally. "Shadow" has a figure standing

> ...*to watch the sun*
> *slip over the world's edge*
> *its white-hot temples burning*
> *where earth and vapour merge,*

a premonition perhaps of the death of the sun and with it, the death of life itself which confronts her:

> *The shadow at my feet*
> *rose upward silently;*
> *announced that it was I;*
> *entered to master me.*

Then it

> *... deepens into fear*
> *of time that falls away,*
> *of self that vanishes*
> *till eyes stare outward blind*
> *on one invading darkness*
> *that brims from earth to mind.*

Life for her had always depended on the earth; it was spiritual because human, human because earthy, coming from the earth, the source of life. With the disappearance of the earth into darkness life seemed threatened. But as she watches, the after-image of the sun appears,

> *burning behind the eye,*
> *single and perilous*
> *but more than memory.*
> *When universe is lost*
> *man on that centre stares*
> *where from the abyss of power*
> *world's image grows and flares.*

Having stared so intently at the setting sun, the image is imprinted on her retina. Thought is not directed but suspended and learns to receive, to receive the power to name and so face the darkness:

> *World's image grows, and chaos*
> *is mastered and lies still*
> *in the resolving sentence*
> *that's spoken once for all.*
> *Now I accept you, shadow,*
> *I change you; we are one.*
> *I must enclose a darkness*
> *since I contain the Sun.*[1]

This is the source of her passion for politics, for poetry, for life against death. For her political involvement had always meant resistance to the inhuman,[2] to the nothingness threatening us not only in nuclear war but in the progressive dehumanisation of a culture devoted to material development. Nevertheless what drove this involvement was not a system of ideas but a passion for life, for the fires of creation which arise even, perhaps especially, from destruction.

A prescient journalist, Claudia Wright, author of a series called "The Big Shots" in the Melbourne *Herald* seems to have understood something of this in her essay on Judith Wright, published in October 1970, "The Woman Who Fights to Save the Earth". She understood the importance of the earth for Judith, though she expressed it with journalistic exaggeration, describing "Calanthe" as an "Aussie *Wuthering Heights* setting"! Nevertheless, she was accurate enough when she wrote that Judith had "created her own environment" there, an environment full of energy: "the whole place sparkles with sun, the smell of the mountain and the sounds of the birds". Judith's passion for the country as a whole comes through also, as she tells the journalist that she has "always been concerned with the treatment of my country . . . you'll find this in my writings. I am bound up with being fifth generation Australian, and was born on the land and worked on the land".

That was her context, and it set her apart from the rage for development going on around her. As the article reported, Judith lived "modestly and unpretentiously", though it also noted the Blackman paintings "in layers everywhere" inside the house, singling out the portrait of Jack.[3] But she was also in tune with the longings of the early 1970s, the "Age of Aquarius", with its opposition to war, concern for civil rights, scorn for rigid views, hope for liberation, a respect for individuals and search for a new set of values. As Judith put it in a student newspaper in March 1971:

> I think there is a chance of deep change in the individual and I think it may be the only chance we have: overthrowing a system which is old-hat. I do not believe in any of the present political systems. [Today, however, there is] a chance of achieving what has to be changed, to bring about a change of feeling.[4]

But to go fast forward, as many wanted to do at the time, also meant forgetting fast, and memory was crucial for her. She would always have a debt to pay to her childhood and would continue to honour her longing to make "a net to catch the unknown world" and to discover the "secret no man knows".[5] She was also troubled that young people seemed to be limited as she had not been, having no access to the living world around them. "A lot of them", she believed, had "gone off the track with heroin" for that reason.[6]

The Vietnam War dragged on, with an increasing number of young men's lives dependent on the lottery of their draft[7] – one of Meredith's boyfriends was on the run, refusing to fight in a war he did not believe in. Judith was sympathetic and "marched, wrote letters and did what she could".[8] But she believed that the answers were ultimately beyond politics, that what needed to be changed was the way we see the world. As she wrote to Shirley Walker some years later:

> I don't think that even scientists any longer regard the physical and the psychic as separate, and all the work being done seems to confirm this – what is the observer, what the observed? Can you tell the dancer from the dance? With the "material" becoming more and more difficult to define, and so many workers even in the sciences now more interested in studying relations than in studying the object itself, ecology rather than taxonomy, the distinctions that used to be made get more and more blurred ... Jack's ... work implied that we are part of a unity with "nature" and that human thought is the development of that relationship.[9]

It was this conviction which made her so passionate in defence of the Great Barrier Reef and continued to involve her in the environmental cause. In 1970 John Sinclair, founder of the Fraser Island Defence Organisation (FIDO), had discovered that a Fraser Island mining lease had been granted, which could destroy magnificent dunes and the life dependent on them, and Judith had rallied also to its defence. These places, together with the forests threatened by woodchipping, the plains around Noosa and the sand of Cooloola were, she felt, part of her inheritance and thus of the fabric of life which sustained her, and she became more and more hostile to the talk of economic and technological "development" which threatened to destroy them. True development meant the increase of life, she wrote in "Letter", a poem for Meredith. It was not a matter of technology or money.

> *I promised you unborn*
> *something better than that –*
> *the chance of love; clarity,*
> *charity, caritas – dearest,*
>
> *don't throw it in. Keep searching.*
> *Dance even among these*
> *poisoned swords; frightened only*
> *of not being what you are –*
>
> *of not expecting love*
> *or hoping truth.*

Safety and security might no longer be possible. But she refused to drop out, to

> *Wipe all the questions*
> *into an easy haze,*
> *a fix for everything?*[10]

She was determined to fight on.

The next issue to confront her in the fight was the Concorde, the new supersonic airliner which Qantas was being urged to buy. Alarmed by the possible dangers posed by its sonic boom to human and animal health, and the destruction to the ozone layer caused by its flying so high, increasing water vapour and thus interfering with the weather and climatic patterns, she got in touch with overseas groups opposed to the Concorde – the Anti-Concorde Project in Great Britain and the Citizens Against Sonic Boom in the United States – who confirmed her fears. A journalist friend in London, Clare Wagner, also kept her supplied with information. What Judith learned from her increased her alarm, and in July 1971 the WPSQ brought out an emergency issue featuring the Concorde as well as the threat of sandmining on Fraser Island and the struggle to save Cooloola. She also spoke that same month to the Association of Science Teachers in Queensland about the dangers posed by the Concorde. In Sydney the Citizens Campaign Against Concorde was formed in February 1972, and Judith spoke at a meeting they organised in July in the Sydney Town Hall.

For her, the aircraft was a symbol of the technology which was destroying the living world. As she wrote to Kathleen McArthur:

> The thing uses titanium for all leading edges and heatable metal, since it carries 90 tons of fuel and is a high fire danger. With that prospect Cooloola would never survive the next ten years ... A fleet of hundreds of Concordes would make hay of [the world's resources of oil and of these metals] ... reserves in no time. Out goes the Barrier Reef.[11]

There would be no resisting the push to exploit the oil resources to be found there, she believed, if this fleet came into being.

Once more there was wide public support, and Judith received numerous letters, one which told her that "I heartily condone your activities". Another, from a Sydney journalist, said that "it gives me strength to know you".[12] Thistle Stead, wife of Christina's naturalist father David Stead, and an ally in other environmental struggles, also expressed support in a personal letter, as well as more publicly in a letter to the *Sydney Morning Herald*.

Opposition to a shiny new piece of machinery, however, especially one which promised to make air travel much faster, was not to become as popular as opposition to mining on the Reef or to woodchipping. Newspaper columnists like Max Harris were enthusiastic about the possibilities the sleek and beautiful-looking aeroplane opened up, and were scandalised by the opposition to "progress" which promised to bring Australians much closer to the rest of the world. Moreover, in contrast with those opposing mining on the Great Barrier Reef or in Kakadu or at Cooloola or on Fraser Island, or woodchipping in the forests, the scientific arguments against the Concorde were complicated and widely disputed. It was also easy to present its opponents as mere Luddites. One man wrote, not very elegantly, to say that he was scandalised by Judith's letter to the *Australian* opposing the Concorde:

"having studied your poetry I was astounded to see the statements attributed to someone, whom I thought capable of more respectable protestation".[13] She was accused of accepting money from United States aircraft manufacturers who stood to lose a great deal if the Concorde was widely accepted.[14]

Judith persisted, and tried to make clear that it was not the technology which troubled her but its consequences. She also believed that the proponents of Concorde were not necessarily disinterested, accusing Max Harris, perhaps not entirely justly, in a letter she wrote in response to his in defence of Concorde in the *Australian*, of wanting to promote "the avant-garde image [of himself as] ... the first Supersonic Jet-Setter".[15] She was also shrewdly aware of the politics involved, suspecting that the French might use the recently signed wheat agreement with Australia to pressure the Australian Government to oblige Qantas to buy the Concorde.

The fact that the Concorde's proposed route to Sydney passed over Central Australia and might thus affect the Aboriginal peoples of the desert, the "wild country" of "Australia 1970" and damage the environment which was so sacred to them, intensified her concerns, especially when the Managing Director of the British Overseas Airways Corporation (BOAC), arguing in favour of Concorde, remarked that even if it did some damage, it would only be to a "few Abos and kangaroos in the desert".[16] Judith had had letters from a white adviser to the Pitjanjarra people telling of their terror when the Concorde flew over their land on a trial flight. One old man, he reported, had "practically gone mad" with terror. Others were nearly deafened by the sonic boom, and the native animals had scattered in terror. She believed that Aboriginal people mattered and was enraged by this indifference to them. They, too, must assert their rights and she wrote to Mary Durack, asking her to mobilise Aborigines as well as the other citizens of Broome and the Kimberley in opposition to the aircraft.[17]

There were many supporters and morale was high. As one of them wrote, half wryly, half cheerfully; "Ah well, Judith, I suppose if we didn't have these community chores to do we'd be wasting our time reading books, sitting in the sun, listening to music, or gossiping to our mates."[18]

Wright's family was also supportive. Her brother, Bruce, and his wife offered her $600 for the cause and the use of their new flat in Sydney as a base for her work there in June. A week or so later, on 14 April, he wrote saying that he had persuaded the local Graziers' Association to send a resolution to the annual conference that government should do nothing about Concorde until unqualified evidence was forthcoming that it would not harm the environment. Peter also offered to raise at least $1000 from the family towards the expense of bringing a speaker from Britain who would argue the case against the Concorde. The Students' Representative Council of the University of New England also offered her space for an article in the student newspaper, putting the anti-Concorde case.

Qantas, too, seemed less than enthusiastic – the aircraft might cut hours off the flight from London but it would be expensive to operate and to buy, so the airline, already feeling the effects of the international move towards lower airfares and increasing oil prices, was cautious. By April Wright was feeling increasingly confident of winning the battle. "Heave ho, my hearty", she wrote to Dick Piesse of the ACF, "the cracks are showing."[19]

But the pace she was setting herself was having its effect. In the same month she had to take to bed with "a temperature like a yo yo" as she told Kathleen McArthur; "I don't know definitely yet what it is I've got. The doctor is coming in to do a blood test today. What a curse."[20] "Black/White", written about this time, is about being knocked out of action briefly by fever:

> *This time I shall recover*
> *from my brief blowtorch fever.*
> *The sweats of living*
> *flood me; I wake again,*
> *pondering the moves of anti and of pro*
> *Back into play I go.*

But it also offers a glimpse of the ambiguity in which she lived, battling for the forces of life but haunted still by death, Jack's death in particular:

> *I'm none too sure exactly why I'm here,*
> *which side I'm playing for –*

> *But still, here's day, here's night*
> *the checkerboard of yes and no*
> *and take and give.*
> *Again I meet you face to face,*
> *which in itself is unexpected grace.*
> *To arms, my waiting opposite –*
> *we live.* [21]

Political as her struggles might seem, they were part of that larger struggle of creation and destruction she had been aware of all her life:

> *Living long is containing*
> *archaean levels,*
> *buried yet living.*
> *Greek urns, their lovely tranquillity*
> *still and yet moving,*
> *directing, surviving.*[22]

Up again after her illness, Judith found herself arguing with the ACF, which had once seemed to promise so much for the environment. She was increasingly uneasy at the way the council, of which she was still a member, included more and more establishment figures, especially businessmen like Baillieu Myer and Don Malcolm, executive of the ICI subsidiary, Fibremaker. She had also been deeply troubled when the foundation had not taken the strong stand she hoped for against the proposal to mine for uranium in Kakadu National Park in the Northern Territory and by the response of her old ally Francis Ratcliffe, still an important figure in the ACF. He advised her to write to Sir Maurice Mawby, Chairman of Directors at Conzinc Rio Tinto, the company concerned with the Mary Kathleen uranium mining, telling her that he was an "extremely good bloke". He was sure, he told her, that she would "get cooperation" from Mawby. In Ratcliffe's view the environmental movement should be the ally and not the antagonist of business: its task was to interest the community in conservation, not to oppose "development", or to go around "peppering governments at State or Federal level; they should be left to deal with environmental issues as they saw best."[23]

Judith, of course, saw things differently. Her position was much more radical. As she wrote in "Conservation as a Concept", what was needed was rather to investigate "the whole basis of the scientific and technological revolution" which had led to the "separation of ourselves from our own background, and the direction of our willed thought upon it as a quantitative, not a qualitative, entity, wholly apart from ourselves".[24] The Concorde issue brought to a head these differences with people like Ratcliffe, and she told the *Sunday Australian* in an interview on 26 March, headed "Poet Judith Wright Gives Duke Concorde Option", that she intended to resign from the ACF unless it protested strongly against the Concorde's planned visit to Australia. As the headline suggested, she was also critical of the Duke of Edinburgh (who was patron of the ACF) for his failure to oppose the Concorde. This was a fairly ingenuous position, of course, since the Concorde was a symbol of British achievement in technology, something that would have been difficult for the Duke to oppose. But Judith's fierce integrity had no time for compromise and her anger increased when she heard that the ACF's scientific committee had met in secret to discuss the Concorde and had issued no report either way.[25]

The ACF council meeting in November 1972 brought things to a head. Despite all her lobbying and all the scientific evidence she had assembled, provided by scientific friends and colleagues like Len Webb, the council still refused to oppose the Concorde. Even the Council of Europe, as she reminded them, had pointed to possible dangerous consequences for the large and arid landmass of Australia. But the majority remained unmoved. For them, the ACF's function was, as Ratcliffe put it, to be a "steadying influence", not to engage in controversy. Feeling that her position was becoming increasingly untenable, Judith told Milo Dunphy of Ecology Action that she felt as if she was "on ice" and might have to resign – "which no doubt will be an enormous relief to many in the ACF top levels".[26] She was not sure that this was the best thing to do tactically, though at the moment she felt there was "practically a military government and curfew" within the organisation and that she was largely ineffectual, though the Director, scientist Dick Piesse, seemed to have some sympathy with her views. In the end she decided to stay on until the annual general meeting the following March at which, she wrote, Prince Philip was "expected to grace us with his august presence. This will mean, I take it, that everyone is expected to keep a suitably reverential hush".[27]

In the meantime she continued to fight the Concorde, telling the foundation's acting director in October that there should be no "compromise with business and government interests on a matter which, if 'leadership' in conservation is in any way the Foundation's aim, there should be no compromise", going on to remark sharply, "Where there can be no compromise, the Foundation should not attempt a compromise."[28] For her, what was needed was leadership. Australians must "formulate a philosophy that will mean we balance our growth with the needs of the future",[29] as she told the *Australian* at the beginning of 1972 as one of a group of "famous Australians" asked to formulate their New Year's wish.

It was a difficult time. She knew that the ACF mattered and that she needed allies in it and was, she told Len Webb in a letter asking him not to resign from the council, "trying to be prudent and listening to everyone".[30] But there were many other issues on which the foundation's position seemed to be equivocal – Lake Pedder in Tasmania, for instance, and woodchipping, especially in the tropical rainforests – so that she was losing respect for and hope in the council, if not in the Foundation as a whole. Unable to compromise any longer, she finally resigned towards the end of the year, which set her free to criticise what she saw as the council's pusillanimity and lack of vision.

But there were environmental crises everywhere. One which also concerned her was the proposed "development" of the area around Westernport Bay in Victoria, and she spoke at a "Save Westernport" rally at the Melbourne Town Hall in March, attended by at least 1700 people. Overpopulation throughout the world was also reaching a crisis point in her view and her concerns were increased when she attended the session on the Consequences of the World's Population Growth at the Australian and New Zealand Association for the Advancement of Science (ANZAAS) Conference in May. This crisis, she thought, was yet another consequence of the "extrovert utilitarianism ... the force behind the classical economy which encourages us to go on blindly climbing the graph without observing the crash ahead".[31] The Federal Government's virtual go-ahead to mining on Aboriginal lands and its support for uranium mining (McMahon had replaced Gorton as prime minister) was yet another example of what she called the "red blooded grab-faith – a faith in the infinite resources of the finite" which in her view threatened life, human life especially, on the planet.

Judith was appalled by a general drift towards inhumanity, a general crisis of value around her. For her, as for many other people at the time, a whole range of issues seemed to be coming together and demanding commitment.

Women's issues were also beginning to figure, and she spoke to the newly formed Women's Electoral Lobby (WEL) in August about the power women could wield as voters when they decided to organise. Her own struggles for independence as a young woman had made her sympathetic to the whole range of needs facing women. In Launceston early in 1972, where she had been after the "Save Westernport" rally to give a talk about poetry, for instance, one questioner asked her views on abortion. She saw no value in imposing her views on others, she said; "only you can tell if you have done the right thing", adding at the same time that she was always "happy to help someone in need" and could give her questioner "the name of a good abortionist".[32]

Public figure though she was, she still found herself involved from time to time with the "intricate dramas in progress, other people's dramas", those of women in particular. There was, for example, a "confused teenager who landed on the doorstep at the beginning of December in 1970 and stayed on until New Year, draining the whisky but getting slightly less confused". When she returned home, however, things got worse and she was committed to a mental hospital, "having run wild and defiant". But she continued writing letters to Judith who thought she would "certainly be back" – a prospect she did not welcome since she was desperately busy. Yet she felt that she could not turn her young friend away if she did appear, resolving at the same time to slip "a mickey finn in the whisky to discourage too much expense".[33]

The same year a woman dying of a brain tumour "entered her life", with a letter saying that she wanted to leave money to the conservation movement. She had had an extraordinary life and family background and had "kept the world at arm's length for ten years". But now, as Judith confided to Barbara Blackman, it seemed she had decided to fall in love with Judith as a final gesture:

> She is now on her final death-bed but I could write many pages about the weird things that happened during these months; she was a regular witch, with terrifying psychic force, had been running a business with shattering success until her brain tumour began, then the Forces turned against her and she could do nothing right and everything happened to thwart her and what was more to damage anyone who tried to help her as well – I was quite terrified and only my constant invocations of the Middle Way, I'm sure, prevented me from getting them as well. People were to have tractor accidents, horse accidents, car accidents etc. all around her as soon as they became indispensable to her plans for the future. I tell you it was impressive.[34]

For the time being, however, the public sphere was less demanding as the tide flowed towards the election of the Whitlam Government at the end of 1972. But Judith continued to be a public figure and in the middle of that year the Melbourne *Sunday Review* suggested her as poet laureate. True, she also had her critics: after she led the anti-Concorde march in Melbourne in March, a headline in the *Sydney Telegraph* shouted "Come Off It, Miss Wright". She also had continuing disagreements with some people who called themselves conservationists. One of these was the journalist George Munster:

> His is a predictably mid-European viewpoint, saying animals should be preserved in zoos and that the preservation of species in some specialist habitats had to be endorsed by academics with specialist interest. [I told him that] he reminded me of some indoor European adolescent carefully putting pins through butterflies. It shut him up.[35]

Judith was in fact more hard-headed than many environmentalists, being aware that, as scientists were beginning to understand, life as a whole constituted a large and complex whole, what Len Webb called a "cooperative maintenance system", threatened, however, by the worldview on which technological society was based, which set subject/object, fact/value, nature/science against one another. Poems like "Geology Lecture", published in *Poetry Australia* in 1971, expressed her dissatisfaction with this division, and her poetry continued to explore and question this opposition ignoring the relationships between different forms of life. "Alive", "Lament for Passenger Pigeons" and "Bid Me Strike a Match and Blow" are typical – the last yet another poem about fire as symbol of creation and destruction. As always, therefore, poetry was her way of understanding herself and the world.

> *Time locks us up in the mind,*
> *but leaves this window, art,*[36]

as she put it in "Picture". But it was poetry, too, which kept her in touch with her senses, reminding her that despite everything,

> *Living is dailiness, a simple bread*
> *that's worth the eating,*

occasionally putting her in touch with a "sudden laser" which "slants . . . through common day",

> *. . . a wine,*
> *a drunkenness that can't be spoken or sung*
> *without betraying it.*

which

> *. . . seems to have nothing to do with things at all,*
> *requires another element or dimension.*[37]

Despite everything therefore, despite the people

> *with sharks in [their] eyes*
> *contracts in [their] hands*
> *and balance sheets*
> *that have to keep climbing*

there was still good news, the knowledge and the hope that

> *for a while longer*
> *my friends*
> *can sing and paint pictures*
> *can love and quarrel*
> *can fall into despair*
> *and come up out of it.*

There was other good news, too. All over the world people were beginning to question the direction of current history. As "Good News" concludes:

> *One crack in a grey wall*
> *can spread*
> *one seed can grow.*
> *Don't you understand*
> *that a minute gained*
> *might mean*
> *everything?*[38]

The crisis itself, too, was provoking new thought. As she wrote in "Conservation as a Concept":

> We're *too conscious* now to be able to revert [to traditional ways of thinking and feeling] … without some further principle emerging in consciousness somehow. To me it can only be a value principle and a value system – and values are bunk to Consciousness II [a reference to current discussions of different kinds of consciousness]. Interesting that a year or two ago there was a UN conference on the place of value in a technological world. I'm waiting for the publication of the papers.[39]

Some scientists were also beginning to pursue this approach, studying the relationship between human beings and the environment, seen as something living; amongst these her friend Len Webb, of CSIRO. The old approach, which he called "autecology", had divided the study of the natural world into a series of separate disciplines, biology, zoology, geology and so on, but the new approach he advocated, "synecology", concentrated on the pattern of the whole area or system which, he argued, has a different quality from the sum of its constituent parts, something beyond mere quantity. This kind of study, he argued, was leading to a "fresh intellectual and moral view of man's relationships and responsibilities towards the environment", corresponding to the "contemporary desire for wholeness" apparent around them but also echoing the insights of contemporary physics and mathematics into the way in which the observer affects what is observed.[40]

It was not only a question of talking about and fighting for the environment but, as Judith put it in "Conservation as a Concept", of coming to understand and live out "the human role as a new obligation for the continued existence of the earth and its doings and beings",[41] meeting in this way what Jack had called "the challenge of reason". It was also a way which helped keep her alive emotionally. Political involvement often makes one doctrinaire, but Judith continued to feel passionate about people.

"Tableau", for instance, is about a young man she glimpsed on the other side of the street.

> *Bent over, staggering in panic or despair*
> *from a post to parking-meter in the hurried street,*
> *he seemed to gesture to me,*
> *as though we had met again; had met somewhere*
> *forgotten, and now for the last time had to meet.*
>
> *And I debated with myself; ought I to go*
> *over the road – since no one stopped to ask*
> *or even stand and look.*

She went.

> *... His almost vanished voice*
> *accepted me; he gave himself to my hold,*
> *(pain, cancer – keep me still).*
> *We leaned on a drinking fountain, fused in the vice*
> *of a double pain; his sweat dripped on me cold.*
>
> *Holding him up as he asked till the ambulance came,*
> *among the sudden curious crowd, I knew*

> *his plunging animal heart,*
> *against my flesh the shapes of his too-young bone,*
> *the heaving pattern of ribs. As still I do.*[42]

Whether or not this actually happened is not the point. What matters is the feeling it expresses. "Entangled in much battle and travel",[43] as she was seeing her latest volume of poetry, *Alive*, through the press, she also kept up a correspondence with a prisoner in Bathurst gaol in New South Wales, a young man interested in poetry, and found time to visit him several times.

Poetry might occasionally have to be set aside, but it lay at the centre of all she was doing, contesting the inhumanity of a world in which, as "Advice to a Young Poet" put it,

> *Your fingers and hands have turned*
> *into hooks of steel?*
> *Your mind's gone electronic*
> *and your heart can't feel?*[44]

As Heidegger, one of the philosophers who had most interested her and Jack, had said, even if "the world's night is now approaching its midnight",[45] we can still dwell upon earth poetically, since to be "fully human is to have a world", to be aware of the "thingly character" of things[46] and of the sheer power of existence.

> *...Poetry that thinks is in truth*
> *the topology of being*[47]

and it was this "topology of being" which had engaged her since childhood.

Sometimes this took her to dark places. "White Night", for instance, expresses a nightmare sense of evil:

> *The hound sobs on the trail,*
> *but the wolf's long dead – long dead*
> *the unseen choice, the need*
> *that led into this night.*
> *Light-years of stars pour in*
> *on to a sleepless bed;*

> *the years fray, the threads weaken,*
> *cloud crosses, corners darken.*
>
> *'The boarhound and the boar*
> *pursue their pattern ..."*
> *but what stars reconcile*
> *the two before they fail?*
> *What long chase closes in*
> *to wreck what helpless prey?*
>
> *Lord, it cannot be I!*[48]

But poetry also helped her keep an ironic view of herself. "To Mary Gilmore", for instance, describes leaving home for one of the many conferences she attended at the time:

> *Having arranged for the mail and stopped the papers,*
> *tied loaves of bread Orlando-like to the tree,*
> *love-messages for birds; suitcase in hand*
> *I pause and regard the irony of me.*
>
> *Supposed to be fifty-six, hair certainly grey,*
> *stepping out much like sixteen on another journey*
> *through a very late spring, the conference-papers packed as*
>   *a half-excuse for a double-tongued holiday.*

Like Mary Gilmore as she remembered her, Judith, too, was "playing/her poet's game as though she'd never be done". But she also knew her place in the scheme of things and accepted it cheerfully if ironically:

> *It isn't far to my grave,*
> *the waiting stone. But still there's life to do*
> *and a taste of spring in the air. Should I sit and grieve,*
> *Mary, or keep the ink running, like you?*[49]

Her public life had not absorbed her private life and she still kept up with the family. In September 1972 a family reunion was held at "Dalwood", the original family home, to commemorate the wedding of

May Mackenzie and Albert Wright there a hundred years earlier. Peter, Judith's younger brother, was organiser, and he wrote to her months before telling her to "put the day in your diary and make sure you're not mixed up with Concorde".[50] The old house was falling down but they would have a barbecue for two hundred outside, catered for by a Ms McGuigan. The current owners of the property welcomed the idea since the publicity would be helpful when they made a public appeal for the restoration of the old house and grounds, and since the Wyndhams were still a distinguished family, the *Sydney Morning Herald* obliged by reporting the occasion.

Family members came from all over Australia, and Judith and her cousin Owen, the oldest of the direct descendants of May and Albert, received the guests. Before the event Judith was less than enthusiastic, telling Kathleen McArthur that "the disastrous effects of the population explosion will be something to see even if they don't all come. But the wine should be good".[51] She played her part in style, however, enjoying the occasion, even if her feelings were a little ambiguous. It was over ten years since the publication of *The Generations of Men*, and with her growing interest in the Aboriginal side of the story of settlement her thoughts were leading her toward the book which would become *A Cry for the Dead*. Nonetheless, her sense of belonging and the memory of those she had loved remained. To the end of life she was to write poems about the family, and her experience of public life had given her a new respect for the values she had learned, especially from her father. Despite everything, she felt, as she had written at the end of *The Generations of Men*, that "a certain stamp" distinguished them, "a mark that singles out even the most distant and rebellious of them for [its] own",[52] marking them off from the rest of the world of competition and self-interest described in "At a Public Dinner":

> *... the champing jaws,*
> *solemnly eating and drinking my country's honour,*
> *my country's flesh. The gravy's dripping red,*
> *a nourishing stew for business.*[53]

It seemed to her at least that they cared nothing for the past or for the country and that, for all their faults, her family had done so. She would, she said, "rather suffer the flames of hell" than be like the opportunists who seemed to her to be running the country now, and attributed her "grey hairs" to the grief of the "lost battles of the last ten years"[54] which she had fought with them. The people she valued were those like John Büsst and Arthur Fenton, who had died during the battle, Kath Walker, Len Webb, Nugget Coombs (whom she was to get to know well in the following years), and, of course, Jack,

> *poets and fighters with their eyes on truth,*
> *swearing like Thomas Traherne, so perfectly*
> *to hate the dull corruption of [others'] greed.*

These represented a "burst of glory in the world and man", and it was to them she turned for sustenance:

> *I call you up, true men, who lived and died;*
> *my dead beloved, my guides, my living friends.*
> *I say your names, I sing you to my side.*[55]

Her friendship with Kath Walker was a special inspiration since it was through her that Judith was learning about Aboriginal culture from the inside. A story in the *Sydney Morning Herald* in March 1972 about the making of a film of an earlier poem, "The Blind Man", featuring the Aboriginal actor Cyril Fisher from Cherbourg Reserve who played the part of the blind man, Yellow Delaney,

> *Landless and loveless [who] went wandering*
> *with his despised white girl, and left no track*
> *but the black mark of a campfire. How can they die*
> *who live without a country?*[56]

noted the "subtle, yet loving manner" in which she talked with him about "the problems of contemporary Australia, racism, pollution and conservation" as they sat on the beach by the war memorial under the fig tree, as in the poem. But in learning from Kath, Judith was also sharing her pain:

> Kath ... has been here on and off for a fortnight [she wrote to Kathleen McArthur in 1972]; the poor woman is in even more a

state of despair over her people's situation than we are of the country's and is rapidly convincing herself that bloody revolution is the only answer. We have long and exhausting bottle-fests while she argues it out. I shall be as much of a new lefty as she is before long.[57]

Kath trusted Judith, suggesting that they write a book together in which she would "think black" and Judith would "think white", looking together for some way of "guiding people out of the mess they're in". Though nothing came of this project, both of them were convinced that the great task was to help Aboriginal people recover a sense of pride in their identity and culture – Judith had already agreed, for instance, to become patron to an Aboriginal organisation, Boornong Mumba, set up on Mount Tamborine, with some help from Judith's connections in the Department for the Arts.[58]

Despite her growing awareness of their suffering, Judith was envious of Aboriginal people's affinity with the land. As she wrote later in a foreword to Alan Marshall's collection of Aboriginal stories, *People of the Dreamtime*, "we [non-Aborigines]...had come here already dispossessed, not only of the countries we came from but from our own inner unity", and now live, as she put it "among a comfortable rubble of material possessions, alone and unbelonging".[59] But she was also prepared to join in their struggle. At the University of Queensland, she supported Abschol, a student organisation which helped Aboriginal people with their studies, and in 1971 she not only gave her name to an essay competition which hoped to increase understanding of their culture among Aboriginal and non-Aboriginal people alike, but also acted as one of the judges. Non-Aborigines were asked to write about "The Meaning of Land to Traditional Aboriginal People" while Aborigines were asked to imagine themselves living in Sydney in 1789, the year after the landing of the First Fleet.

Judith also supported Kath in her attempt to set up a centre on Stradbroke Island for Aboriginal people, where they would also share their culture with other Australians, though Kath mostly fought her own battles. Better off than most of the Aboriginal people who drifted dispossessed and bewildered to Brisbane in search of jobs, Kath still lived not far from her own country, Stradbroke Island, just across the waters of Moreton Bay where she had been born and where her people, the Noonuccal people, had always lived. These rootless ones, she understood, were "truly at the bottom of life in an alien world".[60] That was why she was determined to find a place where their values and thus their hope and dignity could be restored.

From childhood Kath had resisted the idea of assimilation and the assumptions on which it depended: "that Aborigines want to become part of white society, and that white society will let them in on equal terms". Most Aborigines she knew rejected the basic assumptions of white society with what Judith called "a deep turning away", a profound rejection of "the rat race, the grab, the exalting of money and possessions ... [and] the repetitive mechanical work that the consumer society demands".[61] The key was to find a place where they could be themselves. Eventually, after several years' search, Kath found a place on Stradbroke Island, a five-acre block close to the shore of Moreton Bay, not far from where she had grown up, and she determined to get possession of it.

This was not easy, "Queensland being the most South African of states": no Aboriginal person could own land in Queensland nor could anyone purchase it on their behalf. But, at the Federal level at least, concern was growing about their plight. The 1967 referendum had at last recognised Aborigines as citizens and there were attempts to upgrade Federal Aboriginal policies and aim for self-determination rather than assimilation. Prime Minister Harold Holt appointed distinguished public servant, H. C. (Nugget) Coombs, to chair a small body entitled the Council for Aboriginal Affairs to oversee these policies. Nugget and Judith were to become allies, fighting prejudice on behalf of indigenous Australians.

But Canberra was a long way from Stradbroke Island. The block Kath wanted was still enclosed and under the control of Redlands Shire Council, who were unwilling to lease land to Aborigines. Judith had had some dealings with Coombs, who had given evidence as an economist against drilling for oil on the Barrier Reef, and when the Council of Aboriginal Affairs had attempted to negotiate better conditions for

Aborigines with the Queensland Government – a move the Premier, Bjelke-Petersen denounced as "Federal interference" – Judith's contacts with him and with others in Canberra brought a promise of some Commonwealth support. With that, and as a result of strenuous lobbying and much eloquence on Kath's part, the Redlands Council agreed to lease the land to her for a peppercorn rental. True, the conditions were hard. The council wanted the land to revert to its control after twenty years, together with any buildings that might have been erected on it. Kath had made plans for a little theatre and a circle of houses in which the artists and dancers could live, and a museum of Aboriginal culture, but she accepted the conditions since she had little bargaining power and less money with which to fight. She and her friends hoped that by the time the lease expired they would have cleared the legal hurdles and somehow have raised enough money to buy the land.

The settlement was called "Moongalba", the name of a wise old man of the Noonuccal trible, which also meant "sitting down place". It was a success from the beginning as friends and sympathisers, many of them university students, flocked to the island, helping clear the land but leaving the big cypress pines and eucalypts to shelter the birds and possums. They also built a big iron-roofed open shed with a fireplace for meetings and cooking. Non-Aboriginal university students, schoolchildren and families came together here with Aborigines as friends, helping to build the place, sharing talk, singing and plans and learning from one another. Soon other Aboriginal groups, actors and dancers especially, were coming regularly to the island. The Aborigines could feel they were on their land and could enjoy their own culture, and the whites began "to understand as they never otherwise could, what it is to be Aboriginal".[62] Judith came as often as she could. "Moongalba", as she wrote, was

> a place to bring sorrows and problems ... But above all [it] is a place to relax, away from the hostile and critical eyes of white people, in a place Aborigines can feel is their own. The far-off lights of Brisbane are muted by the trees, and people can be themselves, acting out their real lives, singing their own songs, laughing and dancing, miming and learning, and talking freely.

It was especially important for Judith because it was "not a place for policies. Kath has turned to the creative side of life ... This is a meeting place ... for learning, enjoying and living".[63]

The achievement was Kath's, but Judith supported her with her friendship and often financially as well. She also used her influence on "Moongalba's" behalf whenever she could. In June 1975, the *National Times* published her essay on "Moongalba", and Frank Heimans of Film Australia made a film about the place and the friendship which had helped to bring it into being, showing Kath and Judith walking in the bush and along the beach nearby.

In the middle of all the other battles she was engaged in, this friendship meant a great deal. As she wrote in "Two Dreamtimes":

> *Kathy my sister with the torn heart,*
> *I don't know how to thank you*
> *for your dreamtime stories of joy and grief*
> *written on paperbark,*

these stories which took her back to her own childhood but also in a sense prompted her to rewrite it:

> *You were one of the dark children*
> *I wasn't allowed to play with –*
> *riverbank campers, the wrong colour,*
> *(I couldn't turn you white).*

As she realised, she was one of "the conquerors". But with Kath she was able to cross the boundary and to realise in some measure how bad things were for Aboriginal people and share some of their pain:

> *Sitting all night at my kitchen table*
> *with a cry and a song in your voice,*
> *your eyes were full of the dying children,*
> *the blank-eyed taken women,*
>
> *the sullen looks of the men who sold them*
> *for rum to forget the selling,*

> *the hard rational white faces*
> *with eyes that forget the past.*

But what brought them closer together perhaps was a common

> *... grief for a lost country,*
> *the place we dreamed in long ago,*
> *poisoned now and crumbling,*

and their sense of themselves as writers "bought and sold/our songs and stories too" and their common sisterhood,

> *telling sad tales of women*
> *(black or white at a different price).*[64]

In all these ways Kath was becoming for Judith "the person I speak and talk to most easily. I refer things to [her] in my mind", a kind of "touchstone" to whom she mentally referred ideas and projects and from whom she drew many of these ideas.

That may have been why she was not so interested at this stage in the legal arguments for Aboriginal rights, perhaps also because, at the time, there seemed to be little hope in the law. On one occasion, for example, Nugget Coombs invited Judith to lunch with distinguished lawyer Zelman Cowen, then Chancellor of the University of Queensland and later to be Governor General, to discuss the question of Aboriginal land rights. Cowen's views were discouraging. Legally he could not see how Aboriginal rights to land could be allowed since at that stage the doctrine of *terra nullius*, the belief that before the first European settlers arrived the land had been unoccupied, prevailed. In her own mind, however, Judith was already questioning the doctrine as she recalled her childhood

> *... riding the cleared hills,*
> *plucking blue leaves for their eucalypt scent,*
> *hearing the call of the plover,*
>
> *in a land I thought was mine for life*[65]

and knowing, if only unconsciously, that she was owned by the land with which Aboriginal people had lived from time immemorial, not the other way round. As she had written in "At Cooloolah" in the 1950s, "no land is lost or won by wars, for earth is spirit".[66]

In any case Aboriginal issues were beginning to assume a new importance on the national scene. In 1966 the Gurindiji people of Wave Hill in the Northern Territory went on strike in protest against low wages and poor conditions. With mining assuming new importance, the question of Aboriginal rights to the land they still occupied was becoming urgent, especially in the Northern Territory where there were substantial deposits of uranium in the Kakadu area and elsewhere which mining companies hoped to develop. Accordingly, in 1971 the Council for Aboriginal Affairs, led by Coombs, drafted a statement committing the government to acknowledge the right of Aborigines to choose the pattern and determine the pace of future development. Prime Minister McMahon read this statement at a meeting in Cairns of State and Federal ministers concerned with Aboriginal issues. It had little impact. Indeed, Ralph Hunt, Federal Minister for the Interior, issued a counter statement declaring his commitment to traditional policies of assimilation and control.[67]

The majority of McMahon's government, including the minister for the newly established Department of the Environment, Aborigines and the Arts, agreed with Hunt and with his insistence that Australia was "one nation", refusing to acknowledge Aboriginal culture as different and with its own right to respect. Hunt showed little sympathy for Aborigines' claims to the lands they had always occupied, declaring that mining should be permitted on Aboriginal land and that in general mining should have precedence over their claims.

These statements were badly received by Aboriginal people and their supporters at home and abroad, and when the policy was announced on 26th January 1972 – Australia Day! – the London *Times* carried a headline, "Australia's New Rejection of the Aborigines". Not long afterwards, a group of Aborigines set up a tent "embassy" on the lawns outside Parliament House in Canberra as an expression of their feeling that they were aliens in their own country. The government tolerated this until the middle of the year, when, under pressure from its supporters, it gazetted an ordinance prohibiting camping on public lands in the Australian Capital Territory. On 20th July the police moved in and there were angry clashes between them and Aboriginal people and their supporters, with some arrests. Dispersed by force, the Aborigines declared their determination to return, and further violence threatened. But negotiations behind the scenes between the Council for Aboriginal Affairs and the government prevented this, and the Aborigines were allowed to return.[68]

Judith was involved, though at a distance, in this struggle. In April she wrote to her cousin Tina's husband, now Executive Director of the Country Party, imploring him as a "man of conscience" to use his influence on behalf of the Aboriginal people "for the sake of the image Australia has overseas and among ourselves for that matter and for all our consciences now and in the future to try and stop this filthy deal", signing herself "yours in love and fury".[69] Her friendship with Kath and her involvement with organisations like Abschol, which tutored Aboriginal children, had brought her close to their suffering. One of her friends, an Aboriginal woman involved in running Abschol at the University of Queensland, confided to Judith one day she felt she could no longer cope with the "routine of meetings, disappointments etc, and would like ... to get away from this 'rat bag' existence", thinking longingly of the "difference ... when our ancestors roamed this country".[70]

Judith was concerned more widely for racial justice. The tour of the South African rugby team in 1972, the Springboks, became a major issue since the team included no black players – apartheid, the official state policy, extended to sport also. A group of Judith's Brisbane friends decided to protest in an unusual way. They booked Kath Walker into the motel at which the Springboks were staying and then Judith, the Aboriginal pastor Jim Brady and the poet Rodney Hall joined her for dinner, sitting almost next to the South Africans.

Rodney remembered it vividly because he had been part of a large demonstration outside the motel at which the police had charged the demonstrators, trapping them in a cul-de-sac and then manhandling them. But, knowing the area, he knew there was an inconspicuous set of steps at the side of the wall and managed to escape with a few others, arriving somewhat dishevelled at the dinner. But he was pleased to note the South Africans' uneasiness and the dignified demeanour of his friends, who sat on for some time after the footballers had left.[71]

In Australian politics at least change was on its way, as under Gough Whitlam the Australian Labor Party was about to end the long reign of the Conservative parties. Amongst other things, Labor was promising to give more attention to Aboriginal affairs and to the environment, to make the Great Barrier Reef a Marine National Park, to save Lake Pedder in Tasmania, to prevent uranium mining and to bring Australian troops home from Vietnam. When approached, after the election had been announced, to sign an open letter to be published in the national media declaring the need for change and supporting the Labor Party, Judith therefore agreed. The request reached her just as she was about to set off to Sydney, as she wrote wearily, "on another series of hopeless enterprises mixed with exhortations to the converted". She wondered whether anything would come of the letter or whether Labor, once elected, could stand up to the pressure of big business, which seemed determined to override environmental concerns and the claims of Aboriginal people and was working hard and spending a great deal of money to put its case. Conzinc Rio Tinto had even managed to place an advertisement in *Wildlife* claiming that mining benefits the environment.[72] Though the council of the WPSQ demanded an explanation from the advertising agency involved, it was a salutary reminder of the determination of the mining lobby. Government intervention seemed to be the only way to stop them. Besides there were some men Judith respected in the Labor Party and, after all, as she concluded, "one can but try".[73]

The letter duly appeared with a wide range of distinguished signatories, including Sir Macfarlane Burnet, Patrick White, Leonard French, Ken Myer, Bruce Grant, Professor Hedley Bell and Manning Clark. The Brisbane *Courier Mail*, not entirely sympathetic, wrote that its appearance might be "vital to the poll" and that it might well be "one of the most devastating catalysts in the history of Australian politics".[74] Judith also appeared on the stage of the Sydney Opera House with a group of other eminent Australians prepared to show their support at the launch of the ALP campaign.

In December the Labor Party won the election. At the beginning of the year, reminding Whitlam of the bet she had made him thirty years before that one day he would be prime minister, Judith had written to him to say that it was "a long time since we've met – but I have followed what you have done with interest and admiration".[75] His election and the promises which had been made elated her. "There is a new wind blowing," she wrote, "and I hope it won't die down too quickly."[76]

CHAPTER XII

MOVING SOUTH

"It will be cold where you are going."
Yes.

"Moving South",
Collected Poems, p. 386

From now on much of Judith's time was to be spent in Canberra since Whitlam's victory meant that there would be work to be done there. Certainly, like many others, she found the first days of the new Labor Government exciting. In swift succession conscription was abolished, Australian troops were withdrawn from Vietnam, sporting ties with South Africa banned and diplomatic relations set up with the People's Republic of China.

Things moved at a whirlwind pace over the summer as the Department of Defence was reformed – five separate departments being amalgamated into one – inquiries were set up into Aboriginal land rights and into education and a National Aboriginal Consultative Council appointed. Language programs were introduced for ethnic minorities, women were promised equal opportunity and better openings for employment. The new government was also committed to the arts. Early in 1973 an Australia Council was instituted along the lines of the Canada Council to oversee matters to do with literature, theatre, opera, music and the visual arts with Nugget Coombs in the chair. Judith was appointed to it, along with other writers like David Williamson and public intellectuals like Phillip Adams. She was happy with the Council's direction: for the first time, she felt, a writer "could apply for a grant without having one's whole background wrung through the wringer" or questions asked in parliament about one's political views – as had happened under Menzies when "one had to toe the line politically".[1] Now artists rather than politicians were to decide on the merits of applicants and allocate grants.

Environmental issues remained as urgent as ever. In February Ecology Action, whose members, "young and full of fury",[2] had been in the vanguard of the opposition to Concorde, joined with the Campaign to Save Native Forests (which had originated in Western Australia) to fight the woodchipping which was threatening forests throughout Australia. A public meeting was held in the Sydney Town Hall on 18th February, outlining the dangers. The new government, however, was concerned to woo environmentalists and Whitlam instituted a Department for the Environment whose Minister, Moss Cass, attended this meeting in Sydney and promised that no new experiments in woodchipping would be allowed unless the government was convinced that they were in the national interest. Since a study of the woodchip industry by Richard and Val Routley of the Australian National University (ANU) had concluded that the profits were marginal, the workers were badly paid, forest resources were being wasted, the soil was being damaged, animal and plant species destroyed and tourist potential affected, environmentalists believed that this was unlikely and therefore called for an end to woodchipping altogether.

Most State governments, however, remained enthusiastic proponents of development and of woodchipping. In Queensland, environmentalists nevertheless won several victories. Len Webb and his colleague Geoff Tracey demonstrated that the area of forest near Cairns where woodchipping was proposed was much smaller than believed so that the industry could not last more than ten years and would thus be unprofitable. As a result the proposal was quietly dropped. The battle line was fought on several fronts with documents being leaked to the Queensland Opposition, for example. None of this made the environmentalists very popular with the Queensland Government, of course, which characterised them as "green revolutionaries", people with "common affiliations with Communists, [of] moral depravity and god knows what all", according to a letter Judith wrote to Kathleen McArthur, advising and warning that "they've got ASIO in to supply files and information", and thus to "watch your step as I watch mine".[3] Nevertheless the fact that the new Federal Government had created a Department for Environment and Conservation and set up an interdepartmental committee to review environmental issues throughout Australia gave conservationists a new ally and with it a certain respectability.

Things began to move early on this front also. In his policy speech in November 1972 before the election Whitlam had promised to "preserve and enhance the National Estate". Cynics at the time regarded this as a bait to environmentalists. But in May 1973 a Committee of Inquiry was set up, largely at the initiative of Tom Uren. Until this time inquiries into environmental issues had been quite specific, limited to a particular place or issue. But this was to be, to use Judith's phrase, "rather a dashing general inquiry", which included the built-up environment, architecture and places of historical, cultural and social interest, as well as the natural world, and was an attempt to make an inventory of the nation's natural and cultural resources – a necessary first step to their preservation.

She was not particularly sanguine at first about the composition of the committee, the majority of whom came from the National Trust and were thus more concerned with cities and towns than with the land itself. For Judith it was the land which was crucial and her growing friendship with Aboriginal people like Kath Walker made her see the concern with architecture and monuments as "a European thing" and another sign of the way in which we still have not put down our roots properly into the land. As she wrote in "Geology Lecture" we "perch upon" it

> *... now in half a doze*
> *sitting with gently folded hands today;*
>
> *containing all prehistory in our bones*
> *and all geology behind the brain*
> *which in the Modern age could melt these stones*
> *so fiercely, time might never start again.*[4]

Nevertheless she accepted appointment to the committee, which was to be chaired by Mr Justice Hope. The responsible ministers for the inquiry were Tom Uren, Minister for Urban and Regional Development, who became a good friend of Judith's – creating a scandal for one of her relations, a stickler for convention, who disapproved of him not only because he was a Labor politician but also because he wore a waistcoat and bow tie[5] – and Moss Cass, Minister for Environment and Conservation.

Some of Judith's friends also were distressed by her growing involvement with government affairs, though for different reasons. Dorothy Green saw it as a distraction from her real work as a poet, and her literary agent, Alex Shepherd, wrote, begging her not to accept the invitation to join the inquiry. "I agree", he wrote, "that there are a number of carts to be pulled but there are plenty of good horses, Clydesdales even, to do that. It isn't a job for a thoroughbred." Her reply, however, was that the Clydesdales were fully occupied and that, in any case, the committee needed someone known to the conservation movement through Australia. Unconvinced, Shepherd wrote back, telling her of a meeting he had had in the street with Patrick White to whom he had reported Judith's answer. White, he said, had asked him to "tell you there are enough Clydesdales, they just have to be prodded into work. They won't do it otherwise."[6] She paid no attention, however, and spent the next year and a half on the inquiry, determined to do what she could in public life now that there was an opportunity. For her, the thought of calm wisdom, of manageable relationships and of an old age with nothing to say that the future would listen to had to give way to her sense of responsibility to the people and the land she loved.

She was now away a great deal in Canberra or travelling around Australia on inquiry business. At "Calanthe" she had been on her own since Meredith had moved to Canberra to study at the ANU and was soon to go to Japan on a scholarship. She would have had to move away in any case since she had developed an allergy to the rainforest scrub ticks, which might even prove fatal. But Queensland was becoming uncomfortable for Judith for other reasons. John Sinclair, enemy of development on Fraser Island and founder of FIDO, but also a civil servant working in Adult Education had been persecuted, vilified and hounded from his job. Judith found this kind of politics distasteful and felt increasingly the need to work federally.

So she spent less and less time at "Calanthe". When she was there it often seemed as if she no longer quite belonged, now that those she loved were no longer there:

> When we first came
> the house seemed too big,
> then too small,
> now too big again.
> When I'm alone
> it creaks like footsteps.[7]

She had always suspected that perhaps we did not will our lives so much as live out "some inescapable logic in them",[8] as if

> ... Life's still obscure commands
> direct our blood, still salt from far below.[9]

This logic was now directing her south, to the cold from which she had originally come:

> Working today in this subtropical green
> summer extravagance,
> cutting back fleshy stems,
> smelling steam-scented gardenias
> I think of winter.
>
> Last night a chained dog howled
> in the heat of the full moon,
> the old house rustled
> like constantly turning pages.
>
> But far off southward
> a stony ridge lay waiting
> for me to know it ...
> I shall light fires.[10]

More practically, keeping house and looking after the garden took time, and often when she returned from her travels Judith felt overwhelmed by their demands. She had never been a dedicated housewife, but now things, she felt, were getting out of hand:

> I gave in finally today [she wrote to Barbara Blackman on one occasion after returning from Canberra] and asked the local Cleaning Lady to come and do out my toadstool-infected house, and we have been having cups of tea all day, she is a very nice one and doesn't keep coming in as the last one did reproachfully holding out dead mice and fur-filled bottles of 1960 Ketchup, but puts them tidily in the compost instead ... I am currently wrestling with the problems consequent on my deciding to have a Lily-Pool in the garden (leaks in pool, no lilies, drawing bandicoots, mosquitoes and a swelling chorus of happy bullfrogs).[11]

Besides, at home by herself she was defenceless against interruptions which were becoming more and more frequent. In one month, April 1973, for instance, she told a friend that she had "a girl painting my portrait (which will be depressing), a poet reading my books, and his girl friend coming up over Easter", to say nothing of "a mysterious green baby rainforest bird which someone dumped on me to bring up"[12] – a responsibility she took seriously.

Canberra looked increasingly attractive. In those early days of the Whitlam Government it was a centre of intellectual energy, full of lively and intelligent people who seemed to share the ideals she was fighting for. Tom Uren, one of the Labor Left and a major figure in Whitlam's second ministry, was "a one time heavy weight boxer, big, bearlike, with a ready grin". He had been a prisoner of war of the Japanese and hated war and the human misery and destruction it brought as much as Judith did. He, too, had been shocked by the first atomic bombs on Hiroshima and Nagasaki and had opposed nuclear weapons ever after, and with Jim Cairns he had also been prominent in the campaign against Australia's involvement in Vietnam. He was also concerned for the environment, loving the Australian bush, and in his portfolio worked to shape new, more human and beautiful cities, hoping to attract people away from Sydney and Melbourne, which, in his view, were becoming too large and inhuman, to less crowded parts of Australia.[13] So Judith found him sympathetic, especially as he cooperated enthusiastically with the Inquiry into the National Estate.

As poems like "At a Public Dinner" suggest, until now she had been deeply suspicious of politicians and of people in public life, thinking them intent on personal gain, "tired of being asked about tomorrow" and concerned only for profit, "the rising price of uranium, beef and gold".[14] But politicians like Uren seemed to echo the dream of equality for which she admired the poet Harpur and which she saw as characteristic of the best in the Australian tradition. She shared their reforming zeal, convinced, as the New South Wales Humanist Manifesto she signed in October put it, that "traditional moral codes and the new material codes fail to meet the pressing needs of today and tomorrow; (and that therefore) we need radically new human purposes and goals".[15] In her view the new government in Canberra was concerned to find these new purposes and goals to give equal opportunity to all and to care for the environment.

She was also getting to know Nugget Coombs, already one of Australia's most senior and distinguished public servants, sharing his views on public service and responsibility for the common good. Whitlam had made Coombs his special adviser, regarding him not only as a good economist but a man with a deep concern for social justice. Even more importantly, as far as Judith was concerned, Coombs also had a deep and abiding interest in Aboriginal affairs and a determination to further Aboriginal interests. In 1968, following the Referendum of 1967 which had acknowledged Aboriginal people as citizens, he had been appointed Chairman of the Council for Aboriginal Affairs by the Holt Government and had worked on behalf of Aboriginal people under successive governments. In 1968, Aboriginal occupation of their traditional lands was at their lowest ebb, but he remained convinced that, as the centre of Aboriginal culture and values, land was crucial to their well-being and as far as practical must be shared with them by non-Aboriginal Australian society. Like Bill Stanner, Judith's former teacher, whose ABC Boyer Lectures in 1968 broke the same ground, Coombs was determined to end the "long silence" which had all but eliminated Aboriginal voices and interests from national consideration.

Coombs also chaired the new Australia Council and was largely instrumental in having Judith appointed to it, though she also attended Literature Board meetings occasionally. He had long admired her poetry, calling her the "wisest of our poets", and often discussed Aboriginal and environmental issues with her. As they got to know and respect one another, he asked her on occasion to deputise for him when he was unable to fulfil a speaking engagement.

This kind of influence, the ability to button-hole politicians and public servants, was something Judith had not known before. It was tiring and demanding, but she enjoyed it – the habit of command was something she had observed and admired as a child in her grandmother. So, newly confident, in the middle of the first year of Whitlam's Government, she submitted a set of proposals for conserving the national environment and controlling pollution: tax incentives for clearing land should be abolished and farmers and graziers encouraged instead to preserve the native forests; a thorough scientific study should be made of the environmental issues facing the nation; water and air pollution should be monitored with the Ministry of the Environment given extra powers and legislation introduced to penalise irresponsible companies; and finally, the Federal Government should legislate to define and preserve its powers over offshore waters (this would include the waters of the Great Barrier Reef, of course).[16]

This was an extensive shopping list, but it is an index of environmentalists' hopes at the time, which Judith shared. She was also optimistic about the possibilities for change in Aboriginal affairs. Whitlam was personally sympathetic, and the Minister for Aboriginal Affairs, Senator Cavanagh, had acted decisively to prevent Concorde overflying Aboriginal communities in the Centre. Both Cass and Uren were also sympathetic. At this stage even Rex Connor, powerful Minister for Minerals and Energy, seemed to listen to environmentalists, intervening decisively to save the Barrier Reef from oil exploration, as she put it, preventing "one of the companies from slipping a fast one across him", and "stopping all the leaks".[17] Later in October, also at Connor's insistence, the Federal Government took control of the North West Shelf project in Western Australia, arranging to buy the oil and gas and take responsibility for selling them and controlling production.

The devotees of progress were by no means defeated, however – later they were to play a substantial part in bringing down Whitlam's Government. Schemes like the Ord River in Western Australia, which environmentalists like Judith regarded as an "eco bomb", were going ahead, and at the ANZAAS Conference in August of that year West Australian mining entrepreneur Lang Hancock recommended the use of nuclear power for mining and for deepening the Port Hedland harbour. Nevertheless Judith was more optimistic than she had been for some time. At the end of June the Federal Government made a grant of $5000 to the WPSQ for its journal *Wildlife*, something she regarded, not surprisingly, as "a marvellous precedent",[18] and the society's December newsletter praised "sound progress" that had been made during the year with the help of the Ministry of the Environment. True, Lake Pedder was still threatened, but it seemed as if the Great Barrier Reef and the Cooloola sands would be saved; the government seemed to understand what was at stake.

Judith was becoming more of a public figure than ever, and the Brisbane *Courier Mail* proudly proclaimed her "one of the most important women in Australia". This seemed true as far as the environment was concerned. She was also becoming a source of information. In May 1973, for example, the Professor of Geography at the University of New England, Ian Douglas, wrote asking about the state of the rainforests in the Bellingen Valley, information he needed for a paper he was preparing for the forthcoming ANZAAS Conference. He also wanted to know of "any major encroachments ... taking place or likely to take place in Queensland",[19] taking for granted that Judith would know.

The Inquiry into the National Estate took up most of her time and energy. Friends might beg her not to waste on politics the energies she should be giving to her poetry, but Judith's love of the land and loyalty to its needs compelled her, especially as the more she learned about it, the more desperate the environmental situation seemed to her. Quite apart from the threat to the Barrier Reef, the native forests throughout Australia, Lake Pedder in Tasmania and so on, the desperate plight of the Murray–Darling river system was just beginning to be acknowledged. In her view preservation of old buildings and monuments was a secondary matter since our very existence depended on the environment and she lobbied to see to it that two more environmentalists were appointed to the inquiry: Len Webb (whom the committee used as an expert and guide when they visited Fraser Island and the tropical rainforests in North Queensland) and Milo Dunphy (who was in fact an architect but also a founding member of Ecology Action and a staunch ally in the struggle against the Concorde).

The final brief given to the committee had been a comprehensive one and Judith was determined that they would carry it out. They were to inquire into:

(a) national parks, nature reserves and other places for the protection of wildlife, both plants and animals;

(b) buildings and structures, by themselves or in groups, and urban conservation areas, which should be preserved and/or restored for historical, architectural or other reasons;

(c) areas of special scientific interest, including caves and other geological formations;

(d) areas of special archaeological interest including Aboriginal sites;

(e) the coastline;

(f) inland water expanses, rivers, lakes and islands, apart from those to be designated as national parks and nature reserves (see (a) above);

(g) urban parks, including botanical gardens, and other urban areas for the purposes of recreation and amenity;

(h) scenic areas not otherwise included in the above categories.[20]

The first task involved making an inventory, travelling around the country from the Kimberley in Western Australia to the Queensland rainforests and lands, from the New England plateau to Tasmanian forests, and historical buildings in cities and towns. The committee then had to consider "practical policies for protection, restoration and improvement as soon as we can". To help in these tasks they called for submissions which had to be read and assessed. Judith's particular responsibility, she told Len Webb, was to catalogue "'scenic areas', whatever they may be".[21] She was not content just to accept the agenda given them but used her contacts to influence it, arranging for her brother Peter to take her to see an Aboriginal stone ring he had discovered in the Ebor Falls area in New England so that she could report on it, for instance.[22] She also suggested to Inquiry Secretary George Brownbill areas the committee should visit like the Daintree Forest, which was to become famous later in the struggle to save it from the "developers", Fraser Island (she had also already alerted John Sinclair to put in a submission), places along the Queensland coast like the Cooloola area threatened by "development" and the Gulf country below Weipa. Inland, she suggested the brigalow country she loved, which had been one of her father's abiding interests. She recommended to Brownbill that he contact some of her allies in the environmental struggle in Queensland: the President of the Queensland Conservation Council, Peter Stocker, the President of the Littoral Society, Eddie Hegerl, the Secretary of the Noosa Parks Development Association, Arthur Harrold, and others like Kathleen McArthur, still Secretary of the Caloundra branch of the Wildlife Preservation Society, Mrs Joan Wright, President of the Cairns branch of the society, Percy Trezise, an air ambulance pilot but also a dedicated conservationist and President of the Cape York Conservation Council, famous amongst conservationists for his hair-raising aerial tours of endangered areas of coastal land and forest.

All this was demanding enough quite apart from the travel. As Judith told one of her friends, "I move like lightning these days". There were also "loads of bumph to read",[23] something which could be more than usually trying for someone who brought a sharp eye to language. Jargon gave her special pain. At a conference she attended at the time, she was given what was called an "identibadge", "personized and plasticised". Her response was to paste it on to a large piece of paper and label it "verbal pollution".[24] It was another product of the culture she disliked, of

> *masks with false smiles,*
> *bribers, connivers,*
> *smelling of facts*
> *and factories*

> *and underhand money*
> *short-changing the world*[25]

which she was trying to fight. For her, precision was both discipline and goal, the constant obligation she referred to in one of her poems:

> *Searching ourselves in pain, we yet rejoice*
> *that the implacable awaited voice*
> *asks of us all we feared, yet longed, to say.*[26]

Not surprisingly, this took its toll. Like her grandmother, she might seem indomitable and often indefatigable, but her health problems were increasing. Her old hip injury was playing up, and in October she had to have an x-ray, asking her friends to "Keep their fingers crossed"[27] as to its outcome. She was also getting deafer which made for difficulties travelling and trying to communicate with others. According to one friend who accompanied her from time to time, Judith would deal with those difficulties by taking the offensive, announcing her name as soon as she arrived at a hotel or motel, asking for her key and paying the account on the spot, all in one fell swoop, so that no one needed to say anything to her after that.[28] Being deaf made committee work difficult, too, for her colleagues as well as for herself.

But Judith refused to slow down. The situation was urgent, she felt. It might not be much longer that she and her friends

> *[could] sing and paint pictures*
> *[could] love and quarrel*
> *[could] fall into despair*
> *and come up out of it*[29]

since her work with the inquiry confirmed what she had felt writing poems like "Australia 1970", that the country was dying before their eyes as the pressure of developers increased and the cry went up that technology was the answer to all problems. So when Len Webb, concerned for her, urged her to take some time off, she retorted; "'Piano, piano indeed? Fortissimo, fortissimo is more like it."[30] But she felt the strain, as a remark in an earlier letter suggested; "I expect you're sick and tired of your life-time fight for conservation. You're on everybody's rat-bag list and probably feel like a voice in the wilderness." But her faith in the importance of the work was undimmed. "Whatever the cost," as she told Webb a year or so earlier, they must fight on: "don't worry ... we'll beat the bastards if we have to take to the streets with petrol bombs to do it."[31]

With Whitlam as prime minister things might not seem so extreme, but hard work was still required – which was, no doubt, why she had also agreed to sit on the newly constituted Literature Board. The health of the arts had always seemed to her an indicator of the general health of a society. She also believed that the arts had a crucial role to play in a settler society like Australia in which we had still to come to terms with the land and its original inhabitants – hence her admiration for Charles Harpur who had insisted that the real task of settlement was to imagine ourselves into existence by learning from our environment.

Being on the Australia Council kept her in touch, though not always comfortably, with contemporary developments in the literary world. As a writer she was expected to be the writers' champion; in May 1973 A. D. Hope wrote, urging her to use her influence to have members of the Australian Society of Authors (ASA) and the Fellowship of Australian Writers (FAW) appointed to the board.[32] He had heard rumours that "generalists", people like publishers and academics, were to be appointed rather than writers, and he was troubled by this. She agreed, but told him that she did see the wisdom of having a representative of the Department of Foreign Affairs on the board, at least in the early stages, since she or he could help promote Australian artists overseas.[33]

As usual, Judith took her responsibilities seriously, reading widely about kinds of arts funding throughout the world. She was most impressed by the Swedish model which gave special support to writers who had proved themselves to their peers and provided grants to enable them to travel. She also liked their idea of setting up writers' centres in major cities.[34] As a result of her research into these matters, to her surprise, she found herself on a subcommittee for staffing and administration. This was something she was interested in, though she realised that some might think she had sold out writers' interests to join the bureaucrats. She defended herself, telling Geoffrey Blainey that "it is writers I am concerned with", and to defend their rights and interests it mattered to have on the board "people who know where the toothpoint goes and can bring vocal pressure to bear on those who don't". After many years on committees she thought she knew.[35]

It was also important, she believed, "to get certain principles established in the beginning". After that she could "leave with a clear conscience".[36] One principle was to keep renewing the membership of the Council so that it did not fall into the hands of any one group. She thought there ought to be a constant turnover of Council membership, some members to be appointed for one year and some for two – a safeguard if mistakes were made with appointments. She also wanted to keep appointments free from political loyalties – there was pressure from some quarters, for instance, to make sure that Council members were sympathetic to the Labor Party. Judith did not agree, having no problems with writers "stirring the possum".[37] It was something, after all, which she herself had so often done.

She admired Whitlam and believed in his commitment to the arts. She had also had enough of parochialism and the influence of local pressure groups, so she was appalled when a West Australian council member proposed that funding should be returned to the States.[38] The Australia Council was "not power hungry", she wrote, opposing this proposal, but it was important to have a national and international perspective. At the same time she insisted on the need to keep at arm's length from government.[39] Writers must not let themselves be used; it was their independence which made them crucial to the life of a democratic society. When the Australia Council suggested that poets should be asked to write a new national anthem to replace "Advance Australia Fair" she "hastily excused herself".[40] Governments, in her view, should support writers, not coopt them for their purposes.

This commitment to writers and their independence made her see the importance of copyright as a protection not only of their intellectual property but also of their income – something she had always been vitally interested in as she tried to support her family. With Coombs' support she was in the forefront of the struggle to set up a Copyright Council. As she knew from her own experience, writers' incomes had "dropped notably" with the advent of photocopying,[41] and inflation was affecting them also. If they received some income from works copied or borrowed from libraries that would augment their incomes. Australian writers were handicapped, too, by the smallness of the local market and lack of recognition overseas. Their needs, in her view, should therefore come first as far as the Literature Board was concerned, so she was less than enthusiastic about its decision to fund a Chair in Australian Studies at Harvard: "What is the use of giving a million dollars to an American University", she wrote, "if there aren't going to be any [writers]."[42]

She was keenly interested therefore in the last case brought and won by Angus & Robertson on behalf of Frank Moorhouse against the University of New South Wales in April 1974, where there had been extensive copying of Moorhouse's work without any payment to him. She was also involved in the campaign the Australian Society of Authors conducted to collect fees from universities for photocopying. The universities were not "playing fair" and were "hiding behind their students" in this matter, she believed. To strike a blow in this campaign, in August she removed her works from the library of the University of New South Wales in protest and appeared on the ABC to explain why she had done so.

Judith belonged to the Australian Society of Authors, the closest thing to a trade union writers had, and contributed ideas as well as action to their campaign. At a meeting to discuss the matter in Perth, for example, she suggested a token licence fee of $1 to copy a work as a starting point for further negotiations. Later that year she discussed with the ASA ways of preserving royalties paid to Australian writers as local publishers began to respond to international developments and negotiated overseas rights sales. She also carried on a spirited correspondence with her agent, Alex Shepherd, and her own publishers, Angus & Robertson, about the rates they paid.

On another front, she had a long and, on her part, somewhat angry, correspondence with the University of Queensland Press, who were in the process of setting up a Portable Australian Writers series on the model of the very successful series published by Viking in the United States. Wanting to include Judith in the series, the Press had gone ahead and prepared a manuscript, the editor believing that he had her permission. She maintained, however, that she had not been asked, and wrote, somewhat tartly, about the propensity of academics to pick up, consume and profit by creative writers' work, demanding that the manuscript be withdrawn.[43] It was.

As well as these local and sometimes personal issues, she worked hard to promote Australian writing and pushed for government support in schools and the media. Despite this, being a member of the Australia Council did not necessarily make for popularity with other writers, especially with those whose grant applications had been rejected, though she had never been one to socialise much with other writers. There were differences, too, between Council members at times. At one stage early in its existence, when Geoffrey Blainey was Chair, Judith felt "alone except for David Williamson on the upper or hot seat",[44] in her opposition to the majority's views. It was often lonely work. But she had a powerful ally in Coombs, whose reforming idealism and artistic tastes she shared, and when pressure of work obliged him to resign as Chair of the Australia Council at the end of 1973, Judith was one of the people he consulted about the choice of a successor.

They had other interests in common. Coombs was determined to get the Commonwealth to build on the result of the 1967 referendum which had granted citizenship to Aboriginal Australians and to aim at self-determination rather than assimilation[45] – something close to Judith's heart. He was impatient to move, having learned a great deal not only about the deprivations of Aboriginal people but also about their aspirations in his role as Chairman of the Council for Aboriginal Affairs. The government was sympathetic and equally impatient; "Festina Lente", as Judith remarked was "a motto [this new] government has never heard of."[46] In May 1973 the Australia Council and the UNESCO Committee for the Arts (to which she also belonged) sponsored a seminar for Aboriginal people on their arts and cultures and the possibilities of further development. It was held in Canberra but Aboriginal people from all over Australia came together, tribal people who still lived on their traditional lands and those who had been dispersed and to an extent detribalised living in the cities and country towns, though, because of a series of misunderstandings, there were no Torres Strait Islanders. Judith was there at Coombs' suggestion as a member of the Australia Council and of the UNESCO committee. She was pleased to see a large number of Aboriginal people from Queensland and especially pleased that among them was her friend Kath Walker, her "Shadow Sister". As she wrote to one of her friends, it was "a lovely occasion altogether", though she noted that "the number of things they have asked for, and really need, will be quite beyond the Government's capacity to provide". Judith was learning already the limits of a government's good intentions. But "at least we now know what they do want".[47]

Aboriginal people were also beginning to command increasing respect and support. Aboriginal painting and dance were becoming fashionable, and in literature Kath Walker's success had been followed by writers like Kevin Gilbert (who also became a friend), Jack Davis, Robert Merritt, and others. In literature, it was urban Aboriginal people who were prominent – traditional culture was oral, not written. Painting and dance, however, were largely the province of traditional people. As both groups began to meet more often and work together, they drew closer. This Canberra seminar, in particular, marked a giant step forward. Towards the end of proceedings the leaders of the traditional peoples present declared that they would accept all Aboriginal people, whether or not they were "pure blood" or lived according to traditional ways. As Judith recalled, it was "a great breakthrough from many points of view and urban people were nearly weeping for joy. It was a lovely concession altogether."[48] It was to be crucial for the future as Aboriginal people became increasingly united, confident in their abilities, proud of their culture and increasingly energetic in claiming their rights.

A new phase was beginning for sympathisers like Judith. But they also found themselves from time to time caught in the crossfire between Aboriginal claims and the interests of non-Aboriginal groups – pastoralists and miners, but also well-meaning whites. A minor incident occurred when, as a member of the Australia Council, she was asked to go to Nimbin in northern New South Wales where the hippy festival, Australia's answer to Woodstock, had been held. There were allegations that Literature Board funding had been misused, but when she arrived to investigate she also had to consider claims by local Aborigines that the main campsite had been an Aboriginal site, "very sacred with a burial ground".[49] How the matter was resolved we do not know. But the first enthusiastic days of the Whitlam era were over, and problems lay ahead.

There was a break in the middle of 1974 to attend a conference at the East–West Center at the University of Hawaii in Honolulu on "Socioliterature", defined by the organisers as concerned with the ways in which literature "interprets and illuminates human nature, the human condition, the problems of society and [writers'] contribution to international cultural understanding". However sweeping and even pretentious Judith found this, these were issues that had always concerned her. She accepted the invitation, writing that she was "particularly interested in the new upsurge of identity among Australian Aborigines and in the literature – though so far there is not much of it – being produced by Aborigines",[50] and offered a paper on the subject.

This was one of the first papers about Aboriginal writing, and Judith was acutely conscious of the dangers involved, especially the danger of appropriating Aboriginal writing for non-Aboriginal ends. She worked closely with the writers whose work she discussed – Jack Davis, Kevin Gilbert and Kath Walker, writing to them to ask their permission to do so and for their help. When she had written the paper she sent it to Kath for comment and approval. As for the conference itself, Judith had little patience with academic theorising, but she found meeting so many writers from the region exciting, even if she also felt her position as a middle-class Australian woman, a representative of "the humbled powers in defeat", as she put in her poem about the conference. With her sense of history and of the disastrous effect Western ideas and Western power had had on other cultures, she felt her position as a white woman as

> *Round the Pacific's moaning shores,*
> *dirty with gunboats, loud with planes,*
> *the ancient countries stand and wait*
> *longing to take their shape again,*
> *shake off the years of Coca-Cola*
> *and speak in voices of their own*
> *the new-remembered poetry.*

But she enjoyed herself also, as the title of her poem about the conference, "Party with the Gods", suggests:

> *There was Vincent Eri from Niugini,*
> *Albert the writer from Samoa,*
> *Hone the shiningtoothed, the Maori*
> *swinging a sharktooth on a chain,*
> *Hussein, Professor of the Truth,*
> *Fernando from Malaysia.*

From where they sat drinking and dancing, Western culture looked increasingly shoddy;

> *It was the evening and the beer,*
> *the moon on beaches made of money,*
> *the palm-trees in the steamy night,*
> *the animals hooting in the zoo,*
> *the sound of waves from the Pacific,*
> *gave us that dangerous dreaming-fit*

But she was aware of reality also, even as she

> *... watched Hone Tuwhare dancing,*
> *his sharktooth bouncing on his chest.*
> *Outside, the drift of different colours,*
> *the shamed exploited in their T-shirts*
> *advertising coke and dollars*
> *stared through the plateglass in surprise.*
> *The gods are seldom seen in pubs*
> *dancing the haka in Hawaii.*

For a moment here, as sometimes with Kath, it was as if she had crossed a boundary to share the wealth of peoples and cultures which Western culture had tried to destroy, offering a glimpse of a different future:

> *Tyrants departing, could the gods*
> *Come creeping back from forest hideouts?*
> *And who came in but the old gods?*[51]

Their presence was to remain with her, troubling yet also empowering.

She returned to Australia to attend the ANZAAS conference in Perth, arriving on 13th August after the long flight fom Honolulu. It was back to work with a vengeance since she saw the conference as part of her work for the Inquiry into the National Estate, involving four days of intensive lobbying. Finding it more difficult to listen to papers or to join in a general conversation, it had become her practice to take people aside and talk to them personally. This method proved useful in getting her views across, especially as, being deaf, she did most of the talking.

After the conference on 18th and 19th of August, they inspected the forests of the south-west for the inquiry. What she saw left her pretty depressed – John Forrest National Park, for instance, seemed to her "completely worn out ... like a mangy old dog" – since the forests were suffering from "development". Hearings followed in Perth on 20th of August, after which the committee flew to Queensland where she, Milo Dunphy and Keith Vallance were to inspect Fraser Island and after that Cooloola, returning to hearings in Brisbane on 11th and 12th of September.

Not surprisingly, Judith's depression returned, fuelled by exhaustion. "Fact is," she wrote to Len Webb, "I'm losing hope that the human race will ever do anything about its problems before it does away with itself." She was aware of the growing rumbles of environmentalists throughout the world, "small colonies of hopeful bacteria", she called them. But in her view they were "going about things in such an inept manner ... that it seems to do as much harm as good" – enthusiasts near her on Mount Tamborine, for example, were planting pumpkins in the rainforest.[52]

She was also depressed by developments in the ACF, with the council apparently more and more sympathetic to business interests. In July the *National Times* ran a story headed "How An Old Boy Network Mixed Scotch With Rocks At The ACF",[53] suggesting that the foundation was being heavily influenced by a group of businessmen, educated at Scotch College in Melbourne, who had substantial mining interests. Then in October the *Australian* revealed that Commander Michael Parker, former aide-de-camp to Prince Philip but now a prominent Melbourne businessman, had arranged to take the Prince,

Patron of the ACF, on a camping trip in Central Australia. "We're not saying where we're going", the *Australian* reported Parker saying "in a jovial voice", as he emerged from a boardroom lunch at Travelodge Australia where he was a director.[54] Elsewhere it was being thought that Prince Philip might ask the Prime Minister to increase funding to the ACF when they met. But the association with business interests worried people like Judith, who believed that those interests threatened both the environment and Aboriginal people on whose lands most of the mineral deposits were to be found.

Things were not looking good for the Federal Government either. The economy was in trouble, influenced by the world-wide oil crisis and growing inflation. There were scandals amongst its members, too. Jim Cairns' alleged affair with his secretary, Junie Morosi, which led to his being sacked as Treasurer, and the secret loan raising deal with a dubious Pakistani financier, Tirath Khemlani, had badly tarnished the government's reputation. It barely survived the election of 1974.

At the time Judith had little energy for politics since most of the first part of 1974 was given up to editing the report for the National Estate inquiry. Because she was a writer she had been given responsibility for it, but it was a daunting task, "rather like trying to pack an octopus into a matchbox". They had travelled thousands of kilometres, covering most of Australia, and dealt with a wide range and variety of highly contentious issues and had done so "in a considerable hurry"[55] – indeed many of their inspections, she felt, with her usual critical honesty had been "pretty cursory". The report also had to be written in a hurry since Tom Uren, the minister responsible, wanted it finished before the election in May.

Although the work was not entirely left to her, different members of the committee being responsible for writing different sections, the overall task of coordination and organisation was. Quite apart from problems of tact and style involved, this troubled her ethically:

> We had a great deal of material to deal with and a lot of notes but we couldn't be considered experts for the most part. I think Uren had skimmed the top of the environmental movement for the members; it depended more on whether the issue concerned had

got a lot of attention than whether we knew our stuff. I was worried over this ... There were quite a lot of issues which, if we had been challenged on them, might have blown a few holes in what we had to say; but since nobody in the parliament or for that matter in the public knew much about them either, we got off lightly.[56]

Consequently it was a tense time for them all, but especially for Judith. However, she was no respecter of persons and used her authority as editor to pull people into line. On one occasion she even rebuked the Chair, Justice Hope, when she felt he was interfering. In her view, as editor, she was the one to make the decisions about the shape and style of the report, even if the final responsibility fell on the committee, and as a writer she had never been sympathetic to work she thought inferior.

The committee met its deadline and the report was a handsome publication with photographs of natural scenery and significant buildings and national monuments illustrating the nature and condition of the "National Estate". In one critic's opinion, it was "the most visually beautiful official document yet to grind from the open government ... [as well as] one of the more important".[57] But there were problems. It was not clear what the report meant by "cultural significance" or why it mattered, especially if economic arguments could be advanced for pulling buildings down or exploiting the resources of a particular place. One critic complained that aesthetic values were given precedence over questions of human well-being.[58]

For her part Judith was not entirely satisfied that the needs of the environment and of Aboriginal people and their culture had been given their due. Nevertheless, all things considered, she told a friend she was "rather proud" of the report.[59] They had had "a good say on the major issues then beginning to emerge" and had introduced "those questions at governmental level as well as those worrying the electorate then". Although, looking back, she realised that the task they had been given was probably impossible, "at least we anticipated a few problems and left the way open for more".[60] Unfortunately, as the Whitlam Government lurched from crisis to crisis, little was done about their recommendations apart from setting up the Australian Heritage Commission as a Federal body responsible for the National Estate. In any event it was not to be very effective under subsequent governments. "If there had been any chance of getting [the rest of their] ... recommendations implemented", Judith still feels, "the exercise would have been ... useful."[61] Economic interests were increasingly outweighing all other considerations.

But Judith was not one to let issues die. She and Len Webb kept alive the questions about rainforests and the Great Barrier Reef which the report had raised at a conference in Cairns a few years later, and they produced another survey relating to North Queensland, *Rainforest, Reef, Mangroves, Man*, in which they drew on the inquiry's recommendations. Her conviction remained unshaken that the great question was not economic but that of the land itself, as a whole and not just "the cultivated part". "Land is the basis of every nation," she wrote, "and if we have damaged much of it, then the challenge is to restore that and preserve what is left undamaged for the future."[62] Since childhood the land had been part of her and she of it, and as one of her closest friends describes it, this was a "deep umbilical relationship". Whatever she was doing and wherever she was, there seemed to be a "deep and indissoluble connection between her eyes and the landscape".[63] She would continue to fight on its behalf.

Judith was also more and more conscious of the "Dark Ones" she wrote about in one of her poems, the Aboriginal people whose lives and fate were so closely related to the land. She was aware, also, how little many, if not most, other Australians cared about them.

> *On the other side of the road*
> *the dark ones stand.*
> *Something leaks in our blood*
> *like the ooze from a wound.*
>
> *In the town on pension day*
> *mute shadows glide.*
> *The white talk dies away*
> *the faces turn aside.*
> *A shudder like breath caught*
> *runs through the town.*

> *Are they still here? We thought ...*
> *Let us alone.*[64]

But she refused to turn aside. In the midst of all her other activities she was corresponding with a young Queensland Aborigine, Estelle Martin, who had written asking for her help. Estelle's brother, Richard Martin, had been convicted of manslaughter – his sister believed unjustly – and given a savage sentence, and appeals for a retrial or for a review of this sentence were refused. Estelle compared his case with that of Saccho and Vanzetti in the United States in the 1930s. The authorities were not interested in justice in her brother's case either, she believed, but in keeping an Aboriginal leader in prison. "I really am depressed," Estelle wrote, "and tired of fighting. Judith, I never believed that white authority could lie so much about a poor black man who is not a murderer ... He is a leader – no wonder they try to break his spirit."[65] Judith did what she could, but the system, she realised, was weighted against Aboriginal people.

She was growing more angry at the way injustices committed against Aboriginal people and their suffering were being ignored, and the way so many "pale eyes" were turning away from "those dark gutters of grief", the eyes of the "dark ones".[66] As she wrote to Len Webb, "most Australians have been trained to suspect feelings, having been brought up to believe we contain Very Nasty Animals, which have to be kept down; and plenty of us have had very nasty experiences with these animals because we don't know them. Nothing makes the average White Australian Protestant male more uneasy than any display of ordinary (basic) reaction to a situation." This, she thought was a main reason why Aborigines

> seem the lowest of the low to most people and end up in jail. What they do is the equivalent of an uncontrolled Person of the White Lower Classes and therefore deplorable. If we could learn somehow to be ourselves and not to be Norm Everage, there might be a chance of understanding ourselves; as it is, we hoard the whole thing up and it turns to poison and greed.[67]

She did not go to the other extreme either, however, and embrace the cult of the Noble Savage. Judith remained her father's daughter, concerned for practical solutions. Throughout the years she was to do what she could on behalf of Aboriginal people when they asked her to do so – Kath Walker had taught her to be scrupulous in this matter – usually at the political, organisational or financial level.

She had little time for the cult of feeling so popular in the 1970s, largely a result of American influence. Hearing of a group in Cape Cod who called themselves the "New Alchemists", for instance, who were trying new methods of farming using only wind and solar power, she remarked; "Well, if they do set up things like that, come the famines who will come swarming over the wall to loot it all". Nice feelings alone could not overcome the ruthlessness of the powerful. Jack's argument still seemed to her as cogent as ever, that the essential problem was the divorce between intellect and biological or feeling response, and the split somehow had to be healed if society were to become more just and we were to live in an ecologically sustainable way.

Her old disillusionment with politics was returning, especially now that, with the National Estate inquiry finished, she had a little more time to reflect on what was happening. The Whitlam Government seemed to be betraying many of the hopes she and many others invested in it. Though she did agree to appear on the stage of the Sydney Opera House to support the government at the launch of their 1974 election campaign, she was beginning to see Canberra and the political game itself somewhat differently, as increasingly "inhuman ... though there are many I love here". As she put it in one of her "Brief Notes on Canberra":

> *Considered as an ecosystem*
> *Canberra is impossible.*
> *No balance between input and output;*
> *a monoculture community*
> *whose energy goes entirely into organization.*[68]

She was a poet, dedicated to "the process of understanding one's life and its meaning ... That is what life is for". But imagination and this kind of reflective feeling were increasingly being "devalued in favour of the harder values of so called nationalism", especially economic rationalism.[69] The issues which mattered so profoundly to her seemed to be slipping into the background as economic values moved to the fore. The Great Barrier Reef was threatened again, with renewed attacks by "developers" supported by the Queensland Government, which was playing the card of States' rights and trading on growing dislike of the Whitlam Government. A headline in the *Australian* highlighted this trend: "Canberra Rapidly Losing Say Over Off-Shore Oil Search Areas".[70] In Cabinet Moss Cass and Tom Uren, supporters of the environmentalists, were losing ground to the influential Minister for Minerals and Energy, Rex Connor, who was now siding with the developers. After "fourteen years of bloody battle", Judith told Kathleen McArthur wearily, there seemed no end in sight.[71] Not that she would give in. She still put most of her energies into the struggle and at the end of that year minded the WPSQ office during the Christmas break to make up for her many absences during the year.

The long-standing battle over Fraser Island, which had such a special place in her memory, was reaching a climax as Bjelke-Petersen's Government supported the push to exploit the island's mineral sand resources. Whitlam, who had promised to defend the island, was under increasing pressure, both political and economic, and ministers like Connor were gaining the upper hand. People still looked to Judith for help, hoping that now that she was in Canberra so often she might be able to influence the Federal Government. But that was seeming less likely. In April 1975 Milo Dunphy wrote asking: "What on earth to do about Whitlam and Connor and Fraser Island and the Kakadu export licences?"[72] A public statement by the former members of the National Estate Committee and a newspaper advertisement were suggested,[73] and Geoff Mosley of the ACF proposed to Macfarlane Burnet that all those who had signed the letter supporting Whitlam in 1972 now write to him about Fraser Island,[74] reminding him how ecologically significant it was, as the largest sand island in the world, but also how vulnerable.

Judith responded and tried to involve as many other distinguished Australians as she could, writing to Patrick White in March, for instance, and reminding him that their grandfathers had known one another long ago, and telling him that now was the time for them to stand together in defence of the environment. He agreed, remarking that "we are run by sinister powers, inside and outside Australia [and] they have to be fought", though as before, he also warned her that the battle was taking up too much of her time as a writer. Yet he also conceded that "any kind of artist who has been to that island will remain affected by it forever, which is a very good reason for protecting it".[75] He wrote a personal letter to Whitlam, asking him to save the island. His previous novel, *The Eye of the Storm*, had reached its climax on Fraser Island and the novel he was writing at that time, *A Fringe of Leaves*, was based on the story of Eliza Fraser, shipwrecked off the coast, who had lived with the Aborigines on the island and given her name to it. It has a memorable description of her first glimpse of the island:

> Round them shimmered the light, the sand, and farther back, the darker, proprietary trees. Where the beach rose higher, to encroach on the forest, great mattresses of sand, far removed from the attention of the tides, were quilted and buttoned down by vines, a variety of convolvulus, its furled trumpets of a pale mauve.[76]

The ACF also took up the cause, declaring in March that the whole island should be a National Park and given World Heritage listing. Geoff Mosley, the ACF's Executive Director, wrote a letter appealing to the Managing Director of Dillingham-Murphyores, the company planning to mine there, appealing to him to stop the project.[77]

Judith, for her part, wrote to Whitlam, asking him to veto mining proposals, expressing her concern for the government's image and reminding him that "most conservationists are Labor voters".[78] The political argument was a strong one. In the Queensland State election the conservationists were campaigning actively against Bjelke-Petersen's Government, especially in the marginal seats, accusing him of "betrayal" and declaring that they would not be placated until mining was stopped, telling him: "You have let Dillingham's bulldoze your government too far".[79] At the Federal level, however, Whitlam seemed convinced by Connor's arguments in favour of mining. Caucus sided with Cass, the Minister for Environment and Conservation, and as a result Cabinet decided to hold a public inquiry beginning 1st of June. At the same time, however, although no licence was granted, Cabinet gave approval to Dillingham to begin negotiating export contracts. Connor, who had been absent from the Caucus meeting on account of illness, thus managed to get at least part of his way, threatening to resign rather than "be dictated to by the lunatic fringe of a pack of conservationists".

It was a stalemate. As Judith acknowledged, "we all know no government these days, however good its original intentions, can help succumbing to some pressures and compromising some of its assurances".[80] But she kept up the pressure, writing to a number of prominent Australians – MacMahon Ball, David Campbell, Frank Fenner, Leonard French, Bruce Grant, Sir Keith Hancock, Davis McCaughey, Patrick White, Manning Clark, and Ken Myer – encouraging them to express their disapproval of mining to Whitlam. Disillusion was growing. The Prime Minister's "self-centred policies", Hancock wrote, were breeding "cynicism amongst supporters of Labor". Patrick White wrote to Whitlam, attacking him for his backdown:

> I was appalled and depressed ... As well as ruining one of the most beautiful and scientifically unique islands in the world, the move is going to cause no end of trouble to the Labor position by further embittering already disillusioned conservationists in Queensland and elsewhere. Can't something be done, please, to avert the destruction of an island which should be preserved as a national park?[81]

Whitlam's bureaucratic reply – "I want to reassure you as best I can" – did not reassure him. As he said to Nin Dutton, "I'm afraid [Whitlam's] very stubborn. I don't want to end our alliance, but it won't be what it was if he sells out on Fraser Island. I too, can see my way to being stubborn." He also wrote disgustedly to another correspondent that "they seem intent on digging out every dollar there is in the ground, destroying natural beauty which is the only thing we've got in any way distinguished".[82]

In the long run, however, despite everything Fraser Island was saved, thanks to the Queensland Trades and Labour Council which resolved to put a black ban on all activity if mining went ahead – as they had done in the Great Barrier Reef case – and to the High Court which found in favour of FIDO's case against mining. In October 1976, the report the Whitlam Government had commissioned also recommended against mining. The new government, under Malcolm Fraser, accepted this recommendation and, despite opposition from the Queensland Government, mining ceased on 1st January 1977.

Judith was increasingly wondering whether anything would ever reverse the trend of destruction and exploitation which, the more she learned of it, seemed to flow through Australian history. As she wrote in "At a Public Dinner":

> *It was all there in the first step onto land,*
> *the flag raised, the guns fired . . .*
> *. . . Go away, we're tired;*
>
> *we're tired of being asked about tomorrow.*
> *Today the profit. Today the hideous old,*
> *the rising price of uranium, beef and gold*
> *Today, for the dreamers, the totally useless sorrow.*[83]

In April she sent an ancient Japanese poem to Barbara Blackman who was then overseas but shared her feelings. Meredith, studying in Japan, had translated the poem and sent it to her, but she remarked to Barbara that the poem "couldn't have been more apposite" to their present situation.[84]

> *Here and there and all over the place*
> *stirring up sensations –*
> *nothing but guys who like to drink big.*
>   *Fern leaves and clouds*
>   *The world so cold and dark*
> *But suddenly one day*
> *these fellows*
> *will just rot away*
> *Will be carried off with the rain*
> *and afterwards nothing but silent blue ferns*
> *and somewhere*
> *some transparent geologist will record*
> *that this was the coal-age of humanity.*

Judith was also beginning to feel somehow homeless. She had always had a deep feeling for place, but though she still owned "Calanthe" and went back there when she could, she spent much of her time travelling or staying at University House in Canberra – and she had never liked institutional living, however sophisticated. Meredith was not due back from Japan until April 1975; she was enjoying herself learning about traditional Japanese culture. She even had a Buddhist monk boyfriend. But Mount Tamborine no longer seemed to Judith such "a comfortable place to be" as "development" flourished with "revolting plastic flags fluttering all over" and "promotions of all kinds. The captains and kings of industry" were triumphing even here,[85] and right-wing views were spreading amongst their formerly tolerant neighbours. So she felt "in a kind of limbo", a feeling heightened by a family wedding in New England. As she reported it to Barbara Blackman it was

> all very traditional, in a chapel built by an Early Family of great wealth ... Quantities of champagne and all the women my past schoolmates now stout wives of graziers and obviously padded with banknotes. Totally unconversable on any subject but cooking.

She felt an outsider also because of her association with the Labor Government. "Everyone was very delicate but I do not think I am popular with my family. However, I refuse to regard myself as an outcast because of my small-l liberalism, and brazened it out without much trouble." This suspicion against her because of her politics increased her unease; the country, seemed to be "getting terribly polarised".[86]

On 31st May 1975 she turned sixty. Her mood was very different from that of the poem "Turning Fifty". Then, in the kitchen at "Calanthe", she had raised her cup of coffee,

> *dark, bitter, neutral, clean,*
> *sober as morning –*
> *to all I've seen and known –*
> *and this new sun.*[87]

But now she felt she was walking a tightrope:

> *I've cultivated stability*
> *by keeping my horizons straight.*
> *Now of a sudden we're crossing*
> *very mountainous country.*

The way ahead was looking more and more uncertain and it seemed that she would have

> *Late in life, though, to acquire the habit*
> *long unadmired in others*
> *of seeing no further than the pace or two ahead*
> *on a quaking rope.*[88]

True, as another poem suggests, Jack's memory sustained her, but painfully:

> *Space between lip and lip*
> *and space between*
> *living and long-dead flesh*
> *can sometimes seem the same.*
>
> *We strive across, we strain*
> *to those who breathe the air,*
> *to those in memory;*
> *but Here is never There ...*
>
> *and this each human knows:*
> *however close our touch*
> *or intimate our speech,*
> *silences, spaces reach*
> *most deep, and will not close.*[89]

But friends were supportive. Charles and Barbara Blackman returned to Australia, to Sydney, after several years overseas, and organised a birthday party for Judith at Chiron College at Birchgrove, an independent and somewhat unorthodox school they had founded after their return. A newspaper account described the afternoon in the "picturesque and slightly trendy grandeur of the College on the waterfront with students in their blue jeans serving champagne and orange juice or stirring large pots of curry not far from the table crowned with a giant French country wedding cake surrounded by a mountain of profiteroles". Getting guests through the door when Judith was standing nearby was "like asking a toddler to control peak-hour traffic. They cuddled her, swamped her with gifts and fresh wildflowers, then they chatted, reminisced and laughed." Most were friends of many years, some of whom Judith had not seen for a long time. A.D. Hope was there, "chort[ling] happily about the power of alcohol to uninhibit" and Nancy Keesing, pondering a question she had been asked about the punctuation of a poem of one of the English Romantic poets. Gwen Harwood, who had been there though she had not known Judith well then, was a reminder of Brisbane at the end of the war, and painters and musicians mixed with environmentalists, sharing a common friendship.

Although Judith enjoyed the day, it was also an occasion for taking stock. As she told the journalist covering the party: "I think it would be a good idea, now I'm 60, to stop doing all those things people keep wanting me to do. Now I shall do those things I want to do, and I think now is a very good time to start," and she quoted a saying by a Chinese poet:

> Before 40 life is a struggle to get on the right side of fame, fortune and sex. After 70 one is prone to being beset by decline and disease, so between 50 and 60 is the great calm plateau of life, and 60 is the peak.

"Now I can still enjoy my wine and my books and my writing," she went on, "I propose to make my sixties time of calm enjoyment".[90]

It was a "very generous party", and she still has the white umbrella signed by everyone present – the Blackmans' idea. It was also perhaps a moment of the kind she described in "Grace", which

> *... slants a sudden laser through common day.*
>
> *It seems to have nothing to do with things at all,*
> *requires another element or dimension.*
> *No contemplation brings it; it merely happens,*
> *past expectation and beyond intention.*[91]

Writing to Barbara Blackman a week later to thank her and sending "an inadequate quantity of Queensland nuts and chrysanths [chrysanthemums] to express some of my thanks", she said that it "couldn't have been more beautiful".[92]

But then it was back to the round of meetings, a meeting of the UNESCO Arts Committee, for instance, in Canberra, which was "cold, cold, cold", and which seemed to Judith to "produce little but paper". On her way to her aircraft in Sydney she was nearly swept off the tarmac by wild weather. When she returned to Mount Tamborine she found the place crowded with newspaper and radio reporters, "doing a promotion at the behest of demonaical developers – may they spend the afterlife eating dirt and being run over one and all".[93] She was depressed, also, by other developments, especially on Fraser Island, and spent many hours at meetings to plan tactics for the forthcoming enquiry into their developments. To add to the depression, she felt that having been away so often she was no longer pulling her weight as president of the WPSQ, at a time when the Bjelke-Petersen Government's tactics were becoming increasingly tough. John Sinclair, having lost his job as a public servant, was entangled in a complicated court case which threatened to bankrupt him. In comparison, "even the snow and ice" of the south began to look "tempting".[94]

Queensland had been her summer. But now,

> *Doesn't summer*
> *half know itself a cheat, conjuring*
> *all this green foliage*
> *to hide the rocks, the earth*
> *that waits to take it back?*
> *Beauté de diable*
> *its enchanting flesh*
> *already beginning to droop like an old breast*
> *on ribs of bone.*

It was beginning to seem time to return to the cold.

> *...I move*
> *closer towards the pole.*

> *Wind off the mountain snow,*
> *small white-etched trees*
> *leaning in leeward gestures.*
> *I shall step carefully into the acid vapour*
> *of morning frost. At night*
> *I shall light fires.*[95]

In the meantime, since Meredith wanted to stay longer in Japan, Judith decided to visit her there. What she was doing certainly seemed more interesting than the political chores Judith had been involved in, like editing the National Estate report "at top speed so that the relevant pollies can have it before they draft their election speeches". Meredith had been learning to play the Japanese flute from a Zen Buddhist monk, a hermit who lived in the mountains outside Kyoto who occasionally came down to teach selected people to play the flute "and also dances through the streets, playing it in the old style". As well as this and her other studies Meredith, who had learned pottery in Australia, also worked from time to time with potters in a village not far from Kyoto.

In October Judith left for three weeks in Kyoto to stay with Meredith in "her little wood and paper room in the little house she shares with friends", a young man from Oxford, a Japanese dental mechanic and other "odd comers and goers from Buddhist monks to television announcers".[96] For once, she enjoyed the flight. Looking down on the China Sea

> *on archipelagos of sullen pearl*
> *and gaps of ocean flicked by sunlight's fin,*
> *it set me staring downwards into me,*

reminded her, even within the "dragon shell" of the aircraft, that nature was powerful still. She gloried in the

> *... sudden light, the gaps between*
> *terrors, the glow of cloud-tops, crevices*
> *of green serenity. Whimpering, half in love,*
> *I press on the armoured glass to watch you, lean*
> *to your diverse passages, asking what you mean*
> *by those mute and merciful designs of pearl,*

to be answered with a display of power as it "knocked [her] back with a fang-flash and a snarl"[97] of thunder and lightning.

Japan opened out another world. Meredith's current boyfriend, a monk who had "fled his temple on an offshore island and his disapproving family for one last lingering look at freedom represented by Meredith",[98] took them to the monastery of Nanzenj, "a lovely place ... with a holy waterfall and many famous paintings ... [which] specialises in Tigers, not actual but metaphorical, in the paintings, that is".

Meredith had been learning the art of Noh theatre at one of the oldest and most famous schools. It was something of an honour to be accepted, but she was to make her first appearance as the mother in what proved to be "a long sad play" about a family crisis over a younger son who refused to be priest. Judith was invited to attend. Before it, however, Meredith and an English friend, Stephen (whom she was later to marry), spent hours practising, and "the little wood and paper house resounded with extraordinary noises in practice with fans". The actual performance, which lasted all day, took place in a temple, with the audience kneeling or cross-legged on cushions – "hard on my ageing bones but very educative", since "it was odd, to say the least, to observe the daughter of one's blood in kimono and obi singing in strange tones and in a foreign language".[99] During the interval, however, she

> distinguished [herself] by getting locked in a toilet, a difficult situation for one without any Japanese, except for the word Ano, which means Er and was for once quite useful; and was finally let out by a giggly lady whom I managed to signal through a window. To be locked in a Japanese temple lavatory is no mean experience and I am sure the audience of ladies is still retelling the story.[100]

For her part, Meredith sang her way through the play successfully, thus graduating to the next stage of her training.

They also spent a day at a folk festival in a country town not far away, attended by nearly all the local farmers and their wives. The villagers performed temple festival dances and drum rituals with gusto, with many children joining in. One item, Judith thought, seemed "just like 'Oranges and Lemons' in a foreign language", though the children were "perfectly drilled little creatures", reminding her that she was in

Japan, which perhaps was why she especially enjoyed one little boy who "kept putting out his tongue at the audience and looking embarrassed".

The stay was not entirely peaceful, however. The right-wing political movement, Black September, was active at the time, and Kyoto was a centre of their activities. Meredith had to go to the university to collect her scholarship allowance and Judith went with her. Red Army members confronted them at the main entrance, however Meredith knew the ropes, so they went around to another gate and made their way in. Judith was not particularly troubled by those activities, describing them somewhat insouciantly:

> There is a class of sort of failed samurai ... who specialise in the ancient craft of robbery and murder, learn from early babyhood how to navigate themselves underwater for miles and jump rivers and climb castle walls and stand for hours dead still in fields pretending to be scarecrows. A disciplined race even in the lower orders. But I don't think they live on wheatgerm ... they must be a modern modification.[101]

The pollution she saw everywhere was more shocking, and in a poem written later she recalled listening to monks singing by a waterfall, but also being appalled by the state of the river,

> ... *the sweet Kamo*
> *choked with old plastic toys,*
> *tyres and multiple rubbish.*[102]

On the whole, however, she enjoyed Japan, especially the visit to the temple near the grave of a famous woman poet of the tenth century, and another day at a potter's village to meet Meredith's potter friends. They also shopped, worked together in Meredith's "tiny impossible garden", planting ferns "stolen from a nearby mountain" and talked. It would not be easy, she realised, for Meredith to return to life in Australia.

Even for Judith the return was difficult:

> It doesn't matter where you go for escape, bulldozers and gravel trucks and their consequences always follow. We have the whole of the south end of Long Road marked out in lots for development

and no doubt the end of the credit squeeze will mean a rash of awful cottages and brick horrors and the road will be widened or something. Already the last of the gravel-red roads are being bitumised, and North Tamborine shopping centre is a confusion of new roads and new shops. And the Gold Coast approacheth closer and closer.[103]

Shortly afterwards an advertisement in the *Canberra Times* caught her eye. A block of land, 100 acres, part of a 2250 acre cattle station, "Half Moon", near the little settlement of Mongarlowe, 16 kilometres from Braidwood, which was about 80 kilometres east of Canberra, was for sale. The owner, Stewart Harris, an English journalist and for some time Australian correspondent for the London *Times*, was having to sub-divide the property. His children had grown up and moved away, and the property was too large for him and his wife to manage by themselves. He was an environmentalist and, having managed to have the whole area gazetted as a wildlife refuge, made it clear that the new owner would be expected to accept the responsibilities involved. This was no problem for Judith – as someone who came from a pastoral family she understood the pressures which obliged Harris to sell, and liked the place. The fact that, as a journalist, Harris had been sympathetic to the Aboriginal cause helped too. So Judith decided to buy the land and build on it.

For his part, Harris was relieved that she understood his reason for selling and later wrote of the way she appreciated the compromises sometimes forced on the "man on the land". During a severe drought, for instance, he got permission to shoot some of the kangaroos he was supposed to protect, to prevent all of them dying of starvation. He informed Judith that he had used a professional shooter, but was worried about her response. In fact she said nothing. As he got to know her, she became a kind of conscience and he felt her "brooding potentially critical presence" as he sold more blocks, hoping that "she would approve of the new owners' environmental credentials". They were later to become allies on the Aboriginal Treaty Committee, but he remained respectful, seeing her as "a formidable woman ... who would perhaps risk a promising personal relationship ... for a greater, general good".[104]

Judith loved the place. It was the kind of country in which she had grown up in New England, though rougher, possibly colder, and less cultivated, on the edge of the escarpment overlooking the Shoalhaven River. She wrote to Kathleen, telling her that:

> The land is so lovely I can't believe I've got it ... All ironstone quartz conglomerate rocks with all manner of wild flowers. Plenty of roos and wallaroos graze near the house and birds. I swam in the Clear Clean Wild River last time I was there ... So who cares about the chill winds of the Abyss?[105]

She would have liked to give it an Aboriginal name, but the local language had died out and in any case there were few Aboriginal people left in the district. The area had been settled early, in the 1830s, mostly by British officers from India, and they had disposed quite thoroughly of the Aboriginal people as well as of the forests which had originally covered the hills. One of Judith's anthropologist friends came up with a word for "Edge" in the Pitjantjatjara language, but it did not seem right to her to use it here, and so she kept to English.[106]

There was no house on the land, so she was not able to settle there at once. For the time being she continued to live at University House in Canberra while she negotiated with architects and builders about a house and then waited for them to build it.

As a child she had identified with

> ... the sapling's growing-point;
> a gathered strength, a total thrust
> muscling itself, its swirl and sheaf
> to one high clench of folded leaf.
>
> My body answered tiptoe there,
> a central need to rise as high
> as limit, balance, let you go.

But now she was realising that;

> Breadth, form, completion – those depend
> upon a proper symmetry.

> *The length of branch, the stance in space,*
> *what leaf and fruit tree can sustain*
> *dispose around and central strain.*[107]

This house would be her new centre of gravity.

She was still writing, and had managed to do so even in the midst of all her other activities. Though plagued by lack of time "to meditate and work on things" she would still draft a poem, she recalled later, "and by the time I got back to it another poem would be nagging at me".[108] Even at her busiest, poetry remained "a way of seeing where [she was] at a particular time".[109] As she put it on another occasion "you don't know where you are until you know what you are".[110] At the beginning of the decade she had felt that, being a writer, many saw her merely as a "bunny with a plastic sword".[111] But now she was turning back to writing. In 1975 Oxford published a collection of her essays on literature, the environment and Aboriginal issues, *Because I Was Invited,* and her tenth collection of poetry, *Fourth Quarter*, was published the following year.

Its title signalled her sense that she was entering into the last stage of life, but, as the title poem expresses it, defiantly so. It is addressed to the moon, the woman's sign, not at the full, but with a "last lemon-quarter grin". Her fighting spirit remains:

> *I won't resign.*
>
> *Tomorrow you'll be gone*
> *into the black;*
> *but you're just moving on*
> *to make your comeback.*
>
> *I won't be back again*
> *or not this way.*
> *But still there's gold to win*
> *from the mullock's clay.*[112]

It was not an easy collection; as she told Heather Rusden she was trying to "express in it the inexpressible", to "say a few things Jack's work had been pointing to"[113] and there was a new austerity evident in many of the poems. She was also concerned with structure, the arrangement of the poems in the book as a whole. In her view the critics had missed this and the fact that it was based on the mandala, a symbol of wholeness. The poems as a whole were an extended meditation. So there are poems about dreams and growing old, often identifying with the waning moon:

> *Men spy you out with eyes.*
> *Their red brand's on your flank*
> *and they plan colonies*

– a reference, of course, to talk of space travel and the "conquest" of the moon, but also an indication of her feeling for the conquered and oppressed. Hence the conclusion:

> *As for us, your true citizens,*
> *we'll never make it*
> *into those well-controlled*
> *and solar-heated settlements.*[114]

Her life was moving in the opposite direction from the world of technology, moving inwards to respond to the voice to which her poetry had always answered,

> *... the voice ... not our own*
> *and yet its tone's deeper than intimate,*

which speaks the question, "expected and entreated long" which demands one "put all else away"[115] – hence the prayer to the moon, "Chill Domina":

> *... the prayer of age. In my last quarter*
> *let me be hag, but poet.*
> *The lyric note may vanish from my verse,*
> *but you have also found acceptable*
> *the witch's spell –*
> *even the witch's curse.*[116]

This prayer was perhaps answered. Internationally her reputation was growing – over the next few years writers in Italy, Russia,

Yugoslavia and even China wrote asking permission to translate her poetry. She also carried on a long correspondence with a young American, Peter Kaplan, a poet who lived at Wood's Hole, Massachusetts, and earned his living as a waiter at a café for writers and artists; he wrote her letters "full of rainbows and recipes for clam chowder". He told her that he had long admired her poetry, especially their "wonderful intelligence and stamina", and felt a "great spiritual closeness to her" and wanted to publish an American edition of her work. Robert Lowell, he said, still remembered her from the Poetry Expo in Montreal and "even recalled liking your poetry (this in itself is amazing; he tends not to like his contemporaries)".[117] Judith enjoyed these letters for their enthusiasm, their oddity and their feeling for poetry. But Kaplan died suddenly and mysteriously by drowning and nothing came of his proposal. Soon afterwards the American publishers, Houghton Mifflin, published a selection of her poems. Virago Press in England were also interested in doing an English edition, and her work was featured in the *Times Literary Supplement* in a special issue on Australian literature.[118]

In 1975 Judith was awarded the Robert Lee Frost Medallion for poetry and a further Creative Arts Fellowship at the Australian National University, which put her in touch with writers in Canberra. She often attended their Wednesday evening meetings at which they talked about poetry in general as well as their own, though she doubted whether she was very helpful. She had "never regarded the opinions of other writers on what [she] was going to write", regarding poetry as "something you write or don't write. It only comes of itself. Influence from outside is bad as well as easy."[119] Nevertheless many of the younger or newer poets were inspired by her: Barbara Giles, Joyce Lee, David Brooks, Mark O'Connor (another passionate environmentalist), Margaret Diesendorf, Tim Aslanides, Julian Croft, and Peter Skryznecki, who had been teaching in New England and writing poems about the place. She welcomed him in a poem she dedicated to him as a

> *latecomer to my country,*
> *sharer in what I know*
> *eater of wild manna.*[120]

Over the years she also kept up a special correspondence with Silvana Gardner, a poet and painter whose family had come to Australia as refugees. Older poets of her own generation, like Rosemary Dobson, Dorothy Green and A. D. Hope remained friends, and she saw more of them now that she was more often in Canberra. In Queensland she still kept in touch with Elizabeth Perkins and John Bligh, a friend from the days in Brisbane in the late 1940s. She also corresponded with an English poet and Professor of Classics, Martin Robertson, whom she had met in England in 1968, and exchanged poems with him.

Young women especially looked to her as a role model. According to Fiona Capp, Wright "made writing the most natural thing in the world. Her brilliance did not daunt but inspire. She did not set herself up as one of the immortals," though she had been "truly visionary" in her work for the environment and for the Aboriginal cause, as well as in her poetry. For Capp, Vincent Buckley's patronising judgement was both laughable and offensive:

> When [Judith Wright] is content to be a woman, [he wrote] enduring the profound incidents of a woman's life, she is able, paradoxically enough, to transcend her womanliness to be a very fine poet. When she attempts to be not a woman, but a bard, commentator or prophet, she becomes a bit of a shrew which is the worst and most unwomanly of all things that a woman may become.

"What is alright for W. B. Yeats," Capp comments, "evidently, is not alright for Judith Wright even though she has often been likened to him." What especially appealed to young women like her was the fact that, as well as writing powerfully about areas of women's experience seldom explored, Judith had also, as it were, beaten the men at their own game. There was nothing apologetically "feminine" about her and Capp particularly admired her intelligence and her "grim humour".[121]

For Finola Moorhead, too, Judith's work represented a kind of transformation. She had been writing poetry all through her adolescence, but when she read Wright she realised that

> the daydream, the emotionality of belief and hope [of her poems] the grand themes the abstract schemes bore no resemblance to

> [Wright's] clarity. The word-craft, the rhythm, serenity. The authority. Because she was as great as any poet anyway, because I had met her and she was real and honest with me, Judith defined both poetry and the poet.

Moorhead recalls visiting Mount Tamborine in 1973 when she encountered this authority again:

> [She] was reading Patrick White's *The Eye of the Storm* and walked through the house mumbling, "Patrick, Patrick, a noddy is not a gull, it's a tern. They're banksias on Fraser Island not carobs or a cyclone doesn't have an eye ... I realised that for me, like Patrick, the truth of the matter was not necessarily fact. But for the poet, accuracy was essential.[122]

So, too, was her passion and involvement, something previous generations had suspected but which the 1970s generation believed in as Judith did, having always insisted on the connection between literature and life – she admired books like Helen Garner's *Monkey Grip*, which had just appeared, for its physical as well as its intellectual honesty.

Nevertheless the freewheeling 1960s and 1970s were coming to an end. The constitutional crisis precipitated when the Senate, where the Opposition had the majority, refused supply, reached its conclusion on 11th November 1975 when Governor-General Sir John Kerr dismissed the Whitlam Government. Like many others, Judith was stunned by the news, and it was a moment she would never forget. "I knew people whose life's work seemed to fall" with Whitlam, she recalled later. For her, it marked the end of an era since she had felt that if "we ever were going to grow up it might have been under Whitlam". The Vietnam War, for instance, had been an "appalling example" of the way Australian governments allowed themselves to be influenced by overseas interests, Whitlam had put an end to our involvement in it, introducing an independent foreign policy for the first time as well as many other reforms. He had been destroyed, she believed, by those opposed to change. From now on it would be impossible to trust any government.[123]

It was time to make the break – going back to Queensland, where Bjelke-Petersen was still in power, was now like "stepping into a mud hole".[124] The "They" of the poem of that name, who "look like people" but are not, seemed to dominate business and political life there. Her family might have been successful financially and had profited by the process of imperial expansion but they had always played by the rules, she felt. As she put it in a poem she wrote to them about this time, they were like

> *A small stream, narrow but clean,*
>
> *running apart from the world.*
> *Those hills might keep them so,*
> *granite, gentle and cold.*

But now a stream of filth seemed to be running

> *through settlement and town*
> *darkened by chemical silt,*[125]

– the love of money which was threatening to destroy the earth. Going south, back to the cold, she would be returning to her roots in a sense, preserving the best of that tradition.

She was able to sell "Calanthe" to someone she knew would look after it, a retired businesswoman who had helped with management problems at *Wildlife* some years earlier. She promised to keep the name "Calanthe" and the big plank of weathered beech on which Jack had carved it, and to look after the garden they had loved.

There was much to leave behind and many good memories, even of the political struggles. As Judith wrote in her last message to the WPSQ, "some of the best memories of my life will be of the Society and the work we have done together and you yourselves".[126] Most important, however, were the memories of Jack. Not far away, was

> *...the mountain that we climbed*
> *when hand in hand my love and I*
> *first looked through one another's eyes*
> *and found the world that does not die.*
>
> *Wild fuchsia flowered white and red,*
> *the mintbush opened to the bee.*

*Stars circled round us where we lay
and dawn came naked from the sea.*[127]

But now Judith's life lay elsewhere. Meredith had come back from Japan, for the time being at least, to work on her thesis in Canberra, so they would be together again. Builders had started work on the house at "Edge" but it would be sometime before it was finished, so she and Meredith rented an old building, formerly a bank, in nearby Braidwood, "huge [and] cobwebby" though with a "pleasant courtyard at the back", and for some time lived a "kind of caretaker life". Judith rather enjoyed their semi-bohemian existence there:

> We have distributed such possessions as we dare unpack so as to look faintly as if some one is in residence [she wrote to a friend] but we still echo: [there are] plenty of marble mantle pieces and fire places and hot water but little furniture and no carpets.[128]

After her travels over the last decade and living so much at University House, it was good to have a place of her own again and to be "settled at last in this rather crumbly though inspiring building". She was also looking forward to getting back to writing more or less full-time. Mount Tamborine would always be important, and she intended to be buried one day in the little cemetery beside Jack, but in the meantime, as she wrote in "Moving South":

*I'm tired now, summers,
of cutting you back to size.
Where I'm going you will be more succinct;
just time for a hurried embroidery
of bud, leaf, flower, seed
before the snow-winds snip you
to a root's endurance.*

*I may be more at home
observing your quick passages,
stacking up wood
against the length of winter.*[129]

CHAPTER XIII

TOWARDS A TREATY: A JUSTER JUSTICE

> Now brood no more
> On the years behind you
> The hope assigned you
> Shall the past replace,
> When a juster justice
> Grown wise and stronger
> Points the bone no more
> At a darker race.
>
> Kath Walker, from Oodgeroo,
Kathie Cochrane, University of
Queensland Press, Brisbane, 1994

In a way the fall of the Whitlam Government simplified matters. Judith was no longer likely to be asked to serve on government committees nor could she be expected to lobby with more hope of success: her views on mining and "development" generally were too well known for the new Liberal Government in Canberra to listen. Not long after the election, for instance, a friend told her that one of the new ministers had spoken "very ruefully of some attack you made recently, presumably on environmental policies. Obviously they would love to have you on their side".[1] But just as obviously this would not happen as long as they supported "development".

Being something of an outsider made Judith more powerful, however, though in a different way. As one of Isak Dinesen's characters says, "Women, when they are old enough to have done with the business of being women, and can let loose their strength, must be the most powerful creatures in the world."[2] Judith's world might be growing colder and darker but it was also growing simpler, as poems she was writing at this time, like "Easter Moon and Owl", "Patterns" and the dream sequence "Interface", suggest. "Patterns" opens with a sense of having been "too long away, too far"

> *... halfway round the world,*
> *telescoped days and stretched them out again.*
> *New faces, voices, wants; ribbons of roads and air*
> *wound in and then unwound,*
> *drained*
> *answers from blood, hand, mind.*

But now she hoped to return to familiar things:

> *the seven stones*
> *the brown clay jar,*
> *the carved seashell,*
> *still in your former place.*

In them she could recognise familiar patterns and rediscover an "old silence", a "familiar peace/persisting still,"[3] Because society seemed so intent on destruction, she wanted to get back to the kind of constructive and visionary thinking she had done with Jack, whose work, she told Heather Rusden, had given

> us a chance to revise our attitude to the world – [something which most of us seldom face] honestly perhaps never will. He always used to say there perhaps needs to be a total breakdown, a total collapse before anything new can be done. That does not worry me very much.[4]

In comparison even poetry seemed to matter less. However important for her, as she was to write later, poetry was "a marginal pursuit ... except for people like me who haven't been able to escape its orders".[5] Now, after all that had happened over the last decade, she needed to rethink, take the long perspective and move ahead: "I think if one goes back over one's poems, one tends to go back to the same place."[6] She wanted to get in touch again with the natural world, to engage in the kind of encounter registered in earlier poems like "Swamp Plant", "Encounter" and "Platypus".

Here, too, in the natural world, she remembered Jack:

> *However intently sought, it comes back changed:*
> *that clear blond evening on the pastoral hill,*
> *grass gilt by the moon,*
> *the swoop and song of the wires, the hare crouched still,*
> *your hand on mine –*
> *all comes clearly to mind, and all's estranged.*

The last decade had changed her and she was getting old:

> *It's not the past that dies. It's I who die.*[7]

Since the house at "Edge" was still not finished, they were "camping out" in Braidwood. With the spring rains the old bank, "this ancient mansion", seemed to be "falling to pieces more and more", "dropping little plaster messages on the floor and rusting the stove – I'll be thankful to be out of it". She also disliked the weather, "constant brooding cloud and cold feet", though with fewer calls on her time she was "getting some work done from time to time".[8] At Christmas, she and Meredith and some of Meredith's friends went out to "Edge" and camped there, with "much swimming and sunburn". Being on her own land again was "lovely" and she spent much of her time, as she reported to Barbara Blackman, "noting flowers, birds and kangaroos, of which we have numbers – also wombats, which are rather a worry re ticks. I don't know if they have them or not but I like wombats, which I've scarcely met before."[9] She could be more relaxed about Meredith's allergies here, too. They discovered, for instance, when she was stung that she was not allergic to bee-stings, after being stung and sitting "quivering and awaiting death for the first hour or so. It's very interesting to have such a threatened daughter, not a moment's boredom." Meredith herself, however, did not seem particularly worried. Her allergist had told her the only way to get any immunity is to have a needle a week for the rest of her life – and even then it would be six months of needles before she had any result – so she has decided it's not worth it. On the whole I agree.[10]

But environmental concerns remained. Not long after moving to Braidwood, in November 1976, she discovered an application to set up a goldmine at "Half Moon" near "Edge". It was an old goldmining area and the company involved, Alpha Mining, believed that there might still be significant deposits there. So it was back to work for Judith, organising the residents to oppose the application since, quite apart from the damage it would do to the land and its flora and fauna, mining would threaten the Shoalhaven River and the creeks running into it with mercury poisoning.

Her friendship with Kath Walker, "the person I speak to ... most easily", was also keeping her up to date on Aboriginal affairs. "I refer things to Kath in my mind," Judith told Heather Rusden[11] and they would write poems as well as letters to one another – though Judith's "Two Dreamtimes" is the only one to have been published. When she could, Judith would visit Kath at "Moongalba", finding it "a place to bring sorrows and problems" and to relax and be at peace. She describes an evening in spring 1974, for instance, when the Torres Strait Dancers group came from Brisbane for a *kup-mari* (a feast).

> About one hundred people wandered among the trees, and ate meat cooked in banana leaves in an earth oven, with chunks of pumpkin and potato instead of the traditional yams, and fruit drinks. The big Torres Islanders, soft-voiced in a language of their own, gave their traditional songs and dances in a mixture of firelight and spotlight, while the shell-strings tinkled in the breeze round the open-air stage, and the audience crowded around three sides, sitting on the sand, leaning against tree trunks and each other.[12]

Frank Heimans' film, *Shadow Sisters*, about their friendship and about "Moongalba", also gives a glimpse of the life there and of the beauty of the island as they explore it together.

Occasionally, Kath would come to "Edge" to stay with Judith, recovering from illness or from overwork, and they would have "a fine time catching up with one another". "For some reason," Wright wrote, she was "the one person I can connect with all the time ... unpredictable as she is. Everyone else seemed unspontaneous beside her."[13]

With her she was learning about Aboriginal life from the inside. Kath's elder son, Dennis, was an activist like his mother and had already had several brushes with the authorities and had spent time in prison. Her other son, Vivien, an artist and actor, finding life in Brisbane impossible, was to spend years in the United States before returning home in his thirties and dying not long afterwards. Judith was concerned about Kath's health also, writing to her during the winter of 1975 when she was still living at Mount Tamborine:

> I worry about you down there in all this damp weather, catching bronchitis. The tents are good in good weather, not so good in this showery stuff. Any time you need a break in a warm house, come up for a while, you can write here ... Look after yourself Kath and keep writing; it reaches more people than you'd think and we've got only one Kathy Walker. I am keeping the poem [which she had just sent her] in my special treasures and though our shadow cries, still we are tied together in a special way and I love you.[14]

At first it seemed that the Fraser Government would be supportive. The *Aboriginal Land Rights Act* which Whitlam's supportive government had hoped to introduce went through Parliament in 1976. Whitlam had supported the Aboriginal cause, declaring in December 1972 that the "Aborigines are our true link with our region ... a responsibility we cannot escape" and that "we will be judged by our treatment of [them]".[15] In this spirit his government had legislated for equal wages for Aboriginal stockmen and he was sympathetic to Aboriginal land claims, flying to Wattie Creek in the Northern Territory in August 1975 to hand over 3240 square kilometres of Wave Hill Station to the Gurindiji people, saying with some solemnity to their leader: "Vincent Lingiari I solemnly hand to you these deeds as proof in Australian law that these lands belong to the Gurindiji people and I put into your hands this piece of the earth itself as a sign that we restore them to you and your children forever." To this Vincent Lingiari replied in English: "We are all mates now."[16] Fraser, too, seemed to recognise this.

The 1976 *Aboriginal Land Rights (Northern Territory) Act* was a first step. It did not – at that stage legally it could not – acknowledge the prior rights of Aborigines to the land they occupied but Prime Minister Fraser told the first meeting of the new National Aboriginal Conference which he set up in April 1976 that "the key feature of the government's policy is self-management".[17] Moreover, the Act only covered the Northern Territory for which the Federal Government had responsibility; the States were still largely in control of Aboriginal affairs. But it gave some autonomy to the Northern and Central Land councils which it set up, and these councils were given inalienable freehold rights to their traditional lands.

It was a step in the right direction as far as Aborigines were concerned, though there was a long way to go. In 1974 Mr Justice Woodward had presented his report to the Commonwealth Government outlining a basis for the recognition of Aboriginal rights to land and giving them some control over mining on their traditional lands. Mining should be permitted on Aboriginal land, he recommended, but only with their consent and on terms they freely accepted, and their wishes should be overruled only in exceptional circumstances "in the national interest", and then only after a judicial enquiry.[18]

This was an advance on the Blackburn judgment of 1971 in which Mr Justice Blackburn had effectively ruled that Aboriginal people had no real rights to their land under Australian law. In his view there was "no doubt that Australia came into the category of a settled or occupied colony" and that sovereignty was vested in the Crown, so that Aboriginal rights had ceased to exist. But as Stewart Harris noted, "No Aboriginal would accept this finding, certainly not the old men of Yirrkala who still had pellets in [their] body from the fighting days."[19] In the eyes of Aboriginal people their links with the land had never been broken. Blackburn's judgment had been good news, however, for the mining companies Nabalco and Conzinc Rio Tinto, who hoped to exploit the bauxite deposits in the Arnhem Land Reserve. Other companies hoping to mine for uranium in Kakadu and elsewhere were also encouraged.

Nevertheless for the time being public opinion seemed to be sympathetic to Aboriginal claims. In Queensland in 1974 an Aborigine, Neville Bonner, had been elected to the Senate, and shortly afterwards he introduced a motion in the Senate which was passed unanimously, calling for compensation for the indigenous peoples of Australia for their dispossession. The motion stated:

> That the Senate accepts the fact that the indigenous people of Australia, now known as Aborigines and Torres Strait Islanders, were in possession of this entire nation prior to the 1788 First Fleet landing at Botany Bay, urges the Australian government to admit prior ownership by the said indigenous people, and introduces legislation to compensate the people now known as Aborigines and Torres Strait Islanders for dispossession of their land.[20]

Bonner was a conservative, telling the Senate on that occasion that he had "always tried to follow the rule of law and ... [had] counselled many of my young Aboriginal fellows that it is within the walls of this Parliament that the laws are made" and that it was "within the walls of this Parliament that we can bring to the notice of the nation the problems with which we are faced".[21] But the motion was a significant one. Many Aboriginal people were growing impatient, however, amongst them Kath Walker, "a lifetime campaigner against racism who never lost her fierceness", as Lois O'Donoghue, another campaigner, called her. To them it seemed that white Australians would never voluntarily concede their right to the land. As Blackburn had remarked when he appeared for the Arnhem Land people before Mr Justice Woodward, "a great deal of received doctrine has to be upset"[22] before that could happen, most particularly *terra nullius*, the doctrine that Australia had been legally unoccupied before the arrival of European settlers and that the Aborigines did not own the land in the sense acknowledged by British law, a sense based on individual ownership.

But legal moves were afoot to challenge this doctrine. In September 1974, and again in February 1975, Paul Coe for the Aboriginal Legal Service of New South Wales had brought unsuccessful actions in the ACT's Supreme Court to have Aboriginal land ownership recognised in the Northern Territory's uranium country. When he appealed to the

High Court the appeal failed, though narrowly, with two of the five judges supporting it. But the majority view was, as Mr Justice Gibbs put it, that "the contention that there is in Australia an Aboriginal nation exercising sovereignty, even of a limited kind, is quite impossible to maintain".[23]

In international law, however, sympathy was growing for the claims of indigenous people, and in August 1976 Coe wrote to the Secretary General of the United Nations, Kurt Waldheim, seeking an advisory opinion from the International Court of Justice on the Aboriginal claim to land. In 1975 that court had found in favour of the nomadic peoples of the West Sahara, judging that, despite subsequent Spanish colonisation, they "should be considered as having in the relevant period possessed rights, including some rights relating to the lands through which they migrated" and that "these rights constituted legal ties".[24] In November of the same year, two Aborigines landed at Dover on the south coast of England in a small boat – which sank incidentally, but not before they had planted the Aboriginal flag and taken possession of the country. They informed the British Prime Minister, James Callaghan, that they had done so and that their action had been "a replica of the purported British taking of Australian Aboriginal country".[25]

Judith and her friends watched these developments. She also kept in touch with Aboriginal leaders like Kevin Gilbert and Jack Davis in Western Australia with whom she had corresponded about her paper on Aboriginal writing for the East–West Conference in Hawaii. They were looking for international support for their cause; Davis had visited the United States several times and was impressed by the strength of the black movement there. Kath Walker was also involved. She was the Australian delegate to the World Council of Churches' Conferences on Racism held in London in 1969, then in 1972 she was invited to tour and lecture in New Zealand, and was guest lecturer at the University of the South Pacific in Fiji the following year. In 1974 she was Australia's official envoy at the International Writers' Conference in Malaysia.

At the end of that year, on her way to the second World Black and African Festival of Arts and Culture in Tunis, she was also involved in an international incident. The British Airways aircraft on which she was travelling was hijacked in Dubai by a group of Arabs, demanding the release of two Palestinian prisoners in Holland and thirteen in Egypt. One of them, who spoke English, asked Kath whether she was English or Pakistani and was amazed when she said she was an Aboriginal Australian. She also told him that she had some sympathy with their cause but felt that he and his colleagues would be better employed at the Festival of Arts and Culture to which she was going than by hijacking an aircraft. From Dubai they flew to Tunis where the aircraft sat once more for hours on the ground in stifling heat. Some of the passengers were released there, though not those with British passports – ironically, as an Australian, Kath was classified as British. In a second wave of releases she was finally set free however, though there was another irony here which was not lost on her. They were taken from the aircraft in a Black Maria which, as she put it, had been "part of the system used to keep Aborigines firmly under white control, [and] here she was now being rescued in one".[26]

Judith was being educated in the realities of Aboriginal life, of a people systematically "persecuted", as she put it in "Two Dreamtimes",

> *Raped by rum and an alien law,*
> *progress and economics,*[27]

as through Kath, she met other Aborigines. "They are better people than we [are]," she decided, "more open, less demanding and profit-oriented".[28] These views coloured the research she was doing for *The Cry for the Dead*, rewriting the story of her family told in *The Generations of Men* to tell it from the point of view of the Aboriginal people they had dispossessed.

Her concern for the environment also increased her respect for Aboriginal culture. Thus she wrote that in comparison with those of the Aborigines, who "took ecological rather than mathematical laws as their base", she found our patterns of land use and our imposition on the land of a network of strict boundaries and straight lines "ecologically farcical". They were also profoundly destructive. Traditional Aboriginal attitudes to land, she believed, were much more enlightened that those of the "most enlightened conservationists".

But they are "based on a far deeper association with it than any we can claim".[29] "Our history in this land ... has been one of not listening, not understanding, not looking after it" and our tendency "to reverence only what will bring in immediate dollars". But Aborigines had always "lived within their biological means"[30] and were more adult in their attitudes. We tend to

> identify the natural world with Mum, the patient supplier of our childish needs, the wiper-up of all our childish messes, the inexhaustible worker who can always be bullied into working a little harder, supplying a little more,

but they knew they had to respect and obey it. For all of these reasons, she believed, we need to learn from Aboriginal people how to "grow up" in our attitudes to the natural world.[31]

A conservation seminar which she attended in Cairns in June 1976 increased these convictions. She was also interested to learn there more about the ways Aboriginal thinking was linked to the natural world – an idea central to Jack's philosophy which was becoming increasingly accepted. As she told to Len Webb in August:

> I don't think that even scientists any longer regard the physical and the psychic as separate, and all the work being done seems to confirm this – what is the observer, what the observed? can you tell the dancer from the dance? With the "material" becoming more and more difficult to define, and so many workers even in the sciences now more interested in studying relations than in studying the object itself, ecology rather than taxonomy, the distinctions that used to be made get more and more blurred.[32]

Webb was hoping that the Academy of Sciences would recognise the role of Aboriginal culture, especially its care of the environment, and hoped to include a chapter on this subject in the History of Australian Science which the Academy was planning. Judith also respected the practicality of Aboriginal culture and suspected the religiosity, even sentimentality, of some environmentalists in their attitude to it. Nor was she taken by ideas about Aboriginal "spirituality". "I've never strongly felt the need to posit an 'outside' deity", she told Webb, "when there's so much to be discovered about the 'inside', or an absolute when the relative's what we live by; except of course for the cosmos, the dance itself."[33] Having grown up on the land she had no time, either, for sentimentality about the natural world.

> *Beak, claws, knifebright eye,*
> *predator, antagonist,*
> *winds that slash the naked flesh*

were also, she knew, part of its "terms of possibility":

> *traps are set wherever you go.*[34]

She was also meeting other white people involved with the Aboriginal cause. One of these was Bill Stanner who had been a young anthropologist at the University of Sydney when she was an undergraduate and now held the Chair in Anthropology and Sociology at the ANU. His *White Man Got No Dreaming*, the ABC Boyer Lectures published in 1975, was an indictment of the settlers' treatment of Aboriginal Australians, the "long silence" about it and also of the assumptions that had justified and continued to justify notions of white supremacy.

Judith's friendship with Nugget Coombs was to prove even more important. Since the late 1960s he had been involved with Aboriginal affairs in his capacity as a public servant. But by 1976, no longer an adviser to government, he was free to be critical and to strike out in his own direction. Having completed his term as Chancellor of ANU, where he had helped to set up the university's Northern Australian Research Centre to do research into Aboriginal culture and history, he now spent a good deal of his time in the Northern Territory, getting to know Aboriginal people there – aware of the growing interest of mining companies in the mineral resources to be found on their traditional land, he was deeply concerned for their interests.

Even as an adviser to the Whitlam Government in October 1974, Coombs had spoken out about the plight of the Mappoon people of Queensland, whose land was threatened by mining. And in January 1975 he had spoken out about a consortium of financial interests and mining companies which had been formed to exploit the uranium resources of the Territory, especially in the Kakadu area. In 1978 Judith and he were to join forces and set up a committee to work for a treaty with the Aboriginal and Islander peoples of Australia, believing this to be the only way in which their rights could be properly safeguarded.

In the meantime, Judith continued to commute from "Edge" to Canberra for meetings – she had been reappointed to the Council of the ANU – and to visit friends. She had also been given a three-year Senior Writer's Fellowship from the Literature Board, which enabled her to research *The Cry for the Dead* and spend a good deal of time working in the National Library. But since it was always important for her to set what she was reading in its actual physical context, she also made a trip to central Queensland the following year to get a feel for the country and talk to descendants of the pioneers still living in the area. Meanwhile she saw through the press her account of the Great Barrier Reef, *The Coral Battleground,* and was assembling the essays to be published in *Because I Was Invited*.

She was still being invited to literary events also. In February 1976 she was a guest of the Adelaide Arts Festival, and later that year she agreed to be patron of the Armidale Arts Festival and patron of the Christopher Brennan Society – as her poem "Brennan" suggests, she had a special feeling for him,

> *Self-proclaimed companion*
> *of prophets, priests and poets,*
> *walker on earth's last fringes,*
> *haunted lover*
> *of the beckoning darkness,*
> *last Symbolist, poor hero*
> *lost looking for yourself.*[35]

In a sense, she felt increasingly his "journey was our journey".

She was also guest of honour at the PEN International Congress held in Sydney, took part in poetry evenings organised by the ANU Convocation during the winter and later, and opened the Conference of the Australian Universities' Language and Literature Association in

Brisbane – it proved an opportunity to spend time in the State Library in Brisbane looking over records of settlement for *The Cry for the Dead*.

Honours were coming her way, too. In 1976 she was made an honorary Doctor of Letters by her old university, the University of Sydney, in 1977 by Monash University in Melbourne, in 1981 by ANU, in 1985 by the University of New South Wales and by Griffith University in Brisbane, and the University of Melbourne in 1988. She was not particularly interested in these honours and was amused when she arrived in Melbourne to receive her doctorate from Monash and to give the graduation address to be met at the airport by a chauffeur dressed in the university's uniform. But they could be useful in other ways. As a supporter of Aboriginal rights and opponent of "development" she was, as she remarked to Len Webb, "not a respectable member of society, from the present point of view. But the number of doctorates I am accumulating indicates a kind of covert sympathy somewhere". They could also be helpful to the conservation camp where at the moment "morale ... [was] not the best". She concluded that she "had better accept the useless things, if only to increase my tailspin as it were. I am now three doctors and three fellows, quite an academic gathering in myself. Age, age, what it does to you!"[36]

She refused to join the fashion for literary theory, however. For her, literature in general and poetry in particular was a matter of passion and commitment to life in all of its aspects – a view which is evident in the letter she wrote to Peter Skrzynecki thanking him for the "good and moving poems" in his most recent volume, adding:

> I often feel that during the last few years academic reviewers have set themselves up as the only possible patrons and judges of poetry and that the poet is to them the merest producer of something to sharpen their claws on and get a possible promotion from condemning. Certainly no poet's views on poetry gets a hearing in English Departments.[37]

Rather like Patrick White, who had complained that "journalists and teachers rule what intellectual roost there is",[38] she had always been suspicious of academics who tried to dictate to artists, and she went on to tell Skrzynecki about her friend, Rodney Hall, who had recently

Jack with baby Meredith, 1950.
(Courtesy of Judith Wright)

Judith with Jack at "Calanthe", circa 1964.
(Courtesy of Judith Wright)

Jack at "Calanthe", circa 1953.
(Courtesy of Judith Wright)

Judith at "Calanthe", 1965.
(Courtesy of Judith Wright)

Studio portrait of Judith, 1967.
(Courtesy of Judith Wright)

Meredith, Judith and Jack's daughter, 1964.
(Courtesy of Judith Wright)

Rosemary Dobson (left) with Judith at a poetry reading at the Goethe Institute, 1980.

Studio portrait of Judith, 1985.
(Photograph by Attila Kiraly; courtesy of Judith Wright)

Studio Altenburg in Braidwood where Judith and Meredith
lived for a year on leaving Queensland.
(Photograph by Terry Milligan)

Judith Wright, 1996
(Photograph by Terry Milligan)

addressed a group of post-graduate students and been made to feel a "complete non-expert on literature ... or at least considered as such. Long ago," she went on rather grimly, "when there was first discussion of setting up a Chair in Australian Literature, I foresaw just such a situation"[39] – though she did not add that she had herself been approached about accepting that Chair.[40]

To her, life always seemed superior to theory. That was why she was always interested in young poets, their passion and their experimentation. One of these was Michael Dransfield, the young poet who died of a drug overdose in 1973. To her, his promise, his energy and his beauty had seemed to represent all that was hopeful in the early 1970s and she had suggested to the UNESCO Committee that he should represent younger Australian poets overseas. His death, she told Rodney Hall, stood for the tragedy of the collapse of those hopes. But there seemed to be little reason for it, other than the sheer disillusionment which seemed to be settling in around her.[41]

To her, this death seemed to epitomise all that a generation had gone through:

> *When you were dying, we couldn't stop thinking of you,*
> *counting what we had of you,*
> *letters kisses poems.*
> *They tasted chemical-strange. So did the world.*[42]

But in this world, despite her differences with academia, she was still widely regarded as one of Australia's most significant literary figures. She was the first recipient of a Senior Anzac Fellowship, set up in the last days of the Whitlam Government under an agreement between the Australian and New Zealand governments, and took it up in 1976, travelling around New Zealand, appearing at universities and teachers' colleges, meeting writers and publishers, speaking to local people and generally acting as literary ambassador over a period of six weeks.

The first week, from 14th to 21st of May, was spent in Wellington, the capital, where she met the New Zealand Book Council Management Committee, members of the local PEN Club and the Victoria University's honours students and creative writing groups. At these meetings she discussed Australian literature and the work of the Literature Board of the Australia Council, the Australian Society of Authors, the National Book Council and the Copyright Council – one of her special interests. From there she went to Palmerston North and New Plymouth and then on to Auckland for a week. On 7th June she flew to Christchurch where, apart from the usual poetry readings, interviews and meetings, she spent time with the editors of New Zealand's two leading literary magazines, *Landfall* and *Island*, and with Albion Wright of Caxton Press. From 13th to 15th June she was in Dunedin, and then spent her last two days in Kingston and as a tourist, for once, at the nearby Franz Josef Glacier.[43]

It was a strenuous itinerary but, as she told Barbara Blackman, "quite good fun". The cold, her old enemy, was ferocious, however. "I have a different word for cold", she wrote, after her three days in the snows of the Southern Alps which made her think that, after all, "Braidwood's quite a warm place".[44] She enjoyed her meetings with the writers, which were much less formal – one of them described as "featuring (public) grog, dinner and Beethoven"[45] – and thought it a pity that their work was not better known in Australia. She also realised how much the lot of Australian writers had improved in comparison with theirs, thanks to the system of grants set up by the Whitlam Government. On her return she tried to get some New Zealand work published in Australia, and she made a habit of reading some New Zealand poetry whenever she was asked to appear at readings. Using her influence with the Literature Board she also managed to get an agreement between the two countries to make exchange of books between them easier.

During the trip she was pleased to meet again the writer Hone Tuwhare, whom she had first met at the East–West Conference in Hawaii. As she had done at that conference, Judith responded to the vitality and spontaneity she found in the Maori people. In contrast, the Pakeha seemed much more staid, "Thoroughly Nice People", in fact, except for their "prime minister who takes a pride in being a Thoroughly Nasty Person".[46]

A poem tells about one occasion with the "Nice People" at a town in the Southern Island:

> *Such kind uncertain ladies in their best*
> *gather to entertain the visitor.*
> *The local talent stands by the piano*
> *fingering music-pages*
> *criss-crossed with sticky-tape.*
> *They sing "I Love You Truly"*
> *to an audience in neat and nervous rows.*
> *This district*
> *"is essentially one of clear sentiment",*
> *declared the Tourist Bureau publication.*[47]

But behind the niceness she was aware of other things; the threatened power of the natural world and the privilege of panic of mortality, which they seemed to ignore. This ignorance and timidity troubled her. When she read them some of A. D. Hope's work, for instance, poems about

> *age. Passion. Loss, and death*

she noted their uneasiness:

> *They lean a little forward. Faces answer,*
> *"We too have not much time*
> *to find the one in whose lost folds of hair*
> *we long to sleep. Here too the early snows*
> *have already fallen."*
>
> *The single terrible white peak*
> *rears in the window-frame.*
> *It is for tourists. Just a tourist-mountain.*
> *"But sometimes, we too pause*
> *and look, and look away."*
> *So white, it casts a shadow on the day.*[48]

For Judith energy always won out over respectability. So it was the Maoris who attracted her most. As Australians had done, the New Zealand settlers had failed to respect the indigenous culture.

> *Over the forest names*
> *the Maoris left, they have imposed*
> *another country's history*
> *(Palmerston North, New Plymouth).*[49]

But Maori culture seemed to her in tune with the land:

> *Vine-spiralling Maori genealogies,*
> *carved paths through forests*
> *inscribed with life-forms, coded histories*
> *tangled my eyes*
> *never quite able to meet that paua-stare.*

In contrast, the city the settlers had built seemed temporary. Built on a fault line, it

> *...climbs and scrabbles*
> *arguing with contours, trying to keep square,*

vulnerable between

> *...the double fetch of oceans*
> *belting a narrow land. Ridged peaking crawls*
> *of alps topped neat with sundae-snow.*
> *Surge. Pressure. Cracks of farmland*
> *scattered with wool-worms,*
> *sheepyards, wooden houses.*

All of their achievements seemed dwarfed by the natural world they pretended to tame:

> *This sky flies clouds, gulls, ghosts.*
> *Deep down, the world-plates struggle*
> *in strangling quiet on each other.*
> *Offshore, deliberate breakers hit the coasts.*

The Pakeha were mere onlookers. It was the Maoris who were at home here, as the poem suggests:

> *A grizzled man, scotch-eyed, grey-overcoated*
> *stares from the terrace. A straggle of Maori boys*

> *come swinging curls and tangles. Packs*
> *cling like children on their backs.*
> *Around his donegal-granite stance*
> *their laughter parts, loops out*
> *like water spiralling around a stone.*[50]

But Judith also felt an outsider. The country was too small, "all wool and a yard wide, so to speak"[51] – space was always important to her. Another poem describes this sense of being circumscribed:

> *A narrow shelf below the southern alps,*
> *a slate-grey beach scattered with drifted wood*
> *darkens the sullen jade*
> *of Tasman's breakers. Blackbacked gulls*
> *hunt the green turn of waves.*

A girl "with Maori eyes" gathers driftwood, but otherwise

> *But for her smile, the beach is bare.*

A visitor, Wright feels "a one-day stranger here",

> *not knowing even the gulls' language.*

Having been in the presence of the powers of a land very different from her own, she looks therefore for a memento. Her first thought is of a "Maori twine of roots" but she realises that she could not carry it. So she settles for a stone which she finds "in the chant of sea-edge, grind of shingle",

> *a slate-grey oval scrawled with quartz*
> *like a foam-edge, an edge of mountains*
> *white as my hair.*
>
> *I take you this for love, for being alone;*
> *for being, itself. Being that's ground by glaciers,*
> *seas and time. Out of the sea's teeth*
> *I chose it for you, for another country,*
> *loving you, loving another country.*[52]

When she returned home it was winter, metaphorically as well as literally. The work on *The Cry for the Dead* still dragged on, difficult and painful, not just because of the grim stories of settlement she was discovering but also because of the state of the archives in which she was trying to work. In the State Library in Brisbane, for instance, letters and documents to do with atrocities committed against the Aborigines had been removed or mutilated. Pages had been torn out and there were large gaps in the records – evidence of the refusal to face the truth which she was trying to challenge in her book.

Back in Braidwood, the winter seemed to go on and on, "nothing but rain and cold coming from the coast", even in November, and to make matters more depressing, the house at "Edge" was progressing very slowly. The political scene was equally depressing, so much so that in October the *National Times* published a call for a people's convention to discuss ways and means of making the voting system reflect more truly "the political wishes of all Australians".[53] But nothing came of it. With the first anniversary of the dismissal of the Whitlam Government on 11th November 1975 approaching, Judith expressed her feelings in a letter to the *Canberra Times* in which she wrote that:

> The Coalition government seemed to be at the service of the rich, [the] large share holders and the multi-nationals who are fast becoming our economic masters ... [But for their part they show no concern for] our economic independence, our environmental future, the rights of our Aboriginal people, and the social and cultural life of this nation.

Admitting that "all have found cause to criticise the actions of the Whitlam Government", she believed that the way in which it had been overthrown had been disastrous: "The crisis created by the actions of the Governor-General [have] thrown Australians into a bitter polarization which will take a long time to heal ... No responsible political party should take action, whose outcome is so obviously and predictably divisive."[54]

Her family may have been politically conservative but they had always believed in the common good, something Judith thought that the Fraser Government was neglecting in favour of sectional interests. So she readily agreed to speak at the rally, organised by historian and commentator Humphrey McQueen, on the steps of Parliament House on 11th November to commemorate Whitlam's dismissal. But she used the occasion to speak about the environmental crisis – morale was low amongst conservationists since the go-ahead for uranium mining in Kakadu.

Nevertheless there were some encouraging signs on the environmental front. Change was afoot at the ACF, for instance. Sir Garfield Barwick was about to retire as president and Judith had been approached to nominate. She refused, but suggested Nugget Coombs. Initially he was dubious about the value of doing so, but after reflection he agreed and was elected. Under his presidency the foundation took a different direction, beginning by acknowledging what we had to learn about care for the environment from Aboriginal people, and lobbying the Federal Government to hand back Uluru to its Aboriginal owners. Under Coombs' presidency the ACF also declared its opposition to uranium mining in the Northern Territory. Elsewhere, too, conservationists could take heart.

The Federal Government had accepted the findings of a report on Fraser Island commissioned by the previous government but tabled only in November 1976, which recommended against mining there. That year John Sinclair, long-time secretary of the Fraser Island Defence Organisation, was voted the *Australian*'s Australian of the Year – a public commendation for his stand. At the same time, despite widespread public concern and a ban by the four unions involved, the Federal Government confirmed export permits had been granted for existing contracts for the Ranger Consortium mining uranium in the Northern Territory, and in Queensland and Western Australia State governments seemed intent on pushing "development" ahead as fast as possible. Despite some gains, therefore, it was back to the barricades. Conservationists organised protests and wrote letters to politicians and newspapers demanding the cessation of uranium mining in Kakadu. Judith addressed one of these rallies in Canberra, pointing out the dangers involved to Aboriginal culture as well as to the environment. She also signed a full-page advertisement in the *National Times* sponsored by a group of prominent Australians calling on the Federal Government to put a stop to uranium mining.

It seemed, as usual, to be one step forward and one step back. As she wrote to Len Webb, in 1977, it seemed as if they were still "digging [themselves] out of a long dark tunnel". The Fox Royal Commission had not yet reported, but it looked as if mining would be given the go-ahead in Kakadu since the government seemed "determined to get [mining] going under any circumstances". But they would still put up a fight: "bastardi nil carborundum as the Romans used not to say". It was "all very discouraging, like catching a good surfing wave and landing on a rock. Moreover, it leaves you with a nasty way of rejoicing over every problem the government strikes which can't be good for the character."[55]

"Edge" was still not finished.

> No damn plumbers [she told a friend in February] and what there is is too haughty even to keep appointments and I can't very well move there until the plumbing is connected. Otherwise, the plastering and most of the painting are done, the electricity is waiting for the plumber to be finished, and Meredith and friends occasionally put paintbrush to oil-pot to cover the outside walls. It can't be long now but oh gawd, what it's costing.[56]

The unusual design was no doubt part of the cost. She wanted solar power, so the plan was for a row of skylights on the roof. But they were put in wrongly, so the solar unit had to go on the top of the roof. There were advantages in that, however, since she would be able to see the stars at night. But she was getting more and more impatient to move in, especially since it would be "lovely swimming in the river" over the summer.[57]

Her patience was being tried in other ways, too. *The Coral Battleground* was finished and Judith was "sticking pins in Nelson's to get it out as soon as possible before Fraser caves in over the Reef and hands it back to Queensland". On the positive side, however, her latest collection of poems, *Fourth Quarter*, had just appeared. They were poems "meant for meditation" since she was increasingly aware that "you don't know where you are until you know what you are".[58]

In May the first section of the Fox Report, which dealt with the consequences of uranium mining, was released. It was quite specific about the dangers, declaring that "the nuclear power industry was, if unintentionally, contributing to an increased risk of nuclear war". But it did not condemn the industry outright, and the newspapers carried what Judith thought "ecstatic misinterpretations" of what the report "in fact hedged about with many warnings and reservations"[59] had actually said. The Melbourne *Sun* featured the headline "Uranium: It's Yes!", the *Sydney Morning Herald* declared "Way Open To Uranium Sale" and even the usually thoughtful Melbourne *Age* said "Uranium: Cautious Yes". The Commissioners seem to have been troubled by these responses, writing to the minister concerned, the Minister for Environment, Housing and Community Development, pointing out that their findings did not amount to recommendations and should not have been used to support the government's policy, which was in favour of developing the Northern Territory as the "Uranium Province". Investors paid little attention to such cautions and there was a rush of speculation. Mining was about to begin; the genie was out of the bottle.

Poems like the "Interface" sequence published in *Fourth Quarter* gave a glimpse of Judith's feeling that the world was going mad, like the whales in "Interface (III)":

> *Whales die of a sort of madness:*
> *They choose their own beaching.*
> *Watch them come in like liners*
> *under deranged captains.*
>
> *Try to turn such whales aside*
> *back to deep waters –*
> *obstinately, blindly, certainly*
> *they'll find another beach.*
>
> *Death is inside the whale,*
> *some diseased directive,*
> *some inner treachery,*
> *some worm lodged in the brain.*[60]

It may even be that things were "past cure". But, in the meantime, friendship remained.

In May "Edge" was finished at last, and she held a cheerful housewarming party to which old and new friends came to celebrate, amongst them Dorothy Green, Rosemary Dobson and her husband Alec Bolton, Christina Stead, then living at University House in Canberra, the Japanese translator of her poetry, who was working at the ANU, and the poets Roger McDonald and Rhyll McMaster, who lived locally. Celebration was more than ever important now.

At the end of May the second section of the Fox report appeared, to do with Aboriginal attitudes to land and to mining. By now Judith and her friends were convinced by its equivocal tone that Aboriginal claims would be brushed aside, though negotiations between Aborigines and the miners went on for the rest of the year. Judith was profoundly depressed by what was happening, feeling herself "right on the ropes". Part of the depression was a feeling of shame. It was, she told Heather Rusden later, "impossible for anyone to look at that situation and know what had happened without feeling so ashamed you would like to go away and hide your head in a corner".[61]

There was also the threat to the environment involved in uranium mining. The whole system of wetlands on Kakadu, opponents feared, would be polluted and possibly also the underground river system which fed into the great artesian basin of the Centre. Protest meetings and marches continued throughout the year. Judith herself was desperately busy trying to finish *The Cry for the Dead*, but when she was invited to speak at a demonstration in Brisbane in October she agreed, though reluctantly, since when she had left Queensland she had determined to have no more to do with Queensland politics. As patron of the Campaign Against Nuclear Power, however, she felt obligated to accept the invitation, even though laws against demonstration and street marches passed by the Bjelke-Petersen Government made protests dangerous with protestors liable to end in gaol. She felt that she had "too much to do to want to spend time in the watch-house" and warned the organisers that if they attempted a march after the speeches, she would not join them – marches were forbidden though speeches were not.

Nevertheless as she told a friend, "goodness knows who else will accept a speaking assignment bar Kath Walker," so she felt she had to be there,[62] especially as she was determined to speak about Aboriginal and environmental issues as well as uranium mining.

In the event, a number of people did set off to march after the speeches, and the police reacted violently with large numbers of protestors being arrested, amongst them Labor politician Senator George Georges. Judith stuck to her decision not to march and had to watch as protesters were bundled into the paddywagon. The violence troubled her. So, too, did the way the press misreported the occasion. "The march was reported in the English newspapers as being merely an anti-uranium march", she noted, since she had not been the only one to canvass environmental and Aboriginal issues:

> Of course only the violence [was] mentioned [it was] assumed that all anti-uranium marchers go in order to be knocked on the head; so [I] got anxious letters from friends in England asking whether I'd survived. Ah well, such is life without a free press.[63]

When Judith was invited to speak at another demonstration on 11th November, she refused, giving as her excuse that there was a university council meeting that day. In fact, she told a friend, she was getting tired of all the calls on her. All this "come over to Macedonia and help us [was] getting wearisome".[64]

Finishing *The Cry for the Dead*, she thought, would be far more useful than marches and demonstrations. Not long after the Brisbane demonstration she set off again for the Dawson River area to check some final details, hiring a car so that she could be more mobile and less dependant on others. She was afraid that none of the locals would talk to her since her views about history and the treatment of Aboriginal people were by now quite well-known and that perhaps she would have to disguise herself and appear "convincingly harmless".[65]

It was a trip which brought back memories, reminding her of the time just after the war when she and Jack had been "careless and moneyless and could only see the place via train and foot in a hot January".

But in fact it went well. She "met a lot of the 'old hands', aristocratic and otherwise, but [they] didn't take any baits. I did my poodle-faking act very well" and Meredith (who travelled with her) "kept discreetly silent." She "managed to get a fair idea of the country as it is now and [learned] a bit about the recent past". But what she learned was depressing: "They have just about ruined that country; mostly sand underlain with clay, creeks deep in sand and only spear-pumps get water ... a real mess", though she did see "some excellent regrowth ... [the] biggest regrowth on the black soils". By and large, however, she found the mood of the people unsympathetic: "Rural misery flourishes, as do complaints about unions and demands for the troops".[66]

Returning to "Edge", she found that swallows had built over the front door and ants had invaded the kitchen – nature was not always benevolent. She also faced the task of putting all the material she had gathered on to card indexes, which proved demanding and time-consuming. There were endless delays with *The Coral Battleground*, too, as it neared publication and the date, originally scheduled for the middle of the year, was pushed further and further ahead. As she reflected wryly, it seemed to be "one of those years when most of my plans have to be revised and every set date gets changed and I can't get any sense into my progress" – she had had to put off her trip North to accommodate the new publication date, which was finally set for 20th August, "a perfect curse" since she had already promised to be at a seminar on the National Estate to be held at the University of New England on the 23rd. She wanted maximum publicity for the book since, in her view, the Federal Government seemed likely to give in to the Queensland Government's determination to "develop" the Reef, and she hoped that it might have some effect. In fact, when it finally did appear, the response to the book was disappointing. There were few reviews and little public response – she suspected pressure from the Queensland Government and the developers.

Even the weather seemed to be against her, "dry as a sunstruck bone" even in November because there had been "no rain since August"; she was beginning to think that she would have to buy water from the local council to keep her going over the summer. True, she derived some comfort from the thought of a long drought since "the Fraser government [would] probably go out at the end of it ... nothing like misery for changing governments".[67] Meantime she was settling down to work in earnest on *The Cry for the Dead*, which was proving "one helluva job". It helped that Meredith was working on her doctoral thesis, living in the guesthouse at "Edge" and they lived as "monastic (or nunnastic?) a life for most of the week as we can, with interludes of visitors and excursions to Canberra".[68] She interrupted the routine at the end of November, however, to organise a film evening and forum on uranium mining in Braidwood with the local environmentalists. The film they chose was *Oh, What A Lovely War*. There is no record of the reaction, though Judith was a little apprehensive:

> [Local people] don't get much fun, [she told a friend] and may turn up for kicks. They will get a shock if so and no doubt some people won't speak to me afterwards, especially if our swinging electorate finally swings.

But on the whole she thought the attempt would "be worth the odium".[69]

The summer continued hot, though to her relief the drought broke in mid-January so she could now leave the place without fear of bushfires. But the swimming hole in the river was a "standby". It was "a lovely river for swimming" and private enough for skinnydipping. So the previous year, as "local warden", she had "declared the Mongarlowe Bend Pool a nude beach". By the end of the summer, she reported that she and Meredith were "getting quite aquatic; we swim among platypuses no less, and they don't seem to mind".[70] But she found time also to read and think about environmental issues and how they related to the clash between Aborigines and miners in Kakadu. She shared some of these views with Len Webb, who had been sending her articles on the subject:

> Seems to me, as ever, that the real hang up over getting a Conservation Ethic is doing away with the scientific materialist attitude; "nature-as-object versus nature-as-part-of-the-subject": once you switch from the emotional bond to the surroundings, as with so-called savage societies, to the intellectual–analytic separation, maybe there's an operative block between fore-brain and hind-brain or something? Or between the left and right hemispheres? I'm no brain specialist.

She disagreed, however, with Webb's notion that the physical environment is absorbed into the world of human thought. This view, she told him,

> ignores the fact that previously [nature] was absorbed into the world defined by feeling, emotion, what have you; [in contemporary culture] it's switched hemispheres, that's all. It always was part of human life, it only got separated out when it lost its spiritual significance. How we get that back is the real crux: not much chance when the world is run by exploitative interests.[71]

This notion that the key issue was to discover the spiritual, that is, unconscious, intuitive realm if human consciousness and the natural world were to return to a proper relationship, had been one of Jack's key convictions, of course. But in the 1950s and 1960s it had seemed merely speculative. Now, however, it was growing increasingly relevant, and the issue of spiritual or psychic renewal more and more urgent.

The state of the human psyche was affecting the world, and both were changing:

> *The voice of water as it flows and falls*
> *the noise air makes against earth-surfaces*
> *have changed; are changing to the tunes we choose,*

– destructive times. Preoccupied with "metal" and a dirty need for material power and possessions

> *…we have lost the bird, the thing itself,*
> *the sheen of life on flashing long migrations.*
> *Might human music hold it, could we hear?*
> *…*
> *Whatever Being is, that formula*
> *it dies as we pursue it past the word.*
> *We have not asked the meaning, but the use.*[72]

The few politicians who seemed to understand these issues were disappearing from the stage. Gough Whitlam was about to retire from politics, and Judith agreed to be one of the speakers, along with Patrick White and Manning Clark, "at a sort of farewell presentation" held over the Australia Day weekend. In elegaic mood, she saw the occasion as "the old guard's last stand". She also wondered

> what [Gough] will decide to do, poor chap. The ANU is said to be offering him a sort of political-science fellowship, but I can't see him settling down in academia with all that going on just over the lake, it would be refined torture; if Fraser has any sense he will offer him the UN Ambassadorship, but sense is not highly characteristic of this government, nor of this country for the matter of that.[73]

For herself, too, recent events seemed to have "knocked the poetry out of me", though "I struggle on with the prose", continuing to wrestle with *The Cry for the Dead* and in the throes of rewriting the third chapter for the third time – since the present was so shoddy it was less and less "easy to shuck off the past" and her responsibilities to present it.

Disillusion was growing. She had just retired from the UNESCO Committee, reflecting that "UNESCO here is not much worse than UNESCO anywhere I suppose," but glad to be out of it "after four years of totally pointless annual meetings, and that was about it".[74] It was her fourth quarter and she was beginning to feel old, describing a poetry reading in Canberra which had "dredged me and Alec Hope up to dodder through our Early Works, a process which reduced us to a sort of nostalgic paste".[75] So she was in the right mood to speak at a symposium organised by the Brennan Society on "Loss of Faith and Its Implications for the Writers of the 1890s and Beyond". A month or so later she gave a lecture on John Shaw Neilson, a poet she had always admired. During this time, too, she was working on a revision of her monograph on her old favourite, Charles Harpur. So literary matters and causes were taking up a good deal of her time once more. In January she had a battle with the editor of the Harpur monograph, who wanted her to substitute "British" for "English" in the phrase "English penal system". She refused, remarking that the Scots and Irish would agree with her.[76]

It was "a god awful wet winter" and she had money worries also, suspecting that writers' grants would be cut in the Federal budget, which would mean that she would be "back to taws again" financially. She was still struggling with *The Cry for the Dead*, thousands of words "being put back in the wpb from time to time while I try again ... my capacities seem to grow less as time goes on". But on the positive side a "fair-sized selection" of her poems was now on sale in the United States. "So far," she wrote with some gratification, "reviews have been surprisingly pleasant [which meant that] I may have achieved a small market outside this fatuous country".[77]

Inside it, however, things seemed to be going from bad to worse. The Federal Government was cutting university budgets – which involved Judith directly as a member of the University Council. That university, she reported, was

> going under to Fraserism fast – Federal government is changing the Act to get them, and they are informed they are subject to the *Public Service Act* re strikes and therefore any academic can be removed from his job by a stroke of the pen at the Minister's pleasure, nobody will want to do research etc. under the circumstances. O tempora, O mores![78]

As a member of the council she felt she had a responsibility to try to defend the university, but thought that their resistance was getting nowhere. In the meantime, however, she concluded this gloomy letter by remarking that "I must gather meself together and think up a cheerful dish for dinner to console" the young woman staying with her to make a film about "Edge", who was having difficulties filming with the cold, wet weather.[79]

Negotiations over mining in Kakadu dragged on. Nugget Coombs was now spending much of his time in the Northern Territory, keeping Judith in touch with developments. He also told her about some of the bush medicine he was learning about from his Aboriginal friends and sent her some emu bush which, she told Len Webb who was also interested in Aboriginal medicine, "they apparently use as a pick-me-up or something", offering an "ethnobotanical addition" to his knowledge.[80] Coombs kept her up to date with Aboriginal resistance to mining, particularly that of the Northern Land Council under the leadership of Galarrwuy Yunupingu, and with this knowledge she wrote to Prime Minister Fraser urging him not to give way to pressure from the mining industry. The protection of Aboriginal land and their rights to their own culture, she told him, "involved the honour of all Australians", and if the government were to betray them, "I, for one, will be shamed beyond bounds".[81]

In November 1978, however, an agreement was signed and the Ranger Mine given the go ahead. Both Judith and Coombs were angry, believing that not only the Aborigines had been bullied into giving way but also that different groups had been played off against one another. They also believed that the government had taken the miners' side. Coombs expressed his outrage in a letter, which he made public, to the Minister for Aboriginal Affairs:

> I have frequently, throughout my official life, disagreed with the actions of the government of the day, but never before, in the field of domestic policy, have I felt such shame at the way in which policy has been put into effect ... The signatures [of the Aboriginal leaders] have, I believe, been obtained without the processes of clarification and discussion which were promised ... Furthermore, the proceedings ... not merely failed to include representatives of communities vitally concerned but were such as to leave those Aborigines who did participate bewildered and unaware of the significance of what was happening.[82]

For her part Judith wrote a furious letter to the *Australian*. "So, as always, Australia as embodied in [this] Report, has made its choice under the dollar sign – taken thirty pieces of silver despite world criticism." This choice, she declared, would affect "young people of intelligence and conscience", increasing the "rising tide of despair and disaffection [the] sense of communal guilt and bitter resentment towards their elders" which she discerned among them. The report would have consequences far beyond the economy: our treatment of Aboriginal Australians would be "a social and moral issue of feeling all our lives". The hopes many had begun to cherish for more just, intelligent and compassionate attitudes were being crushed and, Judith concluded, referring to A.D. Hope's poem, "Australia", that we were on our way to becoming the "type who will inhabit the dying earth" he had predicted.[83]

But the advocates of mining and nuclear power were cock-a-hoop. Professor Ernest Titterton of the ANU, for instance, attacked the anti-uranium movement in a paper entitled "Nuclear Power and the Anti-Uranium Movement: A Social Problem", which was published in the *ANU Reporter,* adding insult to injury. In response, as a member of the University Council, Judith wrote to the chancellor asking that the matter be discussed by the council, risking the accusation of being an enemy of academic freedom. Titterton's paper, she argued, was bad science and its publication had damaged the university's reputation.

The cold winter was followed by a very hot summer. January 1979 was the hottest on record, and February the second hottest. It was apocalyptic weather, reflected in the poem "Oppositions", about being caught in a summer storm and being reminded of the incident years earlier flying to Armidale with Meredith, then a babe in arms, when

> *From a small plane once I looked down a cliff of cloud*

which "like God to Moses ... exploded into instructions". Fire had always in a sense been her element, and here, "counting heartbeats from flash to crash of thunder", she reflected

> *a long time back we clambered up the shore*
> *and learned to play with fire. Now there's no stopping us.*

She was losing whatever confidence she had in human progress, so the poem concludes with a counter-image of a frog on the shower pipe

> *Small damp peaceful sage with a loony grin*
> *("one minute of sitting, one inch of Buddha") ...*

...

> *Back to the drainpipe, frog, don't follow me.*
> *I'm off to dry my hair by the radiator.*

As she told Len Webb, "I suppose at my age I'm losing hope that the human race will ever do anything about its problems before it does away with itself in the first place," but she refused to give in to what she regarded as the enemies of life. So the poem concludes:

> *I can't believe that wine's warm solaces*
> *don't help the searcher: the poet on the wineshop floor*

was given his revelations. The hermit of Cold Mountain laughs as loudly perhaps – I choose fire, not snow.[84]

Judith was also finding strength and inspiration in Aboriginal resistance. In the Northern Territory the Aboriginal people might be temporarily defeated but they were determined to defend their rights. As Galarrwuy Yunupingu had declared in a speech to the National Press Club on 10th November 1977:

> Our duty is to safeguard Aboriginal land ... not only to protect Aboriginal land, but also to protect the long-term interests of European Australians too, because Aboriginal land is part of Australia. We live on our land, we love it, we are nothing without it. Governments can give away land for short-term gain, financial, economic, even political. We intend to protect that part of Australia which has been entrusted to us.[85]

Resistance was growing throughout Australia. In December 1978, not long after the Ranger project was given the go ahead, Aboriginal and Torres Straits Islander people held a conference at Lismore in New South Wales with the title "Attempt Great Things, Expect Great Things". They aimed to create a national framework for action emphasising their unity and solidarity, and to hammer out common policies and come up with specific programs on health, land rights, self-determination and self-management, determined to claim recognition as a distinct and viable cultural group with their own heritage, language, customs and institutions. They also demanded full ownership of the mineral rights on their lands and compensation for the lands taken from them, and the same rights, privileges, responsibilities and opportunities as other Australians. They would no longer be subject to the patterns of discrimination which had oppressed them for so long, they declared.[86]

Judith supported these claims, writing to the *Sydney Morning Herald* to denounce the way Aboriginal people had been treated not only in the past but in the present in the tactics used to get agreement to mining in Kakadu. It was, she said, "a callous agreement forced on the Aborigines for the most questionable motives for a commodity that may well be the death of us all, and by men whose hands had been soiled by the action ... a disgrace to us all."[87] She also wrote to the Prime Minister in the same terms.

She found herself more and more disgusted when she came to Canberra, describing herself to Len Webb "looking under my eyebrows at the Faces in the Street and cursing every one of them on too many counts to be counted". At "Edge", however, she had an ally in Stewart Harris, who had come to know and respect Aboriginal people and culture in the Northern Territory. One day, discussing the situation with him, she suddenly felt that it had become intolerable. "We've got to do something," she declared. "I'll see Nugget." Coombs was then in Canberra, and, as Harris tells the story, Judith left at once and "drove her little car to Canberra".[88]

That was the origin of the Aboriginal Treaty Committee, as Judith's talk that day with Coombs led to its formation. As she reported to Len Webb a few weeks later:

> A few of us down here are working on the idea of a treaty or agreement in draft form recognising Aboriginal claims to land, self-determination etc. to be proferred by whites for Aboriginal criticism; before the next election (Federal) to be introduced as a private bill by some willing member, not necessarily Labor since frankly Labor's record is good only by accident and perforce.[89]

The original members of the group, apart from Coombs and herself, were Charles Rowley and Bill Stanner, both anthropologists, and Stewart Harris. Barrie Dexter, a diplomat and former Ambassador to Laos was sympathetic but unable to join since he was a public servant, but Dymphna Clark, wife of Manning Clark and a distinguished scholar in her own right, and Diane Barwick, also an anthropologist, became members. Their first action was to sponsor an advertisement in one of the national papers to publicise the idea. The state of Aboriginal affairs seemed to be deteriorating since, despite Fraser's promise to stand by them, apart from its surrender to mining interests in Kakadu, the Federal Government had failed to protect the people of Aurukun and Mornington Island from the Queensland Government's determination to permit mining on their lands. To make matters worse, the first meeting of the newly appointed National Aboriginal Conference in

Canberra in April 1978 seemed to suggest that this body would be as ineffective as those set up by previous governments.

Nevertheless this body supported their initiative and in April it called unanimously for a treaty to be negotiated. After further discussion with them to ensure the support of the Aboriginal community, the committee decided to launch a public campaign, which Coombs did on 2nd June, in a talk on the ABC's "Guest of Honour" program. He told his audience that a basic injustice had to be set right:

> In taking their land we did not merely deprive Aborigines of property. We also took the source of their livelihood, the very foundation of their society, the basis of the rights and obligations on which it was built, and above all the source of the religious convictions which gave purpose and justification to their lives.[90]

The Treaty Committee was made up of busy people so they usually met over lunch at Coombs' flat at University House to discuss plans and circulate papers and information. But they were all convinced that the matter was urgent. As Judith said, Aboriginal people were perhaps "the most tolerant people on earth. But you can also drive people just too far".[91] Recent events at Noonkanbah Station in Western Australia underlined this concern. An American oil exploration company, Amex, urged on by the West Australian Government of Sir Charles Court which provided police protection, had forced its way on to the Aboriginal-controlled station to drill for oil on a sacred site although the traditional owners had refused permission. It was an event which attracted international attention and increased the Committee's determination to empower Aboriginal people.

As Kath Walker said in a paper given at the ANU about this time:

> When the decade started there was optimism and hope in the face of dreadful problems. Despite a good start, the optimism has gone, the hopes have been dashed. Only the dreadful problems remain. My people face dispossession and death and despite the efforts of Aborigines and our white friends like Judith Wright, Nugget Coombs, our future is grim.[92]

A treaty would guarantee the protection of identity, languages, law and culture and, the Committee hoped, restore Aborigines' rights to the land which had been taken from them, or if this was not possible, offer compensation for its loss and the damage done to their traditional way of life. It would also regulate conditions governing mining and grazing and give Aborigines the right to control their own affairs and establish their own associations for this purpose. In this way they would no longer be dependent on the changing policies and whims of governments at State and Federal level.

But first, non-Aboriginal Australia had to be educated. Perhaps their greatest problem, apart from downright racism, was the general ignorance of the injustice of the situation. As a select committee of the British House of Commons had acknowledged as long ago as 1837, the land had been "taken from them without the assertion of any other title than superior force".[93] The legal justification for this appropriation had been the doctrine of *terra nullius*, the legal fiction that Aborigines were too "primitive" to have owned the land in the sense British law recognised and that in law the country was therefore unoccupied. This was the view which generally prevailed, and in his 1974 report on Aboriginal land claims in the Northern Territory, Mr Justice Woodward had reiterated it. The result was that indigenous people had to depend on the often dubious goodwill of governments at the State and Federal level. Until 1967 they were not even recognised as citizens but were regarded as wards of the state, without the right to vote, own property or make decisions of a substantial kind for themselves – in some States they were not allowed to marry without the permission of the Protector of Natives. As the 1997 report on the "Stolen Generation", *Bringing Them Home*, has shown, systematic attempts were also made until that time to destroy their identity and culture by taking children away from their parents and educating them in our ways.

Now, however, indigenous people were beginning to claim their rights. A month or so after Coombs' ABC talk launched the public campaign for a treaty, on 7th August a group of Aborigines – writer Kevin Gilbert, Les Patten, son of a well-known shearer's leader Jack Patten, George Rose and another man, Kevin, who refused to give his surname (probably for fear of the authorities) – pitched a tent on Capital Hill in Canberra where the new Parliament House now stands. They called for a treaty and a bill of rights, describing themselves as the "National Aboriginal Government".

Shortly afterwards, on 26th August, the Treaty Committee's advertisement appeared in the *National Times*, outlining their aims and appealing for donations and public support. This was followed by a press conference and later by another full-page advertisement, this time in the *Australian*. The campaign was underway and for the next few years it was to take up a substantial amount of Judith's time and energy.

At the beginning she was not optimistic about their prospects, writing to Barbara Blackman that "it is all of course quite useless in all likelihood – imagine Court or Banana Petersen submitting to such a thing – but Nugget is getting so despondent that at least one last fling at turning the Australian whites into a human race seems worth it".[94] Friendship with Kath Walker urged her on, as did her sense of family history. In New England in late 1979 or early 1980 this had been brought home to her when she met Bill Cohen, then staying with her brother, Peter, on his property, "Lana". Cohen's father, an important man amongst his own people whom the locals had dubbed "King", had worked for the Wrights at "Wongwibinda". On one occasion, May Wright's diaries described him as appreciatively accompanying them on a family picnic and keeping them supplied with bush tucker.

Cohen was about Judith's age, but when they met he was living in the woolshed on "Lana" doing odd jobs about the place. Talking to him, she came to realise how little she knew of the Aboriginal people who had worked for them and whose land her family had taken from them – "stolen" is the word she used in her essay "Whose Country Is It Anyway?". Though they had grown up in the same area, they had never come to know one another: he was "One of the dark children/[She] wasn't allowed to play with".[95] "There was a whole lot of stuff," she understood, reflecting on their meeting that "he could have said about his childhood which he very decently did not say ... They are more generous than we are. If the same thing had happened to us there would have been scandal and murder." He had been initiated, and was proud of his Aboriginal culture. But he refused to refer to the massacres and injustices of the past, remarking, to her shame, that he did not think this was "Christian".[96]

Cohen wanted to write his autobiography and asked Judith for help. She agreed, advising him, sensibly, to "just write the way you say it".[97] When it was finished she helped him find a publisher and wrote an introduction to the book, which appeared some years later as *To My Delight*. Getting to know him confirmed her belief that her family's fortune was built in large part on Aboriginal labour as well as on their dispossession and that she had therefore a moral responsibility to them. Cohen's dignity and readiness to forgive also impressed her. As she put it, "we had imposed our law on people whose law is far better than ours".[98]

The more she learned about Aboriginal people, the more this view was confirmed. Discussing with Len Webb the organisation of a conference on the wilderness she insisted that Aborigines should be "involved in some more important way than just as local colour for the delegates ... not just [as] Links with our Primitive Past but Pointers to a Better Future kind of thing".[99]

Her commitment to Aboriginal people and their culture went with her sense of the environment. As she wrote to Elizabeth Harrower:

> I have not been an environmentalist in the sense that you have not been a feminist (active stances taken by Martha, both of them) but one's energy and argument derives from the same source, in the end – what all those sociologists call "quality of life". I agree with you, that what really matters is relationship, obvious and oblique, body to earth and heart to mind and the integrity of things created or imagined. I think I'm not a militant partly [from] a temperamental disinclination to force, partly [from] a faith in love and a fear of rage.[100]

In Judith's view Aboriginal culture was on the side of "quality of life", in contrast with our society which, she believed, was dominated by "exploitative interests". "Maybe", as she also told Elizabeth Harrower, this "whole has to break down to start again. But the breakdown is not proving pleasant". She thought that learning from and supporting Aboriginal people, however, might point the way to a better future.

In this way she reflects the strain of "moral anxiety or feelings of disquiet about European colonisation within the conquering culture",[101] which some historians suggest has been present from the beginnings of settlement, and was indeed explicit in the instructions given to the first governor, Arthur Phillip, and to many subsequent governors. It was also implicit in the various attempts made by the British Government to protect the indigenous people from the worst excesses of the settlers. The Treaty Committee drew on this tradition, which may explain why it seemed at first to have widespread support, in Canberra especially. Most of those on the Committee were influential members of the community, both locally and nationally, and the university gave them a small office in the university grounds. Their influence began to spread and support groups grew up throughout the country.

Judith took a break in mid-July for a gathering of writers in Rockhampton in Queensland, "a great line-up of past celebrities, Alec Hope and Xavier Herbert, as well as me," she told Webb, "and we had some very lively panels arguing with each other and a very enthusiastic audience".[102] These were writers she respected. As she had said some years earlier, in a paper on "Books in the Age of Admass", it was too easy for writers to yield to the "mechanised stupidity and mechanised falsity of mass communication", and even poets now often used "the word 'truth' or the word 'freedom' with the same indifference [with which they would] say to a stranger, 'I am pleased to meet you'".[103] But the writers here, she felt, were not like that; they had kept their integrity and sense of responsbility to the past and future as well as the present. While there she was also able to meet local historians and get some useful information for *The Cry for the Dead* – Rockhampton had been the port at which her grandfather had landed when he first went north, as well as the place where he had died and been buried. So she returned with "three large foolscap pads of notes, mostly unintelligible shorthand" to transcribe "before I forget what they are all about".[104]

There were many other demands on Judith's time and energy. In April she was invited to join the board of the feminist publishing house, Sisters, which included Hilary McPhee, Di Gribble, Joyce Nicholson, Sally Milner and Anne O'Donovan. Until now, Judith had not been much involved in the feminist movement, being too busy elsewhere.

But from childhood she had suffered the disadvantages of being a woman in a pastoral family – men got the land and women had to marry a pastoralist if they wanted to stay on the land – and had been conscious of her rights and determined to exercise them. Believing, as she did, that "strong men and women could shape history" (she had seen her grandmother do it and celebrated her power in *The Generations of Men*), she was, Stewart Harris observed, never one "to accept a hopeless personal status", and she also refused to grovel before "technology and science and market forces".[105] She took it for granted that she participated in public affairs in her own right as a human being – at Treaty Committee meetings, one of her colleagues recalls, she would even on occasion reprove her distinguished friend, Nugget Coombs, "pouncing on him when he spoke like a sexist old male".[106] So she was happy to help women writers.

She particularly felt for women who were exploited and oppressed, as poems like "Eve Scolds" and "Eve Sings" make clear. In her relationship with Jack she had declared her independence of convention and conventional morality, and they had worked together as intellectual equals. But her letters show her awareness of the ways in which so many women suffered at men's hands. In his memoir, Stewart Harris, surprised that she enjoyed watching Australian Rules football on television, reports her saying that part of the attraction was "watching men hurting each other", and smiling with satisfaction, adding "for a change".[107] She was always pleased to see justice done. And she was not afraid of standing up for herself. According to Hilary McPhee, one of the reasons she had invited Judith to join the Sisters board was to thank her "as a fellow human being" for one such occasion – a United Nations conference on science and development in Melbourne.

As the *Age* reported this incident, in a story headed "She's No Guru", Judith had attacked what she called "Technological Determinism", in a paper given at the conference, seeing it as an abdication of intellectual and social responsibility". She had also argued that urban life today was dehumanising. This had antagonised the Dean of Science at Monash University, a Professor Swan, who made a more or less personal attack on her, saying that while he "respected her as a poet ... as a guru she was a disaster". He also "angrily challenged her to explain why she was wearing a pseudo-suede jacket and synthetic skirt, both products of technology". This was a charge she thought would not have been levelled at a man and told a reporter that she was "amazed by the emotional level of his outburst",[108] implying that it was misogyny rather than concern for science which had inspired it; as Coombs and several others pointed out, her attack on technological determinism was based on solid evidence.

She was never a doctrinaire feminist, however, believing that the crucial conflict was not between men and women, scientists and poets, but within people, between their creative and destructive impulses. As Eve says to Adam in "Eve Scolds":

> *Each of us wants to own –*
> *you, to own me, but even more, the world;*
> *I, to own you.*

It was this possessiveness and the desire to control and consume, in her view, which was responsible for the state of the world in general and of the environment in particular. As this poem suggests, relations between men and women would always be ambiguous. As Eve concludes:

> *Lover, we've made, between us,*
> *one hell of a world. And yet –*
> *still at your touch I melt. How can there be*
> *any way out of this?*[109]

She might be getting old but she was still passionate. One of the poems written around this time, "Cold Night", is about a strange encounter with a man who came to her door one night.

> *Rain on his face and his hair wet*
> *he looked a refugee from night,*
> *hasty and trembling. One hard kiss*
> *and he fled out to his own house.*

He was, the poem says, someone "scarcely seen before",

> *but walking sometimes on cold nights*
> *the showers strike my naked face*
> *hard, sudden, in a kind of kiss.*[110]

This may never have happened, but the fact that, according to the poem, the man, the neighbours had told her, was dying, points to the kind of erotic rage against death one finds in Yeats' later poetry. Jack's memory was still powerful, as "Twenty-five Years" suggests, with its memory of a

> ... clear blond evening on the pastoral hill,
> grass gilt by the moon,
> the swoop and song of the wires, the hare crouched still,
> your hand on mine.[111]

Watching Meredith, "now a most self-possessed and rather beautiful creature", also reminded her of the body's beauty, and "Woman in Orchard", perhaps her reply to A. D. Hope's poem about Susannah and the Elders, dwells on this beauty and its poignancy, especially in the opening image:

> The woman in the orchard kneels
> to love her body in the pool
> and dream herself for ever young.

But the poem is aware, also, of a "witch's eyes ... watching", aware of all the forces working to make the young woman what

> ... you will be
> and poison what you are.

Nevertheless, it accepts the ambiguities, accepting

> the ugly one you will be,
> the lovely one you are.[112]

Judith was not a jealous old woman; she enjoyed young people in general and Meredith's friends in particular when they came to stay. Over the summer when she was home from Japan they "had good fun and much talk ... lovely walks and sunrises", went on trips to the coast and to parties in Canberra and elsewhere. But Meredith was thinking of staying on in Japan more or less permanently, "obstinately [refusing] to consider" a conventional career. As Judith told a friend with some satisfaction, she preferred "to hang on to the edge of the revolving wheel as best she can and keep herself uncorrupted by the rat-race"[113] – she was her father's daughter. She felt at home in Japan, sharing a house with several foreigners. One of them, an Englishman whom she was to marry the following year, was writing a novel, Judith reported, "which would grace a modern Henry James but will never be published, having just reached its thousandth page already".[114] Another member of the household was a young American woman whom Meredith had just helped through pregnancy and birth in the not very easy circumstances of a Japanese hospital. But remembering her own fierce independence, Judith was prepared to let Meredith live her own life.

Judith had always cherished her own integrity and independence, which made her difficult to deal with at times. She had been looking forward to attending a conference in Cairns in November on the future of the Cape York area, for example, and had canvassed with Len Webb the possibility of involving local Aboriginal people, believing that environmentalists had a great deal to learn from them about care for the land since their attitudes were based "on a deeper and far older association with it than any we can claim".[115] When she discovered that several mining companies had put up the money for the conference, however, she refused to go. She would have nothing to do with them, believing that they were trying to infiltrate the environmental movement and use it for their own ends.

In the meantime "Edge" was a good place to live when she was able to spend time there: "it continues to provide all I ought to need, as the Bible puts it". Her neighbours were congenial: a "Permaculture Family" with two children on the next block downriver, "husband a biologist in Canberra during the week, wife raising every possible kind of domestic creature from donkeys to pigeons on far too little land in order to preserve the rest of the trees etc", and opposite a Dutchman, a weaver and member of the Craft Council. Nearby was the "incipient goldmine which we hope we have kept incipient for the time being at least", but the river where they swam in hot weather flowed at the bottom of the hill and around them lay the bush where kangaroos and native creatures of all kinds lived and flourished.[116]

She had many visitors, especially in springtime when, as she told Kathleen McArthur, people kept ringing and announcing their arrival, as if they were migrating birds. Some visits were especially important.

Kevin Gilbert, who was then living in Canberra, came from time to time in summer to camp and to get on with his writing. This interfered with the nude bathing, but, as Judith said, "Aborigines have a lot more right to [the area] than I do".[117] She would have liked to share the place with Kath Walker, too, but she was busy campaigning for Aboriginal Rights and spending time overseas representing the indigenous peoples of Australia at conferences and arts festivals. In the four months from November 1978 to February 1979 she visited Lock Haven State College in Pennsylvania, Concorde University in Montreal, the Institute of American Indian Arts at Santa Fe in Mexico, and the University of California at Berkeley, and in 1980, to celebrate her sixtieth birthday, Channel 7 in Brisbane featured Kath on the program "This Is Your Life". So there was little time for relaxation. Towards the end of that year, however, she was able to spend a few months at "Edge" recovering from sinusitis, over-work and disillusion. A recent submission to the Federal Department of Aboriginal Affairs asking for financial support for "Moongalba" had been refused, and she was particularly bitter about this since one of the reasons given was that the title to the land was not guaranteed; the fact was that under Queensland law Aborigines could not obtain such a guarantee.

Judith shared Kath's anger and disappointment – she, too, had put a good deal of time and money into the project – but apart from this they "had a fine time catching up with one another", and as always, Judith enjoyed her friend's energy and inventiveness. She had started a business in Melbourne, for instance, anticipating the vogue for Aboriginal art and spent most of the time drawing what Judith called "crazy neo-Aboriginal stuff in sketchbook after sketchbook and writing poems, all the time talking flat out", something she confessed she could not take as a "permanent part of life", however much she enjoyed Kath's company, since "one doesn't get a word in"[118] – something which was often said about Judith as she grew more and more deaf and talked at people.

But Kath's views confirmed her own. In particular, she agreed with her when she wrote:

> As I have travelled throughout the world, I have often thought that one could judge society by the way it treats its racial

minorities. Where a minority was forced to live in squalor, I have seen a squalid society. Where a minority was riddled with disease, I have seen a sick society. Where a minority was without hope, I have seen a nation without hope.[119]

The Cry for the Dead had made Judith so vividly aware of what she called the "blood-stained past", the long and brutal war for possession of the land and of her own family's part in it.[120] But Kath's insistence that Aboriginal people needed to deal with their problems in their own way was also important at this stage as the Treaty campaign continued. As Kath put it later in an interview with Jim Davidson:

[Aboriginal people] have said we want to integrate with [white people], but we don't want to live with them. We don't want to be enemies, we want to be friends, but we don't want to follow their way, because the Aboriginal is starting to realise how much the white man is leading himself to destruction.[121]

Judith agreed, of course, as Coombs and the other Committee members did, that Aboriginal people must be free to go their own way. Stanner was particularly worried on this score, however, since he was afraid that Aboriginal people might be pushed into negotiations which they did not fully understand and be made to conform to our ways. Aboriginal law, he realised as an anthropologist, was different from the European law which had been imposed upon the Aborigines. It was also very complex and differed between the various groups throughout the country. All of these things would have to be taken into account and handled sensitively if their ways were to be respected. Stanner was also afraid of a white backlash when it became clear that Aboriginal values and beliefs would have to be taken into account in any proper kind of negotiations. He was in bad health by this time, and that, combined with his doubts, led him to resign from the Treaty Committee.

The idea was catching on with non-Aboriginal Australians, however, and branches of the Committee were springing up throughout the country. Early in the New Year, Don Dunstan spoke about the need for a Treaty at the National Press Club in Canberra, and on 3rd April the Melbourne *Age* carried an editorial on the subject. At the local level in

Canberra, Charles Rowley, another anthropologist, addressed the subject at a meeting of the ANU Convocation. More and more people seemed to be aware of the need to right at least some of the wrongs committed against indigenous people. A group of academics from the Darwin Community College wrote to the provisional council of the proposed University of the Northern Territory asking that the charter of the new university acknowledge the integrity of Aboriginal knowledge and that an Aboriginal person should be appointed to the interim Senate.[122] The group also wrote to Judith asking for her support, which she agreed to give.

Of all the groups, the most significant proved to be one in Townsville, which originated what came to be known as the Mabo case. Its members included historian Henry Reynolds, a pioneer in the study of the Aboriginal side of the story of settlement, and a young lawyer, Greg McIntyre, who was to be the instructing solicitor in the Mabo case. In their discussions the group decided to organise a conference on land rights and the future of race relations, to be held at James Cook University in Townsville in 1981. This conference saw the beginning of the legal battle of the Meriam people (the people of Murray Island), which reached its conclusion a decade later in the High Court's Mabo decision.

In the meantime, some Aboriginal people were becoming uneasy with the idea of a treaty, as were some members of the Committee. Judith and Coombs were aware how important it was to consult and listen to Aboriginal people and how easy it was to manipulate them. They still remembered with disgust the way the Kakadu agreement had been managed.

It was also difficult to get consensus among various Aboriginal groups. Since there was no one body which represented the views of all indigenous people, it was not clear who or what organisation could sign a treaty on behalf of all indigenous people. Many distrusted the National Aboriginal Council, a creation of government. Obviously, it needed remodelling to make it more representative, but this, too, worried Judith and Coombs since they feared that Aborigines and Islanders would not be given the time they needed to discuss the issue, and that an agreement be forced on them. "Rushing anything through is certain to mean a dirty deal and on the way they have treated the

Northern Land Council etc. over mining it's very clear that dirty deals are the best you can get unless there's a very strong and widespread consensus." They were "crossing [their] fingers" and hoping that the Aborigines would demand "plenty of time".[123]

In other areas confusion was growing. Environmentalists were beginning to disagree about the notion of "wilderness", and some of them seemed to Judith increasingly insensitive to Aboriginal needs and values. Her old ally, Vincent Serventy, published an article in the *Sydney Morning Herald* on 9th January entitled "Luring Back The Animals", which seemed to her to imply that the environment movement only had to do with preserving fauna and flora and nothing to do with Aboriginal people or culture. She disagreed. For her, the real issue, as she wrote to Len Webb, was philosophical, a question of the values by which we live; she believed Aboriginal people could teach us a great deal about respect for life:

> We need something a lot wider than "wildlife" as a subject – it keeps people happy to imagine that if they can still see a magpie about things must be okay, and the world isn't on an exponential suicide jag after all, which, as you know, it is.[124]

The problems she was having with *The Cry for the Dead* increased her sense of frustration. The research was finished but she was having difficulty shaping the material, "chopping off bits here and there like some inefficient butcher with a dragon to be presented in neat joints".[125] The material itself was also depressing, telling a grim story of killings and dispossession.

The effect of all of this was reflected in an interview with the *Sydney Morning Herald*, headed "Judith Wright – In The Wasteland". In it, having decided, as she told Webb, to "blow my top and make it a real aggro session", she gave vent to her most pessimistic feelings, which disturbed many of her friends and supporters. Vincent Serventy wrote: "Please Judith, the soul of the conservation movement must not give up", and Thistle Stead, another long-term ally, wrote in similar terms.[126] Others, however, were less sympathetic. A letter to the editor of the *Herald* declared she had no "love for [her] country". Only a few understood what she was trying to do. Alex Carey was one of these, writing to her that

> having in a lesser way, attempted to influence our society towards saner, less exploitative values and a less befuddled propagandist view of the times [he shared her] deep concern for the evident vulnerability of most ordinary people ... [In his view they were exposed to] even more manipulation by even more ruthless Kissingerian accounts of the great economic centres of power [a manipulation which, he believed, spelled] the end not just of society but of personal relations.

He also expressed his "enduring appreciation for the-quite-literal-integrity of your life and work, of what you have written and what you have done and tried to do".[127] This kind of support was important since there were not many, apart from Len Webb and other close allies like the ANU philosopher Richard Routley and his wife Val, who agreed with Judith's belief that the environmental crisis was part of a larger crisis of value – Jack's view, of course, but a belief that was coming to seem more and more unfashionable as the 1960s and 1970s gave way to the 1980s.

The proponents of economic growth, and their new allies, the economic rationalists, seemed to be winning the battle for public opinion, and the environmentalists were becoming unpopular. In December 1980 they were blamed for the bushfires which swept through the forests of Sydney, killing five firefighters. "These young people lost their lives," one man declared, "just to make sure a few lousy trees stood up."[128] Wright regretted the firemen's deaths, but this kind of division between human and environmental values was something she could not accept. To her, damaging the environment damaged, indeed threatened, human life. At the same time she thought that many environmentalists did not make this link since they had not thought through their position philosophically and were content merely to respond to specific issues. As she wrote scornfully to Webb, commenting on a brochure from the World Wildlife Foundation which someone had sent her, "to convince me there's really something going on", they seemed to her "in a rut so deep [they] cannot see out",[129] and failed to see what was happening. For that reason they failed to see that the real threat lay with economic rationalism. So long as merely economic values prevailed the world would continue to be destroyed. As Coombs had emphasised in a paper at a conference some years earlier, the original meaning of "economy" was "care for the household". The "world is not a factory", Judith insisted, echoing his view, and forests are "not mere collateral", they are valuable in and for themselves. Trees have a right to life as well as human beings who in fact depend on them for their well-being. Even in money terms destruction of the environment was foolish. We should reflect, she wrote to Len Webb,

> in terms of monetary returns from soils which should still be fertile, rivers which would not be silt-laden etc. if we hadn't destroyed the forests in the past. A good calculation of that would be pretty astronomical in its figures ... Could anybody do a calculation of that kind?[130]

She had been reading a good deal about environmental theory generally but felt very gloomy about the Australian situation in particular. Elsewhere it was being suggested that loans for "development" should be conditional on meeting stringent environmental criteria. But here she was "darned if [she could] see any lender – country, bank or finance company – agreeing to the loans on such conditions. They knew all too well where the butter's spread." The only hope seemed to be "evangelization ... but neither governments nor industry are wide open to angels' voices".[131]

The loudest voices seemed to come from the opposite direction, and they were intruding even at "Edge". At the end of 1979 Judith had discovered that another application had been made to prospect for gold, which involved dredging the river at Mongarlowe. She had many other irons in the fire, the Treaty Committee especially, but rallied the neighbours to oppose it. When in the second week of February a hearing was held in the Mining Warden's Court in Sydney, she wrote proudly that "all the inhabitants of Half Moon were there to give evidence, plus the owner of the land, and they ran through 25 tapes, much to the annoyance of the clerk".

It was a marathon hearing, but went in the residents' favour and she was hopeful that they had managed to put paid to such projects. Prospectors still continued to bother them, even after this success, and she still felt embattled against "gold-detectors, hopeful mining applications, and the [already] established mine outside the gate ... Gold-hungry ockers are hard to bear. The place crawls with them." But at least they now had some protection. "Instead of repelling hopeful fossickers with the power of the eye", she and her neighbours were now "able to say that we are a Mining Reserve under Section 24 of the Act, and stun them with legality."[132]

It was a small victory but invigorating.

> I have put on a fresh lease of life and have been rushing up to Townsville to do public meetings, radio talk backs, TV etc., and down to Melbourne to do the same. But was caught in Melbourne by the plane stoppage just as I was on my way to Brisbane for more of it. I had to come back to Canberra by Pioneer bus – truly dreadful, surrounded by knitting grandmothers and chatty talk from the mothers, bearable on their own, but sycophantic giggles at the driver's witticisms were too much for me, and I feigned sleep after the sixtieth attempt to join in. Shan't try buses again.[133]

Her friends thought she was overdoing it, but a sense of urgency, of the need for a treaty with Aboriginal people especially, drove her on. At "Edge" the Aboriginal past, long suppressed and denied, seemed to be returning to haunt her. Exploring the local archives, she had come across the story of Nellie, the last of the local Aboriginal people who had more or less disappeared in the 1880s, wife of "King Billy" who had died before her. After his death she had "succumbed to the drinking habit" (as the local newspaper put it) and had been banished from the town, but her wailing from the fringes of the town had tormented the settlers as long as she lived. She may be the "last old woman" of the poem "River Bend", written about this time, who

> *thin, black and muttering grief,*
> *foraged for mussels, all her people gone.*

Her presence seemed to haunt the place:

> *Last night a dog howled somewhere,*
> *a hungry ghost in need of sacrifice,*

her death imaged in the dead kangaroo by the river, a

> *... slender skeleton*
> *tumbled above the water with her long shanks*
> *cleaned white as moonlight ...*
> *Pad-tracks in sand where something drank fresh blood.*[134]

But poems came much less often now with so much to do:

> *Old Rhythm, old Metre*
> *these days I don't draw*
> *very deep breaths. There isn't*
> *much left to say.*[135]

Nevertheless when they came, they came powerfully, charged with a deeper sense not only of her own mortality but also of the way, as a descendant of a pioneering family, she herself was implicated in the sufferings of the land and the suffering of its original inhabitants. This may be why she was cautious when a film-maker, Frank Harvey, proposed to make a film of *The Generations of Men*. The money was attractive. But on one hand she was afraid that the film might glamorise the story of settlement which, she now realised, had been so costly to Aboriginal people, and on the other, if it emphasised this cost, might offend her "large and critical clan" whose feelings she respected, even though she disagreed with them. Correspondence about the film dragged on over several years but in the end Harvey was unable to find the money to finance it and the proposal fell through.

Meredith came back from Japan to spend the summer of 1981 at "Edge" and once again she and Judith spent a good deal of time together, swimming in the river, walking for miles or driving to the coast and "having long oblique conversations of the kind we go in for"[136] (which her deafness also necessitated). This peace was interrupted by the Treaty Committee Art Show, a fund-raising venture. The idea, which originated early in 1980 when Sidney Nolan offered them a painting to raffle, was to get together a collection of paintings on Aboriginal themes. In April Judith had written to Barbara Blackman, whose husband Charles was a leading painter and who knew a great deal about such things, asking for suggestions about painters who might be approached. Rudy Komon, one of Sydney's best-known dealers, was sympathetic, and they hoped to hold the show at the Blaxland Gallery. At that time "with Court doing his worst to Aborigines at Noonkanbah and elsewhere", they thought that artists would be sympathetic. Barbara was at that time living in Perth, so she hoped she might also be able to "think of some W.A. painters whose consciences are sore".[137]

There was a magnificent response. As well as Sidney Nolan, Arthur Boyd and Fred Williams, many other artists cooperated. Even Brett Whiteley, who, characteristically, had not replied to letters, made a contribution, selling a large work through another gallery after the exhibition was over and sending the money to the Treaty Committee. Dymphna Clark, together with Heather Rusden, the Committee's secretary, was the main person responsible, but all the Committee pitched in, helping to run the exhibition in January. Judith, too, interrupted her time with Meredith and her work on the proofs of *The Cry for the Dead* to spend a day there at the end of January.

The show was a great success financially, contributing $40,000 to the Committee's fund, which, as Judith put it, "made many things possible". The generous support of many distinguished Australian artists was also heartening – when Arthur Boyd's painting failed to sell, for instance, he sent them "large quantities of money to make up for it".[138]

The exhibition helped raise public consciousness as well as funds. Pamphlets explaining the idea of the treaty were on display and many people asked questions about it. True, not everyone who came was supportive. On the day Judith was on duty, one woman responded angrily, telling her that the "Aborigines arrived in Australia so late that we did not owe them anything". Her family arrived in Australia in 1888, she said, "and there were not any Aborigines here then". "Remarkable", Judith commented to Barbara Blackman. For her part, she bought a painting by Ray Cook for Meredith, a Mornington Island scene with "three Aboriginal women standing under palms looking out over a beach and a hazy sea".[139]

The exhibition was timely, too, since the Noonkanbah affair was still dragging on in Western Australia and the Committee was able to help with fares for an Aboriginal delegation to go to Geneva to put the case against the mining company and the West Australian Government to the United Nations. This affair also helped the cause since it highlighted the need for some legal guarantee of the rights of Aboriginal people, the kind of guarantee it was hoped that a treaty would provide.

The most significant event in the year in this respect, however, was the conference at James Cook University in Townsville in August, organised by the local Treaty Committee on "Land Rights and the Future of Race Relations". It had always been the Treaty Committee's view that their task was to make themselves superfluous, and this conference became part of the winding-down process since it was here that the Mabo case first got underway. A meeting was held between two representatives of the Treaty Committee and some of the Meriam (Murray) Islanders. Having heard Nonie Sharp, one of the Treaty Committee members, outline the Blackburn judgment (which had rejected Aboriginal land claims on the grounds that their links with the land were not of the kind recognised in British law) one of them, Flo Kennedy, angrily rejected that view and suggesting taking the State and Federal Governments to court to prove their rights.[140]

The process was to be long and tortuous, but the Townsville conference saw its beginnings and helped determine directions and strategies. Apart from Islander leaders like Flo Kennedy, Reverend Dave Passi and Eddie Mabo, many prominent Aboriginal leaders like Marcia Langton and Shorty O'Neill also attended the conference, as did people from reserves at Cherbourg, Mornington Island and Palm Island and from all over Australia. One old lady, Granny Dolly, believed to be over a hundred, shared her memories of massacres in the early days, and the general sense was that the time had come for indigenous people to assert their claims for justice. Many white supporters were there: Henry Reynolds, Greg McIntyre, Garth Nettheim, Professor of Law at the University of New South Wales and long-time advocate of indigenous rights, and Al Grassby, former minister of the Whitlam Government now involved in multi-cultural and ethnic affairs, and, of course, Nugget Coombs and Judith Wright.

When Coombs heard of Flo Kennedy's suggestion, which had been enthusiastically supported by the meeting on Murray Island, he was excited since the Committee had been looking for a test case, hoping, as Coombs put it, "by judicial process to invalidate the principles on which the Blackburn judgment" had been based.[141] Judith agreed; her paper at the conference had lamented the "deprived and unrecognised state" of Aboriginal and Islander peoples. Outlining the situation in the Kimberley where the local people were "being driven from their homelands ... by the Ashton diamond venture", she argued that this kind of oppression would continue until you have a "watertight and satisfactory treaty at Commonwealth level. Accept nothing from the Commonwealth government," she warned her Aboriginal audience, at the same time reminding them that however "traitorous (it might seem to their own law) ... you have your rights under British law".[142]

Nevertheless this tension between British law and their own was increasing Aboriginal suspicion of the idea of a treaty and was in the long run to bring about the demise of the Committee. On the other hand, pursuing their rights under British law was also to lead, in the Mabo case and later in the case of the Wik people, to victory in the High Court, bringing about significant gains – at least until the election of the Howard Government. In any case, the Treaty Committee was now committed to supporting Aboriginal and Islander people as they pursued their goals in court. Not long after the conclusion of the Townsville conference the long legal battle, first of all in the Supreme Court of Queensland, and then later in the High Court of Australia, began. The conference as a whole also passed a resolution, declaring that all participants and, they hoped, "people of good will" would "contribute to the struggle" for justice for Aboriginal and Islander peoples, asking at the same time that no action be taken in the matter of a treaty without extensive consultation with them. Judith concurred with this. She was losing faith in white society, and living in Canberra, "that chilly and self-contained city" and watching "the chilly Fraser Government" at work, she thought there was less and less chance that much would be done for indigenous Australians. Coombs' links with several land councils in the Northern Territory had made him aware of their distrust of white law. Judith agreed. "We had imposed our law", she wrote, "on people whose law was much better than ours." She also thought that the Minister for Aboriginal Affairs had done a "snow job" when he asked the NAC to find an alternative word to "treaty" – a word whose legal connotations went further than the Fraser Government was prepared to go. They came up with a word for the Yolngu language, "Makarrata". But this singled out one particular language and culture from all the others. Even more troubling, as the Treaty Committee understood, this word did not mean anything like a treaty, a legally binding agreement, but only that "some small disquiet had come to an end".[143] In any case many indigenous people saw the idea of a treaty as a "whitefella" idea. For them, land was the crucial issue and talk of a treaty seemed a distraction.

Internationally, however, indigenous peoples were becoming more self-conscious, pushing their rights to justice and recognition. In April 1982 the World Council of Indigenous Peoples met in Canberra and members of the Treaty Committee were admitted as observers, though neither the media nor the government seemed to recognise its significance. As Judith noted, since the delegates "were all shapes and sizes and [wore] some lovely costumes ... the papers tended to treat it all as a folk festival" instead of a political occasion, but a meeting of peoples from all over the world who had survived contact with the West and were determined to assert their rights made it a memorable and significant gathering. The stories many had to tell were stories of persecution and oppression; Judith found the plight of the indigenous peoples of South America particularly moving, "prison camps, organised shooting and torture – you name it". Contemplating their plight and that of the blacks of South Africa, she even began to think that after all indigenous Australians might not be "the worst-off in the world".[144]

Nevertheless the Australian Government's response to the World Council was disappointing. The National Aboriginal Council (NAC) had hoped to take overseas delegates on a tour of Australia afterwards to meet various indigenous groups throughout the country, but funds were not forthcoming. The Treaty Committee was able to provide a limited amount, but Judith was angry at the government's parsimony, attacking it as "more mean-minded than one would believe".[145] It also seemed to her shameful that several Aboriginal groups from the Kimberley and North Queensland were unable to attend because of the cost.

The occasion did mark "another long step forward on the way for Aboriginal people". Younger Aboriginal leaders like Marcia Langton, Patrick and Michael Dodson and Mick Miller found themselves meeting indigenous leaders from all over the world and learning from and with them. As official proceedings drew to an end, they came together in an unofficial forum running parallel with the official meeting and issued what Judith saw as a "moving statement" about the plight of the indigenous peoples of Australia, one which she hoped might "actually put a bit of stuffing in the Aboriginal council people". True, this was a muted hope since their resolve, as she wrote to a friend, would probably "evaporate as soon as the Minister got them in a corner over their debts to the government". As she concluded, writing from sad experience, "Ah well, from those who have not, all shall be taken, and they know it".[146]

The emergence of confident young leaders, however, suggested to the Committee that the time was coming to bow out and leave indigenous people to deal with governments in their own way, though she and Coombs were troubled by divisions within their ranks. Discredited by its association with a government, for instance, the NAC seemed to be doing nothing to defend Aboriginal rights against the mining companies and pastoralists who were opposing them and seemed to have lost the confidence of most Aboriginal people – Kevin Gilbert accused it of being a mere "puppet body" – and it seemed to be constantly bowing to government pressure, agreeing, for example, not to claim sovereign status for Aboriginal people should any treaty be negotiated. Its hierarchical structure also went against the egalitarian nature of the Aboriginal community. Other groups complained that the NAC was not providing them with enough information about the proposed treaty or Makarrata to make an informed decision.[147]

All of this exacerbated the problems the Treaty Committee was already facing. No doubt many Aboriginal people wanted the formal recognition of their sovereignty which a treaty would provide – Kevin Gilbert had sent letters to ambassadors of the various nations represented in Canberra, for instance, asking them to pay rent to the local people, whose land they were occupying,[148] but there never had been one Aboriginal nation and it was becoming more and more difficult to reconcile the needs and interests of the many different peoples scattered across the country, some still living in traditional ways and others living in cities or country towns as fringe dwellers.

By the middle of the year it became clear to the Treaty Committee that they had reached the end of their usefulness, especially when the lawyer and activist Pat O'Shane, the first Aboriginal person to graduate from Harvard University, repudiated the idea of a treaty at a meeting of Labor lawyers; the Mabo case was also now getting underway. The Committee thought it best to bow out, though they remained ready to help whenever and however they were invited to do so. Judith continued to do what she could. Not long after the Townsville conference, she was asked to join the Committee of the Yiperya Teachers' Training School in Alice Springs which hoped to train Aboriginal students in both Aboriginal and non-Aboriginal ways. Drawing strength, as their prospectus put it, on "40,000 years of cultural survival", they hoped to make their way without government assistance – a hope which proved vain; the Northern Territory Government questioned their right to the land on which the school was built and little other help was forthcoming.[149]

There was much work to be done in raising the consciousness of non-indigenous Australians, and the Treaty Committee began to concentrate on that. "I can never get to the bottom [of most Australians' views]. One minute we are all for everything, next minute someone comes in waving some dollar sign and waves an anti-flag, and we go in that direction."[150] Nevertheless, some people were interested in Aboriginal issues and towards the end of the year the Treaty Committee ran a legal seminar to which a number of Aboriginal people were invited to put their case. As Judith reported it, some of the white lawyers who attended "were pop-eyed with alarm" at the "unanswerable questions" many of the Aborigines asked, "such as, 'Can any white lawyers explain by what right you people came here in the first place?' Lawyers are not equipped to deal with such matters."[151]

The Commonwealth Games in Brisbane in August gave Aboriginal people an opportunity to draw international attention to their plight, though Judith was aware of the forces arranged against them and of attempts being made to cause division amongst Aboriginal people and the Islanders. The Queensland Government organised a Commonwealth Writers' Week to coincide with the games, inviting Aboriginal writers,

Kath Walker amongst them, and non-Aboriginal sympathisers like Judith, to take part and thus give a blessing to the games. Kath accepted and offered visiting writers hospitality at "Moongalba". But Judith refused, and wrote to her friend warning her that she was being used. In her view, Bjelke-Petersen regarded those who were sympathetic to Aboriginal rights as "Communists", seeing them as part of an international conspiracy to destroy Christianity and Christian values. Judith was angry that her refusal to attend had not been publicised, and that in fact her name was used to attract other writers who otherwise might have boycotted the occasion.

The Treaty Committee, however, kept an eye on the situation and, when a number of Aboriginal people were arrested during a demonstration, appealed for funds to put up bail for them. Bjelke-Petersen was outraged, abusing them for supporting "Communists" but undaunted, the Committee proceeded to organise a counter-occasion to the Brisbane Writers' Week, an Aboriginal Film Festival in Canberra.

In all of these ways the Committee felt they were making some impact on non-Aboriginal Australians. The director of the newly appointed authority to oversee the Bicentennial celebrations in 1988 reported that one of the most frequent suggestions for marking the Bicentenary was to sign a treaty with Aboriginal Australians. On the other side, however, mining and pastoral interests were stepping up their attacks on Aboriginal claims, land rights especially, and spending large sums of money on advertising their views. In Western Australia, where the Labor party under Brian Burke had won power by promising Aboriginal land rights – the two northern electorates in which Aboriginal people were the majority held the key to electoral victory – these interests succeeded in destroying the government's resolve, such as it had been. Apart from the churches, few organised groups opposed this propaganda, though Judith believed that the churches should have been doing more. The exception was the Quakers in Western Australia; Judith was a great admirer of Jo Vallentine, a Quaker, who had just become Australia's first Green senator.

Nevertheless some people still hoped that Burke would keep his promise, and at the Federal level Prime Minister Bob Hawke, at an

Aboriginal festival in the Northern Territory, had promised land rights and a measure of self-determination. Stewart Harris's book about the treaty, *It's Coming Yet*, had been published in 1981 and there seemed to be a good deal of support for the idea. Even in 1980, according to Harris, more than 2500 individuals and families were committed supporters and had donated $35,000 for the campaign, almost entirely in small donations – the Committee had "neither canvassed nor received money from business".[152] Heavily committed elsewhere as they were, the Committee decided to disband, believing, perhaps naively, that Hawke would keep his promises about land rights. Coombs, however, who knew about politics from the inside, was worried that Hawke and his government might not be able to resist the pressure from the mining and pastoral lobby. The Committee's funds were beginning to run out, and this also influenced the decision. In any case, as Judith put it, it was time for us "oldies [to] ...gracefully step down and – we hope – hand over everything we have done to the AIAS (Australian Institute of Aboriginal Studies) and to a younger group".[153]

As a last act, however, they decided to use the remaining funds to organise an international conference on "International Law and Indigenous Rights" at the ANU on 21st and 22nd November. Since a recent decision of the World Court had found that the indigenous peoples of the Saharan region in North Africa had not been deprived of rights to their land by the Spanish occupation, it was hoped that Australia's indigenous peoples might be helped by international law. The Federation of Land Councils had already realised this. A conference of this kind seemed "an interesting way to proceed", and an appropriate way to wind up the Committee's work, especially as the Senate Committee on Constitutional and Legal Affairs, to which the Treaty Committee members had given evidence, had concluded that, "however lamentable and mistaken the British view of Aboriginal culture, law and land use may have been, it is now a matter of past history". Indigenous peoples' loss of sovereign power could not, they said, be remedied by *post facto* recognition.

At the conference it was hoped that developing concepts in international law would be used to explore "the real status of Aborigines as people who have not ceded any land or received any compensation for its theft, and on the possibilities of action under international law".[154] Garth Nettheim had an abiding interest in these issues and worked with the Treaty Committee on the organising side.

Internationally, change was in the air. The World Council of Churches was taking an interest in the situation of Aboriginal Australians, and as a result of a report to the Human Rights Commission, *Continuing the Journey: Justice for Aboriginal Australians,* had set up a continuing group within the Australian Council of Churches to monitor events. The International Commission of Justice, the United Nations Human Rights Commission and Amnesty International had all shown "substantial interest" in the report, also signifying that they would take notice of the issues raised according to their own style and procedures. International law perhaps offered the most promising avenue since the International Court of Justice had also recently found against the South African Government, which was claiming control of neighbouring Namibia as a former colony. As Judith said hopefully, it began to seem as if the "attempt to justify the occupation of Australia under the *terra nullius* rule would now be highly risky under [this] now new international legal perspective".[155]

Many international legal scholars signified their interest in the conference. The Hon. Thomas Bayer, for example, Chairman of the Alaska Native Review Commission, wrote saying that he hoped to attend and sent an advance copy of his address to the Inuit Circumpolar Conference. Representatives of Canadian and United States indigenous peoples, as well as many other distinguished international lawyers, attended along with Aboriginal and Islander peoples and Australian lawyers and legal scholars. Thus the conference set the problems facing Aboriginal and Islander peoples in an international context, initiating a significant new stage in their struggles. It was a fitting conclusion to the Treaty Committee's work.

Their final message, written by Chairman Nugget Coombs, appeared in the last issue of *Aboriginal Treaty News*, promising that the Committee members would continue "to press the Commonwealth government to take the steps necessary to a binding, negotiated treaty" and to support Aboriginal campaigns for "material, social and spiritual independence". Shortly afterwards Labor won the Federal election and on 8th December the new Minister for Aboriginal Affairs, Clyde Holding, promised national legislation on land rights to give Aboriginal people inalienable freehold title, protection for sacred sites, control over mining on their land, access to mining royalties and compensation for land which had been taken from them. The situation seemed more hopeful than it had been for a long time.

In the meantime, Judith was still involved in other issues. A respectable public figure, in February she was one of a group of "distinguished Australians" to discuss with the architect the "ethos" of the new Parliament House on which work was soon to begin. She was also appointed to a committee to oversee the setting up of an Australian Peace and Development Institute – a project dear to her heart – and later received a letter from John Langmore, a politician she approved of, thanking her for her work on the committee.[156] Internationally also, she was widely respected. In 1980 she was awarded the Order of the Golden Ark by the Dutch Government, presented to her by the Dutch Ambassador at a ceremony in Canberra, and in May 1982 was invited to the University of Bologna, Europe's oldest university, as a guest lecturer there for a semester. Her other commitments made it impossible for her to accept, but she appreciated the honour. She was awarded yet another honorary doctorate, this time from the ANU, drawing a letter of congratulation from her brother to say how much he admired the "splendid robes" in the photograph she sent him.[157]

Judith no longer had any illusions about public life, however, and was not prepared to take political gestures at their face value. Thus when Queensland Premier Bjelke-Petersen declared the Archer River area a National Park in May 1982 and many environmentalists welcomed the move, Judith thought, shrewdly enough, that it was designed to drive a wedge between them and the Aboriginal people of the area who were claiming the land. "Any further betrayals of that order", she wrote, "and the Aborigines will hate conservationists as much as they hate miners." She despaired of the naivety and ignorance of many environmentalists which left them open to this kind of manipulation. "No attempt at persuasion will apparently get into [their] heads", she told Len Webb, "that Aborigines know more about the care of the environment than they do." They had more right to manage the land, she thought, than any environmentalist. As she reminded Webb, recent discoveries in the area around Lake George near Canberra suggested that their management of the land by fire might date back 120,000 years – "we look pretty silly beside that".[158] She was also troubled by the way environmentalists had used the ancient painting in the caves in the Franklin River area for their own ends during the debate over the dam, angering Aboriginal people.

In August she was invited by the local Survival and Disarmament Group to Albany to speak there on Hiroshima Day. At the last moment local authorities refused them permission to use the hall, booked some weeks earlier, and one of the other speakers was not able to get to the meeting when his flight from Melbourne was cancelled. Judith saw these as "attempts to sabotage" the meeting, remarking ruefully, that if so, it was a "piquing thought" that since she got to the meeting and he did not, she was "not regarded as as dangerous as a male scientist".[159] In May she had spoken at an Anti-Nuclear Conference in Melbourne organised by Joe Camilleri of La Trobe University and also agreed to be a patron of the Victorian Native Forests campaign, even though she thought they "would inevitably be defeated by the bloody-minded foresters and governments (New South Wales and Victoria) determined to do away with every tree". Environmentalists seemed to be getting nowhere "with the pollies and bureaucrats and indeed never will under the present dispensations, whether Labor or Tory", but she was determined to keep battling. In Western Australia the jarrah forests were threatened by bauxite mining, die-back was reaching epidemic proportions and there was talk of more woodchipping, while in Queensland at Teronia a whole forest was endangered. As she noted with some bitterness, the Federal Government's environmental slogan for the year was "Protect Trees Which Protect Us" but "trees are being removed wholesale wherever you look" often merely "to make pulp wrappings for Japanese goods".[160]

Judith continued to be in demand as a writer and received the Australian Women Writers' Award in 1980, addressing the Women Writers' Congress in Melbourne that year. But, as she confided to

Barbara Blackman, the literary scene was "not mine – it never was", and she would have preferred to keep away, "to cultivate my herbs and say nothing to speak of these days on literary matters". In her view far too many writers, in Sydney especially, seemed to spend "most of their time one-upping one another", living by the motto, "get in for your cut as hard as you can". In particular she disliked literary occasions and what she saw as the display and complicity with the status quo they involved. Invited to a poetry reading, for example, she found herself booked into a "huge new mafia-type hotel ... infested by ... foreign parasites ... all Mercedes and bottle-blond attachments, and cosmopolitan accents ... for which they paid $100 for a room and breakfast".[161]

Judith's writerly sympathies belonged to the early 1970s, with writers like Michael Dransfield, whose death had prompted the poem in which she had set his passion, poetry and rebellion against the new generation of crop-headed businessmen:

> *(Cromwell's men*
> *going on missions*
> *against the longhairs),*
> *briefcases packed with our future in even black typing.*[162]

But she was generous to young writers, young women writers especially, and to the local arts community of Braidwood where she often took part in their activities, though not to the extent of joining in the "ethnic old-time dancing" which figured at their Heritage Festival in 1981, organised to raise money for drought relief. She also valued old friends like Barrie Reid (now Director of the State Library of Victoria and editor for a time of *Overland*), Barbara Blackman, Rosemary Dobson, Nancy Keesing, Dorothy Green and Rodney Hall. At poetry readings now she often read the work of other writers, especially Bruce Dawe, whose political concerns echoed her own, Geoffrey Lehmann, or her favourite colonial poet, Charles Harpur, also passionate in his concern for justice.

This concern remained uppermost. As she was to say at the opening of the 1985 Conference of the Association for the Study of Australian Literature, she was a poet and critic "with an axe to grind ...

[C]onservation, Aboriginal rights, human rights, and the defence of freedom of speech ... are as important to me as poetry, and indeed indispensable to the writing of poetry".[163] So, insisting on this, as a guest of the Adelaide Festival in 1982, she took as her topic "The Writer as Social Commentator".

Her address on the occasion of the New South Wales Premier's Book Awards the same year was even more controversial. The subject she chose was "Side Effects of the Literate Society", and the side effect she chose to concentrate on was the destruction of trees; she called on people to recognise the need to preserve the forests. This was controversial enough but she also praised pre-literate cultures like those of the Aborigines, cultures which live by

> fable, legend and myth – which we have despised ... brought up to believe in the documents and only the documents [but which] nourish us still and have survived as the imaginative and symbolic source of all our creative possibilities ... They lie at the basis of the human adventure, where we first came out of the forest with our stone axes, to sit under a tree and tell the story.

On "the brink of self-destruction", these cultures, she argued, remain crucial to our survival.[164] As she told the Women Writers' Congress, for her, poetry, "includes and implies a re-creation of personal, group and national relationships; an empathy or sympathy with others and with the planet itself".[165]

At the book awards, however, she felt a long way from these relationships. The motel she was booked into had "pictures of naked gents on the wall with large feathered bonnets on" – not really her style, she felt – and at dinner she sat with a group of literary academics with only her old friend Nancy Keesing "to leaven the lump". True, she was pleased with the awards (though *The Cry for the Dead*, which had just appeared, was eligible and did not receive a mention). Richard Haese's *Rebels and Precursors* won in the section it belonged to, Peter Carey's *Bliss* in the fiction section and Fay Zwicky's *Kaddish* in poetry – the last, in her view, "a very good book indeed".[166]

Judith was possibly disappointed by the reception of *The Cry for the Dead*, for which she had hoped for so much. It had finally appeared at the end of 1981 after many problems along the way, many of them caused by cultural tensions. The first drawing submitted for the cover, for instance, was an Aboriginal one, but it was dominated by the figure of a white man with an Aboriginal figure fitting into his shape, an image, Judith was told, which expressed "a feeling of confrontation ... of one race ... being disrupted by another". But she thought that the picture was likely to be misunderstood and was in any case uneasy about using the work of an Aboriginal artist. "Even though the artist may be long dead," she wrote to the editor, "there's a system of belonging which makes them still part of the culture."[167] In the event the drawing was not used. There were also ethical problems with the maps and the editor was troubled by the "shocking number of references" – around 2500 of them. Judith insisted, however, that scrupulous scholarly accuracy was essential.

The reviews were good. In the *Sydney Morning Herald* Axel Clark called it "a lament for all the dead – for all the black and white people, for the stock and for the flora and fauna – destroyed in the pastoral invasion she describes".[168] Edward Kynaston, writing for the *Australian*, called it "a strong, sombre book ... a grim warning ... a poet's priceless truth".[169] In the *Age*, however, Eric Rolls criticised her failure to make recommendations about what might be done to remedy "the helplessness of most Aboriginal communities" and blamed her for "opting out" of her responsibilities.[170] Judith was stung by this criticism, pointing out that this was the business of the Federal Government and directing attention to the work of the Treaty Committee under the guidance of Nugget Coombs, "by far the wisest and most experienced ex-public servant who had dealt with Aborigines and their problems".[171]

Peter Pierce voiced the general consensus that the book marked a "radical ... departure ... from the dutiful, admiring accounts of pastoral expansion" which had been the rule and was "subversive for the ammunition it [gave] to Aborigines fighting for political recognition and material compensation";[172] the *History Teachers Journal* of Victoria recommended it as a text for matriculation in Australian History for this reason. But the book did not sell well and was remaindered. In a sense this was no surprise. As the Foreword pointed out, there was a general "bias against the idea of Aboriginal resistance" since it contradicted the myth of peaceful settlement, so that it was "not a popular note to strike." In his review in the *Times Literary Supplement*, Randolph Stow made a similar point, noting that "one closes [the book] with feelings of despondency … which most Australian writers do not like to entertain".[173] Judith herself suspected foul play, feeling that the publishers had not done enough to publicise the book. She also suspected that many conservatives, possibly even her own family, saw her as a "traitor" for writing as she did and had done their best to kill the book. On the other side, however, a letter to the *Age*, rejoiced that she had "rejoined the ranks of the indignant".[174] For her, personally, it had been an important exercise. She had revisited her own traditions, discovered "much terrible material" which had been suppressed, and in her own way made some amends for it, even if in the process, as one of her friends remarked, she had been "making the natives restless".[175]

In 1985 she would be seventy. Over the last few years she had had a resurgence of energy but this had led her, she realised, to "do too much, which I am prone to". She did not know "how I manage to be at most of the things I agree to do". But now, she confessed, half-facetiously, half-seriously, to Barbara Blackman, she was beginning to feel "old and tottery", though "still in the field despite a few disabilities".[176] These disabilities, her deafness especially, were increasing and her eyesight was also failing. Many of her friends, too, were ill. John Büsst's sister, Phyl, who had been a staunch and generous ally during the battle to save the Great Barrier Reef, was seriously ill, and Judith worried that life was becoming unendurable for her. She was finding visits increasingly "daunting" and sometimes melancholy since most of her friends, she told Len Webb (with some exaggeration), seemed to have "gone overseas or gone melancholy mad or something".[177]

One of her last poems, "Rockpool" expresses a sense of being somehow at the end of an era:

> *My generation is dying, after long lives*
> *swung from war to depression to war to fatness.*[178]

History's pain was not diminishing either. "Victims" reflects on the pain of many migrants:

> *...ageing now, some dead.*
> *In the third-class suburbs of exile*
> *their foreign accents*
> *continue to condemn them*

as their memories remained of wars and concentration camps, humiliations and sufferings unimaginable to their children who

> *have put on, over the years*
> *a delicate cloak of fat.*[179]

At the same time many people seemed to be retreating into themselves, dreaming of "getting rid of politicians and bureaucrats and [becoming] Pluralist Anarchists", as she put it.[180] But she herself had no intention of giving up. For one thing, loyalties to the past kept her going and the abiding sense of nothingness which must be contested, the continuing dialogue she wrote about in a poem written after Jack's death, the dialogue

> *made out of plus and minus,*
> *zero and number...*
>
> *Flick off the conscious switch,*
> *there's Nothing, sprung*
> *out of its secret place behind the world.*[181]

This nothingness must be contested to the end.

CHAPTER XIV

PHANTOM DWELLING

> I've no wish to chisel things into new shapes.
> The remnant of a mountain has its own meaning.
>
> "Rockface",
> *Collected Poems*, p. 420

"Time and trouble will tame an advanced young woman," Dorothy Sayers wrote, "but an advanced old woman is uncontrollable by any earthly force".[1] Many women live more or less private lives, being married and looking after children. Judith had done this in the 1950s and early 1960s. But then she had moved into public life, into the game of mirrors described in "Glass Corridor", walking down a hall of reflecting mirrors through

> *a swaying maze of gestures*
> *eastways, westways.*
>
> *Who knows which I am,*
> *this criss-cross evening –*
> *or how many?*[2]

Now she was more or less single. With the ending of the work of the Treaty Committee her strenuous involvement in public life was nearly over, and she was spending more time at "Edge".

She was now almost totally deaf and her eyes seemed to be giving out also; in August 1983 there was talk of an operation for cataracts.

As she remarked to Barbara Blackman: "Everyone flees from those they are afraid are going to ask for something, especially sympathy. The only answer is independence", concluding, however, that "all in all I am thankful to be deaf and curmudgeonly" rather than "blind and sociable".[3] But friendship, as always, remained important, and passion also; her life would never come to a tidy ending, however much

> *Gravity's drag, time's wear, keep pressing downwards,*
> *moving loose stones downslope, sinking hills like wet*
>   *meringue,*

and subject her to its pressures. She might

> *... move more slowly this year, neck falling in folds,*
> *pulses more visible; yet there's a thrust in the arteries*

but this poem, "Pressures", tells of the joy at seeing an old and much loved friend again:

> *Blood slows, thickens, silts – yet when I saw you*
> *once again, what a joy set this pulse jumping.*[4]

At "Edge", too, which reminded her of "the way New England used to be",[5] she could draw strength from the living world around her. The task of the poet, for her, had always been to make clear to herself and thus to others the crucial temporal and abiding questions, and in this task she had always depended on nature, believing with Heidegger that to be fully human is to dwell upon the earth, to have a world and that:

> *The world's darkening never reaches*
> *to the light of Being*[6]

glowing there. She had known this in the rainforest:

> *The forest drips and glows with green.*
> *The tree-frog croaks his far-off song.*
> *His voice is stillness, moss and rain*
> *drunk from the forest ages long.*

> *We cannot understand that call*
> *unless we move into his dream,*
> *where all is one and one is all*
> *and frog and python are the same.*[7]

At "Edge", in a colder and more austere landscape, she was still aware of this abiding power. Even

> *Walking here in the dark my torch lights up*
> *something massive, motionless, that confronts me.*[8]

There was more time for reflection here also, though she did not look for comfort in any easy belief.

> I prefer not to talk in terms of the "gods" which are temporary and objectified [she wrote] ... but if you've read Jung ... you'll know that what he calls God ... is approximately what you mean by truth and that his view of wholeness ... includes the female principle as essential though unfortunately we're changing only very slowly.[9]

Rather, like the older Yeats, she was more and more aware of the energies, the energy and savagery of things. "Rockpool" expresses this sense:

> *I hang on the rockpool's edge; its wild embroideries:*
>
> *admire it, pore on it, this, the devouring and mating,*
> *ridges of coloured tracery, occupants, all the living,*
>
> *the stretching of toothed claws to food, the breeding*
> *on the ocean's edge. "Accept it? Gad, madam, you had*
>   *better."*[10]

Dr Johnson's stoic phrase which concludes the poem points to the courage which sustained her. But Johnson would also have approved of the ethical passion which precluded self-pity. She was feeling more and more the stranger she had felt as a child, estranged from the majority of people around her who seemed increasingly preoccupied with the "business of money-making, money-having and money-spending". But like Dr Johnson, she looked outwards rather than inwards, though what she saw was not his kind of monumental Christian God but something more elemental and more defiant.

> *Today's white fog won't lift above the tree-tops.*
> *Yesterday's diamond frost has melted to ice-water*

she wrote in "Winter", and the cold had cut through much that had once protected her:

> *These hundreds of books on the shelves have all been read*
> *but I can't force my mind to recall their wisdom.*

> *Let's drink while we can. The sum of it all is Energy,*
> *and that went into the wood, the wine, the poems.*[11]

But she had not turned her back on society. Coombs's prediction was being swiftly fulfilled as miners and pastoralists put pressure on the Hawke Government and in Western Australia, under Brian Burke, another Labor Government succumbed to them almost entirely. By October 1984 the press was saying that the time for federal legislation for Aboriginal land rights was past. In any case, they reported, rights would have to be limited to "a set of principles". The future of the mining veto, even the limited veto granted under the Northern Territory legislation, was also in doubt.[12] Nor were governments doing much to help Aboriginal people put their case. On television, West Australian Aboriginal leader Rob Riley complained that they were being forced to counter the propaganda campaign against land rights mounted by the mining industry without any financial help. Lack of finance, he told a Senate subcommittee in May, even prevented the NAC Makarrata subcommittee from consulting with Aboriginal groups, let alone commission any research on the matter. In November, giving the Curtin Memorial Lecture in Perth, Coombs had condemned what he saw as the abdication of responsibility in this respect by government, and later that month he and nearly a hundred other eminent Australians, of which Judith was one, published an advertisement in the press calling on the government to stand by its earlier promises to Aborigines.[13]

For the moment, however, there seemed little that could effectively be done at government level since the Minister for Aboriginal Affairs, Clyde Holding, had recently told Aborigines: "We would like to recognise all your rights, but our white constituents won't let us".[14] This seemed to put paid to ideas of a treaty, especially as far as Aborigines were concerned. As Judith wrote to Len Webb later, "the problems inherent in Aborigines dealing on any level with governments have put [the idea of a treaty] out of court for some of them – at least White Australian governments as they are".[15] Judith and Coombs saw their point, but still felt that a treaty was the only final answer since it would give them official standing – a view which subsequent developments confirmed.

In the meantime the Committee decided that a book should be written about the movement for a treaty, and Judith was asked to write it. Working almost non-stop she finished the book, *We Call for a Treaty*, within the year. But it was an even more difficult process than usual since each chapter had to be circulated amongst Committee members for comment as it was finished. This was something which, as a writer, she found very difficult and would never ask of anyone else (she waived her right to read this biography chapter by chapter, for instance). Somehow the book was finished, more or less to everyone's satisfaction.

Writing it she had had to spend a good deal of time in Canberra, using the resources of the Institute of Aboriginal Studies to whom the Treaty Committee had handed over most of its records. After the peace of "Edge" she did not enjoy this return to communal life, finding

> living in my corridor at University House during the week ... rather awful; I've had accountancy seminars, management seminars, mining company conferences, secret sessions of the Hope Commission guarded by security personnel (can't call them people) and many other horrors going on just beside my room ... But at least it is cheap and close to the Institute for work and has a good selection of wine in the bottleshop. Can't complain I suppose. I don't feel I belong to that ambience nevertheless.[16]

When the book was completed, they found it difficult to get a publisher – as she often did, Judith suspected that powerful interests were working against them – but they eventually found one.

Other activities continued. In November 1983 she gave the keynote address at the ACF National Conference in place of Nugget Coombs, who was ill. Petra Kelly, heroine of the German Greens, also spoke at the conference and David Bellamy, another world figure of the environmental movement, gave the after-dinner speech. Australian environmentalists felt more and more a part of the world movement, and at home the Federal Government had stopped the damming of the Franklin River in Tasmania and 98.5 per cent of the Great Barrier Reef had been declared a Marine National Park.

Judith's environmental activities, however, were entering into a new phase. On 20th September the WPSQ celebrated its twentieth anniversary, and as one of the society's founders and president for over a decade, she was a guest of honour. The celebration was held at the Botanic Gardens at Mount Cootha, followed by the annual general meeting in the Gardens Theatrette which the current president, Don Henry, got through, as he had promised he would in his invitation, "as speedily as possible".[17] It was a cheerful occasion, complete with birthday cake, and Judith was able to meet many of her old friends. She was especially pleased to see again the poet Silvana Gardner, with whom she had corresponded for years, whose spontaneous spirit and lyrical paintings had brought light into dark moments.

For the celebration she stayed with Len and Doris Webb and had long discussions with Len, now retired from the CSIRO but a research fellow at Griffith University. Like her, he was working at what she called – possibly ironically – the "Ecological–Humanist–Ecoethicist Pole"[18] of the environmental movement. "Rainforest", which she had sent to Webb in September 1983, gives a sense of what this meant: the forest, like the world generally, could be properly understood only by those who had experienced and shared in its life. She no longer believed, as she told him, "that value judgements can be made on a theoretical basis, they involve a level below that if they are to work".[19] As the poem puts it,

> We with our quick dividing eyes
> measure, distinguish and are gone.
> The forest burns, the tree-frog dies,
> yet one is all and all are one.[20]

What we need to do is "to learn the language of the forest – that is deep ecology". Biophysical facts should be set within this more profound dimension of experience, familiar to so-called "primitive" peoples but not to Western culture. Decision-makers in particular ought to be aware of the "non quantifiable values" it thus opens up.[21] With economic rationalism becoming more and more fashionable, even or perhaps especially at government level, this was a vain hope, of course. But Judith found it comforting to discuss her ideas with Len and Doris, who were also thinking along similar lines.

From childhood the state of the natural world had affected her. The bad drought of the early 1980s reminded her of the droughts of the 1940s and 1950s which had seemed to her then part of the conflagration of war, ending with the fire storms of German cities and the annihilation of Hiroshima and Nagasaki:

> *In my sixty-eighth year drought stopped the song of the river,*
> *sent ghosts of wheatfields blowing over the sky.*
>
> *In the swimming-hole the water's dropped so low*
> *I bruise my knees on rocks which are new acquaintances.*

But the dust, blurring the "daybreak moon", had taken her further back, reminding her of the face of her mother, the Euridyce figure of her childhood, moving away from her towards death, her face looking "through a grey motor-veil" like the moon "blurred in a gauze of dust". It seemed a world without shadows, transparent to the sources of light and fire:

> *Fallen leaves on the current scarcely move.*
> *But the azure kingfisher flashes upriver still.*
>
> *Poems written in age confuse the years.*
> *We all live, said Bashō, in a phantom dwelling.*[22]

This sense of mortality was borne in on her not just when she looked at the natural world but as she watched her friends growing older. Dick Roughsey, for instance, an Aboriginal Queensland painter who had been part of the struggle for the Great Barrier Reef, Cooloola and the rainforests, was dying of cancer, "just about transparent but very tranquil and apparently in no pain".[23] In other ways, too, there were signs of "gravity's drag, time's wear". The old family Wyndham home, "Dalwood", already in disrepair in 1972 when the family had celebrated the centenary of May Mackenzie's marriage to Albert Wright, was now in danger of collapsing entirely, and at the end of 1984 a public appeal was made to save it. Judith was invited to join the trust set up to look after the money raised. But she refused, saying that she would be "embarrassed to be seen supporting celebrations of the early settlers. The Aborigines would think it more appropriate that the money should go to them not restoring a colonial house – quite right".[24]

Family memories kept returning. The next year, Judith received a letter from a friend of her Aunt Weeta, who had taught French for years at New England Girls' School but was now back in London, recalling Weeta's love for her niece and her pride in her achievements.[25] The memory returned of this aunt and of her life at "Wongwibinda", the loneliness, for instance, which Judith had sensed as a child (though not all the details were accurate – Weeta was not eighty-three when she died):

> *I had an aunt who lived*
> *much of her life alone.*
> *We are alike,*
> *glad when guests have gone,*
> *though often glad*
> *also of company.*
> *She died at eighty-three.*
> *No one was there.*
> *Do you need help to die?*
> *Shall I?*[26]

At "Edge" she watched the seasonal flocking of the birds, red rosellas, black cockatoo, magpies, currawongs and swallows

> *All of them flocked together,*
> *crying aloud, knowing*
> *the end of autumn*

and the coming of winter. Her thoughts turned to people she had loved who were no longer with her:

> *At the end of autumn*
> *I too – I want you near me,*
> *all you who've gone, who scatter*
> *into far places or are hidden under*
> *summer-forgotten gravestones.*[27]

Nevertheless she did not take refuge in thoughts of transcendence, which, she told Len Webb, she found "a difficult word",[28] preferring to focus on life and her part in it, destructive as well as creative.

The poems she was writing at the time, the last she was to publish, were inspired by the Persian form, the ghazal, lyrics usually about love and wine, though often mystically understood, from five to twelve lines, though she did not try to imitate the original in which every line had to repeat the same line. They were poems about energy and transfiguration into the larger life of the cosmos:

> *who wants to be a mere onlooker? Every cell of me*
> *has been pierced through by plunging intergalactic*
>   *messages,*[29]

Judith was finding it hard to cope with the cold winters at "Edge", however, and problems with her eyes were making it dangerous to drive, so she was thinking of moving back to Braidwood. She loved the bush and its life, and wanted "her place" looked after properly when she moved, so she began exploring the possibility of giving the house and land to the university to be used as a research station – there were rare birds and flowers in the area. The problem was that, unless she handed it over lock, stock and barrel, which she did not want to do, the house and land would still be regarded as an asset for taxation purposes, should she need to apply for a pension later on. Her books and what they earned under the Public Lending Rights agreement and from the new *Copyright Act* still provided her main source of income, though she also had a pension from the Australia Council, and she needed to be careful. Exasperated, she wrote to a friend that "giving things away is more time and trouble than selling them".[30]

She was also getting more of her papers together to place in the National Library – she had already deposited some the previous year – and was trying to organise Jack's papers into another book. Given the fact that *The Structure of Modern Thought* had not sold well, she was unlikely to find a publisher for it. All this was forcing her to look back, and an approach by a prospective biographer pushed her further in this direction. Disliking the idea of someone else writing her life, she decided to anticipate the "self-proposed biographer ... by doing at least some of the job myself by getting in ahead of her. As I simply don't want my biography written ... an autobiography seems the only answer, but what a nuisance."[31] From then on she worked intermittently at this autobiography, in between all the other things she was doing.

Amongst these was a request from Geoffrey Blainey to write an essay on Australian landscape for *Daedalus*, the journal of the American Academy of Arts and Sciences. The issue as a whole, Blainey wrote, was about the question, "What makes Australia tick?" and "Why does it operate as it does?". Judith accepted but she was not very happy with the subject she was allotted, which was "landscape". This, she said in her essay, was a very limited concept and sprang from what she saw as the "irreconcilable difference of viewpoint" between ourselves and the land's original inhabitants, the Aborigines. For them "every part of the country ... every mark and feature was numinous with meaning". But the notion of landscape implies a division between the self and the land. In contrast with Aborigines what non-Aboriginal people "see in the landscape", she thought, was "partial, inadequate and temporal vision, reflecting our own interests". She also lamented the loss of the Aboriginal vision. In her view there were "few places left in Australia where this ancient relationship to the land has not been fractured and destroyed", so that where Uluru (Ayers Rock) is for Aboriginal people a sacred place and centre of the land itself, for us it is a tourist centre.

The title of her essay, "Landscape and Dreaming", indicates the way she tackled the subject, reflecting on the differences between the two approaches to the land and then looking at the land itself with a poet's eye, with a sense of awe at its variety and significance and at the dangers which threaten it from our mindless exploitation of its material resources. The essay concluded on a note of hope, if also of challenge:

> A growth of attachment on grounds not wholly economic is perceptible already, and may finally bring the two viewpoints a little closer if real action is taken to heal the wounds we have dealt both to the land and its original owners.[32]

The American editor, Stephen Graubard, was sympathetic. In correspondence he had worried that there was no essay on Aboriginal Australians, aware of a "new sensibility among Australians" which made such an essay necessary, and asked her to suggest someone to write it. She suggested the historian Henry Reynolds, but he was unable to do it, so that when the volume finally appeared there was no essay on Aboriginal Australians. But Judith's essay at least highlighted the importance of their culture. It also refused to conform for the sake of conforming to the accepted pieties and write about the preservation of Australian landscape, as the editor had suggested, emphasising instead its destruction at the hands of white settlers whose "ignorance and contempt stands between us and the story of the millennia that preceded the European arrival ... [though] now a little of the truth is emerging".[33]

Nor was Judith entirely biddable when the contributors (who included Geoffrey Blainey, Leonie Kramer, Zelman Cowen, Manning Clark, Donald Horne and Hugh Stretton) met for dinner in Melbourne in April 1984 to make final arrangements for publication. According to others present, she had a heated argument with Geoffrey Blainey and "nearly came to blows" with Richard Walsh (at that stage Managing Director of Angus & Robertson, her publishers) over remarks he had made about Aborigines which, she said, "suggested he had never been outside Sydney as far as [they] were concerned". She felt that she had been "more critical than polite" since she was not entirely easy about the whole enterprise; with its large budget and the lavish dinner, it seemed to her to be "one of those exercises only Americans could afford".[34] But she confessed that she had not been able to resist the offer of $1000 for her essay,[35] nor perhaps the honour of being invited – she had recently written to a friend that she had "reached the age where nobody wants me to write anymore except forewords to their or their daughters' books".[36] Her deafness may also have contributed to her touchiness. Nevertheless Stephen Graubard felt that she made "a great contribution" to the meeting and the discussion.

As far as poetry was concerned she was writing much less and much more austerely:

> *I used to love Keats, Blake,*
> *Now I try haiku*
> *for its honed brevities,*
> *its inclusive silences.*
>
> *Issa. Shiki. Buson. Bashō.*
> *Few words and with no rhetoric.*
> *Enclosed by silence*
> *as is the thrush's call.*[37]

But try as she might "to see without words", as the living creatures around her did, she could not; she lived, as she had always done, "through a web of language".[38]

In 1984 she was awarded the Asan World Prize for poetry and invited to India, where she had always had many admirers, for the presentation. For health reasons she was unable to make the long flight, so the award was presented by the India High Commissioner at a ceremony in Canberra. She and Jack had always been interested in Hindu philosophy, and she had good memories of her visit there some years earlier. She had also corresponded over the years with a number of Indian scholars and writers, and Shiva, the lord of fire and of the cosmic dance, had figured and continued to figure in her poetry, so it was an honour she appreciated. Despite her many political activities she had always taken the long view, as Jack had:

> Politics aren't the only thing. It's like concentrating on the rash and forgetting to treat the measles ... Politics are the froth on the top of the cauldron ... not what makes the water boil. The really important thing is to find out why the water is boiling – and the really difficult thing.[39]

It was disappointing, therefore, not to be able to go to India again, especially as politics in Australia, "the froth on the top of the cauldron", were becoming more distasteful.

In June 1984 her friend Sylvia Monk, an environmentalist and champion of Aboriginal people who lived on the Gold Coast in Queensland, received a death threat. The local newspaper, the *Gold Coast Bulletin,* reporting the incident, quoted from a letter she had received: "If you like the filthy Asians, why don't you go to their stinking countries. Germs like you must be destroyed before you destroy Australia with your filthy Asians and Niggers".[40] Violence seemed to be on the increase. Even in the more temperate south Judith also believed that she was "suffering interference from parties unknown in her phone calls and correspondence".[41] In July her car was broken into in the carpark of the National Park near the coast where she had left it to go walking. The window was smashed, and she lost her credit cards, driver's licence, car registration, everything else in the wallet and $80 holiday spending money, but she suspected foul play as well as robbery.[42] She also thought that deliberate attempts had been made to sabotage the Albury–Wodonga Hiroshima Day Rally that year, and in July 1984, back in Albury again, she told her listeners that they should all be afraid of what the Opposition were trying to do and the ways in which they were trying to do it. Queensland seemed to her to be particularly bad and she could not go there "any more without finding my face in a fixed snarl".[43]

As far as Aboriginal people were concerned, mining companies were spending millions of dollars to turn popular opinion against land rights. But there was some concern at government level. In May the former secretary of the Inquiry into the National Estate, George Brownbill, now working for the Department of Aboriginal Affairs, wrote asking Judith to contribute an article to counter the anti-Aboriginal propaganda appearing in the media as part of a counter-campaign.[44]

In the Northern Territory in July the Northern Land Council had given in to pressure from mining and other interests and agreed to mining in Kakadu. Rightly or wrongly, Judith saw this as the work of "corruption and bribery" and "threats practised" on some of the Council's members, writing angrily that Aboriginal people "are no less subject to intimidation and pressure than we are" and, she added also, more dependent on government funding. They had had "very arrogant treatment from people who should have known better", concluding that the whole white community, not just those immediately involved, must face up to our responsibilities to indigenous Australians.[45]

In South Australia the push was on to mine for uranium at Roxby Downs while in Queensland the battle to save the Daintree Rainforest was raging; Judith wrote to Len Webb that it looked as if it would be "going the way of all rainforests in Queensland". Not that she intended giving in: "we never learn not to try to buck the system, it seems",[46] as she said. On Daintree Day she was at a festival for the environment in Cairns, speaking with senators Bob Brown and Margaret Reynolds, and Geoff Mosley of the ACF. Aboriginal people were involved also and Aboriginal dancers supplemented what the speakers had to say.

Judith was, as she put it, "still a pretty busy old person",[47] writing "ferocious articles on Hawke", for instance. "All politicians without exception have my deep-purple witch's curse," she told Barbara Blackman, "and I wish it would work for once. [But] I'm afraid nuclear missiles have outdated such things long ago."[48] She was no longer as hopeful as she had been during the battle for the Great Barrier Reef, thinking that with all the forces arranged against them "we're never likely to win anything any more". Her letters to the paper, she complained, were not being published, suspecting that this was because the Liberals were "on the racist lurk". "A shabby dictatorship emanating from Queensland" seemed to be approaching, and she wrote with concern of a piece of graffiti she had noticed on a recent visit in the centre of Canberra.

> A notice ... [asked] "ARE WE READY FOR A GREEN PARTY IN AUSTRALIA". "NOT ON YOUR LIFE: NO YOU FUCKING GREEN WEEDS" replied the populace in spray paint. This in Canberra, what elsewhere? Very like my memory of Germany in 1937.[49]

"Where, oh where, is the fire and glitter in our day?" she lamented.[50] The Labor Party, too, seemed to have betrayed its principles. She had recently attended their National Conference, spending

> a freezing wet day or two in Canberra glaring at Labor politicians in the Lakeside lobby ... surrounded by wet woolly people

alternately glaring at the Right and the Centre Left and screaming applause at the Left, without of course any effect except possibly pneumonia on their return.[51]

Her deafness as well as her principles must have made her a difficult presence.

But her motto was still *nil desperandum* and she continued challenging the status quo, telling members of the ACF at their annual general meeting that there should be an Aboriginal member of the council, for instance. In August, opening the annual conference of the Association for the Study of Australian Literature at the University of New England, she also made an attack on the current vogue of literary theory. It was, she thought, part of the utilitarian and materialistic trend of the times which had no time for poetry or philosophy. In her view, as always, the key question was one of values. As she had put it in *Because I Was Invited*, the "dangerous division [lies] ... not between Arts and Science, but between our idea of ourselves and our real nature",[52] which in her view was intimately related to the rest of creation and beyond the power of merely rational analysis. "The Current of events which forms the life-stream of the individual escapes ... fixation and description."[53] The crucial question, therefore, was to find ways of combining the intuitive, emotional and aesthetic dimension with the intellectual and ethical. Literary theory seemed to Judith "radio-active territory" because there was, she thought, "too much theory and too much self-consciousness. Fear of the critics and theorists are bad for the poet".[54] Her paper did not please everyone, and was not published, as such addresses usually were, in the Society's journal, *Notes and Furphies*. But she remained defiantly of her own opinion. In any case she had never been entirely at her ease in the academy. For her, poetry was not an intellectual game; it had a cosmic as well as a political and social dimension – in common with Aboriginal myths. As she wrote in "Words, Roses, Stars",

> ... *words are human; language comes and goes*
> *with us, and lives among us. Not absurd*
> *to think the human spans the Milky Way.*

> *Baiame bends beside his crystal stream*
> *shaded beneath his darker cypress-tree*
> *and gives the gift of life, the endless dream,*
> *to Koori people, and to you and me.*

It was this life she had always served, and this language,

> *plucked by a path where human vision went.*[55]

As she had put it, more prosaically, in 1989: "poetry has to show a way down into, back and beyond or it's not poetry", which, she thought, was the reason why "at a time when none of us want to look at the reality of ourselves, such poetry isn't welcome to anyone".[56]

In fact she was finding more interest in her ideas amongst scientist friends like Len Webb and Val Plumwood, at that stage Professor of Environmental Philosophy at Macquarie University. Most literary critics and academics did not seem interested, and literary theory seemed to her to be taking them in the opposite direction, making them complicitous with a culture she saw as exploitative and destructive.[57]

There were lighter moments. She continued to entertain friends at "Edge" and with some of them saw Max Gillies' satiric revue, *A Night of National Reconciliation*, and enjoyed it hugely. During the year, too, she sat for her portrait by Judy Cassab as part of the series Cassab was doing on eminent Australians – one wonders whether she spoke to Judy Cassab, a refugee from Hungary, about what she had seen there in 1937.

In the midsummer of 1985 bushfires raged around the Shoalhaven River, though they did not reach "Edge". But Judith felt for the land in this "burned-out summer", torn apart by miners looking for gold and then by cattle grazing and haunted by memories of the fate of its Aboriginal inhabitants:

> *This place's quality is not its former nature*
> *but a struggle to heal itself after many wounds.*
>
> *Upheaved ironstone, mudstone, quartz and clay*
> *drank dark blood once, heard cries and the running of feet.*

But in the long run she believed,

> *Scabs of growth form slowly over the rocks.*
> *Lichens, algae, wind-bent saplings grow,*

admiring the tenacity she saw in nature and in its creatures even in this dry summer:

> *All day the jenny-lizard dug hard ground*
> *watching for shadows of hawk or kookaburra.*
>
> *At evening, her pearl-eggs hidden, she raked back earth*
> *over the tunnel, wearing a wide grey smile.*[58]

But she was not so sure about the survival of human beings.

The Hawke Government had been narrowly re-elected, though the appearance of the Nuclear Disarmament Party was a heartening sign, winning a degree of electoral support and in Western Australia even managing to get Jo Vallentine into the Senate. Despite this, there seemed little prospect of a change in government attitudes to Aboriginal land rights. Meeting in January, Aboriginal leaders strongly condemned Hawke's failure to keep his promises, and threatened embarrassing action in the Bicentennial year unless the situation improved. Following this, in February the NAC issued a pamphlet, *Minimum Expectations of National Land Rights Legislation*, demanding the right of a veto on mining and unconditional restoration of traditional lands. Also in February, Kevin Gilbert circulated an appeal to non-Aboriginal Australians, explaining the basis of his people's claim to the land: "Sovereignty is ours," he wrote. "It has not been changed by invasion and sovereignty must never be changed by invasion" – a point, he noted, which Margaret Thatcher, Britain's Prime Minister, had made during the Falklands War to refute the claim the Argentinian Government had made as a result of their invasion of the Islands. But Gilbert saw little hope for his people in a treaty or Makarrata which he saw as merely "a trick", believing that the government had no intention of acceding to Aboriginal claims. Instead, he was looking to international sanctions, calling on the world community to "cease making trade agreements with Australia until Aboriginal sovereignty is recognized and protected by international law". He also demanded a National Summit on Land Rights.[59]

The Federal Government, however, paid little attention, giving in to pressure from the Burke Government in Western Australia, which had introduced legislation to deny Aborigines the right of veto and permanent ownership of what land they had – the best they could hope for was leasehold. Thus, when on 20th February the Federal Government released its proposed model for land rights it was soundly rejected by most Aborigines. Clearly uneasy, the government dissolved the NAC in May, promising to replace it with a more effective organisation. Just as clearly dissatisfied, not long afterwards 600 Aborigines from all over the country converged on Parliament House in a peaceful but angry protest.

There may have been a certain grim satisfaction in all this for members of the Treaty Committee. But it was clear, as most commentators were pointing out, that the mining and pastoral interests were winning the battle for public opinion and there seemed to be little they could do about it. But they had at last found a publisher for *We Call for a Treaty* – Collins Dove. In the meantime leaders of the mining industry, like Hugh Morgan, continued to attack Aboriginal claims and Aboriginal culture; he characterised it as "paganism, superstition, fear and darkness", something which "good Christians should disapprove of".[60]

So it was perhaps not surprising that in the middle of the year Judith went down with a fierce bout of flu and had to take a break, spending several days on Heron Island on the Great Barrier Reef, though, as she wrote, she was careful there to avoid "US millionaires and Gladstone yobbos".[61] She was still vividly aware of her body, of having

> *kept [her] skinful of red*
> *on this hinged scaffold of bone*
> *(with all due gratitude*
> *to the help of medical science) . . .*
>
> *We have held off the enemy*
> *and welcomed the friend and lover;*
> *it has been a long alliance.*[62]

But she was beginning to feel her age.

Divisions within the environmental movement did not help. The idea of "wilderness" in particular was still causing trouble. In the 1960s and 1970s environmentalists had fought to have National Parks set aside as "wilderness" areas. But as Aboriginal people began to assert their claims to these areas, they were being resisted by some environmentalists who saw them as intruders since they thought of "wilderness" as a place where nobody lived, or should live. This had never been an Aboriginal view, of course. For them every person had an intimate sacred relationship to and responsibility for the land on which he or she lived, and every part of the country had been looked after in this way.

As Judith was quick to point out, the views of environmentalists who wanted wilderness areas to be empty areas were thus profoundly offensive to the indigenous peoples who had looked after and cared for the land over so many thousands of years. In her view, Aborigines should be given responsibility for wilderness areas, not excluded from them. This view suffered a setback when the Aboriginal people of the Daintree area supported the building of the road through the forest. As she said to Len Webb, this was the result "of their miserable situation and should not be held against them",[63] and in any case they had always been practical in their attitudes to the land. With her pastoral background, she was suspicious of attitudes to the land which were merely romantic – as she thought the attitudes of some environmentalists were – and she accepted that the Daintree people might have reasons for their decision. The struggle for Aboriginal rights was not becoming any easier, but she remained dedicated to the cause, sending the proceeds of the sale of her papers to the National Library – $1800 – to the National Federation of Land Councils, for instance. Many of the documents included in these papers, collected during her research for *The Cry for the Dead*, she reflected, related to "the invasion of Central Queensland", so that it was appropriate to give the money earned from their sale to Aboriginal people.

Problems were looming in the Bungle Bungle and in the Kimberley generally in Western Australia, where there was talk of increasing tourism as well as of exploiting the mineral resources. The discovery of diamonds there was troubling, especially as the Australian Government was encouraging the interest of the South African diamond companies. It will mean "transferring South African problems to Northern Australia", she wrote.[64]

Judith saw the conflict between Aborigines and environmentalists as "a ghastly situation if ever there was one!"[65] but she did not hesitate in her loyalty. In her view, the opposition of groups like the Wilderness Society to Aboriginal occupation of National Parks

> adds up to a confirmation and endorsement of the *terra nullius* judgement ... [which] has resulted, over the last two hundred years, in dispossession, destruction and the denial of all human rights to Aborigines, has turned all Aboriginal land in Australia over to destructive interests, and is the chief stumbling block to justice and reconciliation.[66]

She had had a "yarn with Vin Serventy", inclined to the Wilderness Society position, she reported. He had "been complaining about Aborigines using their privileges of hunting and cutting down trees in Kakadu" but she thought that her "gently put remonstrances" had had some effect since he now seemed "more or less fired with the idea of indigenous rights in at least some parks".[67] She also managed to get Tasmanian environmentalists to set up a committee to consider the matter, indifferent as ever to the unpopularity which made her "that woman ... always sticking her head in places she's got no business in",[68] as a friend of her brother Peter described her – not entirely ingenuously perhaps since he had recently invested in a woodchipping venture.

Her interest in the environmental movement had always been intellectual, not merely emotional. It was this which had inspired the battle to save the Great Barrier Reef:

> What was being fought for was in effect an environment alien to human occupation and full of creatures largely unknown to most people. [We had] no commitment to cuddly koalas and symbolic kangaroos, but just to ... abstract old truth and beauty, and against the mad machine![69]

This involved a process in which the self is seen in relation to the natural world and "the narrow, corporeal self is transcended, and a wider, non-corporeal 'Self' realised" – the kind of process reflected in the poems she was writing at the time like "Rainforest", "Hunting Snake", "Fox" and "Epacris". Not everyone found this appealing. As one writer observed, this made ecology a "grim science"[70] since identifying with the natural world also meant suffering with it from the wounds inflicted on it by "development" – as she had always done. It also meant letting go of the merely personal and individual, identifying with the impersonality expressed in a poem published years before in 1959, with "the candid staring of the lake" which

> *holds what's passing and forgets the past.*
> *Faithful to cloud and leaf, not knowing leaf nor cloud,*
> *it spreads its smooth eye wide for something's sake.*

Even then, however, she had understood that "my meaning's what you are".[71]

That, of course, is why her opposition to the concept of "progress" had always been so passionate because that concept made human will and desire the centre of the universe. "The technological explosion and the economic thinking that has supported it have been based on false premises about the resources of the planet." Like Paul Ehrlich whom she then went on to quote, she believed that "the growth mania in developed countries [was rather] ... the creed of the cancer cell",[72] essentially destructive. It was this belief which inspired and sustained her long career as an environmentalist, peace activist and supporter of Aboriginal claims, and she still believed as much as ever in these causes. As she had written in a passage quoted by Len Webb in *Wildlife* in 1985:

> There is no stronger force than emotion, if it is well based and directed. For it is feeling that establishes values, and if we are ever to move from economic values to a reassertion of ecological values our feelings and sympathies must be engaged first ... This is not to say that an ecological value-system by itself would be enough, or that we can do without an intellectual, thought-out,

basis for it. Far from it, the scientific and intellectual revision of
our priorities is urgently necessary and has indeed been the basis
for the new movement of feeling.[73]

Now, though, Judith was moving towards the austerity she had prayed for in a poem written in the 1950s:

Let the stream of my life run muted,
and a pure sleep unbar
my every depth and secret.

I wait for the rising of a star
whose spear of light shall transfix me –
of a far-off world whose silence
my very truth must answer.[74]

Almost totally deaf, she was becoming more solitary. She was positive about this, having always "been either a cat that walked by myself or on the fringes of other people's lives and in strict camouflage", and telling Barbara Blackman that it was "rather an advantage ... I can close my door and ignore visitors entering". But she felt the loss. On another occasion, for example, she wrote to Barbara who had quoted someone who said that being deaf was really no great deprivation,

I can assure him that it just ain't so. In fact it removes more than
a whole dimension and I'm thankful for hearing aids, however
inadequately they represent the outer world of sound. I can,
however, remember a world when I could hear things all around
me instead of just in one ear if then, and so I'm lucky compared
to one who never heard birds, for example, singing in trees at
different heights and distances.[75]

She turned seventy on 31st May 1985. On her sixtieth birthday she had written a poem, "Counting in Sevens", speculating on turning seventy, reflecting that, throughout her life,

... with every added seven,
some strange present I was given.[76]

Now that she was seventy, she decided that the gift was silence: she would write no more poetry. Her body had always spoken in her poetry, now it was getting tired, and it was time to go with its rhythms:

> *Counting in seven-year rhythms I've lost nine skins*
> *though their gradual flaking isn't so spectacular.*
>
> *Holding a book or a pen I can't help seeing*
> *how age crazes surfaces. Well, and interiors?*
>
> *You ask me to read those poems I wrote in my thirties?*
> *They dropped off several incarnations back.*[77]

Walking was no longer easy – her old hip injury caused pain – her sight as well as her hearing was failing, and driving at night, when headlights were likely to blind her, and in strong sunlight was difficult. The problem was diagnosed as retinal scarring – probably the result of days on the beach when she was an undergraduate – which had intensified the problem of cataracts.

Poetry for her had always come "from a level you don't know about"[78] and she had never regarded it as her own possession. Now, drawn to silence, she would let the world speak, watching as

> *Eastward, Mount Budawang*
> *deliberately releases*
> *stars, moon and sun*
> *upward by night or day, one following one;*

rolling out its "lengthened strip of black calligraphy".[79]

She had been reading Bashō, the Japanese haiku poet to whom Meredith had introduced her, and she quoted two of his sayings to Len Webb at the beginning of May, just a few weeks before her birthday:

> "All who have achieved real excellence in any art, possess one thing in common, that is, a mind to obey nature, to be one with nature, throughout the four seasons of the year."

"Go to the pine if you want to learn about the pine, or to the bamboo if you want to learn about the bamboo and in doing so you must lose your subjective preoccupations with yourself. Otherwise you impose yourself on the object or do not learn."[80]

In this silence perhaps

... the word that, when all words are said,
shall compass more than speech. The sun is gone;
draws on the night at last; the dream draws on.[81]

One of her letters shows her drawn into this dream:

Returning from an hour of wandering and wood-gathering ... as I came up the hill with my armful a flight of eight crimson rosellas swept through the trees and landed to drink at my bird-bath, with mud splash and chatter and the black cockatoos who came with the rains have been gathering in the trees round the house with those loud raucous cries; and outside the gate after the rain there sprang up six incredible fungi about the size of a washing-up bowl, dark brown and shiny. They are called Boletus Portentous, and I have never heard of them before.[82]

More practically – and this was the reason she gave to most people – Judith was too busy speaking and writing about Aboriginal rights and the environment and collecting essays for the book which was to become *Born of the Conquerors* to have time for poetry. As Aboriginal people felt they belonged to the land rather than owned it, she now felt that she belonged to the causes she had served for so long which had to do with the world and its peoples, and that she should give her remaining energies to them. "Prose", she explained to Heather Rusden, "is the natural vehicle of argument and reaches more people, and what I had to say was urgent."[83]

She remained passionately concerned about politics, believing that the world was "in a very dangerous state". She was particularly disturbed by the visits of United States ships, "nearly every one [of which in her view] ... carries nuclear weapons,"[84] and would have liked to join the demonstration at Pine Gap, the United States communications base outside Alice Springs though she was unable to do so.

In 1986 the nuclear reactor at Chernobyl in the USSR exploded, sending its deadly fumes across Europe. The nightmare of nuclear destruction which had haunted Judith since the first explosions at Hiroshima and Nagasaki returned:

> *"Brighter than a thousand suns"* – *that blinding glare*
> *circled the world and settled in our bones.*[85]

In November the same year, a fire broke out in the Sandoz G. G. chemical factory in Basle, Switzerland, flooding the Rhine with lethal chemicals.

Governments and traditional political parties generally seemed to be doing little about the situation. Judith was furious with the Labor Party; "We are not going to stop working, to sit quiet while the party of betrayal pretends it hasn't betrayed us and pretends it isn't involved in furthering that nightmare … We're going to change things. The cause of life is stronger than our opponents think."[86] The Democrats invited her to join them, but she was to write later to Cheryl Kernot, who was then their leader, "I don't join parties, just support and oppose individual parties' actions". She admired the "tenacity of spirit" the Democrats were showing "in opposing the worst manoeuvring against the interests of Aborigines and the environment",[87] but chose instead to join the Nuclear Disarmament Party, the nuclear threat being uppermost in her mind at the time.

In August, her friend Dorothy Green and a younger colleague, David Headon, organised a Conference at the Australian Defence Force Academy in Canberra, "Imagining the Real: Writing in a Nuclear Age", at which Judith gave a paper. The issue seemed a crucial one to her. Like many others she had been disturbed by the findings, just released, of the Royal Commission on the atomic tests the British had conducted at Maralinga in the 1950s – they had troubled her at the time but now the full truth was coming out – and was particularly enraged at the way in which the lives of Aboriginal people of the area had been callously ignored as if they hardly counted as people.

There seemed to be threats everywhere. At "Edge" what Judith called "the blasted mine" near her boundary had "struck enough gold for them to apply for the rest of the area right up to [her] boundary and possibly put up a small mining village till they [ran] out of it". She was "fighting to prevent them draining their mud on to 'Edge' at least".[88] A recent study at Monash University had found that mercury was highly toxic and that if mining went ahead it would threaten the local water supply and the survival of a rare breed of fish, the Macquarie perch, which lived in the local streams and rivers.[89] Led by Judith, the local residents were up in arms and a series of public protest meetings were held.

The Ecopolitics Conference at Griffith University in August 1986, which Len Webb had helped to organise, brought Judith back to the question of Aboriginal rights with a paper on "The Landless People and Their Rights to Land".[90] As she tackled it she dealt, amongst other things, with the issue of the wilderness and the conflict between Aborigines and some environmentalists which had arisen, putting the case for Aboriginal management of wilderness areas. She argued in particular that the traditional peoples of Kakadu in the Northern Territory and of the Bungle Bungle in the Kimberley should be given control of these areas, and that a lease-back arrangement should be implemented in the Bungle Bungle.[91] White graziers and farmers, she pointed out, had done substantial damage to the land whereas the Aborigines had looked after it for thousands of years. These areas, she emphasised, were of particular environmental significance, so that allowing their traditional owners to care for them would benefit Australians generally as well as constitute "a model for European–Aboriginal cooperation".[92]

Most Aboriginal people, she noted, still regarded the land we had taken from them as theirs, and quoted a recent statement of the Northern Queensland Land Council:

> *Two hundred years soon to break our law.*
> *Two hundred years soon, we make war.*
> *Don't you think it's time for peace?*
> *Pay the rent.*
> *Sign the lease.*[93]

She and friends like Nugget Coombs had been following this case with interest since it supported the view that territory occupied by peoples whose culture and law was different from those of the West could not be regarded as *terra nullius* and that its indigenous inhabitants therefore had rights to the land recognisable in law. This view was to influence the findings of the majority of the High Court judges in the Mabo case some years later.

In the meantime there were some minor concessions made by the Federal Government, which had jurisdiction over the Jervis Bay area and had introduced the Aboriginal Land Grant (Jervis Bay Territory) Bill, granting inalienable freehold ownership to the Wreck Bay Aboriginal community. True, there were few non-Aboriginal interests involved here so that, except for the Aboriginal community involved, this did not represent a major victory. More significant was the handover in November of Uluru to its traditional owners despite "the outcry by rednecks", some of whom alleged that the Aborigines had not always been there and that their claims were fabricated. As Judith noted, better informed than they were, the journals of the explorer Ernest Giles, the first white man to see the Rock, clearly refuted that view.

None of these concessions, however, changed her conviction that the government had "sold out" as far as Aborigines were concerned. Coombs felt just as strongly and in March he wrote once more to the Prime Minister, Bob Hawke, accusing him of a "betrayal of trust" as far as Aboriginal Australians were concerned. The basis of the argument for land rights, he wrote, was a matter of justice, though "our failure to recognise [their just rights] long ago has created conditions which justify actions based on compassion also". The real issue, in his view, was a matter of justice. "Let there be no doubt about it", he asserted, "the occupation of Australia ... was in international law, illegal."[94] Judith agreed, though she put it even more strongly, on another occasion: "We have a very wicked history, and we have a very wicked present situation", and should therefore "face up to our responsibilities under international law and under any proper sense of justice".[95]

The question was what could be done. There was some talk of reviving the Treaty Committee, but three of the original members had died, some of the others were ill, and all were heavily engaged elsewhere. Besides, the results of a survey of attitudes to Aborigines commissioned by the Department of Aboriginal Affairs suggested that even a government more dedicated to justice for Aboriginal people than the Hawke Government seemed to be would find it politically difficult to support Aboriginal claims.

> It would be easy to despair at the extent of ignorance, intolerance and misunderstanding uncovered by our research towards Aborigines generally and land rights more specifically, [the writers of the survey wrote]. [These attitudes seemed to be] founded on lack of knowledge and understanding [and] compounded by underlying fear and prejudice.[96]

Judith continued to be troubled, too, by the population explosion throughout the world. Despite the popular view that Australia was relatively "empty", her knowledge of the land convinced her that the continent was already overpopulated and that we were putting pressure on the environment which it could not sustain. This was confirmed by evidence brought forward at a conference on migration at the Australian National University in September. Closer to home, she was angered by what she saw as Bjelke-Petersen's latest move, an attack on the industrial rights of workers of the South-eastern Queensland Electricity Board who then went on strike to protest against his legislation. Judith sent a message to their protest meeting: "With you in spirit and in protest against repressive legislation. Queenslanders must win back their democratic rights. Writers and artists are especially threatened whenever civil liberties are violated."[97] If it was true that you "need to get on with the world", she remarked, "you can't ever agree with it"[98] – and in this, as on other occasions, she did not, or at least not with the world Bjelke-Petersen inhabited.

> *My generation is dying, after long lives*
> *swung from war to depression to war to fatness.*

but she clung to her values, even as she acknowledged reality:

> *I watch the clams in the rockpool, the scuttle, the crouch –*
> *green humps, the biggest barnacled, eaten by seaworms.*
>
> *In comes the biggest wave, the irresistible*
> *clean wash and backswirl. Where have the dead gone?*[99]

Judith's eyesight was continuing to fail, and in the middle of the year she was faced with the threat of cancer. In October of 1986 she had tests for a lump in her breast and wrote to Kathleen McArthur – the only person she told about it – that it might "mean trouble".[100] The growth was malignant and there would have to be an operation, though she had to wait until a bed was available – there were long waiting lists in Canberra. In the meantime she was trying to clear her correspondence and making arrangements with a young woman she had befriended some years earlier when she was a confused teenager to come to "Edge" to look after her while she was recuperating after the operation.

Still, despite everything, she wrote to Kathleen "one bashes on".[101] She was not particularly troubled by the thought of death – as she had said after Jack's death: "death's part of life – dammit"; and as a country child she had learned about "the deathly side of life". At "Edge" she reflected on this:

> Birds are rushing everywhere feeding their mates and their young – my swallows are being driven to distraction by four babies – and I've two blue tongues, let alone all the little jacky lizards plus, of course, the kookaburras trying to catch the latter. Lucky we're all food for something in the end.[102]

As she put it in "Winter":

> *The paths that energy takes on its way to exhaustion*
> *are not to be forecast. These pathways, you and me,*
>
> *followed unguessable routes. But all of us end*
> *at the same point, like the wood on the fire,*
>
> *the wine in the belly. Let's drink to that point – like Hafiz.*[103]

(Hafiz was a Persian poet she had been reading and who had inspired the form these last poems took, the ghazal.)

"Communication", published in 1970, had come from an earlier spell in hospital and a meeting with a "three day friend on the edge of dying". They had

> ...*talked out to each other*
> *our separate pains, deeper than strangers do*...
>
> *Die as we must, we two were then related*
> *in human honesty and suffering.*[104]

But no poems came from this time in hospital. Judith's friends were deeply concerned, realising how much many people depended on her. Manning Clark, for instance, sent her a telegram: "Fight on, we all need you. [You are] ... a gift to our generation."[105]

The operation was successful, though for some time afterwards writing was difficult since the nerves of her shoulder had been affected by the surgery. This was a major problem since she wrote about twenty-five letters a week, to say nothing of other writing. But she managed to get an electronic typewriter which made things a little easier. By the beginning of the next year, 1987, she was more or less recovered, though she wrote to Kathleen McArthur at the end of March:

> It's not an operation I'd really recommend if it were not a necessity but I'm back on course again with a bit of trouble with a right arm that won't do much. But I've made very good progress. They caught the thing very early. Had good T.L.C. (tender loving care) and housekeeping for six weeks after my release from hospital by [a young friend] who turned up at Tamborine aged twelve, having run away from home, now doing a Mature Age Arts degree in Adelaide after many adventures. Luckily she was starting her vacation and arrived at my place to look after the house and me – a nice case of casting your bread on the waters.[106]

It took more time to recover her energy, however. Aboriginal issues were her first priority and here she kept in touch largely through Nugget Coombs who was spending even more of his time in the Northern Territory – he had recently had pneumonia and Canberra winters were dangerous for him. He had been at the conference in Kununurra organised by the ANU under its public affairs program to discuss the relationship between Aboriginal people and economic development in the north-west, which was attended by academics, lawyers, teachers, film-makers, journalists, politicians (including one cabinet minister), park rangers and representatives of the mining industry as well as a large number of Aboriginal people. The conference felt that it would be difficult to reconcile the interests of Aboriginal and Torres Strait Islander peoples on the one hand, and the interests of economic development and conservation on the other. However it was thought to be crucial to acknowledge the original and continuing ownership of the land by indigenous people and that this should be guaranteed by Federal legislation. The conference also condemned the West Australian Government of Brian Burke, which had set up a royal commission on Aboriginal land rights and then ignored its findings, calling on the Federal Government to use its authority to ensure that the Aboriginal peoples of Western Australia be guaranteed their rights to the land.[107]

Judith was in agreement, of course, and one of the first articles she published after her operation in the environmental journal *Bogong* reminded readers of the debt any environmentalists owed to the indigenous peoples who had cared for the land for so long. She knew, too, that Aboriginal people were angry with what they saw as Labor's betrayal and sympathised with this anger. There was also a certain bitter pleasure in the way some Aboriginal leaders were now speaking about the idea of the treaty, even if it was no longer on the political agenda. In May, for example, Patrick Dodson, director of the Central Land Council, described by the *Bulletin* as the "voice of reason" amongst Aboriginal leaders, called once again for a treaty, warning the government that Aboriginal people were getting tired of the "hard slog" to achieve justice. Labor should not take their support for granted, he said, since Hawke's Government seemed to be doing even less for them than Fraser's – he had at least acknowledged their need for land. Highlighting this growing anger, Tasmanian Aboriginal leader Michael Mansell had recently visited Libya looking for support, and there were threats of boycotting the Bicentennial celebrations the following year. Dodson's article concluded with a similar threat.[108] In June, back at work, Judith attended the ANZAAS Conference, speaking on the relationship between Science, Conservation and Ethics and a month later was at a seminar on population at the ANU entitled "How Many More Australians? – The Resource and Environmental Conflict". The Minister for Immigration, Chris Hurford, had announced an increase in the number of migrants, but Judith and most of the people at the seminar opposed this, believing that Australia was already over- rather than under-populated. They were not opposed to migrants, she insisted, but the land was worn out and our demands on it were too high. She contrasted the way we see nature and its resources as expendable, to be exploited for our profit and pleasure, with the Aboriginal belief that human life is intimately bound up with the land's well-being, concluding, as usual, that if we were to avoid destroying ourselves we must change our attitudes and values.[109]

As the Bicentennial year drew closer, however, the Aboriginal cause seemed to be making some slight headway. In June the ALP Conference affirmed the need for an agreement or treaty with Aboriginal and Islander peoples, though some felt that the government should wait until Aboriginal people themselves asked for it.[110] In the same month Prime Minister Bob Hawke flew to the Barunga Festival in the Northern Territory and, influenced perhaps by the force of the feeling he met among Aboriginal people there, actually promised a treaty – a promise made famous by one of the songs of the Aboriginal band Yothu Yindi and pursued over the years by Aboriginal leaders like Galarrwuy Yunupingu, Chairman of the Northern Land Council.

This was a political minefield on both sides. Negotiations, if they ever took place, would be long and, for the Aboriginal people, expensive, since they would need to talk with one another and send representatives from all over Australia. In August Judith agreed to act as coordinator for all the groups, supporting their cause in the Canberra area and trying to raise money to help. The government, however, was caught in a dilemma, afraid of the pressures from mining and pastoral interests and aware of the survey which indicated the electoral unpopularity of any attempt to grant land rights, while understanding also that international attention was being focused on Australia on account of the treatment of our indigenous peoples. "It's a Catch 22," Judith observed. If the government did not "get some kind of agreement our name will be even more mud in the international arena than it is at present"[111] – but at the same time they would probably lose votes by doing so. Several overseas journalists had recently visited her at "Edge" to interview her on the matter since she was well known for her views.

In November the sympathetic Minister for Aboriginal Affairs, Gerry Hand, lost his portfolio. Judith was angry, seeing this as a response to pressure from those opposed to the Aboriginal cause. She wrote to Len Webb that Hawke would not "find it so easy to escape": the Bicentenary would allow the Aborigines to make their point powerfully and embarrassingly. She herself had decided not to have anything to do with the Bicentenary – as Patrick White had also – and wrote happily about a poster she had just seen in Canberra saying "Don't Celebrate 88, Support a Sovereign Treaty 88. Don't Celebrate Land Theft and Murder".[112] At the end of 1988, the Aboriginal activist Burnum Burnum was to pay tribute to her for her support throughout the year, writing that "Judith Wright has great energy. She loves Aboriginal people".

She still had standing in the wider commuity also – in some quarters she was called "a cultural treasure". A play, *Growing Up With Judith*, had just been written by Jane Ahlquist, who wrote to her saying that she hoped to get it performed and sent her the manuscript. Garth Welsh of the West Australian Ballet also wrote asking permission to choreograph one of her poems to Jack, "Love Song in Absence". She was honoured internationally also. In April Tom Shapcott, who had been one of the young Brisbane poets she had inspired in the 1960s, and was now Executive Director of the Literature Board, arranged for a translation to be made of some of the poems from her last collection *Phantom Dwelling*, to be read at the International Poetry Festival in Strega, Yugoslavia; this was especially pleasing since she felt that the critics had not really understood or appreciated these poems. But Judith was not prepared to settle down and become a Cultural Monument. When Bobbi Sykes, Aboriginal writer and activist, told her that she had not been given the grant she had applied for from the Literature Board,[113] Judith was extremely angry and wrote to say so. She was angry, too, when Mark O'Connor, an environmental ally as well as fellow nature poet, failed to get the grant he had applied for to write a series of poems about the Great Barrier Reef. She wrote in protest to the *Sydney Morning Herald* which headed her letter: "How Australian Is The Australia Council?"[114]

But that summer was peaceful, with Meredith home from Japan for a few weeks. Her mood was also influenced by the recent meeting between United States President Ronald Reagan and the Russian leader Mikhail Gorbachev, which seemed to promise an end to the Cold War. All her life Judith felt she had been living in the shadow of war but perhaps now a change was beginning. As usual, she spent Christmas in New England, although her brother Bruce was not well. His daughter gave a party for him and his wife Sheila to celebrate their seventieth birthdays. Judith was feeling more in tune with family. "At our age", she wrote, "we have to meet when we can", especially as on the whole they had now "learned to forgive each other for the way we differ".[115] The poem she wrote for them put it this way:

> *With so much past in common,*
> *on the whole we forgive each other*
> *for the ways in which we differ –*
> *two old men, one older woman.*
> *When one of us falls ill,*
> *the others may think less*
> *of today's person, the lined and guarding face,*
>
> *than of a barefoot child running careless through*
> *long grass where snakes lie, or forgetting*
> *to watch in the paddocks for the black Jersey bull.*[116]

It was a good party, since there were old friends there as well, including one who, like her, was now almost totally deaf. For this reason they could, she felt, "understand one another",[117] just as later Barbara Blackman was to observe an instant rapport between Judith and the photographer Axel Poignant, who was also deaf: "They looked into one another's eyes. They knew one another".[118]

In the general mood of understanding Judith gave them all, as Christmas presents, Bill Cohen's autobiography. His life, after all, "sort of meshes in with ours". His father, Jack Cohen, had helped with the mustering at "Dyamberin", her Uncle Owen's property, and had thus been part of her childhood. "Early pastoral life made you depend on people who could help you out and were available in time of trouble."[119] She was beginning to realise that, if they had been part of the process of colonisation, "our hands show little blood" in comparison with those who now ruled the country and the economy, "what swells over us now",

> *the heave of the great corporations*
> *whose bellies are never full.*

On the whole:

> *At best, the men of our clan*
> *have been, or might have been,*
> *like Yeats' fisherman.*
> *A small stream, narrow but clean,*
>
> *running apart from the world.*[120]

In this mood, afterwards she hired a car and drove to Mount Tamborine, following the route she, Jack and Meredith had taken so many times. It proved a difficult trip, however, since the car had not been properly serviced and she had to stay overnight at Warwick. The purpose of the trip was to check on a report she had heard that Jack's gravestone had been tipped over, but she found it still upright, beside the grave of his old friend, "Have-A-Chat" the busdriver. This was where she would finally come, too, one day, and "in a packet" be buried beside him.[121]

From the graveyard she drove slowly past "Calanthe", almost invisible behind its lantana hedge, but there was no one at home. The new owner had claimed to be a gardener but to Wright that day the garden seemed "like great overgrown botanical gardens". She was told, too, that the old carpet snake who had lived in the roof had died:

> *Houses and bodies:*
> *both limiting factors,*
> *shelters, educators,*
> *subject to alteration*
> *by the inhabitants*
> *under their own conditions.*[122]

The National Park they had loved and fought for, however, was in good condition, though down below the skyscrapers of the Gold Coast looked to her "like rotten teeth".[123] She had also hoped to visit an Aboriginal friend, Ysola Best, who had set up a Cultural Centre on the Mountain to recover and preserve local Aboriginal history and culture. Ysola was away, but returning to the mountain reinforced her determination, as she told Kathleen McArthur, to "dodge all temptations to do with the bloody Bicentennial".[124]

Returning to Mount Tamborine she was aware of the process of life she had written about leaving "Calanthe", pouring

> ... *through doors and telephone, comings and goings.*
> *People attract and direct*
> *that current, are its transformers,*
> *stations in space and time. We choose or reject*
>
> *what passes us on the streams that circle the world ...*
> *A kind of weaving*
> *goes on all the time in houses, its pattern*
> *determined by the years of taking and giving.*

She had lived here with those she loved, enclosed in "our portion of time, our pattern of making". And this memory strengthened her:

> *To live, to work together in intimate peace*
> *is to prove in the dark the quality of light.*[125]

The Bicentennial year, 1988, had begun, however, and "the quality of light" needed protection. The former members of the Treaty Committee decided to put the $2000 royalties from *We Call For a Treaty* towards an advertisement during the year, calling for a treaty. But otherwise Judith's boycott was so absolute that she would not even join in the Aboriginal march through Sydney, though she would be "certainly cheering" them. She was also refusing all interviews by journalists and in January she disappeared with Meredith "into the depths of Tasmania beyond the reach of the 'Celebration of the Nation'. What rot that is!"[126] Her only hope, as she told a friend, was that

"Aboriginal sabotage will be effective" and that we might begin to recognise their claims to sovereignty.[127]

They found the Tasmanian mountains and forests very beautiful, though they did not enjoy the sight of the logging trucks, "dragging out as many logs as they could find for fear of new declarations". Nor did they enjoy the echoes of the past, the convict brutalities of Port Arthur and the grim history of the attempt to wipe out the Aboriginal peoples of the island. As she had written in "The Dark Ones",

> *the night ghosts of a land*
> *only by day possessed*
> *come haunting into the mind*
> *like a shadow cast.*[128]

The touristic veneer of the place troubled them also, and they left with impressions of "a sad but lovely island full of haunts and terrors suitably tamed by the National Trust into tea rooms and craft shops etc".[129]

These impressions may have influenced what she had to say in Perth, where she had been invited to speak at a literary luncheon on "The Writer as Activist". She chose to speak about her favourite, Charles Harpur, the son of convicts, his father an Irishman transported at the age of twenty-four for armed robbery – "sixty pounds of bacon, four gallons of yeast and a sum of money were involved" – and his mother at thirteen or fourteen for "stealing two yards of dress material from her mistress".[130] His family, she told her prosperous audience, would not have regarded property as sacred or seen our definitions of "crime" or divisions of class as indisputable. Praising Harpur's "fiercely principled stand" against privilege and injustice, and noting the consequent unpopularity and neglect of his work, she drew a parallel with the Aboriginal writers who were beginning to appear: Kath Walker (who in 1988 had taken her tribal name, Oodgeroo Noonuccal), Kevin Gilbert, Jack Davis, Colin Johnson (who was to follow Kath's example and become Mudrooroo Nyoongah), Archie Weller, Bobbi Sykes, and many others.

> These new writers [she told her audience] belong to a people we don't even legally recognise as a people, but who insist on their

separate reality and their right to their own voices and their own view of us and our critical pretensions.[131]

Going on to attack the "dead weight of our conventional academicism" which had ignored these writers and the powerful interests "opposed to Aboriginal self-determination and self-expression", she concluded by calling for a "partisan and activist art" like Harpur's, for too long "excluded from our canons". She believed, she said, as Harpur did, that poetry should be "the vehicle of earnest purpose, the audible expression of the inmost impulses of [the poet's] moral being".[132] "I don't think [the lecture] made me popular with anyone", she told Kathleen McArthur, "but at our age what's a little unpopularity?". In fact she was probably pleased at being able to show her colours since she was angry at recent developments in the State. "I wasn't there to congratulate C.R.A. for invading National Parks and Aboriginal land anyway" – as they had just done in the Rudall River National Park. Judith was rather pleased with herself at being "stupid enough" to challenge people in this way. She was recovering her energy, able once again to "do too many things".[133]

In May she got her final clearance from the surgeon, which made her ebullient, writing to Kathleen McArthur: "We've won a few fights with the sharks in our time". In this mood she felt even "entitled to read a few novels".[134]

There is not much evidence, however, that she did so. She was still busy writing to politicians, to New South Wales politician Barrie Unsworth, for example, congratulating him on his opposition to woodchipping. "The planet is now hanging by a few threads from its last resources", she wrote, "and the forests are of importance far beyond their immediate area ... Jobs will not be of much moment to us when the air and waters are dying; and only principled action will hold back disaster."[135] Her running battle was also continuing with environmentalists who were, in her view, insensitive to Aboriginal claims and needs, to which she felt they were making only a token response. She was trying to attack the complacent view of history being celebrated in the Bicentenary.

Although during the year she had only been asked to do "the occasional speech", the ACF Conference in the middle of the year gave her a public opportunity. In her paper she pointed out the destruction that two hundred years of white occupation had caused and quoted from an earlier paper by Nugget Coombs, "Matching Ecological with Economic Realities", in which he reminded his audience that "being economical" meant making best uses of limited resources – as Aboriginal people had done by matching their values to the needs of the land: "the essence of hunter gathering is to leave enough for the next time".[136] Instead of continuing this history of exploitation, she told her audience, we must enter into dialogue with Aboriginal people and find a new set of values. She concluded by putting before them what Coombs, in his earlier paper, had called "A New Decalogue", which proposed, amongst other things, that: "Thou shalt have no other gods before the Finite Environment. Thou shalt not live on capital. Thou shalt not lust after resources at disequilibrium prices"[137] – not exactly a popular view in the Age of Economic Rationalism.

Judith was also critical of the way in which the monument built as a Bicentennial project at Longreach in Queensland, The Stockman's Hall of Fame, had ignored the Aboriginal contribution, calling it "The Stockman's Hall of Infamy". In the north in the early days, she knew from her research, it had been impossible to keep European stockmen, so that the pastoral industry had largely relied on Aboriginal stockmen. As she put it: "the P. B. A. [Poor Bloody Aboriginal] population did most of the pastoralists' dirty work, wholly or partly unpaid, and got no encomiums in that building for their blood and sweat."[138] Once more, she felt, their contribution had been written out of white settler history.

"I just look at [people]", she told Heather Rusden, "and say, for God's sake, they don't know what they are doing to themselves." As Jack had argued, history would destroy those who did not interrogate it: "Once you're set on a course its movement drags you along with it. So you can't feel angry with people but with the way history is pulling us inexorably to the edge"[139] – as it was doing, she believed, with the environmental crisis, the population explosion and the power technology has given us to destroy ourselves if not the world. Once it had gained momentum, this movement was very difficult to stop and could only be halted by determined, principled, intelligent and visionary people. But there were, Judith feared, none of them left in the Labor party where, in her view, there was no longer any place for "people of really good faith".[140] In elections now she voted Green, Democrat or Independent – in the 1983 election Kath Walker had stood for the Democrats, and though she was not successful, her nomination seemed to Judith a sign of good faith on the Democrats' part.

She was now thoroughly disillusioned with politics, though she still believed passionately in democracy, which allowed her to think, speak and act as she did. She wanted others to be equally critical, writing that "unless and until people wake up, and kick out their governments, kick out their multinational companies, and change their priorities in life, [things] ... will continue to get worse".[141] As she told the audience at the Forestry Exhibition she opened in August, current society was "a vast machine built for nothing more than the consumption of the earth" and the only way to check it was to reimagine the world, changing our values, and seeing things in a holistic rather than analytic way, thinking of forests, for example, "not as just trees, but as a support system for all life" – as she remarked on another occasion, trees, too, had "a right to life".[142]

During the year she had been in correspondence with John Seed, an ecologist who worked with Joanna Macy in the United States, and a group of other environmentalists. They were hoping to organise a "Council of All Beings" at which they would attempt to work out a new set of values which would "re-earth" people, and they invited Judith to it. She would have liked to go but, apart from her problems with air travel, she was by now so deaf that it would have been impossible to take part. But she was very interested in what they were doing, seeing it as part of the development Jack had hoped for in which "thought becomes conscious of itself as thinking", development which seemed to her to open up an "immense perspective" and to mark the possibility of the quantum leap in language he had been looking for. She saw parallels between their approach, based on empathy with the rest of creation rather than merely thinking about it, and Aboriginal culture.[143]

These were not popular views, however. Judith was finding herself less and less in tune with the general mood, and a piece she was asked to write for the Melbourne *Herald* on "What I Would Say to the Prime Minister" did not appear. Perhaps because her advice was too much for people to stomach – almost certainly so for Prime Minister Bob Hawke:

(1) Stop believing what Billionaires tell you. (2) Give the young a say and some hope. (3) Change education which is today biased towards the status quo. (4) Set up a strong Press Council. (5) Stop forest clearance. (6) Fund the search for sources of alternative energy. (7) Conduct research into the limits of population in this country. (8) Put a stop to uranium mining. (9) Cease to live by a philosophy which makes economics the supreme value. (10) Pay our debts to Aboriginal people. (11) Resign.[144]

But she could also still write lyrically, as she did in "Gone Bush 1989", an essay describing the district around "Edge" between the Little River and Mount Budawang, which she loved. By now a part of the local community, she also took part in the Braidwood Festival which was held in the latter part of the year, though she was equivocal about the visits to some of the old properties which were also a feature of the Festival. "Such large estates," she wrote to Len Webb, "their magnificent colonial homesteads ooze 'Thornbirds' in every pore."[145] She saw things more and more through Aboriginal eyes and had not forgotten Oodgeroo's words:

> This is my land. I have always said that, even as a child. The white people used to say to Dad: "That girl walks this land as though she thinks it's hers." Dad wouldn't say anything – he'd just walk home and tell me that Mrs So-and-so said you walk this land as though you think it's yours. "It is mine, isn't it?" and he'd say, "Yes girl, and don't you forget it."[146]

Judith was still close to her and her family. In January Oodgeroo's elder son, Dennis, sentenced to two and a half years for "entering a dwelling with intent to commit an indictable offence," wrote to her asking for help. In his view he had been "illegally arrested", not only because he had not actually committed an offence by entering the house of a former girlfriend, but also because he claimed that white law had no jurisdiction over him, "a Noonuccal person of Quandamooka". It was the question of sovereignty again. White people had never signed a treaty with his people, he declared, but had taken the land by force, and therefore he did not recognise their law. Judith saw his point but, "born of the conquerors" as she was, she knew the attitudes of most white people, and had no hope that his argument would be accepted by the courts. White law "is a poor instrument for you and your people", she told him, though she thought that the Mabo case, then proceeding on its long and tortuous but eventually victorious way, might help them. But she also believed that "the initiatives of Aborigines", such as his, "would be important" in resolving the question of sovereignty also, concluding by assuring him that his people had "more sympathisers than ever".[147]

In this vein, in June 1989 the surviving members of the Treaty Committee considered sponsoring another advertisement calling for a treaty and approached a number of eminent Australians asking for their support. Malcolm Fraser, whose record on Aboriginal affairs now seemed to her much better than Hawke's, was sympathetic, and the writer Tom Keneally also offered to sign. But Garth Nettheim, Professor of Law at the University of New South Wales and a strong champion of the Aboriginal cause, doubted whether an advertisement was the best approach at the moment, particularly as some potential signatories, Morris West, for instance, were not completely in sympathy with the idea of a treaty, regarding it as "too extreme".[148] Others were beginning to have doubts also. In an editorial later that year, the usually sympathetic *Canberra Times* worried that, even if it were to happen, the treaty might prove to be a debacle, pointing out that Hawke's Government had done nothing to provide Aboriginal people with advice, lawyers or money for consultations throughout the country. At the same time, however, it acknowledged the sympathy of "people of goodwill in the general community" and indicated that some gesture was called for. In the event the advertisement did not go ahead, and for the time being there seemed little that could be done, pending the outcome of the legal action being taken by the Murray Island people.

The environmental movement also seemed to her "stuck in the old rut of clamouring over what is happening without doing work on forward planning and research questions".[149] She had never had much sympathy with romantic gestures, telling Len Webb that she was

> growing weary [of these invitations] ... to go to the Eden blockade so-called and get myself arrested for publicity purposes ... I refuse to risk my valuable breathing apparatus in the Eden lockup so long as I can do better work at the desk [she had been writing a series of articles and sending them to journals like *Habitat* and to environmentalists like Philip Toyne and her old friend and ally Milo Dunphy for them to use]. But perhaps I will have to resign myself sooner or later if I can't get sense out of the Federal government.[150]

She was also still arguing with the Wilderness Society, which, in her view, failed to understand Aboriginal people and their needs – they seemed to imply that "only we invaders have rights".

She was unhappy, too, with her publishers, Angus & Robertson, recently taken over by Rupert Murdoch's News Limited. They wanted to reprint her two last volumes, *Alive* (1973) and *Phantom Dwelling* (1985), separately. But she was not happy with this arrangement. They had not sold well and *Phantom Dwelling* in particular had not been well received; in her opinion there had been only one review which had understood what she was trying to do. But she did not want poems from these two volumes included in the updated edition of her *Collected Poems,* which was also being planned, and she appealed to the Australian Society of Authors for help. For the time being she won her point, and the *Collected Poems* did not appear until 1994. Though she was no longer writing poetry it had always mattered very deeply to her. To most people she knew, it seemed

> a marginal pursuit, probably, except people like me ... haven't been able to escape its order and have, in my seventy-fifth year, published too many poems to repent and change my ways as long as there's anything in me which is rapidly ceasing to be the case. Age, not reluctance, prevents writing except in prose (even that is not easy) ... Poetry I think, has never been ... a doer ... It is an expression of *being,* of where one is at the time not a political or otherwise active entity ... So-called progress is deterministic and appears to have its bit between its teeth prevents reading as [we] might.[151]

But perhaps she was exaggerating. She still continued to receive numerous letters like the one which arrived from a schoolboy and began: "Dear Miss Wright, I think your poems are the greatest". Practicality seems to have overwhelmed feeling in her response to this tribute, however, since she annotated it, "no stamp, no reply"[152] – she usually replied to all correspondence. As she had written to English friend, Martin Robertson, also a poet, some years earlier:

> *When all the living's done*
> *it's poems that remain.*
> *All that is personal, said Yeats,*
> *soon rots*
> *unless packed in ice and salt.*[153]

The personal, too, remained and she enjoyed a visit towards the end of the year from Laurie Hope, another friend from the days at Mount Tamborine in the 1940s and 1950s, reminding her of his memories of Meredith as the little girl he had painted in the garden at "Calanthe". But it was clear that soon she would have to make another move; leave "Edge" and go and live in Braidwood. Summer was coming but her life was moving towards autumn,

> *Autumn swings earth round sun*
> *at the invisible lasso's end,*
> *turning this latitude south and winterward.*[154]

In May 1990 she would be seventy-five: "Only in silence the word, only in dark the light, only in dying life: bright the hawk's flight as an empty sky."[155]

CHAPTER XV

I CHOOSE FIRE – NOT SNOW

...the poet on the wineshop floor

was given his revelations. The hermit of Cold Mountain
laughs as loudly perhaps – I choose fire, not snow.

"Oppositions",
Collected Poems, p. 422

"Seventy-five is apparently an awesome age", Judith was to write when she reached that age. "Well, we want to go to eighty."[1] She was still hanging on at "Edge" since she loved the place, with its trees and birds, the kangaroos and wallabies nibbling in the garden, the life of the bush going on around her and the river below. She could look out on them from inside through the glass wall which faced towards the river and was lit by a skylight from above. Outside in a sense was also Inside, as it had never been at "Wallamumbi". Inside, too, were the paintings and the artefacts she had collected over the years and books everywhere, stacked or standing or lying about. She liked entertaining friends here with good wine, good food and good talk – though since she could not hear them properly, this was either talk among themselves or monologues from her, though they were sympathetic listeners. In summer they could go swimming in the river below.

True, the winters were harsh. Some years earlier, however, after visiting a relative in a geriatric hospital, she had declared that she would "crawl out and lay [herself] across a railway line" rather than submit to the indignities there. "The world ain't what [she] had hoped it might be on the way to becoming",[2] but she would go on living, questioning and fighting to the end:

> *Old age and winter are said to have much in common,*
> *Let's pile more wood on the fire and drink red wine.*

> *Freedom, as Janis Joplin sang, can be "just another*
> *word for nothing left to lose".*[3]

The country here reminded her of New England. So when she gave an interview to the *Canberra Times* in March 1994 her mind went back to childhood:

> As a poet you have to imitate somebody, but since [as a child] I had a beautiful landscape outside that I loved so much and was in so much ... it was my main subject from the start ... It comes to me naturally ... Most children ... are brought up in the "I" tradition these days – the ego, it's me and what I think. But when you live in very close contact with a large and splendid landscape as I did you feel yourself as a good deal smaller than just I.[4]

Opening a Forestry Exhibition four and a half years earlier in August 1989 she also remembered this landscape, recalling the fate of the splendid red cedars which had grown on the edge of the escarpment, "the grandeur of those trees, their architecture, the hanging gardens of ferns and orchids" and the birds. They had been destroyed by the timber cutters, and she recalled "the red wounds in the soil – bleeding in every rainfall – that took their place".[5] But here at "Edge" the bush was healing itself after being scarred by mining at the end of the nineteenth century and, to a lesser extent, by grazing. It was therefore a good place to be.

It was also a good place to be reminded of the task she and Jack had set themselves. It is all too easy in old age, as Yeats said, to come to a cul-de-sac in which

> *...all seems evil until I*
> *Sleepless would lie down and die.*

But as the bush around her, threatened but living still, reminded her:

> ... *That were to shirk*
> *The spiritual intellect's great work,*
> *And shirk it in vain. There is no release*
> *In a bodkin or disease,*
> *Nor can there be work so great*
> *As that which cleans man's dirty slate.*[6]

But death was "marshalling his armies" around her, as it had done long ago during the war.[7] Her old teacher and ally, Bill Stanner, had died at the end of 1987, and she had missed him in her battles to convince the Wilderness Society of the needs of Aboriginal people.[8] Then Oodgeroo's younger son, Vivien, died in February 1991, aged thirty-eight, and was buried with his ancestors at "Moongalba", and Oodgeroo herself fell seriously ill shortly afterwards with shingles and trigeminal neuralgia.[9]

> In public Oodgeroo had always remained strong, resilient and ready at all times to be provocative, with a piercing wit and a menacing intellect. But the loss of a son who was taking on his mother's weapon of language and adding to it with his very substantial artistic talent was almost too much to bear.[10]

Dorothy Green, too, "the last remaining sage",[11] was ill and was to die in mid-1991. But perhaps the closest blow was the death of Judith's younger brother, Peter: driving alone along the New England Highway, he had suffered a sudden and fatal heart attack and his car had veered across the road, striking another vehicle coming in the opposite direction, though fortunately the other driver was not seriously injured.[12] Peter had always been her little brother, born when their mother was ill and, never as strong or aggressive as the rest of the family, he had shared something of her feeling for the environment. A man possessed of that "marginal sort of grace" which, she felt, had softened "our arrogant clan", he had been one of those

> *like Yeats' fisherman.*
> *A small stream, narrow but clean.*[13]

Now the time had come to sing the "Dies Irae", as she had predicted.[14] But it was yet another loss. "Sometimes", as she wrote to Barbara Blackman, she felt that she "stuck out now like a shag on the rock" with so many of her friends dying or already dead.[15]

There was little comfort to be gained from the wider scene, either. Global warming was now being accepted as a fact, and Judith saw the signs all around her. When her "resident swallows", which bred there every year, returned "Edge" in 1991, for example, they failed either to build or breed. She was also troubled by the effects of the population explosion and by the fact that nobody seemed to her to be doing much about it. So when Len Webb accepted an invitation to attend a conference on the environment in Rome organised by the Vatican, she was critical, reminding him of the Pope's opposition to birth control.[16]

Generally the world seemed to her to be in an even greater mess than ever, and she wrote gloomily to Kathleen McArthur:

> What a fearful gam we're in, and apparently unable to recognise it ... All the financial newspapers can talk about is the price of even lower prices for uranium and what a pity it is. But mankind is as mad as a cut snake.[17]

As far as Aboriginal affairs were concerned, many people were still suspicious of their claims to land rights in national parks, thinking that no one should intrude on the "wilderness". That year even the WPSO, which had meant so much to Judith in the past, came out in opposition to them. She was "trying at a distance to pull a bit of weight but deafness is a serious handicap and age and comparative poverty". As we have seen, she was scornful of these environmentalists and disappointed by their stand, writing to a correspondent that she could not summarise their arguments because she did not understand them.[18] At best their position seemed to her sentimental, at worst, racial prejudice. She was also enraged by the latest Queensland scheme to set up a rocket port for space launches in the Cape York region, a scheme which would affect Aboriginal people.[19] Though she had hoped for something better from him after the long reign of Bjelke-Petersen, the new Labor Premier, Wayne Goss, had given his blessing to the scheme.

At the beginning of that year, 1990, she had planned a "lengthy wander" from May to July, the cold months at "Edge", to North Queensland first and then to the Centre around Alice Springs to visit the Pitjantjatjara people and see her friend Nugget Coombs who was with them at the time. She had been invited by Warren Showdon MP, and his wife, to stay with them, but it also seemed a good opportunity to get material for a series of articles on land degradation in areas which had been abandoned by white people and then handed back to the original Aboriginal owners to see what they could do with it – "without money or advice, of course".[20]

In fact, Judith got no further than Townsville where she attended a conference at James Cook University, sparked off by the talk of the Cape York Space Port and a "new outbreak of tourism" in the area, about the future of remote Aboriginal Islander communities. There she heard of new threats of oil drilling on the Great Barrier Reef, which was quite enough to prevent her from taking a holiday, even though she no longer felt that she had much influence on the public scene.

There were new people in power in Canberra and, she told Barbara Blackman,

> the demand from officials upon me is not high (I am not noted for going the way other people want me to) but the sudden broaching to of the ship of state in view of heavy seas ahead is adding to my jobs, nevertheless, and I am pushing other barrows whose wheels aren't working well. (I like mixing all possible metaphors, now that chaos is fashionable.)[21]

As she remarked to Len Webb, however, "old poets never die, they just blaze away".[22] When the Gulf War began, despite her sense that nobody now listened to her, she wrote a strong letter to Prime Minister Hawke who had committed Australian warships to support the United States in the Gulf War without consulting Cabinet. Hawke's Principal Private Secretary replied. But his reply did not satisfy her, and she wrote back saying that the point of her letter had not been taken: she had not merely questioned the wisdom of the decision to involve Australian forces, she said, she had also raised "constitutional questions concerning the procedures used in despatching ships to alien territory"

– which were "quite unwarrantably hasty".²³ She and Michael Denborough of the Nuclear Disarmament Party also issued a press statement along the same lines, but it was not taken up by the media. Undaunted, she also wrote to the Governor-General, Bill Hayden, asking him as Commander-in-Chief to stop the commitment of Australian ships. He told her that he had no power in the matter.²⁴ The shadows, she remarked to Barbara Blackman, seemed to be falling all the other way.²⁵

She was also appalled by the massacre in Tianamen Square in Beijing in the previous year and worried about the fate of Dr Tang Zhengquin from Guangzhou (Canton), her Chinese translator, since she had not heard from him for some time and feared for his safety. The anthology she had done for Angus & Robertson, supposed to have been published in March, had been delayed and she had not yet received her complimentary copies or, more to the point, the second advance on her royalties payment.²⁶ There were also some problems with her Emeritus Fellowship from the Australia Council since in the previous year she had earned too much from her writing to qualify for it.²⁷

Nevertheless there was some good news. The Australian National University was talking more enthusiastically about using "Edge" for research since the project conducted there the previous year had earned its chief investigator the university medal and a scholarship to Cambridge.²⁸ Oodgeroo, too, was better and much more cheerful, and the first elections for the Aboriginal and Torres Strait Islander Commission (ATSIC), set up by the Hawke Government to administer Aboriginal affairs, were to be held in November. Many Aboriginal people believed that its real purpose was to undermine the demand for land rights – and Judith was inclined to agree with them – but friends like Oodgeroo were hopeful, even enthusiastic, about the new initiative, and she was pleased for them.

Judith was still trying to convince environmentalists that they should listen to Aboriginal people and respect their culture; it was bad enough to have to deal with ignorance and prejudice in the general population, but even more depressing when allies seemed to turn into enemies. On her return from North Queensland, she told Len Webb that she had not found anyone there favourably disposed to Aboriginal claims,²⁹ she felt betrayed by these environmentalists, particularly by the members of the WPSQ. Their misunderstanding of Aboriginal culture, she believed, was the result of "Machiavellian machinations" by those in power, especially in Queensland, designed to "set the Greens against the blacks and the Greens in turmoil amongst themselves". But she also thought that the environmentalists' devotion to what they saw as "the 'cardinal principle' of absolute protection of Nature's wild life" meant that they had "no room in [their] world for any new kind of vision ... nor any other ethic than [their] own".[30]

In the meantime she had been working on Jack's papers, still hoping to get another book from them. It seemed increasingly clear to her that his ideas were "coming to sombre fruition ... with the breakdown of the world-picture",[31] and this breakdown, she thought, accounted for the narrow-mindedness she found amongst some environmentalists and their conviction of the exclusive rightness of their own values. Quite apart from Jack's influence, as a poet she had always been "concerned with the true stature of things",[32] and questioned accepted attitudes and values. Much of 1991 was taken up with arguments, especially with the WPSQ with whom she no longer felt that she could identify. In her disappointment she judged them more harshly probably than they deserved, seeing them "rather as an arm of the bureaucracy than a leader of ... enlightened and forward-looking opinion". But she felt that she could not "let these people get away with [the] kind of misinformation" they seemed to her to be spreading.[33] "Anyone trying to stop me from talking has a job ahead," she told Webb, "I have to stand up and get independent sooner or later." She decided to resign from the society she had founded and served for so long. Len Webb and others tried to dissuade her, but she was determined. Her blood was up, as the conclusion to her letter to him made clear: "So, as the body put it in the old story, 'Pigs,' I says, 'and sweeps out.'"[34]

Her anger was increased by the fact that, in contrast, the ACF had issued a draft policy on Aboriginal and Islander rights and was working to bring environmentalists and indigenous peoples closer to one another. She might as, she told a correspondent, be "sick of dealing with ... rednecks over Aboriginal land rights", but she was more and more convinced of the importance of the issue: "the Aborigines own the bloody country that's what".[35]

She was not pleased either by the Act setting up a National Council for Reconciliation to work to bring Aboriginal and non-Aboriginal Australians together in preparation for the Centenary of Federation in 2001. She thought it "as bad as they come", a mere public relations exercise, and advised Len Webb to refuse if he were invited to join the Council. "It will do nobody any good least of all the perpetrators of it."[36] The idea seemed to her a distraction from the crucial issues of land and sovereignty and it was absolutely necessary, she believed, "to drag our minds towards such problems before the end of the century", though, she added, in Queensland this would involve "unprecedented speed of thought".[37] This jaundiced view may have come from the fact that when she wrote the letter she was ill, "underwater, so to speak, with incipient pneumonia" with her temperature soaring. She could only hope, she told Webb, that "Gaia has a good recipe for human stew".[38]

She recovered, but only to be enraged again, this time by a television program about Cape York, "Cape of Dreams", broadcast on a commercial channel, which represented Aboriginal people as cannibals. She was so angry and so determined to make some amends that, for once, she agreed to be interviewed on land rights by a visiting Finnish journalist and gave him her opinion of the ignorance, prejudice and sheer malice of those responsible.

To make matters worse, her hearing that year took "a very sharp downturn" so that she was now virtually incommunicado except by phone, which had an amplifier attached to it, adding decibels to her hearing aid. Even then, the problem was to hear the phone when it rang in the first place: "I don't often hear it," she wrote, "unless I'm right beside it." As she told a correspondent, however, she was also "relieved by this physical let-out as I'm having hell's delight dealing with Queensland rednecks over Aboriginal land rights. I'm probably much safer at the typewriter than I would be in Cape York!"[39] So she was resigned to her growing isolation:

> I don't mind. It's not a disability to me really because I'm a writer, you see and I think quite a lot of writers would be happy to be deaf. Indeed, if I ever manage to write anything more it'll be because I'm not listening.[40]

Nevertheless, looking back at the end of November, she seemed to have experienced "an unprecedentedly awful three months", and she feared "that the chaos principle has already won": she had been seriously ill, resigned from the WPSQ after nearly thirty years, felt that things were going from bad to worse for Aborigines and for the environment, and the world situation seemed more and more desperate. "The transitional monsters of exploitation" were, she felt "riding on our backs". The only hope, she still believed, was a transformation of value: "we might just come out of it all with a new origin of species – and about time too".[41]

But some positive things had happened, too. Her collection of essays on Aboriginal affairs, *Born of the Conquerors*, published by the Aboriginal Studies Press in Canberra, was launched by the Minister for Aboriginal Affairs, Robert Tickner, on Budget Eve, and Cassandra Pybus, editor of *Island* magazine, had commissioned an essay from her on the Mabo case, which was then nearing the end of its long series of hearings. As its title, "A Shaft of Light: The Murray Islands Case", suggests, her tone was positive. The *Federal Racial Discrimination Act* of 1975, she pointed out, ratified the United Nations Declaration Against Racial Discrimination in the framing of which the Australian delegate in the years immediately after World War II, Dr Herbert Evatt, had taken a leading part. This Act now obliged the Australian Government to take action against States practising discrimination: the Queensland Act dealing with Aboriginal affairs, for instance, was in clear breach of our obligations under the Covenant as was the *Queensland Coastal Islands Declaratory Act* of 1985, which retrospectively extinguished any native title that may have existed before the annexation of the outer Torres Strait Island in 1879 – their response to the early stages of Eddie Mabo's claims. True, it was not always easy to get the *Racial Discrimination Act* to work in favour of Aboriginal people. In 1981, for example, an Aboriginal delegation from the Queensland reserves had scraped up enough money to go to Canberra to make that case. But, "in that chilly and self-contained city, the chilly Fraser government did little to give them hope".[42] Nevertheless she believed that changes were on their way.

The conference at James Cook University in Townsville at which the Mabo case originated in August 1981 had asked "why the Federal government had failed to carry out its stated policies and how it could be persuaded to do so". In Judith's view the Mabo case was the most significant of these strategies and when at last it moved to the High Court from the Queensland Supreme Court "for many people, an almost hopeless situation began ... to crack open, and a wall which seemed to have no door began to split apart".[43] That hope was that the High Court might dispose at last of the legal fiction of *terra nullius* and acknowledge Aboriginal ownership of the land. In private, writing to Len Webb, Judith put it more strongly. The question, she said, was whether or not "we ... go into this imbroglio with a long outdated view of ownership of the country and an arrogant nineteenth-century attitude to Aboriginal claims". If so, "we are already discredited".[44] But at last things seemed to be moving. The United Nations declared 1992 the Year of Indigenous Peoples, and it was opened in Australia in November 1991 by Paul Keating (who was to succeed Bob Hawke as Prime Minister a month later) with a speech in Redfern, centre of Sydney's Aboriginal community. In it Keating apologised to the indigenous peoples of Australia on behalf of all non-indigenous Australians for the injustices they had suffered. We must, he said, set aside "unconstructive emotions" like guilt and "open our hearts" to indigenous Australians. Especially with the Mabo decision about to be handed down, he said, the year could be "an historic turning point, the basis of a new relationship between indigenous and non-Aboriginal Australians".[45]

Certainly there were some hopeful signs. Columnist P. P. McGuinness, for example, not noted for his radical views, had written earlier in the year, as Judith reported him, that "something like a treaty ... [wasn't] a no-no any more".[46] Opposition to land rights was still strong. Indeed, as Judith observed to Webb, reinforcements seemed to be arriving: "the South African situation is overwhelming us with rich refugee arrivals" who would, she feared, "try to take us over in turn ... The Aborigines are suffering accordingly".[47] She was also suspicious of the rhetoric which was flowing so freely that year. Preferring deeds to words, as the year drew to an end she sent a fax to the Aboriginal community of the area around Braidwood offering to "pay the rent as far as my income allows",[48] that is, to pay them an annual amount for being on their land.

The heartening signs continued. "There is already a lot brewing in places like South America," she wrote, "over 600 years' celebration of Columbus' arrival".[49] A World Summit of Indigenous Peoples had been called by the United Nations, and non-government organisations concerned with indigenous peoples were to hold their own summit concurrently. Judith suggested to Webb that he and his colleagues at Griffith University organise a similar gathering in Australia, inviting the Indian woman Vandasa Shiva, whose ecological writings had impressed her. Although nothing came of that suggestion, there was growing sympathy for the Aboriginal cause and a growing readiness to make common cause with them, even in places like the Northern Territory where Nugget Coombs, with whom she was in frequent contact, was trying to set up a Forum for Indigenous People, partly funded by the Northern Territory Administration and partly by the ANU's Northern Australia Research Unit with which he had had a long involvement.

Aboriginal people were also taking action themselves. In Canberra, several representatives of the Wiradjuri, Ngunarval and Arrente people, Ian Williams, Isabel Coe, Harold Williams and Sonya Laughton, had occupied Old Parliament House on Australia Day 26th January. When they were charged with trespassing, their counsel argued for a stay of proceedings in the Magistrate's Court on the grounds that his clients had appealed to the International Court of Justice, arguing further that since the land had always belonged to the Aboriginal and Islander peoples and, for lack of a treaty, still did so, they could not be accused of trespass since this was still their land.[50] Quoting High Court Judge Lionel Murphy, counsel pointed out that,

> the history of the Aboriginal people is that they have been the subject of unprovoked aggression, conquest, pillage, rape, brutalisation, attempted genocide and systematic and unsystematic destruction of their culture as aforesaid with acts of barbarism.[51]

The objection was not sustained, but the point had been made.

With her failing eyesight, Judith was finding it difficult to read, but she was interested in these legal and constitutional issues, aware that they were likely to become crucial, especially if a favourable finding in the Mabo case revived the idea of a treaty. In May she sent Webb a paper by a Canadian lawyer, Peter Jull, an expert in indigenous rights advising the Torres Strait Islanders who were demanding independence. She realised that these international precedents were important.

But she was aware that powerful interests were arrayed against them, worrying that her correspondence with Coombs and other high profile friends and colleagues was being intercepted not just by ASIO but also by "the kind of surveillance practised by the lords of industry".[52] She informed Coombs in June that she had destroyed much of their correspondence in her "nice new raging hot stove ... I have to protect my friends and my daughter against the rogues and traitors to whom the letters were of interest".[53] Police violence against demonstrators protesting against the AIDEX Trade Exhibition of weapons in Canberra added to her fears that people who opposed powerful economic interests might be in danger. Nevertheless as she also told Coombs, "we can only stand on what we have done against the current".[54]

But however much she might rail against the Establishment, she was by no means an outsider. This same year, 1992, she was awarded the Queen's Medal for Poetry, the first Australian to receive the award. The British Poet Laureate, Ted Hughes, who had long admired her work, had written earlier asking her permission to propose her for the medal[55] and she had agreed. But the actual award came as a surprise. She had no real interest in such honours, but she realised that they could be useful politically to lend a certain respectability to the causes she was involved in. Besides, though she was no monarchist, she felt that the Queen had "done a very good job in a most difficult forty years",[56] and agreed to come to Canberra in February when the Queen would be there on a state visit to receive the award at her hands. By that time, Judith had become completely deaf, but it was pointed out that all she had to do was to be there, so she agreed to come with Meredith accompanying her. The Queen was very gracious and Judith took to her, in fact, reporting that:

She seemed to me quite a nice, ordinary kind of lady. She made quite a nice joke: the medal had a beautiful naked Muse on the back and the Queen's face on the other, and she pointed to herself – meaning she was the model for both.[57]

Judith's deafness was also a kind of protection since it was difficult for journalists to interview her – she had never liked such interviews. But she did tell them, somewhat ingenuously, that it was "a pretty medal". Some of her Aboriginal friends, Kevin Gilbert especially, were unhappy that she had accepted an award from the Queen of England. But she explained that the prestige it gave her might be helpful to their cause, remarking with some amusement "how many people, Republican or otherwise, noticed the Queen's medal as against the other awards" she had received, adding that it had already fended off "a few of the crazies".[58]

Her reputation was still high internationally, and that year Virago revived the idea of an English edition of her *Collected Poems* which would also feature excerpts from *The Generations of Men*, some short stories and essays on poetry, the environment and Aboriginal issues – a kind of Portable Judith Wright. Her experience with the earlier Portable Edition, attempted by University of Queensland Press without (she said) proper consultation, made her hesitant, but the thought of being published in England was attractive. She suggested including selections from *We Call for a Treaty*, only to be told it would have "very little currency" in the United Kingdom[59] – which was probably true enough; it had not done well even in Australia. In the upshot nothing came of this proposal. In the meantime another collection of her essays, *Going On Talking*, was published by a small Sydney publisher, Butterfly Books.

She felt at times now as if she was seen more as a literary monument than as an actual writer, though she was in fact writing less and less: "You need to be young to get the proper impulse to write," as she said to Heather Rusden. "I don't know if the muse is interested in me any more. I have probably done all I can in poetry ... Unless I've got this pull I don't even try to write."[60] She was invited to be a patron of the newly instituted Queensland Writers' Centre, together with

Oodgeroo, David Malouf, Bruce Dawe, Thea Astley and Geoffrey Dutton, and was also interviewed by Dinny O'Hearn for the "Bookshow" on SBS television. Her deafness made this a difficult business, but they solved the problem by having O'Hearn pass the written questions to her while the camera was moved away.

Judith's deafness was cutting her off more and more from others, especially from the lighter side of life. In December, for instance, the editor of Sydney University's student newspaper, *Honi Soit*, of which she had once been a sub-editor, invited her to launch the first issue for 1993 during Orientation Week. She refused, saying that she was too busy as well as too deaf.[61] In the same month she refused an offer to make a film with Oodgeroo for Iguana Films, who wanted to celebrate the friendship between the two women. Once more Judith's excuse was that she was over-worked: "I cannot spare any time, quite frankly, for anything that does not look in any way useful – indeed urgent – for the cause of Aboriginal rights, and this seems at best irrelevant." She and Oodgeroo had made their film *Shadow Sisters* years ago with Frank Heimans of Film Australia, she said, and they were now both "exhausted". Perhaps it was also that, as for Yeats in old age, all things seemed to be turning into questions or perhaps she was exhausted by the great rock of mortality, and now had little wish, as she put it in "Rockface", to "chisel things into new shapes".[62] But it is clear that she would have liked to spend time again with Oodgeroo, beginning her letter to her: "Dear Oodgeroo, in fact very dear, though we don't meet".[63]

Other people kept pressing. During 1992 she was approached by a Sydney littérateur, Clayton Joyce, who had just edited a collection of essays on Patrick White, *A Tribute to Patrick White*, and wanted to do the same for her. She had contributed to the tribute to White, claiming fellowship with him, as a relation and another "dissident from that sheepfold, a country-bred descendant of country people who had slipped out of the net",[64] so she felt that she could hardly object to Joyce's new proposal. For a variety of reasons the volume did not eventuate but the response from her friends was enthusiastic, and Kathleen McArthur, Stewart Harris, Finola Moorhead, Oodgeroo, Heather Rusden and Bruce Dawe all contributed essays.

In Judith's view, however, this was no time to relax and bask in the admiration of others, there were still battles to fight. As she wrote later to Len Webb, she had "never sought academic splendour or even respectability; I just hover on the fringes with my sting well out".[65] In February there was a minor skirmish when Australia Post proposed closing the Braidwood Post Office for reasons of economy. She had no sympathy with economic rationalists – calling them the "Conrats". She had grown up with notions of public service and a reverence for and identification with life and a commitment to its future which scorned mere individualism and insisted on responsibility to others as well as to the place in which she was born and lived, and her friendship with Nugget Coombs had strengthened these feelings. Thus while saving the post office in a small country town might not have seemed a major issue to many people, it mattered to her. As she wrote to the local newspaper, the *Tallangatta Times*, the post office was "an essential public service. It belongs to us, the people. If it goes, we have failed a major test to ourselves and to the future".[66] They passed that test, however, at least for the time being, and the post office stayed.

There was also a larger battle to fight. A proposal was afoot to dam the Shoalhaven River – Judith's river, as she thought of it – to supplement Sydney's water supply, its advocates pointing to the needs of Sydney's rapidly expanding population and waxing lyrical about the size of the proposed dam, five times the volume of Sydney Harbour. But size had never impressed Judith, and as for the needs of a growing city, she was caustic about the failure to control the world's and Australia's population. As far as the dam was concerned, two main issues worried her, very specific and local: first that the flooding involved would revive the danger of mercury poisoning from the tailings of the old gold mines around Mongarlowe and then that the ecology of the region would be damaged or destroyed. As she put it, attacking the proposal in an essay called "The Destruction of Two Rivers", the "lovely rivers of the southern tablelands" with the fish, animals and vegetation which depended on them would be destroyed merely to supply water "free to Sydney to be polluted and wasted".[67] It is not clear how she actually saw the needs of Sydney's growing population being met. But that was not her business, and for her principles were more important than pragmatic needs. In any case she had never been an admirer of cities and objected to the way their needs were given priority over the needs of the land itself and the people on the land. For her, these rivers and streams were valuable in and for themselves and what she called the "terrifying rise of population in the world" was no justification for destroying them.

In this she was supported by Nugget Coombs. Although he was a distinguished economist he was passionately concerned for the common good. For him, economics therefore ought to concern itself not just with money-making and development of the earth's resources but with managing "the household of the earth itself, [and caring] for it in its relatedness". Controlling population was a crucial part of this care: if the environment was not to be destroyed, "the first and most essential prescription was control of population growth".[68] Judith agreed, and her love for and knowledge of the land added to her concern. In fact, she argued, Australia was not "a big country, but one of the most arid and infertile ... with a limit in inland areas set inexorably by lack of water and a high evaporation rate".[69]

The population issue was rapidly becoming another passion. "Nothing works while population spins giddily upwards," she wrote to Webb, "bureaucrats multiply, subtract and divide, and the whole thing goes downhill with dizzying speed."[70] She had already attended several conferences and seminars in Canberra on the subject of the world population crisis and on the need to control its growth. On the practical level, she had also joined Children by Choice, a movement to which Len Webb's wife, Doris, had introduced her. In her view the larger life of the earth demanded our continual loyalty:

> *We with our quick dividing eyes*
> *measure, distinguish and are gone.*
> *The forest burns, the tree-frog dies,*
> *yet one is all and all are one.*[71]

These long-term issues seemed to her to matter more than short-term political ones. So when, later in the year, Prime Minister Keating began to push the idea of a Republic she refused to be distracted.

> I'll be interested in a republic [she said] when I see some sign that the republican movement is interested in the fact that we are none of us likely to live more than twenty-five years unless there is a major change in our way of doing so. I have more to do than bother about republicans until then.[72]

As Jack had always said, what mattered was to get the general picture first and not to spend too much time on specific parts of it.

In March the little hearing she had disappeared. She was, she wrote, suddenly "walled off from technology and nature's noises, all at once".[73] Over the years she had learned to cope with deafness, and this had meant that she had never been really sociable. But that had not worried her so much so long as she had books and a few good friends, and she had even made a kind of virtue out of it, saying that being deaf had been important for her poetry since it had put her in touch with her inner voice: "to write a poem which really grabs you you have to become practically unconscious of everything else". She had also kept in touch with friends through her letters – Barbara Blackman, for one, found this "word-woven intimacy" more comfortable than meeting in the flesh[74] since talking with her always involved shouting or writing messages on paper. But the total extinguishment of all sound was not easy. Fortunately, Meredith was with her, home on vacation from Japan. They decided that it would be a good idea for Judith to learn sign language, but nothing much came of that – she was too busy and few people could understand or use it.

For someone who "live[d] through a web of language",[75] she felt more than ever out of touch with "whatever they define as the world these days... TV, modern political awfulness". But she was also more than ever disgusted with the direction the world seemed to be taking, especially on Aboriginal issues: "Really I think all whiteys are potentially Ku Klux Klan, or practically all; as far as I'm concerned the only goodies are the friends of my own age who are rapidly dying off ... I see very few capable of taking their place," she wrote, asking Len Webb to "stick around, will you?",[76] since he was one of the "goodies".

This depression may also have had physical causes since Judith's eyesight was deteriorating so much that she would soon have to give up driving. When her driver's licence ran out the next year, she thought she would probably not pass the eyesight test. This meant that she would have to leave "Edge", though she put a brave face on it, writing that "if I haven't run out myself at seventy-eight I'll be prepared to shift to the local bin for the Frail Aged", adding, however, that maybe that would not happen "while she could still wield a typewriter"[77] and keep herself part of political and literary conversation.

She was still wielding her typewriter to some effect. Apart from all her other correspondence, she produced, desktop-published and circulated *Network News*, a publication intended for supporters of Aboriginal rights in general and in particular for small Aboriginal bodies which needed to keep up to date with what was happening. The final edition appeared in January just before the Mabo decision was handed down.[78] She also kept on writing letters about issues which concerned her, notably the environment. Since environmentalists in New South Wales seemed to be getting nowhere and were short of money, time and support, she now looked to the Victorians whose research program on the actions of the foresters she admired but also found "hair-raising. Illegal logging, illegal roading, cans of deadly poison left on logging sites, trees dozed into creekbeds, the lot."[79] So she was now writing and lobbying on their behalf.

In the meantime she was coming to terms with the possibility of blindness. There were many activities she would have to give up, and it seemed as if she might not be able to complete her autobiography (which she had been working on intermittently) and would have at last to give in and allow someone to write her biography. Several people had already requested permission, which she had refused. She had grown used to living in silence, but as a poet her eyes had delighted in what they had seen. At "Edge", as at "Calanthe", she had absorbed the details of the world about her: sun orchids, violet stick insects, lichen, moss and fungus, the caddis fly which drowned in her wine glass, the eyes of a fox suddenly fixed in the headlights of her car, "staring and snarling back", the tiny clusters of whitebeard heath in flower, the epacris,

> *Grey-green, as high as a hand*
> *beside that lichened stone,*
> *... clenched pale buds*
> *no bigger than river-sand,*[80]

a hunting snake

> *Head-down, tongue flickering on the trail*
> *[questing] through the parting grass*

as

> *sun glazed his curves of diamond scale,*[81]

and the flocks of birds, black cockatoos, rosellas, magpies, currawongs and swallows in the trees around her.

She loved the place, and also had "very good neighbours, and more friends than neighbours, in this neighbourhood", as she wrote, "and as for wind and cold ... I'm a New Englander by birth and a Braidwoodian from choice". She enjoyed solitude, being able to live in a place in which "I don't have to encounter the crazies (crouched behind the Half Moon gate and its various prohibitions)". But her disabilities were making life here "too much to handle",[82] so she would soon have to move back into Braidwood. Before she did so, however, she wanted to see to it that the place would be properly looked after. She had already offered the property to the ANU for research purposes and at her urging, no doubt with some help from Nugget Coombs who was still connected with the university as a Research Fellow, a committee had been set up to consider how it might be used. Judith hoped that it might be used for teaching. Environmental education seemed to her to demand the kind of experience of the natural world she had had as a child, and students might have something like that at "Edge". She was sceptical about courses in which students of the environment saw nature, as she put it, "through a windscreen darkly, or a course in biology".[83] She also hoped that the university would do its civic duty in the area – during the debate on the Shoalhaven dam she had written asking them to send a representative to the public meeting to protest against it.

The winter, a hard one, sharpened her resolve to move. Initially Meredith had hoped to find her a house in town, but those negotiations fell through, and they had to settle for something else. Arranging things in Australia, Meredith found, was often exasperating. Since she lived mostly in Japan, she could "never understand why all the things she organises in Australia go paralytic until she comes back and blows them apart". As Judith saw it, for that reason, "we deserve our economic fate, this is how the rot sets in".[84]

When Meredith returned from Japan in September she helped her mother move into Braidwood, into a "nice little (though rather too little) flat" across the lawn from the old bank in which they had lived when they first arrived from Queensland, which was now an art gallery and craft shop, the Studio Altenberg. There was a vegetarian café at the back run by local artists, where she could have her meals, if she wished. The flat had originally been the stable for the "long-departed bank manager's" horses, though she noted, "the horses had every comfort; ...the stable is very well upholstered by the present owners and an interesting study in the archaeology of the Horse Age". The people who ran the gallery and the café, writers and craftspeople, were already friends, so she settled in "with sighs of relief after the cold and grey winter ... I am much happier with good coffee and good friends so close I must say",[85] making the best of things.

Moving is always melancholy. As she had written after the move from Queensland in a poem called "Unpacking Books":

> *Traherne said nothing had been loved as much*
> *as it deserves. Though growing old I lament*
> *too few answers to beauty's sight and touch,*
> *too many words.*[86]

So it seemed a good idea, before Meredith returned to Japan, to make the trip to the Centre she had planned the previous year – they would meet Coombs there, and the special vastness of the land in the Centre would restore her spirits. Meredith did a lot of walking on the trails around the MacDonnell Ranges near Alice Springs while Judith relaxed and enjoyed an "ecstatic amount of sun". They also drove through other national parks in the area, most of them part of the Ross River cattle station, and, as Judith observed, "showing it". The National Parks Authority had been trying to regenerate the area, with mixed success, however, since there were still cattle there, and cattle were "the most destructive factor in just about everything that ever happened in the region, no two ways about it".[87] As a descendant of cattlemen she felt some responsibility for this, believing, as she told Webb, in what she called "Morphic Resonance", the linking and repetition of forms in nature. Through her ancestors, she felt herself part of this process of destruction. As she had written in "For a Pastoral Family":

> *What swells over us now is a logical spread*
> *from the small horizons we made –*
> *the heave of the great corporations*
> *whose bellies are never full.*[88]

At least, however, she had been and still was trying to make some amends to the Aboriginal owners who had cared for the land long before this process had begun.

From Alice Springs they flew north to Darwin to visit Coombs and drive with him to Kakadu. For years Judith had been concerned about the fate of the people of that area and for their land as the miners forced their way in to develop the mineral resources, but a friend had urged her to go and see what was happening for herself and realise how urgent the matter was. The place was "wearing out", he told her, "and the trad owners are wondering why on earth they entered into that agreement with the N. T. and Fed services". After being there Judith understood their feelings but she was also appalled by the damage tourists were doing to the beautiful and fragile environment, especially "the people who raged through it in four-wheel drives!".[89] Her feeling for the land had always been maternal, and here a beautiful area, cared for by its Aboriginal owners over thousands of years, was being ravaged by unthinking white people. Earlier in the year when another friend had written that he was about to visit a place in far north Queensland, she had written that "it sounds like the kind of place that I personally shiver at the thought of even visiting, shame and fear combining to make me feel a few hundred thousand years out of place".[90] She came away from Kakadu with similar feelings and returned to Braidwood more concerned than ever.

Nevertheless the highlight of the year, the High Court's decision in the Mabo case, gave her and others like her new hope. The judges reassessed the legal justification for our invasion and occupation of the country, *terra nullius*, the notion that the country had been unoccupied, or at least that the indigenous peoples' ideas of land ownership were so different that in effect they did not occupy the country in our legal terms. In the light of the evidence presented on behalf of Eddie (Koiki) Mabo and his fellow appellants from the island of Meriam (Mer), however, the High Court found it clear that this was not so. They had occupied the land and cultivated it without interruption for hundreds of years. In this case the fiction that the land was unoccupied in our terms could not be upheld.

Normally, the Court conceded, they would not have had the right to question the fundamental assumptions about property and settlement on which Australian society rests. But in the light of the history of occupation, which Justices Deane and Gaudron called a "national legacy of unutterable shame"[91] and of Australia's international obligations enshrined in the *Racial Discrimination Act*, the majority found the concept of *terra nullius* discriminatory, unjust and unconscionable.

> Judged by any civilised standard [Justice Brennan wrote], such a law is unjust and its claim to be part of the common law to be applied in contemporary Australia must be questioned ... [I]t is imperative in today's world that the common law should neither be nor be seen to be frozen in an age of racial discrimination.[92]

The government concurred. Prime Minister Keating hailed it as "an historic decision", declaring that Mabo was "an issue that the country could not ignore ... morally" and "an opportunity to heal a source of bitterness", claiming that it "may [even] have the potential to work a miracle" and urging Australians "to bring the dispossessed out of the shadows". He intended, he said, to introduce an "act" or "process" whereby Australians would "recognise and make amends for [the] past wrongs which we [have] failed to see".[93]

As for Judith, she was pleased but not ecstatic. She wrote triumphantly on her Christmas cards, "No more *terra nullius*",[94] but shrewdly (as it proved) she did not believe that there was the public support or even, despite the Prime Minister's support, the political will to carry through the consequences of the High Court's decision to guarantee Aboriginal people right to the lands they still occupied and make some compensation to those who had been dispossessed. She knew by experience the strength of the opposition which would be marshalled against it and remained pessimistic about the situation. "Optimistic? I don't know what that word means," she had written a year or so earlier. In her view "you either get along with the world [or you don't]. You can't ever agree with it",⁹⁵ and that she could not do so long as Aboriginal people "starve, hang themselves in custody and outside it, and sit in gutters crying their eyes out while the world whirls by".⁹⁶

She had always been suspicious of sentimentality and of mere "do-gooders", remarking ironically on the way "we all want to save the world in spite of its reluctance to be saved", and had few illusions left about politicians and the political process, doubting that there would be any real change since the interests of miners and large landowning interests were threatened. "What a ghastly race we are to be sure," she wrote, "I'm much happier with (myself)".⁹⁷ She chose the way Yeats had written about:

> *Hearts with one purpose alone*
> *Through summer and winter seem*
> *Enchanted to a stone*
> *To trouble the living stream.*⁹⁸

Christmas 1992 marked the end of another stage. This year Judith did not go as she had always done to New England, but went instead to stay with a niece and her friends at Merimbula on the coast. It was an uncomfortable trip since her "crook leg" made it difficult for her to sit in one position for long, and after the four-hour drive from Braidwood she arrived "the same shape as the car seat",⁹⁹ and it was some time before she could stand upright. Nevertheless she had no intention of becoming old and decrepit so a few days later, tired of sitting at home, she climbed down a cliff path. But unfortunately this had "awful results for [her] bony structure", and she had to resort to the physiotherapist on her return to Braidwood – "a consoling process at least", though, characteristically gloomy, she added, "what good may come of it I cannot tell".

Her arthritis was troubling her also, though she was determined not to become a cripple, forcing herself every day to walk "grimly" to the post office – which was still there – "to keep [her] muscles in working order".¹⁰⁰ She had the added incentive that she had been invited back to

Central Australia in 1993 and intended to get there, even though at times "the idea of moving any further than between the bed and the desk gets rather out of reach". It was difficult too, to get out to "Edge" to see the place again, though she managed that from time to time with the help of friends. Yet despite all these difficulties she believed she was better off in Braidwood living "in a converted stable with a broken-down typewriter than out there (in the larger world) with the wolf-pack and its nastiness".[101]

That nastiness seemed to be growing. As she had feared and predicted, hostility to Aboriginal land rights seemed to be increasing rather than diminishing as a result of the Mabo judgment. The historian Geoffrey Blainey, for instance, had declared that it had the potential to split the country:

> We could well end up with two permanent systems of land tenures and the genesis of two systems of government [he wrote]. Aboriginal lands form almost a continuous corridor from the Arafura Sea to the Southern Ocean, with only tiny breaks in continuity ... One large Aboriginal area has the rainfall and general capacity to support a nation of many millions at East Asian standards ... To grant land rights ... is also to weaken ... the real sovereignty and unity for the Australian people.[102]

Hugh Morgan of Western Mining went even further, declaring that the High Court's judgment contained "the seeds of territorial dismemberment of the Australian continent and the end of the Australian nation as we have known it".[103] There were also attacks on the High Court itself led by the conservative politician Peter Costello who accused it of being "unelected and unrepresentative" and of usurping the role of Parliament and of "unilaterally changing the law".[104] Judith was depressed but not surprised by these responses, and the fact that these critics proclaimed the idea of "one law, one people, one destiny".[105] Throughout her life she had been suspicious of any kind of compulsory behaviour and had valued diversity. For her, and for friends like Coombs, the moral tradition of justice the High Court had evoked in its judgment was far more important than economic considerations.

On the positive side, however, Prime Minister Paul Keating continued to support the decision. Acknowledging the long history of dispossession as our "National shame", he praised the High Court for its recognition of the "fundamental truth", that our indigenous peoples who belonged to "the oldest culture in the world" had "lived with the land for thousands of years".[106] He also signalled his determination to push ahead with legislation that would allow Aboriginal people to claim land under the terms of the High Court's judgment, and make compensation to those who could not do so, and moved responsibility for Aboriginal Affairs to the Department of Prime Minister and Cabinet, declaring that his government was committed to "land rights title, the reconciliation process, the issue of a treaty, and Aboriginal aspirations to be recognised in the Constitution".[107] On the Aboriginal side, Lois O'Donoghue, Chairperson of ATSIC, welcomed this "recognition that the rights of indigenous Australians are central to the issue of our country's national identity and its place in the world".[108]

Judith made little reference to these promises in her correspondence, perhaps because of her suspicion of politicians but also because she felt more and more detached from a society in which, as she saw it, "the only contribution worth considering (for most) is More and Grab-While-the-Money-Lasts ... (and) depth-and-meaning concepts seem like distraction from the issues in hand". To her this was short-sighted nonsense: in her view the continued existence of human life was threatened unless we changed our values and our way of living and she raged against the general ignorance of a situation. We were, she thought, like frogs in a saucepan on a stove: "the heat is on the frog (but) it doesn't really notice".[109]

Personal losses added to her gloom. In April the Aboriginal writer and activist Kevin Gilbert died. She had admired him for his struggles and for the difficulties he had overcome and had tried to support him, and she mourned for him, feeling the injustice of his death. As she said to Barbara Blackman, able men like him could not be spared: there are "so few of them, so many of us and with such power".[110] Gilbert had suffered a great deal at the hands of the white man's law and done much for his people, both in his writing and in his political activity, and he would be badly missed. Even more painful, however, was the news from

Queensland in August that Oodgeroo was very ill, dying of multiple cancers in Greenslopes Hospital where Jack had died.

She had only a few weeks to live, Judith was told, but was not suffering greatly and was unafraid. The hospital staff cared for her lovingly and her room was filled with friends and relations who came to see her, and with flowers from well-wishers.[111] Dennis, her surviving son, and his ex-wife Patty, who loved Oodgeroo, were with her when she died at 6.30 a.m. on Thursday 16th September. She was buried at "Moongalba" under the trees beside her other son, Vivien, and a baby granddaughter who had died not long before her.

Judith was not able to get to Brisbane to see Oodgeroo or to be at the funeral but her friend's death was a deep loss. She and Oodgeroo had not seen much of one another over the past few years – they were both involved in too many things to have time to spare. But they had known one another since the 1960s and had shared many things together – poetry, friendship and, above all, their struggles for the Aboriginal cause. Oodgeroo's poetry had also meant a great deal to Judith since Oodgeroo was her kind of poet, not narrow or self-absorbed (as Judith thought so much contemporary poetry was), but passionate, expansive and committed since it grew out of a community of experience. She had also learned a great deal from Oodgeroo about Aboriginal people from the inside. As she recalled, before meeting Oodgeroo she

> had always, and so had [Jack], felt awfully embarrassed about being white, let's put it that way, because you can't get in touch with people you've wronged ... It's very difficult indeed. Both of us did what we could; we used to employ Aborigines when there were any around to employ, which was seldom, and so on, and Jack was very good at talking to Aboriginal people, better than I was, so when I met Kath ... I was absolutely fascinated by her beauty and her bravery.[112]

There had been some Aboriginal people in New England during her childhood, of course. But there had been "no chance of getting in touch with them ... we were on their land. It wasn't possible to talk to them on any kind of equal terms", and as she grew older she realised this more intensely, realising "how hated we were – we really are hated, you know, and that in itself puts an awful barrier between you and anybody".[113]

But Kath (as she was then) had accepted Judith and paid her the compliment of talking straight:

> She said what she thought and she was always very clear in her denunciation and anything like that so I could go along with anything she said and understand it. Very important that.[114]

Judith remembered her wondering, for instance, "why white men are like they are? A question I couldn't properly answer."[115] But they had also shared many other things together. Driving with her in search of a place for her Centre, for instance, Judith had experienced something of the prejudice and hatred directed against Aboriginal people and touched the history of settlement in a different way.

She also owed to Oodgeroo the discovery of the real depth and breadth of Aboriginal culture since Kath/Oodgeroo wrote from the experience of Aboriginal people who had not been supposed to exist, the "fringe dwellers", the so-called "half-castes" who lived not on their own land but on the fringes of white society and often looked as if they were merely poor whites. Through her, Judith entered into a different and less romantic world than the world of traditional people and was enriched by the friendship of many of the people who lived there – people like Kevin Gilbert, for example.

It was a friendship based on mutual understanding, appreciation and honesty. But, according to Oodgeroo, it went deeper than that. In the last major public lecture she gave, the Goossens Lecture delivered at the Sydney Opera House on 9th June 1993, only a few months before she died, she said that she felt that she and Judith had been "sisters in another Dreamtime a long, long time ago".[116] She had always felt, she said, that Judith's poem, "Canefields", with its opening image of the "coloured girl" who "leans on the bridge/folding her sorrow into her breast",[117] was about her and that they had met in this way, before they met physically. On their first meeting, too, Judith had told her about the occasion which had sparked off the poem "Bora Ring": riding on the family property in 1943 she had come on the deserted bora ring, and was so upset by the sense of loss which overwhelmed her that she turned her horse and went home at once to write a poem about it.[118] They were so close that at one stage, in 1969, Kath had suggested that they write a book together, with herself "thinking black" and Wright "thinking white", trying to "guide people out of the mess they're in".[119] But Kath also spoke of Judith's generosity. As she told Jim Davidson, when she first told her about her dream of setting up her own Aboriginal Centre, Judith "was marvellous ... she just allocated $5000 and said, 'Go, do it'."[120]

Together the two of them had contested white prejudice, ignorance and fear; Judith remembered the dinner she and a group of friends had organised with Kath and the Aboriginal pastor Jim Brady, for instance, in the dining room of the motel in Brisbane at which the Springboks were also dining during their tour of Australia in the 1970s. Judith had also helped Kath's son, Dennis, in his encounters with the police, trying to find lawyers to help, lobbying and writing letters on his behalf. But she had rejoiced too, in Kath's growing fame and influence, and when invited to lunch with the Governor-General in 1988 at the World Expo in Brisbane, she had taken Kath (by this time Oodgeroo) with her as her guest. Always, however, she had learned from her, during the nights they had sat over a bottle of Scotch at "Calanthe" in the late 1960s and whenever they met afterwards.

Long before the Mabo decision Kath had taught her just what land rights really meant. As she had put it in 1986:

> There is a ridiculous assumption that we want Australia back. We don't want it back, but by God, we want a piece of it. We don't want one square inch of land owned by whites. We are talking about Crown land. We don't want to be rich, but we want the comfort of some security.[121]

She thus gave Judith an understanding of the real significance of the Mabo case. As she said after Oodgeroo's death: "If we are willing to acknowledge that we are on [the Aborigines'] land and we have done them wrong, they feel better. In that respect the air has cleared." She was also "glad that Oodgeroo [had] lived to see it, because we used to talk about how dreadful the thing was",[122] and now something had happened to mitigate the situation.

It had been her friend's "despair over her people's situation" in the 1960s which, as she said to Kathleen McArthur, went much deeper even than her despair over the destruction of the environment, which had pushed her into involvement in the issue in the first place. Writing after one of their "bottle fests" at "Calanthe", she told Kathleen then that she would soon be "as much a new lefty as she is before long".[123] They shared a profound integrity also. In 1988 Oodgeroo returned the MBE she had been awarded in 1970 as a protest against the celebration of the Bicentenary, as Judith was to return her honorary doctorate from the University of Queensland when the university gave an honorary doctorate to the former Queensland Premier, Bjelke-Petersen.

It was a strange friendship, between one "born of the conquerors" and one of those her ancestors had dispossessed. But it was a friendship which Judith was proud of and needed, based as it was on her memories of the land and of her childhood

> ... *riding the cleared hills*
> *plucking blue leaves for their eucalypt scent,*
> *hearing the call of the plover,*

and her grief for what was happening to this "lost country". This, she realised, had led her to appreciate what had happened to the land's people also. As she told Kath,

> *If we are sisters, it's in this –*
> *our grief for a lost country,*
> *the place we dreamed in long ago,*
> *poisoned now and crumbling*

once "peopled by tribes and trees", now

> *doomed by traders and stock exchanges,*
> *bought by faceless strangers.*

But – and this was perhaps an equally powerful connection – they also shared "sad tales of women" bought and sold, "black or white at a different price".[124]

With Oodgeroo's death something very important had died and another connection with the "easy Eden dreamtime" of Judith's childhood was severed. But she mourned, too, the honesty with which Oodgeroo had spoken to her about the "knife between us" and about the "cruel faces" of Judith's "righteous kin", but also the "secret kindness" with which she said those things. "Oh she was beautiful", as Judith said, looking back "My God she was beautiful, a marvellous woman, and so articulate too".[125]

For that reason Judith agreed to write a tribute to her for both the *Sydney Morning Herald* and the *Australian*, and spoke to the ABC "7.30 Report" crew who arrived in Braidwood by helicopter, more or less unannounced, for the interview. Perhaps the best summary of Oodgeroo's significance for her is in these lines from one of Oodgeroo's poems, "A Song of Hope", which Judith quoted in her essay for a collection in Oodgeroo's honour:

> *Look up, my people,*
> *the dawn is breaking,*
> *The World is waking*
> *To a bright new day,*
>
> *Where no one defame us*
> *No restriction tame us,*
> *Nor colour shame us,*
> *Nor sneer dismay.*[126]

"Time [had] not changed that hope", Judith said, and she, too, continued to find "in this old culture ... renewal, as well as hospitality and beauty, art and faith in the present and future."[127]

That was probably why, barely a week after Oodgeroo's death, on 22nd September, Wright wrote to Bobbi Sykes suggesting that Sykes organise a lecture tour by a group of Aboriginal women, rather than men (who, she noted, seemed to be the ones doing all the talking), to explain the idea of land rights to non-Aboriginal Australians. Bobbi Sykes, who, like Pat O'Shane had graduated from Harvard, had been a special protegée of Oodgeroo's, who had written to her while she was still in Harvard, telling her to "do what you've got to do, girl, and hurry home. I'm waiting for you".[128] Now Judith was asking her to carry on Oodgeroo's work. As usual, however, she was practical as well as idealistic, backing her suggestion with hard cash to meet the expenses of the trip, offering from $8000 to $10,000, which she hoped to raise by selling some of the paintings she and Jack had bought in the early days from young artists like Charles Blackman, Laurence Hope, Sidney Nolan and others who had since become famous. In the meantime, she enclosed a preliminary cheque, promising that she would "most willingly keep on funding [their efforts] as long as I can, in admiration of black women themselves".[129] At the same time she became a member of Tasmanian Aboriginal leader Michael Mansell's Provisional Aboriginal Government.[130]

Throwing in her lot with the Aboriginal cause in this way, she knew, was not likely to make her popular, especially with people in power. Asked to use her influence on behalf of Barrie Reid, who was then seriously ill and whom several other friends wanted to see given an honorary doctorate (like his contemporary Charles Osborne who had just been honoured by the University of Queensland), for instance, she was doubtful whether she could be any help:

> I am in the pooh nationally [she wrote] because of my support and public statements on the Aboriginal question ... You see what broken reeds you are relying on. I know nobody at ANU worth knowing and even these are too old to be much use ... I am an old woman; and that's no recommendation for anything in the academic field.[131]

She was also still angry with environmentalists who did not respect Aboriginal culture and claims. Even if it seemed that these people won "every time they can scoff at such out-of-date notions", she declared, "I don't give up the struggle". In her view they were quite simply ignorant of the fact that

> [we] all live and die together, however much we hope we are separate from Nature ... Most people live in cities and regard Nature as something beside the road to the beach, nothing to do with them unless they can use it as a place to throw bottles.[132]

Being an environmentalist, she thought, demanded "a different way of living", though, as she wrote to an old ally in the movement, Milo

Dunphy, many were content merely "to criticise ... dreadful new developments instead of jacking up and demanding" something different. She herself had long ago given up the "preservation concept", being persuaded that, as Marx had put it, the task was not just to understand the world but to change it. Jack had long ago convinced her that the system of thought and of value by which we in the West are living and had been living for the last three or four hundred years would not stand up to epistemological scrutiny since it was based on a series of impostures and logical fallacies. This conviction, however, gave her the decisiveness, the ability to contemplate disaster with strong nerves, which still made her, as she ruefully admitted, "a sort of guru to ... many people who want help, advice, reassurance, etc. and other things".[133]

She had always, after all, been fascinated by fire. "Bid Me Strike a Match and Blow", written in the 1970s, had expressed her sense of its power in the image of its "final dance" as the world catches fire:

> *Trees rise in it; whole dying forests rise,*
> *whole peoples made of flame*
> *storm upwards and are gone:*
> *flights of death-ridden birds,*
> *the fur and fear of blazing animals.*
> *Earth's sap and emerald*
> *die in a central gold;*
> *drawn tall to dervishes of smoke they rise.*

But, as the same poem makes clear, fire also makes for transformation and purification:

> *The speech of fire is all an upward prayer,*
> *evangel to convert*
> *to primal purity*
> *all pasts that die,*
> *all time's long error and black history*
> *to be a speck of carbon in the sky.*[134]

Even in old age this fire still burned in her, and her impatient courage still spoke to many people. Barbara Blackman remarked, in fact, that it seemed to her to offer a protection from the shadow which seemed to her and many others to be enveloping Australia as the 1980s wore on.[135]

In some quarters Judith was being called, somewhat sentimentally, "Australia's living treasure", and the Australian branch of the writers' international organisation, PEN, proposed her for the Nobel Prize for Literature. She, too, could stand in the company of major writers who had set themselves against the current of their times in the name of a larger vision of humanity. The idea did not appeal to her. "I've told them all to stop it," she said. "I've got quite enough to do without having to cope with that stuff too. I'm happy to have no handles. Give yourself a handle and somebody pulls it." Instead of proposing her for awards, she thought people should stop and think about the way they lived and where the world might be going.[136]

She was still convinced that Jack's philosophy held the key to many of the problems facing us. Mere social change was not the answer, she told Webb. What was necessary was the kind of rethinking Jack had called for and she sent him a copy of *The Structure of Modern Thought* with the hope that he would get

> more out of it than most do. If we have indeed, as he argued, been following a track that's cyclical in thought without noticing the fact, getting to the same place over and over again may finally provide a Eureka effect. But though it's clear enough to me, nobody I know has understood it. It is of course a symptom of our frustration that we keep on doing the same thing over and over again without finding the exit.[137]

Nevertheless she liked to think that others were beginning to think along his lines. *How Are We To Live?* by the young Monash philosopher Peter Singer, echoed many of Jack's intuitions, and her friend Val Plumwood, now teaching in the United States and a leading eco-feminist, had drawn on his ideas about the dangers of dualism and of the division between human beings and the natural world in an essay on "Wilderness Scepticism and Wilderness Dualism". In it she also developed the argument Judith had been making for some time to groups like the Wilderness Society, that "wilderness" ought not be seen as a place devoid of human beings but one in which human beings and nature come together.[138] In Judith's case, however, nature was pressing its claims hard. "Commitments seem to increase with age", she wrote, "while capacity lessens; I get far too many requests to do things", though her deafness, now total, provided some protection; "an excellent excuse to keep out of trouble", she called it.[139]

In one week, for example, she received invitations to give a keynote address for a women's conference on the Republic and another for a conference on Australian Literature in Guongzhou, China, and a letter asking her to write an introduction for a book. She refused them all since, apart from her failing energies and deafness, she was less and less interested in mere talk. As she told Len Webb who had sent her a scientific paper to read:

> I am trying to get past the theory to the practical implications ... Nor do I think that theory ever shifted a brick. One of the worst features of post-modernity (if that is what we are suffering from) is this academic approach, usually quarrelsome and always self aggrandising, where there are real jobs to be done in the real world (but then, as I think I said, there are many modes of reality and finding the one you think is real (REALITY! Loud cheers!) is a highly contentious process.[140]

"Few are experienced enough in the difference between an object of scholarship and a matter of thought," she concluded.

Jack had known this. Those who met him recall the way he interrogated every idea of every situation, moving

> ... entire
> into the very core of concentration,[141]

and in one of her poems she had prayed for this kind of precision:

> *Let me be sure and economical as the rayed*
> *suns, stars, flowers, wheels: let me fall as a gull, a hawk*
>
> *through the confusions of foggy talk,*
> *and pin with one irremediable stroke –*
> *what? – the escaping wavering wandering light,*
> *the blur, the brilliance; forming into one chord*

> *what's separate and distracted; making the vague hard –*
> *catching the wraith – speaking with a pure voice.*[142]

Where others might prefer easy and comforting opinions and fashionable ideas as they grew older, she was still prepared to think strenuously. For one thing, she had always had a strong belief in the existence of evil. "I have lived long enough to know the truly human is also anti-human," as she told a friend about this time. "I believe in the devil ... God isn't on our side and neither is Gaia." The motto many liberals lived by, "let conscience be your guide", seemed to her suspect therefore: "How did we get a conscience anyway and where does it get its imprimatur?" Nor was she prepared to accept sentimental talk about the earth, what she called the cult of "Mum – that exploited old lady with a fellow-feeling for Gaia" who was in fact a bastion of the status quo, and probably worked "in the armaments industry or at least doing the job of cleaner or computer operator".[143] She preferred to

> *Cast a cold eye*
> *On life, on death.*[144]

"We've given ourselves over to greed and materialism, lust and hatred," she told journalist Richard Glover. "We know we're going to cook or choke to death if we go on as we are – but still we don't do anything. Greed wins out every time."[145] It was not a good world for poetry with its

> *...ancient vow to celebrate lovelong*
> *life's wholeness, spring's return, the flesh's tune.*[146]

The next year, however, a small book of some of her poems which had been translated into Japanese by Meredith and a colleague, published by the National Library, was launched at the Adelaide Festival. Judith was, she said, "inordinately flattered",[147] perhaps even heartened by this. It was probably true, as she said to a friend, that

> books are no longer favoured as a means of communication. I should be on video, I'm assured, though I am already [a video had been made about her and her work for the Australia Council] with little apparent effect. Nobody can stand the sight of print, it seems. Well so perish all civilisations, ours is now overdue for that.[148]

But poetry still existed and was still valued, by a few people at least:

> *There's an essential music still, a moon*
> *where no man's landed.*[149]

Soon afterwards, too, the revised edition of her *Collected Poems* appeared, to be greeted with enthusiasm and respect.

For her, poetry had always been of a piece with a concern for justice. As she had written in "Unpacking Books", dedicated to fellow poet, Derek Walcott, in the midst of the

> *legacies of dead empires, the bitter taste*
> *of warring faction, the natal land's slow death,*
> *all energy, fertility, fruit ripped out to waste ...*
>
> *poets keep an oath to hold and praise*
> *what lives beyond the power-dreams of England, America,*
> > *Spain.*[150]

So it was appropriate that the same year, 1994, she won the Human Rights Award for her poetry. Equally appropriately, from her point of view at least, the main award for Human Rights went to Bobbi Sykes for her work for her people – Judith had been one of the people who nominated her for the award.

In her day-to-day life Judith was part of the Braidwood community. In many ways it was not a usual country town since a number of writers, artists and craftspeople lived in and around the town, and the proprietors of the Studio and Café Altenburg kept an eye on her in her flat across the lawn. True, some more conservative townspeople disliked her activism and her outspoken opinions – on one occasion, for example, it was proposed that she be asked to speak at a tree-planting ceremony the council was organising. But the majority disagreed; they did not want controversy.[151] That year there had been a police raid on a property not far from "Edge", whose counter-cultural occupants had been growing marijuana and the people of Braidwood were perhaps trying to be extra careful. She herself suspected that she was under surveillance for her political views, so the council's decision did not surprise her. But she was never troubled by opposition, nor did she mind being alone:

> *We are old companions, self. We can go on,*
> *sometimes in love, sometimes lonely*
> *with the old pang, the old delight,*
> *the living balance between*
> *waking and sleep.*[152]

Friendships were still precious, however. She saw less and less of Nugget Coombs with whom she had worked since the 1970s in the early days of the Australia Council, then on the Treaty Committee and subsequently battling for Aboriginal rights, since he now spent most of his time in the Northern Territory and she regretted that. His health also was failing, so even though she found travel difficult and painful with her hip problems and arthritis, when Meredith returned for her mid-summer break they flew to Darwin to see him – he was very fond of Meredith. They spent "a splendid day or two" in Kakadu being rowed along the Alligator River by two of the Aboriginal rangers, one of whom was the son of Bill Neidjie, Aboriginal leader and philosopher. They also spent some time at the Northern Australian Research Unit of the ANU in Darwin with the anthropologist Deborah Bird Rose, whose *Dingo Makes Us Human* Judith regarded as "one of the best insights into Aboriginal thinking and living that I have come across".[153]

On their return to Braidwood she stayed with Meredith at "Yuen", the name she gave to the property she had bought in relatively unspoiled bushland on the Mongarlowe road not far from "Edge". This was something of a return home and she enjoyed pottering about, helping Meredith set up a native garden and planting it for the coming season before she returned again to Japan. After that Judith returned to Braidwood, which was changing, too – it was becoming something of a tourist centre, especially for Canberra people who would stop on their way through to Bateman's Bay on the coast or stay for the weekend in one of the guesthouses or at the original post office, the first building in the town, now an elegant motel with a fine restaurant. In November Steele Rudd's *On Our Selection* was filmed in the picturesque town, and there was much excitement amongst the locals. But Judith was not keen on these developments and kept out of the way.

The retinal scarring which was affecting her eyesight meant she could now see very little and had to type in capitals – "at the top of my voice", she put it, if she was to see what she had written.[154] However, as she had told an interviewer the previous year, "You can adapt to almost anything so long as you've a purpose in life, something you are doing". She made the best of things, remarking that she thought "quite a lot of people who have disabilities are rather pleased to retire into them from time to time". She had done this with her deafness, realising that it gave her a certain power, enabling her to "command the conversation, free of verbal distractions or interruptions while those around her had to listen",[155] and now she treated her failing eyesight in the same way, telling a friend that she was "about to give up as much writing as I can in favour of enjoying the rest of my years".[156] Not being able to see, she thought, would also help her preserve the feeling for people and the world which, in her view, many people were losing as a result of their addiction to television, a medium which she regarded as "insensitive and gaudy, denying viewers the chance to do their own interpreting or experiencing of life", forcing on them instead "selected interpretations of the world" which allowed "no room for criticising, softening or explaining". Now that she did not have "to hear (or see) it any more", she declared she felt "free".[157]

These feelings may explain why, pressed by an interviewer to choose one of her poems which was special to her, she chose "Request to a Year", a poem about detachment. It tells of her great-great-grandmother on one of their holidays in Switzerland, sitting high up in the Alps looking down to see from "a difficult distance" the second of her sons balanced on an ice floe in the river far below drifting towards a waterfall.

> *Nothing, it was evident, could be done;*
> *and with the artist's isolating eye*
> *my great-great-grandmother hastily sketched the scene.*

Luckily his sister, who was on the riverbank, reached out "a last-hope alpenstock" to him which he grasped. But what the poet admired was her great-great-grandmother's stoic calm, the fact that "The sketch survives to prove the story by".[158]

Perhaps this detachment appealed to her especially now since, to add to her other problems, she had developed angina – "which makes another good excuse", she said, "to stick at home and [not] ... go gallivanting anywhere else".[159]

By and large she stuck to this resolution, writing, for example, that she had been invited to "A Poet's Something" in Canberra and that "someone threatens to come and pick me up chair and all", but that she would "stoutly resist all attempts to move her". She was, she said, "perfectly happy with a typewriter and a heater and rug in winter time and a few loved visitors at weekends and intended to stay at home".[160] She had never been much interested in reputation, having always done what she thought she ought to do rather than what was expected of her, and in her view "to age disgracefully is far better than the alternative". "All in all" she felt "well enough equipped to enter [her] eightieth year."[161]

Nevertheless it was also a melancholy time. Stewart Harris, from whom she had bought the land at "Edge" and who had worked with her on the Treaty Committee, died in November. Recalling the past became more painful:

> *All those sights, smells and sounds we shared*
> *trailing behind grey sheep, red cattle,*
> *from Two-rail or Ponds Creek*
> *through tawny pastures breathing pennyroyal.*
> *In winter, sleety winds bit hands and locked*
> *fingers round reins. In spring, the wattle.*[162]

Public life still intruded from time to time, however. In the new year she received the A. A. Phillips Award of the Association for the Study of Australian Literature. The award represented an act of appreciation of her as one of Australia's leading writers, and someone who had for some time been one of the society's patrons – its current president, Shirley Walker, was also the author of a fine study of Judith's poetry.

The A. A. Phillips Award was made only occasionally for a work or an author considered to have made an outstanding contribution to Australian literary studies. The citation in her case was generous, noting the wide range of her writing, poetry, criticism, biography, short stories, essays, social history and stories for children, but also praising "her lifelong commitment, in all her writing and in her public life, to Aboriginal and environmental issues".

> In her writing [it went on] Judith Wright has gone a long way to create an Australian identity which is fully cognisant of the intersection of past and present, the individual and the community, women and men, love and hate, and above all, the relationship between the environment and its inhabitants.

It also spoke of her "sensitive and insightful articulation of the complex relationships between black and white Australians" and honoured her for having been "consistently ahead of her time ... an always courageous thinker, writer and speaker on issues of individual and national significance", and for recognising the link between creative and critical writing and seeing them as "forces for social change". Anyone interested in the cultural history of Australia in the second half of this century, it concluded, might well take her as a "central example of Australia's intellectual, political and psychical trajectory".[163]

She was unable, however, to come to Armidale to accept the award in person – the conference was to be in July, midwinter, and travel was difficult. Deafness, which had "kept [her] away from [their] door at Conference times" in the past, was also a continuing problem. But she wrote accepting the honour with "joy and thanks", though privately she confessed to some amusement: "All of a sudden I am regarded as somehow more respectable. (Awards, medals etc. make a difference to the bourgeois mind.) It has brought old acquaintances and relatives about my ears in a big way".[164]

In March 1995 a successful cataract operation enabled her to rejoice in being able to see trees, flowers, birds and the landscape clearly again. There was other good news, too: the doctors also found that the effects of the retinal scarring were less serious than they had thought originally, so that she was no longer immediately threatened with blindness. She could relax a little, especially as she now had a part-time secretary to help her with her correspondence.

In September a Sydney actress, Dawn Langman, staged a performance of some of her poems with the assistance of one of Judith's Canberra friends, Anne Edgeworth, who directed it and wrote to tell her about the performance. An Adelaide musician, Beckie Llewellyn, provided music, some of it her own, as a bridge between the separate poems and occasionally to accompany them – there was marimba music from the Caribbean to introduce "Unpacking Books", dedicated to Derek Walcott, for instance. The setting was striking, Edgeworth told her, with the stage projecting out beyond the proscenium arch into the audience. On the right was the poet's study with its books, typewriters, bookshelves and papers, and on the opposite side what was supposed to be outdoors where the actress who was playing the poet moved around. Behind, at the back of the stage, a group of eurythmists, "dream workers", Edgeworth called them, appeared from time to time to dramatise "the imaginative energies working in the poet's being".[165]

There were two performances of the work and on the second night an almost capacity audience gave the performers a standing ovation. It was one of the first programs of the kind in Australia and most found it a powerful experience, especially its last moments, an interpretation of the poem she had written for Jack McKinney, "For One Dying". Those in the audience who knew the poet herself and her own growing frailty found this moving, from the opening lines:

> *Come now; the angel leads.*
> *All human lives betray,*
> *all human love erodes*
> *under time's laser ray;*

to the conclusion:

> *Renew the central dream*
> *in blazing purity,*
> *and let my rags confirm*
> *and robe eternity.*
>
> *For still the angel leads.*
> *Ruined yet pure we go*
> *with all our days and deeds*
> *into that flame, that snow.*[166]

As director, Edgeworth had insisted that there should be no music for these last lines and only the minimum of movement, so that the poem ended "in absolute stillness as the lights and cyclorama slowly faded into darkness".[167] As "Four Quartets", one of Jack's favourite poems, puts it,

> ... As we grow older
> The world becomes stranger, the pattern more complicated
> Of dead and living.[168]

Oodgeroo, too, was still part of this pattern – when her arthritis was particularly bad Judith would use an Aboriginal cure, a bush plant Oodgeroo had told her about.

At the beginning of winter her brother Bruce, two and a half years younger than she, died suddenly of a stroke after being well enough to come to Braidwood to celebrate her eightieth birthday in May. She was now the last one left of her immediate family. Many of her friends, too, were ill: the poet John Bligh, an old friend from her days in Queensland in the 1940s and 1950s, had had a stroke, as had Nugget Coombs. He had been brought from Darwin to Concord hospital in Sydney where Judith visited him in November. She found it a painful visit, writing to Len Webb after she had seen him: "Don't take that track if you can help it".[169]

As she confided to him on another occasion, she seemed to be "going through one helluva time ... not only with all those damn anniversaries stirring me up but with old friends dying and going into hospital for the last time",[170] quoting what Dorothy Green had said to her: "Old age is not for sissies". A major earthquake in Japan with its epicentre at Kobe where Meredith worked had also worried her. Meredith actually lived in Kyoto, which was less badly affected, and had been there at the time, but even there she had had a narrow escape when her bookshelves collapsed and her furniture was thrown about by the shocks of the quake, though she herself emerged unscathed.

The earthquake, Judith thought, was yet another sign that, as one of her Aboriginal friends put it, "the earth was angry". Despite everything, therefore, she kept on working to save it. That year, 1995, when *The Generations of Men* was republished, she donated the proceeds to Greenpeace. It was fitting, she thought, that a book about her ancestors who had been part of the process of colonisation and thus of the destruction of the environment it had involved should help finance a group working to save it.

At a more personal level, she was pleased that year to be asked to write the entry on Jack McKinney for the *Dictionary of National Biography* – the first time he was included and a recognition at last of his significance as a thinker. "This", as she had written in her poem about their pilgrimage to the grave of her grandfather, Albert Wright, "is what the dead desire – their meaning."[171]

But she did not stay pious for long. The new Chair of the Australia Council, Hilary McPhee, announced radical changes to the Council's funding programs which seemed to her and also to the Australian Society of Authors to threaten the livelihood of many established writers. The current range of fellowships was to be replaced by a series of once-only two-year fellowships, with the emphasis on young writers and the system of peer assessment was to be changed substantially.[172] Since Nugget Coombs, the main architect of the Council when it was first set up under Whitlam, was ill and "out of the battle", she felt, that out of loyalty, "those who were on the original Council ought to be out there defending his creation, and I am one of them".[173]

So it was back to the old round of letter-writing, arguing and lobbying, though she no longer had the contacts and influence she had once had. Nevertheless some of the more extreme proposals were for the time being abandoned, and some of the anxieties of older writers assuaged.

Judith was trying to compile a list of all the organisations and programs in which she had been involved with Coombs, not only as a tribute but also because it seemed important to her to keep alive the vision of public service by which he had lived. She loathed the "Conrats" who seemed to her to be running the country, not just because of their destructive effects on people and on the environment but also because they represented for her the culmination of the process of colonisation and money-making she had come to question so profoundly. As she had said in an interview with the *Canberra Times* the preceding year, this process was selfish as well as destructive:

> Everything we did when we came was to advance our personal fortunes at the cost of the land. There was never any thought that the land itself deserved anything. Quite the reverse. Once you'd cleared the Aborigines off it was yours to do what you liked with. Ownership and of course once you'd made your fortune you could get out and a lot of them did, too. So really our whole history has been exploitation.[174]

She and her friends, especially Coombs, had shared a different vision of justice and of equal opportunity for all.

Even as a child she had been unable to accept the tranquil inhumanity which had no concern for the less powerful and less successful so that she had found her work with him deeply satisfying. She realised, of course, how difficult it was to turn around a tradition of exploitation – "that's what it amounts to"[175] but she had been determined to try. That was why she was "going on talking" (the title of her latest collection of essays), believing still that people and the land were valuable in and for themselves, choosing that part of her inheritance against the entrepreneurial spirit which was also part of it. At the same time she recognised that it was the latter which had prevailed: "we never came because we wanted to own something beautiful, we came because we wanted to own or exploit a place for our own personal fortunes and it's not easy to get around that".[176]

She was, she said, getting as "lame as a one-legged duck" and was often subject to bad migraines. But she had read a book by Oliver Sacks which helped her cope with them, since it offered a marvellous explanation of "all those strange things that [used to] happen" when she had a headache. The coloured lights and strange shapes she saw, for example, were not, as she feared, signs of hallucination, but natural phenomena with physiological causes. She now found them interesting rather than troubling and told Barbara Blackman, "I no longer fear I'll die of it".[177]

Christmas that year was peaceful since she spent a fortnight more or less alone at "Edge", "my soul home in the eucalyptus forest ... away from [the] tourists and English trees and daffodils" of Braidwood.[178] The weather was chilly and rainy, but friends came for lunch from time to time and later on her sister-in-law, Peter's wife, Jane came to stay. She felt more relaxed than she had been for some time, telling friends that she had "virtually given up tweaking tails", admitting also, however, that "the tails I sometimes still tweak are all in election mode now anyway"[179] – a Federal election was in the offing. But this mood did not last long. The Conservative parties won the Federal election by a large majority, which in her view did not bode well, either for Aboriginal people or the environment. In March, back in Braidwood, she invited Val Plumwood there to discuss what could be done to save the local forest which seemed to have been "dedicated to the timber industry"[180] by the powers that be.

On the positive side, Angus & Robertson had decided to republish *The Coral Battleground*, originally published by Nelson in 1977, to celebrate the twentieth anniversary of the Great Barrier Reef Authority, whose appointment had been one of the achievements of the battle to save the Reef. Judith had recently had another heart attack, but was "recuperating on a diet of pills and sprays", she told Len, but this news pleased her and she wrote that she was "hoping for the spring" and for the book's appearance.[181] Her Foreword to this edition reflects these hopes:

> There are not many success stories in the attempts we make to save especially important elements of the natural world from our own greeds and needs ... But the story of the rescue of the Great Barrier Reef still throws a light on the present and gives hope for the future, and because of the rescue many people have been able to experience and enjoy the marvellous stretch of sea and reefs and islands, and the intricate patterns of living beings, which make up its existence.[182]

She did not mention them here, but thoughts must have gone to those who had fought with her and were now dead, people like John Büsst and Arthur Fenton. As she had written in one of her later, autumnal, poems:

> *At the end of autumn*
> *I too – I want you near me,*
> *all you who've gone, who scatter*
> *into far places or are hidden under*
> *summer-forgotten gravestones.*[183]

There was good news, too, from her friend Ysola Best at Mount Tamborine. The Aboriginal Cultural Centre she had set up to record and celebrate her people's past and present in the area was flourishing, providing a background of the Aboriginal story of the region over centuries.

In July, however, Judith had another heart attack and spent some time in hospital. She was alone when it happened, but had the presence of mind to ring the local hospital asking them to send an ambulance for her. She did not enjoy being in hospital but was grateful for the care. Soon afterwards Meredith came back for her mid-year break, so Judith was able to convalesce at "Yuen" amongst the trees and birds. The attack, however, had left her exhausted and she was daunted by the "piling up of correspondence, jobs and faxes appealing for everything from money to signing appeals for human rights problems".[184] From now on, she realised, she would have to be careful, and this warning was underlined by a series of minor attacks later in the year.

Judith was "driven and despondent" about the political situation, too. One of the first acts of the new Howard Government had been to attack ATSIC, accusing its members of irregularities in its financial dealings and setting up an extended investigation. The investigation's report, when it appeared, found that ATSIC was better run and more financially responsible than most other government departments but the damage had been done in the public's mind – the report was not publicised nearly as widely as the allegations. To add to her worries she believed that mining and pastoral interests were gearing up for a new attack on Aboriginal rights.

Certainly times seemed to be changing and, in her view, returning to the 1950s' mood of charge and counter-charge. Prime Minister Howard gave a speech in Adelaide attacking what he called "the black armband school of history" in which the sufferings of Aboriginal people were acknowledged – implicitly attacking what she had tried to do in *The Cry For the Dead*. But perhaps the most unpleasant event had to do with a feature article published in the Brisbane *Courier Mail* in September in which it was alleged that the historian Manning Clark had been a Soviet agent. Judith had known him well – he had been for some time President of the Fellowship of Australian Writers in Canberra and an admirer of her work, and his wife, Dymphna, who had been a member of the Treaty Committee, was also a good friend. Judith was outraged by the allegations.

To many the episode was more farcical than anything else, arising originally, it seemed, out of a remark by the poet Les Murray that he had seen Clark wearing the Order of Lenin medal at a public dinner. The allegations were more or less disproved, but it was a distressing incident, especially for his family and friends. The attack on someone no longer alive and so no longer able to defend himself affronted Judith's sense of decency: "The dead can't speak", she reminded a journalist, commenting on the affair. Besides, it seemed a crude attempt to rewrite the past: "most of the names [now being bandied about] ... are ... unfamiliar to today's readers but their reputations were being attacked".[185] This world in which she now found herself seemed to have lost even the "marginal sort of grace" with which she had been brought up.

As well as disgusting her, the incident brought back old fears of persecution. She had long believed that her work for the environment and for Aborigines had made her powerful enemies who would stop at nothing to discredit anyone who got in their way, and she was convinced also that ASIO kept an eye on her: to be involved in these issues, she believed, was "more than enough" to warrant its attention,[186] and this attention, she believed, was thorough. She also remembered from her researches for *The Cry For the Dead* how facts inconvenient to the Establishment had been suppressed and documents removed from archives. In January, for instance, she had written to someone wanting to do similar research into the treatment of Aboriginal people, warning her that "libraries had been combed through by unseen hands" to remove documents which told of atrocities committed against Aborigines. Sometimes, she wrote, she felt that "not only libraries, but whole institutions, are involved in *suggestio veri* and *suggestio falsi*" – even at this late postwar date. So the attack on Clark seemed to her a "mad revival which seemed to have its own 'agenda' of the nasty 1950s". After all these years and all her hopes, she felt "pretty damn sick of" what she saw as a return to ignorance, prejudice and fear.[187]

Shortly afterwards, however, she herself was involved more directly when the *Canberra Times* revealed that she and Jack had also been on

ASIO's files in the 1950s among people labelled as communists or communist sympathisers. She was very angry. Many of the other names on the list were writers like Mary Gilmore, Walter Murdoch, Kenneth Slessor and Alan Marshall, whom no sensible person would suspect of being communists. Others like Frank Hardy and Judah Waten had been members of the Party – for what that was worth – and the Christesens and the Palmers were known for their left-wing views.

There was an irony in these allegations, too, since she and Jack had refused to have anything to do with the atmosphere of charge and counter-charge. Judith took the attack seriously. The journalist who broke the story had hoped to show the extent and absurdity of 1950s witch hunts, and told her that his "pen [was] at her command".[188] But she faxed back to him: "These be deep waters unless you know a good deal about the background of the Cold War and McCarthyism", believing also that "those days are far from dead".[189] She saw the incident as "part of an attack by powerful interests", and in her case, she thought, a punishment for the republication of *The Coral Battleground* which had attacked those interests and told of victory over them.

She defended herself vigorously, therefore, writing to the *Canberra Times* and later to the *Australian Book Review,* declaring that she had never been a communist or a communist sympathiser. As she put it in the *Canberra Times*:

> Living as I was on a one-acre farmlet on Tamborine Mountain with a small daughter (four years old at the time) with a living to earn for her and for Jack McKinney, her father, a war pensioner from World War I with severe health problems including shellshock, I had no time for politics and little interest in them.[190]

She had been disgusted then, as she was now, by the "outburst of political hatred fuelled ... by ... McCarthyism ... and our dependence on America", which meant that "anyone slightly out of the way was suspect; I was a writer, Jack a philosopher, who better to snarl at". These hatreds seemed to be reviving – or being revived – and it did not bode well for the future.

The affair rolled on. Further allegations were made that a Russian agent, Surkov, who had come to Queensland in the 1950s, supposedly on the invitation of James Devaney, had also visited the McKinneys at "Calanthe", thus implying their communist sympathies. Judith had no recollection of this visit but remarked somewhat tartly that

> dozens of right-wing visitors [had also] pushed themselves into our company via the British Council ... including Stephen Spender, da Madariaga, the Priestleys and others for whom I had to cook lunches [adding with an exasperated sigh] ... and we even rose to a bottle of wine if obtainable.[191]

The whole affair seemed to her to have "its own agenda" which was worrying. "In these times", she told readers of the *Australian Book Review*, "it becomes necessary for anyone who remembers Cold War days – and no doubt many who don't – to watch their steps."[192] It also increased her disillusionment with politics. As a result, despite her sympathy for the family, she did not sign the letter protesting against the attack on Manning Clark: "politics after all", she said, "has got us into all our trouble". Besides, she feared she was in danger of becoming a "Token Signatory".

The world seemed to be going backwards and the fear expressed in poems like "They", written in the 1970s, returned:

> *They look like people*
> *that's the trouble.*

It is

> *Only afterwards*
> *when you're alone*
> *you realize what you said*
> *what the bargain was*
>
> *you hear the click*
> *as they say well thanks so much*
> *and go off*
> *to file the evidence*
>
> *exactly like the click*
> *in the telephone receiver.*[193]

Her health was a problem also, since she was afraid that stress might bring on another heart attack. Eventually the fuss died down but it left an unpleasant taste.

Judith's friends were supportive. One, who had been at university and had travelled with her through Europe in 1937 and now lived in Canberra, wrote to the *Canberra Times*, pointing out ASIO's lack of credibility. She, too, she wrote, had recently discovered that she had featured in their files. But most of their information about her and her family was wildly inaccurate – "a slapdash job!".[194]

There was bad news from the Great Barrier Reef at this time, too. Pollution and tourism were increasing and a "development" at Hinchinbrook was spreading silt and pollution further into the waters of the Reef, threatening the life there. The dugong population, affected by this pollution and overfishing, had fallen eighty per cent between 1987 and 1994. Overall, too, the picture was grim, especially as a phenomenon called the Black Line, which had proved deadly to coral elsewhere in the world had begun to appear. To complete the gloomy picture, North Queensland back-benchers, members of the Coalition which controlled Federal Parliament, angered by an increase in the tourism levy, were demanding a review of the powers of the Great Barrier Reef Marine Park Authority.[195] These powers had been one of the positive signs Judith mentioned in her new Foreword to *The Coral Battleground*, and in the wake of the Mabo decision the Authority had begun widening its scope to recognise the prior claims of indigenous peoples, the Reef's original inhabitants and original users. Coalition politicians, however, opposed these claims and wanted to give a green light to "development" and tourism.

There was also bad news in October from Kakadu where Energy Resources of Australia (ERA) was, Judith was told, "being aggressive and threatening"[196] in its dealings with the traditional owners. She was not surprised since, in her view, the Howard Government's sympathies lay with the miners. But she felt increasingly helpless as she watched the small gains which had been made for Aboriginal rights and the environment being eroded. This distress was almost physical: she felt that she was suffering from some great "heart pain, world pain" and everyone of good will "should be suffering [it also] by now".[197] The strange weather being experienced throughout the world, record cold spells and storms in the northern hemisphere and extreme heat in the south, accompanied by storms and extraordinary swings of temperature also depressed her, seeming to be further signs of impending disaster. "Our nice new government is not going to do a thing about it either."[198]

She was not an admirer of John Howard, who seemed to her unable to face "Reality and the problems thereof".[199] Quite apart from what she saw as his lack of concern for Aboriginal and environmental issues she was angered by his attack on the public service: "Canberra (the city and the government) is already bled white", she wrote gloomily to Webb in May.[200] But things were to become worse.

After a long delay, the High Court handed down its decision on the Wik case early in 1997. The indigenous people of the Cape York area – in which Judith and various friends had long taken an interest – had appealed to the High Court to determine whether or not the grant of a pastoral lease extinguished their rights to their traditional lands, and the Court found in their favour. These rights, their judgment read, might indeed survive these grants so long as they were not inconsistent with the rights of the pastoralists though in case of conflict the pastoralists' rights would prevail.

Moderate as this judgment seemed to be, it provoked an outburst on the part of some pastoralists, especially the National Farmers' Federation and the mining industry. Prime Minister John Howard had earlier declared that his government would abide by the verdict of the Court – not a very surprising statement from a responsible politician – but to Judith, as to many Aboriginal sympathisers, the government seemed less than sympathetic to the Aboriginal cause. A sustained attack on the High Court began also, led by the Premier of Queensland, Rob Borbidge, and Premier Richard Court of Western Australia, supported by farmers and many pastoralists. The High Court was again accused of usurping the role of Parliament, as it had been in the Mabo case. Thirteen years earlier, in 1983, Judith had written an essay entitled "Whose Country is it Anyway?" which concluded by saying that "Aboriginal land rights, and the Conservation movement, are two of the most important shifts towards enlightenment in our time".[201] Now this enlightenment seemed to be in retreat and the barbarians (or Conrats) seemed to be in charge.

The emergence of Pauline Hanson, an independent member of Parliament whose attacks on Aboriginal people and Asian migration had brought about a revival of racism, further disgusted and depressed Judith. Nearly twenty years earlier, in her introduction to Alan Marshall's collection of Aboriginal stories, quoting Laurens van der Post condemning the attitude of many whites to the indigenous peoples of Africa, Judith had pointed to

> "the peril of man when divorced from the first things in himself" – the peril of the loss of meaning in life. Cut off by accumulated knowledge from the heart of his own living experience, he moves among a comfortable rubble of material possessions, alone and unbelonging, sick, poor, starved of meaning.

She had then gone on to draw a parallel with Australia: "It seems to me that this is a most accurate description of the lives of non-Aboriginal Australians in a country to which they know they have no abiding title nor depth of relationship".[202] All they seemed intent on, she thought, was money; but the results were increasingly destructive for the land, its Aboriginal inhabitants, and society itself, which was becoming increasingly polarised. This state of alienation and meaninglessness seemed to be the mood of the moment.

Part of her anger came from the kind of aristocratic disdain Yeats had also felt for such people,

> ...*the sort now growing up*
> *All out of shape from toe to top,*
> *Their unremembering hearts and heads*
> *Base-born products of base beds.*[203]

But for her it was also fuelled by ethical passion.

She wrote to the *Canberra Times* on Australia Day 1997 that this Australia Day would be for her "by far the most shameful I can remember in my long life", declaring that we were rapidly replacing South Africa in the world's perception and that "if we 'white Australians' wish to escape the fate of South Africa – let alone the condemnation of our own consciences – we must step forward and say so".[204]

For all that she still believed, she said, that "the world is ... a bloody wonderful place" and still saw herself "as pretty damn fortunate, really". She had "been able to do so many things [she] wanted to do" and many of the causes she had fought for, like the Great Barrier Reef campaign, the struggle to save Fraser Island and the Inquiry into the National Estate, had had "at least some sort of useful outcome ... Even if only for dodging the slings and arrows" she felt "a happy person as far as I can be".[205] The way the world seemed to be going also depressed her – environmental destruction, wars and rumours of wars, disease and the increasing gap between rich and poor throughout the world – but she remained tough-minded, remarking to Len Webb that while he kept "bashing the unknown" with speculation about metaphysical matters, "the rest of us try to get a handle on the known".[206] "I am a neutral observer in these matters," she told him on another occasion. "God hasn't yet vouchsafed me a vision, nor has science for that matter."[207]

She was not optimistic that humanity would survive, and was even less optimistic about the future of Western civilisation. Nevertheless she remained determined to "play a match against the age's mind"; to "storm my limits like a jaguar's cage".[208] She had always believed in style and had no intention of merely letting her life unravel. That, in Yeats' words, would be

> *...to shirk*
> *The spiritual intellect's great work,*
> *and shirk it in vain.*[209]

Life in Braidwood was becoming physically more and more difficult and isolated. It was, she felt, "time I moved, with miners sharpening their teeth all around the poor little stable [where she lived] and unspeakable deeds being pondered".[210] In March Meredith found her a flat in Canberra and she moved there at the end of the month.

Canberra had seemed a strange place when she first moved there from Mount Tamborine:

> *Considered as an ecosystem*
> *Canberra is impossible.*

> *We the robbers robbed in turn,*
> *selling [our] land on hire-purchase;*
> *what's stolen once is stolen again*
> *even before we know it.*[214]

A poem published in *Southerly* in 1962 had prayed:

> *Let love not fall from me though I must grow old.*
> *To see the words fade on the fading page,*
> *to feel the skin numbing in fold on fold,*
> *the mind and the heart forgetting their holy rage ...*
>
> *Let me not watch in spite, caring no more,*
> *but let my heart's old pain tear me until I bleed.*[215]

She had always been the champion not of things as they are but as they might be, and despite everything she was still prepared to look ahead. As she had written to Rosemary Dobson a few years earlier:

> Times are very different from what we knew or expected in the 'forties and 'fifties and beyond. I don't look at them with any pleasure – but who knows, all these brutalities may pass and breakdowns everywhere may be what we need to change ourselves utterly as is now necessary – but into what? Some things are now in the daylight which weren't then; some are hidden that ought not to be and things are coming out that weren't available before – I have been reading the texts for chaos, even the mathematics and geometry, which somehow seem more comprehensible than ordinary mathematics; and that is something new and gives me hope we might win out yet.[216]

The work of imagination she had been engaged in all her life remained, she still belonged to the "raging kin", the thinkers and artists she had known and to their attempt, to

> *...shape eternity*
> *into earth's image, make the unseen seen*
> *in forms of immutable jade.*[217]

She could still rejoice in these forms, even if she herself was no longer fashioning them in words. So when Rosemary Dobson sent her a copy of *Collected Poems* which had recently appeared, the gift turned a day in which she felt miserable

> with heavy cold into a thing of joys and sorrows instead of merely resentment and coughing ... All the poems have come back to me as they were when I first read them, and with their very taste and sound. I don't know why putting everything together makes everything new, but it does.

The "clear-water and white wine joys of reading [these] poems"[218] gave her new life.

> *If we've a heaven or hell, art's daemon will announce*
> *to my arriving soul in either one,*[219]

as she had said in one of her poems of the 1970s. *The Coral Battleground* had been republished, and with *Born of the Conquerors* and both *Collected* and *Selected Poems* also in the bookshops, a new story in the National Library magazine for March 1997, and *The Nature of Love* due to be reissued in May with two earlier stories, she felt "like an author again rather than an Old Grey Mare".[220]

Friendship still gave her joy. Another pleasure poems gave her, she told Rosemary Dobson, was the memories they brought back of the days when Dobson had been a poetry editor at Angus & Robertson and Judith was just beginning to publish with them. She recalled

> so many good things: visiting you upstairs in Castlereagh Street, putting as much of both of you in that anthology as I dared (remember, poetry wasn't supposed to be for women?), getting called down for it; seeing you again when I came to Sydney and stayed with Beatrice and she gave that party after we'd both had babies, and discussing how poetry and babies came from the same place; and reading the books as they came out ... It's all still there, with more added.[221]

There was grief in friendship also. She grieved in particular for Nugget Coombs, with whom she had shared so much, who was now frail and incapacitated by a series of strokes. Her cousin, John Rowland, diplomat and poet, died in 1997, and she was spending time in her little flat going through the family papers he had left her. But she was determined to pay her tribute to the past and was getting back to work on her autobiography.

Jack's memory was still with her. "I doubt whether I'd have been able to do anything without [him]," she told Len Webb, "We had that sort of relationship, we meshed". Meeting him had confirmed her life's direction, and she had no longer felt a stranger with him. "We were working on the same lines – 'what the hell are people doing, and why are they doing it?' ... When he came into the equation, I really started to be able to write."[222] Most of all, with him she had learnt about love,

> *that verb at whose source all verbs*
> *take fire and learn to move.*[223]

As she wrote in "In Praise of Marriages":

> *Not till life halved, and parted*
> *one from the other,*
> *did time begin, and knowledge;*
> *sorrow, delight.*
> *Terror of being apart, being lost,*
> *made real the might.*
> *Seeking and finding made*
> *yesterday, now and tomorrow.*
> *And love was realized first*
> *when those two came together.*[224]

If, as Yeats said, an old man or woman

> *... is but a paltry thing,*
> *A tattered coat upon a stick, unless*
> *Soul clap its hands and sing and louder sing*
> *For every tatter in its mortal dress.*[225]

She had no illusions about life, though she was determined to stand firm. "I do believe in virtue," she told Len Webb, "despite seldom encountering it in real life, any more than spirituality." But she also believed in "the existence of vice, personified by multinationals, ASIO and much else in the field. These are not abstract".[226] Recent events had made her more and more aware of this. She felt under surveillance still: "Pine Gap circles the globe and peers into every nook and cranny ... even my handwriting is probably an open book to you."[227]

But not everything was grim. In Canberra her friends were "rallying round, quite enough to make one believe in 'emotional intelligence'"[228] – a concept she had been discussing with Len Webb. She scouted "intimations of mortality", having "been there and back and [having] nothing to report".[229] But like the great-great-grandmother whose detachment she praised in "Request to a Year", written during the Korean War, she increasingly saw the world from what the poem called "a difficult distance".[230]

> The first of June will see me embarked on my 83rd year [she wrote in March 1997], so who cares – not me. As the years pass I get more giggly it seems ... Be a Buddhist, it gives perspective.[231]

"Climate change is well on the way", and the Howard Government seemed to her intent on destroying much that she had fought for. But

> nothing lasts forever and my personal goddess is Chaos (who if you remember is the oldest of the gods and only Love is held coeval with him/her – see the quotation before the text of *Woman to Man* ...[232]

The last poem in the 1971 edition of her *Collected Poems* had struck a similar note:

> *Now I accept you, shadow,*
> *I change you; we are one.*
> *I must enclose a darkness*
> *since I contain the Sun.*[233]

But the last poem in the later and final edition, which appeared in 1994, extends this, taking us deeper into the mystery of fire, the element of creation and destruction which had engaged her throughout her life. The poem invokes the fires "brighter than a thousand suns", the "blinding glare" of the first atomic bombs which had annihilated Hiroshima and Nagasaki. But, it reflects,

> *Perhaps the dark itself is the source of meaning.*

Certainly, it is the reality of our times and of her life:

> *Human eyes impose a human pattern,*
> *decipher constellations against featureless dark*

as

> *Round earth's circumference and atmosphere*
> *bombs and warheads crouch waiting their time.*

The pattern of things is always, and must be, larger than anything we can understand or control:

> *All's fire, said Heraclitus; measures of it*
> *kindle as others fade. All changes yet all's one.*

> *We are born of ethereal fire and we return there.*
> *Understand the Logos; reconcile opposing principles.*

The world had not gone in the direction she and Jack had hoped for, having, it seemed, become darker and more violent. The tradition she had inherited had almost ceased to exist, but that, too, had to be accepted.

> *Well, Greek, we have not found to road to virtue.*
> *I shiver by the fire this winter day.*

But she would go on looking steadily at the world before her:

> *The play of opposites, their interpenetration –*
> *there's the reality, the fission and the fusion.*[234]

Let "Song for Winter", written in the 1950s speak the last word:

> *All we have made was made by what we do not know*
> *and the worn tool is rusted and grows old.*
> *Now that truth strips us naked to the winter's blow*
> *give us your depthless dark, your light brighter than the*
>   *brightness of the air.*[235]

NOTES

INTRODUCTION

1 Owen Barfield, *Poetic Diction*, Faber, London, 1951
2 "Bora Ring", *Collected Poems 1942–1985*, Angus & Robertson, Sydney, 1994, p. 8 (hereafter C.P.)
3 Jim Davidson, *Sideways From The Page: The Meanjin Interviews*, Fontana/Collins, Sydney, 1983, p. 396
4 "Two Dreamtimes", C.P., p. 316
5 Davidson, p. 396
6 Hélène Cixous & Catherine Clément, *La Jeune Née Paris*, Union Général d'Edition, (translated by Betsy Wine as *The Newly Born Woman*, Manchester University Press, Manchester, 1986). See also the introduction to the thought of Hélène Cixous in Toril Moi, *Sexual/Textual Politics*, Methuen, London, 1985
7 C. J. Jung, *Modern Man In Search Of A Soul*, New York, Harvest Books, 1933, pp. 196–9 (This is a book which, Judith says, influenced her and her husband Jack.)
8 Carolyn Heilbrun, *Writing A Woman's Life*, Ballantyne Books, New York, 1988, p. 124

CHAPTER I: THE GENERATIONS OF MEN

1 C.J. Jung, *Modern Man In Search of a Soul*, Harcourt Brace, New York, 1933, p. 98
2 Judith Wright, Autobiography, unpublished manuscript in Wright's possession, p. 1 (henceforth A.)
3 Judith Wright, "The Marks" in Judith Wright, *Collected Poems 1942–1985*, Angus & Robertson, Sydney, 1994, p. 373 (henceforth C.P.)
4 A., p. 1
5 ibid.
6 Paul Ricoeur, *Oneself as Another*, Chicago University Press, London, 1992, p. 2
7 ibid., p. 33
8 "The Marks", C.P., p. 374
9 A., p. 2
10 Jean Newall and Margaret Wright, *Under the Friendly Walls 1895–1995: A Centenary Publication*, New England Girls' School, Armidale, 1995, p. 14
11 Sean Hand, *The Levinas Reader*, Blackwell, Oxford, 1993, p. 82
12 C.P., p. 118
13 To me, May 1996
14 "For a Pastoral Family", II, "To My Generation", C.P., p. 407
15 Judith Wright, *The Generations of Men*, Oxford University Press, Melbourne, 1965, p. 3 (henceforth Generations); reprinted 1998, ETT Imprint, Sydney
16 ibid., p. 2
17 ibid., p. 8
18 ibid., p. 6
19 ibid., p. 9

20 ibid., p. 23
21 Phillip A. Wright, *Memoirs of a Bushwhacker*, University of New England, Armidale, 1971, p. 3 (henceforth Bushwhacker)
22 Generations, p. 24
23 ibid., p. 53
24 ibid., p. 90
25 ibid., p. 129
26 ibid., p. 134
27 ibid., p. 144
28 ibid.
29 "For New England", C.P., p. 22
30 Generations, pp. 162–3
31 ibid., p. 26
32 ibid., p. 201
33 ibid., p. 232
34 ibid., p. 3
35 ibid., p. 8
36 Bushwhacker, pp. 12–13
37 ibid., pp. 23
38 ibid., p. 25
39 ibid., pp. 28–9
40 ibid., p. 33
41 Fax from Judith Wright to me, 3 December 1996
42 ibid.
43 ibid.
44 A., p. 8
45 "Wedding Photograph, 1913", C.P., pp. 326–7
46 Interviews with Judith Wright, Oral History Collection of the National Library of Australia. Interviewer, Heather Rusden, TRC 2202, I/7 (henceforth O.H.)
47 Bushwhacker, p. 34–5
48 ibid., p. 45
49 ibid., pp. 70–1
50 ibid., p. 39
51 ibid.
52 ibid., pp. 40-2
53 "For a Pastoral Family, I, To My Brothers", C.P., p. 406
54 "For a Pastoral Family, II, To My Generation", C.P., p. 407

Chapter II: The World and the Child

1 O.H., I/19
2 Told to me by Mrs Tina Lister
3 "Wedding Photograph, 1913", C.P., p. 326
4 ibid., p. 327
5 A., p. 9
6 O.H., I/1
7 ibid.
8 A., p. 2
9 ibid.
10 ibid., p. 4
11 ibid., p. 3
12 ibid., pp. 5–6

13 ibid., p. 3
14 Bushwhacker, p. 72
15 O.H., I/20
16 Bushwhacker, p. 72
17 "The World and the Child", C.P., p. 37
18 A., p. 6
19 To me, February 1996
20 A., p. 11
21 ibid.
22 ibid.
23 ibid., p. 4
24 Paul Ricoeur, *Oneself as Another*, University of Chicago Press, London, 1992, p. 105
25 Judith Wright, *Born of the Conquerors*, Aboriginal Studies Press, Canberra, 1991, p. 29
26 O.H., I/12
27 "South of My Days", C.P., p. 20
28 "Northern River", C.P., p. 6
29 Born of the Conquerors, p. 30
30 "Bora Ring", C.P., p. 8
31 Born of the Conquerors, p. xi
32 According to Peter's wife, January 1996
33 A., p. 9
34 O.H., I/19
35 "The World and The Child", C.P., pp. 36–7
36 "To a Child", C.P., pp. 106–7
37 A., p. 12
38 ibid.
39 In conversation with me, August 1995
40 O.H., I/9
41 ibid.
42 ibid.
43 O.H., I/10
44 ibid.
45 ibid.
46 A., p. 4
47 Judith Wright, *The Coral Battleground*, Angus & Robertson, Sydney, 1996, p. 1 (henceforth C.B.)
48 O.H., I/3
49 In conversation with me, August 1995
50 "Falls Country", C.P., p. 328
51 "The Garden", C.P., p. 35
52 Generations, p. 231
53 ibid., p. 224
54 ibid., p. 233
55 O.H., I/11
56 "Bachelor Uncle", C.P., p. 192
57 "Remembering an Aunt", C.P., p. 234
58 O.H., II/3
59 "Remembering an Aunt", C.P., p. 235
60 ibid.
61 A family story passed on to me
62 O.H., I/1
63 A., p. 6
64 "Child and Wattle-tree", C.P., p. 31

CHAPTER III: DO NOT WEAKEN FOR THEIR GRIEF: DO NOT GIVE IN

1 "Wedding Photograph, 1913", C.P., p. 327
2 Bushwhacker, p. 99
3 ibid.
4 "Wedding Photograph, 1913", C.P., p. 327
5 "The Child", C.P., p. 34
6 ibid.
7 *New England Girls' School Chronicle*, Christmas 1931, p. 8
8 ibid., p. 28
9 ibid., Christmas 1932, p. 25
10 O.H., I/19
11 "Save the First Dance", unpublished manuscript in the National Library, B50, F370
12 O.H., I/19
13 See Kelvin Grose and Jean Newall, *So Great a Heritage: A History of New England Girls' School*, Allen & Unwin, Sydney, 1990; and Jean Newall and Margaret Wright, *Under the Friendly Walls, 1895–1995: A Centenary Publication*, New England Girls' School, Armidale, 1995
14 O.H., I/19
15 *New England Girls' School Chronicle*, June 1932, p. 17
16 "Save the First Dance", pp. 3–4
17 O.H., I/18
18 "Save the First Dance", p. 5
19 C.P., p. 18
20 O.H., I/20
21 A., pp. 51–2
22 ibid.
23 In conversation with me, Braidwood, May 1995
24 Owen Wright, *Wongwibinda*, University of New England Press, Armidale, 1985, p. 26
25 A., p. 18
26 Information kindly given to me by Mrs Caroline Mitchell
27 A., p. 18
28 ibid., p. 19
29 O.H., II/1
30 O.H., II/2
31 A., p. 21
32 George Eliot, *Middlemarch*, Penguin, London, 1965, p. 846
33 A., p. 21
34 O.H., II/2
35 A., p. 20
36 ibid.
37 ibid., p. 21
38 Shirley Walker, *Flame and Shadow: A Study of Judith Wright's Poetry*, University of Queensland Press, Brisbane, 1991, p. 8
39 A., p. 23
40 O.H., II/20
41 Donald Horne, *The Education of Young Donald*, Angus & Robertson, Sydney, 1967, p. 199; reprinted 1998 in *An Interrupted Life*, HarperCollins, Sydney
42 To me, Braidwood, May 1995
43 A., p. 21
44 O.H., II/20
45 Jim Davidson (ed), *Sideways From the Page: The Meanjin Interviews*, Fontana/Collins, Sydney, 1983, p. 395

46 A., p. 18
47 O.H., II/21
48 A., p. 20
49 ibid., p. 21
50 *Women's College Magazine*, May 1935, p. 15
51 O.H., II/21
52 "The Moving Image", C.P., p. 3
53 To Kathleen McArthur, May 1958
54 "The Surfer", C.P., p. 21
55 *Poet's Choice 1974*, Island Press, Sydney, 1974, pp. 30–1
56 "The Surfer", C.P., p. 21

CHAPTER IV: WHERE IS HOME, ULYSSES?

1 To me, Braidwood, 5 May 1995
2 O.H., II/1
3 "For New England", C.P., p. 22
4 ibid.
5 ibid.
6 O.H., II/2
7 ibid.
8 O.H., II/3
9 "The Remittance Man", C.P., p. 10
10 A., p. 3
11 This poem does not appear in the Collected Poems. It can be found in *Meanjin*, 2, 1, 1943, p. 16
12 "Letter to a Friend", C.P., pp. 56–7
13 O.H., II/3
14 O.H., I/4
15 O.H., II/3
16 O.H., I/4
17 A personal memoir in the National Library B32 F238, p. 4 (henceforth Memoir)
18 O.H., II/4
19 A., p. 58
20 ibid., p. 31
21 ibid.
22 Memoir, p. 1
23 ibid.
24 ibid., p. 2
25 A., p. 32
26 O.H., II/8
27 ibid.
28 ibid.
29 "For New England", C.P., p. 22
30 *Australian National Review*, 1 January 1938, p. 37
31 A., p. 59
32 ibid., p. 55
33 ibid.
34 ibid.
35 ibid., p. 57
36 O.H., I/14
37 A., p. 58
38 O.H., I/10

39 P. R. Stephensen, *The Foundations of Australian Culture: An Essay Towards National Self Respect*, Allen & Unwin, Sydney, 1986, p. xv (Introduction by Gary Munro)
40 ibid.
41 *Australian National Review*, 4, 22, 1938, pp. 53–4
42 A., p. 59
43 ibid., p. 60
44 O.H., I/17
45 O.H., I/18
46 ibid.
47 ibid.
48 A., p. 60
49 ibid.
50 O.H., I/18
51 *Australian Quarterly*, 10, 2, June 1938, pp. 80–1
52 A., p. 61
53 ibid.
54 Memoir, p. 3
55 ibid.
56 ibid.
57 ibid.
58 ibid.
59 ibid.
60 Memoir, B12, F97
61 A., p. 65
62 O.H., I/19
63 A., p. 60
64 ibid., p. 39
65 A., p.66
66 *Southerly* 1, 4, 1940, p. 24
67 A., p. 67
68 ibid., pp. 41–2
69 Oral History Tape "On Being Deaf", to Heather Rusden, National Library of Australia
70 A., p. 43
71 ibid.
72 A., p. 44
73 ibid., p. 47
74 ibid., pp. 47–8
75 "The Company of Lovers", C.P., p. 7
76 "The Moving Image", C.P., p. 3

Chapter V: South of My Days . . .

1 A., p. 68
2 ibid.
3 "The Moving Image", C.P., pp. 3–4
4 O.H., I/27
5 All of the stories appeared in the *Sydney Morning Herald* during April 1942, the month Wright left Sydney
6 C.P., p. 4
7 A., p. 69
8 ibid.
9 ibid., p. 116

10 ibid., p. 69
11 ibid., p. 70
12 Interview with Marion Firth, *Canberra Times*, 19 March 1994, p. 3
13 *Bulletin*, 10 January 1943, p. 12
14 A., p. 69
15 "Waiting", C.P., p. 9
16 "Soldier's Farm", C.P., p. 11
17 A., p. 71
18 *Southerly*, Volume 1, Number 2, April 1940, p. 17
19 Meanjin Archives (henceforth M.A.), 4 January 1943
20 A., p. 71
21 ibid.
22 ibid., p. 72
23 "Dust", C.P., p. 23
24 "The Moving Image", C.P., p. 3
25 *Sydney Morning Herald*, 21 November 1942, p. 7
26 A., p. 72
27 "The Trains", C.P., p. 12
28 "Address on the Occasion of the Phillip Wright Prize", University of New England, no date, National Library (henceforth N.L.) B19, F136
29 A., p. 77
30 Owen Wright, *Wongwibinda*, University of New England Press, Armidale, 1985, p. 78
31 Jim Davidson (ed), *Sideways From The Page: The Meanjin Interviews*, Fontana/Collins, Sydney, 1983, p. 406
32 "Bora Ring", C.P., p. 8
33 Papers of Judith Wright, N.L., MS5781, Box 7, F54
34 A., p. 77
35 N.L., B19, F127
36 A., p. 73
37 ibid.
38 Letter to Clem Christesen, M.A., 7 February 1944
39 ibid.
40 O.H., I/8
41 "Sonnet", C.P., p. 16
42 "The Moving Image", C.P., p. 3
43 Judith Wright, *Because I Was Invited*, Oxford University Press, Melbourne, 1975, p. 12
44 Lynne Strahan, *Just City and the Mirrors: Meanjin Quarterly and The Intellectual Front 1940–1965*, Oxford University Press, Melbourne, 1984, p. 7
45 ibid.
46 *Meanjin*, Volume 1, Number 1, 1940, p. 5
47 Strahan, pp. 5–6
48 M.A., 23 February 1943
49 M.A., 23 February 1943
50 "Waiting", C.P., p. 9
51 M.A., 15 January 1944
52 M.A., 1 September 1943
53 M.A., 15 January 1944
54 "Dust", C.P., pp. 23–4
55 A., p. 116
56 ibid., p. 117
57 ibid., p. 76
58 C.P., pp. 1–3
59 ibid.

Chapter VI: "Senses that Spoke and Mind that Shaped a World"

1 "Waiting", C.P., p. 9
2 "The Trains", C.P., p. 12
3 A., p. 117
4 ibid., p. 118
5 ibid., p. 118–9
6 ibid., p. 82
7 ibid., p. 83
8 ibid., p. 82
9 O.H., I/19
10 A., p. 87
11 ibid., p. 120
12 M.A., 21 August 1985
13 N.L., B50, F370
14 A., p. 87
15 ibid., p. 88
16 ibid.
17 "The Moving Image", C.P., p. 4
18 A., p. 94
19 ibid., p. 88
20 ibid., p. 87
21 ibid., p. 99
22 M.A., 7 February 1944
23 A., p. 83
24 ibid., pp. 83–4
25 O.H., II/5
26 ibid.
27 O.H., II/7
28 O.H., II/1
29 A., p. 84
30 ibid.
31 Barbara Blackman, "Brisbane in the Barjai Days", an unpublished manuscript kindly lent to me by the author
32 M.A., 25 November 1945
33 O.H., I/19
34 Blackman, "Brisbane in the Barjai Days"
35 "The Moving Image", C.P., p. 3
36 M.A., 19 May 1945
37 Lynne Strahan, *Just City and the Mirrors: Meanjin Quarterly and the Intellectual Front, 1940–65*, Oxford University Press, Melbourne, 1984, p. 21
38 *Meanjin*, Volume 4, Number 1, Autumn 1945, p. 2
39 "Country Town", C.P., p. 13
40 "The Moving Image", C.P., p. 4
41 A., p. 104
42 ibid.
43 These stories were given to me by Judith Wright and Barbara Blackman
44 J. P. McKinney, *The Crucible*, Angus & Robertson, Sydney, 1935, p. 16
45 ibid., p. 42
46 ibid., p. 49
47 A., pp. 100–1
48 ibid., p. 101
49 ibid., p. 89

50 ibid., p. 100
51 M.A., undated
52 ibid.
53 ibid.
54 ibid.
55 ibid.
56 "The Moving Image", C.P., pp. 4–5
57 ibid., p. 5
58 "The Vision", C.P., p. 262
59 A., pp. 108–9
60 J. P. McKinney, *The Structure of Modern Thought*, Chatto & Windus, London, 1971, p. 48
61 A., p. 100
62 J. P. McKinney, *The Challenge of Reason*, Mountain Press, Brisbane, 1950, p. 91 (henceforth Challenge)
63 M.A., December 1943
64 M.A., 27 January 1944
65 A., p. 109
66 ibid., p. 83
67 ibid., p. 85
68 ibid., p. 83

Chapter VII: The Gateway

1 Geoffrey Blainey, "Home, Sweet (and Sour) Home", *Australian Magazine*, 19–20 August 1995, p. 13
2 A., p. 129
3 O.H., IV 1/12
4 Blainey, p. 12
5 "Night after Bushfire", C.P., p. 37
6 "Pain", C.P., p. 30
7 "Spring after War", C.P., p. 33
8 To me
9 O.H., IV 1/12
10 Douglas Stewart, *Norman Lindsay: A Personal Memoir*, Nelson, Sydney, 1975, p. 34
11 O.H., IV 1/12
12 To Judith Wright, 21 August 1985, M.A.
13 Challenge, p. 98
14 ibid., p. 99
15 ibid.
16 ibid., p. 106
17 To me, February 1995
18 A., p. 84
19 O.H. IV 2/11
20 "The Builders", C.P., p. 45
21 "Birds", C.P., p. 86
22 To me, February 1995
23 According to member of the family to whom I have spoken
24 "All Things Conspire", C.P., p. 93
25 "The Flame-tree", C.P., p. 95
26 "The Unborn", C.P., p. 47
27 To me, February 1995
28 Helen Wilcox, Keith McWatters, Ann Thompson, Linda Williams (eds), *The Body and The Text; Hélène Cixous, Reading and Teaching*, Harvester Wheatsheaf, London, 1990, p. 51

29 In conversation with me, February 1995
30 N.L., B7, F52
31 "The Unborn", C.P., p. 48
32 "Woman to Man", C.P., p. 27
33 To Christesen, 9 October 1945, M.A.
34 To Christesen, 24 October 1945, M.A.
35 To Christesen, 21 Nobember 1945, M.A.
36 *Bulletin*, 16 October 1946, p. 2
37 Douglas Stewart, *Bulletin*, 16 August 1946
38 To Christesen, 1 May 1945, M.A.
39 To Christesen, 18 September 1946, M.A.
40 To Christesen, 29 October 1946, M.A.
41 Barrie Reid to Christesen, 11 April 1951, M.A.
42 Patrick White, *Flaws in the Glass*, London, Cape, 1981, p. 104 (© Patrick White Estate)
43 C. J. Jung, *Modern Man in Search of a Soul*, New York, Harcourt Brace, 1933, p. 196
44 "The Bones Speak", C.P., p. 53
45 N.L., B44, F382
46 "Night after Bushfire", C.P., p. 37
47 "Stars", C.P., p. 52
48 Owen Barfield, *Poetic Diction*, London, Faber, 1951, p. 36
49 ibid., p. 32
50 ibid., p. 33
51 ibid., p. 75
52 Vincent Buckley, "The Poetry of Judith Wright", in *Essays in Poetry: Mainly Australia*, Melbourne University Press, Melbourne, 1957, p. 175
53 C.P., p. 26
54 "Midnight", C.P., p. 59
55 "To a Child", C.P., p. 106
56 A., p. 119
57 "Half-caste Girl", C.P., p. 19
58 C.B., p. 1
59 "The Morning of the Dead", C.P., pp. 207–10
60 Generations, p. 26
61 "The Morning of the Dead", C.P., pp. 207–10
62 O.H. III, 2/71
63 Generations, pp. 32–3
64 To Christesen, 14 December 1949, M.A.
65 ibid.
66 "The Promised One", C.P., p. 102
67 "A Song to Sing You", C.P., p. 103
68 "Dark Gift", C.P., p. 71
69 "Ishtar", C.P., pp. 101–2
70 To Kathleen McArthur, 11 January 1950
71 To Kathleen McArthur, 3 January 1950
72 "Waiting Ward", C.P., p. 104
73 To Judith Wright, 21 August 1985, M.A.
74 "Letter", C.P., p. 285
75 To Barbara Blackman, 3 January 1950
76 To Judith Wright, 21 August 1985
77 A., p. 121
78 N.L., B28, F208
79 "Habitat", IX, C.P., p. 308
80 "Flame-tree in a Quarry", C.P., p. 60

81 Theodor Adorno, *Minima Moralia: Reflections from a Damaged Life*, Verso, London, 1994, p. 25
82 "Flame-tree in a Quarry", C.P., p. 60

Chapter VIII: Change and Distance

1 Elizabeth Harrower, *The Long Prospect*, Angus & Robertson, Sydney, 1958, p. 109; reprinted 1995, ETT Imprint, Sydney
2 A. p. 159
3 To Christesen, 26 May 1950, M.A.
4 To me, May 1996
5 To Christesen, 14 May 1946, M.A.
6 To Christesen, 28 November 1947, M.A.
7 Peter Luck, *This Fabulous Century*, Lansdowne Press, Melbourne, 1985, p. 214
8 To Christesen, 30 July 1952, M.A.
9 To Christesen, 17 November 1953, M.A.
10 To Christesen, 12 November 1954, M.A.
11 Fax to me, 21 February 1996
12 To Christesen, 12 November 1954, M.A.
13 ibid.
14 ibid.
15 A., p. 129
16 ibid., p. 132
17 "Habitat", IX, C.P., p. 308
18 To Kathleen McArthur, no date, 1953
19 "Habitat", III, C.P., p. 299
20 "Habitat", II, C.P., p. 298
21 A., p. 125
22 ibid., p. 127
23 To Kathleen McArthur, 3 May 1957
24 To Kathleen McArthur, 12 March 1957
25 A., p. 126
26 Barbara and Charles Blackman, "Jack McKinney", *Bulletin*, 17 December 1966, p. 27
27 According to Barbara Blackman, October 1996
28 A., p. 127
29 "The Poet", C.P., p. 206
30 According to Barbara Blackman, October 1996
31 *Bulletin*, 17 December 1966, p. 27
32 A., p. 158
33 Vivien South (ed), *The Letters of Vance and Nettie Palmer*, National Library of Australia, Canberra, 1977, p. 223
34 According to the Blackmans, *Bulletin*, 17 December 1966, p. 27
35 Challenge, p. 106
36 According to the Blackmans, *Bulletin*, 17 December 1966
37 A., p. 136
38 To Kathleen McArthur, 12 November 1959
39 To Kathleen McArthur, 15 January 1957
40 To Kathleen McArthur, 8 May 1956
41 To Kathleen McArthur, 13 March 1986
42 *Sydney Morning Herald*, 19 June 1958
43 To Kathleen McArthur, 8 May 1956
44 A., p. 139

45 Drusilla Modjeska, *Exiles at Home: Australian Women Writers 1925–45*, Angus & Robertson, Sydney, 1981, p. 177
46 ibid.
47 ibid., p. 191
48 To Kathleen McArthur, 12 August 1954
49 A., p. 140
50 *Cleo*, December 1972
51 To Kathleen McArthur, 24 February 1959
52 ibid.
53 ibid.
54 To Kathleen McArthur, 9 May 1955
55 To Kathleen McArthur, Easter Sunday, 1955
56 Drusilla Modjeska, *The Orchard*, Macmillan, Sydney, 1994, p. 4
57 O.H., II, I/25
58 A., p. 153
59 ibid.
60 A., p. 131
61 ibid.
62 "Two Songs for the World's End", C.P., p. 107
63 A., p. 133
64 ibid., p. 154
65 "The Precipice", C.P., p. 120
66 Quoted by Joseph Rotblat, "Declaring War on War Itself", *Guardian Weekly*, 4 February 1955
67 A., p. 161
68 *Language*, 1, 1, 1951, p. 1 (National Library, B44, F321)
69 ibid., p. 6
70 Theodor Adorno, *Minima Moralia: Reflections from a Damaged Life*, Verso, London, 1994, pp. 27–8
71 "The Harp and the King", C.P., p. 156
72 ibid., p. 158
73 Fax to me, 16 March 1996
74 In conversation with me, 22 February 1995
75 "Unknown Water", C.P., pp. 109–10
76 Owen Barfield, *Poetic Diction*, London, Faber, 1951, p. 52
77 ibid., p. 75
78 ibid., p. 26
79 A., p. 136
80 Antonie Donat, "François Ponge and the Problem of the Epos", University of Queensland Papers, Faculty of Arts, Brisbane, 1, 6, 1963, p. 37
81 ibid., p. 36
82 ibid.
83 ibid.
84 In conversation with me, February, 1950
85 "For Precision", C.P., p. 129
86 Structure, p. 86
87 "Gum-trees Stripping", C.P., p. 133
88 "The Two Fires", C.P., p. 120
89 "Two Generations", C.P., p. 124
90 "The Vision", C.P., p. 262
91 Barbara Blackman, *Glass after Glass: Autobiographical Reflections*, Viking/Penguin, Ringwood, 1997, pp. 30–1
92 A letter to me, November 1996
93 In conversation with me, January 1997

94 A., pp. 129–30. I owe the other biographical details to Ross Keating, *The Life and Poetry of Francis Barbazon*, unpublished PhD thesis, University of Sydney, 1997
95 Fax to me, 23 October 1996
96 Fax to me, 5 November 1996
97 To Kathleen McArthur, 16 April 1954
98 To Kathleen McArthur, 11 July 1951
99 To Kathleen McArthur, 12 November 1959
100 To Kathleen McArthur, 15 March 1954
101 Kathleen McArthur, "A Tribute to Judith Wright", submitted to Clayton Joyce but unpublished, National Library, B64, F467 (henceforth "Tribute")
102 To Kathleen McArthur, 7 June 1955
103 In conversation with me, February 1996
104 Judith Wright, *Preoccupations In Australian Poetry*, Oxford University Press, Melbourne, 1966, p. xi (henceforth Preoccupations)
105 To Kathleen McArthur, Easter Sunday, 1955
106 To Kathleen McArthur, 12 May 1955
107 Judith Wright, "At The Point", in *Born of the Conquerors*, Aboriginal Studies Press, Canberra, 1961, p. 153
108 To Kathleen McArthur, 16 September 1954
109 "At The Point", p. 154
110 To Kathleen McArthur, 10 September 1955
111 According to Barbara Blackman, October 1996
112 "Tribute", p. 5
113 "Sandy Swamp", C.P., p. 88
114 "Tribute", p. 5
115 Judith Wright, "A Philosophy of Urban Wildlife", Address at the Annual General Meeting of the Wildlife Preservation Society of Australia, Sydney, 1976, p. 6, N.L., B50, F 372
116 A., p. 127
117 ibid., p. 158
118 ibid., p. 145
119 "Seven Songs from a Journey", C.P., p. 135
120 ibid., p. 137
121 A., p. 126
122 "Night", C.P., p. 136
123 "Sea-beach", C.P., p. 138
124 "The Prospector", C.P., p. 136
125 Judith Wright, "The Weeping Fig" in *The Nature of Love*, Melbourne, Sun Books, 1966, p. 137; reprinted in 1997 by ETT Imprint, Sydney.
126 A., p. 178
127 "At Cooloolah", C.P., pp. 140–1
128 "Seven Songs From a Journey", "Mount Mary", C.P., p. 138
129 Preoccupations, p. xviii
130 ibid., p. xvii
131 ibid., p. xxi
132 ibid., p. xviii
133 ibid., p. xix
134 ibid., p. xvii
135 To Kathleen McArthur, 14 October 1951
136 To Kathleen McArthur, no date
137 "At the Point", p. 154
138 ibid., p. 155–6
139 ibid., p. 156
140 A., p. 158

141 ibid., p. 157
142 "Double Image", C.P., p. 196
143 A., p. 149
144 To Kathleen McArthur, 20 August 1956
145 To Kathleen McArthur, 5 October 1956
146 "Old Woman's Song", C.P., p. 194
147 "Age to Youth", C.P., p. 195
148 A., p. 129
149 ibid.
150 ibid.
151 "In Praise of Marriages", C.P., p. 152

Chapter IX: Shadow

1 "Turning Fifty", C.P., p. 252
2 To me, May 1995
3 Barbara Blackman in conversation with me, October 1996
4 To Barbara Blackman, 10 July 1956
5 ibid.
6 To Kathleen McArthur, 18 September 1956
7 To Kathleen McArthur, 5 October 1956
8 To Kathleen McArthur, 2 February 1957
9 To Barbara Blackman, 18 March 1966
10 "For One Dying", C.P., p. 259
11 "The Vision", C.P., p. 262
12 Introduction to Eunice Hanger, (ed.) *Three Australian Plays*, University of Queensland Press, Brisbane, n.d., p. 18
13 ibid., p. 20
14 To Kathleen McArthur, 24 March 1960
15 To Barbara Blackman, 10 July 1960
16 ibid.
17 To Kathleen McArthur, 13 January 1961
18 ibid.
19 ibid.
20 O.H., II 2/3
21 "Conservation as a Concept", *Wildlife Newsletter,* 16 August 1968
22 *Sydney Morning Herald*, 18 June 1966
23 To Barbara Blackman, 25 April 1959
24 ibid.
25 To Kathleen McArthur, 28 September 1953
26 ibid.
27 To Barbara Blackman, 25 April 1959
28 "The Encounter", C.P., p. 220
29 To Barbara Blackman, 12 July 1964
30 "The Curtain", C.P., p. 216
31 Barbara Blackman to me, October 1996
32 To Kathleen McArthur, 4 July 1962
33 "The Other Half", C.P., p. 215
34 To Barbara Blackman, 12 July 1964
35 "Homecoming", C.P., p. 228
36 "Power", C.P., p. 222
37 "Autumn Fires", C.P., p. 211

38 O.H., IX 1/14
39 "The Vision", C.P., p. 263
40 O.H., IX, 1/15
41 "Reading Thomas Traherne", C.P., p. 206
42 O.H., IX, 1/15
43 O.H., VI, 1/17
44 O.H., VI, 1/18
45 "Love Song In Absence", C.P., p. 262
46 "The Vision", C.P.,p.263
47 In conversation with me, February 1996
48 Barbara Blackman, *Glass After Glass: Autobiographical Reflections*, Viking/Penguin, Melbourne, 1997, p. 31
49 O.H., VI, 1/17
50 "Wings", C.P., p. 284
51 In conversation with me, February 1996
52 "The Vision", C.P., p. 263
53 "Eurydice in Hades", C.P., p. 264–5
54 "For One Dying", C.P., p. 259–60
55 "Turning Fifty", C.P., p. 252
56 "Habitat", IX, C.P., p. 309
57 "Habitat", VI, C.P., p. 305
58 "Rosina Alcona to Julius Brenzaida", C.P., p. 282–3
59 *Australian Women's Weekly*, 16 December 1964
60 In conversation with Rodney Hall, February 1997
61 Kathie Cochrane, *Oodgeroo*, University of Queensland Press, Brisbane, 1994, p. 165 (henceforth Cochrane)
62 ibid., p. 166
63 ibid.
64 ibid., p. 172
65 ibid., pp. 172–3
66 ibid., p. 173
67 ibid.
68 N.L., B71, F511
69 In conversation with me, May 1996.
70 ibid.
71 Preoccupations, p. xix
72 J. P. McKinney, *The Structure of Modern Thought*, Chatto & Windus, London, 1971, p. 65
73 "Advice to a Young Poet", C.P., p. 269–70
74 N.L. B44, F382
75 *Sydney Morning Herald*, 13 November 1965, p. 20
76 J. P. McKinney, *The Challenge of Reason*, Mountain Press, Brisbane, 1950, p. 7
77 O.H., VII, 2/5
78 "Tool", C.P., p. 266
79 *Australian Women's Weekly*, 16 December 1964
80 To Kathleen McArthur, 23 December 1964
81 O.H., VII, 2/11
82 *Courier Mail*, 3 November 1964
83 *Sydney Morning Herald*, 3 November 1964
84 Evan Jones, *Nation*, 16 May 1964
85 *Courier Mail*, 4 September 1967
86 R. F. Brissenden, "Judith Wright's Art", *Australian*, 5 November 1966, p. 8
87 Dorothy Green, "Judith Wright's Recurrent Debate," *Canberra Times*, 8 October 1966, p. 11

88 O.H., VII, 1/20
89 "At A Poetry Conference, Expo '67", C.P., p. 270 (henceforth "At A Poetry Conference")
90 O.H., VIII, 1/22
91 *Montreal Gazette*, 9 September 1967
92 "At A Poetry Conference", C.P., p. 270
93 *La Prerse* (Montreal) 7 September 1967 (my translation)
94 ibid.
95 ibid.
96 ibid.
97 *Toronto Telegraph*, 9 September 1967
98 ibid.
99 "At A Poetry Conference", C.P., p. 271
100 *Toronto Star*, 11 September 1967
101 "At A Poetry Conference", C.P., p. 272
102 N.L., B32, F242
103 "At A Poetry Conference", C.P., p. 272
104 O.H., VII, 1/23
105 Antoine Denat, "François Ponge and the New Problem of the Epos", University of Queensland Papers, Faculty of Arts, Volume 1, No 6, University of Queensland Press, Brisbane, 1963
106 "Fire Sermon", C.P., p. 276
107 "Flame-tree in a Quarry", C.P., p. 60
108 "The Flame Tree Blooms", C.P., p. 287
109 "Massacre of the Innocents", C.P., p. 278
110 "Christmas Ballad", C.P., p. 277
111 "Weapon", C.P., p. 281
112 O.H., VI, 2/6
113 "The City", C.P., p. 275
114 O.H., VII, 1/14
115 Letter from Vincent Serventy to Judith Wright, 22 October 1965. In the WPSQ Archives (henceforth Archives)
116 From Francis Ratcliffe, 11 July 1967, N.L., B15, F102
117 To Francis Ratclife, 11 July 1967, N.L., B15, F102
118 To Kathleen McArthur, 7 June 1967
119 To Barbara Blackman, 18 March 1966
120 C.B., p. xiv
121 ibid.
122 ibid., pp 2–3
123 ibid., p. 4
124 ibid., p. 6
125 ibid.
126 ibid.
127 To Kathleen McArthur, 12 March 1962
128 C.B., pp. 3–4
129 Frank Kermode, *The Sense of An Ending*, Oxford University Press, New York, 1962, p. 102
130 C.B., p. 4
131 Len Webb to Judith Wright, 8 May 1982
132 C.B., p. 4
133 ibid., p. 6
134 "Australia 1970", C.P., p. 287–8
135 C.B., pp 8–9
136 ibid., p. 9
137 ibid., pp. 11–14

Chapter X: Look at the News From the Other Capitals

1 O.H., IX, 1/26
2 "Tool", C.P., p. 266
3 O.H., IX, 1/26
4 "The City", C.P., p. 275
5 "Letter", C.P., p. 285
6 Judith Wright, "Conservation as a Concept", *Wildlife Newsletter*, 16, 3, 1968, p. 7
7 To Brian Sweeney, 27 December 1967
8 ibid.
9 O.H., IX, 2/1
10 O.H., IX, 2/3
11 ibid.
12 *Quadrant*, January/February 1968
13 O.H., IX, 2/4
14 C.B., p. 28
15 O.H., II, 2/4
16 O.H., IX, 2/7
17 O.H., IX, 2/9
18 To Kathleen McArthur, 29 May 1968
19 O.H., IX, 2/8
20 O.H, X, 1/1
21 O.H., X, 1/3
22 ibid.
23 O.H., X, 1/5
24 O.H., X, 1/6
25 To Kathleen McArthur, 29 May 1968
26 O.H., X, 1/12
27 O.H., X, 1/13
28 To Judith Wright, N.L., B28, F212, 21 June 1968
29 C.B., p. 28
30 Kathleen McArthur, "A Tribute to Judith Wright", p. 3 (henceforth "Tribute")
31 "Jet Flight over Derby", C.P., p. 279
32 "Wings", C.P., p. 284
33 "The Flame-tree Blooms", C.P., p. 287
34 "Massacre of the Innocents", C.P., p. 278
35 O.H., IX, 2/8
36 To Kathleen McArthur, 27 November 1968
37 To Frank Eyre, N.L., B28, F212, 18 August 1968
38 To Qantas, N.L. B28, F212, 8 November 1968
39 "Australia 1970", C.P., p. 287
40 C.B., p. 29
41 Kathleen McArthur, "Tribute", p. 3
42 "Cooloola – A Scandal", *Newsletter of the Caloundra Branch* of the WPSQ, 11 November 1969, p. 3, N.L., B7, F17
43 ibid.
44 ibid.
45 ibid., p. 1
46 ibid., p. 3
47 ibid., p. 2
48 "At Cooloolah", C.P., p. 140
49 Born of the Conquerors, p. 30
50 "Cooloola – A Scandal", p. 2

51 *Newsletter of the WPSQ*, June 1970, N.L., B7, F17
52 N.L., B7, F17
53 O.H., XVI, 1/3
54 *Australian*, 26 November 1969
55 To Kathleen McArthur, 9 February 1966
56 To Barbara Blackman, 18 October 1968
57 ibid.
58 ibid.
59 C.B., p. 31
60 C.B., p. 43
61 ibid.
62 *Australian*, 25 October 1969, p. 15
63 C.B., p. 50
64 "Conservation as a Concept", p. 7
65 *Australian*, 26 November 1969
66 "Conservation as a Concept", p. 6
67 C.B., p. 91
68 ibid., p. 102
69 ibid., p. 50
70 ibid., p. 54
71 ibid., p. 107
72 ibid., p. 108
73 ibid., p. 54
74 ibid., p. 55
75 *Sydney Morning Herald*, 10 January 1970
76 Letter to the Minister, N.L., B28, F213, 14 January 1970
77 Dorothy Green to Judith Wright, N.L., B28, F213, 9 March 1970
78 C.B., p. 108
79 ibid., p. 109
80 "Jet Flight over Derby", C.P., p. 279
81 To Len Webb, 7 June 1979
82 ibid.
83 ibid.
84 "The Dead Astronaut", C.P., p. 280
85 To Len Webb, 7 June 1979
86 Because I Was Invited, p. vi
87 *Australian*, 30 April 1970
88 Finola Moorhead, "A Tribute to Judith Wright", unpublished manuscript, p. 2
89 N.L., B16, F112, 27 July 1970
90 N.L., B17, F118, August 1970
91 N.L., B17, F118
92 ibid.
93 ibid.
94 C.B., p. 96
95 ibid., p. 103
96 ibid., p. 188
97 ibid.
98 ibid., p. 161
99 ibid., p. 104
100 ibid., p. 188
101 ibid., p. 170
102 ibid., p. 172
103 ibid., p. 191

104 ibid., p. 187
105 O.H., XII, 1/3
106 "Wedding Photograph, 1913", C.P., p. 326
107 Bushwhacker, p. 117
108 "Wedding Photograph, 1913", C.P., p. 327
109 "The Slope", C.P., p. 336
110 On a card shown to me
111 "Communication", C.P., p. 289
112 "The Unnecessary Angel", C.P., p. 291

Chapter XI: A Kind of Weaving

1 "Shadow", C.P., p. 292
2 Jean-François Lyotard, *The Inhuman: Reflections on Time*, Polity Press, London, 1991, pp. 6–7
3 *Herald* (Melbourne), 2 September 1970
4 *On Dit*, N.L., B18, F126
5 "The World and the Child", C.P., p. 36
6 O.H., IX, 1/18
7 ibid.
8 O.H., IX, 1/19
9 To Shirley Walker, 14 August 1976
10 "Letter", C.P., p. 285
11 To Kathleen McArthur, 1972 (undated)
12 N.L., B2, F12, 17 March 1972
13 N.L., B2, F12
14 N.L., B2, F12, 25 March 1972
15 N.L., B2, F12, 3 April 1972
16 O.H., X 1/9
17 ibid.
18 N.L., B2, F12, 4 April 1972
19 N.L., B2, F12, 16 April 1972
20 To Kathleen McArthur, 4 April 1972
21 "Black/White", C.P., pp. 335–6
22 "Rosina Alcona to Julius Brenzaida", C.P., p. 282
23 N.L., B15, F102, 3 November 1965
24 Judith Wright, "Conservation as a Concept", *Wildlife Newsletter*, Number 19, August 1968, p. 4
25 N.L., B1, F4, 19 July 1972
26 N.L., B1, F5, November 1972
27 N.L., B1, F4, November 1972
28 N.L., B1, F5, 16 October 1972
29 *Australian*, 2 January 1972
30 N.L., B1, F4
31 To Len Webb, 27 August 1972
32 *Launceston Express*, 25 March 1972
33 To Barbara Blackman, 12 March 1971
34 ibid.
35 N.L., B1, F3, 19 November 1972
36 "Picture", C.P., p. 331
37 "Grace", C.P., p. 331
38 "Good News", C.P., p. 334
39 "Conservation as a Concept", p. 3
40 Len Webb and Bill Williams "Synecology – Cinderella Finds Her Coach", *New Scientist*, 26 July 1973, pp. 195–6

41 "Conservation as a Concept", n.p.
42 "Tableau", C.P., pp. 325–6
43 N.L., B28, F208, 20 March 1972
44 "Advice to a Young Poet", C.P., p. 269
45 Martin Heidegger, *Poetry, Language, Thought*, Harper Colophon, New York, 1975, p. 93
46 ibid., p. 20
47 ibid., p. 12
48 "White Night", C.P., p. 324
49 "To Mary Gilmore", C.P., p. 321
50 N.L., B28, F208
51 To Kathleen McArthur, 22 August 1972
52 Generations, p. 233
53 "At a Public Dinner", C.P., p. 312
54 To Kathleen McArthur, undated 1972
55 "The Slope", C.P., p. 336
56 "The Blind Man", I, "Dust in the Township", C.P., p. 62
57 To Kathleen McArthur, 16 September 1972
58 N.L., B64, F420
59 Born of the Conquerors, p. 13
60 ibid., p. 4
61 ibid.
62 ibid.
63 ibid., p. 7
64 "Two Dreamtimes", C.P., pp. 315–8
65 ibid., p. 316
66 "At Cooloolah", C.P., p. 140
67 H.C. Coombs, *Kulimna: Listening To Aboriginal Australians*, Australian National University Press, Canberra, 1978, pp. 12–13
68 ibid., pp. 15–18
69 N.L., B28, F208
70 N.L., B28, F208, 16 April 1972
71 In conversation with Rodney Hall, January 1997
72 N.L., B28, F208
73 N.L., B28, F208
74 N.L., B28, F208, 16 April 1972
75 N.L., B28, F208, 22 December 1972
76 To Kathleen McArthur, 10 January 1973

Chapter XII: Moving South

1 O.H., V, 1/9
2 To Kathleen McArthur, 18 January 1972
3 ibid.
4 "Geology Lecture", C.P., p. 323
5 N.L., B4, F31
6 N.L., B14, F209
7 "Habitat", I, C.P., p. 298
8 Because I Was Invited, p. 85
9 "Geology Lecture", C.P., p. 323
10 "Moving South", C.P., p. 386
11 To Barbara Blackman, 12 March 1971
12 ibid.

13 Alan Reid, *The Whitlam Venture*, Melbourne, Hill of Content, 1976, pp. 71–2
14 "At a Public Dinner'" C.P., pp. 312–13
15 N.L., B19, F135
16 N.L., B14, F209
17 O.H., XIV, 1/1
18 N.L., B4. F31
19 N.L., B18, F133
20 N.L., B15, F107
21 To Len Webb, 11 June 1973
22 ibid.
23 To Len Webb, 29 May 1973
24 This was either the 1972 ANZAAS Conference in Sydney or the First National Conservation Study Conference in Canberra in 1973
25 "Good News", C.P., p. 334
26 "Poem and Audience", C.P., p. 210
27 N.L., B15, F107, 16 October 1975
28 According to Heather Rusden
29 "Good News", C.P., p. 331
30 To Len Webb, 14 July 1973
31 To Len Webb, N.L., B16, F115, 21 September 1972
32 N.L., B25, F185, 12 May 1973
33 N.L., B25, F185, 15 May 1973
34 N.L., B25, F185, 9 February 1973
35 To Geoffrey Blainey, N.L., B25, F185, 9 February 1973
36 ibid.
37 ibid.
38 N.L., B25, F185
39 N.L., B25, F185, 7 March 1973
40 N.L., B25, F185
41 ibid.
42 N.L., B22, F161
43 N.L., B20, F155
44 N.L., B25, F185, 24 April 1973
45 Tim Rowse, "Post War Australia: A Personal History", *Island*, 12 September 1982, p. 16
46 To Len Webb, 25 February 1973
47 To Len Webb, 29 May 1973
48 O.H., XI, 1/16
49 To Len Webb, 29 May 1973
50 N.L., B24, F178
51 "Party with the Gods", C.P., pp 350–1
52 To Len Webb, 9 July 1973
53 *National Times*, 9–14 July 1973
54 *Australian*, 1 October 1973
55 Fax to me, 22 June 1996
56 ibid.
57 Ross King, "Hobbies, The National Estate and Equity", p. 64
58 ibid.
59 To Kathleen McArthur, 17 November 1974
60 Fax to me, 22 June 1996
61 ibid.
62 N.L., B31, F237

63 According to Barbara Blackman, 29 October 1996
64 "The Dark Ones", C.P., pp. 354–5
65 N.L., B46, F34, undated 1974
66 "The Dark Ones", C.P., p. 355
67 To Len Webb, 9 July 1973
68 "Brief Notes on Canberra", VIII, "Ecological Comment", C.P., p. 354
69 Judith Wright, Foreword to *Collected Poems 1942–1985*
70 *Australian*, 8 December 1973
71 To Kathleen McArthur, 17 November 1973
72 N.L., B16, F116, 10 April 1975
73 ibid.
74 N.L., B16, F116, 17 April 1975
75 N.L., B16, F116, 24 April 1975
76 Patrick White, *A Fringe of Leaves*, London,Cape, 1976, p. 324 (© Patrick White Estate)
77 N.L., B16, F110, 10 April 1975
78 N.L., B16, F110, 14 April 1975
79 N.L., B16, F110, May 1975
80 To Professor Andrews, N.L., B16, F110, 21 April 1975
81 David Marr, *Patrick White: A Life*, Sydney, Random House, 1991, p. 550 (Letter © Patrick White Estate)
82 ibid., p. 551
83 "At a Public Dinner", C.P., p. 312
84 To Barbara Blackman, 12 April 1974
85 To Barbara Blackman, 15 June 1975
86 To Barbara Blackman, 12 November 1974
87 "Turning Fifty", C.P., p. 252
88 "Tightropes", C.P., p. 343
89 "Space Between", C.P., pp. 314–15
90 *Australian*, 9 June 1975, p. 3
91 "Grace", C.P., p. 331
92 To Barbara Blackman, 15 June 1975
93 ibid.
94 ibid.
95 "Moving South", C.P., p. 386
96 To Barbara Blackman, 12 November 1974
97 "For the Quaternary Age", C.P., p. 363
98 To Barbara Blackman, 12 November 1974
99 ibid.
100 ibid.
101 ibid.
102 "At Cedar Creek", C.P., p. 380
103 To Barbara Blackman, 12 November 1974
104 Stewart Harris, "A Tribute to Judith Wright", unpublished manuscript
105 To Kathleen McArthur, 19 December 1975
106 O.H., XII, 1/10
107 "Growing-point", C.P., p. 366
108 O.H., XI, 1/20
109 ibid.
110 O.H., VI, 1/24
111 To Len Webb, 12 March 1973
112 "Fourth Quarter", C.P., p. 341
113 O.H., VI, 1/24
114 "Easter Moon and Owl", C.P., pp. 341–2

115 "Poem and Audience", C.P., p. 210
116 "Easter Moon and Owl", C.P., p. 342
117 N.L., B26, F191
118 *Times Literary Supplement*, 9 March 1976
119 O.H., XI, 1/20
120 "Falls Country", C.P., pp 328–9
121 N.L., B48, F362
122 Finola Moorhead, "A Tribute to Judith Wright", unpublished manuscript
123 O.H., XI, 1/2
124 To Barbara Blackman, 15 June 1975
125 "For a Pastoral Family", V, "Change", C.P., p. 409
126 In the archives of the WPSQ, Brisbane
127 "This Time Alone", C.P., p. 260
128 To Kathleen McArthur, 19 January 1975
129 "Moving South", C.P., p. 387

CHAPTER XIII: TOWARDS A TREATY: A JUSTER JUSTICE

1 N.L., B33, F240, March 1976
2 Carolyn Heilbrun, *Writing a Woman's Life*, Ballantyne Books, New York, 1988, p. 128
3 "Patterns", C.P., pp. 376–7
4 O.H., VI, 1/23
5 To Barbara Blackman, 10 October 1978
6 ibid.
7 "Twenty-five Years", C.P., p. 377
8 To Barbara Blackman, 24 June 1976
9 ibid.
10 ibid.
11 O.H., XIV, 2/11
12 Born of the Conquerors, p. 7
13 To Barbara Blackman, 1 March 1980
14 To Kath Walker, 11 August 1975
15 Stewart Harris, *It's Coming Yet*, The Aboriginal Treaty Committee, Canberra, 1979, p. 31 (henceforth Harris)
16 ibid., p. 24
17 ibid., p. 57
18 ibid.
19 ibid., p. 24
20 ibid., p. 5
21 ibid., p. 6
22 ibid., p. 24
23 ibid., p.25
24 ibid., p. 26
25 ibid., p. 25
26 Kathie Cochrane, *Oodgeroo*, University of Queensland Press, Brisbane, 1994, pp. 105–10
27 "Two Dreamtimes", C.P., p. 317
28 O.H., XV, 1, 23
29 Born of the Conquerors, p. 47
30 ibid., p. 98
31 To Len Webb, 9 July 1978
32 To Len Webb, 12 August 1978
33 To Len Webb, 9 July 1978
34 "Case-moth", C.P., p. 365

35 "Brennan", C.P., p. 403
36 To Len Webb, November 1976
37 To Peter Skrzynecki, November 1978
38 Patrick White, "The Prodigal Son", *Australian Letters*, I, 1
39 To Peter Skrzynecki, November 1978
40 According to Barbara Blackman, October 1996
41 According to Rodney Hall, January 1997
42 "Remembering Michael", C.P., p. 355
43 Judith Wright, "Report on Visit to New Zealand Under Senior Anzac Fellowship, 1976, N.L., B24, F180
44 To Barbara Blackman, 24 June 1976
45 ibid.
46 ibid.
47 "Four Poems from New Zealand", III, "Entertainment", C.P., p. 395
48 ibid.
49 "Four Poems from New Zealand", II, "In The Railcar", C.P., p. 394
50 "Four Poems from New Zealand", I, "From the Wellington Museum", C.P., p. 393
51 To Barbara Blackman, 24 June 1976
52 "Four Poems from New Zealand", IV, "The Beach at Hokitika", C.P., p. 396
53 *National Times*, 13 October 1977
54 *Canberra Times*, 1 February 1977
55 To Len Webb, 1 November 1977
56 To Len Webb, February 1977
57 ibid.
58 O.H., XIV, 1/5
59 To Len Webb, undated
60 "Interface (III)", C.P., P. 345
61 O.H. XVIII, 1/22
62 To Len Webb, 5 July 1977
63 ibid.
64 To Len Webb, 23 July 1977
65 To Len Webb, 22 November 1977
66 To Len Webb, 4 November 1977
67 To Len Webb, 4 January 1978
68 To Len Webb, 28 January 1978
69 To Len Webb, 22 November 1977
70 To Len Webb, 28 January 1978
71 ibid.
72 "Lament for Passenger Pigeons", C.P., p. 319
73 To Len Webb, 28 January 1978
74 ibid.
75 To Len Webb, 12 May 1978
76 ibid.
77 To Len Webb, 17 June 1978
78 ibid.
79 ibid.
80 N.L., B29, F221
81 N.L., B46, F347
82 *Australian*, 24 October 1978
83 N.L., B36, F272
84 "Oppositions", C.P., p. 422
85 N.L., B36, F272
86 ibid.

87 Cutting in N.L., B46, F347, undated
88 Stewart Harris, "A Tribute to Judith Wright", unpublished manuscript, p. 2, (henceforth "Tribute")
89 To Len Webb, 1 March 1978
90 "Tribute", p. 61
91 To Barbara Blackman, 10 June 1979
92 Cochrane, p. 95
93 "Tribute", p. 3
94 To Barbara Blackman, 10 June 1978
95 "Two Dreamtimes", C.P., p. 315
96 N.L., B44, F331
97 ibid.
98 ibid.
99 To Len Webb, 3 August 1979
100 N.L., B30, F222
101 Nonie Sharp, *No Ordinary Judgement*, Aboriginal Studies Press, Canberra, 1996, p. 16 (henceforth Sharp)
102 To Len Webb, 3 August 1979
103 "Books in the Age of Admass", in *Going on Talking*, p. 4
104 To Len Webb, 3 August 1979
105 "Tribute", p. 3
106 According to a Treaty Committee member
107 "Tribute", p. 5
108 Cutting in N.L., B24, F181, no date
109 "Eve Scolds", C.P., p. 359
110 "Cold Night", C.P., p. 375
111 "Twenty-five Years", C.P, p. 377
112 "Woman in Orchard", C.P., p. 375–6
113 To Len Webb, 1 March 1986
114 ibid.
115 ibid.
116 To Barbara Blackman, 17 February 1980
117 ibid.
118 O.H., VIII, 1/14
119 Cochrane, pp. 112–13
120 O.H., VIII, 1/14
121 Jim Davidson (ed.), *Sideways From the Page: The Meanjin Interviews*, Fontana/Collins, Sydney, 1983, pp. 57–8
122 N.L., B47, F356
123 To Barbara Blackman, 10 June 1980
124 To Len Webb, 9 November 1980
125 ibid.
126 N.L., B36, F276
127 ibid.
128 ibid.
129 To Len Webb, 1 March 1980
130 ibid.
131 To Len Webb, 18 April 1980
132 ibid.
133 ibid.
134 "River Bend", C.P., p. 146
135 "Brevity", C.P., p. 143
136 To Barbara Blackman, 6 March 1981

137 To Barbara Blackman, 1 April 1980
138 To Barbara Blackman, 12 December 1981
139 ibid.
140 Sharp, p. 23
141 ibid.
142 ibid.
143 Harris, p. 38
144 To Barbara Blackman, 12 December 1981
145 O.H. XIV 1/27
146 To Barbara Blackman, 12 December 1981
147 N.L., B47, F354
148 ibid.
149 ibid.
150 To Len Webb, 29 March 1982
151 ibid.
152 Harris, p. 242
153 To Len Webb, 14 April 1982
154 Harris, p. 242
155 To Len Webb, 22 August 1982
156 N.L., B38, F296
157 ibid.
158 To Len Webb, 15 May 1983
159 N.L., B50, F372
160 ibid.
161 To Barbara Blackman, 19 August 1982
162 "Remembering Michael", C.P., pp. 355–6
163 Going on Talking, p. 37
164 ibid., p. 34
165 ibid., p. 27
166 To Barbara Blackman, 19 August 1982
167 N.L., B9, F70
168 *Sydney Morning Herald*, 30 January 1982
169 *Australian*, 22–24 January 1982
170 Cutting in N.L., B13, F99
171 ibid.
172 ibid.
173 ibid.
174 ibid.
175 ibid.
176 To Barbara Blackman, 8 January 1984
177 To Len Webb, 29 March 1982
178 "Rockpool", C.P., p. 419
179 "Victims", C.P., p. 402
180 To Barbara Blackman, 16 March 1983
181 "Dialogue", C.P., p. 313–14

CHAPTER XIV: PHANTOM DWELLING

1 Carolyn Heilbrun, *Writing A Woman's Life*, Ballantyne Books, New York, 1988, p. 124
2 "Glass Corridor", C.P., p. 418
3 To Barbara Blackman, 8 May 1980
4 "Pressures", C.P., p. 424
5 O.H., XVIII, 11/3

6 Martin Heidegger, *Poetry, Language and Thought*, Harper Colophon, New York, 1971, p. 4
7 "Rainforest", C.P., p. 412
8 "Rockface", C.P., p. 420
9 To Len Webb, N.L., B34, F254, 9 May 1983
10 "Rockpool", C.P., p. 419
11 "Winter", C.P., p. 425
12 Harris, p. 110
13 Born of the Conquerors, p. 54
14 ibid., p. 55
15 To Len Webb, 11 September 1983
16 To Barbara Blackman, 1 August 1983
17 To Len Webb, 11 September 1983
18 To Len Webb, 21 January 1983
19 To Len Webb, 25 October 1982
20 "Rainforest", C.P., p. 412
21 To Len Webb, 27 September 1983
22 "Dust", C.P., p. 424
23 To Len Webb, 2 May 1984
24 N.L., B48, F363
25 N.L., B30, F228
26 "Habitat", C.P., p. 306
27 "Seasonal Flocking", C.P., p. 405
28 To Len Webb, 21 January 1983
29 "Connections", C.P., p. 422
30 To Barbara Blackman, 29 June 1982
31 To Barbara Blackman, 23 September 1984
32 Stephen Graubard, *Australia: The Daedalus Symposium*, Angus & Robertson, Sydney, 1985, pp. 32–3
33 ibid., p. 31
34 O.H., XVI, 2/5
35 O.H., XVI, 2/3
36 To Barbara Blackman, 16 May 1984
37 "Brevity", O.H., p. 413
38 "Summer", C.P., p. 421
39 To Sylvia Monk, 28 June 1984
40 *Gold Coast Bulletin*, 28 June 1984
41 To Sylvia Monk, 28 June 1984
42 To John Bligh, 1 August 1984
43 To Barbara Blackman, 13 July 1984
44 N.L., B46, F347
45 N.L., B46, F347, 5 July 1984
46 To Len Webb, 1 August 1984
47 ibid.
48 To Barbara Blackman, 28 October 1984
49 ibid.
50 ibid.
51 To Barbara Blackman, 1 August 1984
52 Because I Was Invited, p. 41
53 ibid., p. 168
54 Going on Talking, p. 36
55 "Words, Roses and Stars", C.P., p. 411
56 N.L., B49, F364
57 To Len Webb, 1 October 1984

58 "Summer", C.P., p. 421
59 N.L., B46, F346
60 N.L., B46, F351
61 To Len Webb, 30 June 1985
62 "The Marks", C.P., p. 374
63 To Len Webb, 17 April 1985
64 To Len Webb, 12 September 1985
65 To Len Webb, 30 June 1985
66 Born of the Conquerors, p. 149
67 To Len Webb, 1 October 1984
68 ibid.
69 ibid.
70 P. R. Hay, "The Environmental Movement: Romanticism Reborne", *Island*, 29, Summer 1986, p. 11
71 "The Lake", C.P., p. 189
72 Judith Wright, quoted by Len Webb, "Modern Affirmations of Ecological Ethics", *Wildlife Australia*, Autumn 1985, p. 31
73 ibid.
74 "The Pool and the Star", C.P., p. 92
75 To Barbara Blackman, 25 June 1981
76 "Counting in Sevens", C.P., p. 385
77 "Skins", C.P., p. 423
78 O.H. XVII, 2/1
79 "Mountain", C.P., p. 413
80 To Len Webb, 3 May 1985
81 "Sonnet", C.P., p. 16
82 To Barbara Blackman, 6 March 1981
83 O.H., XVII, 2/1
84 O.H., XVII, 2/1
85 "Patterns", C.P., p. 426
86 N.L., B61, F446
87 ibid.
88 N.L., B77, F555
89 Judith Wright, "The Case History Of A Shocker", pp. 3–4, N.L., B77, F555
90 N.L., B45, F339
91 ibid.
92 ibid.
93 Born of the Conquerors, p. 77
94 N.L., B62, F455
95 OH, XVIII, 1/23
96 N.L., B66, F476
97 N.L., B62, F452
98 O.H., XVII, 1/18
99 "Rockpool", C.P., p. 419
100 To Kathleen McArthur, 18 October 1985
101 ibid.
102 To Kathleen McArthur, 4 January 1986
103 "Winter", C.P., p. 425
104 "Communication", C.P., pp. 289–90
105 N.L., B42, F320
106 To Kathleen McArthur, 31 March 1987
107 N.L., B58, F423
108 N.L., B59, F428

109 N.L., B61, F449
110 N.L., B66, F476
111 To Len Webb, 12 November 1987
112 ibid.
113 N.L., B49, F366
114 ibid.
115 O.H., VIII, 1/1
116 "For A Pastoral Family" VI, "Kinship", C.P., p. 410
117 To Len Webb, 12 November 1987
118 In conversation with me, October 1996
119 O.H., VIII, 1/11
120 "For a Pastoral Family", V, "Change", C.P., p. 409
121 To Len Webb, 11 January 1988
122 "Habitat", IV, C.P., p. 309
123 To Kathleen McArthur, 3 January 1988
124 ibid.
125 "Habitat", IV, C.P., p. 309
126 To Kathleen McArthur, 3 January 1988
127 ibid.
128 "The Dark Ones", C.P., p. 354
129 To Kathleen McArthur, 3 January 1988
130 Born of the Conquerors, p. 128
131 ibid., p. 133
132 ibid.
133 To Kathleen McArthur, 29 May 1988
134 ibid.
135 N.L., B54, F396
136 N.L., B50, F371
137 N.L., B50, F371
138 To Len Webb, 28 August 1988
139 O.H., XVII, 1/11
140 O.H., XVI, 2/2
141 N.L., B50, F371
142 N.L., B45, F344
143 N.L., B50, F372
144 N.L., B50, F373
145 To Len Webb, 19 June 1989
146 Cochrane, p. 48
147 N.L., B47, F358
148 N.L., B66, F477
149 To Len Webb, 19 June 1989
150 ibid.
151 N.L., B42, F321
152 N.L., B60, F438
153 "To M.R.", C.P., p. 382
154 "Backyard", C.P., p. 397
155 Starhawk, quoted in Carol Pearson, *The Hero Within*, Harper San Francisco, 1989, p. 122

CHAPTER XV: I CHOOSE FIRE – NOT SNOW

1 To Barbara Blackman, 5 June 1990
2 To Barbara Blackman, 10 June 1986
3 "Winter", C.P., p. 425

4 To Marion Firth, *Canberra Times*, 19 March 1994
5 N.L., B50, F372
6 W.B. Yeats, "The Man and The Echo", *Collected Poems*, Macmillan, London, 1971, pp. 393–4
7 "The Company of Lovers", C.P., p. 7
8 To Len Webb, 1 December 1987
9 To Len Webb, N.L., B55, F404, 12 July 1991
10 Cochrane, p. 151
11 To Barbara Blackman, 4 March 1990
12 To Len Webb, N.L., B55, F404, 12 July 1991
13 "For A Pastoral Family", "Change", C.P., p. 409
14 "For A Pastoral Family", "Pastoral Lives", C.P., p. 409
15 To Barbara Blackman, 12 July 1991
16 To Len Webb, 20 November 1991
17 To Kathleen McArthur, 28 October 1990
18 N.L., B61, F443
19 N.L., B61, F443
20 To Kathleen McArthur, 28 October 1990
21 To Barbara Blackman, 4 March 1990
22 To Len Webb, 21 October 1991
23 N.L., B71, F552, 1 December 1990
24 ibid.
25 To Barbara Blackman, 4 March 1990
26 ibid.
27 N.L., B62, F450
28 To Len Webb, 21 October 1991
29 ibid.
30 ibid.
31 To Len Webb, 16 January 1990
32 Because I Was Invited, p. 193
33 To Len Webb, 8 September 1991
34 To Len Webb, 13 September 1991
35 ibid.
36 To Len Webb, 28 October 1991
37 To Len Webb, 8 September 1991
38 To Len Webb, N.L., B75, F561, 4 July 1991
39 ibid.
40 To Elizabeth Lawson, 28 October 1991
41 ibid.
42 Fax to me, August 1996
43 Judith Wright, "A Shaft Of Light", *Island*, Number 47, Winter 1991
44 N.L., B55, F403, 20 November 1991
45 Bain Attwood (ed), *In the Age of Mabo: History, Aborigines and Australia*, Sydney, Allen & Unwin, 1996, p. 71
46 To Len Webb, 17 April 1991
47 ibid.
48 N.L., B75, F542, 3 November 1992
49 To Len Webb, 3 March 1992
50 N.L., B62, F455
51 Harris, p. 3
52 To Len Webb, 3 May 1992
53 N.L., B62, F455, 18 June 1992
54 ibid.
55 N.L., B60, F430, 5 January 1991

56 N.L., B70, F502
57 ibid.
58 N.L., B70, F502, 9 March 1992
59 O.H., XVII, 1/28
60 ibid.
61 N.L., B73, F529, 26 October 1992
62 "Rockface", C.P., p. 420
63 N.L., B64, F470
64 Clayton Joyce (ed), *A Tribute to Patrick White*, Angus & Robertson, Sydney, 1991, p. 12
65 To Len Webb, 4 May 1993
66 *Tallangatta Times*, N.L., B75, F555, 6 February 1992
67 Judith Wright, "The Destruction of Two Rivers", N.L., B60, F430
68 Born of the Conquerors, p. 119
69 ibid., p. 121
70 To Len Webb, 15 April 1992
71 "Rainforest", C.P., p. 412
72 To Len Webb, 6 March 1995
73 ibid.
74 Barbara Blackman, *Glass After Glass: Autobiographical Reflections*, Ringwood, Viking/Pengin, 1997, p. 297
75 "Summer", C.P., p. 421
76 To Len Webb, 15 April 1992
77 To Len Webb, 3 May 1992
78 Network of News For Supporters of Aboriginal Rights, Number 6, January 1992
79 To Len Webb, 3 June 1992
80 "Epacris", C.P., p. 415
81 "Hunting Snake," C.P., p. 411
82 To Len Webb, 14 August 1992
83 ibid.
84 To Barbara Blackman, 30 December 1992
85 To Len Webb, 16 September 1992
86 "Unpacking Books", C.P., p. 388
87 To Len Webb, 14 August 1992
88 "For a Pastoral Family", III "For Today", C.P., p. 407
89 To Len Webb, 14 August 1992
90 To Len Webb, 3 June 1992
91 Attwood, p. 71
92 ibid., p. 12
93 ibid., p. xxxii
94 To Len Webb, undated
95 O.H., XVII, 1/18
96 To Len Webb, 30 December 1992
97 ibid.
98 Yeats, "Easter 1916", *Collected Poems*, p. 204
99 To Len Webb, 30 December 1992
100 ibid.
101 To Len Webb, 4 April 1993
102 Attwood, p. 89
103 ibid., p. 90
104 ibid., p. 91
105 ibid., p. 90
106 ibid., p. 118
107 ibid.

108 ibid.
109 To Len Webb, 20 June 1993
110 To Barbara Blackman, 4 April 1993
111 Cochrane, p. 156
112 To Marion Firth, *Canberra Times*, 9 March 1994
113 ibid.
114 ibid.
115 ibid.
116 Cochrane, p. 218
117 "Canefields", C.P., p. 137
118 Cochrane, p. 217
119 N.L., B64, F470, 8 September 1969
120 Jim Davidson (ed), *Sideways from the Page: The Meanjin Interviews*, Fontana/Collins, Sydney, 1983, p. 64
121 Adam Shoemaker, *Oodgeroo: A Tribute*, p. 150
122 To Kathleen McArthur, undated
123 ibid.
124 "Two Dreamtimes", C.P., pp. 315–18
125 *Canberra Times*, 9 March 1994
126 Cochrane, p. 182
127 ibid.
128 N.L., B73, F528, 22 September 1993
129 ibid.
130 N.L., B78, F566, 18 October 1993
131 To Len Webb, 16 May 1993
132 To Milo Dunphy, 20 June 1993
133 To Len Webb, 5 January 1993
134 "Bid Me Strike a Match and Blow", C.P., pp. 322–3
135 In conversation with me, September 1996
136 To Len Webb, 5 April 1994
137 To Len Webb, 5 January 1993
138 Val Plumwood, "Wilderness Scepticism and Wilderness Dualism", in J. Callicot and M. Nelson (eds), *The Great New Wilderness Debate*, University of Georgia Press, Atlanta, 1996, p. 19
139 To Len Webb, 5 January 1993
140 ibid.
141 "The Vision", C.P., p. 263
142 "For Precision", C.P., p. 129
143 To Len Webb, 9 June 1994
144 Yeats, "Under Ben Bulben", C.P., p. 401
145 Richard Glover, *Sydney Morning Herald*, 26 June 1993
146 "Unpacking Books", C.P., p. 388
147 To Len Webb, 3 March 1994
148 ibid.
149 "Unpacking Books", C.P., p. 389
150 ibid.
151 According to a local resident
152 "After The Visitors", C.P., p. 378
153 To Len Webb, 14 July 1994
154 To Kathleen McArthur, 6 June 1994
155 *Canberra Times*, 19 March 1994
156 To Len Webb, 14 July 1994
157 ibid.
158 "Request to a Year", C.P., p. 152

159 To Barbara Blackman, 12 March 1994
160 ibid.
161 ibid.
162 "For a Pastoral Family", VI, "Kinship", C.P., p. 410
163 *Notes and Furphies; Bulletin Of The Association For The Society of Australian Literature*, Number 35, October 1995, p. 3
164 To Barbara Blackman, 16 June 1994
165 Anne Edgeworth to Judith Wright, 19 September 1995
166 "For One Dying", C.P., pp. 259–60
167 To Judith Wright, 19 September 1995
168 T.S.Eliot, *Four Quartets*, "East Coker", V, Faber and Faber, London, p. 22
169 To Len Webb, 30 November 1995
170 To Len Webb, 9 November 1995
171 "The Morning of the Dead", V, "The End", C.P., p. 209
172 *Australian Author*, 24, Summer 1996, p. 4
173 Fax to me, 20 October 1995
174 *Canberra Times*, 19 March 1994
175 Going on Talking, p. 105
176 ibid.
177 To Barbara Blackman, 24 January 1996
178 ibid.
179 ibid.
180 To Barbara Blackman, 2 March 1996
181 To Len Webb, 17 August 1996
182 C.B., p. ix
183 "Seasonal Flocking", C.P., p. 405
184 To Anne Edgeworth, 20 September 1996
185 *Sydney Morning Herald*, 10 October 1996
186 To Len Webb, 18 October 1996
187 To Elizabeth Lawson, 21 January 1996
188 Fax from Norman Abjorson to Judith Wright, 9 October 1996
189 Fax to Norman Abjorson, 9 October 1996
190 *Canberra Times*, 25 October 1996
191 ibid.
192 *Australian Book Review*, December/January 1996/97
193 "They", C.P., p. 349
194 Cecily Parker in the *Canberra Times*, 29 October 1996
195 *Australian*, 6 November 1996
196 Fax to me, 15 November 1996
197 To Len Webb, 8 January 1997
198 ibid.
199 ibid.
200 To Len Webb, 7 May 1997
201 Born of the Conquerors, p. 49
202 ibid.
203 Yeats, "Under Ben Bulben", *Collected Poems*, p. 400
204 *Canberra Times*, 23 January 1997
205 To Len Webb, 8 January 1997
206 ibid.
207 To Len Webb, 17 December 1996
208 "Envy", C.P., p. 383
209 Yeats, "The Man and the Echo", *Collected Poems*, p. 394
210 To Len Webb, 11 February 1997

211 "Brief Notes on Canberra", VII, "Ecological Comment", C.P., p. 351
212 Fax to me, 28 April 1997
213 *Canberra Times*, 24 April 1997
214 "Two Dreamtimes", C.P., p. 316
215 "Prayer", C.P., p. 229
216 To Rosemary Dobson, N.L., B42, F319, undated
217 "Envy", C.P., p. 383
218 To Rosemary Dobson, 2 September 1991
219 "Envy", C.P, p. 383
220 To Len Webb, 8 January 1997
221 To Rosemary Dobson, 15 June 1997
222 To Len Webb, 8 January 1997
223 "Wishes", C.P., p. 225
224 "In Praise of Marriages", C.P., p. 152
225 Yeats, "Sailing to Byzantium", *Collected Poems*, p. 217
226 To Len Webb, 3 March 1997
227 ibid.
228 ibid.
229 ibid.
230 "Request to a Year", C.P., p. 152
231 To Len Webb, 3 March 1997
232 ibid.
233 "Shadow", C.P., p. 292
234 "Patterns", C.P., p. 426
235 "Song for Winter", C.P., p. 91

INDEX

NOTE: JW=Judith Wright. Titles of books, journals and films appear in *italics*. Titles of poems appear in "double" quotation marks, and titles of articles and essays appear in 'single' quotation marks.

Aboriginal and Torres Strait Islander
    Commission 473, 513
Aboriginal Cultural Centre,
    Mount Tamborine 513
Aboriginal Film Festival, Canberra 414
*Aboriginal Land Rights (Northern Territory)
    Act* 362–3
Aboriginal Studies Press 476
Aboriginal Treaty News 416
Aborigines
    Aboriginal Treaty Committee 54, 349,
        390–3, 395, 401, 402, 408–17, 459, 465
    Albert Wright's interest in 8, 141–2, 143–4
    as stockmen 93, 254, 462
    assimilation policy 305
    atrocities against 376
    censoring of early accounts of treatment 514
    civil rights movement 217
    conference in Lismore (1978) 389
    Coombs works for self-determination 328
    depicted as cannibals on
        Cape of Dreams 475
    dispossession of 10–11, 187–8, 191, 364, 401
    Elkin's and Stanner's study of 54
    gain citizenship in 1967 referendum
        217, 319
    Howard criticises "black-armband school of
        history" 513
    ignored in nuclear tests 168
    impact of Concorde on 290
    in Brisbane 107
    in JW's childhood 32
    in Mount Tamborine region 158
    in New England area 27, 30
    in the work of JW 93–4, 188–91
    "invade" Britain 365
    JW on the white perception of 336, 451
    land rights 308–9, 313, 362–3, 364–5,
        389, 413–18, 427, 440, 449–51, 454, 455,
        492, 518
    leaders criticise Hawke 440
    lecture tour by Aboriginal women 497–8
    literature 330
    Mary Gilmore's feelings for 74
    massacres of 8, 92–3
    McKinney's attitude towards 162
    medicine 386
    mining on land of 295, 363
    occupation of National Parks 443
    occupation of Old Parliament House 478
    painting and dance popularised 329
    pitch tent on Capital Hill 393
    removal of children from parents 392, 522
    seminar in Canberra (1973) 328–9
    sovereignty 464–5
    spiritual beliefs 132
    strike at Pilbara 254
    strike by Gurindiji people 309
    tent embassy, Canberra 309–10
    unable to own land in Queensland 305
    Walker establishes Moongalba 306–7
    white law versus Aboriginal law 464–5
    white perceptions of (1938) 68–9
    wilderness versus Aborigines 403, 417–18,
        442, 443, 449, 466, 471, 498–9, 500
    Woodward Report on 363
    Wreck Bay community granted freehold 450
Abschol 304, 310

Academy of Sciences 367
Adams, Philip 313
Adelaide Festival of Arts 245, 274, 369, 420, 502
Adorno, Theodor 150–1, 171
"Advice to a Young Poet" (Wright) 220, 300
"After the Visitors" (Wright) 504
Age 72, 379, 396–7, 401, 421, 422
"The Age of Anxiety" (Auden) 123
"Age to Youth" (Wright) 197
Ahlquist, Jane 456
AIDEX Trade Exhibition 479
The Air-conditioned Nightmare (Miller) 170, 207–8
Air Raid Precautions Centre 82–3, 85
Alaska Native Review Commission 416
Albert by-election (1970) 273
aliens, in Australia 80
"Alive" (Wright) 297
Alive (Wright) 300, 466
"All Things Conspire" (Wright) 130–1
Alpha Mining 361
American Academy of Arts and Sciences 433
American troops, in Australia 103, 109
Amex 391
Amnesty International 416
Anderson, John 51, 75
Angry Penguins 108
Angus & Robertson 134, 178, 327, 434, 466, 473, 512, 524
Anthology of Australian Poetry 166
Anthony, Doug 264
anti-Semitism 65, 75
ANU Reporter 387
ANZAAS Conferences 294, 321, 454
apartheid 310
Archer River, Queensland 417
Argonaut's Club 48
Argus 113
Armidale Arts Festival 369
Armidale School 42, 44
Armistice Day (1918) 2–4
Arrente people 478
Arthurs and Marthas (conservative writers) 109
Asan World Prize, for poetry 435
ASIO 155, 314–15, 479, 514–17
Aslanides, Tim 353
Association for the Study of Australian Literature 419, 438, 506–7
Association of Science Teachers, Queensland 289
Astley, Thea 110, 134, 481
"At a Poetry Conference, Expo '67" (Wright) 224, 225, 227, 228
"At a Public Dinner" (Wright) 302, 319, 341
"At Cedar Creek" (Wright) 348
"At Cooloolah" (Wright) 190, 260
atomic bombs 111, 120–1, 124, 127, 167–8, 318, 448, 527
ATSIC 473, 513
Auchterlonie, Dorothy *see* Green, Dorothy (née Auchterlonie)
Auden, W.H. 64, 122
"Australia 1970" (Wright) 239, 258, 324
Australia Council 313–14, 320, 325–6, 328–9, 372, 510
"Australia" (Hope) 387
Australia Post 482
Australian 241, 264–5, 266–8, 294, 332–3, 387, 393, 421, 497
The Australian Aborigines ... (Elkin) 132
Australian Book Review 515, 516
Australian Broadcasting Commission (later Corporation) 70, 152, 154, 241, 266
Australian Committee for Cultural Freedom 155
Australian Conservation Foundation
    Barwick as president of 275
    campaigns to save Fraser Island 339
    Coombs as president of 377
    holds symposium about Barrier Reef 265
    JW addresses National Conference 429, 461–2
    JW as a foundation member 211, 233–4
    JW pushes for Aboriginal member of 438
    JW threatens to resign from 293
    old boy network in 332–3
    policy on Aboriginal rights 474
    policy towards Concorde 293–4
    Ratcliffe's view of role of 292
    WPSQ affiliates with 234
Australian Council of Churches 416
Australian Council of Heritage Trusts 366
Australian Defence Force Academy 448
Australian Heritage Commission 334
Australian Institute of Aboriginal Studies 415
Australian Labor Party 155, 311–12, 417, 437–8, 455
    see also Hawke government; Whitlam government
Australian National Review 69, 73–4, 75, 96–7, 108, 109
Australian National University 369, 473, 478, 504
Australian Peace and Development Institute 417

Australian Quarterly 72, 73, 75, 78, 97
Australian Security Intelligence Organisation 155, 314–15, 479, 514–17
Australian Society of Authors 325, 327, 372, 466, 510, 521
Australian Universities' Language and Literature Association 369
Australian Women's Weekly 222
autecology 298
"Autumn Fires" (Wright) 210
Avis Rent-A-Car 240
Avon Downs (property) 7, 11

Baba, Meher 176
"Bachelor Uncle" (Wright) 34
"Backyard" (Wright) 467
Bacon, Francis 137
Badger, Colin 117
Badgery, Colin 75
Ball, McMahon 340
Ballad Bookshop 134
Barbazon, Francis 176–7
Barbour, Lyndall 55
Barfield, Owen 126, 136–7, 173
Barjai 109–10, 134, 175
Barnard, Marjorie 177
Barnes, Dr (medical researcher) 240
Barry, John 269
Barunga Festival 455
Barwick, Diane 390
Barwick, Garfield 275, 377
Bashō 446–7
bauxite mining 418
Bayer, Thomas 416
Baylebridge, William 223
Bean, C.E.W. 112
The Beatles 208–9, 222
Because I Was Invited (Wright) 351, 369, 438
Bedford, Randolph 104
Bell, Hedley 311
Bellamy, David 429
Bert (property developer) 183–4
Best, Ysola 459, 513
Betjeman, John 178
Bicentenary (1988) 414, 440, 454, 456, 459, 461
Bickham (property) 7, 9
"Bid Me Strike a Match and Blow" (Wright) 297, 499
Bigg, Alfred Edward 17
Bigg, Ethel *see* Wright, Ethel (née Bigg)
Bigg, Henry Edward 16
Birch, Charles 238

"Birds" (Wright) 129–30
Birds (Wright) 174
Bjelke-Petersen, Joh
  approves land-clearing 187
  attacks civil rights 243
  claims sympathy with Aboriginal writers 414
  conservationists campaign against 339
  declares Archer River area a national park 417
  expediency over development of Cooloola 262
  industrial policy 451
  JW on 437
  long reign of 243, 248, 355
  receives honorary doctorate 496
  resents Federal intervention 306
Black Line 517
Black September 348
"Black/White" (Wright) 291–2
Blackburn, Justice 363, 364, 409, 410
Blackman, Barbara (née Patterson)
  as member of the Barjais 109–10
  friendship with JW 419
  gives JW a birthday party 343–4
  gives JW tablecloth 153
  JW asks advice of re painters 407, 408
  JW's correspondence with 200–1, 206–7, 208, 234, 263, 276–7, 296, 341, 342, 345, 372, 393, 408, 419, 471, 472, 473, 484, 492, 511
  looks after Calanthe for JW 175, 195–6
  moves to Melbourne 134–5
  notices rapport between JW and Poignant 457
  on Jack McKinney 161, 162
  on JW's impatient courage 499–500
Blackman, Charles
  as a painter 198, 407, 498
  contributes painting to Barrier Reef fund 269
  gives JW a birthday party 343–4
  looks after Calanthe for JW 175, 195–6
  moves to Melbourne 134
  on Jack McKinney 161, 162
  suffers Brisbane's provincialism 135
  wishes to see Barrier Reef 234
Blainey, Geoffrey 124, 326, 328, 433, 434, 491
Blake, William 1
Blaxland Galleries 408
Bligh, John 354, 509
"The Blind Man" (Wright) 303
Bliss (Carey) 420

Bogong 454
Bolton, Alec 380
"The Bones Speak" (Wright) 135–6
Bonner, Neville 364
A Book of Australian Verse 176
Bookshow (television program) 481
Boornong Mumba 304
"Bora Ring" (Wright) 93–4, 219, 494–5
Borbridge, Rob 518
Borcheu, George 110
Boreen Point 182–3, 192–3
Born of the Conquerors (Wright) 447, 476, 524
Bourke, Robert O'Hara 113
Boyd, Arthur 134, 135, 171, 408
Boyer Lectures 319
Brady, Jim 310, 495
Braidwood 486–7, 504
Braidwood Festival 464
Breedon, Kay 231
Breedon, Stan 231, 233
Brennan, Chris 274
Brennan, Justice 489
"Brennan" (Wright) 369
"Brevity" (Wright) 407, 435
"Brief Notes on Canberra" (Wright) 337, 521
"Brigalow Country" (Wright) 187–8
Bringing Them Home 392
Brisbane 102–7
Brisbane Public Library 116
Brissenden, R.F. 223–4
British Broadcasting Corporation 163
British Overseas Airways Corporation 290
Brontë sisters 216
Brooks, David 353
Brown, Bob 437
Brown, Cecil 85
Brownbill, George 323, 436
Buckley, Vincent 137, 170, 220, 221, 354
"The Builders" (Wright) 129
Bulletin 30, 73, 96, 97, 108, 154, 189, 206
"Bullocky" (Wright) 133
Bungle Bungle 442, 449
Burke, Brian 414–15, 427, 441, 454
Burnet, Macfarlane 265, 311, 338
Burnum Burnum 456
Burraston, Mr (stockman) 16
The Bush (O'Dowd) 133
"The Bushfire" (Wright) 136
Büsst, Alison 236, 238, 250, 267–9, 278, 303, 422
Büsst, John 236, 238, 240, 241, 253–5, 258, 277–9, 512

Cairns, Jim 318, 333
Calanthe (house) 149–50, 153, 158–9, 175, 215–16, 244–5, 255–6, 263, 286, 317–18, 356, 458–9
"A Call to Arms" (Wright) 44
Callaghan, Barry 226–7
Callaghan, James 365
Camilleri, Joe 418
Campaign Against Nuclear Power 380–1
Campaign to Save Native Forests 314
Campbell-Brown, Kathleen 249
Campbell, David 108, 340
Canberra Times 349, 376, 465, 469, 510–11, 515, 517, 519, 521
"Canefields" (Wright) 188, 494
Cape of Dreams (television program) 475
Cape York Space Port 471, 472
Capp, Fiona 354
Captain Quiros (Spender) 156
Carcanet Press 480
Cardale, Grace 61
Carey, Alex 403–4
Carey, Peter 420
Carson, Rachel 237
"Case-moth" (Wright) 368
Cass, Moss 314, 316, 320, 338, 339
Cassab, Judy 439
Cato, Nancy 276
Cavanagh, Senator 320
Caxton Press 372
Centenary of Federation 475
Central Intelligence Agency 155
Central Land Council 363
Ceylon 14–15
Chalker, Ted 24
The Challenge of Reason (McKinney) 162–3
Chamberlain, Neville 63, 75
Chatto & Windus 280
chemical accidents 448
Chernobyl 448
Chifley government 154
"Child and Wattle-tree" (Wright) 36–7
"The Child" (Wright) 39–40
Children by Choice 483
China 154, 313
Chiron College, Birchgrove 343–4
Christesen, C.B.
   accused of being a communist 155, 156–7, 515
   as editor of *Meanjin* 74, 98–100, 107–9, 112, 117
   as radio broadcaster and poet 96–7
   character 107–8

correspondence with JW 89
falls out with JW 117
invites JW to stay in Brisbane 103
McKinney's correspondence with 118, 119, 122, 129
negotiates over JW's first collection of poetry 132–3
personal library 116
publishes *The Moving Image* 153
Christesen, Nina 103, 107, 155, 156–7
"Christmas Ballad" (Wright) 230
Christopher Brennan Society 369, 385
Citizens Campaign Against Concorde 289
"The City" (Wright) 232, 242, 243–4
Clark, Axel 421
Clark, Dymphna 390, 408, 514
Clark, Manning 112, 257, 311, 340, 384, 434, 453, 513–14
Cleo 166
Clouston, Brian 231, 232
Clunies-Ross, Jeannie 73
coal miners' strike (late 1940s) 154
Coe, Isabel 478
Coe, Paul 364–5
Coffs Harbour 86
Cohen, Bill 393–4, 457
Cohen, Jack 93, 457
"Cold Nights" (Wright) 397
Cold War 182, 457, 515, 516
Collected Poems (Wright) 197, 221, 284, 466, 480, 524, 526
Collected Works (Shelley) 31
Collins Dove 441
Collinson, Laurie 110
colonialism 154
Columbia University demonstration 252
Comfort, Alex 112, 133
Commitee for Un-American Activities 155
Commonwealth Games, Brisbane (1982) 413
Commonwealth Repatriation Training Scheme 125
Commonwealth Writers' Week, Brisbane (1982) 413
"Communication" (Wright) 282–3, 452–3
communism and anti-communism 111, 145, 154–7, 515
Communist Party of Australia 155, 515
"The Company of Lovers" (Wright) 83, 470
"Conch-shell" (Wright) 131
Concorde 288–91, 293–4, 296, 320
Conference on Land Rights and the Future of Race Relations (1981) 522
"Connections" (Wright) 432

Connell, Des 236
Connell, Joe 258
Connor, Rex 320–1, 338, 339–40
conscription 19
conservation *see* Australian Conservation Foundation; environmentalism; Wildlife Protection Society of Queensland
'Conservation as a Concept' (Wright) 293, 298–9
conservatism 134–5
Continental Shelf (Living Natural Resources) Act (1968) 264
Continuing the Journey . . . 416
Conzinc Rio Tinto 262, 292, 311, 363
Cook, Ray 408
Cooloola 259–63, 289, 321, 332
"The Cooloola Conservation Song" 261–2
Coombs, Nugget
  accuses Hawke of betrayal of trust 450
  as chair of Australia Council 313, 320
  as leader of Council for Aboriginal Affairs 309
  as member of Aboriginal Treaty Committee 54, 390–1, 393, 401, 402, 409–10, 412, 415, 421, 428
  at Kununurra Conference 453–4
  elected president of ACF 377
  fights for Aboriginal rights 319, 328
  friendship with JW 303, 319, 482, 504
  gives evidence against drilling Barrier Reef 305–6
  health problems 509, 510, 524–5
  invites JW to lunch with Cowan 308
  involvement in Aboriginal issues after Whitlam 368–9
  JW speaks in place of at ACF 429
  on the meaning of economy 405, 462
  opposes Ranger uranium mine 387
  rebuked by JW for sexism 396
  rebukes government on Aboriginal affairs 427
  spends time in Northern Territory 386, 453, 504
  supports establishment of Copyright Council 326
  supports JW's case against technological determinism 397
  tries to organise indigenous people's summit 478
  view of economics 483
  visited by JW in the Northern Territory 472, 488
  Whitlam's praise for 319

writes final report of indigenous rights
conference 416–17
Copyright Act 432
Copyright Council 326–7, 372
The Coral Battleground (Wright) 234–5,
278–9, 369, 378, 382, 512, 517, 524
Cornford, John 64
Costello, Peter 491
Council for Aboriginal Affairs 305–6, 309,
310, 319
Council of All Beings 463
"Counting in Sevens" (Wright) 445
Country Press Association 113
"Country Town" (Wright) 112–13
Country Towns (Wright) 204
Courier Mail 223, 263, 311, 321, 513
Court, Charles 391, 393, 408
Court, Richard 518
Cowen, Zelman 308, 434
Cowling, G.H. 72–3
CRA 461
Crawford, Alan 55
Croft, Julian 353
The Crucible (McKinney) 114–15
The Cry For The Dead (Wright)
  acknowledges Aboriginal suffering in 513
  as a rework of *Generations of Men* 191,
  302, 366
  JW struggles to write 380–2, 385, 403, 408
  receives no mention at book awards 420
  research for 94, 132, 369, 370, 376, 395, 401,
  442, 514
  reviews of 420–2
cult of feeling 337
"The Curtain" (Wright) 209
Czechoslovakia 252

Dad and Dave 115
Daedalus 433–4
Daintree Rainforest 323, 437, 442
Dalwood (property) 5–6, 13, 301–2, 431
Dark, Eleanor 73
"Dark Gift" (Wright) 146–7
"Dark Ones" (Wright) 335–6, 460
Darwin, Charles 53
Darwin Community College 402
Davidson, Jim 401, 495
Davis, Jack 329, 330, 365, 460
Dawe, Bruce 245, 419, 481
"Dawn Wail" (Walker) 219
The Day the Mountains Played (Wright) 204
de Basil Ballet 74
de Gaulle, Charles 248

"The Dead Astronaut" (Wright) 273
Deane, Justice 489
Delpratt, Madeleine *see* Wright, Madeleine
  (née Delpratt)
Democratic Labor Party 155, 198
Democrats 448
Denat, Antoine 228
Denborough, Michael 473
Depression 47, 48–9, 59, 70, 115
'The Destruction of Two Rivers' (Wright)
482–3
Devaney, James 108, 516
Deveson, Anne 521
Dexter, Barrie 390
"Dialogue" (Wright) 423
diamond industry 442–3
Dicksinson, Sallie 8
Dictionary of Australian Biography 510
Diesendorf, Margaret 353
Dillingham-Murphyores 339
Dinesen, Isak 358–9
Dingo Makes Us Human (Rose) 504
The Dinton-Dalwood letters 13, 62
Dobson, Rosemary 108, 354, 380, 419,
523, 524
Dodson, Michael 411
Dodson, Patrick 411, 454
Dolly, Granny 409
Donnie (Aboriginal boy) 193–4
"Double Image" (Wright) 195
Dougan, John 16
Douglas, Ian 321
Dransfield, Michael 371, 419
Duhig, Dr (*Meanjin* patron) 117
Dumolo, Miss (headmistress) 43
Duncan-Kemp, A.M. 232
Dunphy, Milo 293, 322, 332, 338, 466, 498–9
Dunstan, Don 401
Durack, Elizabeth 179
Durack, Mary 179, 290
"Dust" (Wright) 91, 100, 430
Dutton, Geoffrey 481
Dutton, Nin 340
Dyamberin (property) 32, 457

"Earth" (Wright) 74
East-West Conference, Hawaii (1974)
330–1, 372
"Easter 1916" (Yeats) 490
"Easter Moon and Owl" (Wright) 352, 359
"Ecological Comment" (Wright) 521
Ecology Action 293, 314, 322
economic rationalism 404–5, 430, 482, 522

Ecopolitics Conference,
    Griffith University 449
Edge (property) 349–50, 378, 382–3, 386, 390,
    399, 405, 406, 425–6, 431–2, 448–9, 452,
    473, 486, 511
Edgeworth, Anne 507–9
Education Lending Right scheme 521–2
Edward VII, King of England 13–14, 60
Egremont, Lord 280
Ehrlich, Paul 444
Einstein, Albert 170
Elder, Ann 245
Eldershaw, M. Barnard 73
"Eli, Eli" (Wright) 134, 135
Eliot, George 49
Eliot, T.S. 51, 55
Elizabeth, Queen of England 479–80
Elkin, P.R. 54, 97, 132
Encounter 156
"The Encounter" (Wright) 208, 360
Endean, Bob 268
Endre (Hungarian friend of JW) 66, 67, 76–8
Energy Resources of Australia 517
environmentalism
    see also Australian Conservation
        Foundation; Wildlife Protection Society
        of Queensland; Wright, Judith, as an
        environmentalist; *specific issues, e.g.*
        Great Barrier Reef
    clashes with economic rationalism 404
    wilderness versus Aborigines 403, 417–18,
        442, 443, 449, 471, 498–9, 500
"Envy" (Wright) 520
"Epacris" (Wright) 444, 485
Ern Malley affair 108
Essay on Money (FitzGerald) 73
"Eurydice in Hades" (Wright) 214
Evatt, H.V. 74, 476
"Eve Scolds" (Wright) 396, 397
"Eve Sings" (Wright) 396
The Eye of the Storm (White) 339, 355
Eyre, Frank 178, 257

Falklands War 440
"Falls Country" (Wright) 32–3, 353
Federal Racial Discrimination Act (1975) 476
Federation, fiftieth anniversary of 152
Fellowship of Australian Writers 325, 513
feminism 395–7
Fenner, Frank 265, 340
Fenton, Arthur 255, 267, 277, 279, 303, 512
Fenton, Hilda 267
FIDO 287, 316, 340

Film Australia 307
"Fire Sermon" (Wright) 229
Fisher, Cyril 303
Fitton, Doris 55
FitzGerald, R. D. 73, 89
Five Senses (Wright) 223
"The Flame-tree Blooms" (Wright)
    229–30, 256
"Flame-tree in a Quarry" (Wright) 150,
    151, 229
"The Flame-tree" (Wright) 131
Flashpoint 257
Fleay, David 186, 231, 232
Flying Fox and Drifting Sand (Ratcliffe) 233
"For a Pastoral Family" (Wright) 20, 356, 457,
    458, 470, 488, 506
For love alone (Stead) 60
"For New England" (Wright) 10, 59,
    60–1, 68
"For One Dying" (Wright) 201–2,
    214–15, 508
"For Precision" (Wright) 174, 501–2
"For the Quaternary Age" (Wright) 346–7
Forshaw, Thelma 110
The Foundations of Australian Culture
    (Stephenson) 73
"Four Poems from New Zealand" (Wright)
    373–5
"Four Quartets" (Wright) 509
"Fourth Quarter" (Wright) 351
Fourth Quarter (Wright) 351, 378
Fox Royal Commission 378–9, 380
"Fox" (Wright) 444
Franco, Francisco 57
Franklin, Miles 30, 42, 74, 166
Franklin River 418, 429
Fraser, Eliza 145, 339
Fraser government 410–11
Fraser Island 143–5, 287–9, 316, 322, 323,
    332, 338–41, 345, 377
Fraser Island Defence Organisation 287,
    316, 340
Fraser, Malcolm 341, 363, 386, 465
Frénaud, Andrè 225
French, Leonard 311, 340
A Fringe of Leaves (White) 145, 339
Fizelle, Rah 74

Gallagher, Myrtle 115, 119
"The Garden" (Wright) 33
Gardner, Silvana 354, 429
Garner, Helen 355
Gaudron, Justice 489

The Generations of Men (Wright)
   Albert Wright's musings in 9, 10, 139, 141, 143–4
   based on grandparents' diaries 89
   included in *Collected Poems* 480
   JW on her family's "certain stamp" 302
   JW receives grant to write 130
   JW seeks publisher for 178
   JW struggles to write 164, 204
   May Wright as heroine of 6, 396
   republished (1995) 509–10
   rework of for *Cry For the Dead* 191
"Geology Lecture" (Wright) 297, 315, 317
George VI, King of England 60
Georges, George 381
German Emergency Fellowship Society 53
Germany 63, 75, 78, 80
Gibbs, Justice 365
Gibbs, May 30
"The Gift of Life" (Wright) 40
Gilbert, Kevin 329–30, 365, 392, 400, 412, 440, 460, 480, 492, 494
Gilchrist, Hugh 55
Giles, Barbara 353
Giles, Ernest 450
Gill, Billie 236
Gillies, Max 439
Gilmore, Mary 74, 78, 149, 177, 301, 515
"Glass Corridor" (Wright) 424
global warming 471
Glover, Richard 502
Gold Coast Bulletin 436
'Gone Bush 1989' (Wright) 464
"Good News" (Wright) 297–8, 323–4
Gorbachev, Mikhail 457
Gorton, John 254, 264, 269, 274, 279, 295
Goss, Wayne 471
Grace Leven Prize for poetry 145
"Grace" (Wright) 297, 344
Grano, Paul 74, 109
Grant, Bruce 311, 340
Grassby, Al 409
Grassle, Fred 258
Grattan, Harley 73, 74, 89
Graubard, Stephen 434
Graves, Robert 64
Great Barrier Reef
   campaign to save 234–41, 244, 247, 253–5, 263–70, 321, 338, 443
   declared a Marine National Park 280, 429
   increasing development on 517
   JW publishes *Coral Battleground* 382
   JW raises questions about 335
   JW submits proposal for 320
   JW's first visit to 139
   mining for oil on 472
   pro-mining survey of 258
   public opinion turns against mining 273
   Royal Commission into mining of 276–80
Great Barrier Reef Committee 258, 268
Great Barrier Reef Marine Park Authority 512, 517
Great Waterfront Strike 19
Green, Dorothy (née Auchterlonie)
   attends JW's housewarming party 380
   death 470
   friendship with JW 419
   implores JW to spend more time writing 270, 316
   JW rents old room of 103
   on dualism of human consciousness 224
   on old age 509
   organises conference at Defence Force Academy 448
   sees JW in Canberra 354
   works at ABC 70
Green, H.M. 89
Greenpeace 509
Gribble, Di 395
Griffith University 370
Grigson, John 64
"Growing-point" (Wright) 350–1
Growing Up With Judith (Ahlquist) 456
Guernica (Picasso) 63
Gulf War 472
"Gum-trees Stripping" (Wright) 174
Gurindiji people 309, 362–3

Habitat 466
"Habitat" (Wright) 150, 158–9, 215–16, 284, 317, 431, 458, 459
Haese, Richard 420
Hafiz 452
Haley, Martin 74
"Half-caste Girl" (Wright) 94, 138
Half Moon 382–3, 405–6
Hall, Beth 228
Hall, Rodney 176, 217–18, 228, 270, 271–2, 310–11, 370–1, 419
Hancock, Keith 340
Hancock, Lang 253–4, 321
Hand, Gerry 456
Hanger, Eustice 202–3
Hanson, Pauline 519
Hardy, Frank 515
Harrold, Arthur 323

"The Harp and the King" (Wright) 134, 152, 171–2
Harpur, Charles 178, 204–5, 275, 280, 319, 325, 385, 419, 460–1
Harris, Max 108, 289, 290
Harris, Stewart 349, 363, 390, 396, 415, 481, 506
Harrison, Ruth 257
Harrower, Elizabeth 152–3, 394
Hart-Smith, William 108
Harvey, Frank 407
Harwood, Gwen 344
Have-A-Chat (bus driver) 158, 211–12
Havel, Wacek 226
Hawke, Bob 415, 437, 450, 455, 463–4, 472
Hawke government 427, 429, 440, 450, 454, 465, 473
Hayden, Bill 473
Headon, David 448
Hegerl, Eddie 236, 268, 323
Heidegger, Martin 300, 425
Heimans, Frank 307, 361, 481
Henry, Don 429
Herakleites 4
Herald 286, 463
Herbert, Xavier 395
Hereford Society 12
Heritage Festival, Braidwood 419
Hermes 55
Heron Island 441
High Court 488–9, 491, 492, 518, 522
Hinchinbrook 517
"The Histeridae" (Wright) 201
History of Australia (Roberts) 50
History Teachers Journal 421
Hitler, Adolf 56, 63, 66, 75, 78, 80
Holding, Clyde 417, 428
Holmes, Macdonald 79
Holt, Harold 236, 238–9, 254, 305
Holt, Jan 46
Holt, Zara 250
"Homecoming" (Wright) 210
Honi Soit 55, 56, 481
Hope, A.D.
  at JW's sixtieth birthday party 344
  at poetry reading with JW 385
  at writers' conference in Rockhampton 395
  favours Great Tradition of literature 220, 221
  friendship with JW 354
  JW quotes poem of 387
  JW reads work of 373
  published in *Australian National Review* 74
  published in *Hermes* 55
  urges JW to promote writers' cause 325
  visits JW at Calanthe 176
Hope, Justice 315, 334
Hope, Laurence 110, 135, 153, 175, 467, 498
Hopkins, Gerard Manley 51
Horne, Donald 52, 434
Houghton Mifflin 353
How Are We to Live? (Singer) 500
Howard government 410, 512, 513, 517–18, 521–2
Howard, John 513, 518, 522
Howarth, Guy 51, 110
Hudson, Flexmore 108
Hughes, Ted 479
Human Rights Commission 416
Humanist Manifesto 319
Hungary 198
Hunt, Ralph 309
"Hunting Snake" (Wright) 444, 486
Hurford, Chris 455

Iguana Films 481
"In Praise of Marriages" (Wright) 198, 525
Indian philosophy 176–7, 228, 270, 271, 435
Indonesia 154
Inquiry into the National Estate 315, 319, 322–3, 332
Institute of Aboriginal Studies, Canberra 428
"Interface" (Wright) 359, 379
International Commission of Justice 416
International Congress of Writers, Madrid (1937) 64
International Court of Justice 365
International Law and Indigenous Rights Conference, Canberra 415–17
International Poetry Festival, Yugoslavia 456
International Writers' Conference, Malaysia (1974) 365
Isherwood, Christopher 64
"Ishtar" (Wright) 147
Island 372, 476
It's Coming Yet (Harris) 415

J. Walter Thompson (company) 70–1, 106, 266
Jacaranda Press 218, 231, 232
Jacob, Helen 253
James Cook University 278, 402, 409–10, 472
James, Francis 222–3
Japan 81–2, 85, 346–8
Jedda (film) 192
Jeogla (property) 12, 87, 95, 160
Jervis Bay 450

"Jet Flight over Derby" (Wright) 255, 258, 271
Jindyworobak movement 68–9, 89, 94, 108
Joe (Aborigine) 193–4
John Forrest National Park 332
Johnson, Colin 460
Johnson, Lyndon 217
Johnson, Samuel 426–7
Jones, Evan 223
Jons, Neil 265
Joyce, Clayton 481
Jull, Peter 479
Jung, Carl 135, 138, 212

Kaddish (Zwicky) 420
Kakadu National Park
   Aboriginal land rights 309
   Blackburn judgment encourages
     prospective miners 363
   consortium of companies formed
     to exploit 369
   government approves mining 377,
     378, 386–7
   JW argues for Aboriginal occupation of 449
   JW denounces tactics of mining
     companies 389
   JW visits with Coombs 488, 504
   mining company accused of aggressive
     tactics 517
   Northern Land Council agrees to
     mining 436
   possible effects of mining on 380
   proposal to mine uranium in 292
Kaplan, Peter 353
Keating, Paul 483, 489, 492
Keesing, Nancy 344, 419, 420
Kelly, Petra 429
Kendall, Henry 275
Keneally, Tom 465
Kennedy, Flo 409
Kennedy, Robert 252
Kernot, Cheryl 448
Kerr, John 355
Kevin (Aboriginal activist) 392–3
Keyes, Sidney 110
Khemlani, Tirath 333
Kierkegaard, Soren 94
Kimberley 442
Kindon (property) 19
King Billy (local Aborigine) 406
King, Martin Luther 252
King of the Dingoes (Wright) 95, 178–9, 204
Kipling, Rudyard 30
Kitchener, Lord 14

Knight, George 231
Koestler, Arthur 112
Komon, Rudy 407–8
Kramer, Leonie 176, 270, 271, 434
Kununurra Conference 453–4
Ky, Phan Van 226
Kynaston, Edward 421

Lahey, Romeo 231, 232
Lake Pedder 294
"The Lake" (Wright) 444
"Lament for Passenger Pigeons" (Wright)
   297, 384
Lamington National Park 231
land degradation 100, 472
land rights *see* Aborigines
Landfall 372
'Landscape and Dreaming' (Wright) 433–4
Lang, Jack 49
Langman, Dawn 507
Langmore, John 417
Langton, Marcia 409, 411
Language 170–1
Latham, John 155, 157
Laughton, Sonya 478
Layton, Irving 225
Lee, Joyce 353
Left Book Club 75
Lehmann, Geoffrey 419
Leichhardt, Ludwig 91
Leopold, Aldo 205
"Letter to a Friend" (Wright) 63
"Letter" (Wright) 148–9, 244, 288
Levertov, Denise 225, 227
Levinas, Emmanuel 4
Lindsay, Norman 30
Lingiari, Vincent 362–3
Lippiatt and Company 273, 276
literary theory 438
Literature Board, Australia Council 325–6,
   372, 456
Littoral Society 236, 239, 240, 253, 263, 266
Llewellyn, Beckie 508
Lola (Aboriginal woman) 193, 194
Lona (property) 393
London Commitee for Cultural Freedom 156
London Magazine 110, 134, 251
Louat, Mrs (landlady) 48, 49
"Love Song in Absence" (Wright)
   212–13, 456
Lovell, Nigel 55
Lowell, Robert 224, 353
Lyon, Miss (teacher) 3–4

Mabo case
  concept of *terra nullius* 450, 488–9
  genesis of 409
  High Court finds in favour of Aborigines 488–9
  JW on importance of 465, 477
  McIntyre as instructing solicitor 402
  Queensland extinguishes native title in response to 476
  reactions to High Court decision 491–2
  significance of 410, 495
  Treaty Committee defer to 413
Mabo, Eddie 409, 476, 489
MacArthur, Douglas 85, 100, 105
Mackenzie, Arthur 6, 138
Mackenzie, Arundell 11, 34
Mackenzie, May *see* Wright, May (née Mackenzie)
Mackenzie, Weeta (née Wyndham) 6
Macneice, Louis 64
Macy, Joanna 463
The magic pudding (Lindsay) 30
Mailer, Norman 224
"The Maker" (Wright) 131
Malaysia 154
Malcolm, Don 292
Malinowski, Bronislaw 53
Malley, Ern 108
Malouf, David 481
"The Man and the Echo" (Yeats) 469–70, 520
Manifold, John 176, 217–18
Mansell, Michael 454, 498
Mansfield, Katherine 208
Maoris 372, 373–5
Mappoon people 368
Maralinga 448
"The Marks" (Wright) 2, 441
Marshall, Alan 176, 192, 304, 515, 519
Martin, Estelle 336
Martin, Richard 336
Marx, Karl 56, 499
"Massacre of the Innocents" (Wright) 230, 256
Mawby, Maurice 292
McArthur, Kathleen
  accused of being in pay of communists 259
  cares for Meredith while JW in hospital 195
  co-founds Wildlife Protection Society 205, 231
  essay on JW 481
  explores Noosa area 185–6
  fights Cooloola sand mining proposal 259, 262
  fights to save Great Barrier Reef 267
  friendship with JW 179–82
  JW confides in re illness 452
  JW recommends Miller's book to 208
  JW's correspondence with 147, 159, 164, 166, 201, 204, 247, 248, 289, 291, 302, 338, 350, 399, 453, 461, 471
  on the conservation movement 255
  secretary of WPSQ 323
  writes for *Wildlife* 231
McAuley, James 55, 156, 170, 220–1, 245, 270, 271, 272
McCallum, Margot 70
McCallum, Mungo 50
McCarthy, Joe 155, 515
McCaughey, Davis 340
McDonald, Roger 380
McFadyen, Ellen May 30
McGuffog, Sister 46
McGuigan, Ms (caterer) 302
McGuinness, P.P. 477
McIntyre, Greg 402, 409
McKinney, Jack
  as a father 149
  buys house at Boreen Point 184
  buys panel van 184–5
  character 111–12, 119, 122
  death and funeral 210–12
  declining health 200–4, 204, 206, 210–11
  defends friendship with JW 117–18
  driving tours 185–7
  early life 113–14
  enjoys company of artists 175–6
  enlists in light horse in World War I 113–14
  entry in *Dictionary of Australian Biography* 510
  environmental concerns 186
  explores Queensland with JW 138, 143–5
  family background 113
  first marriage 115
  impact of war on 129
  JW on 116–17, 120–1
  Kathleen McArthur on 180
  life at Calanthe 153, 158, 159–60, 162
  marries JW 209
  meets JW 111
  meets Stephen Spender 156
  moves into JW's house 125–6, 128
  on language 174
  personal charm 161–2
  philosophical work and ideas 115–16, 118–22, 126–7, 163, 170–1, 182, 230, 287, 359, 463, 474, 499, 500
  portrait by Blackman 175

publishes first book 162–3
publishes in *Mind* 163, 201
publishes second book 134
reaction of JW's family to 129–30
under ASIO surveillance 155, 514–15
visits daughter on Palm Island 195
writes *The Crucible* 114–15
writes play at Boreen Point 202–3
McKinney, Lucy 119, 139, 162, 195
McKinney, Meredith
   admired by JW 398
   at Boreen Point 184
   at school 164, 206, 215
   ballet lessons jeopardised 201
   birth 131, 148–9
   buys property 504
   childhood friendship with Aborigines 192–3
   falls out of cot 200
   finds JW flat in Canberra 521
   finds JW house in Braidwood 486–7
   first pony 153–4
   flies through cyclone 169
   flies to Darwin with JW 504
   friend of fights conscription 287
   friendship with Nettie Palmer 177
   gets driving licence 263
   gives mother strength 172
   goes crazy over the Beatles 208–9
   health problems 160, 168, 211, 316, 360–1
   holidays with JW after father's death 212
   in Central Australia 487
   in England 251–2
   in India 246, 270, 272
   in Italy 246
   in Japan 341, 346–8, 509
   in Paris 247–50
   in Scandinavia and Holland 247
   in South Africa 253
   in Tasmania 459–60
   JW buys painting for 408
   JW worries about 196
   Laurie Hope's memories of 467
   lives in hotel in Inverell with JW 204
   love of the sea 182
   Pacific cruise with JW 244
   receives book from Kathleen McArthur 179
   relationship with mother 158
   rents house in Braidwood with JW 357
   sits for final school exams 228
   studies at ANU 316
   takes a year off in Brisbane 256
   translates JW's poems into Japanese 502
   visits home from Japan 398–9, 407, 457, 487, 513
   wins Commonwealth Scholarship 244
   works on doctoral thesis 382–3
McLeod, Don 254
McMahon, William 279, 295, 309
McMaster, Rhyll 380
McMichael, Don 240–1
McPhee, Hilary 395, 396, 510
McQueen, Humphrey 377
Meanjin
   founded by Christesen 74, 96–7
   JW donates money to 98–9
   JW publishes in 63, 83, 96, 119, 169, 171
   JW works as secretary at 107–9, 117
   JW's interest in as a literary journal 96–9
   McKinney publishes in 111
   moves to Melbourne 134
   on an engaged literature 112–13
   origin of name 97
Medawar, Pat 265
Melbourne University Press 178
Menzies, Robert 155, 178, 198, 234, 314
Merritt, Robert 329
Middlemarch (Eliot) 49
"Midnight" (Wright) 137–8
Midyim (property) 179
migration 451, 455, 477, 519
Miller, Arthur 170
Miller, Henry 207–8
Miller, Mick 411
Milner, Sally 395
Milosz, Czeslaw 225
Mind 163, 201
Minimum Expectations of National Land Rights Legislation 440
mining *see* bauxite mining; sand mining; uranium mining
Minnie (nurse) 32, 93
The Mockers (Boyd) 135
Modern Man in Search of a Soul (Jung) 135
Modjeska, Drusilla 167
Monash University 370
Monk, Sylvia 436
Monkey Grip (Garner) 355
Monkman, Kitty 235
Monkman, Noel 235–6
Moongalba (settlement) 306, 361, 400, 414, 470
Moorhead, Finola 257, 275, 354–5, 481
Moorhouse, Frank 327, 521
Morgan, Hugh 441, 491
"The Morning of the Dead" (Wright) 139–43

Morosi, Junie 333
Mosley, Geoff 338, 339, 437
"Mount Mary" (Wright) 191
Mount Tamborine *see* Calanthe; Quantum est
Mountain Press 163
"Mountain" (Wright) 446
Mountbatten, Lord 105
"The Moving Image" (Wright) 57, 83, 85, 86, 101, 102, 113, 120, 122
The Moving Image (Wright) 132–3, 153
"Moving South" (Wright) 313, 317, 345–6, 357
Mudie, Ian 74
Mudrooroo *see* Johnson, Colin
Muller, Bernie 209
Munster, George 296
Murdoch, Nina 48, 51
Murdoch, Rupert 466
Murdoch, Walter 515
Murphy, Lionel 478
Murray Islanders 409–10
Murray, Les 514
Mussolini, Benito 56, 246
My Brilliant Career (Franklin) 30, 42
Myer, Baillieu 233, 292
Myer Foundation 233
Myer, Ken 311, 340

Nabalco 363
"Nameless Flower" (Wright) 185
Nation 206
National Aboriginal Conference 363, 390–1
National Aboriginal Consultative Council 313
National Aboriginal Council 402, 411, 412, 427, 440, 441
National Book Council 372
National Council for Reconciliation 475
National Farmers' Federation 518
National Federation of Land Councils 415, 442
National Library 442
National Security Act 80
National Times 307, 332, 377, 393
National Trust 315
native title 476
The Nature of Love (Wright) 204, 524
Nazism 65–6, 75
Neidjie, Bill 504
Neilson, John Shaw 108–9, 257, 263, 275, 385
Nellie (Aborigine) 406
Nelson 512
Neruda, Pablo 226
Nettheim, Garth 409, 416, 465
Network News 485

New Alchemists 337
New England Girls' School 42–3
New England Tableland 27
New Guard 49
New Guinea 85, 86, 91, 92
New Land, New Language 164
New South Wales Premier's Book Awards 420
New State Movement 128
The New York Journal of Philosophy 196
New Zealand 371–5
New Zealand Book Council Management Committee 371
News Limited 466
Newton, Isaac 175
Ngunarval people 478
Nicholson, Joyce 395
"Nigger's Leap" (Wright) 93–4
"Night after Bushfire" (Wright) 124, 136
A Night of National Reconciliation (revue) 439
"Night" (Wright) 189
Nimbin festival 329–30
Nixon, Cecily 52, 61, 62, 65
Nolan, Sidney 134, 145, 153–4, 176, 198, 407–8, 408, 498
Nookanbah Station 391, 408
The Noonans (radio serial) 115
Noonuccal, Oodgeroo *see* Walker, Kath
Noosa 185
North West Shelf project 320–1
Northern Land Council 363, 386, 403, 455
"Northern River" (Wright) 27
Notes and Furphies 438
nuclear accidents 448
Nuclear Disarmament Party 440, 448, 473
Nulalbin (property) 7–10, 143, 179

O'Connor, Mark 353, 456
Odet, Clifford 51
O'Donoghue, Lois 364, 492
O'Donovan, Anne 395
O'Dowd, Bernard 133
Oh, What A Lovely War (film) 383
O'Hearn, Dinny 481
oil exploration 255
oil spills 258, 266, 268
"Old Woman's Song" (Wright) 197
On Our Selection (Rudd) 504
O'Neill, Shorty 409
"Oppositions" (Wright) 388–9, 468
The Orchard 167
Ord River project 320–1
O'Rourke, Patricia Maria Therese 110
Orrell, John 231, 232

Ortt-Saeed, Jocelyn 246
Osborne, Charles 110, 134, 251, 498
O'Shane, Pat 413
"The Other Half" (Wright) 209
The Other Half (Wright) 223–4
Overland 183
overpopulation 294
Oxford University Press 178, 192, 257

Packer, Kerry 206
"Pain" (Wright) 124
painting 134
Palmer, Helen 64
Palmer, Nettie 64, 149, 155, 162, 166, 177, 515
Palmer, Vance 64, 73, 112, 155, 177, 203, 515
Paris uprising (1968) 247–50
Parker, Michael 332–3
Partridge, Eric 51
"Party with the Gods" (Wright) 330–1
Passi, Dave 409
Passmore, John 51
pastoral leases 518, 522
Patten, Jack 392
Patten, Les 392
"Patterns" (Wright) 359, 448, 527
Patterson, Barbara *see* Blackman, Barbara (née Patterson)
Patterson, Dr (member for North Queensland) 268
Patterson, Mrs (Barbara's mother) 209
Pearl Harbor 81
Pedder, Lake 321
PEN International Congress 369
People of the Dreamtime 304
Perkins, Charles 217
Perkins, Elizabeth 244, 354
Perkins, Mr (teacher) 4
Perry, Grace 110
Petrov Royal Commission 155, 156–7
"Phaius Orchid" (Wright) 185
Phantom Dwelling (Wright) 456, 466
Philip, Prince, Duke of Edinburgh 233, 276, 293, 332–3
Phillip, Arthur 395
photocopying 327
Picasso, Pablo 63
"Picture" (Wright) 297
Piddington, Margaret 71
Pierce, Peter 421
Piesse, Dick 291, 293
Pine Gap 448, 526
Plath, Sylvia 169, 170

"Platypus" (Wright) 360
Plumwood, Val 439, 500, 512
"Poem and Audience" (Wright) 324, 352
"The Poet" (Wright) 161–2
Poetic Diction (Barfield) 126, 136, 173
Poetry Australia 297
Poetry Folio 133
Poet's Corner 1974 57
Poignant, Axel 457
Ponge, François 173, 228
"The Pool and the Star" (Wright) 445
population growth 451, 483
"Power" (Wright) 210
"Prayer" (Wright) 523
"The Precipice" (Wright) 169–70
Preoccupations in Australian Poetry (Wright) 109, 178, 181, 191, 197, 204, 216, 220
"Pressures" (Wright) 425
Preston, Margaret 74, 166
"The Promised One" (Wright) 146
"The Prospector" (Wright) 189
protest movement (1960s) 217, 224–5, 227, 252
Public Lending Rights scheme 432, 521–2
publishing, in Australia 72–3
Purkiss, Jack 24, 85
Pybus, Cassandra 476

Qantas 288, 290, 291
Quadrant 247
Quakers 414
Quantum est (house) 126, 130, 149, 153
Queensland Coastal Islands Declaratory Act 476
Queensland Institute of Engineers 275
Queensland Trades and Labour Council 267–8, 340

racial discrimination 476, 489
Racial Discrimination Act 489
Rainforest, Reef, Mangroves, Man 335
"Rainforest" (Wright) 425–6, 429, 444, 483
Range the Mountains High (Wright) 204
Ranger uranium mine 377, 387
Ratcliffe, Francis 233–4, 292, 293
"Reading Thomas Traherne" (Wright) 212
Reagan, Ronald 457
Realist Writers 217
Rebels and Precursors (Haese) 420
Reconciliation Convention (1997) 522
Red Army 348
Reed, John 134, 176
Reed, Sunday 134, 176

Reid, Barrie 105, 109–11, 126, 134, 148–9, 154, 176, 419, 498
"Remembering an Aunt" (Wright) 35–6
"Remembering Michael" (Wright) 371, 419
"The Remittance Man" (Wright) 62
"Request to a Year" (Wright) 505, 526
Reynolds, Henry 402, 409, 434
Reynolds, Margaret 437
Riley, Rob 427
The River and the Road (Wright) 7, 204
"River Bend" (Wright) 406–7
Roberts, Stephen 50
Robertson, Constance 70
Robertson, Martin 354, 467
Robinson, Roland 192
"Rockface" (Wright) 424, 426, 481
"Rockpool" (Wright) 422, 426, 451
Roff, C. 231
Rolls, Eric 421
Rose, Deborah Bird 504
Rose, George 392
Rose (JW's great aunt) 149
Rosie (Aboriginal girl) 193–4
"Rosina Alcona to Julius Brenzaida" (Wright) 216
Ross, Paddy 93
Roughsey, Dick 430–1
Routley, Richard 314, 404
Routley, Val 314, 404
Rowland, Claude 34–5
Rowland, John 525
Rowley, Charles 390, 402
Roxby Downs 437
Royal Commissions
   mining on the Barrier Reef 273, 276–80
   uranium mining in Kakadu 378–9, 380
Rudall River National Park 461
Rudd, Steele 504
Rusden, Heather 221, 245, 351, 361, 380, 408, 462, 480–1
Russell, Bertrand 170, 201
Russell, George 270, 271
Rutherford, Lord 78

Sacks, Oliver 511
Sadler, Professor 54–5
"Sailing to Byzantium" (Yeats) 525
sand mining 259–60
Sandoz G.G. 448
"Sandy Swamp" (Wright) 185
Satre, Jean-Paul 112
Sayers, Dorothy 424
School Chronicle 40, 43

Scotch College, Melbourne 332
Scott, Peter 250
"Sea-beach" (Wright) 189
"Seasonal Flocking" (Wright) 432, 512
Seed, John 463
Seghers, Pierre 225–6
Selected Poems (Wright) 524
Semmler, Clement 221
Senate Select Committee on Offshore Petroleum Resources 269
Serventy, Vincent 233, 267, 403, 443
Sesquicentenary 68, 73
"Seven Songs from a Journey" (Wright) 187–8, 188, 189, 190–1
7:30 Report (television program) 497
Shadow Sisters (film) 361, 481
"Shadow" (Wright) 284–5
Shapcott, Tom 176, 456
Shapiro, Karl 109
Sharp, Nonie 409
Shaw Neilson, John *see* Neilson, John Shaw
Shelley, Percy 31
Shepherd, Alex 316, 327
Shoalhaven River, proposal to dam 482–3
Showdon, Warren 472
Silent Spring (Carson) 237
Sinclair, John 287, 316, 323, 345, 377
Singer, Peter 500
Sisters (publishing house) 395
"Skins" (Wright) 446
Skryznecki, Peter 353, 370
Slessor, Kenneth 89, 515
"The Slope" (Wright) 282, 303
Snowy River Hydro-Electric Scheme 152
So They Played Together 72
social class, in Australia 71, 106–7
Socrates 163
"Soldier's Farm" (Wright) 89
"A Song of Hope" (Walker) 497
"A Song to Sing You" (Wright) 146
"Sonnet" (Wright) 96, 447
South Africa 310, 477
South-eastern Queensland Electricity Board 451
"South of My Days" (Wright) 27, 84
Southerly 80, 523
"Space Between" (Wright) 343
Spain 64
Spasshat, Angela 16–17
Spasshat, Mabel 17, 36
Spasshat, Percy 16–17
Spender, Stephen 97, 156, 178, 516
"Spring after War" (Wright) 124–5

Springboks tour (1972) 310, 495
Sri Lanka *see* Ceylon
St John, Edward 245
Stammer, David 231
Stanner, Bill 54, 319, 368, 390, 401, 470
"Stars" (Wright) 136
State Library of Brisbane 376
Stead, Christina 60, 71, 380
Stead, David 289
Stead, Thistle 289, 403
Stephen (Meredith McKinney's friend) 347
Stephens, A.G. 70
Stephenson, P.R. 73
Stewart, Douglas 96, 126, 133, 206
The Stirling Castle (ship) 145
Stocker, Peter 323
Stockman's Hall of Fame, Longreach 462
Stow, Randolph 422
Stradbroke Island 304–5
Strahan, Lynne 97
Stretton, Hugh 434
The Structure of Modern Thought (McKinney) 134, 174, 251, 280, 433, 500
Studio Altenberg 486–7, 503
"Summer" (Wright) 435, 439–40
Sun 379
Sunday Review 296
"The Surfer" (Wright) 57, 58
Surkov (Russian agent) 515–16
Swallowfield (property) 36
"Swamp Plant" (Wright) 360
Swan, Professor (Monash Dean of Science) 396–7
Sydney, in the late 1930s 71–2
Sydney Mail 30, 40, 89
Sydney Morning Herald
  JW considers job at 70
  JW denounces treatment of Aborigines in 389–90
  JW writes protest letter to re grants 456
  JW's tribute to Oodgeroo 497
  JW's writes pessimistic article for 403
  on JW 165, 223, 303
  on uranium mining 379
  publishes anti-Concorde letters 289
  publishes anti-South African letter 245
  publishes Blackman's painting of the Reef 269
  publishes JW's work 96, 206
  reports commememoration of wedding anniversary 302
  reviews *A Cry For the Dead* 421
  Serventy's article on wilderness 403
  verse debate with A.D. Hope in 221
Sydney University Dramatic Society 55
Sykes, Bobbi 456, 460, 497, 503
Symbolists 173
synecology 298–9

TAA 240
"Tableau" (Wright) 299–300
Tallangatta Times 482
Tasmania 460
Telegraph (Toronto) 226, 227
Temperley, Dora *see* Wright, Dora (née Temperley)
Tennant, Kylie 245
terra nullius 308, 364, 392, 416, 450, 477, 488–9
Thalgarrah (property) 16, 17, 20, 36, 90
Thatcher, Margaret 440
"They" (Wright) 356, 516
This Day Tonight (television program) 237
This Is Your Life (television program) 400
"This Time Alone" (Wright) 356–7
Thompson, J. Walter *see* J. Walter Thompson (company)
Tianamen Square massacre 473
Tickner, Robert 476
"Tightropes" (Wright) 343
Times 309
Times Literary Supplement 353, 422
Titterton, Ernest 387–8
"To a Child" (Wright) 29, 138
"To A.H., New Year 1943" (Wright) 63
"To Mary Gilmore" (Wright) 301
"To M.R." (Wright) 467
To My Delight (Cohen) 394
Tony (JW's travel companion) 62–3, 81
"Tool" (Wright) 221–2, 242–3
Torres Strait Dancers 361
Torres Strait Islanders 479
Torrey Castle (ship) 258
Toyne, Philip 466
Tracey, Geoff 233, 236, 314
trade unions 154, 267–8, 270, 276, 340
Traherne, Thomas 212
"The Trains" (Wright) 92
Treaty Committee Art Show 407–8
"Tree Grave" (Walker) 219
Tresize, Percy 323
A Tribute to Patrick White (Joyce) 481
Tucker, Albert 134, 176
"Turning Fifty" (Wright) 199–200, 215, 342
Tuwhare, Hone 372
Twelfth Night Theatre 202

"Twenty-five Years" (Wright) 360, 398
"Two Dreamtimes" (Wright) 307–8, 361, 366, 496, 523
"The Two Fires" (Wright) 168, 173, 174
The Two Fires (Wright) 4
"Two Generations" (Wright) 175
"Two Songs for the World's End" (Wright) 168–9

Uluru 450
"The Unborn" (Wright) 131–2
"Under Ben Bulben" (Yeats) 502, 519
UNESCO Committee for the Arts 328–9, 345, 371, 385
United Nations 477, 478
University of Melbourne 370
University of New England 128, 196–7, 221
University of New South Wales 327, 370
University of Queensland 216–18
University of Queensland Press 327–8, 480
University of Sydney 50–8, 370
University of the Northern Territory 402
University of the South Pacific 365
"Unknown Water" (Wright) 172–3
"The Unnecessary Angel" (Wright) 283
"Unpacking Books" (Wright) 487, 502, 503, 508
Unsworth, Barrie 461
uranium mining 292, 295, 309, 363, 377–80, 386–7, 389–90, 436–7
Uren, Tom 315–16, 318, 319, 320, 333, 338

Vallance, Keith 332
Vallentine, Jo 414, 440
Vallis, Val 220, 257
values 298–9
van der Post, Laurens 519
Vaughan Williams, Ralph 53
Vena Park (property) 10
"Victims" (Wright) 422–3
Victorian Native Forests campaign 418
Vietnam war 154, 198, 217, 224–6, 228–30, 243, 252, 313, 355
Viking 327
Virago Press 353
"The Vision" (Wright) 121, 202, 211, 213, 214, 501

Wagner, Claire 288
Wain, Barry 241, 278
Waiting for Lefty (Odet) 51
"Waiting Ward" (Wright) 147–8
"Waiting" (Wright) 88–9, 99, 102

Walcott, Derek 503, 508
Waldheim, Kurt 365
Waldock, Professor (English lecturer) 50
Walker, Dennis 362, 464–5, 493, 495
Walker, Kath
  appears on *This Is Your Life* 400
  as a writer 218–19, 358, 460
  as patron of the Queensland Writers' Centre 481
  attends International Writers' Conference 365
  attends seminar in Canberra (1973) 329
  attends World Council of Churches conference 365
  attitude to the land 464
  campaigns for Aboriginal rights overseas 400–1
  consulted by JW about conference paper 330
  dies from cancer 493
  essay on JW 481
  establishes Moongalba 305–7
  fights against racism 364, 365
  friendship with JW 188, 260–1, 303–4, 308, 310, 315, 337, 361, 362, 393, 400, 493–7
  invited to Commonwealth Writers' Week 413–14
  loses her son 470
  on dispossession of Aborigines 391
  on hijacked aircraft 365–6
  optimistic about ATSIC 473
  rejects assimilation policy 305
  returns MBE in protest 496
  stands as a Democrat 463
Walker, Patty 493
Walker, Shirley 287, 506
Walker, Vivien 362, 470
Wallamumbi (property) 12, 17, 18, 22–3, 32, 86, 95, 160
Walsh, Richard 434
Ward, Ada 104
Ward, Eddie 74
Ward, John 104
Ward, Val 105
Warner, Rex 110
The Waste Land (Eliot) 51, 55
Waten, Judah 515
Wave Hill strike 309
The Way of the Whirlwind (Durack) 179
"We Are Going" (Walker) 218–19
We Call For a Treaty (Wright) 428, 441, 459, 480
"Weapon" (Wright) 230

weapons exhibition 479
Webb, Doris 429, 483
Webb, Len
  appointed to Inquiry into National
    Estate 322
  as an environmentalist 429
  collaborates with JW on reef survey 335
  concerned over JW's health 324
  exposes woodchipping miscalculation 314
  friendship with JW 303
  helps organise Ecopolitics Conference 449
  idea of cooperative maintenance system 297
  JW lends McKinney's book to 500
  JW on 237–8
  JW quotes Bashō to 446–7
  JW's correspondence with 272, 332, 336,
    367–8, 370, 378, 383, 388, 390, 395, 403,
    405, 418, 422, 428, 432, 442, 456, 472,
    474, 482, 484, 509, 512, 520, 525–6
  meets JW 233
  on ACF Council 294
  on the Daintree Rainforest 437
  opposes Concorde 293
  organises wilderness conference 394
  presents evidence of Cooloola's
    importance 260
  proposes new approach to environmental
    study 298–9
  quotes JW in *Wildlife* 444–5
  recruits John Büsst 236
  supports JW's view of environmental
    crisis 404
  sympathy with JW's ideas 439
  tries to dissuade JW from resigning from
    WPSQ 474
"Wedding Photograph, 1913" (Wright) 17, 21,
  22, 38, 281
Wedgwood, Camilla 53
Weller, Archie 460
Welsh, Garth 456
Wesson, Alf 184, 203
West Australian 245, 253
West Australian Ballet 456
West, Morris 465
Westernport Bay, Victoria 294
White man Got no Dreaming (Stanner) 368
"White Night" (Wright) 300–1
White, Patrick
  at Whitlam's farewell 384
  avoids Bicentenary 456
  dislikes JW's 1965 poem 199
  inspiration for *A Fringe of Leaves* 145
  Joyce's tribute to 481
  JW criticises matters of fact in work of 355
  JW writes to 340
  on journalists and teachers 370
  on the "country of the mind" 191, 220
  on the unconscious 135
  opposes JW's involvement in government
    affairs 316
  opposes mining on Fraser Island 338–9, 340
  signs letter against South African
    regime 245
  stays in London during World War II 67
  supports Labor in 1972 311
  tires of aimlessness 117
  upset by JW's talk of literary doldrums 223
Whitehouse, F.W. 260
Whiteley, Brett 408
Whitlam, Gough
  creates Department of Environment 314
  election campaign (1972) 311
  institutes inquiry into national estate
    315, 322–3
  JW ponders future of 384–5
  JW's admiration for 326
  JW's first meeting with 223
  policy on Fraser Island 338, 339–40
  praises Coombs 319
  signs letter against South African
    regime 245
  supports Aboriginal cause 362
  sympathy for change 320, 325
  wins 1972 election 312
Whitlam government
  declares Barrier Reef a National Park 280
  dismissed by Kerr 355, 376
  early reforms 313–14, 318
  gives grant to *Wildlife* 321
  internal scandals 333
  re-elected (1974) 333
  sets up Australian Heritage Commission 335
  vacillates over Barrier Reef 338
'Whose Country is it Anyway?' (Wright) 518
Wik case 410, 518, 522
"Wild Flower Plain" (Wright) 185
wilderness areas 442, 443, 449
Wilderness Society 443, 466, 470, 500
Wildlife 211, 231–3, 311, 321
Wildlife Protection Society of Queensland
  campaigns to save Cooloola 262
  concern over degradation of Barrier Reef
    235–6, 239, 240
  invited to affiliate with ACF 234
  JW as president 205–6
  JW co-founds 205, 231

JW minds office 338
JW resigns from 474
JW's parting message to 356
opposes Concorde 288
prepares case for Royal Commission 273–4, 276
queries advertisement in *Wildlife* 311
receives grant for journal 321
stall at Brisbane Exhibition 266
twentieth anniversary 429
William (dog) 95
Williams, Fred 408
Williams, Harold 478
Williams, Ian 478
Williams, Susannah 53
Williamson, David 313, 328
Win (JW's cousin) 90
"Wings" (Wright) 213–14, 256
"Winter" (Wright) 427, 452, 469
Wiradjuri people 478
The Wisdom of the Ancients (Bacon) 137
"Wishes" (Wright) 525
Witnesses of Spring (Neilson) 257
"Woman in Orchard" (Wright) 398
"Woman to Child" (Wright) 131, 137
"Woman to Man" (Wright) 131, 132, 137
Woman to Man (Wright) 131, 133–4, 137
Women Writers' Congress 420
Women's College, University of Sydney 50, 52, 53, 55
Women's Electoral Lobby 275, 295
Wongwibinda (property) 9–10, 11–12, 33–4, 90, 393, 431
woodchipping 264, 294, 314, 461
Woodward, Justice 363, 392
"Words, Roses, Stars" (Wright) 438–9
"The World and the Child" (Wright) 21, 24, 28–9, 38
World Council of Churches' Conferences 365
World Council of Indigenous Peoples 411–12
World Court 415
World Poetry Conference, Montreal (1967) 223–8, 271
World Summit of Indigenous Peoples 478
World War I 19
World War II 78, 80–5, 91–2, 100, 102–3, 105, 111, 112, 123–4
World Wildlife Fund 404
Wright, Albert (JW's grandfather) 6, 7–11, 34, 61, 139–42, 143–4, 302, 431, 510
Wright, Albion 372
Wright, Arthur (JW's uncle) 9, 12, 19
Wright, Bertie (JW's uncle) 9

Wright, Bruce (JW's brother) 87, 95, 100, 104, 119, 457, 509
Wright, Cecil (JW's uncle) 12, 19, 33, 47
Wright, Claudia 286
Wright, Dora (née Temperley, JW's stepmother) 39
Wright, Elsie (JW's auntie) 9, 34, 67
Wright, Ethel (née Bigg, JW's mother) 1, 15–20, 21–2, 30, 31, 38, 39, 89
Wright, Fred (JW's great-uncle) 7
Wright, Jane (JW's sister-in-law) 511
Wright, Joan 323
Wright, Judith
see also titles of specific books and poems
AS A SUPPORTER OF ABORIGINAL RIGHTS
   agrees to act as coordinator for proposed treaty 455
   angry over Hand's dismissal 456
   as member of Aboriginal Treaty Committee 390–1, 393, 401, 402, 409–10, 412–13, 428
   attends World Council of Indigenous Peoples 411–12
   attitude to land rights 449, 477
   avoids Bicentenary 456, 459
   campaigns for racial justice 310
   criticises Bicentenary 456, 459–60, 462
   declines to produce book of Aboriginal legends 192
   deplores Howard government policy 513, 518–19
   donates money to Land Council 442
   enraged by *Cape of Dreams* broadcast 475
   gets sick of dealing with rednecks 474
   helps counter advertising by mining companies 436
   helps Estelle Martin 336
   helps set up Moongalba 304, 307
   learns about Aborigines 192, 260–1, 303, 366–7, 394, 493–4, 495
   left no time for poetry 447
   notes growing support for indigenous peoples 365
   offers to pay rent to Braidwood Aborigines 477–8
   on oppression in the Kimberley 410
   on the perception of blacks by whites 336
   pessimism over Aboriginal issues 489–90, 492
   produces *Network News* 485
   refuses to attend Cairns conference 399

refuses to attend Writers' Week 414
refuses to join trust to restore
　　Dalwood 431
sells paintings to finance lecture
　　tour 498
sends Webb paper on indigenous
　　rights 479
speaks at Canberra demonstration 522
speaks at Townsville conference 522
suggests Aboriginal member of ACF 438
suggests lecture tour by Aboriginal
　　women 497–8
supports Aborigines' rejection of
　　McMahon's policy 310
supports Abschol 304
supports land claims for Kakadu 386–7,
　　389–90
tries to organise indigenous people's
　　summit 478
urges Hawke government to honour
　　promises 427

AS A WRITER
　　Aborigines in the work of 93–4, 188–91
　　as perceived by other poets 353–5
　　attacks literary theory 438
　　attends Adelaide Festival of Arts 245,
　　　　274, 369, 420
　　attends ANZAAS Conference 454
　　attends conference in Honululu 330–1
　　attends Perth Festival 245
　　attends World Poetry Conference in
　　　　Montreal 223–8, 271
　　attends writers' meeting in
　　　　Rockhampton 395
　　begins first novel 89
　　cautious about film of *Generations
　　　　of Men* 407
　　childhood poems 40–1
　　Claudia Wright's article on 286
　　corresponds with poet prisoner 300
　　debates McAuley in *Sydney Morning
　　　　Herald* 221
　　decides to stop writing poetry 446
　　declines request to make film 481
　　deposits papers in National Library
　　　　433, 442
　　difficulty in writing poetry 166–7, 257
　　English edition of *Collected Poems*
　　　　mooted 480
　　establishes Mountain Press 163
　　finds a publisher for McKinney's book 251
　　first poem published 30
　　helps Cohen find publisher 394
　　helps McKinney with philosophical work
　　　　118–19, 120
　　helps *Meanjin* financially 98–9
　　international reputation grows 352–3, 386
　　introduced to poetry by mother 30
　　invited to Bologna University 417
　　literary luncheon in Perth 253
　　media portrayal of 223
　　meets Stephen Spender 156
　　patron of Armidale Arts Festival 369
　　poems published in Japanese 502
　　publication of anthology delayed 473
　　publishes first collection of poems 132–3
　　publishes in *Australian National Review*
　　　　73–4
　　publishes second collection of poems
　　　　133–4
　　publishes tenth collection of poetry 351–2
　　re-issues of work 524
　　reaction to Ern Malley affair 108
　　rebukes University of Queensland Press
　　　　327–8
　　receives grant to write family history
　　　　130, 138, 145
　　reputation as poet grows 95–6, 177–8
　　researches family history 61–2, 89
　　researches Harpur in Mitchell Library
　　　　204–5
　　returns to writing (1975) 351–2
　　revised edition of *Collected Poems*
　　　　released 503
　　short stories 105–6
　　shrugs off Nobel Prize proposal 500
　　sits on Literature Board 325–6
　　speaks at *Barjai* meeting 110–11
　　speaks at NSW Premier's Book
　　　　Awards 420
　　stage performance of work 507–8
　　translations of poetry 353, 456
　　view of the poet's role 98, 220–1, 225,
　　　　274, 419–20, 438–9, 461
　　wooed by the Establishment 155
　　works on autobiography 433, 485, 525
　　works on manuscripts 204
　　works on McKinney's papers for second
　　　　book 474
　　works on Neilson manuscript 257, 263
　　writes *Birds* for daughter 174
　　writes for *Bulletin* 154
　　writes for *Daedalus* 433–4
　　writes for *Honi Soit* 55
　　writes last poems in Persian form
　　　　432, 452

writes McKinney's entry for biographical dictionary 510
AS AN ACTIVIST
  angered by Howard's policies 518
  becomes interested in politics 56–7
  burns correspondence with Coombs 479
  concern over technology 206
  confronts Minister for Justice 269
  declines to help Christesen during Royal Commission 156–7
  despairs over Hawke and the Labor Party 437–8, 448, 462–3
  disillusioned with politics 337, 516
  fights for retention of lending right schemes 521–2
  fights to save local post office 482
  helps set up Australian Peace and Development Institute 417
  letter to Hawke not published 463–4
  opposes Concorde 288–91, 293–4, 296
  opposes conscription 287
  opposes Harvard chair in Australian Studies 327
  political inclinations 74–5, 100, 111, 155, 156–7, 207–8, 286–7, 463
  political work takes precedence over poetry 275
  returns honorary doctorate in protest 496
  signs Humanist Manifesto 319
  signs letter against South African regime 245
  speaks against nuclear power 380–1
  speaks against nuclear tests 418, 448
  speaks at commemoration of Whitlam dismissal 377
  supports call for Labor government (1972) 311
  supports Queensland strikers 451
  under ASIO surveillance 155, 514–17
  works for copyright justice 326–8
AS AN ENVIRONMENTALIST
  as member of committee of Inquiry into National Estate 315–16, 320–4, 332, 333–4
  as member of committee to discuss new Parliament House 417
  at WPSQ anniversary 429
  becomes involved at Mount Tamborine 218
  campaigns for national park at Noosa 185–6
  co-founds Wildlife Protection Society 205, 231
  decides to devote herself to conservation 256
  disagreements with other environmentalists 296–7, 403, 418, 442, 443, 465–6, 473–4
  disappointed by ACF inaction 292–3
  donates royalties to Greenpeace 509–10
  environment inspections 332
  fights against uranium mining 377
  fights to save Daintree Forest 437
  fights to save Fraser Island 287–8, 339–40
  fights to save Great Barrier Reef 234–6, 239–41, 244, 247, 250–1, 254–5, 258, 264–5, 267, 269–70, 273–4, 276, 279, 287, 335, 338, 382, 443, 512
  foundation member of ACF 233
  gives up preservation concept 499
  hears reports of woodchipping 264
  JW's self-definition 394
  lobbies for environmentalists 485
  on Council of ACF 294
  on Queensland's slash and burn mentality 261
  opens Forestry Exhibition 463
  opposes Concorde 288–91, 293, 294
  opposes damming of Shoalhaven River 482–3
  opposes empty wilderness 443
  opposes further immigration 455
  opposes mining at Cooloola 259–60, 262–3
  opposes mining at Half Moon 361, 405–6, 448–9
  opposes mining in Kakadu 292
  opposes progress 444
  opposes technological determinism 396–7
  opposes tree removal in Mount Tamborine 275–6
  opposes visits by nuclear ships 447
  patron of Victorian Native Forests campaign 418
  presented with bouquet at bush picnic 276
  president of the WPSQ 205–6, 211
  public appearances 237, 275, 321
  reservations about ACF council 292
  speaks at Ecopolitics Conference 449
  submits environmental proposals to Whitlam government 320
  sums up successes 520
  visits Coombs in Northern Territory 472, 488

writes 'Conservation as a Concept' 293,
    298–9
writes for *Wildlife* 231
EDUCATION
    attends business college 69–70
    awkwardness at school 42, 43, 44–5
    boards at New England Girls' School
        42–5
    tutored by governesses 29–30
    University of Sydney 47–58
EMPLOYMENT
    appointed university statistician 43, 125
    as member of Australia Council 313, 320,
        325–9
    as member of Council of the ANU 369,
        386, 388
    becomes professor's secretary 79
    falls out with Christesen 117
    finds first job 70–1
    loses job to a man after war 125
    takes job at Sydney Town Hall 81–2
    teaches at University of Queensland
        216–18, 219–20, 242
    works at *Meanjin* 107–8
    works for Universities Commission 104–5
HEALTH PROBLEMS
    arthritis 490
    cancer 282, 452
    deafness 24, 81, 92, 125, 180, 200, 324,
        332, 422, 424, 434, 445, 457, 475,
        479–80, 481, 484
    develops angina 506
    failing eyesight 422, 424, 446, 452, 479,
        484–5, 505
    fever 291
    heart attacks 512, 513
    hip injury 324, 446
    influenza 441
    migraines 511
    successful cataract operation 507
    undergoes surgery 452–3, 461
HONOURS AND AWARDS
    A.A. Phillips Award 506–7
    Asan World Prize for poetry 435
    Australian Academy of Humanities
        Fellowship 274
    Australian Women Writers' Award 418
    Creative Arts Fellowship 353
    Encyclopaedia Britannica Literary prize
        222–3
    Fellowship with Australia Council 473
    first poetry prize 40
    Grace Leven Prize 145

has portrait painted 439
honorary doctorates 196, 200, 216,
    370, 417
Human Rights Award for poetry 503
Order of the Golden Ark 417
patron of the Queensland Writers' Centre
    480–1
Poetry Society of Great Britain prize 222
Queen's Medal for Poetry 479–80
Robert Lee Frost Medallion 353
Senior Anzac Fellowship 371
three-year fellowship 369
LECTURES AND BROADCASTS
    addresses Fellowship of Australian
        Writers 257
    ANZAAS conference 454–5
    at University College 176
    at University of New England 196–7
    Brennan Society symposium 385
    Chris Brennan Memorial Lecture 274
    Commonwealth Literary Fund Award
        lecture 223
    for Adult Education 161
    for the ABC 154, 159–60
    keynote address at ACF conference 429
    public lecture in Brisbane 203–4
    tour of Queensland coast 276
OPINIONS AND BELIEFS
    compares India and Australia 271
    defends Nolan's painting 134
    dislike of colonialism 67–8
    dislike of patriotism 64, 78
    loathing for jargon 323
    on a conservation ethic 383
    on abortion 295
    on academics 370–1
    on consciousness 172–3
    on death 26, 212, 213, 284–5, 452
    on development 348–9
    on emotion 444–5
    on evil 502, 526
    on exploitation 510–11
    on gods 273, 426
    on individual change 286–7
    on landscape 469
    on materialism 519
    on McKinney's work 359
    on nuclear testing 168
    on overpopulation 483
    on progress 207, 238
    on public perception of Aborigines 336
    on religion 36
    on republicanism 484

on teaching poetry in schools 245
on television 505
on television interviews 237
on the Beatles 209, 222
on the Fraser government 376
on the literary scene 419
on the personal meaning of poetry 351, 360, 466
on the poet's role 98, 220–1, 225, 274, 419–20, 438–9, 461
on the relationship to nature 367
on the writer as activist 460–1
on theory 501
on war 124–5, 230–1
on women 137, 166
PERSONAL LIFE
   affinity with New England landscape 88
   apprehension over increasing violence 436
   as a feminist 395–7
   as a mother 153–4, 164–5, 243
   at eighty years 506
   at seventy years 445–6
   at sixty-eight years 429–30
   attends dying grandfather 90
   attends wedding commemoration at Dalwood 301–2
   birth 1, 20
   buys Half Moon and builds house 349–50
   buys house at Boreen Point 184
   buys house in Mount Tamborine 125
   buys second house in Mount Tamborine 149–50
   checks McKinney's gravestone and Calanthe 458–9
   childhood 21–37, 38–47
   choice of reading at Calanthe 170
   convalesces at Yuen 513
   depressed by the human race 332, 502, 520
   drives to New England on Black Friday 79–80
   early awareness 1–3
   early reading 30–1
   family conservatism 5
   feels an outsider at family wedding 342
   first pregnancy 145–8
   flies through cyclone 169
   friendship with Coombs 504
   friendship with Kath Walker 260–1, 307–8, 315, 361, 362, 393, 400, 493–7
   friendship with Kathleen McArthur 179–82
   grieves for Kath Walker 493, 496–7
   grieves for McKinney 212–15
   has driving accident 186–7
   helps others in need 295–6
   horseriding accident 45–6
   impatient to move into Edge 378
   importance of family to 280–1
   learns about Japanese culture 342
   learns to ride 24
   life at Calanthe 153, 158–60, 165–6, 167, 263, 286, 316, 317–18
   life at Edge 382–3, 390, 399, 406, 425–6, 431–2, 448–9, 452, 468–9, 486
   lives in Braidwood 491, 503, 504, 520
   lives in Brisbane 100–10, 118–19
   lives in Darlinghurst 72
   lives in flat in Canberra 521
   marries McKinney 209
   meets McKinney 111
   moves from Braidwood to Canberra 520–1
   moves into Edge 380
   moves to Braidwood from Edge 486–8
   moves to flat in Brisbane 215–16
   moves to Sydney 48–50
   offers Edge to ANU 486
   pitches camp in swimsuit 204
   receives financial windfall 209
   recuperates on Heron Island 441
   relationship with Jack McKinney 116–17, 120–1, 126, 128, 129–30, 163–4, 525
   relationship with mother 21–2
   rents house in Braidwood 357
   rents out house at Boreen Point 203
   returns to Calanthe after McKinney's death 255–6
   returns to Edge for Christmas 511
   returns to New England (1942) 84–101
   second pregnancy 195–6
   self-assertiveness 396–7
   sells Calanthe 356
   sixtieth birthday party 343–4
   starts poultry farm 160–1
   stays at University House, Canberra 342, 350, 428
   stays with Meredith at Yuen 504
   takes break after McKinney's death 212
   unable to join women's forces 92
   uses Aboriginal medicine 509
   visits Moongalba 306–7
   worries about McKinney's health 201–2, 204, 206–7, 210

TRAVELS
 driving tours 185–7
 in Britain (1937) 59–64
 in Britain (1968) 250–2
 in Central Australia 487–8
 in Europe (1937) 65–7
 in Europe (1968) 246–50
 in India (1970) 270–3
 in India and Pakistan (1967) 246
 in Japan 346–8
 in Kakadu 504
 in New Zealand 371–5
 in Queensland 139, 143–5, 381–2, 472
 in South Africa 253
 in Sri Lanka 67–8
 in Tasmania 459–60
 in the East Indies 31
 returns from Europe (1937) 67–8
 starts out on cruise 244
 to Port Hedland 253–4
Wright, Madeleine (née Delpratt, JW's auntie) 12, 32, 47
Wright, Max 14
Wright, May (née Mackenzie, JW's grandmother)
 as a formidable mother-in-law 19–20
 as matriarch 33–4
 attends coronation of Edward VII 13
 brings out orphans from England 23
 commemoration of wedding anniversary 302, 431
 death 36
 family history 6
 left a widow with five children 10–11
 life at Nulalbin 8–9
 life at Wongwibinda 9–10, 12, 33–4
 meets and marries Albert Wright 8
 on "King" Cohen 393
 picnics with stockmen 93
 prospers 12
 provides for JW's education 47
 reads poetry to JW 89
 tells JW of the Wyndhams 61
 treasures Dinton-Dalwood letters 62
Wright, Owen (JW's uncle) 302, 457
Wright, Peter (JW's brother) 1, 291, 302, 323, 393, 470

Wright, Philip Wentworth (JW's great-grandfather) 6–8
Wright, Phillip (JW's father)
 accompanies JW to Sydney 48
 as overseer of defence in New England 83, 86, 87, 92, 95
 as public figure in New England 128
 attitude to Aborigines 93
 birth 9, 11
 death 280
 declining health 204
 learns stories from Aboriginal nurse 32
 loyalty to family tradition 12
 marries Ethel Bigg 15–16
 pushes for New England National Park 231
 relationship with Judith 21
 remarries 38–9
 sells land for JW's education 47
 suggests JW write novel on family history 89
 summarises his life 281
 supports JW's work to save Barrier Reef 280
 takes over family business 19
 travels overseas 13–15, 17–18
 writes autobiography 7, 281
Wright, Sheila (JW's sister-in-law) 457
Wright, Tina (JW's cousin) 21, 32, 42, 45, 60, 67, 80, 213
Wright, Weeta (JW's auntie) 9, 30, 32, 34–6, 39, 90, 431
Wurms, Father 192
Wyndham, George 5–6, 13, 61
Wyndham, Margaret 5–6, 13, 61
Wyndham, Weeta *see* Mackenzie, Weeta (née Wyndham)

Year of Indigenous People 477
Yeats, W.B. 354, 426, 469–70, 490, 502, 519, 520, 525
Yiperya Teachers' Training School 413
Yomiuri (submarine) 264
Yothu Yindi 455
Young, Ruth 43
Yuen (property) 504, 513
Yunupingu, Galarrwuy 386, 389, 455

Zhengquin, Tang 473
Zwicky, Fay 420